BEFORE WATCHMEN

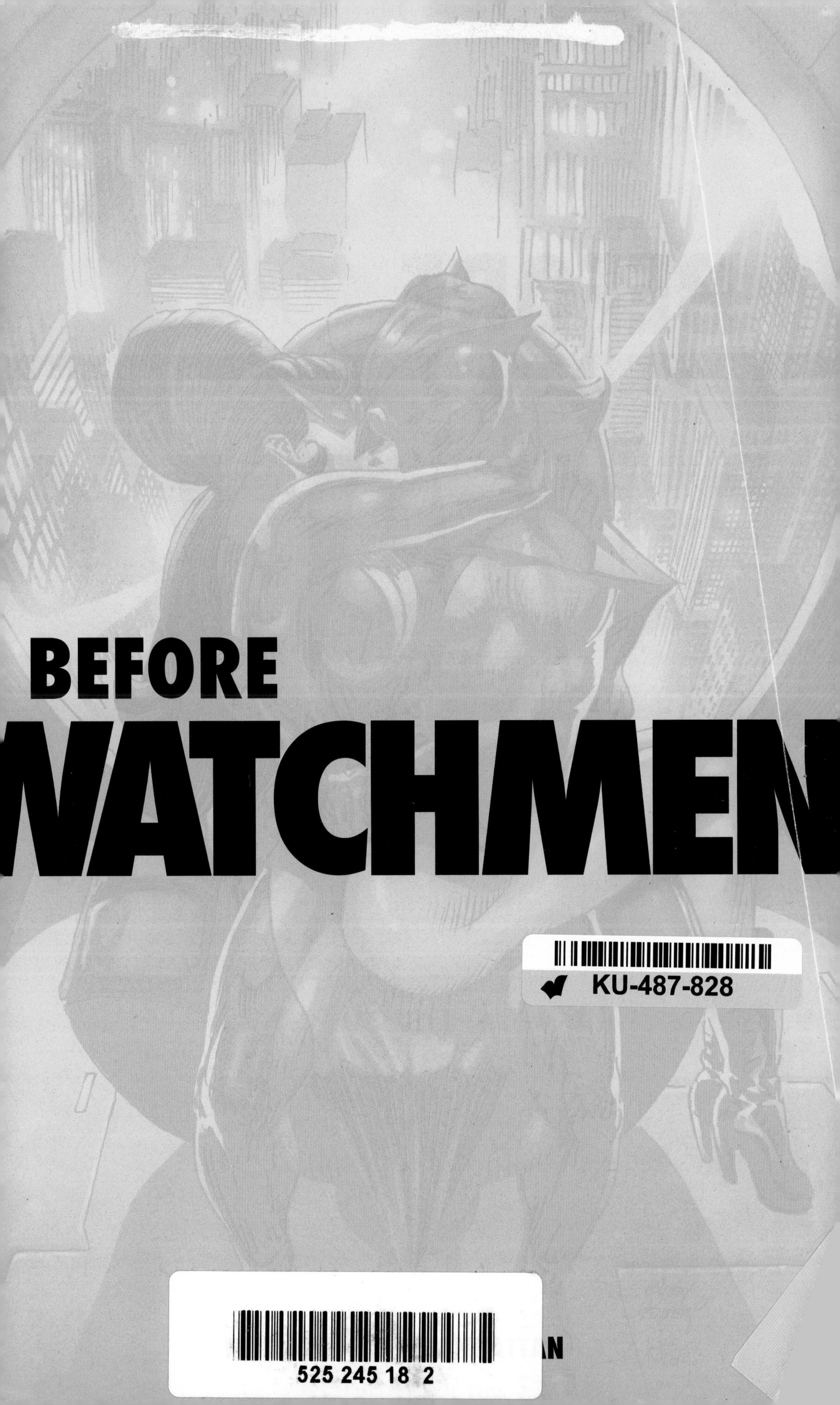

BEFORE

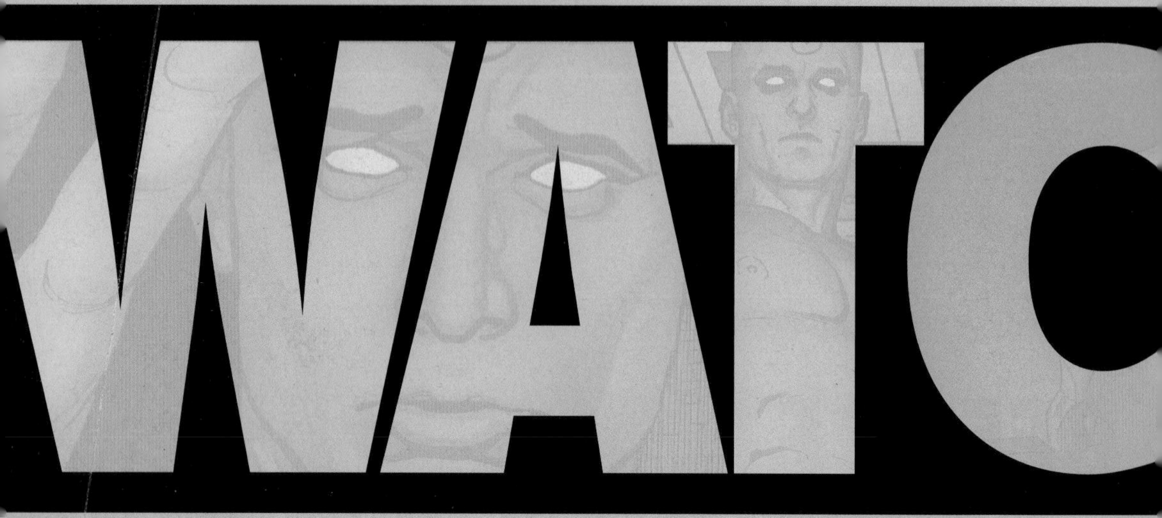
WATC

NITE OWL • DR. MANHATTAN

J. MICHAEL STRACZYNSKI
writer

ANDY KUBERT
JOE KUBERT
BILL SIENKIEWICZ
ADAM HUGHES
EDUARDO RISSO
artists

BRAD ANDERSON
LAURA MARTIN
TRISH MULVIHILL
colorists

STEVE WANDS
NICK NAPOLITANO
CLEM ROBINS
letterers

ANDY KUBERT, **JOE KUBERT** and **ADAM HUGHES**
with **BRAD ANDERSON** and **LAURA MARTIN**
cover artists

Watchmen created by
ALAN MOORE and **DAVE GIBBONS**

MARK CHIARELLO WILL DENNIS Editors – Original Series
CHRIS CONROY MARK DOYLE Associate Editors – Original Series
CAMILLA ZHANG Assistant Editor – Original Series
PETER HAMBOUSSI Editor
RACHEL PINNELAS Assistant Editor
ROBBIN BROSTERMAN Design Director – Books
ROBBIE BIEDERMAN Publication Design

BOB HARRAS Senior VP – Editor-in-Chief, DC Comics

DIANE NELSON President
DAN DIDIO and JIM LEE Co-Publishers
GEOFF JOHNS Chief Creative Officer
JOHN ROOD Executive VP – Sales, Marketing & Business Development
AMY GENKINS Senior VP – Business & Legal Affairs
NAIRI GARDINER Senior VP – Finance
JEFF BOISON VP – Publishing Planning
MARK CHIARELLO VP – Art Direction & Design
JOHN CUNNINGHAM VP – Marketing
TERRI CUNNINGHAM VP – Editorial Administration
ALISON GILL Senior VP – Manufacturing & Operations
HANK KANALZ Senior VP – Vertigo & Integrated Publishing
JAY KOGAN VP – Business & Legal Affairs, Publishing
JACK MAHAN VP – Business Affairs, Talent
NICK NAPOLITANO VP – Manufacturing Administration
SUE POHJA VP – Book Sales
COURTNEY SIMMONS Senior VP – Publicity
BOB WAYNE Senior VP – Sales

Cover design by CHIP KIDD

SUSTAINABLE
FORESTRY
INITIATIVE

Certified Chain of Custody
20% Certified Forest Content,
80% Certified Sourcing
www.sfiprogram.org
SFI-01042
APPLIES TO TEXT STOCK ONLY

Library of Congress Cataloging-in-Publication Data

Straczynski, J. Michael, 1954-
    Before Watchmen : Nite Owl/Dr. Manhattan / J. Michael Straczynski, Adam Hughes, Joe Kubert.
       pages cm. — (Before Watchmen)
    "Originally published in single magazine form in Before Watchmen: Nite Owl 1-4, Before Watchmen: Dr. Manhattan 1-4, Before
Watchmen: Moloch 1-2."
    ISBN 978-1-4012-4514-6
    1. Graphic novels. I. Hughes, Adam T. II. Kubert, Joe, 1926-2012. III. Title. IV. Title: Nite Owl/Dr. Manhattan.
    PN6728.W386S77 2013
    741.5'973—dc23
                                      2013009136

BEFORE WATCHMEN

NITE OWL
writer – J. MICHAEL STRACZYNSKI penciller – ANDY KUBERT
inkers – JOE KUBERT & BILL SIENKIEWICZ colorist – BRAD ANDERSON
letterer – NICK NAPOLITANO

DR. MANHATTAN
writer – J. MICHAEL STRACZYNSKI artist – ADAM HUGHES
colorist – LAURA MARTIN letterer – STEVE WANDS

MOLOCH
writer – J. MICHAEL STRACZYNSKI artist – EDUARDO RISSO
colorist – TRISH MULVIHILL letterer – CLEM ROBINS

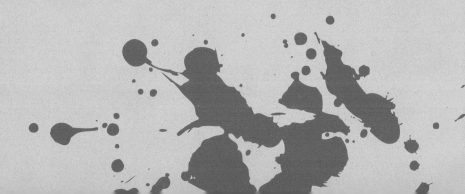

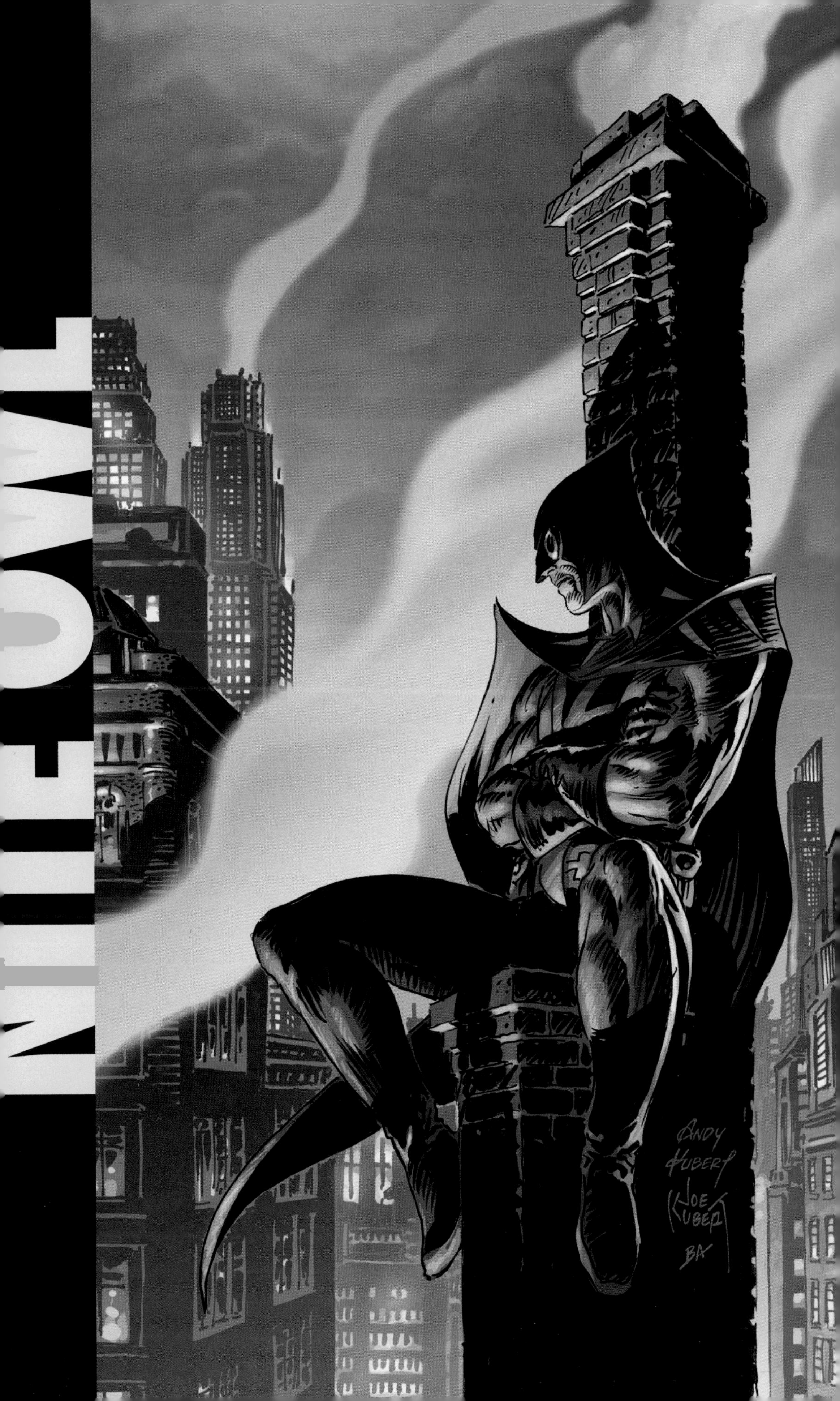
NITE OWL
ANDY KUBERT
JOE KUBERT
BA

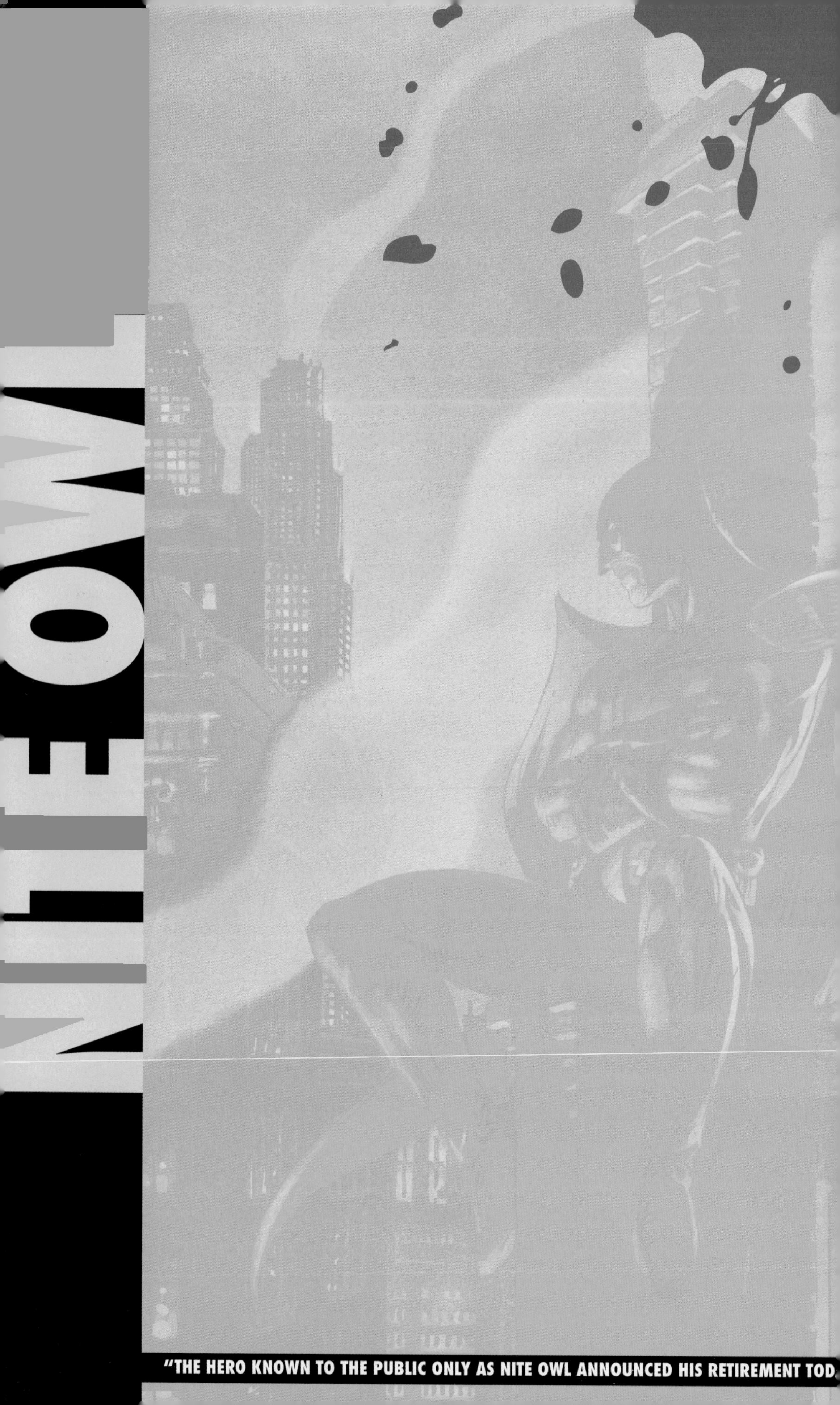
NITE OWL
"THE HERO KNOWN TO THE PUBLIC ONLY AS NITE OWL ANNOUNCED HIS RETIREMENT TOD

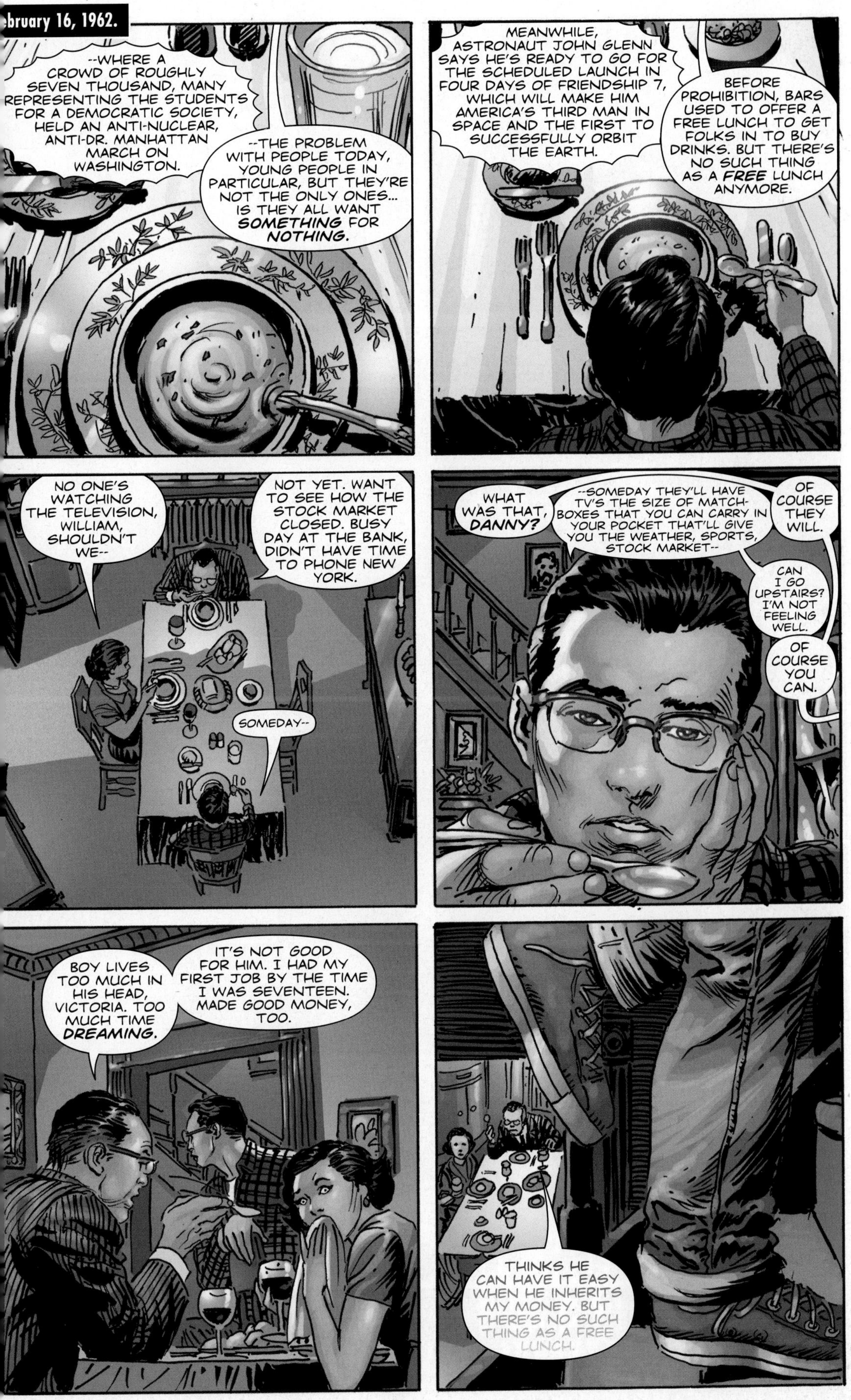

ebruary 16, 1962.
--WHERE A CROWD OF ROUGHLY SEVEN THOUSAND, MANY REPRESENTING THE STUDENTS FOR A DEMOCRATIC SOCIETY, HELD AN ANTI-NUCLEAR, ANTI-DR. MANHATTAN MARCH ON WASHINGTON.
--THE PROBLEM WITH PEOPLE TODAY, YOUNG PEOPLE IN PARTICULAR, BUT THEY'RE NOT THE ONLY ONES... IS THEY ALL WANT SOMETHING FOR NOTHING.
MEANWHILE, ASTRONAUT JOHN GLENN SAYS HE'S READY TO GO FOR THE SCHEDULED LAUNCH IN FOUR DAYS OF FRIENDSHIP 7, WHICH WILL MAKE HIM AMERICA'S THIRD MAN IN SPACE AND THE FIRST TO SUCCESSFULLY ORBIT THE EARTH.
BEFORE PROHIBITION, BARS USED TO OFFER A FREE LUNCH TO GET FOLKS IN TO BUY DRINKS. BUT THERE'S NO SUCH THING AS A FREE LUNCH ANYMORE.
NO ONE'S WATCHING THE TELEVISION, WILLIAM, SHOULDN'T WE--
NOT YET. WANT TO SEE HOW THE STOCK MARKET CLOSED. BUSY DAY AT THE BANK, DIDN'T HAVE TIME TO PHONE NEW YORK.
SOMEDAY--
--SOMEDAY THEY'LL HAVE TV'S THE SIZE OF MATCH-BOXES THAT YOU CAN CARRY IN YOUR POCKET THAT'LL GIVE YOU THE WEATHER, SPORTS, STOCK MARKET--
WHAT WAS THAT, DANNY?
OF COURSE THEY WILL.
CAN I GO UPSTAIRS? I'M NOT FEELING WELL.
OF COURSE YOU CAN.
BOY LIVES TOO MUCH IN HIS HEAD, VICTORIA. TOO MUCH TIME DREAMING.
IT'S NOT GOOD FOR HIM. I HAD MY FIRST JOB BY THE TIME I WAS SEVENTEEN. MADE GOOD MONEY, TOO.
THINKS HE CAN HAVE IT EASY WHEN HE INHERITS MY MONEY. BUT THERE'S NO SUCH THING AS A FREE LUNCH.

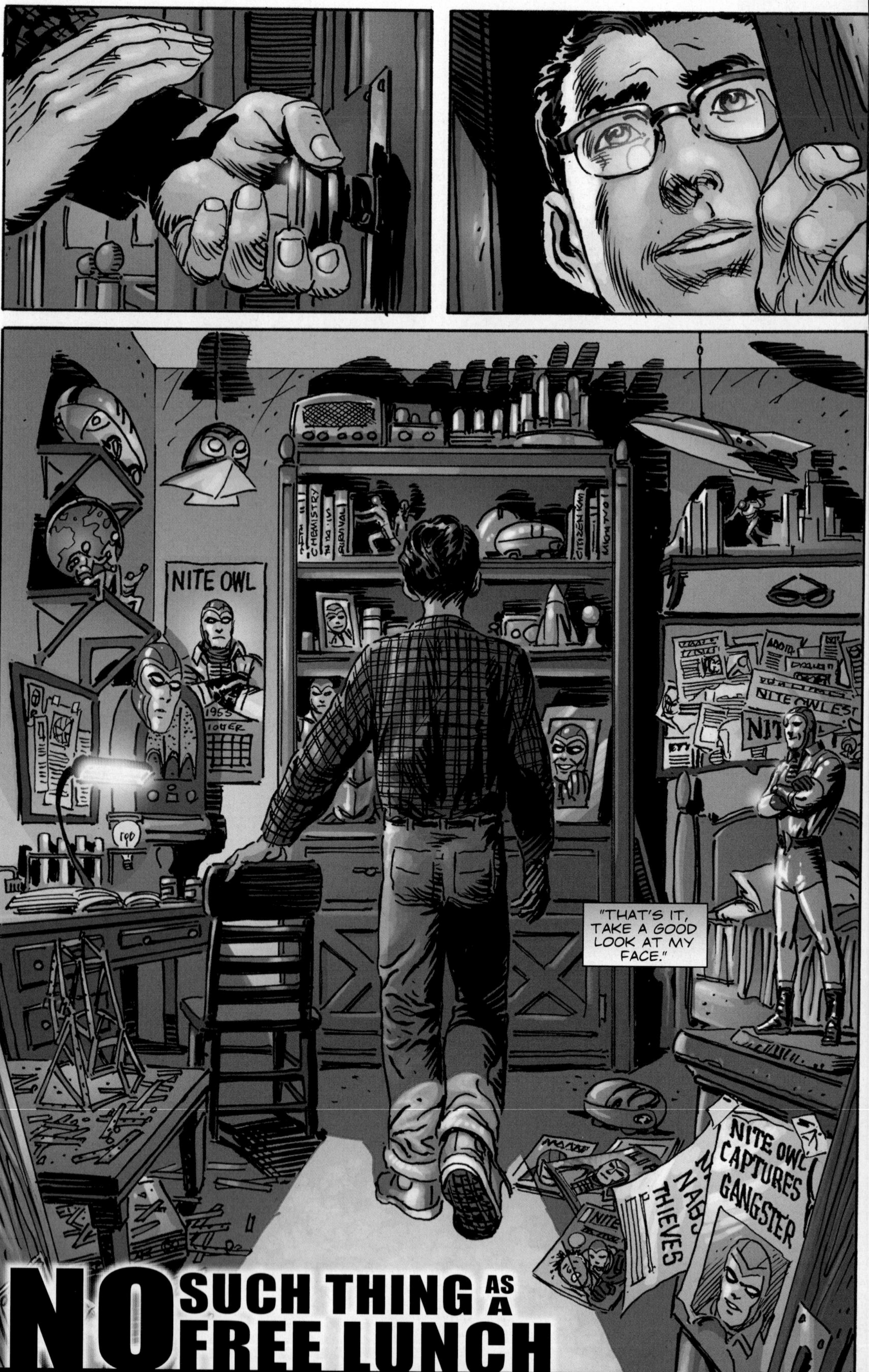
NITE OWL
"THAT'S IT, TAKE A GOOD LOOK AT MY FACE."
NITE OWL CAPTURES GANGSTER
THIEVES

NO SUCH THING AS A FREE LUNCH

J MICHAEL STRACZYNSKI–WRITER • ANDY KUBERT–PENCILS
JOE KUBERT–INKS • BRAD ANDERSON–COLORS • NICK NAPOLITANO–LETTERS
CAMILLA ZHANG – ASST. EDITOR • MARK DOYLE – ASSOC. EDITOR • WILL DENNIS – EDITOR
ANDY KUBERT, JOE KUBERT & BRAD ANDERSON-COVER • KEVIN NOWLAN, JIM LEE WITH SCOTT WILLIAMS & ALEX SINCLAIR-VARIANT COVE
WATCHMEN CREATED BY ALAN MOORE & DAVE GIBBONS

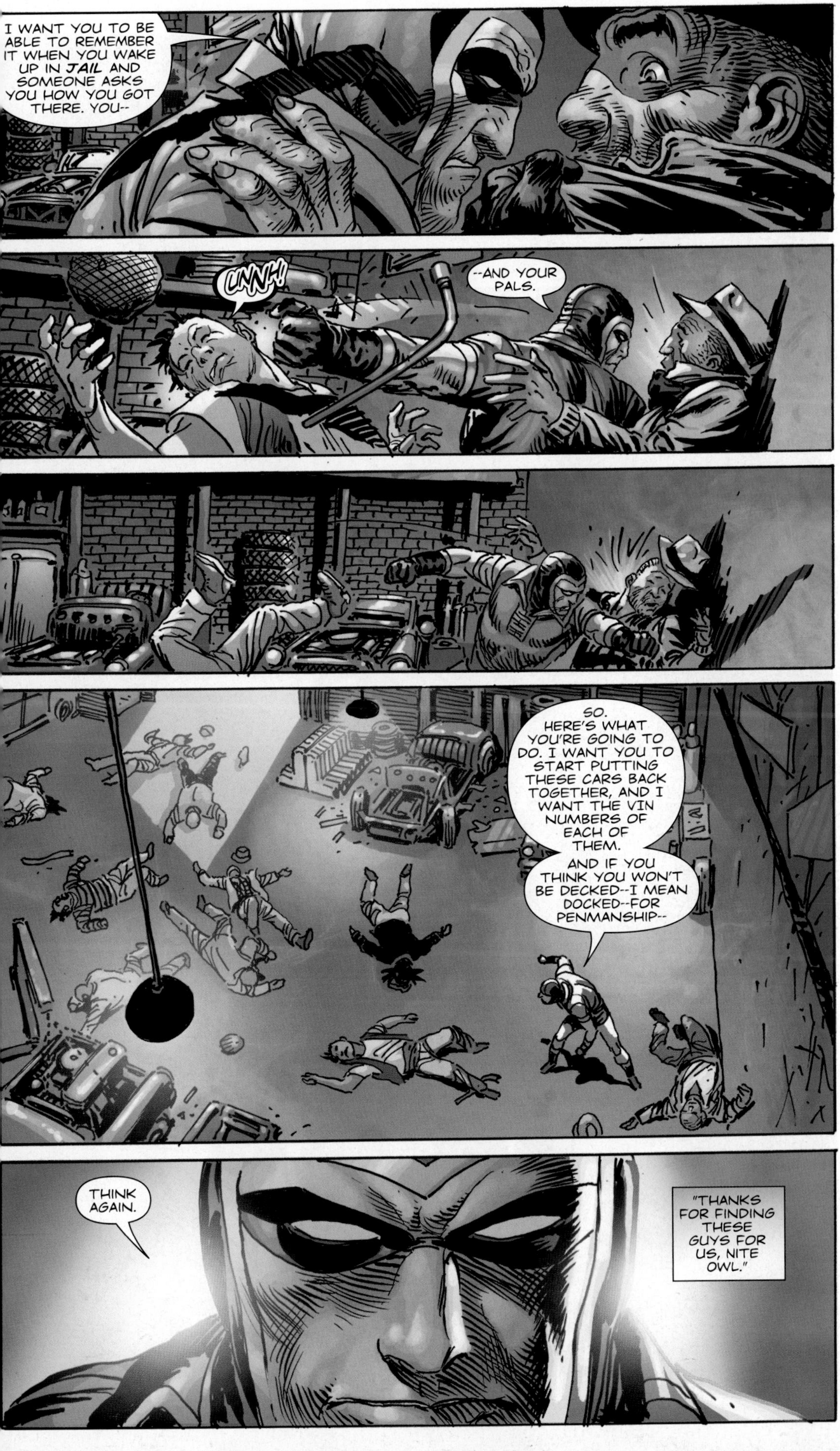
I WANT YOU TO BE ABLE TO REMEMBER IT WHEN YOU WAKE UP IN *JAIL* AND SOMEONE ASKS YOU HOW YOU GOT THERE. YOU--
UNNH!
--AND YOUR PALS.
SO. HERE'S WHAT YOU'RE GOING TO DO. I WANT YOU TO START PUTTING THESE CARS BACK TOGETHER, AND I WANT THE VIN NUMBERS OF EACH OF THEM.
AND IF YOU THINK YOU WON'T BE DECKED--I MEAN DOCKED--FOR PENMANSHIP--
THINK AGAIN.
"THANKS FOR FINDING THESE GUYS FOR US, NITE OWL."

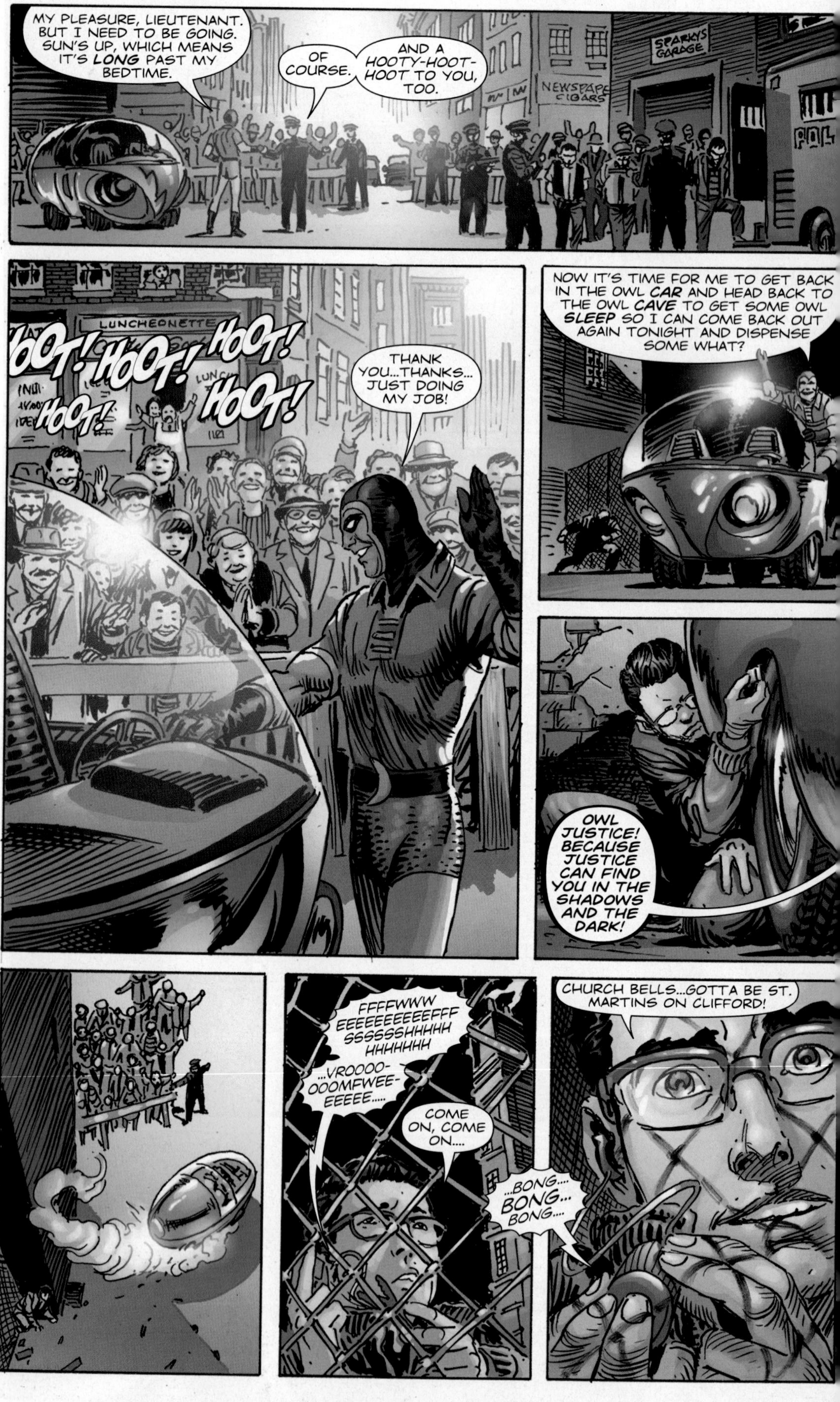
MY PLEASURE, LIEUTENANT. BUT I NEED TO BE GOING. SUN'S UP, WHICH MEANS IT'S LONG PAST MY BEDTIME.
OF COURSE.
AND A HOOTY-HOOT-HOOT TO YOU, TOO.
SPARKY'S GARAGE
LUNCHEONETTE
HOOT! HOOT! HOOT! HOOT! HOOT!
THANK YOU...THANKS... JUST DOING MY JOB!
NOW IT'S TIME FOR ME TO GET BACK IN THE OWL CAR AND HEAD BACK TO THE OWL CAVE TO GET SOME OWL SLEEP SO I CAN COME BACK OUT AGAIN TONIGHT AND DISPENSE SOME WHAT?
OWL JUSTICE! BECAUSE JUSTICE CAN FIND YOU IN THE SHADOWS AND THE DARK!
FFFFWWW EEEEEEEEEEFFF SSSSSSHHHHHH HHHHHHH
...VROOOO-OOOMFWEE-EEEEE.....
COME ON, COME ON....
...BONG... BONG... BONG....
CHURCH BELLS...GOTTA BE ST. MARTINS ON CLIFFORD!

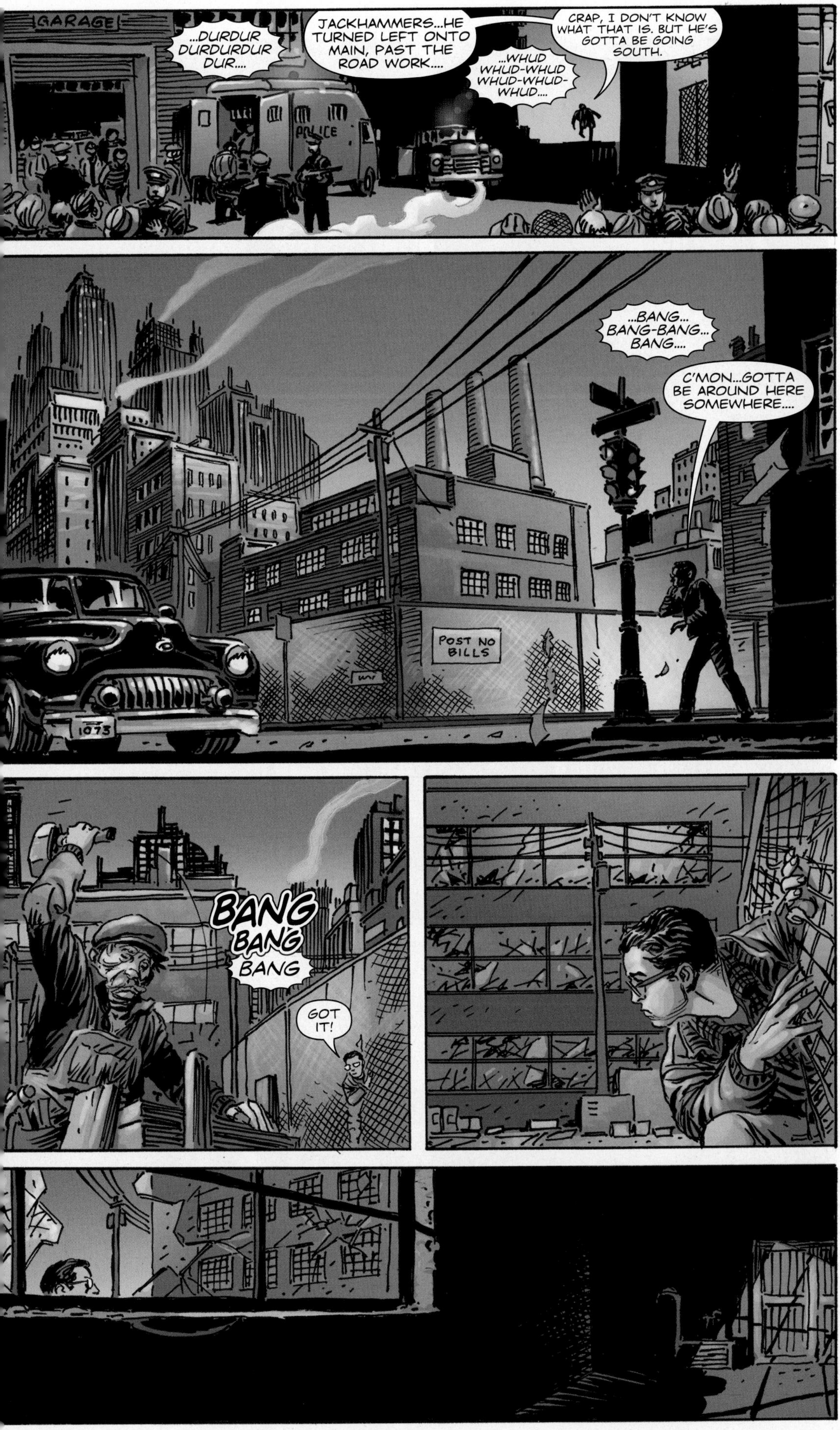
GARAGE
...DURDUR DURDURDUR DUR....
JACKHAMMERS...HE TURNED LEFT ONTO MAIN, PAST THE ROAD WORK....
...WHUD WHUD-WHUD WHUD-WHUD-WHUD....
CRAP, I DON'T KNOW WHAT THAT IS. BUT HE'S GOTTA BE GOING SOUTH.
POLICE
...BANG... BANG-BANG... BANG....
C'MON...GOTTA BE AROUND HERE SOMEWHERE....
POST NO BILLS
1073
BANG BANG BANG
GOT IT!

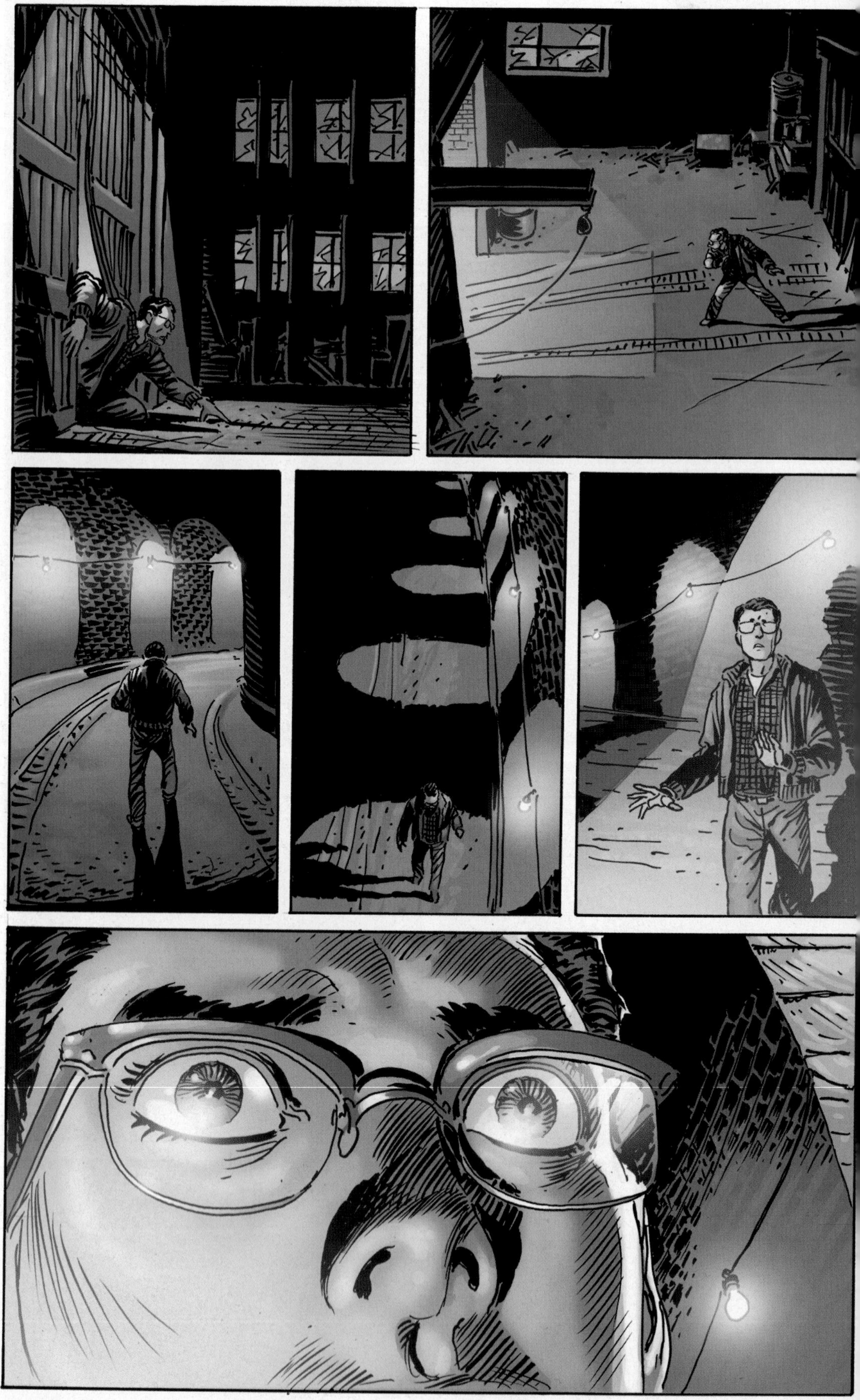

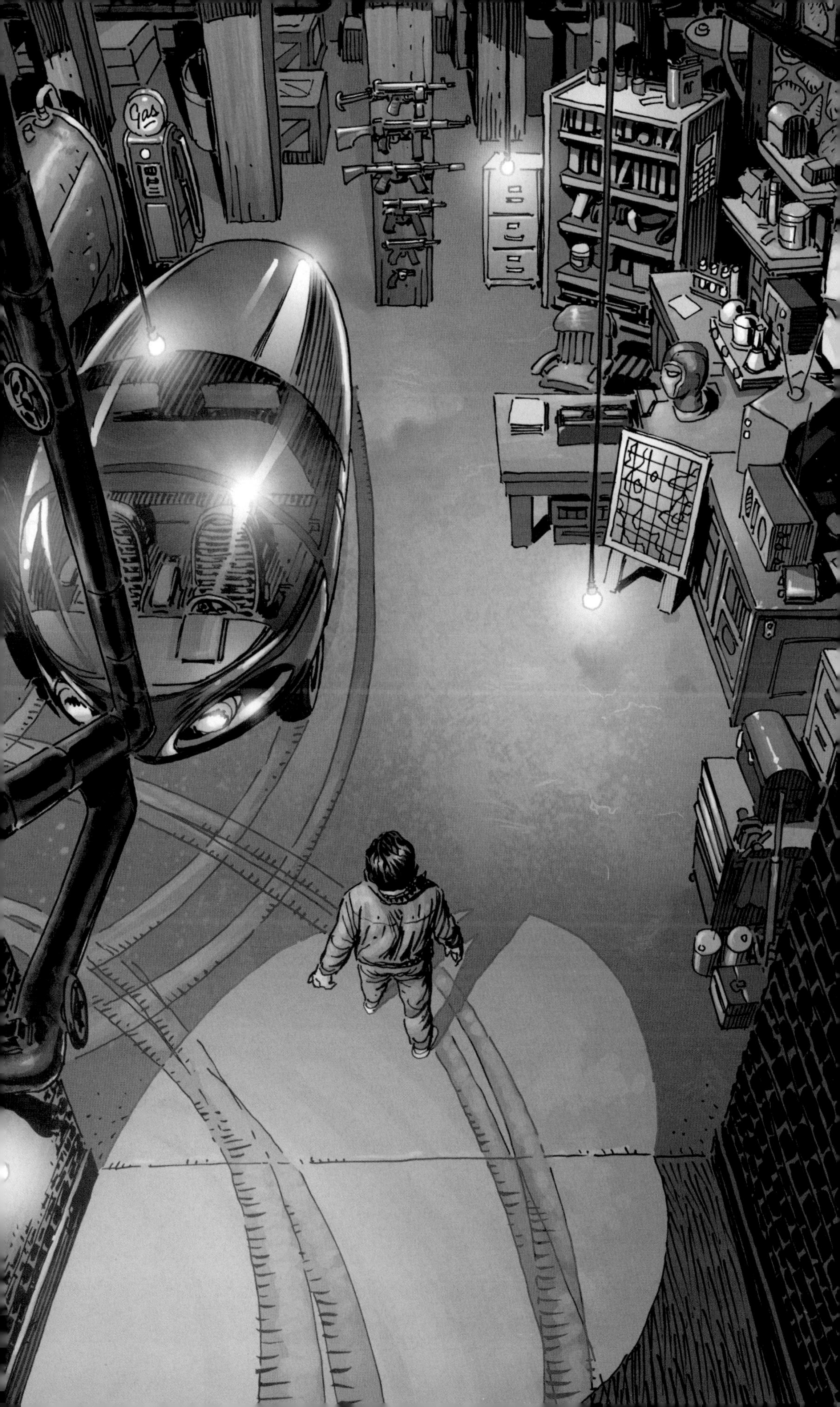
Gas

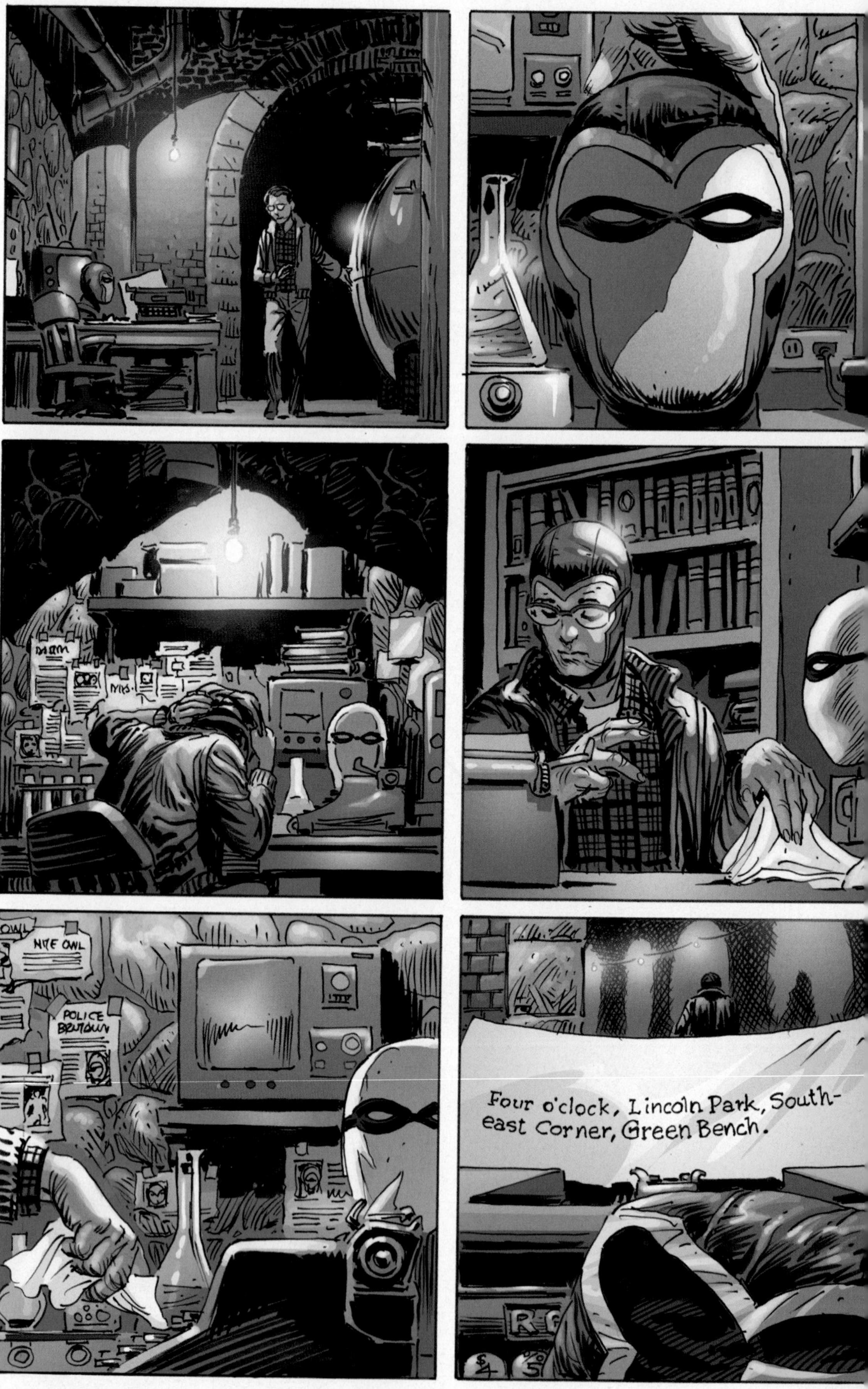
NITE OWL
POLICE
Four o'clock, Lincoln Park, South-
east Corner, Green Bench.

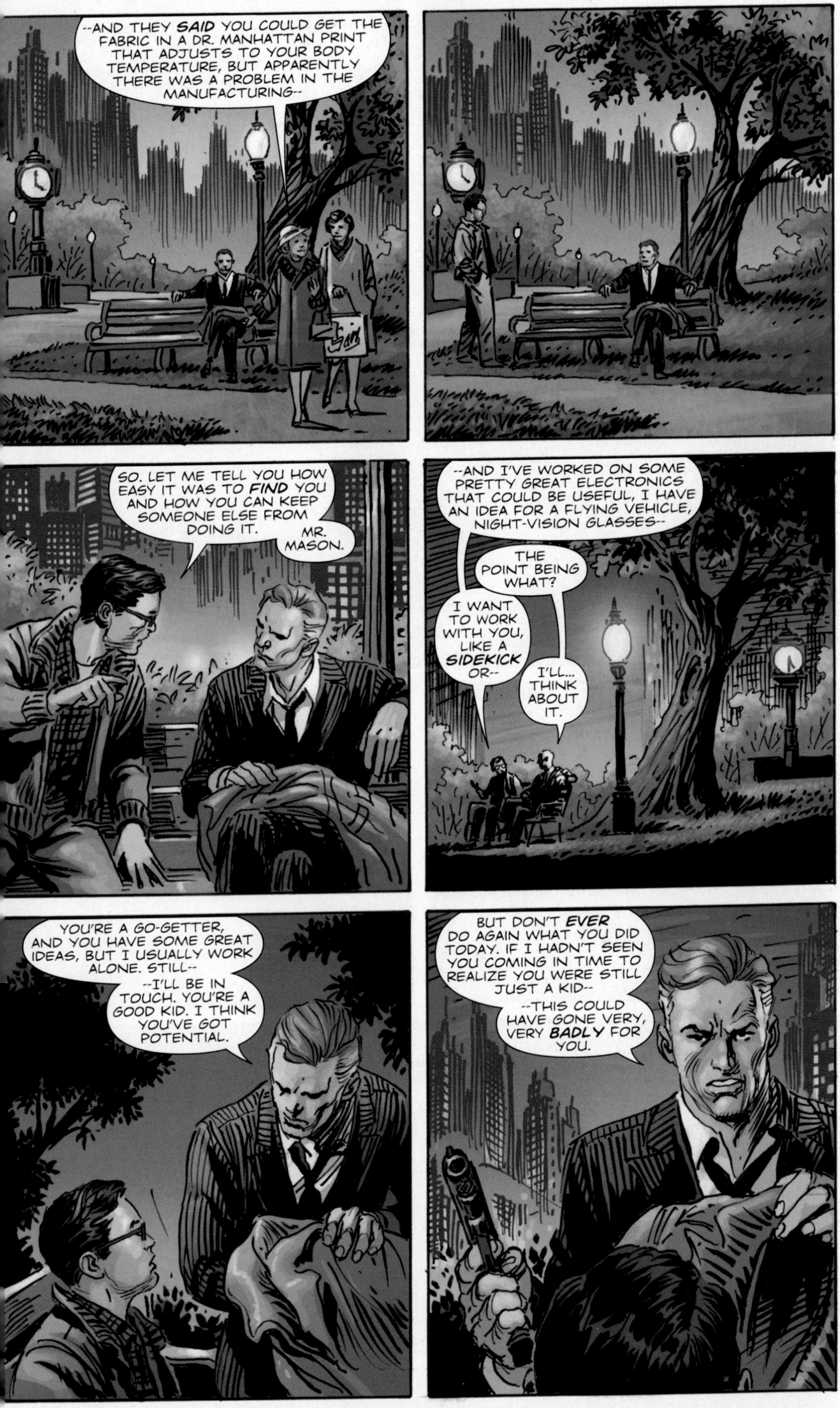
--AND THEY SAID YOU COULD GET THE FABRIC IN A DR. MANHATTAN PRINT THAT ADJUSTS TO YOUR BODY TEMPERATURE, BUT APPARENTLY THERE WAS A PROBLEM IN THE MANUFACTURING--
SO. LET ME TELL YOU HOW EASY IT WAS TO FIND YOU AND HOW YOU CAN KEEP SOMEONE ELSE FROM DOING IT.
MR. MASON.
--AND I'VE WORKED ON SOME PRETTY GREAT ELECTRONICS THAT COULD BE USEFUL, I HAVE AN IDEA FOR A FLYING VEHICLE, NIGHT-VISION GLASSES--
THE POINT BEING WHAT?
I WANT TO WORK WITH YOU, LIKE A SIDEKICK OR--
I'LL... THINK ABOUT IT.
YOU'RE A GO-GETTER, AND YOU HAVE SOME GREAT IDEAS, BUT I USUALLY WORK ALONE. STILL--
--I'LL BE IN TOUCH. YOU'RE A GOOD KID. I THINK YOU'VE GOT POTENTIAL.
BUT DON'T EVER DO AGAIN WHAT YOU DID TODAY. IF I HADN'T SEEN YOU COMING IN TIME TO REALIZE YOU WERE STILL JUST A KID--
--THIS COULD HAVE GONE VERY, VERY BADLY FOR YOU.

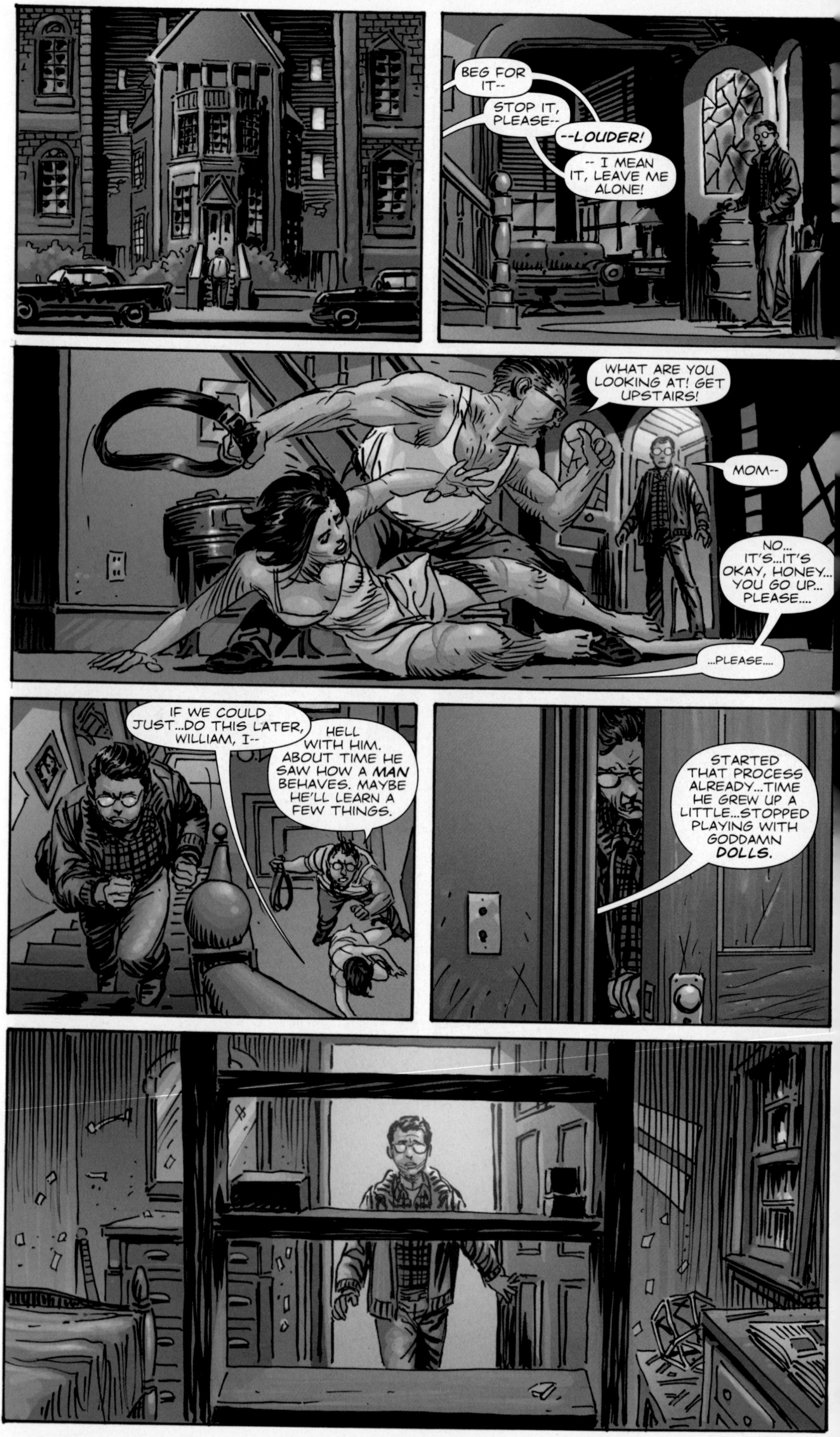
BEG FOR IT--
STOP IT, PLEASE--
--LOUDER!
-- I MEAN IT, LEAVE ME ALONE!
WHAT ARE YOU LOOKING AT! GET UPSTAIRS!
MOM--
NO... IT'S...IT'S OKAY, HONEY... YOU GO UP... PLEASE....
...PLEASE....
IF WE COULD JUST...DO THIS LATER, WILLIAM, I--
HELL WITH HIM. ABOUT TIME HE SAW HOW A MAN BEHAVES. MAYBE HE'LL LEARN A FEW THINGS.
STARTED THAT PROCESS ALREADY...TIME HE GREW UP A LITTLE...STOPPED PLAYING WITH GODDAMN DOLLS.

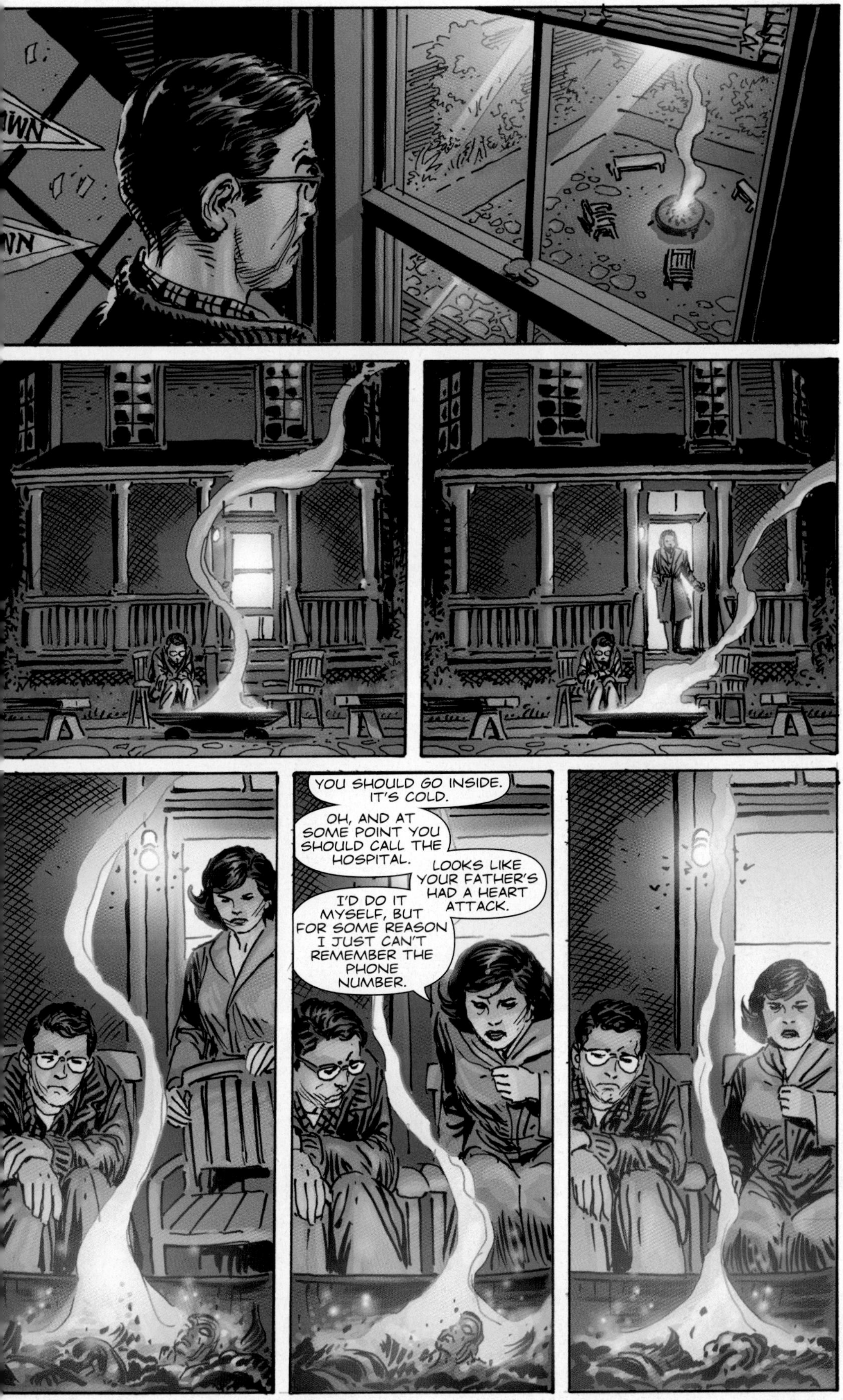
YOU SHOULD GO INSIDE. IT'S COLD.
OH, AND AT SOME POINT YOU SHOULD CALL THE HOSPITAL.
LOOKS LIKE YOUR FATHER'S HAD A HEART ATTACK.
I'D DO IT MYSELF, BUT FOR SOME REASON I JUST CAN'T REMEMBER THE PHONE NUMBER.

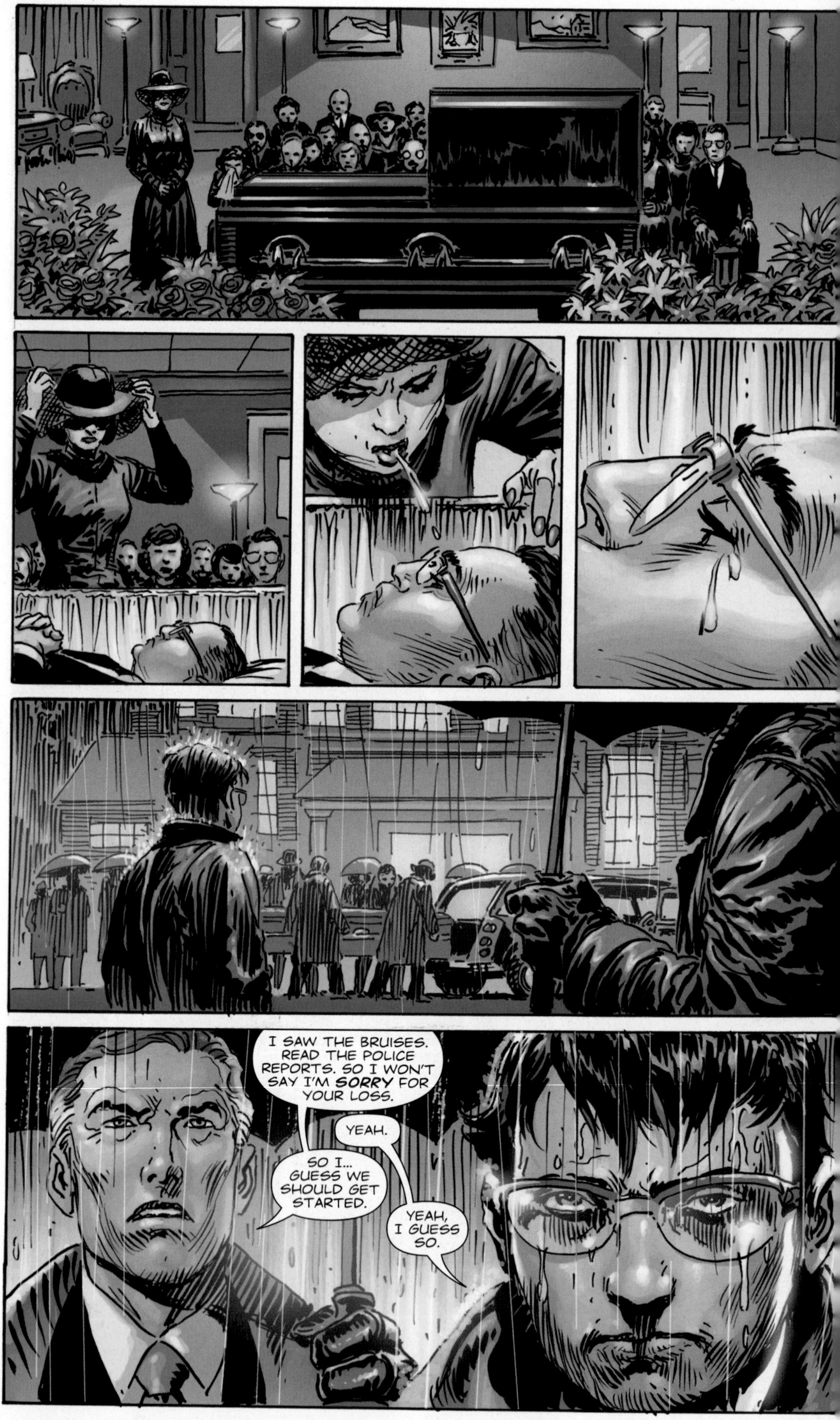
I SAW THE BRUISES. READ THE POLICE REPORTS. SO I WON'T SAY I'M **SORRY** FOR YOUR LOSS.
YEAH.
SO I... GUESS WE SHOULD GET STARTED.
YEAH, I GUESS SO.

I DON'T WANT TO BE CALLED OWLIE--
--OR OWL-BOY, OR OWL-KID.
YOU WON'T.
WOULDN'T DREAM OF IT. NOW STOP DROPPING YOUR LEFT OR I'LL TAKE YOUR HEAD OFF.
--AND THE THRUST SHOULD BE ENOUGH TO ALLOW FOR VERTICAL TAKE-OFF AND LANDINGS.
YOU **SURE** YOU CAN AFFORD THIS?
MY BIRTHDAY WAS YESTERDAY. I SIGNED THE PAPERWORK ON THE TRUST. I CAN AFFORD TO BUY SEVERAL SMALL SOUTH AMERICAN TOWNS.
DON'T. WE HAVE NOWHERE TO PUT THEM.
AND HAPPY BIRTHDAY.
LEGIT OR CROOKED?
CROOKED.
WHY?
UNLOADING AT NIGHT. NO CUSTOMS GUYS AROUND, PROBABLY PAID OFF. TRUCKS WAITING FOR THEIR LOADS DON'T HAVE SHIPPING COMPANY NAMES ON THEM.
FITS YOU BETTER THAN IT DOES ME, AND I WAS NEVER ABLE TO GET THE NIGHT VISION THING RIGHT--
I CAN FIX THAT. BUT ISN'T THIS A LOT LIKE YOUR HEADPIECE? I DON'T WANT TO CONFUSE PEOPLE--
AND THAT MAY NOT BE A BAD THING.
WHAT DOES THAT--
NOTHING... JUST TALKING.
I'M TIRED. WE'LL CALL IT A NIGHT. I'LL NEED A DAY OR TWO OFF, CATCH UP ON A FEW THINGS.
ANYTHING WRONG?
YEAH--

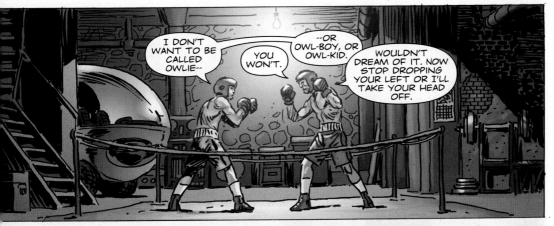

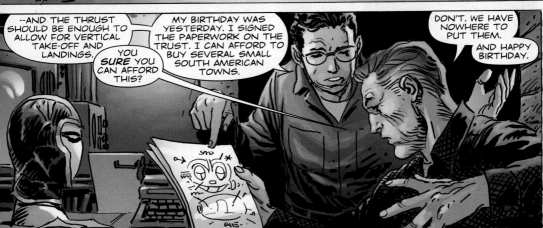

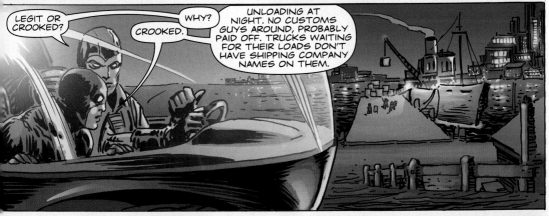

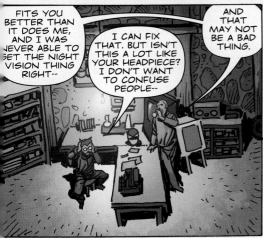

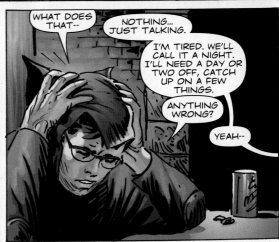

May 12, 1962

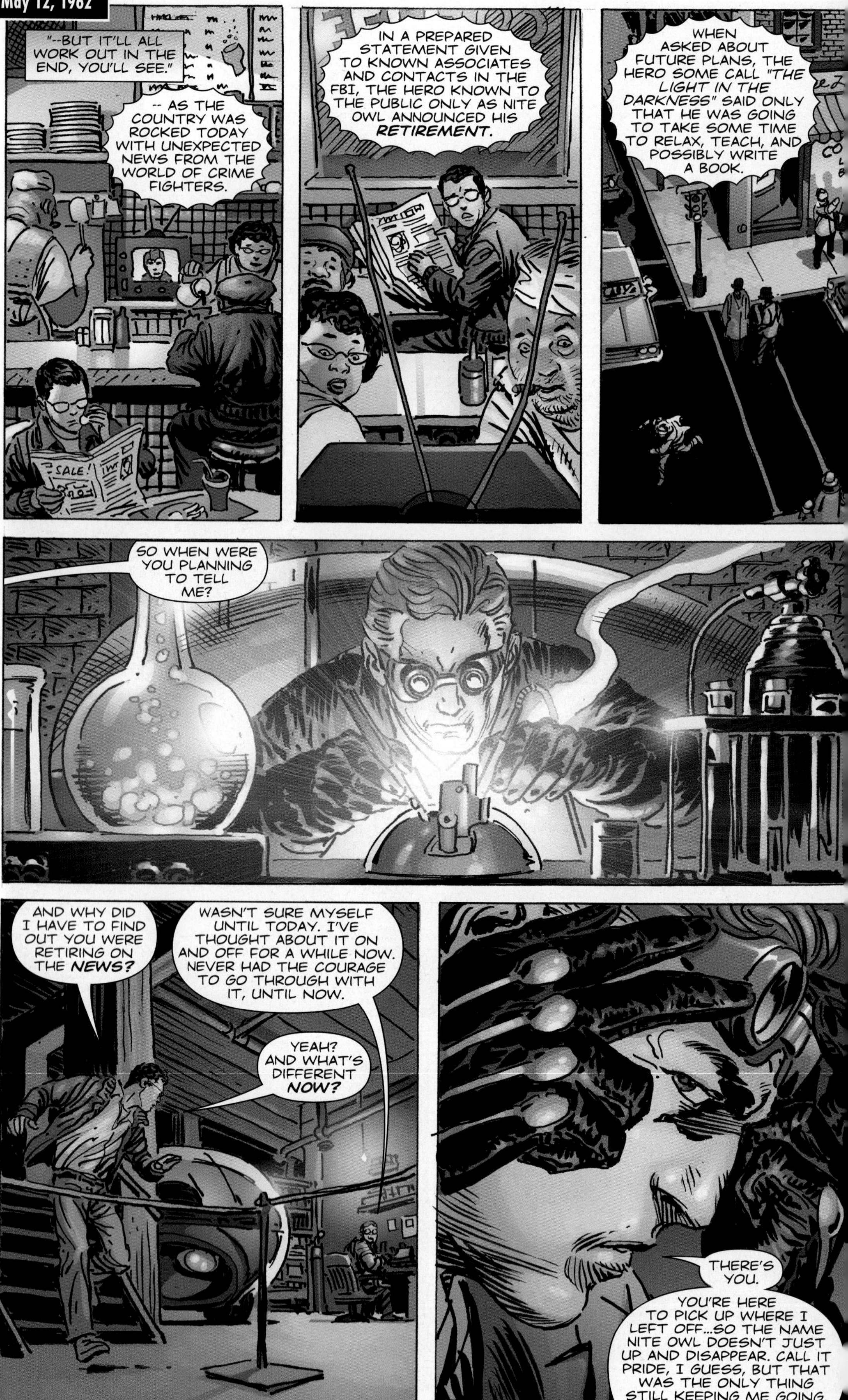
"--BUT IT'LL ALL WORK OUT IN THE END, YOU'LL SEE."
-- AS THE COUNTRY WAS ROCKED TODAY WITH UNEXPECTED NEWS FROM THE WORLD OF CRIME FIGHTERS.
SALE!
IN A PREPARED STATEMENT GIVEN TO KNOWN ASSOCIATES AND CONTACTS IN THE FBI, THE HERO KNOWN TO THE PUBLIC ONLY AS NITE OWL ANNOUNCED HIS RETIREMENT.
WHEN ASKED ABOUT FUTURE PLANS, THE HERO SOME CALL "THE LIGHT IN THE DARKNESS" SAID ONLY THAT HE WAS GOING TO TAKE SOME TIME TO RELAX, TEACH, AND POSSIBLY WRITE A BOOK.
SO WHEN WERE YOU PLANNING TO TELL ME?
AND WHY DID I HAVE TO FIND OUT YOU WERE RETIRING ON THE NEWS?
WASN'T SURE MYSELF UNTIL TODAY. I'VE THOUGHT ABOUT IT ON AND OFF FOR A WHILE NOW. NEVER HAD THE COURAGE TO GO THROUGH WITH IT, UNTIL NOW.
YEAH? AND WHAT'S DIFFERENT NOW?
THERE'S YOU.
YOU'RE HERE TO PICK UP WHERE I LEFT OFF...SO THE NAME NITE OWL DOESN'T JUST UP AND DISAPPEAR. CALL IT PRIDE, I GUESS, BUT THAT WAS THE ONLY THING STILL KEEPING ME GOING.

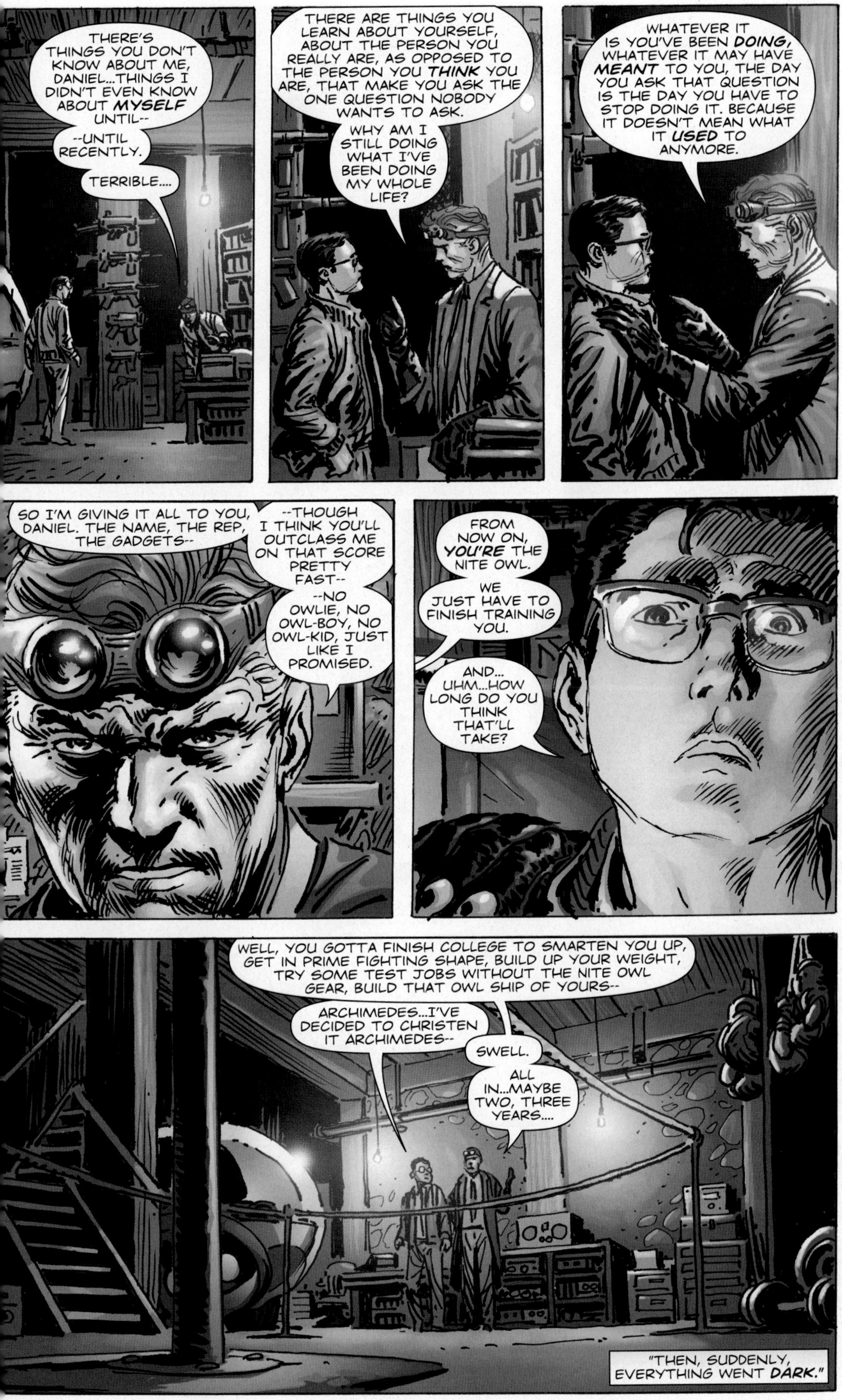
THERE'S THINGS YOU DON'T KNOW ABOUT ME, DANIEL...THINGS I DIDN'T EVEN KNOW ABOUT MYSELF UNTIL--
--UNTIL RECENTLY.
TERRIBLE....
THERE ARE THINGS YOU LEARN ABOUT YOURSELF, ABOUT THE PERSON YOU REALLY ARE, AS OPPOSED TO THE PERSON YOU THINK YOU ARE, THAT MAKE YOU ASK THE ONE QUESTION NOBODY WANTS TO ASK.
WHY AM I STILL DOING WHAT I'VE BEEN DOING MY WHOLE LIFE?
WHATEVER IT IS YOU'VE BEEN DOING, WHATEVER IT MAY HAVE MEANT TO YOU, THE DAY YOU ASK THAT QUESTION IS THE DAY YOU HAVE TO STOP DOING IT. BECAUSE IT DOESN'T MEAN WHAT IT USED TO ANYMORE.
SO I'M GIVING IT ALL TO YOU, DANIEL. THE NAME, THE REP, THE GADGETS--
--THOUGH I THINK YOU'LL OUTCLASS ME ON THAT SCORE PRETTY FAST--
--NO OWLIE, NO OWL-BOY, NO OWL-KID, JUST LIKE I PROMISED.
FROM NOW ON, YOU'RE THE NITE OWL.
WE JUST HAVE TO FINISH TRAINING YOU.
AND... UHM...HOW LONG DO YOU THINK THAT'LL TAKE?
WELL, YOU GOTTA FINISH COLLEGE TO SMARTEN YOU UP, GET IN PRIME FIGHTING SHAPE, BUILD UP YOUR WEIGHT, TRY SOME TEST JOBS WITHOUT THE NITE OWL GEAR, BUILD THAT OWL SHIP OF YOURS--
ARCHIMEDES...I'VE DECIDED TO CHRISTEN IT ARCHIMEDES--
SWELL.
ALL IN...MAYBE TWO, THREE YEARS....
"THEN, SUDDENLY, EVERYTHING WENT DARK."

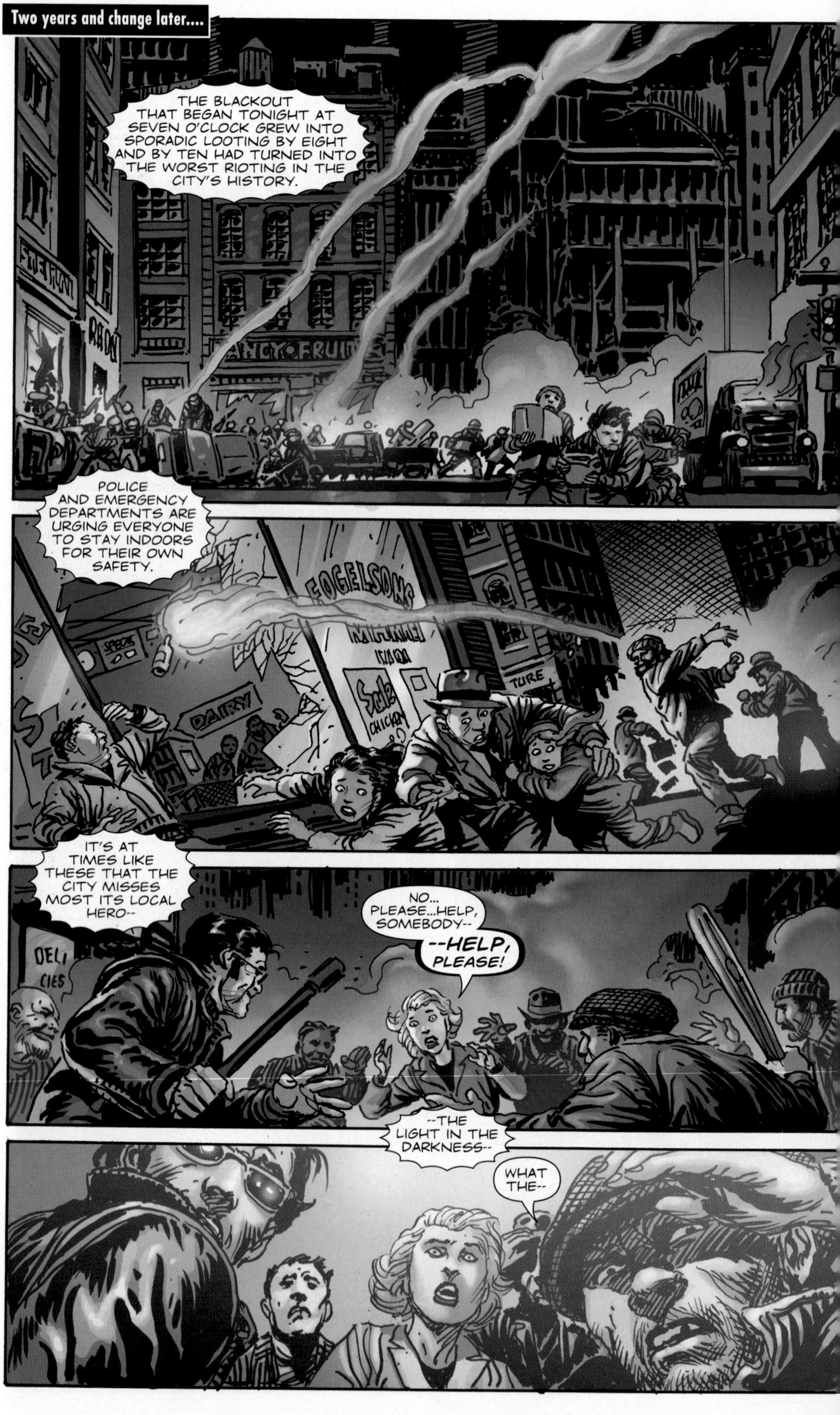
Two years and change later....
THE BLACKOUT THAT BEGAN TONIGHT AT SEVEN O'CLOCK GREW INTO SPORADIC LOOTING BY EIGHT AND BY TEN HAD TURNED INTO THE WORST RIOTING IN THE CITY'S HISTORY.
FANCY FRUIT
POLICE AND EMERGENCY DEPARTMENTS ARE URGING EVERYONE TO STAY INDOORS FOR THEIR OWN SAFETY.
FOGELSONS
DAIRY
IT'S AT TIMES LIKE THESE THAT THE CITY MISSES MOST ITS LOCAL HERO--
DELI CIES
NO... PLEASE...HELP, SOMEBODY--
--HELP, PLEASE!
--THE LIGHT IN THE DARKNESS--
WHAT THE--

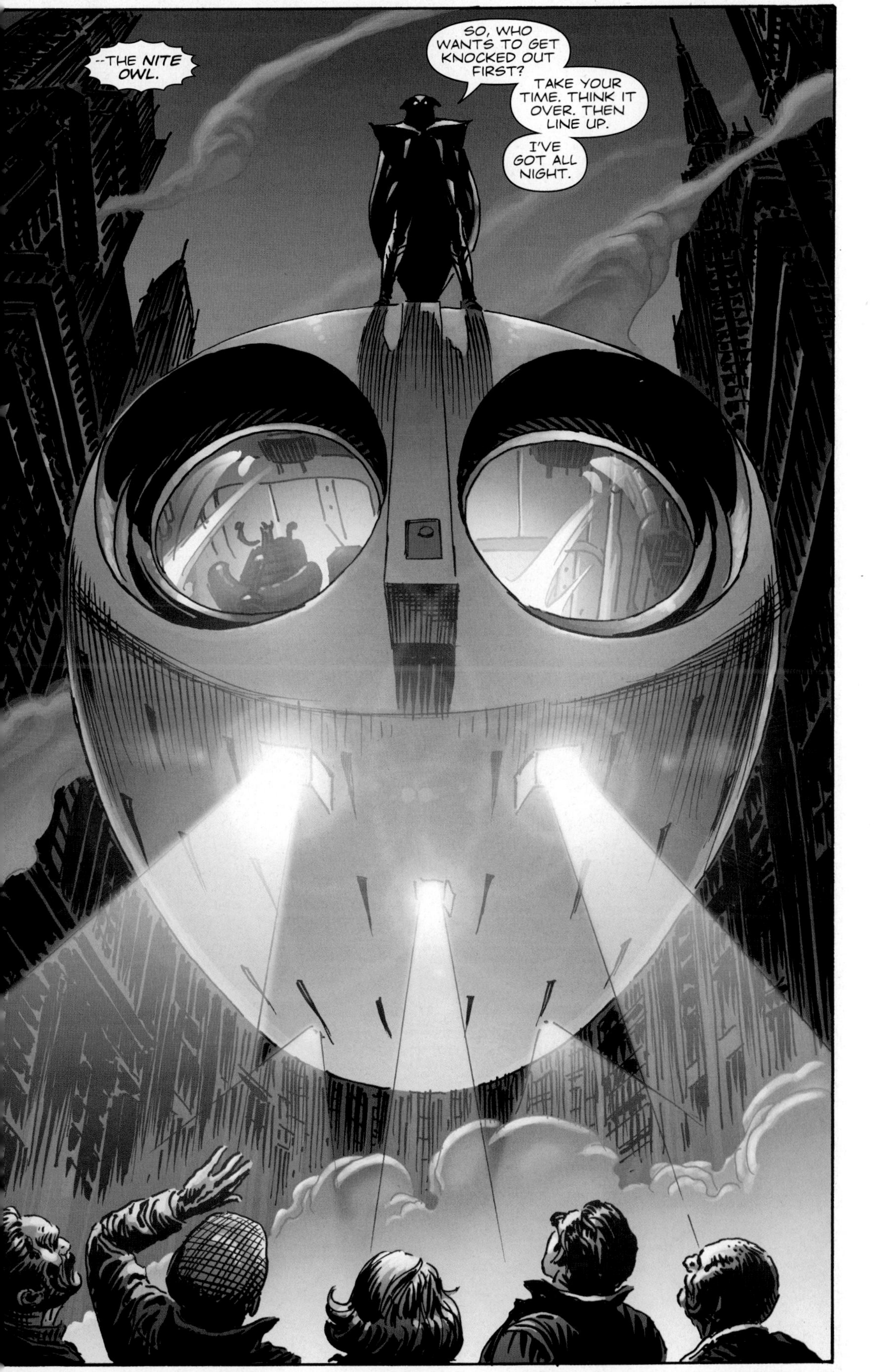
--THE NITE OWL.
SO, WHO WANTS TO GET KNOCKED OUT FIRST?
TAKE YOUR TIME. THINK IT OVER. THEN LINE UP.
I'VE GOT ALL NIGHT.

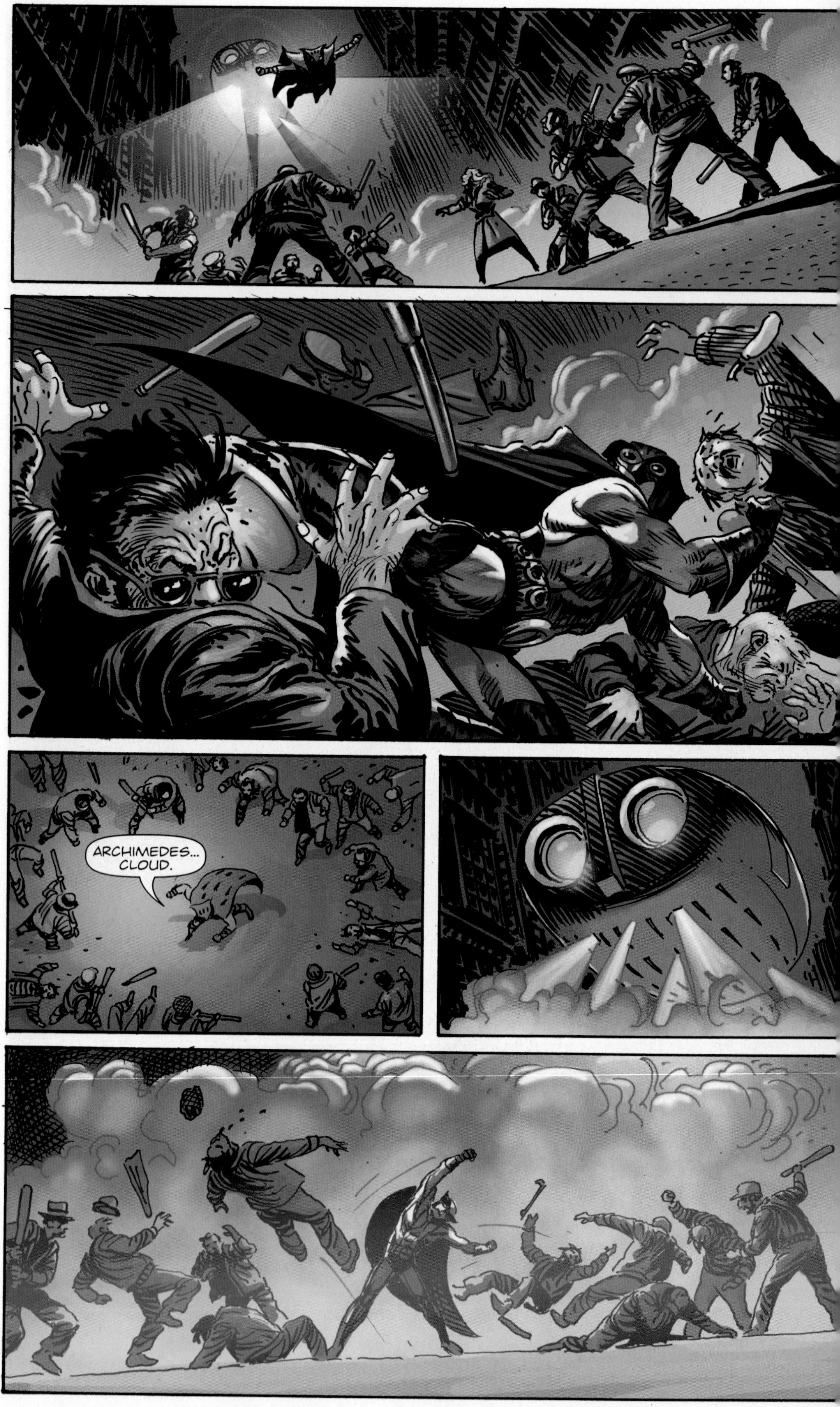
ARCHIMEDES... CLOUD.

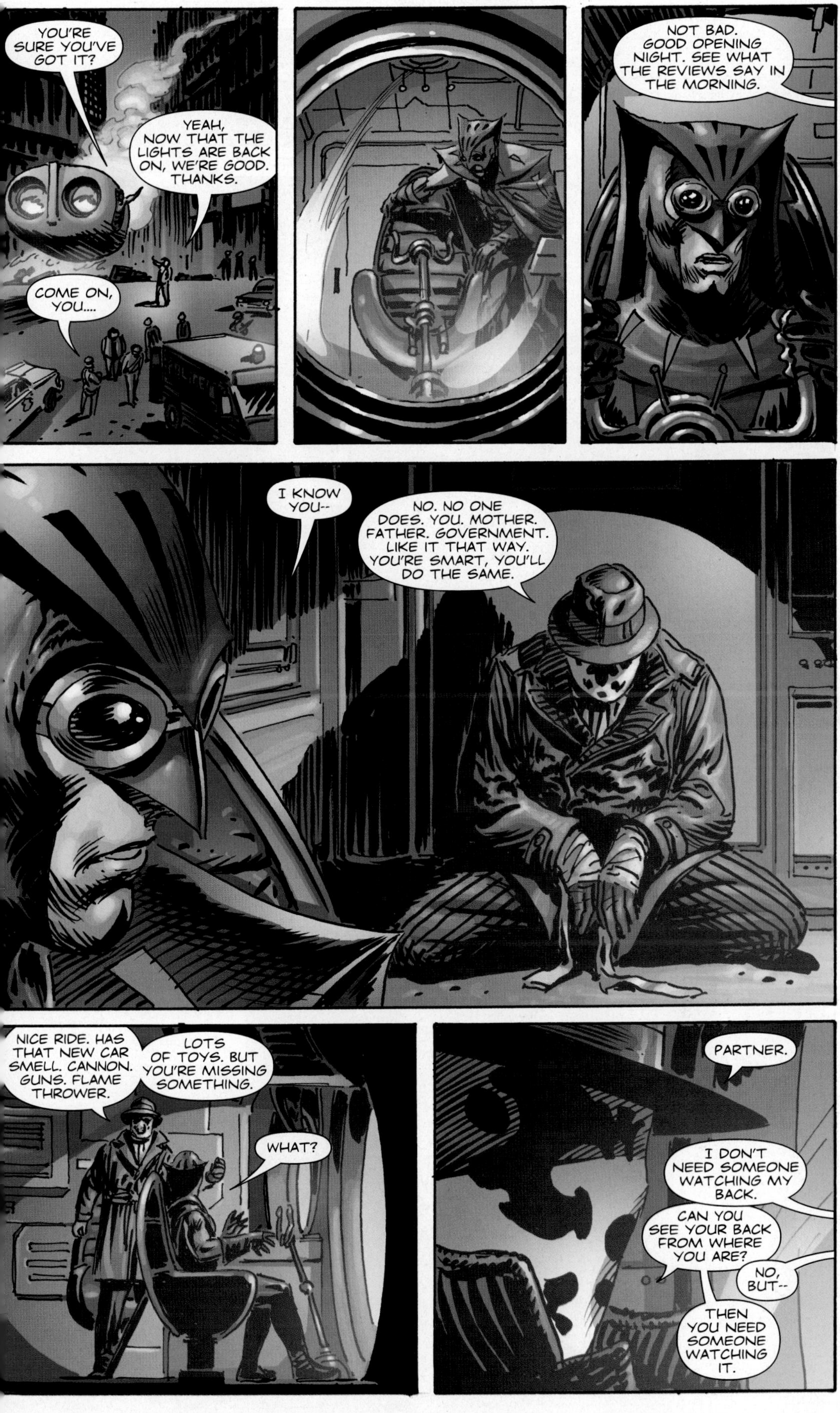
YOU'RE SURE YOU'VE GOT IT?
YEAH, NOW THAT THE LIGHTS ARE BACK ON, WE'RE GOOD. THANKS.
COME ON, YOU....
NOT BAD. GOOD OPENING NIGHT. SEE WHAT THE REVIEWS SAY IN THE MORNING.
I KNOW YOU--
NO. NO ONE DOES. YOU. MOTHER. FATHER. GOVERNMENT. LIKE IT THAT WAY. YOU'RE SMART, YOU'LL DO THE SAME.
NICE RIDE. HAS THAT NEW CAR SMELL. CANNON. GUNS. FLAME THROWER.
LOTS OF TOYS. BUT YOU'RE MISSING SOMETHING.
WHAT?
PARTNER.
I DON'T NEED SOMEONE WATCHING MY BACK.
CAN YOU SEE YOUR BACK FROM WHERE YOU ARE?
NO, BUT--
THEN YOU NEED SOMEONE WATCHING IT.

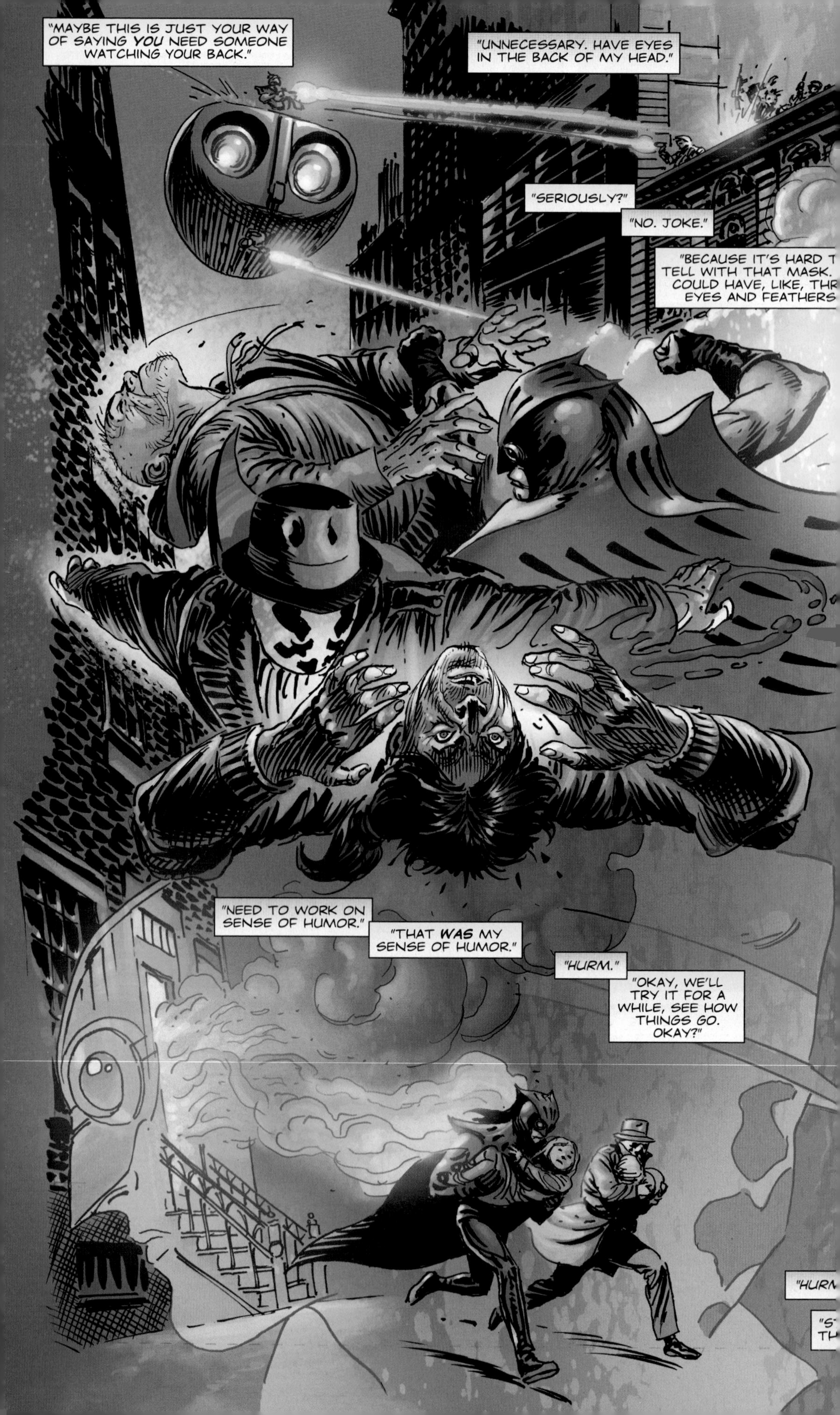
"MAYBE THIS IS JUST YOUR WAY OF SAYING YOU NEED SOMEONE WATCHING YOUR BACK."
"UNNECESSARY. HAVE EYES IN THE BACK OF MY HEAD."
"SERIOUSLY?"
"NO. JOKE."
"BECAUSE IT'S HARD T
TELL WITH THAT MASK.
COULD HAVE, LIKE, THR
EYES AND FEATHERS
"NEED TO WORK ON SENSE OF HUMOR."
"THAT WAS MY SENSE OF HUMOR."
"HURM."
"OKAY, WE'LL TRY IT FOR A WHILE, SEE HOW THINGS GO. OKAY?"
"HURM

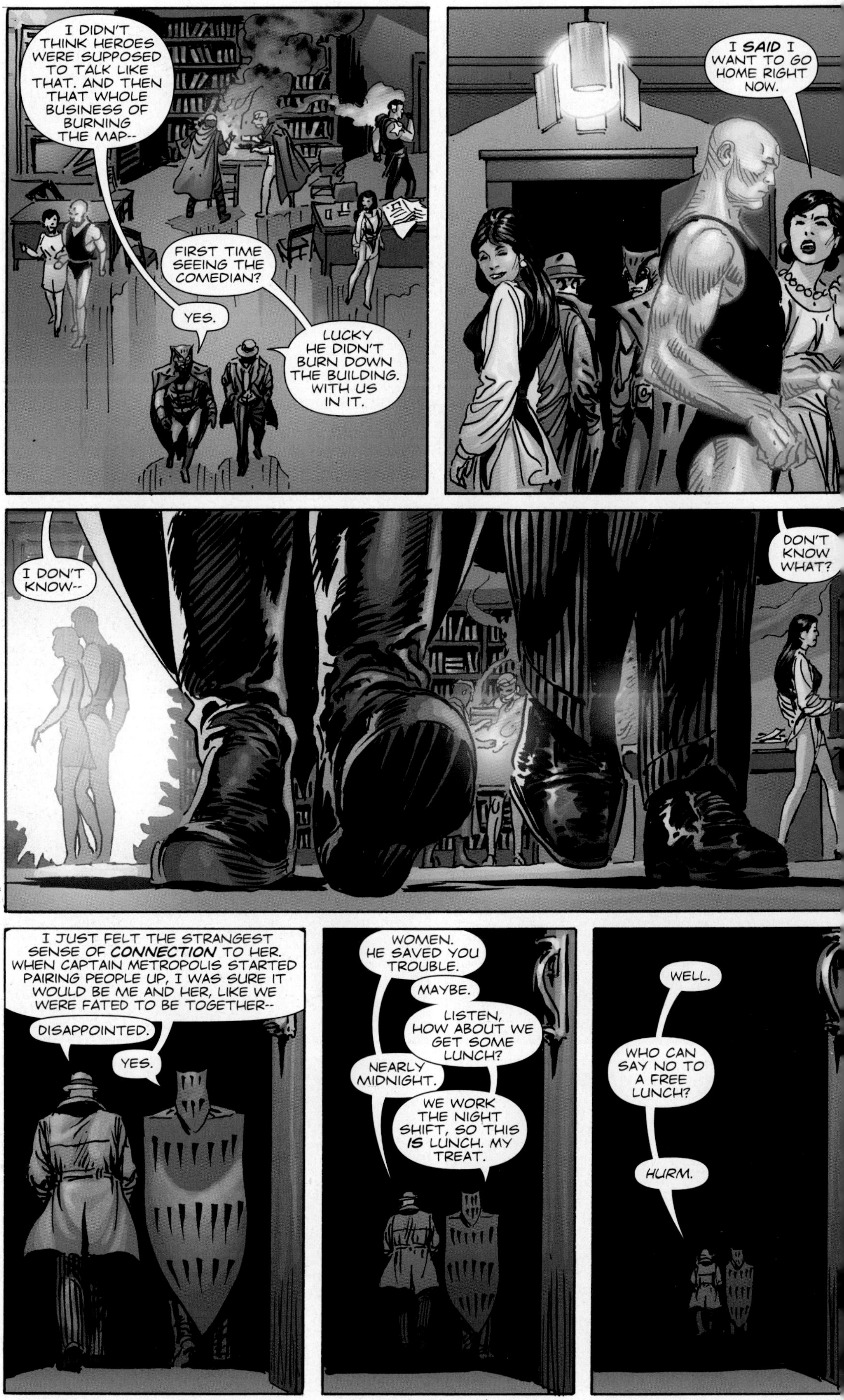
I DIDN'T THINK HEROES WERE SUPPOSED TO TALK LIKE THAT. AND THEN THAT WHOLE BUSINESS OF BURNING THE MAP--
FIRST TIME SEEING THE COMEDIAN?
YES.
LUCKY HE DIDN'T BURN DOWN THE BUILDING. WITH US IN IT.
I **SAID** I WANT TO GO HOME RIGHT NOW.
I DON'T KNOW--
DON'T KNOW WHAT?
I JUST FELT THE STRANGEST SENSE OF **CONNECTION** TO HER. WHEN CAPTAIN METROPOLIS STARTED PAIRING PEOPLE UP, I WAS SURE IT WOULD BE ME AND HER, LIKE WE WERE FATED TO BE TOGETHER--
DISAPPOINTED.
YES.
WOMEN. HE SAVED YOU TROUBLE.
MAYBE.
LISTEN, HOW ABOUT WE GET SOME LUNCH?
NEARLY MIDNIGHT.
WE WORK THE NIGHT SHIFT, SO THIS **IS** LUNCH. MY TREAT.
WELL.
WHO CAN SAY NO TO A FREE LUNCH?
HURM.

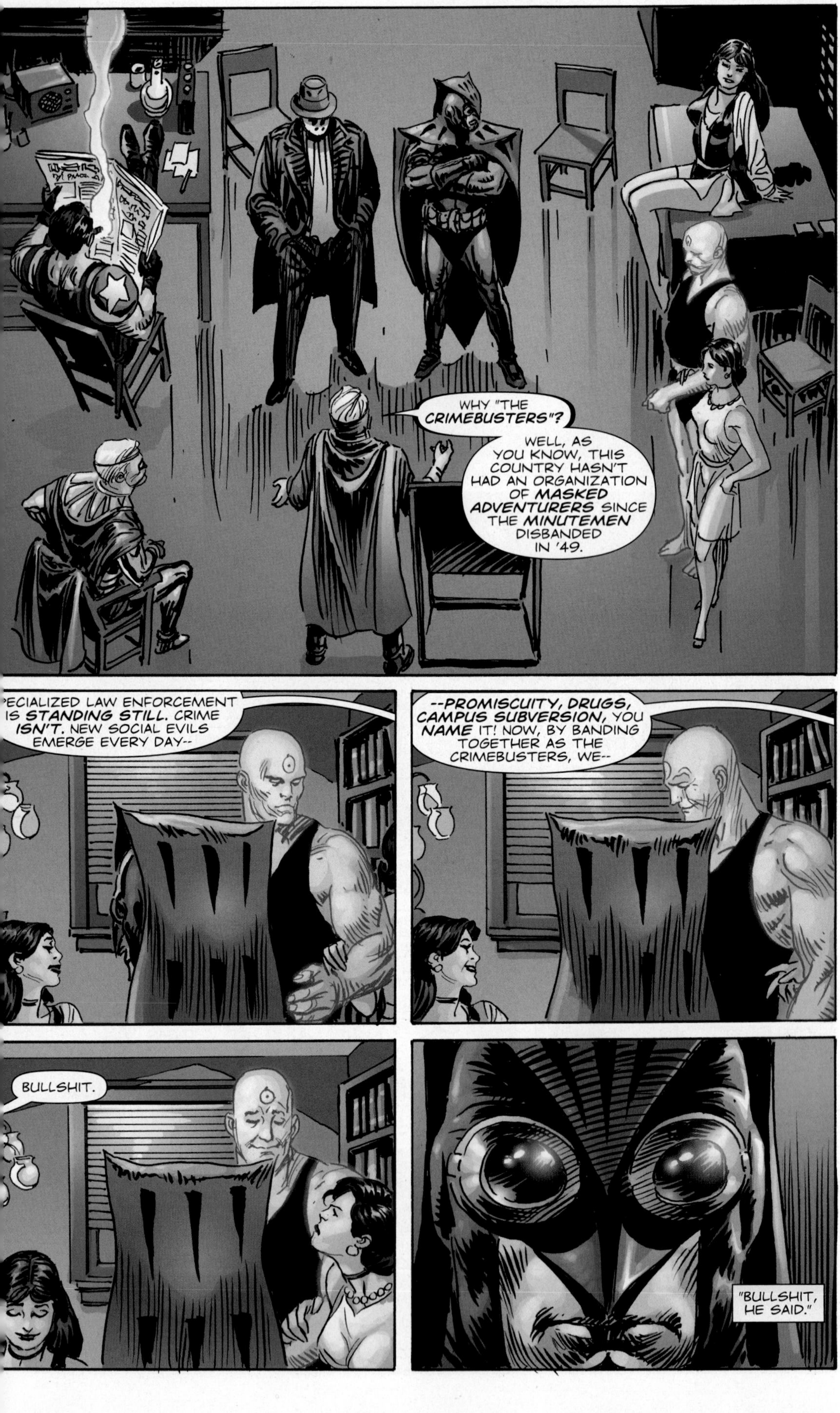
WHY "THE CRIMEBUSTERS"?
WELL, AS YOU KNOW, THIS COUNTRY HASN'T HAD AN ORGANIZATION OF MASKED ADVENTURERS SINCE THE MINUTEMEN DISBANDED IN '49.
PECIALIZED LAW ENFORCEMENT IS STANDING STILL. CRIME ISN'T. NEW SOCIAL EVILS EMERGE EVERY DAY--
--PROMISCUITY, DRUGS, CAMPUS SUBVERSION, YOU NAME IT! NOW, BY BANDING TOGETHER AS THE CRIMEBUSTERS, WE--
BULLSHIT.
"BULLSHIT, HE SAID."

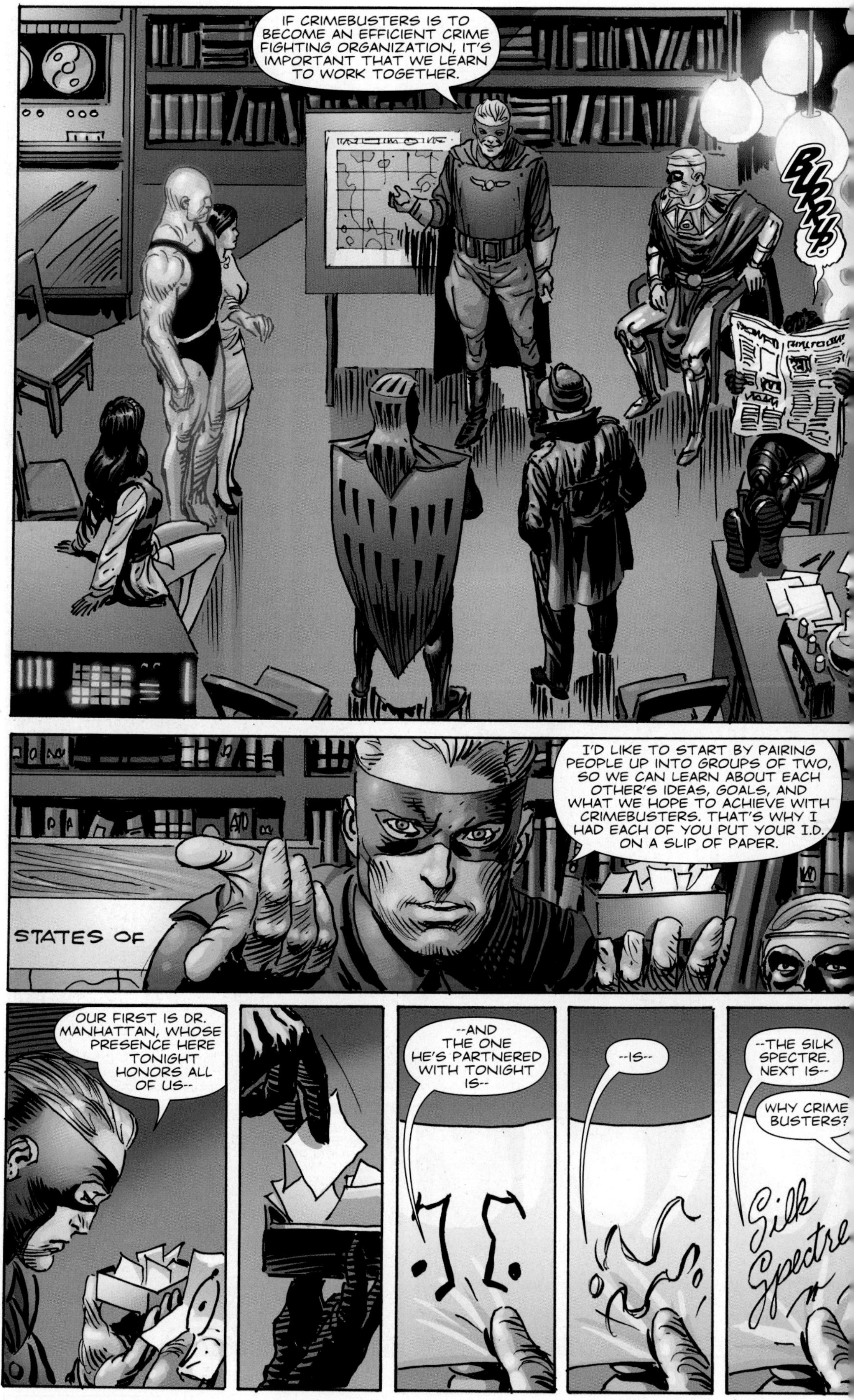
IF CRIMEBUSTERS IS TO BECOME AN EFFICIENT CRIME FIGHTING ORGANIZATION, IT'S IMPORTANT THAT WE LEARN TO WORK TOGETHER.
BURRRP.
I'D LIKE TO START BY PAIRING PEOPLE UP INTO GROUPS OF TWO, SO WE CAN LEARN ABOUT EACH OTHER'S IDEAS, GOALS, AND WHAT WE HOPE TO ACHIEVE WITH CRIMEBUSTERS. THAT'S WHY I HAD EACH OF YOU PUT YOUR I.D. ON A SLIP OF PAPER.
STATES OF
OUR FIRST IS DR. MANHATTAN, WHOSE PRESENCE HERE TONIGHT HONORS ALL OF US--
--AND THE ONE HE'S PARTNERED WITH TONIGHT IS--
--IS--
--THE SILK SPECTRE. NEXT IS--
WHY CRIME BUSTERS?
Silk Spectre

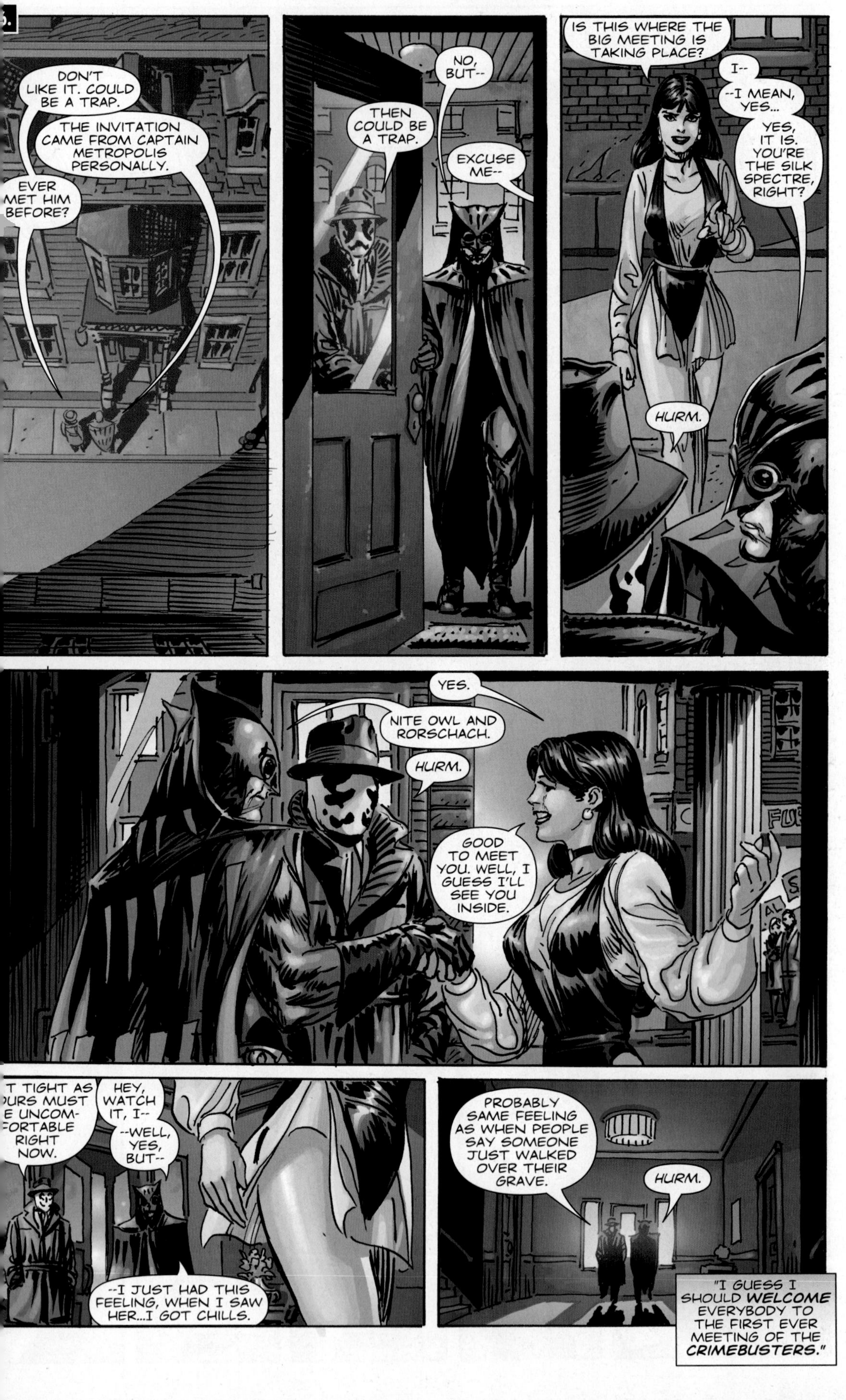

DON'T LIKE IT. COULD BE A TRAP.
THE INVITATION CAME FROM CAPTAIN METROPOLIS PERSONALLY.
EVER MET HIM BEFORE?
NO, BUT--
THEN COULD BE A TRAP.
EXCUSE ME--
IS THIS WHERE THE BIG MEETING IS TAKING PLACE?
I--
--I MEAN, YES...
YES, IT IS. YOU'RE THE SILK SPECTRE, RIGHT?
HURM.
YES.
NITE OWL AND RORSCHACH.
HURM.
GOOD TO MEET YOU. WELL, I GUESS I'LL SEE YOU INSIDE.
T TIGHT AS URS MUST E UNCOM-FORTABLE RIGHT NOW.
HEY, WATCH IT, I--
--WELL, YES, BUT--
--I JUST HAD THIS FEELING, WHEN I SAW HER...I GOT CHILLS.
PROBABLY SAME FEELING AS WHEN PEOPLE SAY SOMEONE JUST WALKED OVER THEIR GRAVE.
HURM.
"I GUESS I SHOULD WELCOME EVERYBODY TO THE FIRST EVER MEETING OF THE CRIMEBUSTERS."

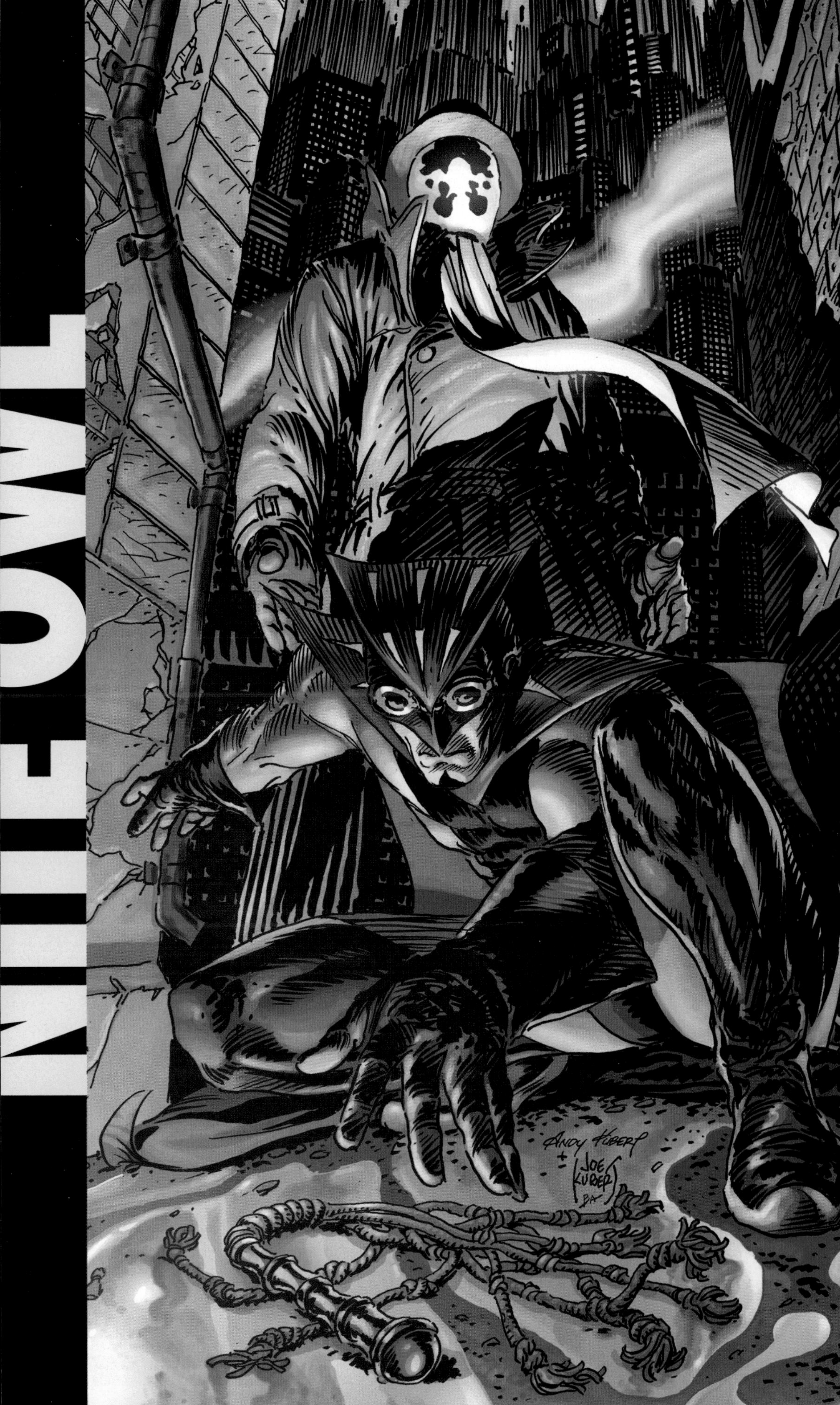
NITE OWL
ANDY KUBERT
+
JOE KUBERT
BA

NITE OWL

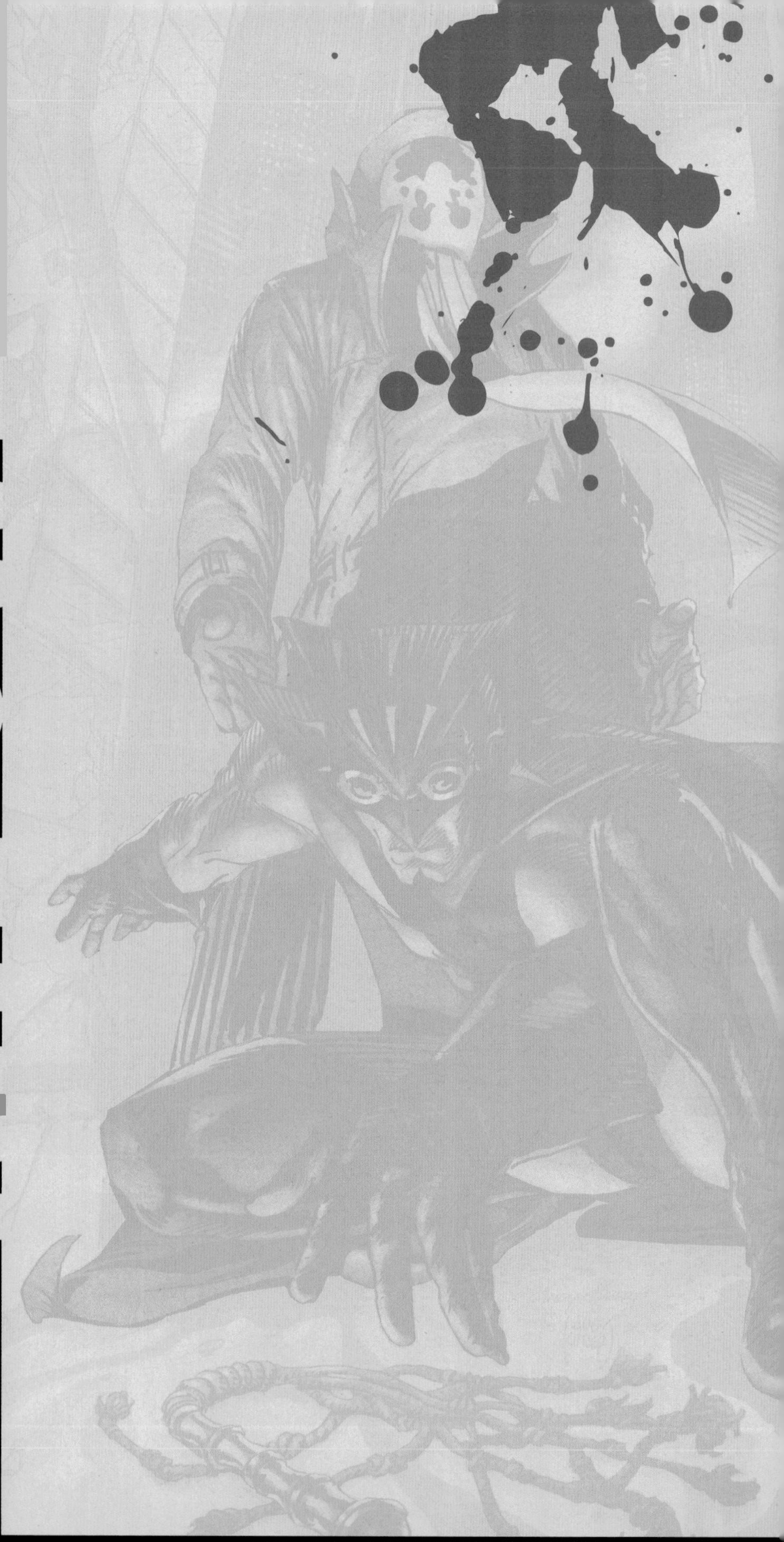

"THEY RUN...I LIKE IT WHEN THEY RUN."

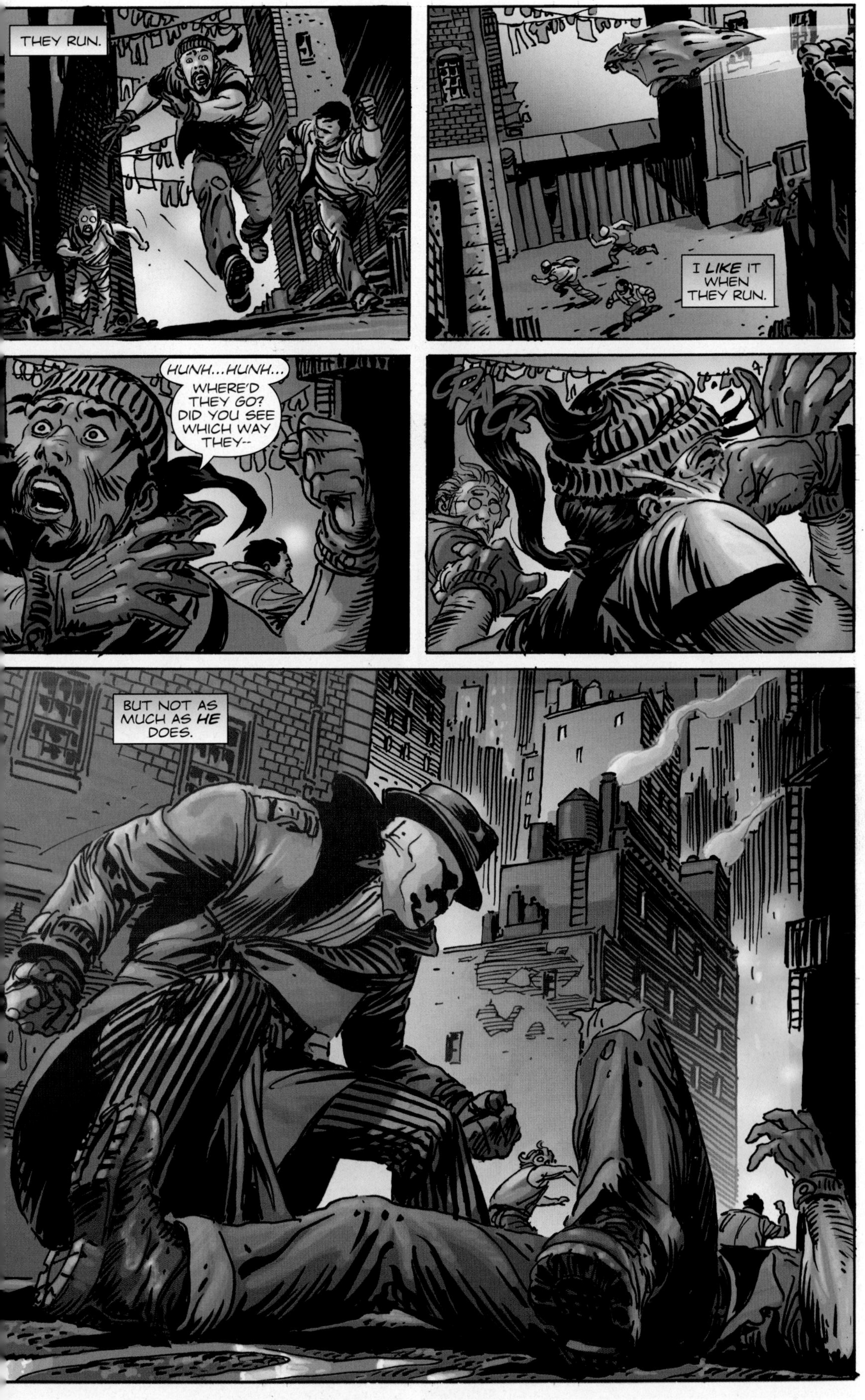
THEY RUN.
I LIKE IT WHEN THEY RUN.
HUNH...HUNH... WHERE'D THEY GO? DID YOU SEE WHICH WAY THEY--
CRACK
BUT NOT AS MUCH AS HE DOES.

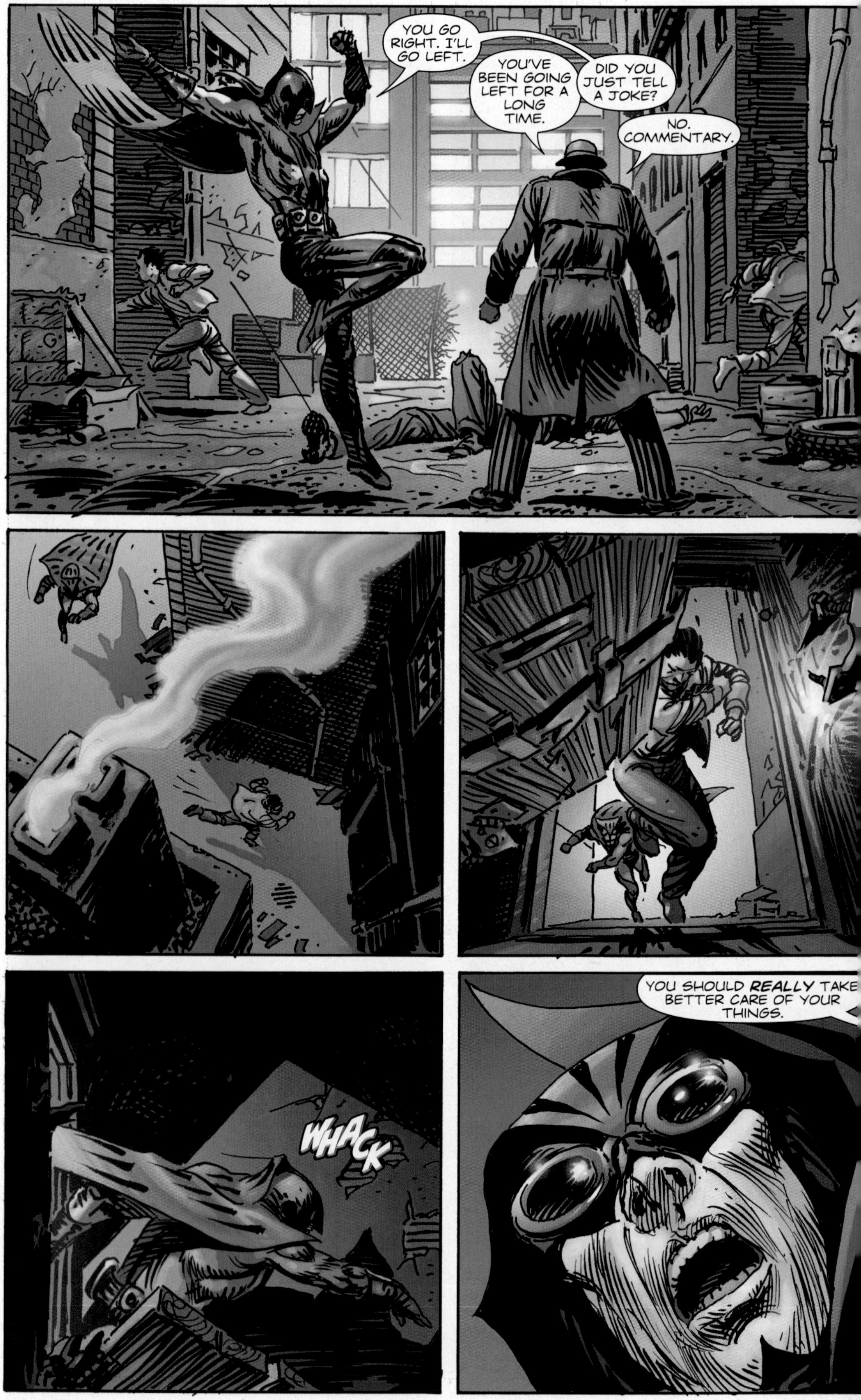
YOU GO RIGHT. I'LL GO LEFT.
YOU'VE BEEN GOING LEFT FOR A LONG TIME.
DID YOU JUST TELL A JOKE?
NO. COMMENTARY.
WHACK
YOU SHOULD REALLY TAKE BETTER CARE OF YOUR THINGS.

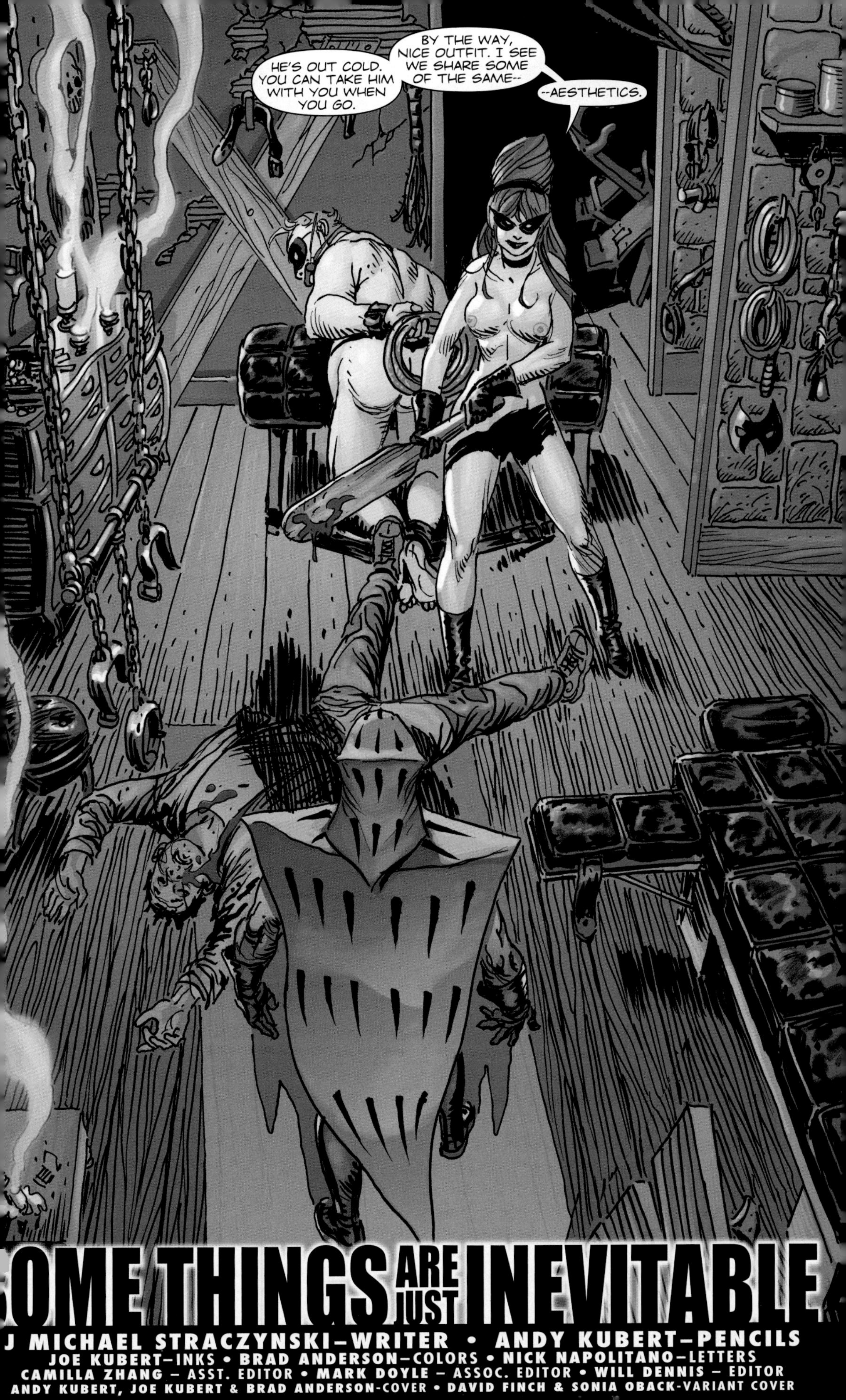
HE'S OUT COLD. YOU CAN TAKE HIM WITH YOU WHEN YOU GO.
BY THE WAY, NICE OUTFIT. I SEE WE SHARE SOME OF THE SAME--
--AESTHETICS.

OME THINGS ARE JUST INEVITABLE

J MICHAEL STRACZYNSKI–WRITER • ANDY KUBERT–PENCILS
JOE KUBERT–INKS • BRAD ANDERSON–COLORS • NICK NAPOLITANO–LETTERS
CAMILLA ZHANG – ASST. EDITOR • MARK DOYLE – ASSOC. EDITOR • WILL DENNIS – EDITOR
ANDY KUBERT, JOE KUBERT & BRAD ANDERSON-COVER • DAVID FINCH & SONIA OBACK-VARIANT COVER

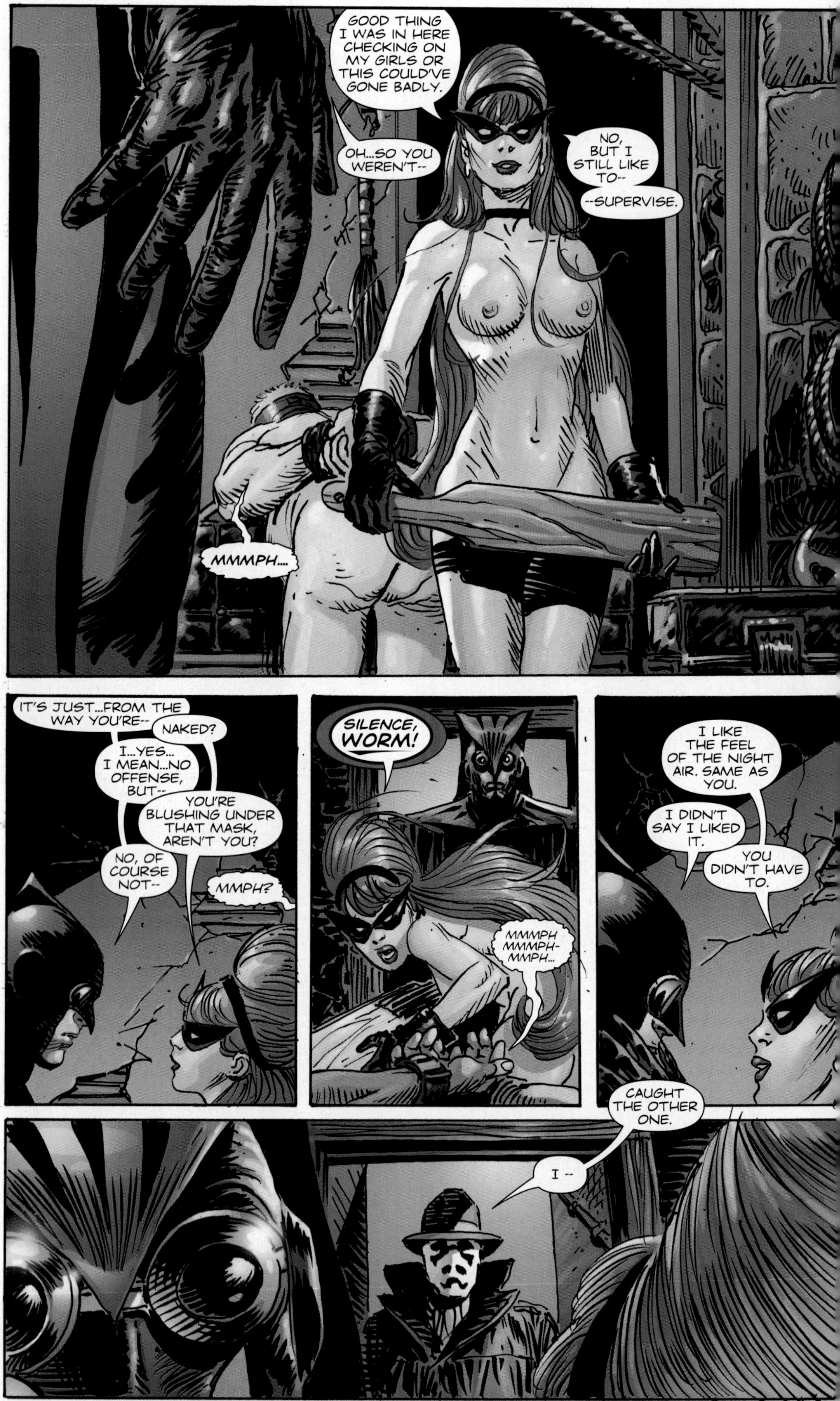

GOOD THING I WAS IN HERE CHECKING ON MY GIRLS OR THIS COULD'VE GONE BADLY.
OH...SO YOU WEREN'T--
NO, BUT I STILL LIKE TO--
--SUPERVISE.
MMMPH....
IT'S JUST...FROM THE WAY YOU'RE--
NAKED?
I...YES... I MEAN...NO OFFENSE, BUT--
YOU'RE BLUSHING UNDER THAT MASK, AREN'T YOU?
NO, OF COURSE NOT--
MMPH?
SILENCE, WORM!
MMMPH MMMPH-MMPH...
I LIKE THE FEEL OF THE NIGHT AIR. SAME AS YOU.
I DIDN'T SAY I LIKED IT.
YOU DIDN'T HAVE TO.
CAUGHT THE OTHER ONE.
I --

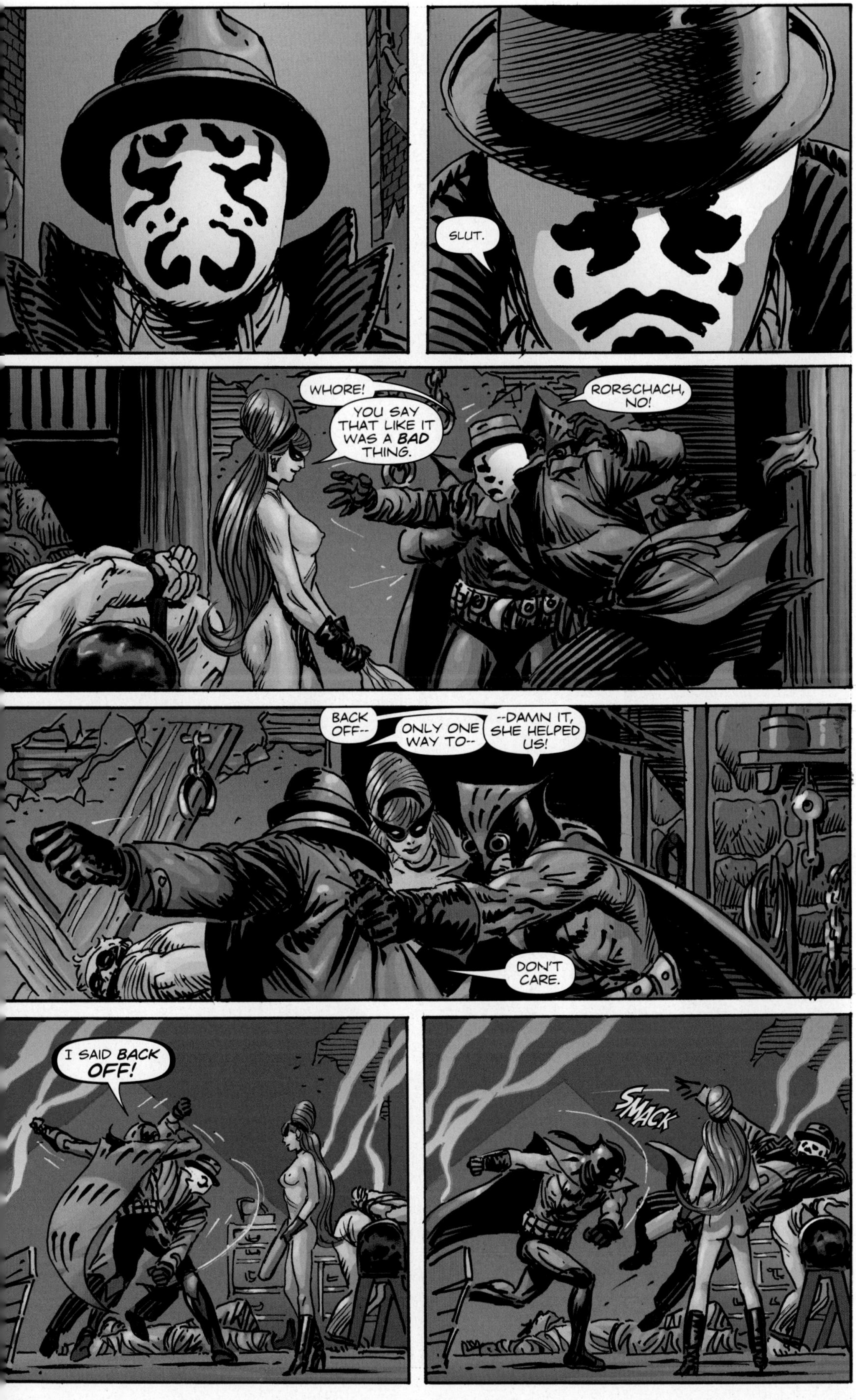
SLUT.
WHORE!
YOU SAY THAT LIKE IT WAS A BAD THING.
RORSCHACH, NO!
BACK OFF--
ONLY ONE WAY TO--
--DAMN IT, SHE HELPED US!
DON'T CARE.
I SAID BACK OFF!
SMACK

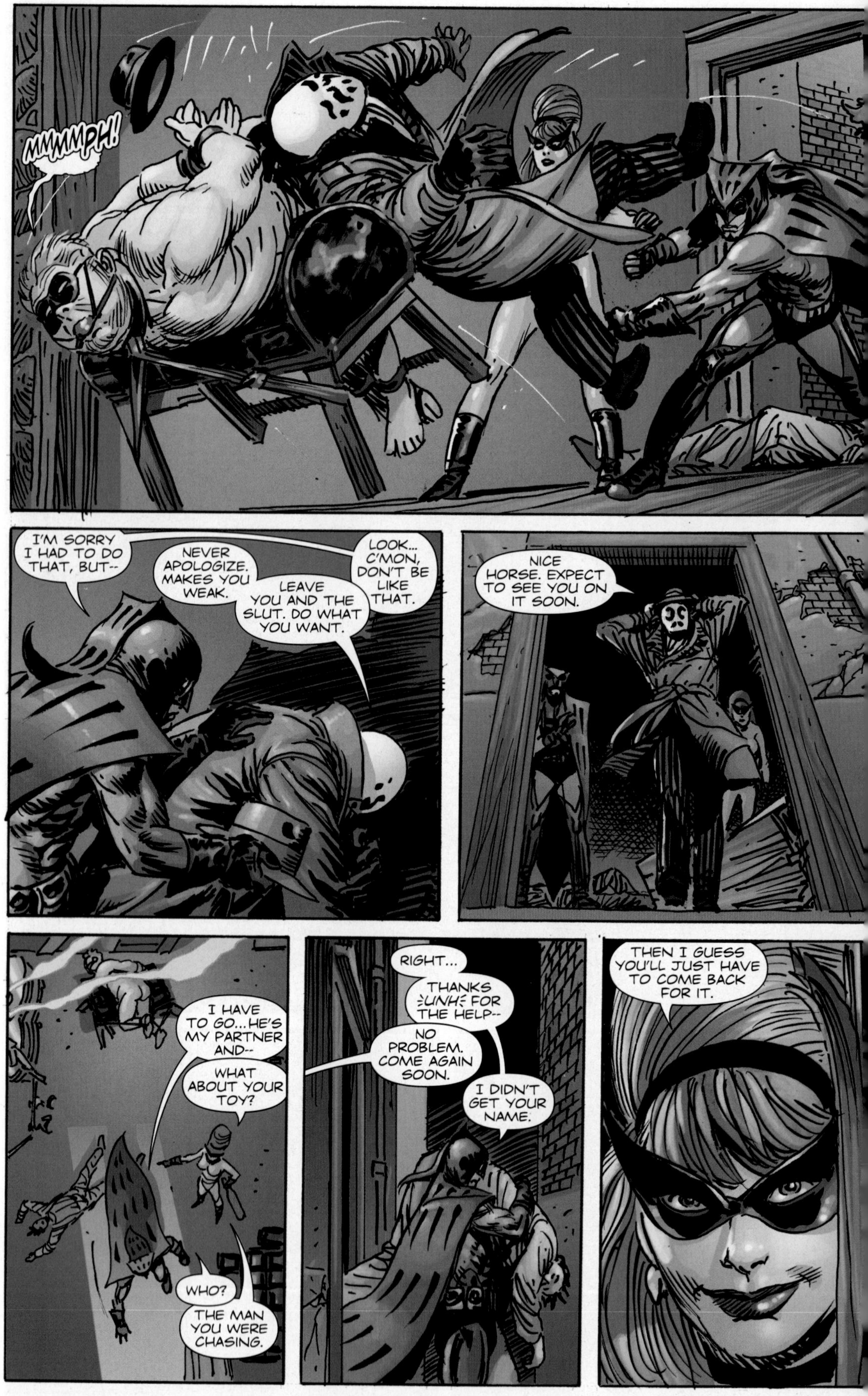
MMMMPH!
I'M SORRY I HAD TO DO THAT, BUT--
NEVER APOLOGIZE. MAKES YOU WEAK.
LEAVE YOU AND THE SLUT. DO WHAT YOU WANT.
LOOK... C'MON, DON'T BE LIKE THAT.
NICE HORSE. EXPECT TO SEE YOU ON IT SOON.
I HAVE TO GO...HE'S MY PARTNER AND--
WHAT ABOUT YOUR TOY?
WHO?
THE MAN YOU WERE CHASING.
RIGHT...
THANKS UNH FOR THE HELP--
NO PROBLEM. COME AGAIN SOON.
I DIDN'T GET YOUR NAME.
THEN I GUESS YOU'LL JUST HAVE TO COME BACK FOR IT.

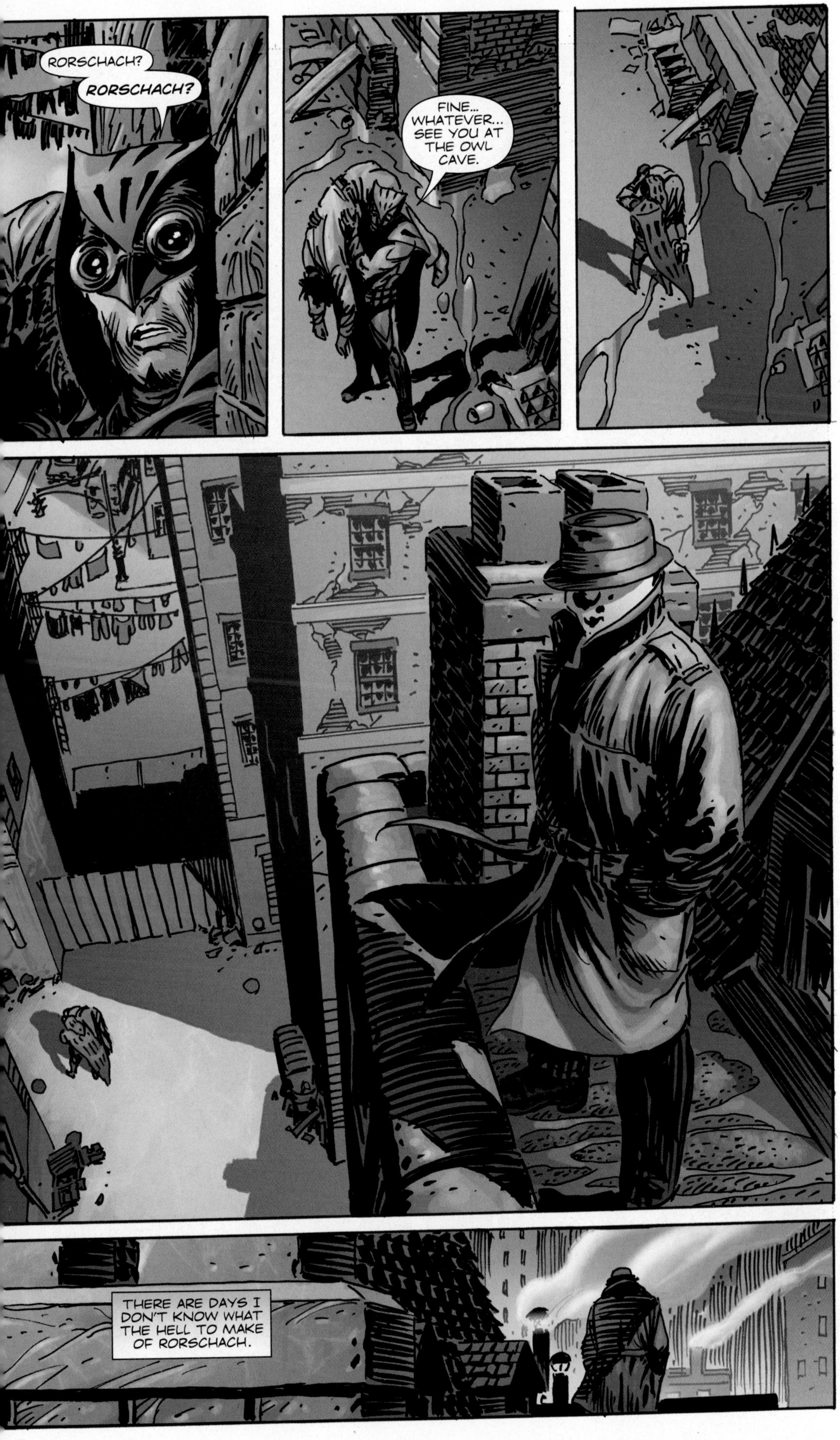
RORSCHACH?
RORSCHACH?
FINE... WHATEVER... SEE YOU AT THE OWL CAVE.
THERE ARE DAYS I DON'T KNOW WHAT THE HELL TO MAKE OF RORSCHACH.

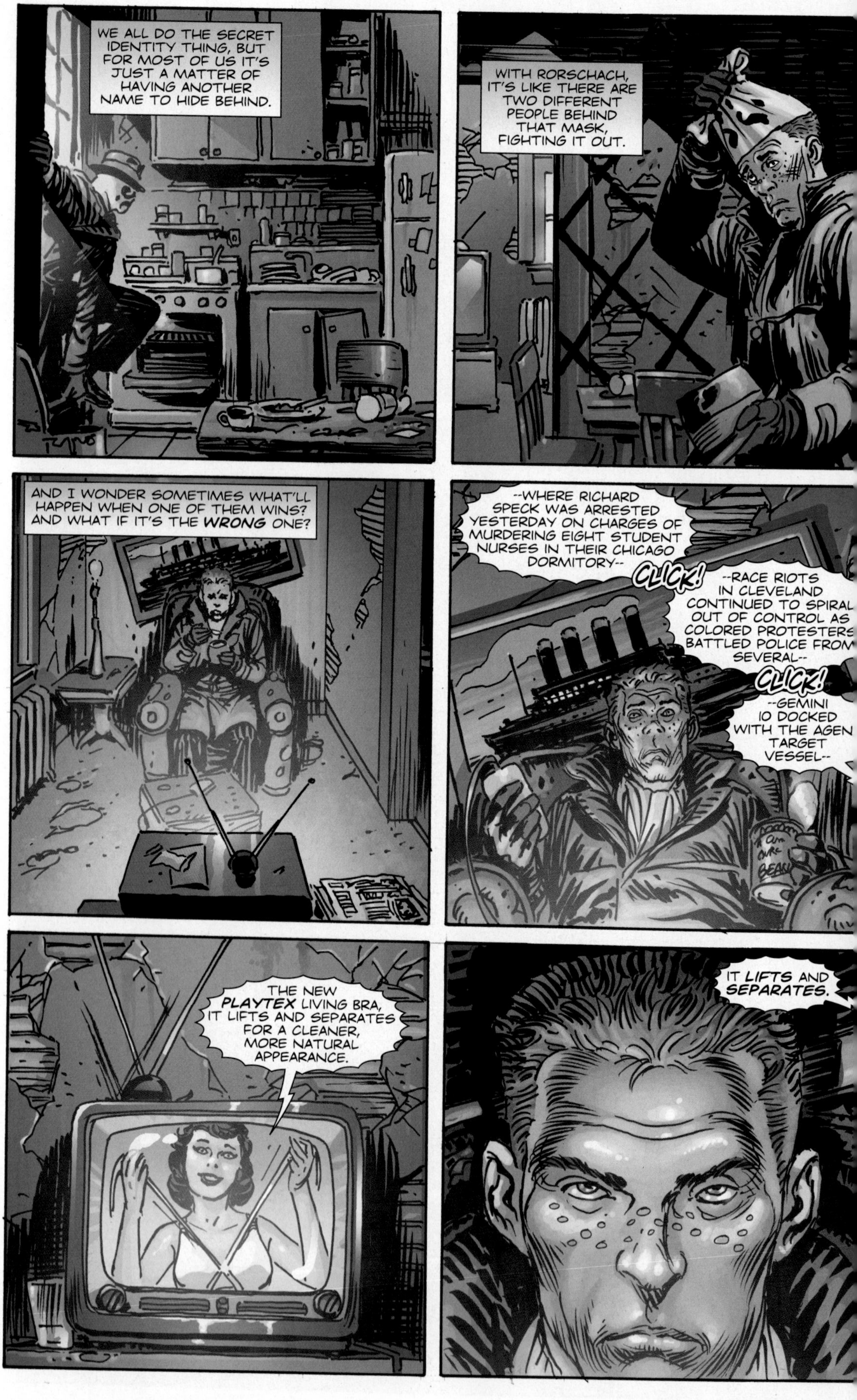
WE ALL DO THE SECRET IDENTITY THING, BUT FOR MOST OF US IT'S JUST A MATTER OF HAVING ANOTHER NAME TO HIDE BEHIND.
WITH RORSCHACH, IT'S LIKE THERE ARE TWO DIFFERENT PEOPLE BEHIND THAT MASK, FIGHTING IT OUT.
AND I WONDER SOMETIMES WHAT'LL HAPPEN WHEN ONE OF THEM WINS? AND WHAT IF IT'S THE WRONG ONE?
--WHERE RICHARD SPECK WAS ARRESTED YESTERDAY ON CHARGES OF MURDERING EIGHT STUDENT NURSES IN THEIR CHICAGO DORMITORY--
CLICK!
--RACE RIOTS IN CLEVELAND CONTINUED TO SPIRAL OUT OF CONTROL AS COLORED PROTESTERS BATTLED POLICE FROM SEVERAL--
CLICK!
--GEMINI 10 DOCKED WITH THE AGEN TARGET VESSEL--
THE NEW PLAYTEX LIVING BRA, IT LIFTS AND SEPARATES FOR A CLEANER, MORE NATURAL APPEARANCE.
IT LIFTS AND SEPARATES.

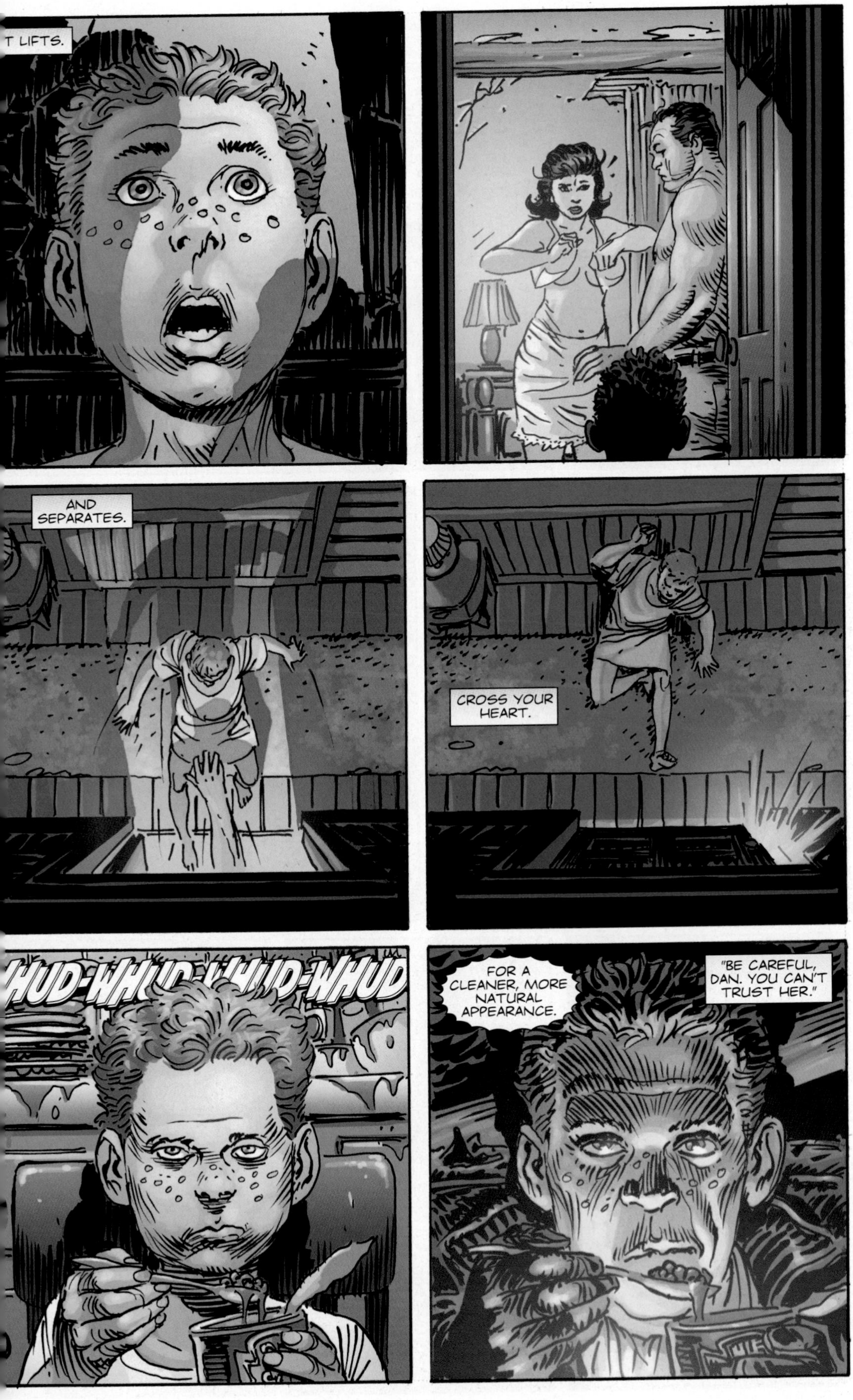
T LIFTS.
AND SEPARATES.
CROSS YOUR HEART.
HUD-WHUD-WHUD-WHUD
FOR A CLEANER, MORE NATURAL APPEARANCE.
"BE CAREFUL, DAN. YOU CAN'T TRUST HER."

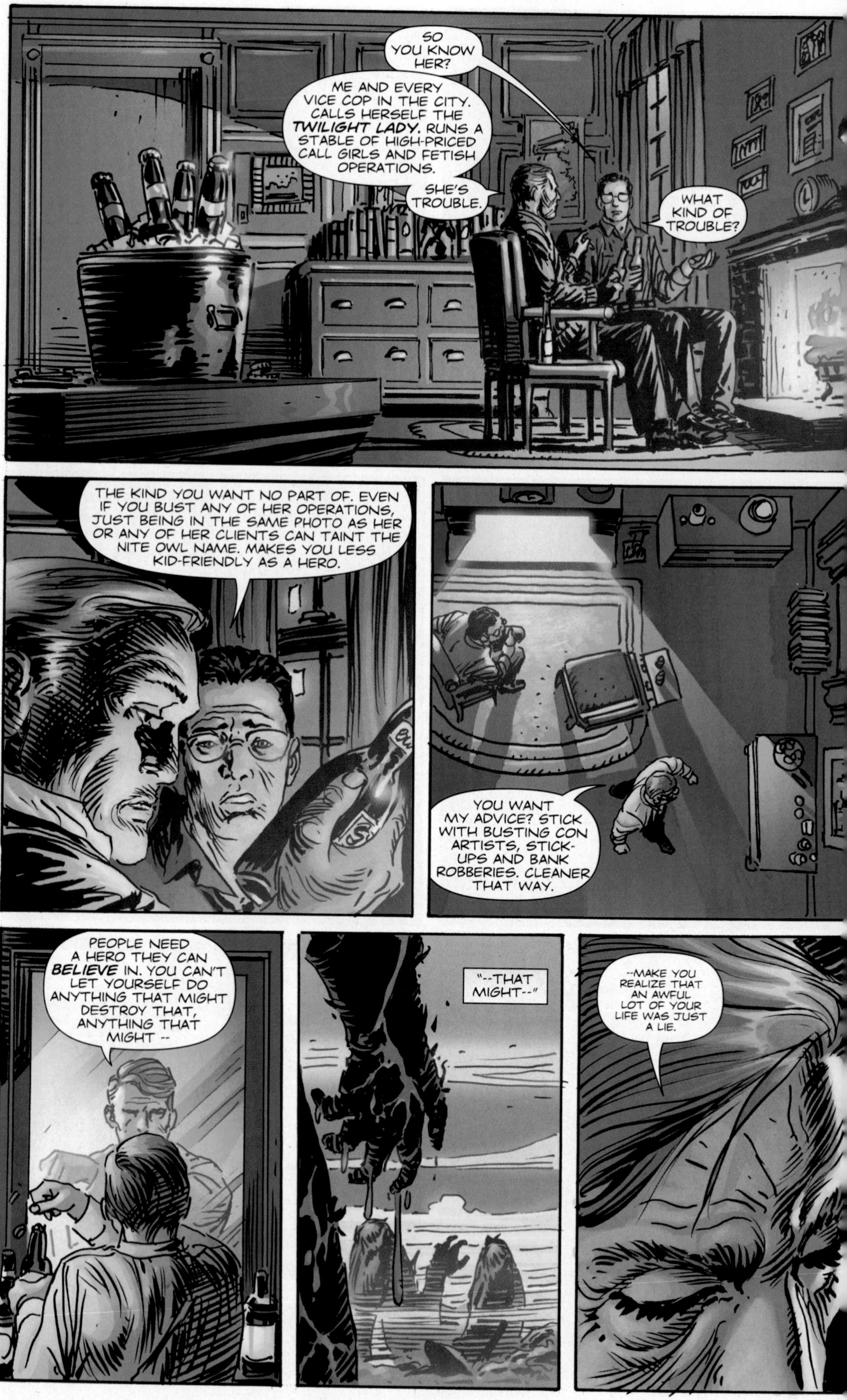
SO YOU KNOW HER?
ME AND EVERY VICE COP IN THE CITY. CALLS HERSELF THE TWILIGHT LADY. RUNS A STABLE OF HIGH-PRICED CALL GIRLS AND FETISH OPERATIONS.
SHE'S TROUBLE.
WHAT KIND OF TROUBLE?
THE KIND YOU WANT NO PART OF. EVEN IF YOU BUST ANY OF HER OPERATIONS, JUST BEING IN THE SAME PHOTO AS HER OR ANY OF HER CLIENTS CAN TAINT THE NITE OWL NAME. MAKES YOU LESS KID-FRIENDLY AS A HERO.
YOU WANT MY ADVICE? STICK WITH BUSTING CON ARTISTS, STICK-UPS AND BANK ROBBERIES. CLEANER THAT WAY.
PEOPLE NEED A HERO THEY CAN BELIEVE IN. YOU CAN'T LET YOURSELF DO ANYTHING THAT MIGHT DESTROY THAT, ANYTHING THAT MIGHT --
"--THAT MIGHT--"
--MAKE YOU REALIZE THAT AN AWFUL LOT OF YOUR LIFE WAS JUST A LIE.

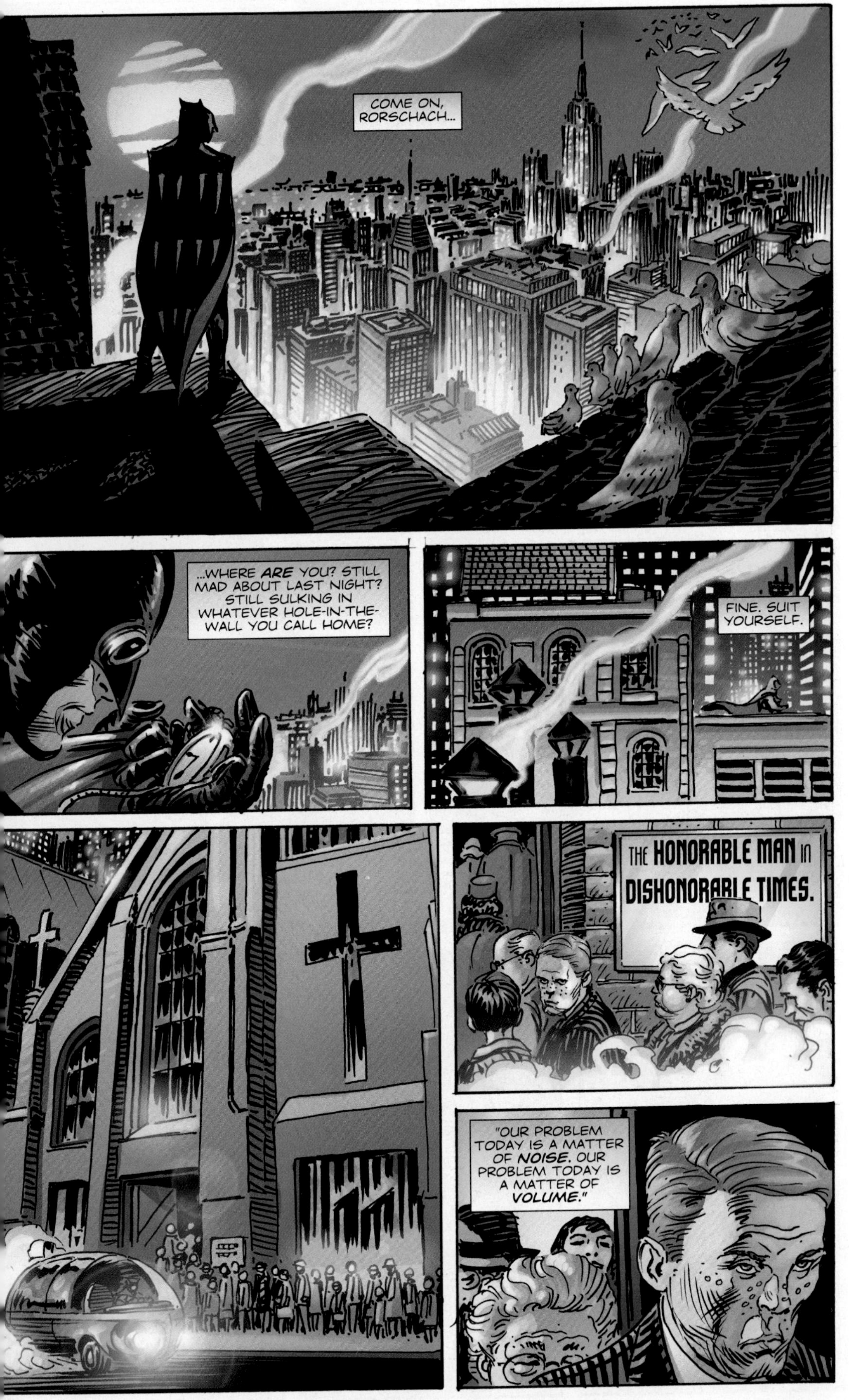
COME ON, RORSCHACH...
...WHERE *ARE* YOU? STILL MAD ABOUT LAST NIGHT? STILL SULKING IN WHATEVER HOLE-IN-THE-WALL YOU CALL HOME?
FINE. SUIT YOURSELF.
THE HONORABLE MAN IN DISHONORABLE TIMES.
"OUR PROBLEM TODAY IS A MATTER OF *NOISE*. OUR PROBLEM TODAY IS A MATTER OF *VOLUME*."

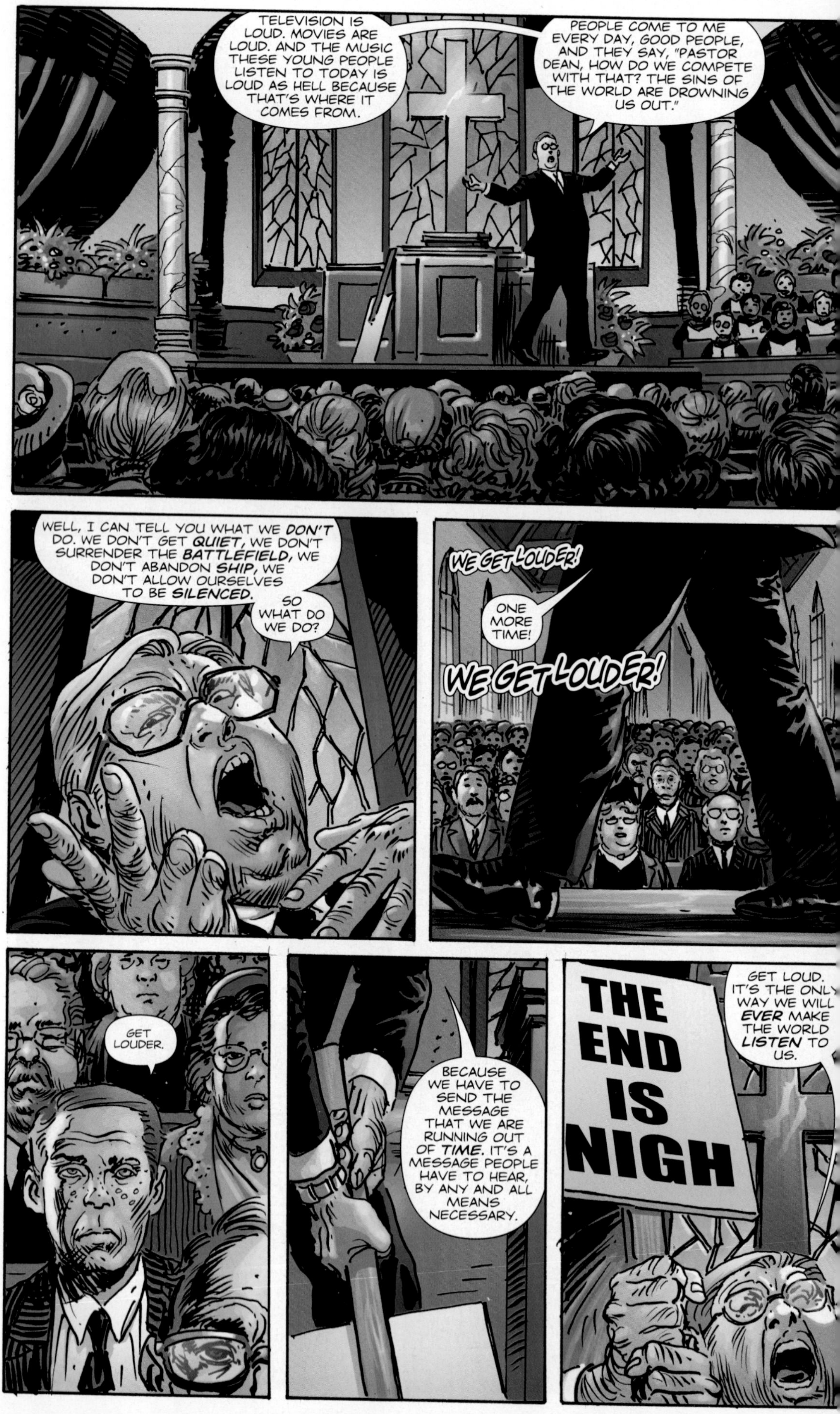

TELEVISION IS LOUD. MOVIES ARE LOUD. AND THE MUSIC THESE YOUNG PEOPLE LISTEN TO TODAY IS LOUD AS HELL BECAUSE THAT'S WHERE IT COMES FROM.
PEOPLE COME TO ME EVERY DAY, GOOD PEOPLE, AND THEY SAY, "PASTOR DEAN, HOW DO WE COMPETE WITH THAT? THE SINS OF THE WORLD ARE DROWNING US OUT."
WELL, I CAN TELL YOU WHAT WE DON'T DO. WE DON'T GET QUIET, WE DON'T SURRENDER THE BATTLEFIELD, WE DON'T ABANDON SHIP, WE DON'T ALLOW OURSELVES TO BE SILENCED.
SO WHAT DO WE DO?
WE GET LOUDER!
ONE MORE TIME!
WE GET LOUDER!
GET LOUDER.
BECAUSE WE HAVE TO SEND THE MESSAGE THAT WE ARE RUNNING OUT OF TIME. IT'S A MESSAGE PEOPLE HAVE TO HEAR, BY ANY AND ALL MEANS NECESSARY.
THE END IS NIGH
GET LOUD. IT'S THE ONLY WAY WE WILL EVER MAKE THE WORLD LISTEN TO US.

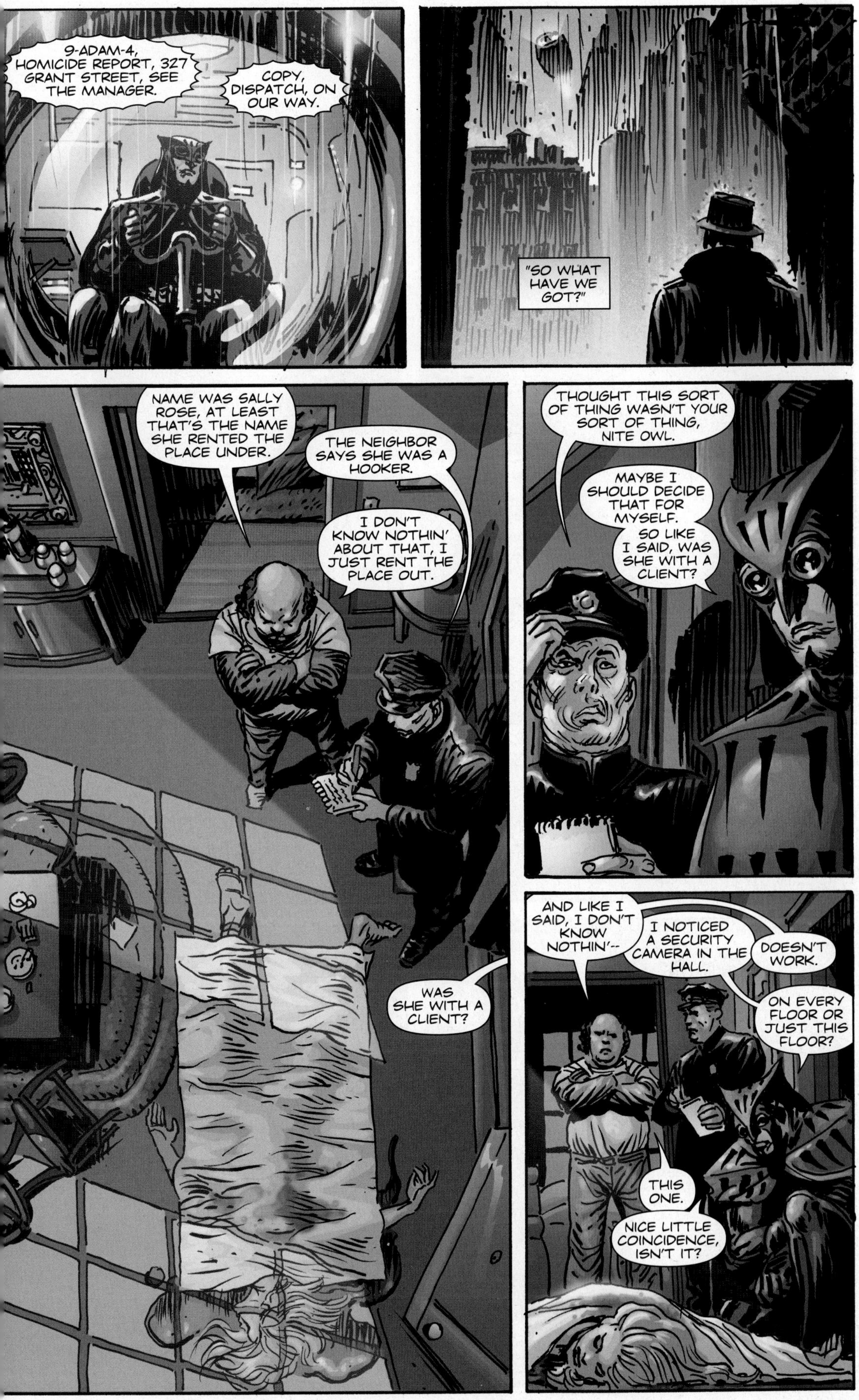
9-ADAM-4, HOMICIDE REPORT, 327 GRANT STREET, SEE THE MANAGER.
COPY, DISPATCH, ON OUR WAY.
"SO WHAT HAVE WE GOT?"
NAME WAS SALLY ROSE, AT LEAST THAT'S THE NAME SHE RENTED THE PLACE UNDER.
THE NEIGHBOR SAYS SHE WAS A HOOKER.
I DON'T KNOW NOTHIN' ABOUT THAT, I JUST RENT THE PLACE OUT.
WAS SHE WITH A CLIENT?
THOUGHT THIS SORT OF THING WASN'T YOUR SORT OF THING, NITE OWL.
MAYBE I SHOULD DECIDE THAT FOR MYSELF.
SO LIKE I SAID, WAS SHE WITH A CLIENT?
AND LIKE I SAID, I DON'T KNOW NOTHIN'--
I NOTICED A SECURITY CAMERA IN THE HALL.
DOESN'T WORK.
ON EVERY FLOOR OR JUST THIS FLOOR?
THIS ONE.
NICE LITTLE COINCIDENCE, ISN'T IT?

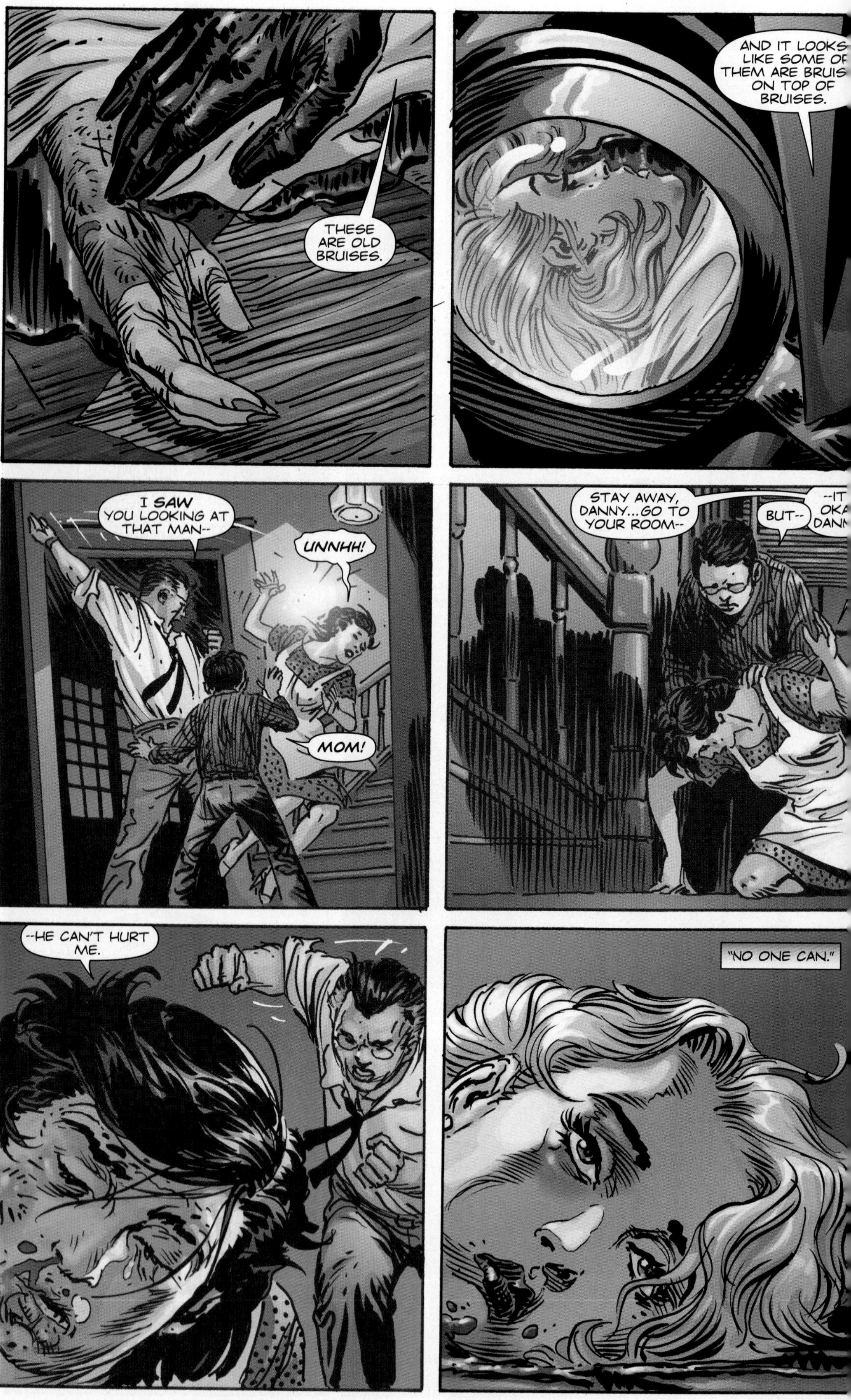
THESE ARE OLD BRUISES.
AND IT LOOKS LIKE SOME OF THEM ARE BRUIS ON TOP OF BRUISES.
I SAW YOU LOOKING AT THAT MAN--
UNNHH!
MOM!
STAY AWAY, DANNY...GO TO YOUR ROOM--
BUT--
--HE CAN'T HURT ME.
"NO ONE CAN."

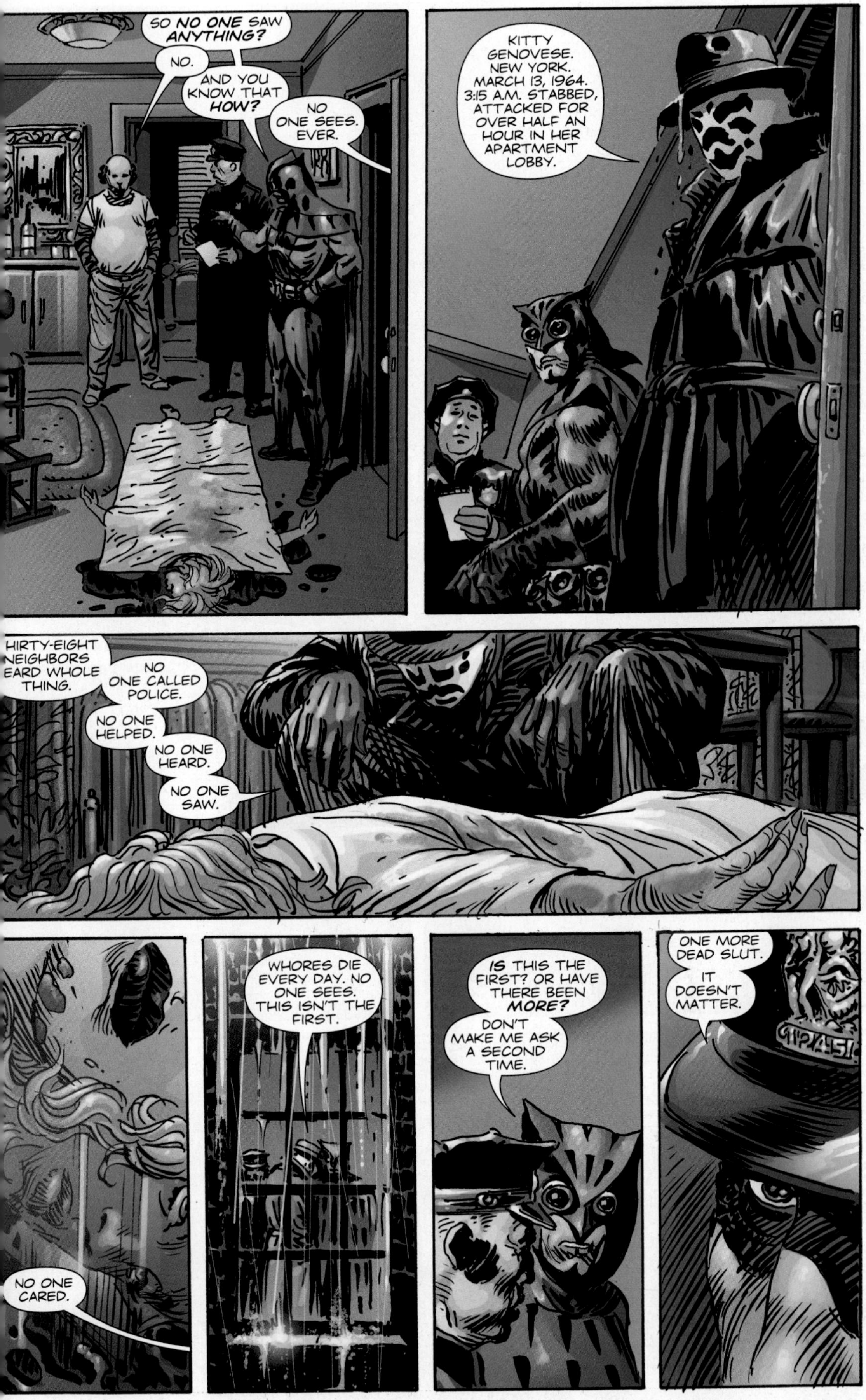
SO NO ONE SAW ANYTHING?
NO.
AND YOU KNOW THAT HOW?
NO ONE SEES. EVER.
KITTY GENOVESE. NEW YORK. MARCH 13, 1964. 3:15 A.M. STABBED, ATTACKED FOR OVER HALF AN HOUR IN HER APARTMENT LOBBY.
HIRTY-EIGHT NEIGHBORS EARD WHOLE THING.
NO ONE CALLED POLICE.
NO ONE HELPED.
NO ONE HEARD.
NO ONE SAW.
NO ONE CARED.
WHORES DIE EVERY DAY. NO ONE SEES. THIS ISN'T THE FIRST.
IS THIS THE FIRST? OR HAVE THERE BEEN MORE?
DON'T MAKE ME ASK A SECOND TIME.
ONE MORE DEAD SLUT.
IT DOESN'T MATTER.

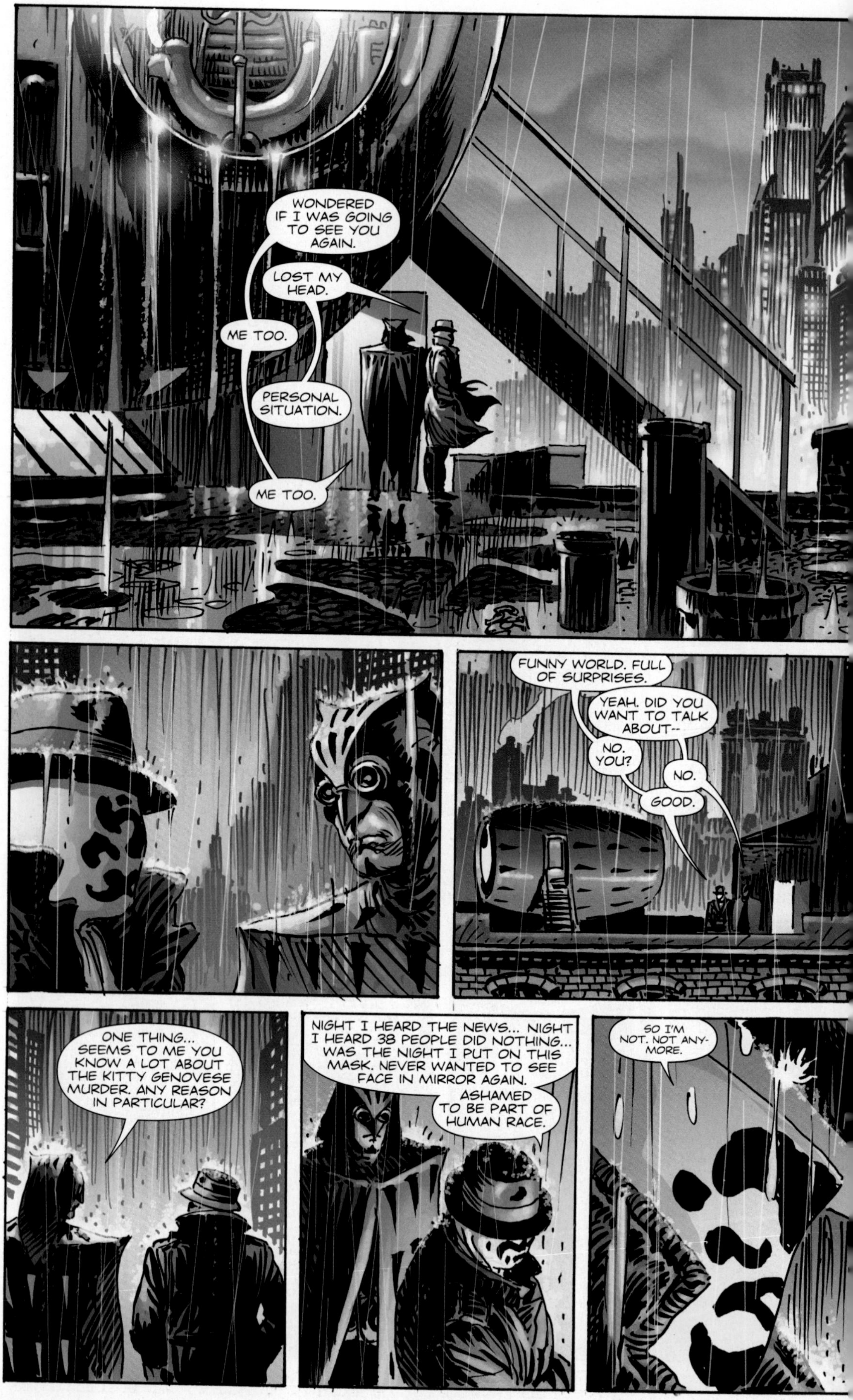
WONDERED IF I WAS GOING TO SEE YOU AGAIN.
LOST MY HEAD.
ME TOO.
PERSONAL SITUATION.
ME TOO.
FUNNY WORLD. FULL OF SURPRISES.
YEAH. DID YOU WANT TO TALK ABOUT--
NO. YOU?
NO.
GOOD.
ONE THING... SEEMS TO ME YOU KNOW A LOT ABOUT THE KITTY GENOVESE MURDER. ANY REASON IN PARTICULAR?
NIGHT I HEARD THE NEWS... NIGHT I HEARD 38 PEOPLE DID NOTHING... WAS THE NIGHT I PUT ON THIS MASK. NEVER WANTED TO SEE FACE IN MIRROR AGAIN.
ASHAMED TO BE PART OF HUMAN RACE.
SO I'M NOT. NOT ANY-MORE.

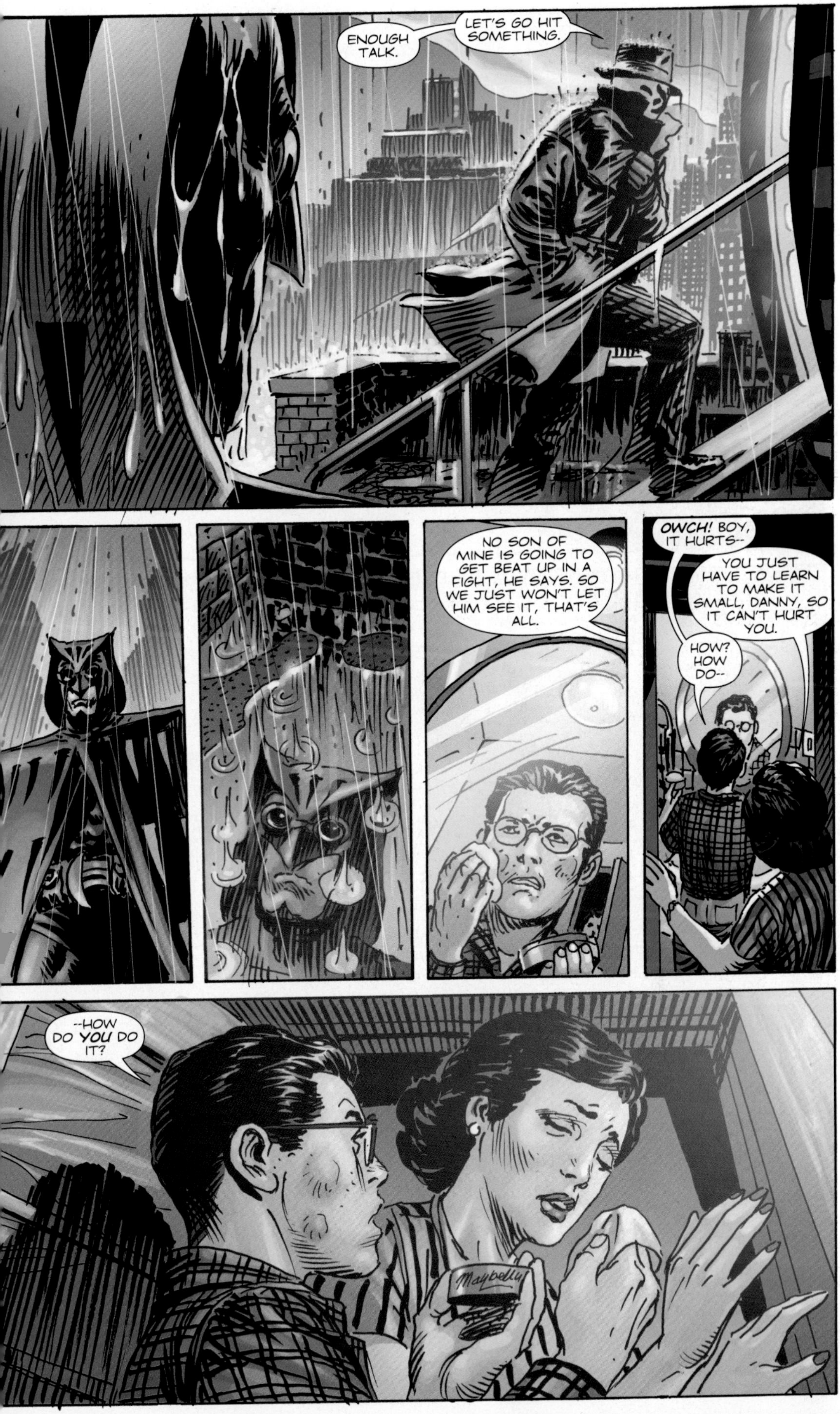
ENOUGH TALK.
LET'S GO HIT SOMETHING.
NO SON OF MINE IS GOING TO GET BEAT UP IN A FIGHT, HE SAYS. SO WE JUST WON'T LET HIM SEE IT, THAT'S ALL.
OWCH! BOY, IT HURTS--
YOU JUST HAVE TO LEARN TO MAKE IT SMALL, DANNY, SO IT CAN'T HURT YOU.
HOW? HOW DO--
--HOW DO YOU DO IT?
Maybelline

YOU HAVE TO FIND A PLACE DEEP INSIDE WHERE NOBODY CAN TOUCH YOU OR HURT YOU. IT CAN BE SOMETHING YOU REMEMBER, SOMETHING HAPPY--

--SOMETHING THAT MAKES YOU ANGRY--

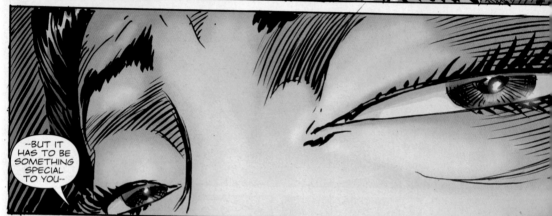

--BUT IT HAS TO BE SOMETHING SPECIAL TO YOU--

"--THAT YOU CAN PUT BETWEEN YOURSELF AND THE *DRAGON*."

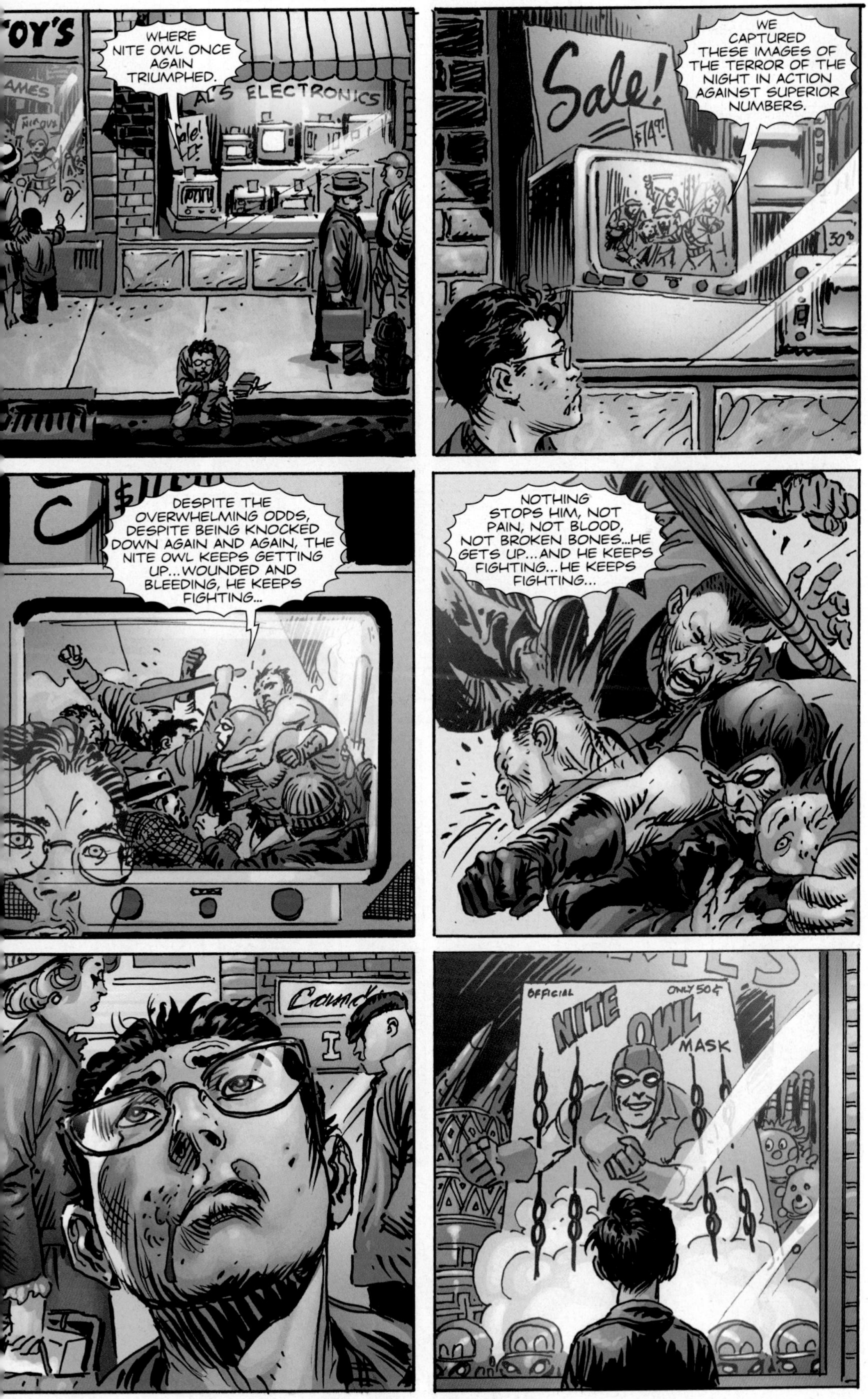

OY'S
AMES
WHERE NITE OWL ONCE AGAIN TRIUMPHED.
AL'S ELECTRONICS
Sale!
WE CAPTURED THESE IMAGES OF THE TERROR OF THE NIGHT IN ACTION AGAINST SUPERIOR NUMBERS.
$74.97
DESPITE THE OVERWHELMING ODDS, DESPITE BEING KNOCKED DOWN AGAIN AND AGAIN, THE NITE OWL KEEPS GETTING UP...WOUNDED AND BLEEDING, HE KEEPS FIGHTING...
NOTHING STOPS HIM, NOT PAIN, NOT BLOOD, NOT BROKEN BONES...HE GETS UP...AND HE KEEPS FIGHTING...HE KEEPS FIGHTING...
OFFICIAL
ONLY 50¢
NITE OWL
MASK

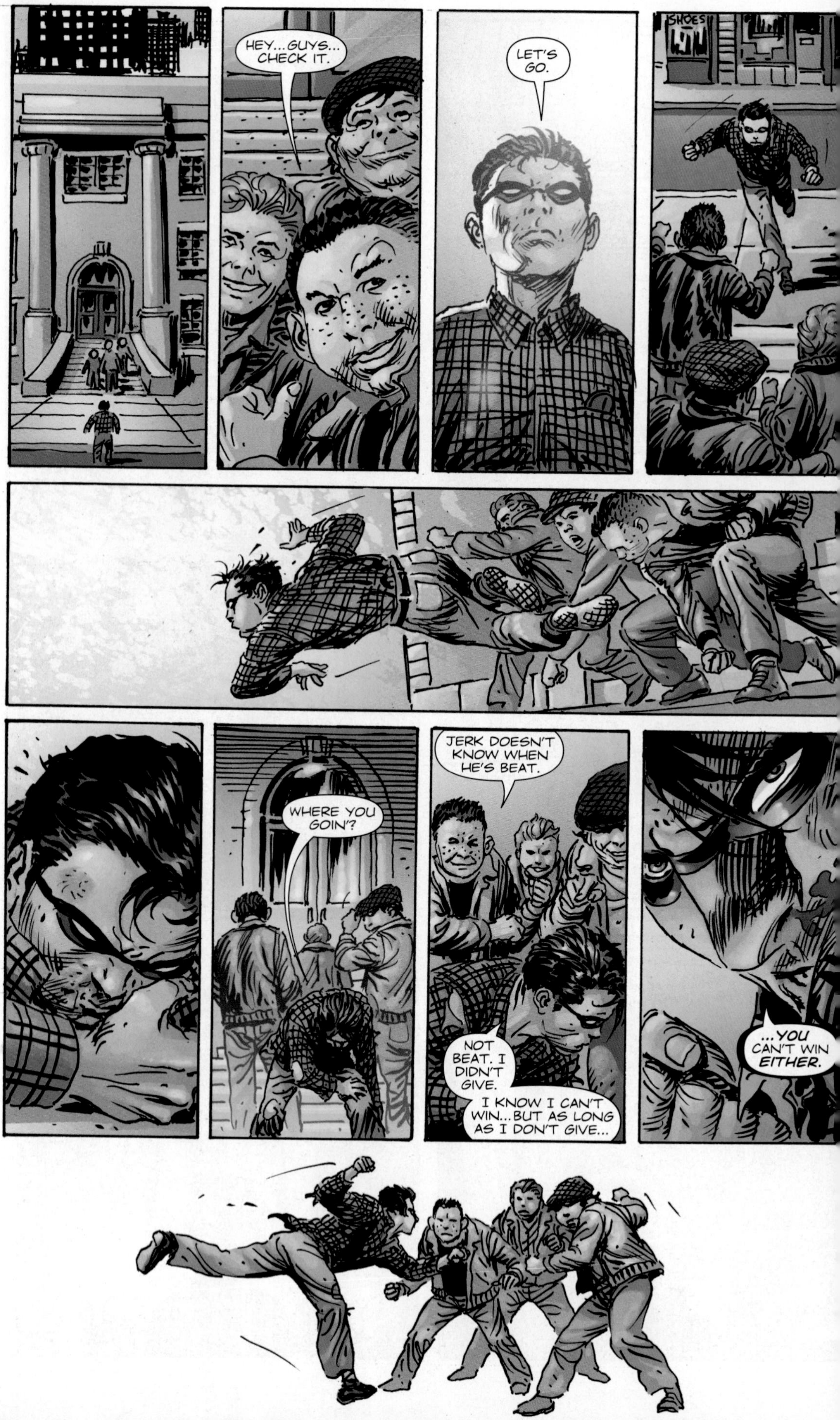
HEY...GUYS...
CHECK IT.
LET'S
GO.
WHERE YOU
GOIN'?
JERK DOESN'T
KNOW WHEN
HE'S BEAT.
NOT
BEAT. I
DIDN'T
GIVE.
I KNOW I CAN'T
WIN...BUT AS LONG
AS I DON'T GIVE...
...YOU
CAN'T WIN
EITHER.

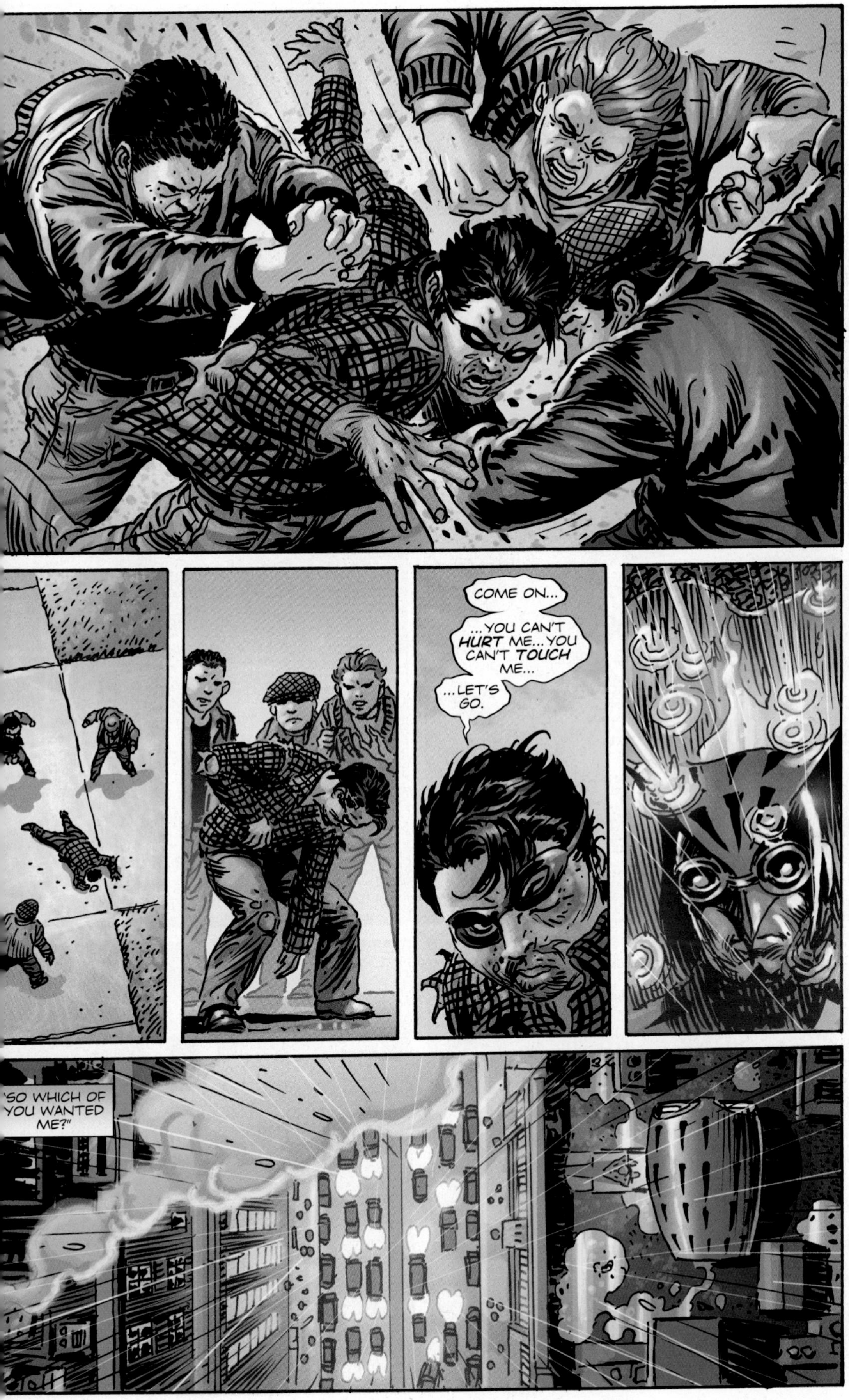
COME ON...
...YOU CAN'T HURT ME...YOU CAN'T TOUCH ME...
...LET'S GO.
"SO WHICH OF YOU WANTED ME?"

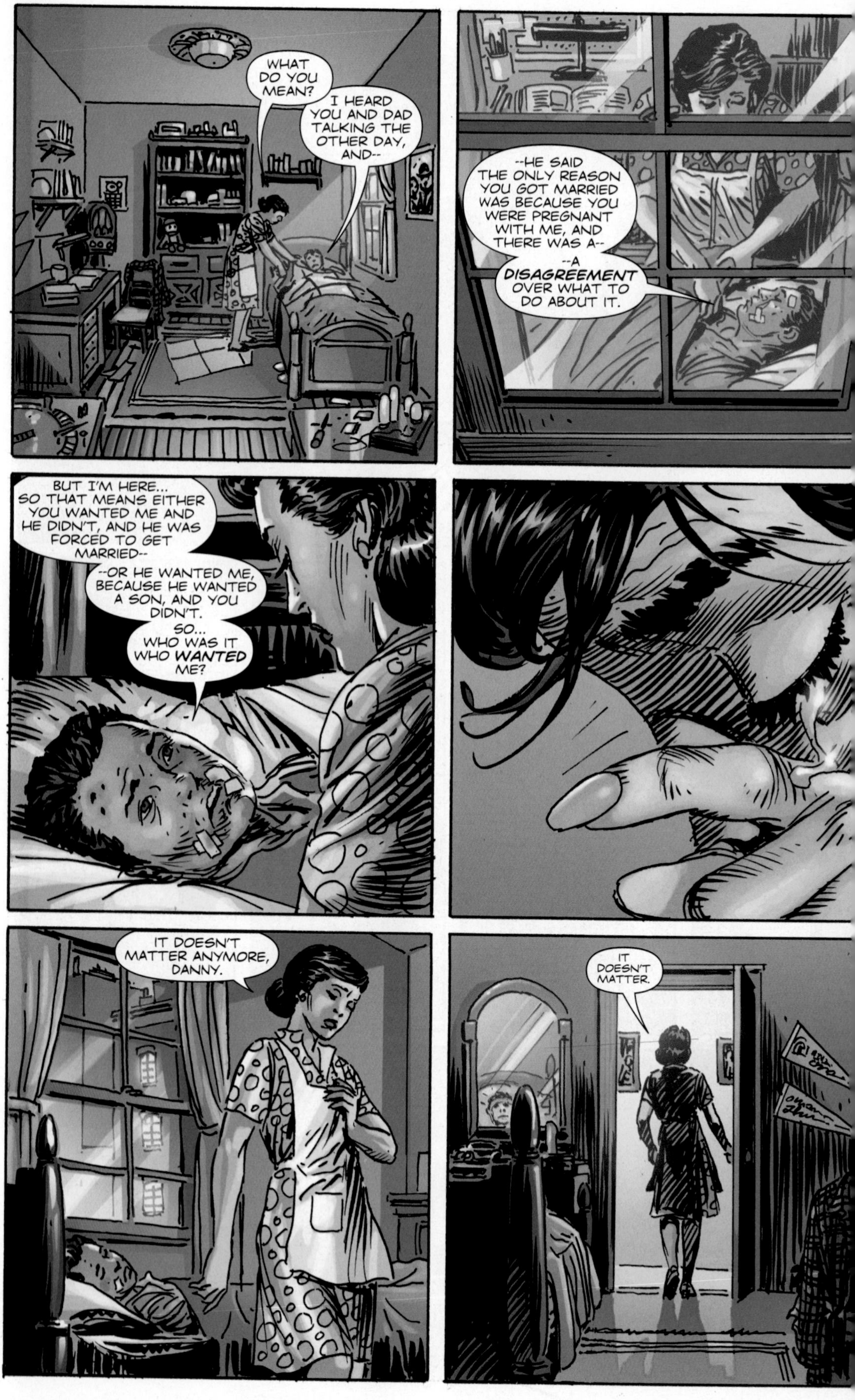
WHAT DO YOU MEAN?
I HEARD YOU AND DAD TALKING THE OTHER DAY, AND--
--HE SAID THE ONLY REASON YOU GOT MARRIED WAS BECAUSE YOU WERE PREGNANT WITH ME, AND THERE WAS A--
--A *DISAGREEMENT* OVER WHAT TO DO ABOUT IT.
BUT I'M HERE... SO THAT MEANS EITHER YOU WANTED ME AND HE DIDN'T, AND HE WAS FORCED TO GET MARRIED--
--OR HE WANTED ME, BECAUSE HE WANTED A SON, AND YOU DIDN'T.
SO... WHO WAS IT WHO *WANTED* ME?
IT DOESN'T MATTER ANYMORE, DANNY.
IT DOESN'T MATTER.

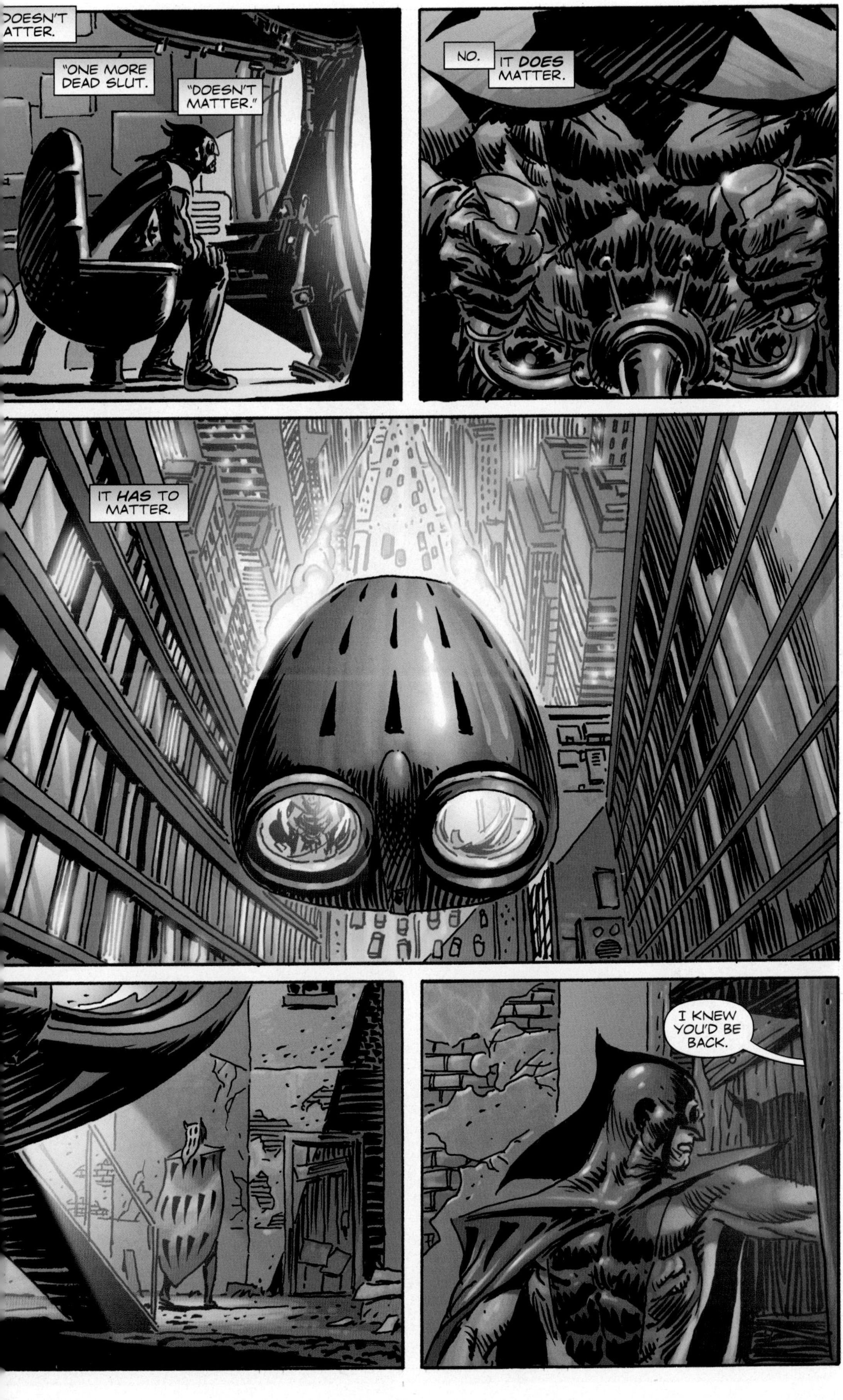
DOESN'T MATTER.
"ONE MORE DEAD SLUT.
"DOESN'T MATTER."
NO.
IT DOES MATTER.
IT HAS TO MATTER.
I KNEW YOU'D BE BACK.

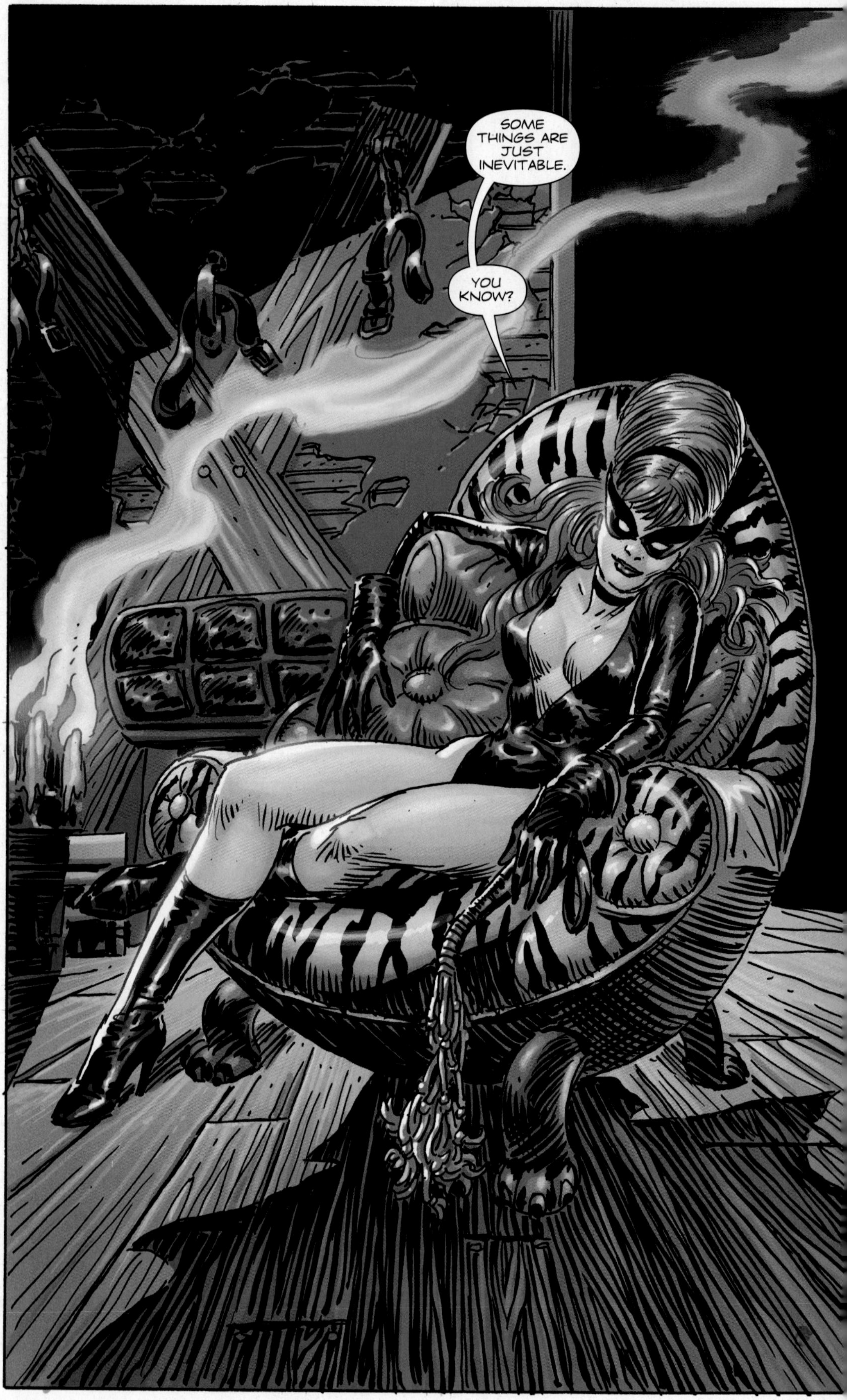
SOME THINGS ARE JUST INEVITABLE.
YOU KNOW?

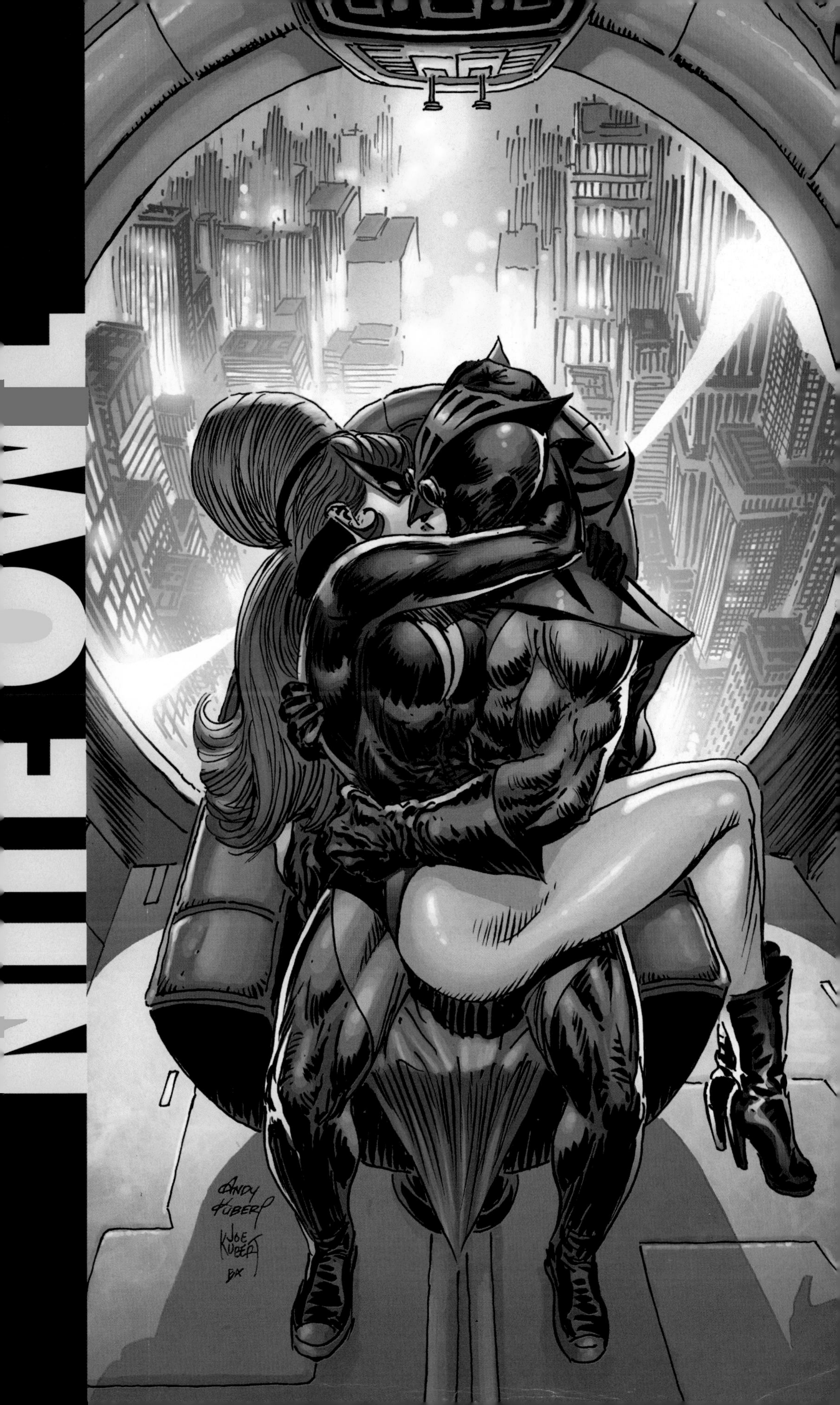
NITE OWL
ANDY KUBERT
JOE KUBERT
BIX

NITE OWL

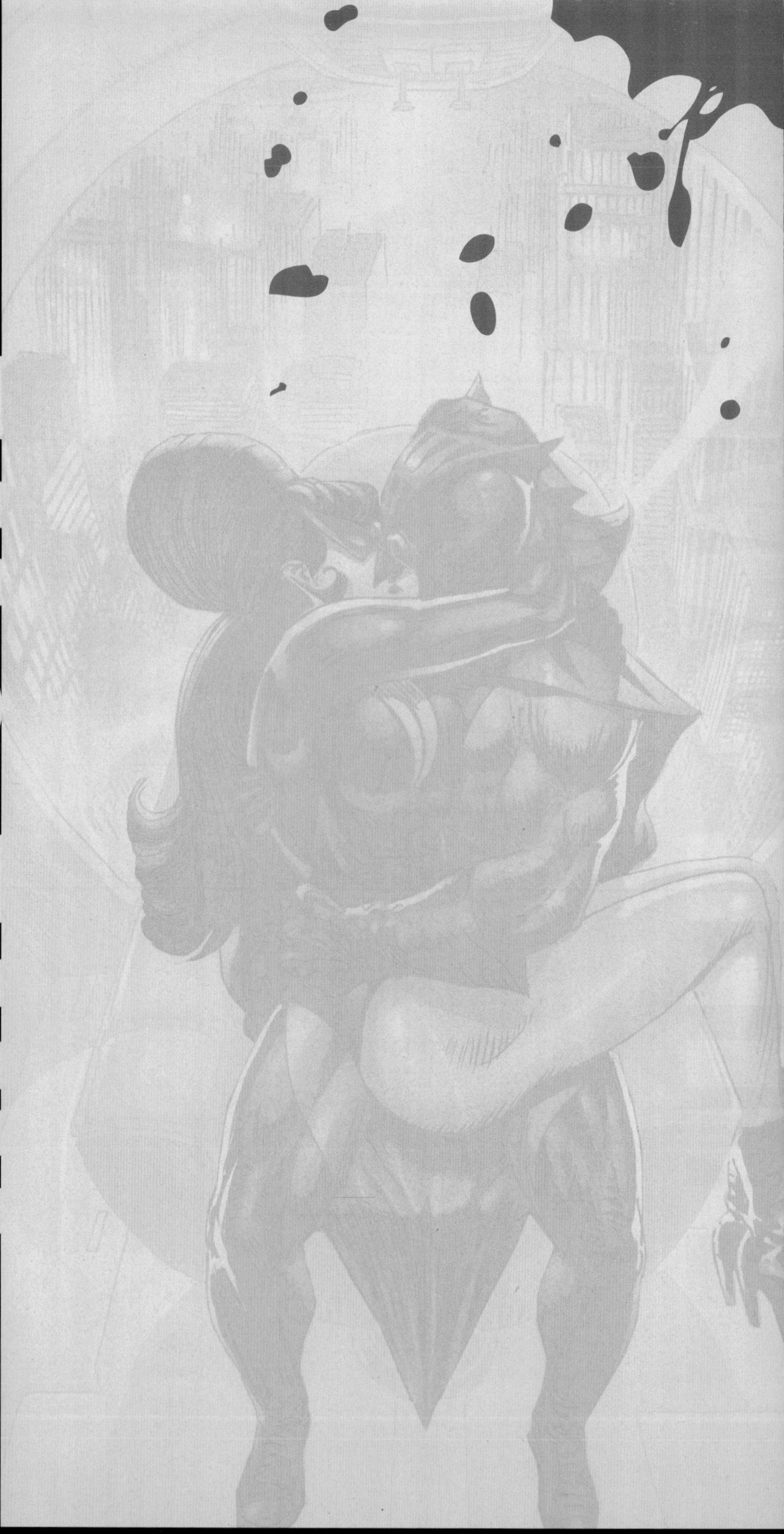

"A MAN LIKE YOU LOVES A MYSTERY."

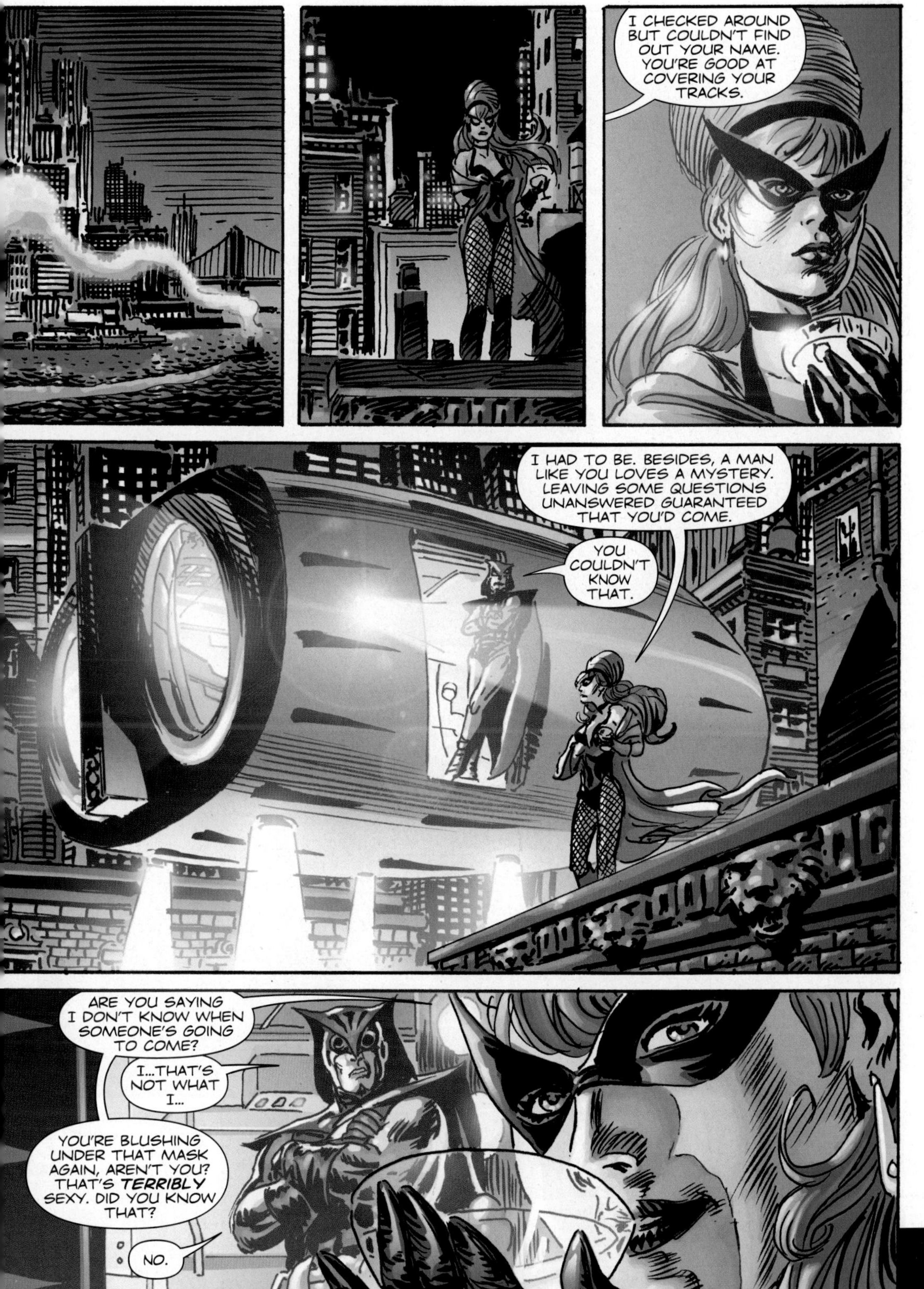
I CHECKED AROUND BUT COULDN'T FIND OUT YOUR NAME. YOU'RE GOOD AT COVERING YOUR TRACKS.
I HAD TO BE. BESIDES, A MAN LIKE YOU LOVES A MYSTERY. LEAVING SOME QUESTIONS UNANSWERED GUARANTEED THAT YOU'D COME.
YOU COULDN'T KNOW THAT.
ARE YOU SAYING I DON'T KNOW WHEN SOMEONE'S GOING TO COME?
I...THAT'S NOT WHAT I...
YOU'RE BLUSHING UNDER THAT MASK AGAIN, AREN'T YOU? THAT'S *TERRIBLY* SEXY. DID YOU KNOW THAT?
NO.

THANKS FOR COMING

MICHAEL STRACZYNSKI–WRITER • ANDY KUBERT–PENCILS
JOE KUBERT & BILL SIENKIEWICZ–INKS • BRAD ANDERSON–COLORS • NICK NAPOLITANO–LETTERS
CAMILLA ZHANG – ASST. EDITOR • MARK DOYLE – ASSOC. EDITOR • WILL DENNIS – EDITOR
ANDY KUBERT, JOE KUBERT & BRAD ANDERSON-COVER • CHRIS SAMNEE & MATT WILSON-VARIANT COVER

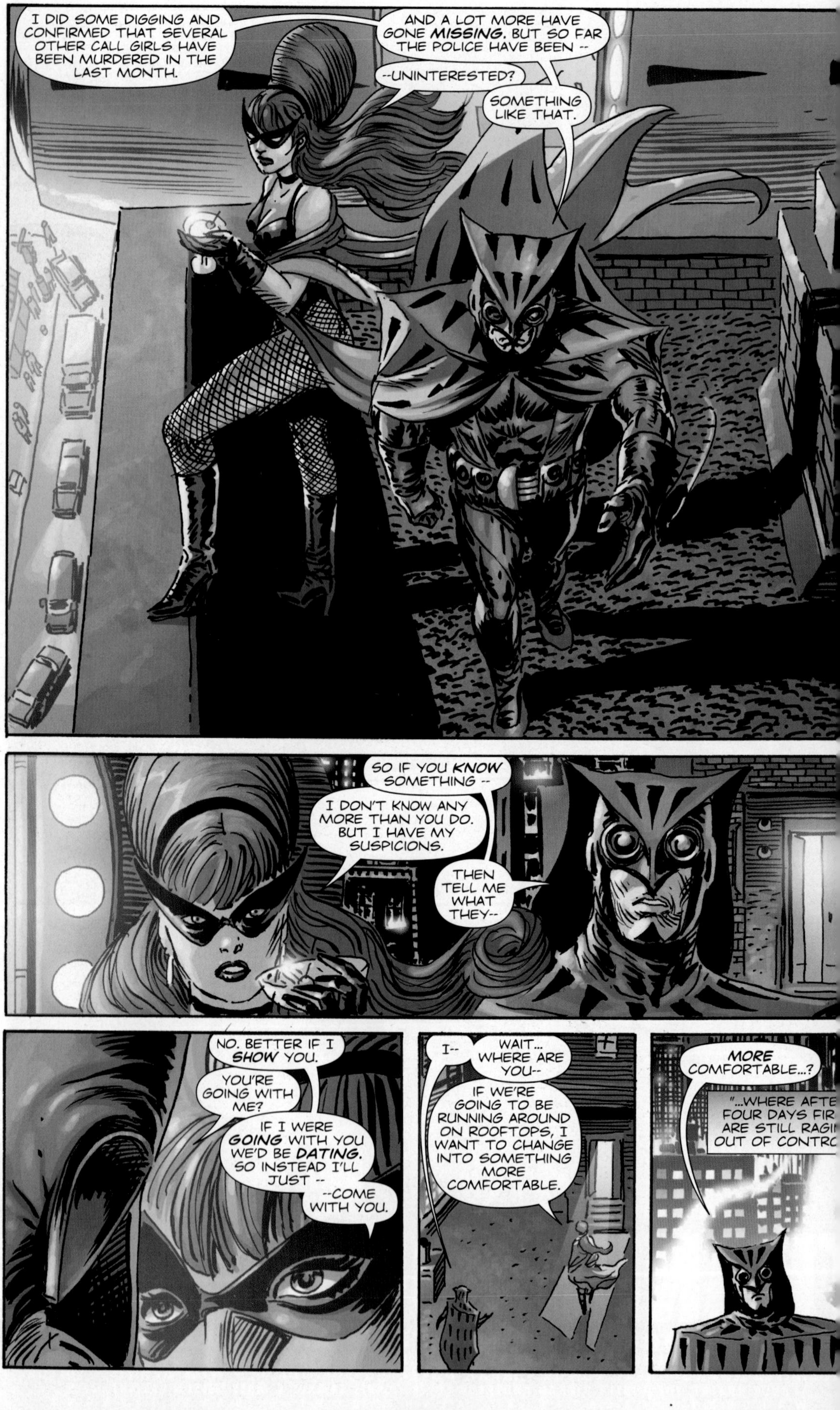
I DID SOME DIGGING AND CONFIRMED THAT SEVERAL OTHER CALL GIRLS HAVE BEEN MURDERED IN THE LAST MONTH.
AND A LOT MORE HAVE GONE MISSING. BUT SO FAR THE POLICE HAVE BEEN --
--UNINTERESTED?
SOMETHING LIKE THAT.
SO IF YOU KNOW SOMETHING --
I DON'T KNOW ANY MORE THAN YOU DO. BUT I HAVE MY SUSPICIONS.
THEN TELL ME WHAT THEY--
NO. BETTER IF I SHOW YOU.
YOU'RE GOING WITH ME?
IF I WERE GOING WITH YOU WE'D BE DATING. SO INSTEAD I'LL JUST --
--COME WITH YOU.
I--
WAIT... WHERE ARE YOU--
IF WE'RE GOING TO BE RUNNING AROUND ON ROOFTOPS, I WANT TO CHANGE INTO SOMETHING MORE COMFORTABLE.
MORE COMFORTABLE...?
"...WHERE AFTE
FOUR DAYS FIR
ARE STILL RAGI
OUT OF CONTRO

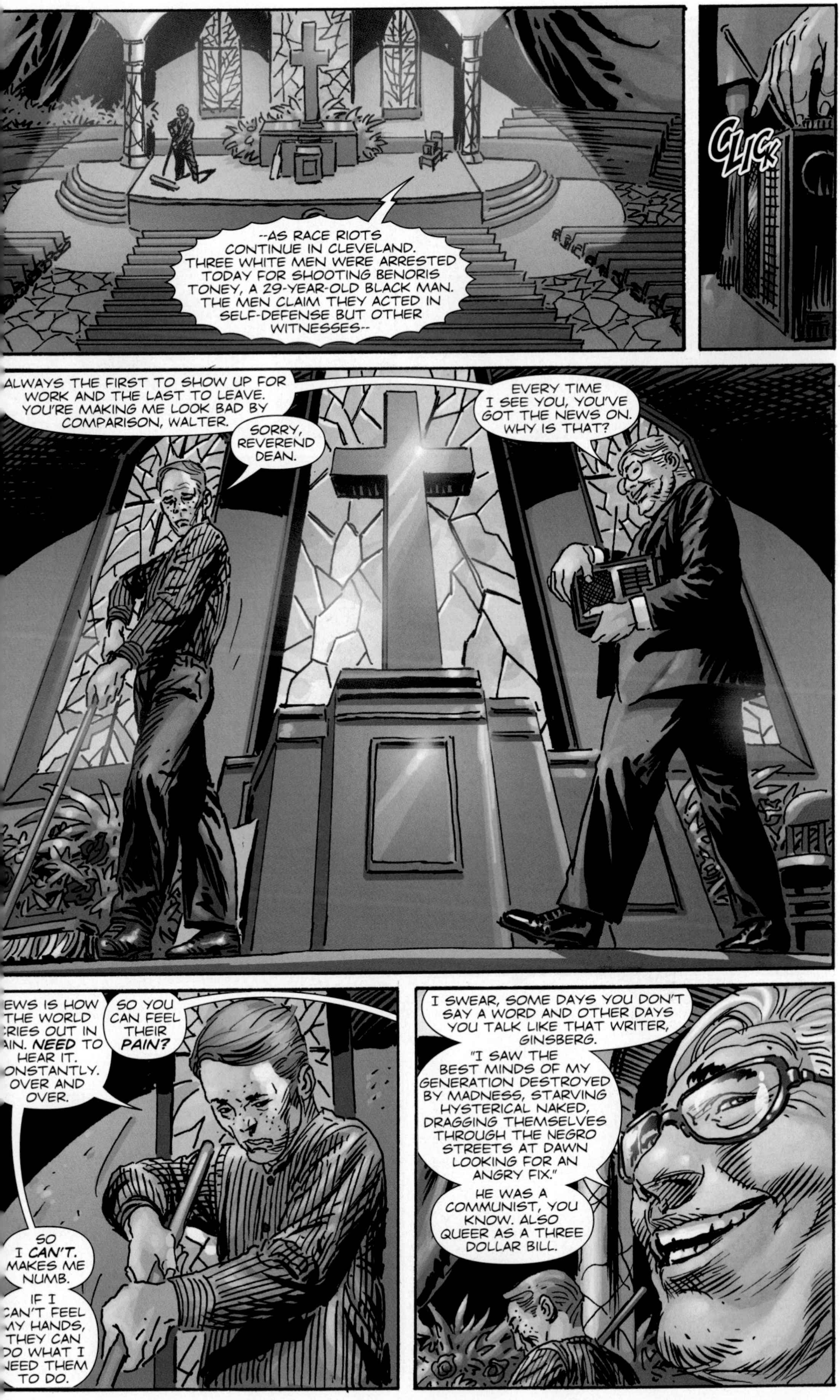
--AS RACE RIOTS CONTINUE IN CLEVELAND. THREE WHITE MEN WERE ARRESTED TODAY FOR SHOOTING BENORIS TONEY, A 29-YEAR-OLD BLACK MAN. THE MEN CLAIM THEY ACTED IN SELF-DEFENSE BUT OTHER WITNESSES--
CLICK
ALWAYS THE FIRST TO SHOW UP FOR WORK AND THE LAST TO LEAVE. YOU'RE MAKING ME LOOK BAD BY COMPARISON, WALTER.
SORRY, REVEREND DEAN.
EVERY TIME I SEE YOU, YOU'VE GOT THE NEWS ON. WHY IS THAT?
SO YOU CAN FEEL THEIR PAIN?
EWS IS HOW THE WORLD CRIES OUT IN AIN. NEED TO HEAR IT. ONSTANTLY. OVER AND OVER.
SO I CAN'T. MAKES ME NUMB.
IF I CAN'T FEEL MY HANDS, THEY CAN DO WHAT I NEED THEM TO DO.
I SWEAR, SOME DAYS YOU DON'T SAY A WORD AND OTHER DAYS YOU TALK LIKE THAT WRITER, GINSBERG.
"I SAW THE BEST MINDS OF MY GENERATION DESTROYED BY MADNESS, STARVING HYSTERICAL NAKED, DRAGGING THEMSELVES THROUGH THE NEGRO STREETS AT DAWN LOOKING FOR AN ANGRY FIX."
HE WAS A COMMUNIST, YOU KNOW. ALSO QUEER AS A THREE DOLLAR BILL.

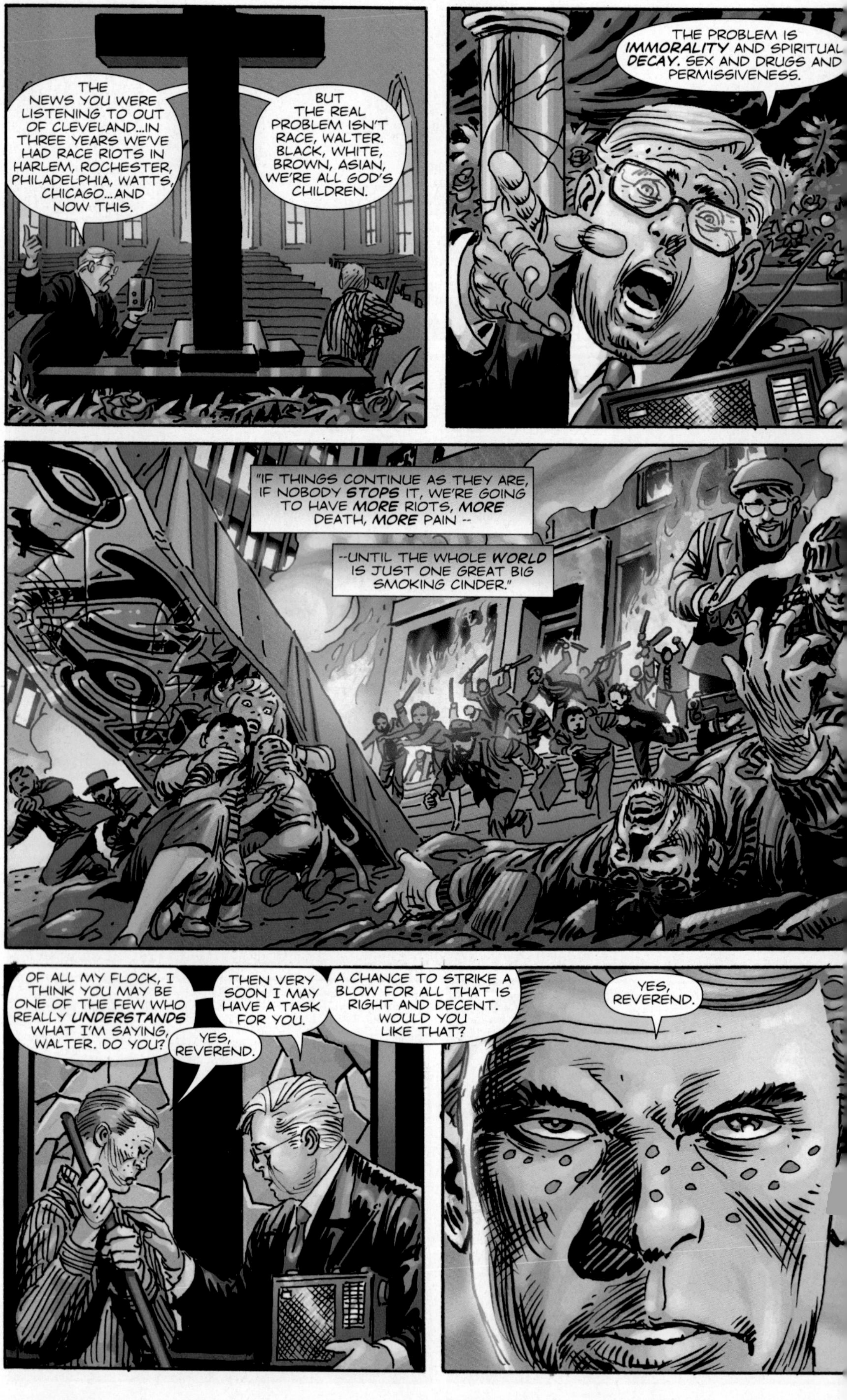

THE NEWS YOU WERE LISTENING TO OUT OF CLEVELAND...IN THREE YEARS WE'VE HAD RACE RIOTS IN HARLEM, ROCHESTER, PHILADELPHIA, WATTS, CHICAGO...AND NOW THIS.
BUT THE REAL PROBLEM ISN'T RACE, WALTER. BLACK, WHITE, BROWN, ASIAN, WE'RE ALL GOD'S CHILDREN.
THE PROBLEM IS IMMORALITY AND SPIRITUAL DECAY. SEX AND DRUGS AND PERMISSIVENESS.
"IF THINGS CONTINUE AS THEY ARE, IF NOBODY STOPS IT, WE'RE GOING TO HAVE MORE RIOTS, MORE DEATH, MORE PAIN --
--UNTIL THE WHOLE WORLD IS JUST ONE GREAT BIG SMOKING CINDER."
OF ALL MY FLOCK, I THINK YOU MAY BE ONE OF THE FEW WHO REALLY UNDERSTANDS WHAT I'M SAYING, WALTER. DO YOU?
YES, REVEREND.
THEN VERY SOON I MAY HAVE A TASK FOR YOU.
A CHANCE TO STRIKE A BLOW FOR ALL THAT IS RIGHT AND DECENT. WOULD YOU LIKE THAT?
YES, REVEREND.

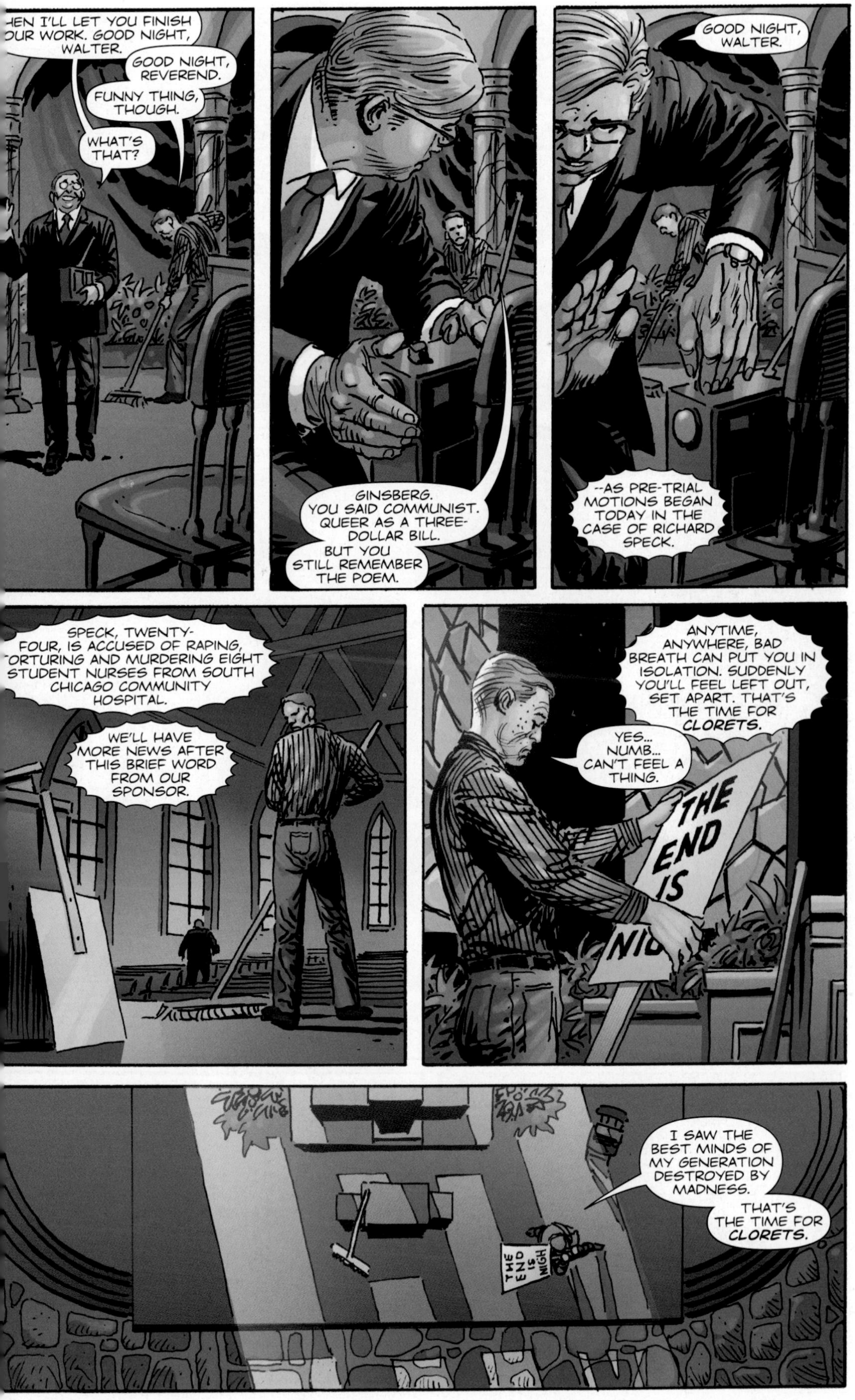

HEN I'LL LET YOU FINISH OUR WORK. GOOD NIGHT, WALTER.
GOOD NIGHT, REVEREND.
FUNNY THING, THOUGH.
WHAT'S THAT?
GINSBERG. YOU SAID COMMUNIST. QUEER AS A THREE-DOLLAR BILL.
BUT YOU STILL REMEMBER THE POEM.
GOOD NIGHT, WALTER.
--AS PRE-TRIAL MOTIONS BEGAN TODAY IN THE CASE OF RICHARD SPECK.
SPECK, TWENTY-FOUR, IS ACCUSED OF RAPING, TORTURING AND MURDERING EIGHT STUDENT NURSES FROM SOUTH CHICAGO COMMUNITY HOSPITAL.
WE'LL HAVE MORE NEWS AFTER THIS BRIEF WORD FROM OUR SPONSOR.
ANYTIME, ANYWHERE, BAD BREATH CAN PUT YOU IN ISOLATION. SUDDENLY YOU'LL FEEL LEFT OUT, SET APART. THAT'S THE TIME FOR CLORETS.
YES... NUMB... CAN'T FEEL A THING.
THE END IS
I SAW THE BEST MINDS OF MY GENERATION DESTROYED BY MADNESS.
THAT'S THE TIME FOR CLORETS.
THE END IS NIGH

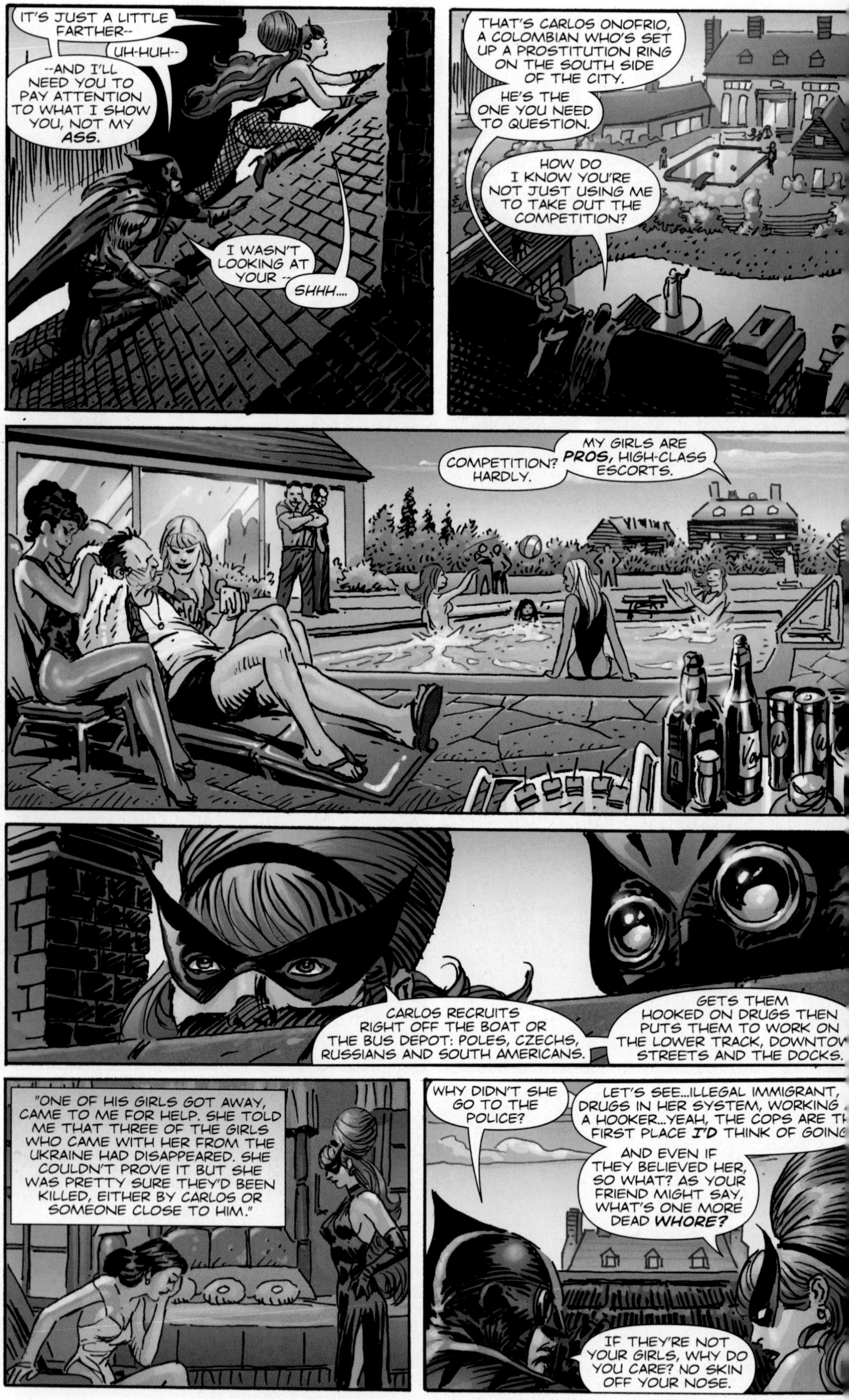
IT'S JUST A LITTLE FARTHER--
UH-HUH--
--AND I'LL NEED YOU TO PAY ATTENTION TO WHAT I SHOW YOU, NOT MY ASS.
I WASN'T LOOKING AT YOUR --
SHHH....
THAT'S CARLOS ONOFRIO, A COLOMBIAN WHO'S SET UP A PROSTITUTION RING ON THE SOUTH SIDE OF THE CITY.
HE'S THE ONE YOU NEED TO QUESTION.
HOW DO I KNOW YOU'RE NOT JUST USING ME TO TAKE OUT THE COMPETITION?
COMPETITION? HARDLY.
MY GIRLS ARE PROS, HIGH-CLASS ESCORTS.
CARLOS RECRUITS RIGHT OFF THE BOAT OR THE BUS DEPOT: POLES, CZECHS, RUSSIANS AND SOUTH AMERICANS.
GETS THEM HOOKED ON DRUGS THEN PUTS THEM TO WORK ON THE LOWER TRACK, DOWNTOW STREETS AND THE DOCKS.
"ONE OF HIS GIRLS GOT AWAY, CAME TO ME FOR HELP. SHE TOLD ME THAT THREE OF THE GIRLS WHO CAME WITH HER FROM THE UKRAINE HAD DISAPPEARED. SHE COULDN'T PROVE IT BUT SHE WAS PRETTY SURE THEY'D BEEN KILLED, EITHER BY CARLOS OR SOMEONE CLOSE TO HIM."
WHY DIDN'T SHE GO TO THE POLICE?
LET'S SEE...ILLEGAL IMMIGRANT, DRUGS IN HER SYSTEM, WORKING A HOOKER...YEAH, THE COPS ARE TH FIRST PLACE I'D THINK OF GOING
AND EVEN IF THEY BELIEVED HER, SO WHAT? AS YOUR FRIEND MIGHT SAY, WHAT'S ONE MORE DEAD WHORE?
IF THEY'RE NOT YOUR GIRLS, WHY DO YOU CARE? NO SKIN OFF YOUR NOSE.

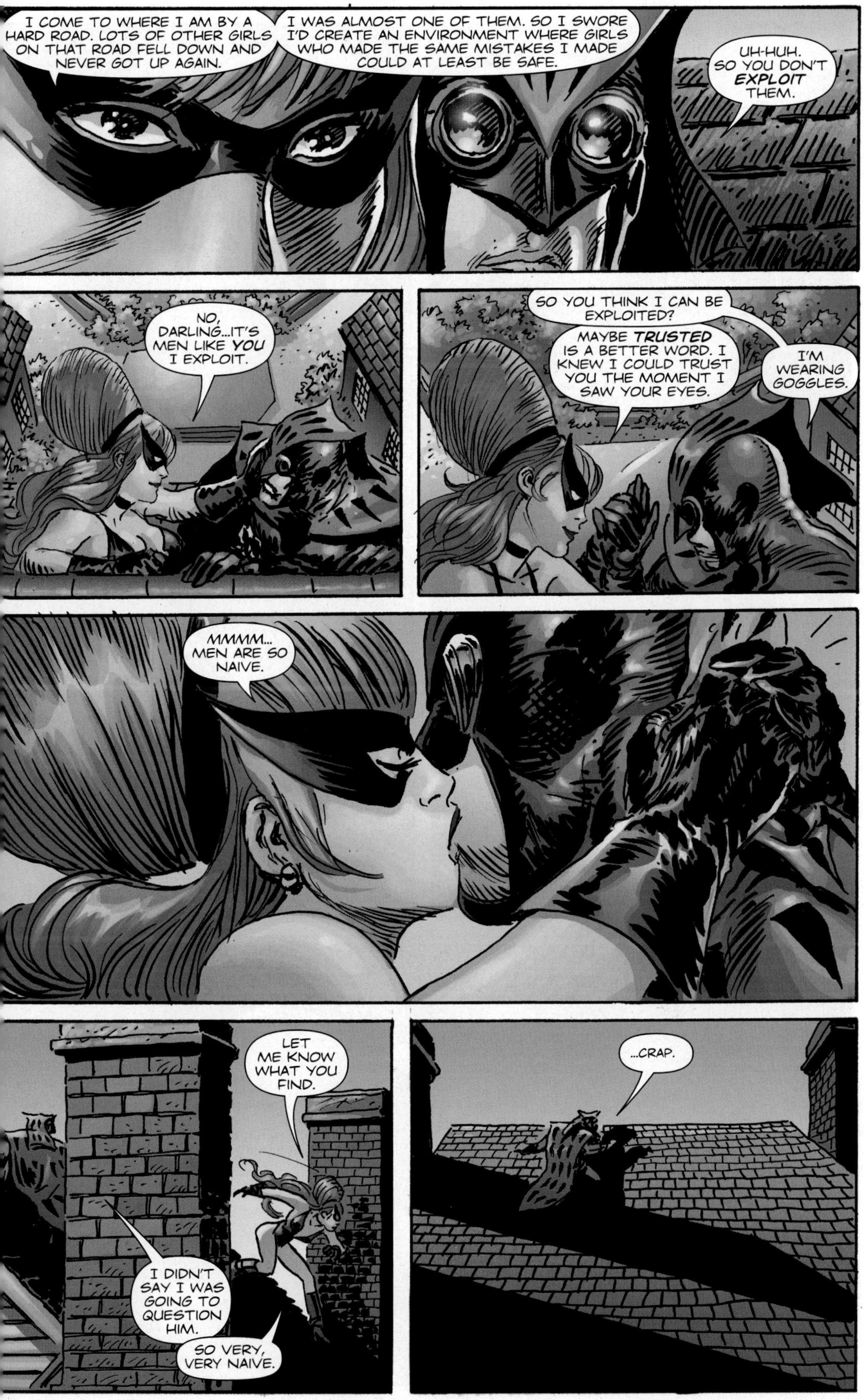
I COME TO WHERE I AM BY A HARD ROAD. LOTS OF OTHER GIRLS ON THAT ROAD FELL DOWN AND NEVER GOT UP AGAIN.
I WAS ALMOST ONE OF THEM. SO I SWORE I'D CREATE AN ENVIRONMENT WHERE GIRLS WHO MADE THE SAME MISTAKES I MADE COULD AT LEAST BE SAFE.
UH-HUH. SO YOU DON'T EXPLOIT THEM.
NO, DARLING...IT'S MEN LIKE YOU I EXPLOIT.
SO YOU THINK I CAN BE EXPLOITED?
MAYBE TRUSTED IS A BETTER WORD. I KNEW I COULD TRUST YOU THE MOMENT I SAW YOUR EYES.
I'M WEARING GOGGLES.
MMMM... MEN ARE SO NAIVE.
LET ME KNOW WHAT YOU FIND.
I DIDN'T SAY I WAS GOING TO QUESTION HIM.
SO VERY, VERY NAIVE.
...CRAP.

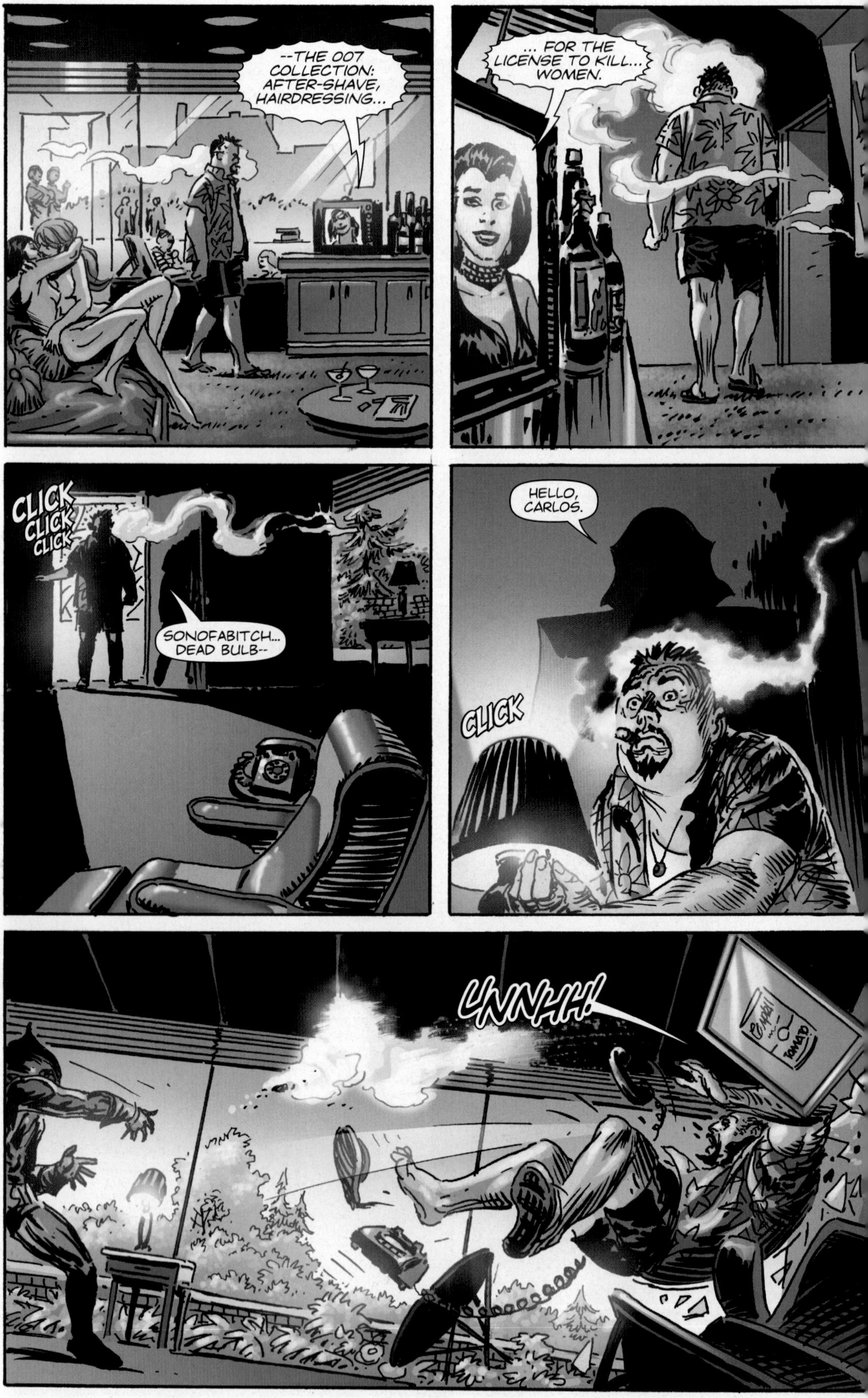
--THE 007 COLLECTION: AFTER-SHAVE, HAIRDRESSING...
... FOR THE LICENSE TO KILL... WOMEN.
CLICK CLICK CLICK
SONOFABITCH... DEAD BULB--
HELLO, CARLOS.
CLICK
UNNH!

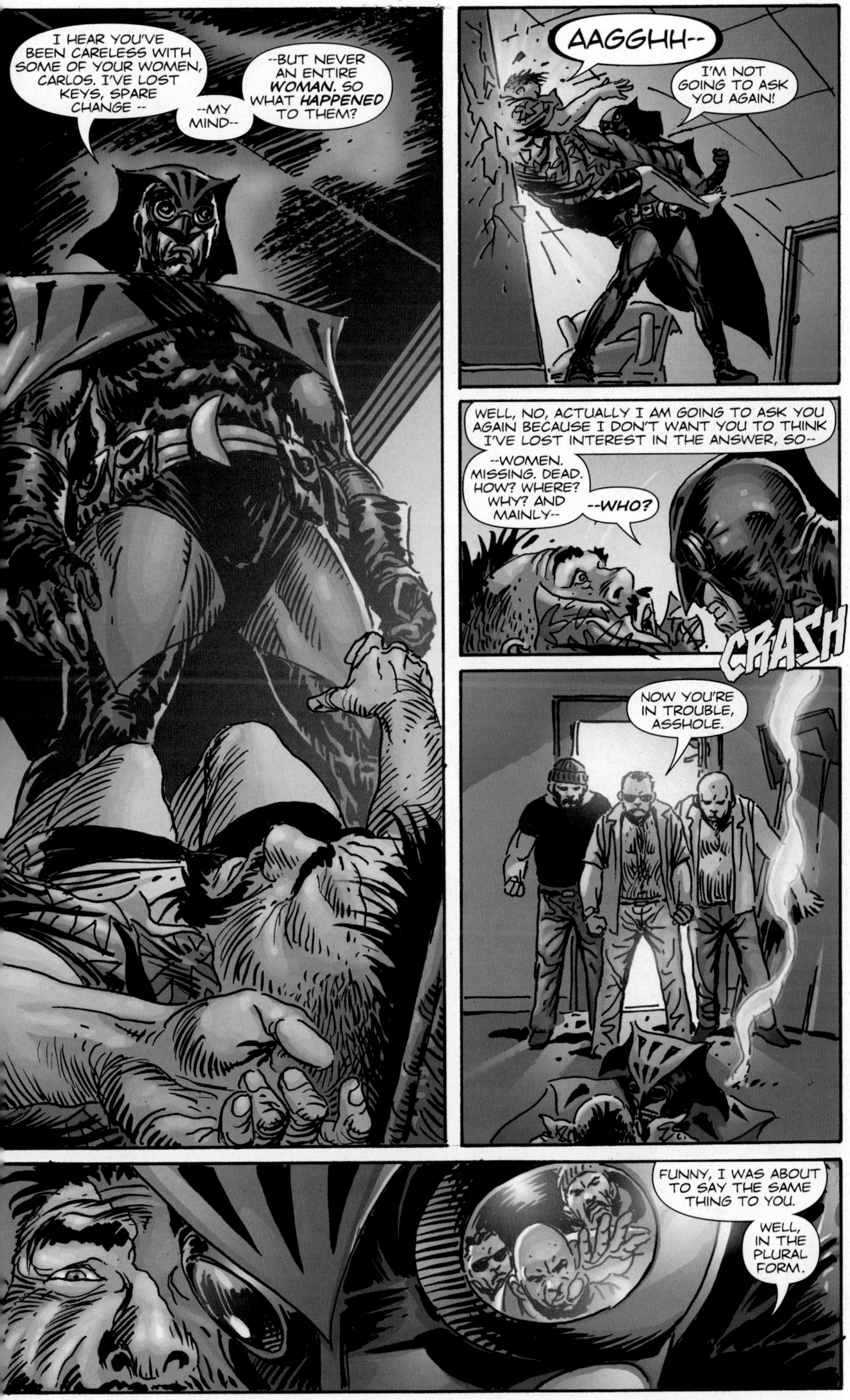
I HEAR YOU'VE BEEN CARELESS WITH SOME OF YOUR WOMEN, CARLOS. I'VE LOST KEYS, SPARE CHANGE --
--MY MIND--
--BUT NEVER AN ENTIRE **WOMAN.** SO WHAT **HAPPENED** TO THEM?
AAGGHH--
I'M NOT GOING TO ASK YOU AGAIN!
WELL, NO, ACTUALLY I AM GOING TO ASK YOU AGAIN BECAUSE I DON'T WANT YOU TO THINK I'VE LOST INTEREST IN THE ANSWER, SO--
--WOMEN. MISSING. DEAD. HOW? WHERE? WHY? AND MAINLY--
--**WHO?**
CRASH
NOW YOU'RE IN TROUBLE, ASSHOLE.
FUNNY, I WAS ABOUT TO SAY THE SAME THING TO YOU.
WELL, IN THE PLURAL FORM.

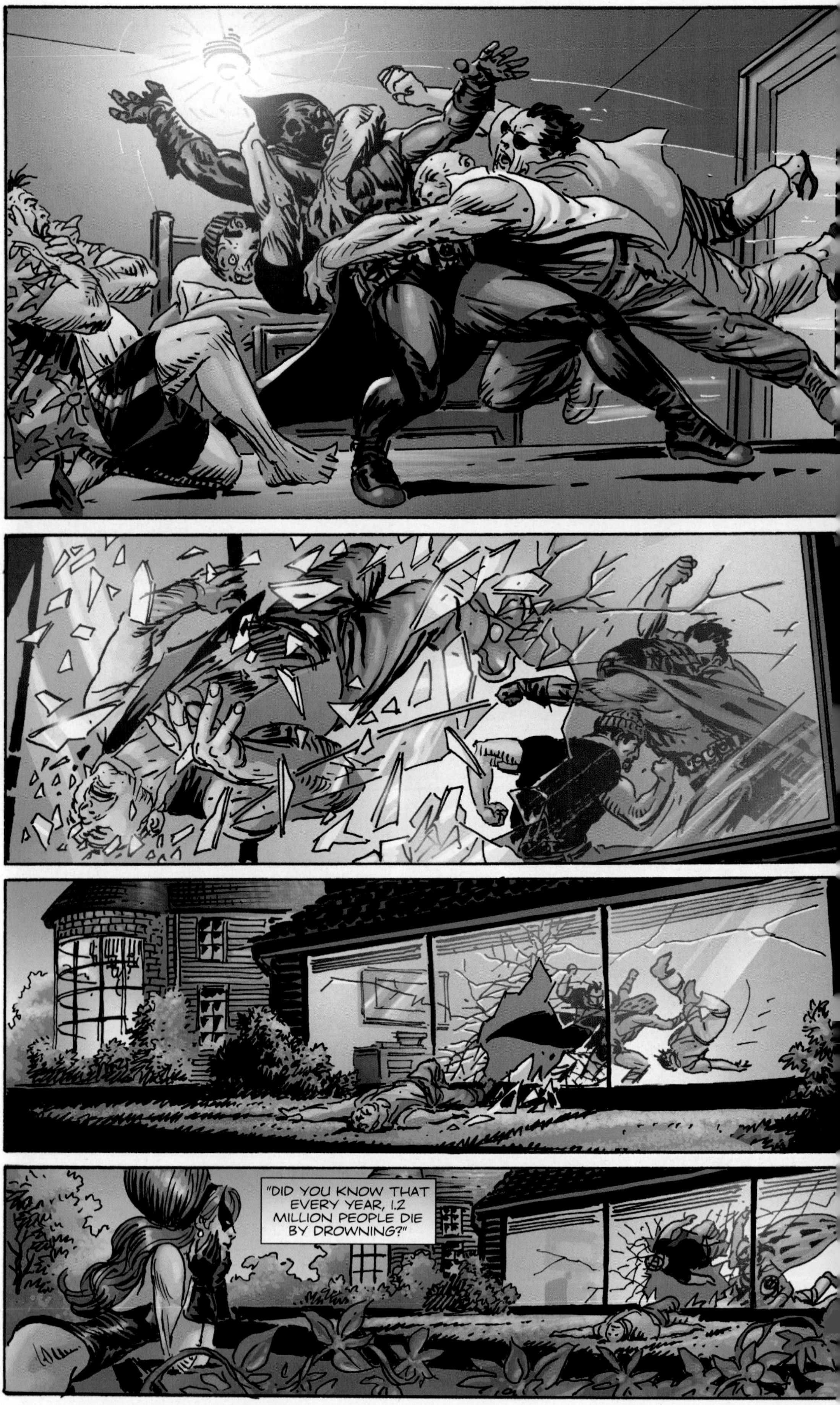
"DID YOU KNOW THAT EVERY YEAR, 1.2 MILLION PEOPLE DIE BY DROWNING?"

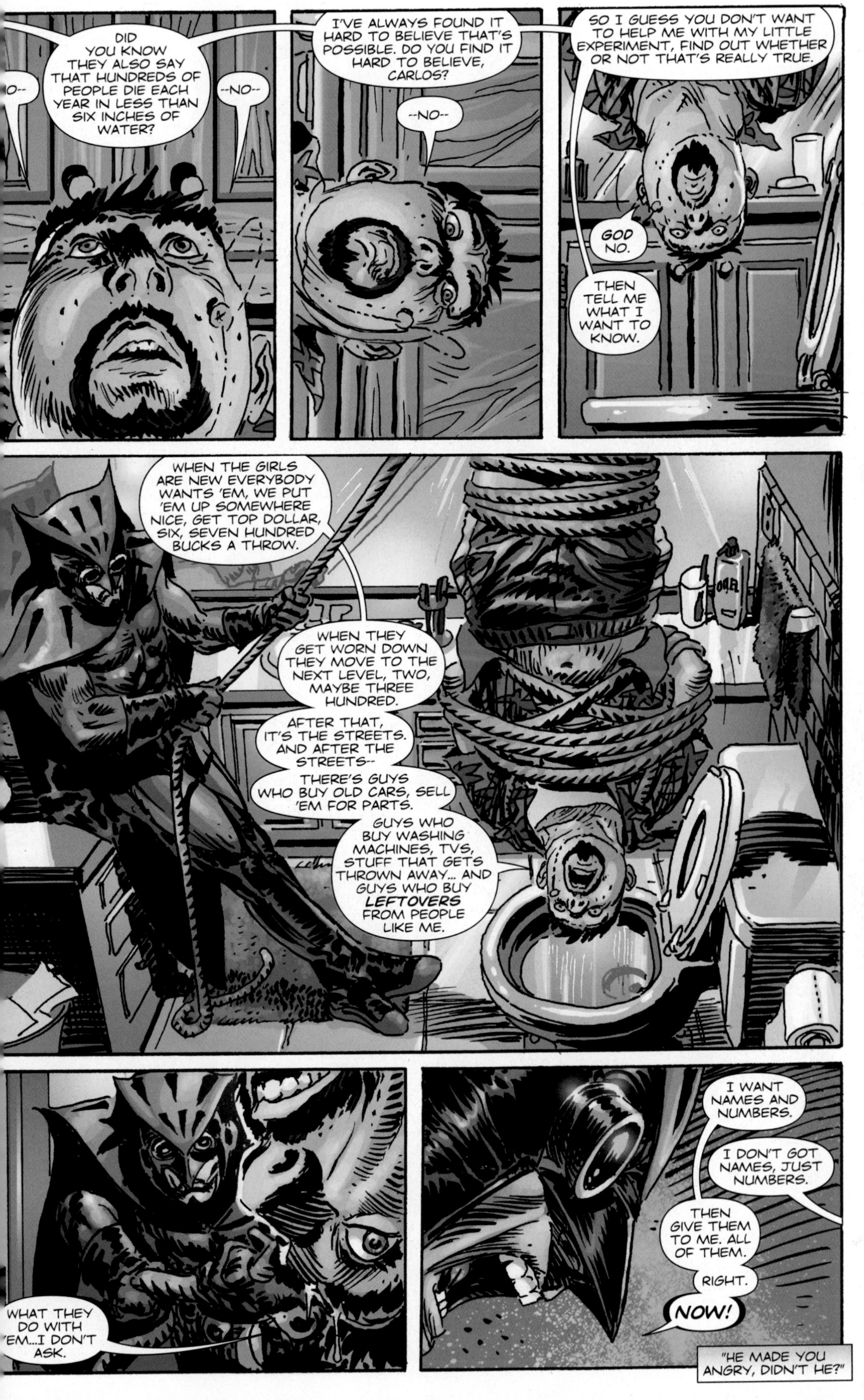

O--
DID YOU KNOW THEY ALSO SAY THAT HUNDREDS OF PEOPLE DIE EACH YEAR IN LESS THAN SIX INCHES OF WATER?
--NO--
I'VE ALWAYS FOUND IT HARD TO BELIEVE THAT'S POSSIBLE. DO YOU FIND IT HARD TO BELIEVE, CARLOS?
--NO--
SO I GUESS YOU DON'T WANT TO HELP ME WITH MY LITTLE EXPERIMENT, FIND OUT WHETHER OR NOT THAT'S REALLY TRUE.
GOD NO.
THEN TELL ME WHAT I WANT TO KNOW.
WHEN THE GIRLS ARE NEW EVERYBODY WANTS 'EM, WE PUT 'EM UP SOMEWHERE NICE, GET TOP DOLLAR, SIX, SEVEN HUNDRED BUCKS A THROW.
WHEN THEY GET WORN DOWN THEY MOVE TO THE NEXT LEVEL, TWO, MAYBE THREE HUNDRED.
AFTER THAT, IT'S THE STREETS. AND AFTER THE STREETS--
THERE'S GUYS WHO BUY OLD CARS, SELL 'EM FOR PARTS.
GUYS WHO BUY WASHING MACHINES, TVS, STUFF THAT GETS THROWN AWAY... AND GUYS WHO BUY ***LEFTOVERS*** FROM PEOPLE LIKE ME.
WHAT THEY DO WITH 'EM...I DON'T ASK.
I WANT NAMES AND NUMBERS.
I DON'T GOT NAMES, JUST NUMBERS.
THEN GIVE THEM TO ME. ALL OF THEM.
RIGHT.
NOW!
"HE MADE YOU ANGRY, DIDN'T HE?"

YES. BUT I GOT WHAT I NEEDED. SIX PHONE NUMBERS. I'LL RUN THEM DOWN, SEE WHAT I CAN FIND. I--

AND YOU WANTED TO *HURT* HIM, DIDN'T YOU?

-- YES.

I'VE FOUND THAT MEN EITHER LOVE AND DEFEND WOMEN WHO REMIND THEM OF THEIR MOTHERS OR ATTACK AND HATE WOMEN WHO REMIND THEM OF THEIR MOTHERS. I FEEL SOME CONFLICT IN YOU.

DID SHE PROTECT YOU? OR LEAVE YOU TO THE WOLVES?

MY MOTHER WASN'T A--

I DIDN'T SAY SHE WAS. BUT SHE WAS USED AND ABUSED, WASN'T SHE?

I...HOW DID WE END UP IN YOUR BEDROOM?

MEN USE MONEY OR FORCE TO TRY AND MAKE US SERVE THEM, TURN US INTO WHORES. WHEN IT WORKS, SOME OF US TURN THE LIGHTS OFF, SO WE DON'T HAVE TO THINK ABOUT WHAT WE'RE DOING.

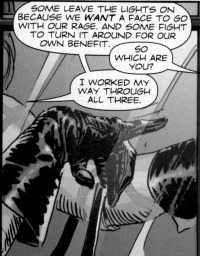

SOME LEAVE THE LIGHTS ON BECAUSE WE *WANT* A FACE TO GO WITH OUR RAGE. AND SOME FIGHT TO TURN IT AROUND FOR OUR OWN BENEFIT.

SO WHICH ARE YOU?

I WORKED MY WAY THROUGH ALL THREE.

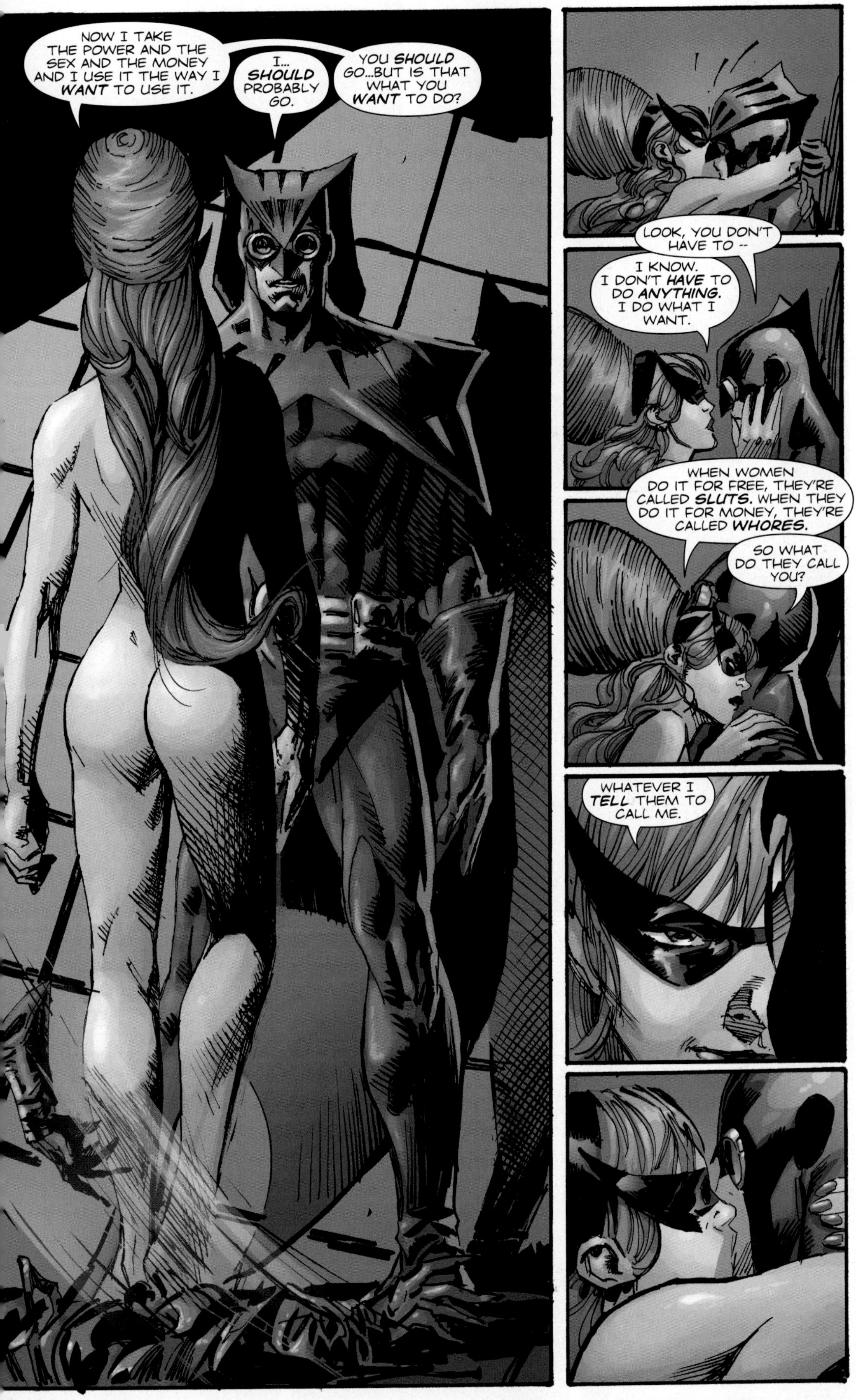
NOW I TAKE THE POWER AND THE SEX AND THE MONEY AND I USE IT THE WAY I WANT TO USE IT.
I... SHOULD PROBABLY GO.
YOU SHOULD GO...BUT IS THAT WHAT YOU WANT TO DO?
LOOK, YOU DON'T HAVE TO --
I KNOW. I DON'T HAVE TO DO ANYTHING. I DO WHAT I WANT.
WHEN WOMEN DO IT FOR FREE, THEY'RE CALLED SLUTS. WHEN THEY DO IT FOR MONEY, THEY'RE CALLED WHORES.
SO WHAT DO THEY CALL YOU?
WHATEVER I TELL THEM TO CALL ME.

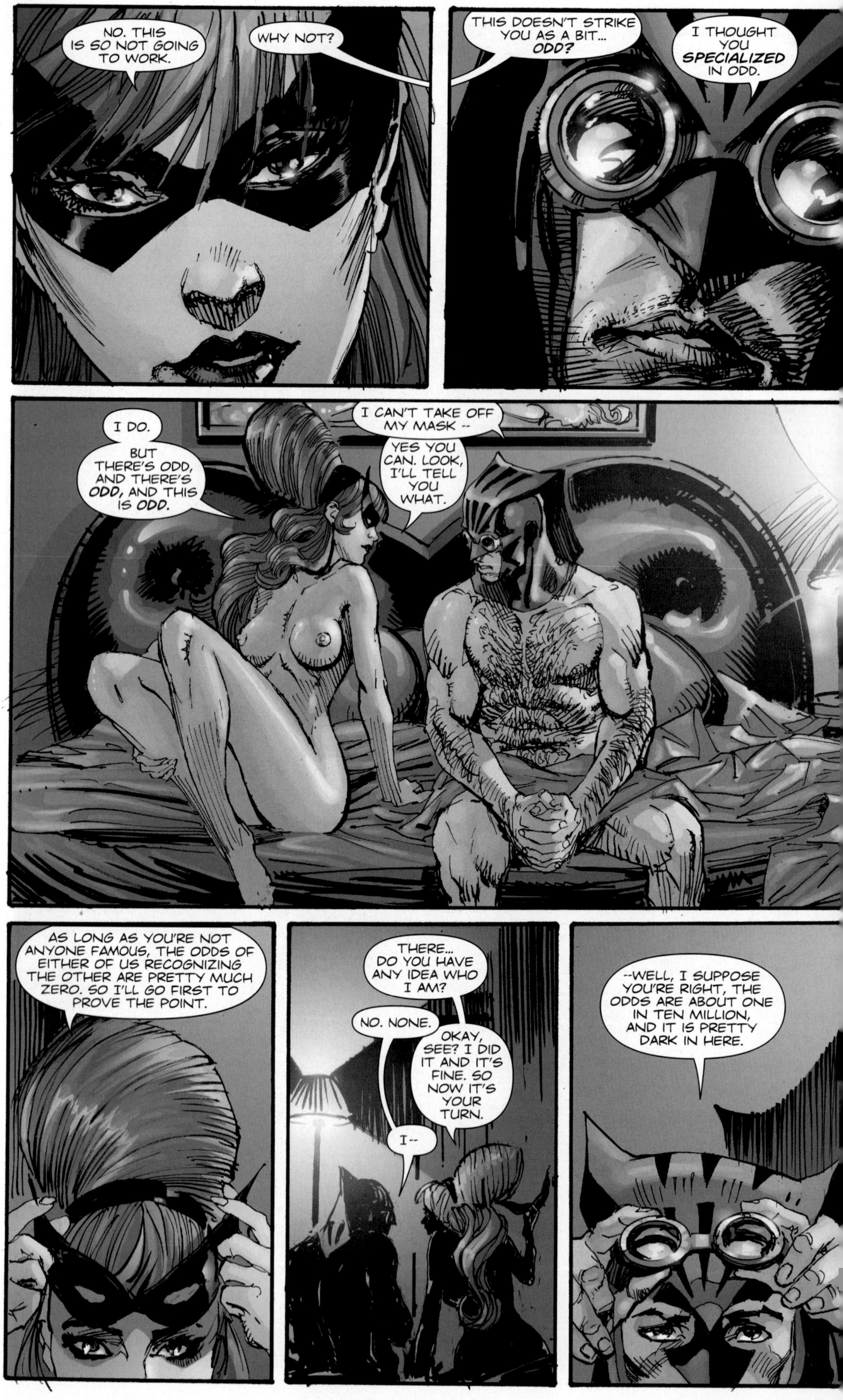
NO. THIS IS SO NOT GOING TO WORK.
WHY NOT?
THIS DOESN'T STRIKE YOU AS A BIT... ODD?
I THOUGHT YOU SPECIALIZED IN ODD.
I DO.
BUT THERE'S ODD, AND THERE'S ODD, AND THIS IS ODD.
I CAN'T TAKE OFF MY MASK --
YES YOU CAN. LOOK, I'LL TELL YOU WHAT.
AS LONG AS YOU'RE NOT ANYONE FAMOUS, THE ODDS OF EITHER OF US RECOGNIZING THE OTHER ARE PRETTY MUCH ZERO. SO I'LL GO FIRST TO PROVE THE POINT.
THERE... DO YOU HAVE ANY IDEA WHO I AM?
NO. NONE.
OKAY, SEE? I DID IT AND IT'S FINE. SO NOW IT'S YOUR TURN.
I--
--WELL, I SUPPOSE YOU'RE RIGHT, THE ODDS ARE ABOUT ONE IN TEN MILLION, AND IT IS PRETTY DARK IN HERE.

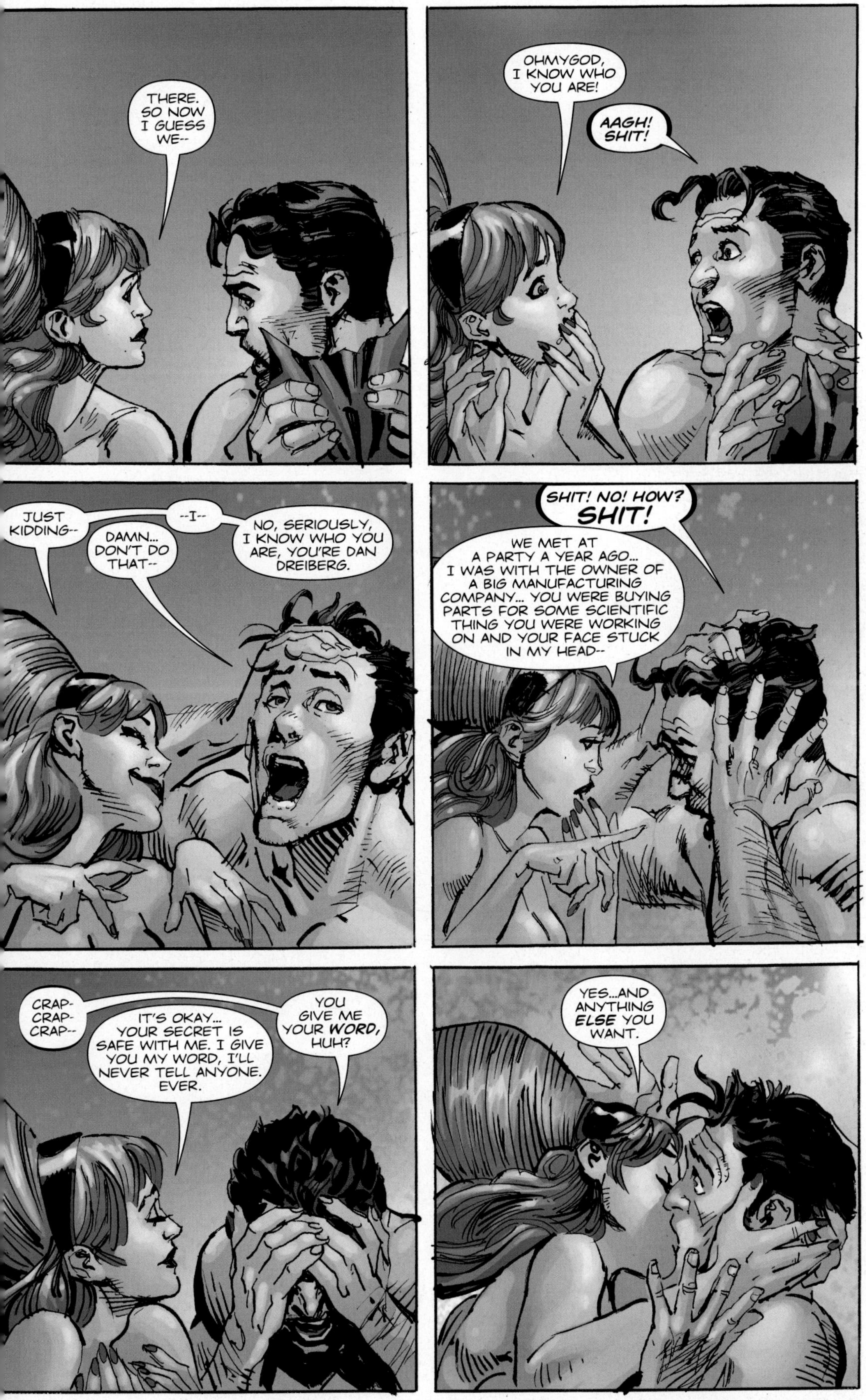
THERE. SO NOW I GUESS WE--
OHMYGOD, I KNOW WHO YOU ARE!
AAGH! SHIT!
JUST KIDDING--
DAMN... DON'T DO THAT--
--I--
NO, SERIOUSLY, I KNOW WHO YOU ARE, YOU'RE DAN DREIBERG.
SHIT! NO! HOW? SHIT!
WE MET AT A PARTY A YEAR AGO... I WAS WITH THE OWNER OF A BIG MANUFACTURING COMPANY... YOU WERE BUYING PARTS FOR SOME SCIENTIFIC THING YOU WERE WORKING ON AND YOUR FACE STUCK IN MY HEAD--
CRAP-CRAP-CRAP--
IT'S OKAY... YOUR SECRET IS SAFE WITH ME. I GIVE YOU MY WORD, I'LL NEVER TELL ANYONE. EVER.
YOU GIVE ME YOUR WORD, HUH?
YES...AND ANYTHING ELSE YOU WANT.

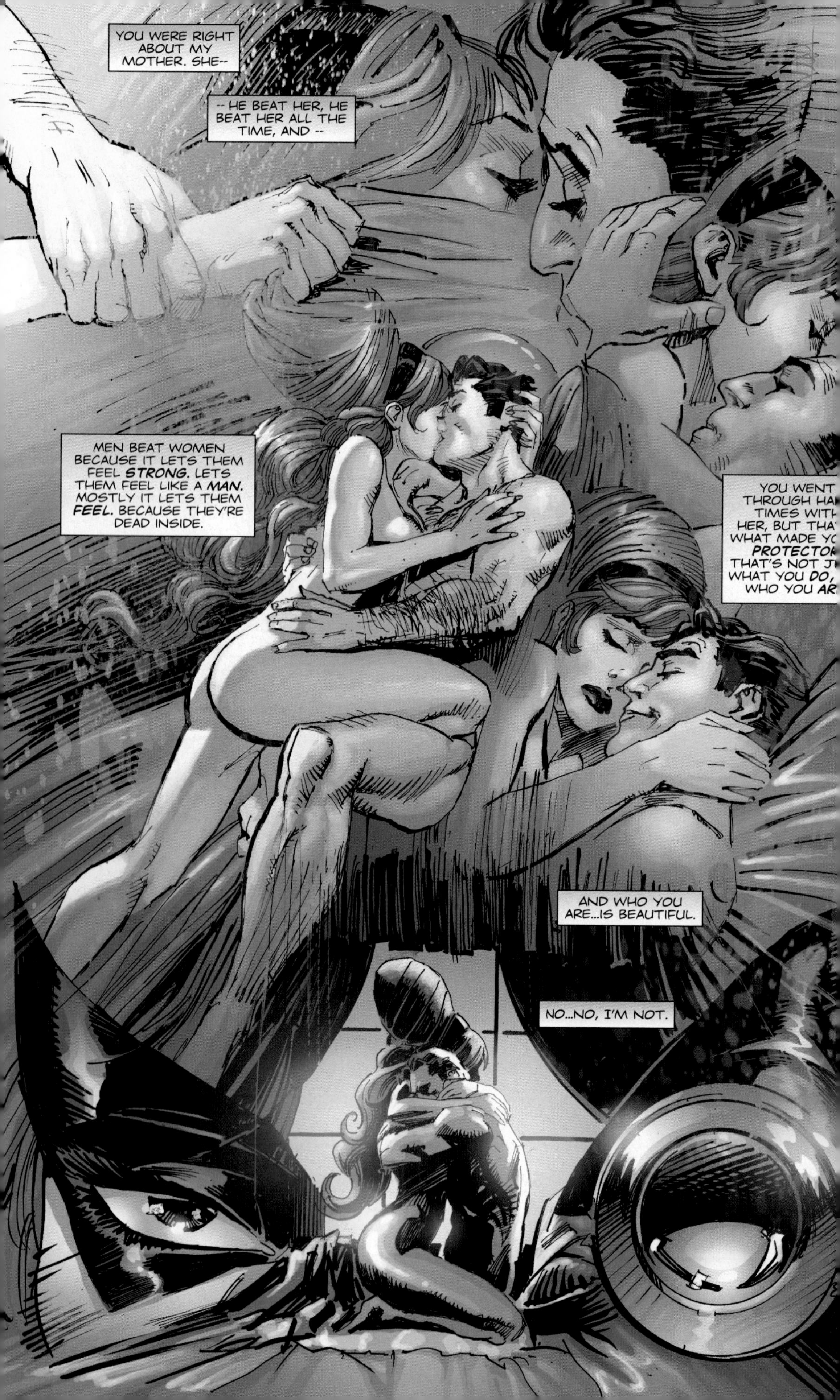
YOU WERE RIGHT ABOUT MY MOTHER. SHE--
-- HE BEAT HER, HE BEAT HER ALL THE TIME, AND --
MEN BEAT WOMEN BECAUSE IT LETS THEM FEEL **STRONG.** LETS THEM FEEL LIKE A **MAN.** MOSTLY IT LETS THEM **FEEL.** BECAUSE THEY'RE DEAD INSIDE.
YOU WENT THROUGH HA TIMES WITH HER, BUT THA WHAT MADE YO **PROTECTOR** THAT'S NOT J WHAT YOU **DO,** WHO YOU **AR**
AND WHO YOU ARE...IS BEAUTIFUL.
NO...NO, I'M NOT.

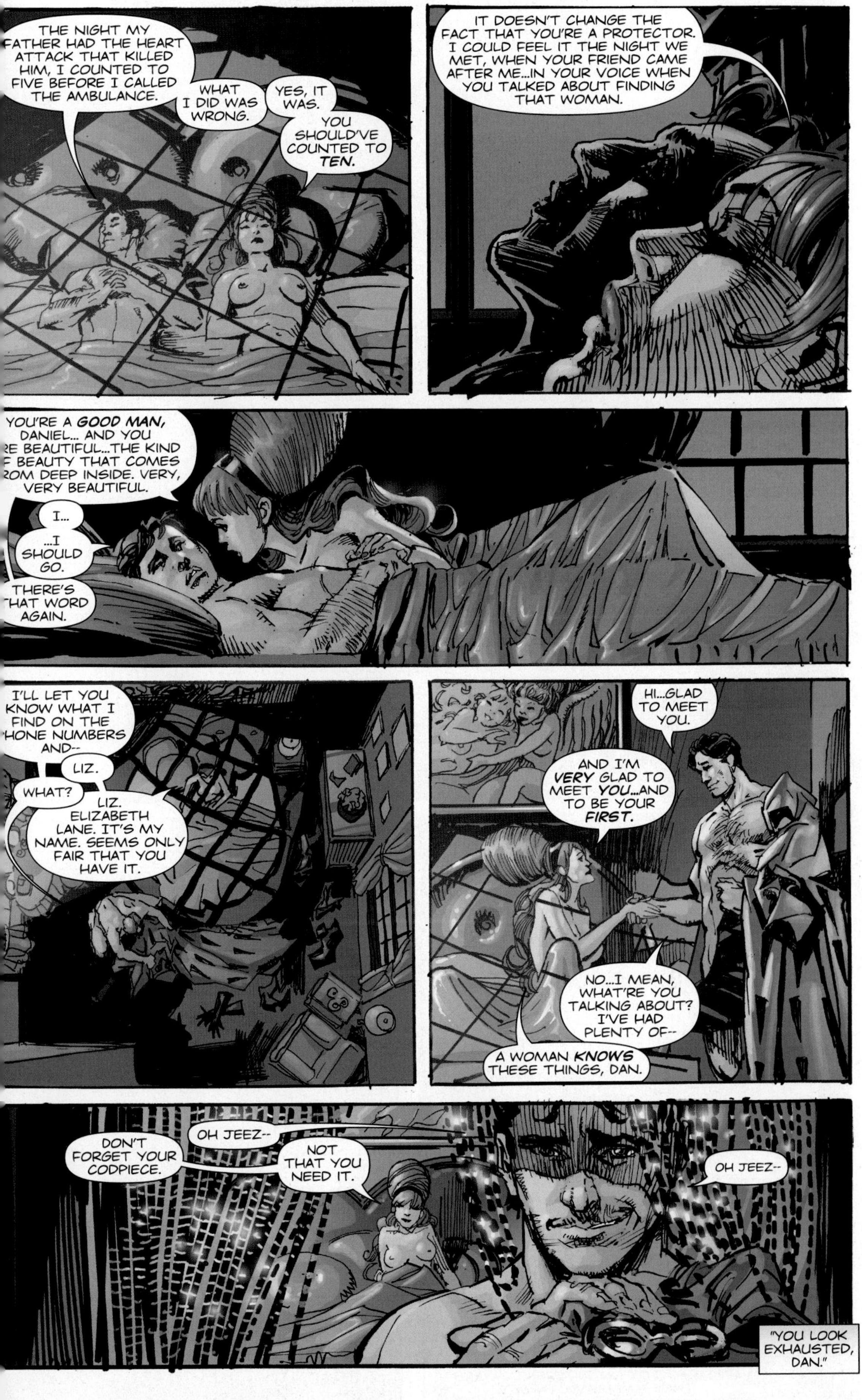
THE NIGHT MY FATHER HAD THE HEART ATTACK THAT KILLED HIM, I COUNTED TO FIVE BEFORE I CALLED THE AMBULANCE.
WHAT I DID WAS WRONG.
YES, IT WAS.
YOU SHOULD'VE COUNTED TO TEN.
IT DOESN'T CHANGE THE FACT THAT YOU'RE A PROTECTOR. I COULD FEEL IT THE NIGHT WE MET, WHEN YOUR FRIEND CAME AFTER ME...IN YOUR VOICE WHEN YOU TALKED ABOUT FINDING THAT WOMAN.
YOU'RE A GOOD MAN, DANIEL... AND YOU RE BEAUTIFUL...THE KIND F BEAUTY THAT COMES ROM DEEP INSIDE. VERY, VERY BEAUTIFUL.
I...
...I SHOULD GO.
THERE'S HAT WORD AGAIN.
I'LL LET YOU KNOW WHAT I FIND ON THE HONE NUMBERS AND--
LIZ.
WHAT?
LIZ. ELIZABETH LANE. IT'S MY NAME. SEEMS ONLY FAIR THAT YOU HAVE IT.
HI...GLAD TO MEET YOU.
AND I'M VERY GLAD TO MEET YOU...AND TO BE YOUR FIRST.
NO...I MEAN, WHAT'RE YOU TALKING ABOUT? I'VE HAD PLENTY OF--
A WOMAN KNOWS THESE THINGS, DAN.
DON'T FORGET YOUR CODPIECE.
OH JEEZ--
NOT THAT YOU NEED IT.
OH JEEZ--
"YOU LOOK EXHAUSTED, DAN."

YOU KNOW ME, HOLLIS, ALWAYS UP ALL NIGHT WORKING.

YOU ON A CASE?

YEAH. I MEAN, MAYBE. WE'LL SEE.

THREE ANSWERS TO ONE QUESTION. *IMPRESSIVE.*

I'M RUNNING DOWN SOME PHONE NUMBERS ON A...*POSSIBLE* CASE. MOST OF THEM HAVE TURNED INTO DEAD ENDS, BUT ONE OF THEM LED TO A PAY PHONE DOWNTOWN.

WHICH MEANS IT'S *ANOTHER* DEAD END--

"-- SINCE *ANYBODY* COULD'VE USED THAT PHONE. YOU NEED ROUND-THE-CLOCK SURVEILLANCE, WHICH WE DON'T HAVE. YOU'VE GOT NOTHING."

"NOT NECESSARILY."

I'VE FOUND A MOLECULAR POLYMER EXTRACT THAT MAY LET ME SEPARATE THE LAYERS OF OIL AND FINGERPRINTS THAT COVER THE RECEIVER.

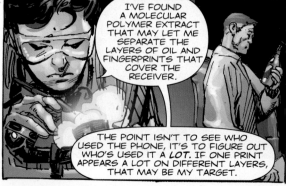

THE POINT ISN'T TO SEE WHO USED THE PHONE, IT'S TO FIGURE OUT WHO'S USED IT A *LOT.* IF ONE PRINT APPEARS A LOT ON DIFFERENT LAYERS, THAT MAY BE MY TARGET.

I THOUGHT YOU SAID YOU WEREN'T GOING TO DRINK BEFORE NOON ANYMORE--

I'M NOT. AH. OPTICAL ILLUSION, THEN...?

SOMETHING LIKE THAT.

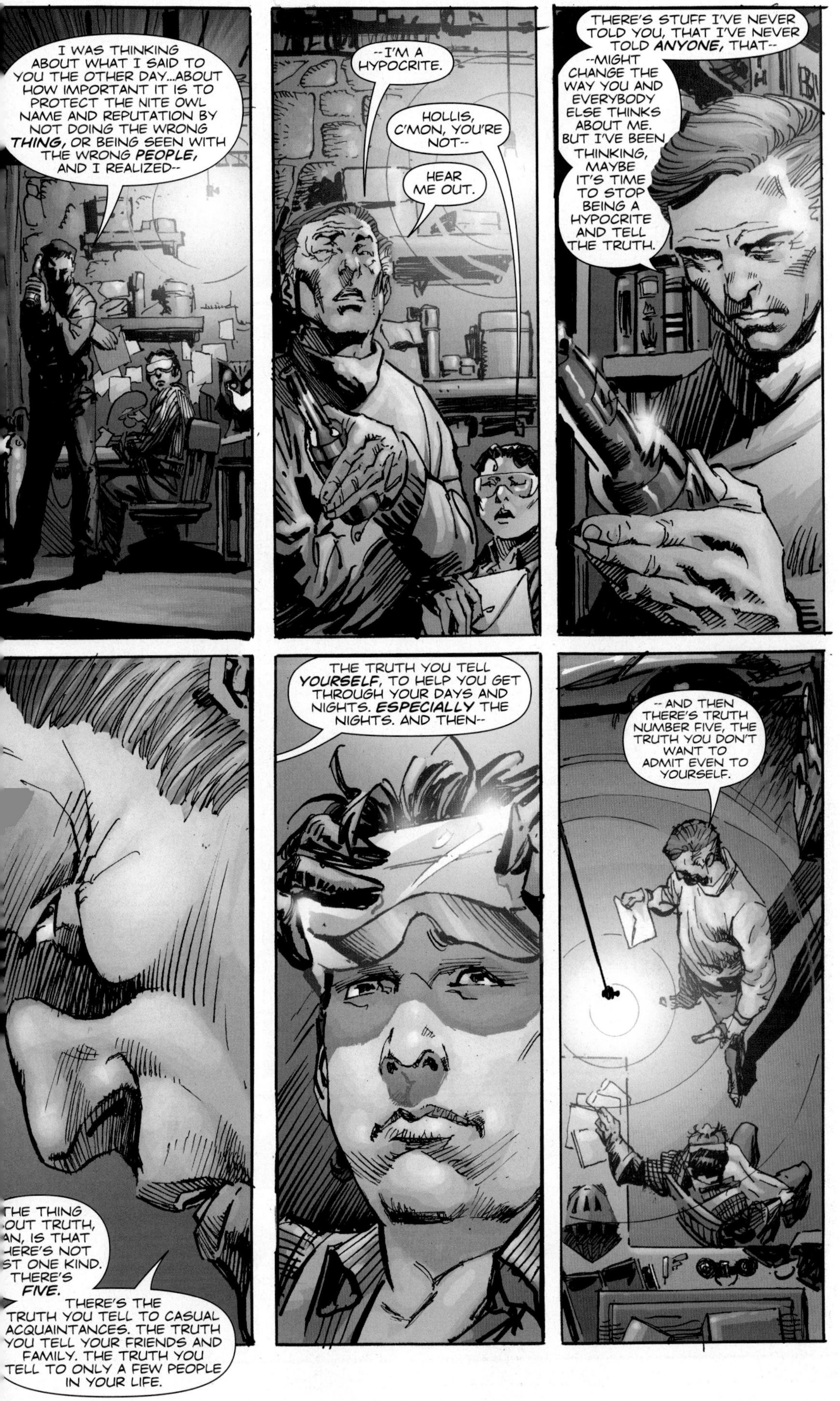
I WAS THINKING ABOUT WHAT I SAID TO YOU THE OTHER DAY...ABOUT HOW IMPORTANT IT IS TO PROTECT THE NITE OWL NAME AND REPUTATION BY NOT DOING THE WRONG THING, OR BEING SEEN WITH THE WRONG PEOPLE, AND I REALIZED--
--I'M A HYPOCRITE.
HOLLIS, C'MON, YOU'RE NOT--
HEAR ME OUT.
THERE'S STUFF I'VE NEVER TOLD YOU, THAT I'VE NEVER TOLD ANYONE, THAT--
--MIGHT CHANGE THE WAY YOU AND EVERYBODY ELSE THINKS ABOUT ME. BUT I'VE BEEN THINKING, MAYBE IT'S TIME TO STOP BEING A HYPOCRITE AND TELL THE TRUTH.
THE THING OUT TRUTH, AN, IS THAT HERE'S NOT ST ONE KIND. THERE'S FIVE.
THERE'S THE TRUTH YOU TELL TO CASUAL ACQUAINTANCES. THE TRUTH YOU TELL YOUR FRIENDS AND FAMILY. THE TRUTH YOU TELL TO ONLY A FEW PEOPLE IN YOUR LIFE.
THE TRUTH YOU TELL YOURSELF, TO HELP YOU GET THROUGH YOUR DAYS AND NIGHTS. ESPECIALLY THE NIGHTS. AND THEN--
-- AND THEN THERE'S TRUTH NUMBER FIVE, THE TRUTH YOU DON'T WANT TO ADMIT EVEN TO YOURSELF.

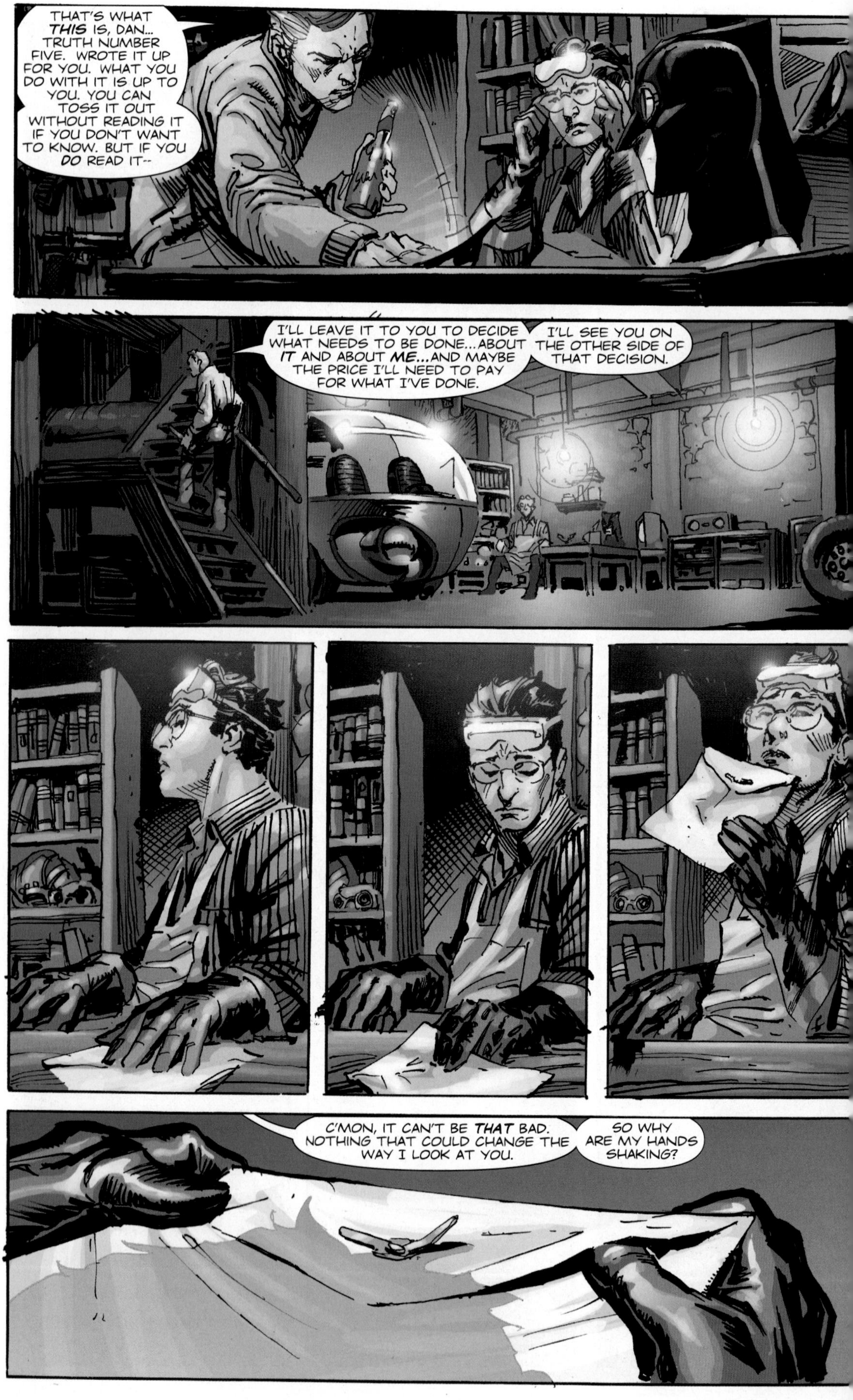
THAT'S WHAT THIS IS, DAN... TRUTH NUMBER FIVE. WROTE IT UP FOR YOU. WHAT YOU DO WITH IT IS UP TO YOU. YOU CAN TOSS IT OUT WITHOUT READING IT IF YOU DON'T WANT TO KNOW. BUT IF YOU DO READ IT--
I'LL LEAVE IT TO YOU TO DECIDE WHAT NEEDS TO BE DONE...ABOUT IT AND ABOUT ME...AND MAYBE THE PRICE I'LL NEED TO PAY FOR WHAT I'VE DONE.
I'LL SEE YOU ON THE OTHER SIDE OF THAT DECISION.
C'MON, IT CAN'T BE THAT BAD. NOTHING THAT COULD CHANGE THE WAY I LOOK AT YOU.
SO WHY ARE MY HANDS SHAKING?

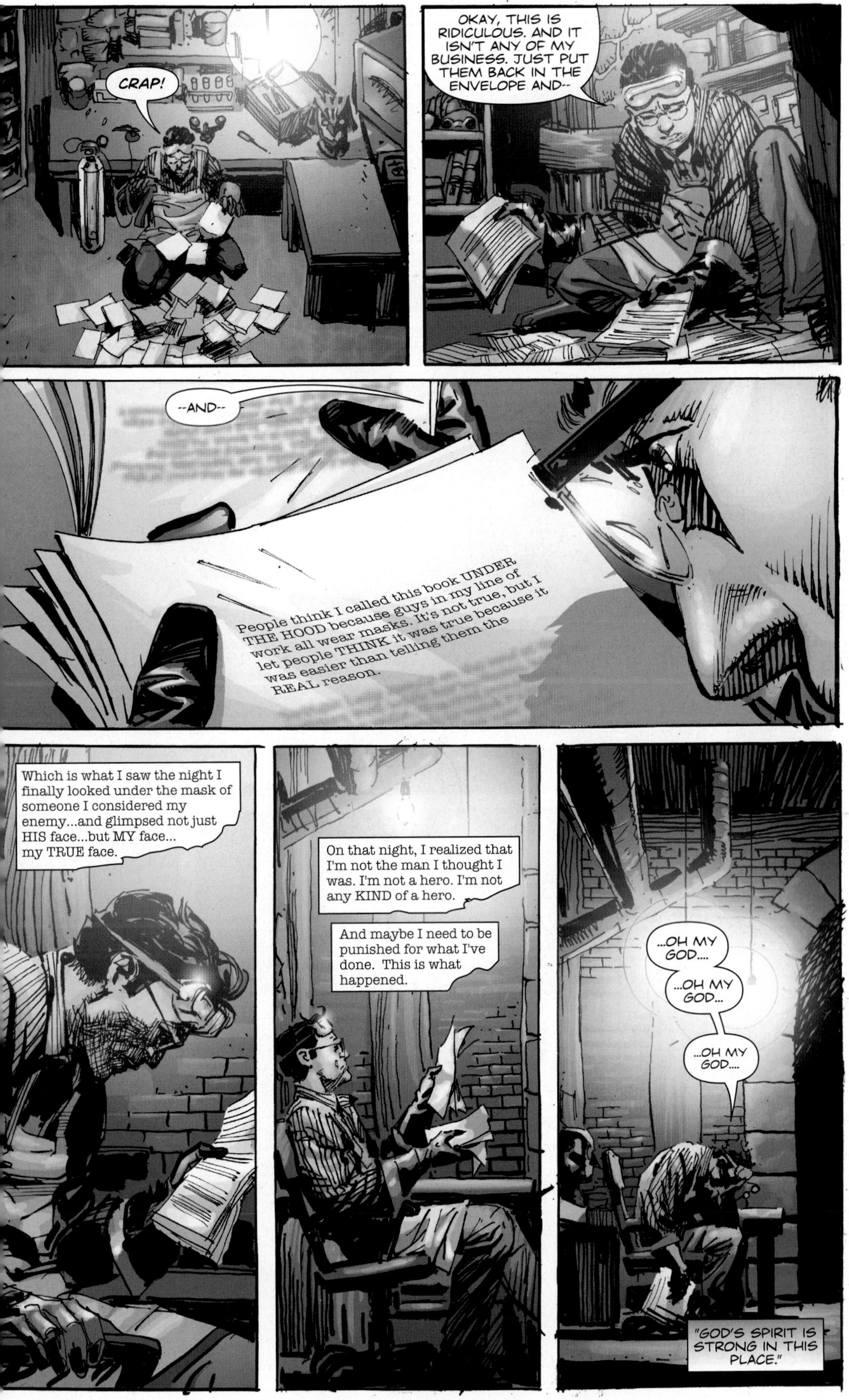
CRAP!
OKAY, THIS IS RIDICULOUS. AND IT ISN'T ANY OF MY BUSINESS. JUST PUT THEM BACK IN THE ENVELOPE AND--
--AND--
People think I called this book UNDER THE HOOD because guys in my line of work all wear masks. It's not true, but I let people THINK it was true because it was easier than telling them the REAL reason.
Which is what I saw the night I finally looked under the mask of someone I considered my enemy...and glimpsed not just HIS face...but MY face... my TRUE face.
On that night, I realized that I'm not the man I thought I was. I'm not a hero. I'm not any KIND of a hero.
And maybe I need to be punished for what I've done. This is what happened.
...OH MY GOD....
...OH MY GOD...
...OH MY GOD....
"GOD'S SPIRIT IS STRONG IN THIS PLACE."

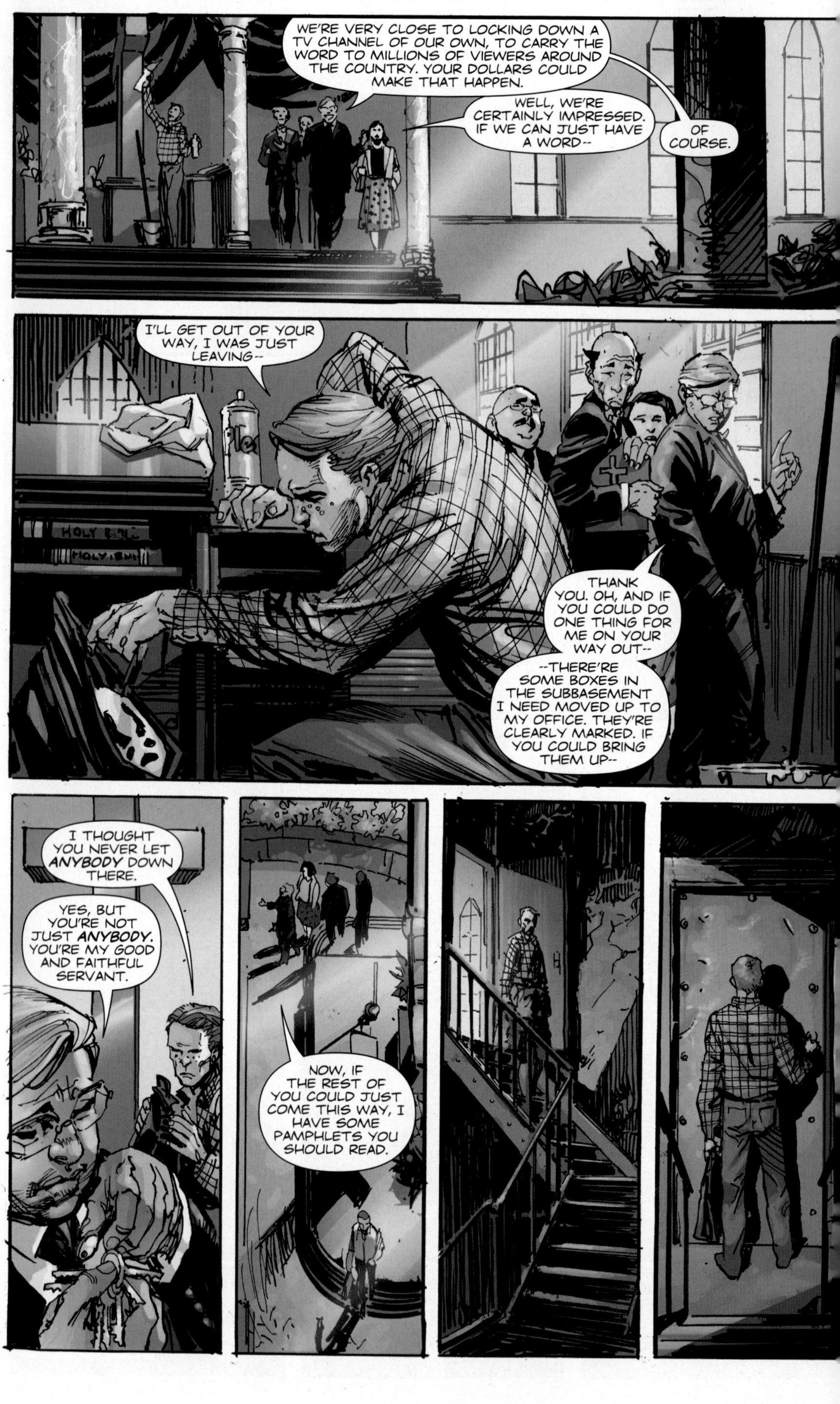
WE'RE VERY CLOSE TO LOCKING DOWN A TV CHANNEL OF OUR OWN, TO CARRY THE WORD TO MILLIONS OF VIEWERS AROUND THE COUNTRY. YOUR DOLLARS COULD MAKE THAT HAPPEN.
WELL, WE'RE CERTAINLY IMPRESSED. IF WE CAN JUST HAVE A WORD--
OF COURSE.
I'LL GET OUT OF YOUR WAY, I WAS JUST LEAVING--
HOLY BIBLE
HOLY BIBLE
THANK YOU. OH, AND IF YOU COULD DO ONE THING FOR ME ON YOUR WAY OUT--
--THERE'RE SOME BOXES IN THE SUBBASEMENT I NEED MOVED UP TO MY OFFICE. THEY'RE CLEARLY MARKED. IF YOU COULD BRING THEM UP--
I THOUGHT YOU NEVER LET ANYBODY DOWN THERE.
YES, BUT YOU'RE NOT JUST ANYBODY. YOU'RE MY GOOD AND FAITHFUL SERVANT.
NOW, IF THE REST OF YOU COULD JUST COME THIS WAY, I HAVE SOME PAMPHLETS YOU SHOULD READ.

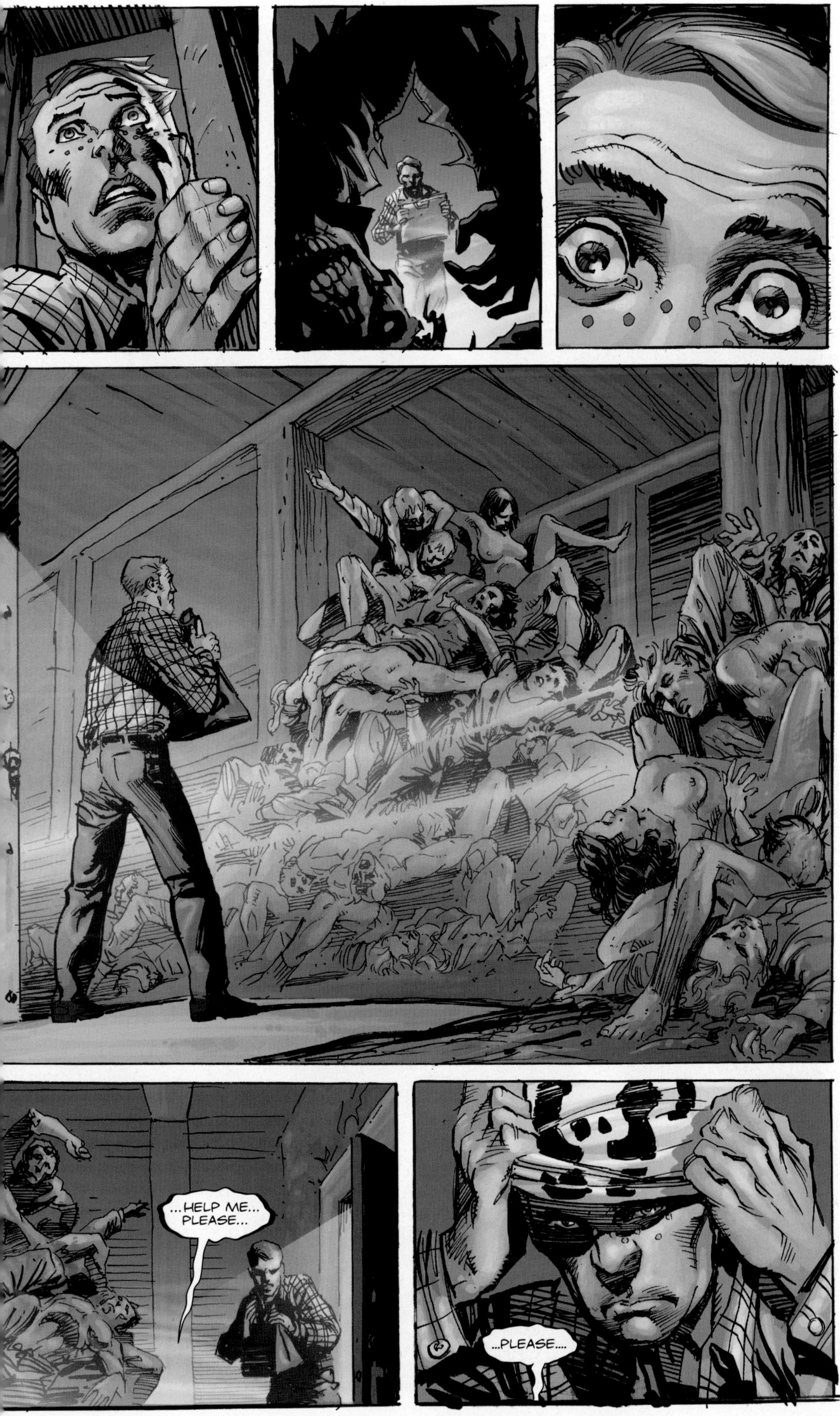
...HELP ME...
PLEASE...
...PLEASE....

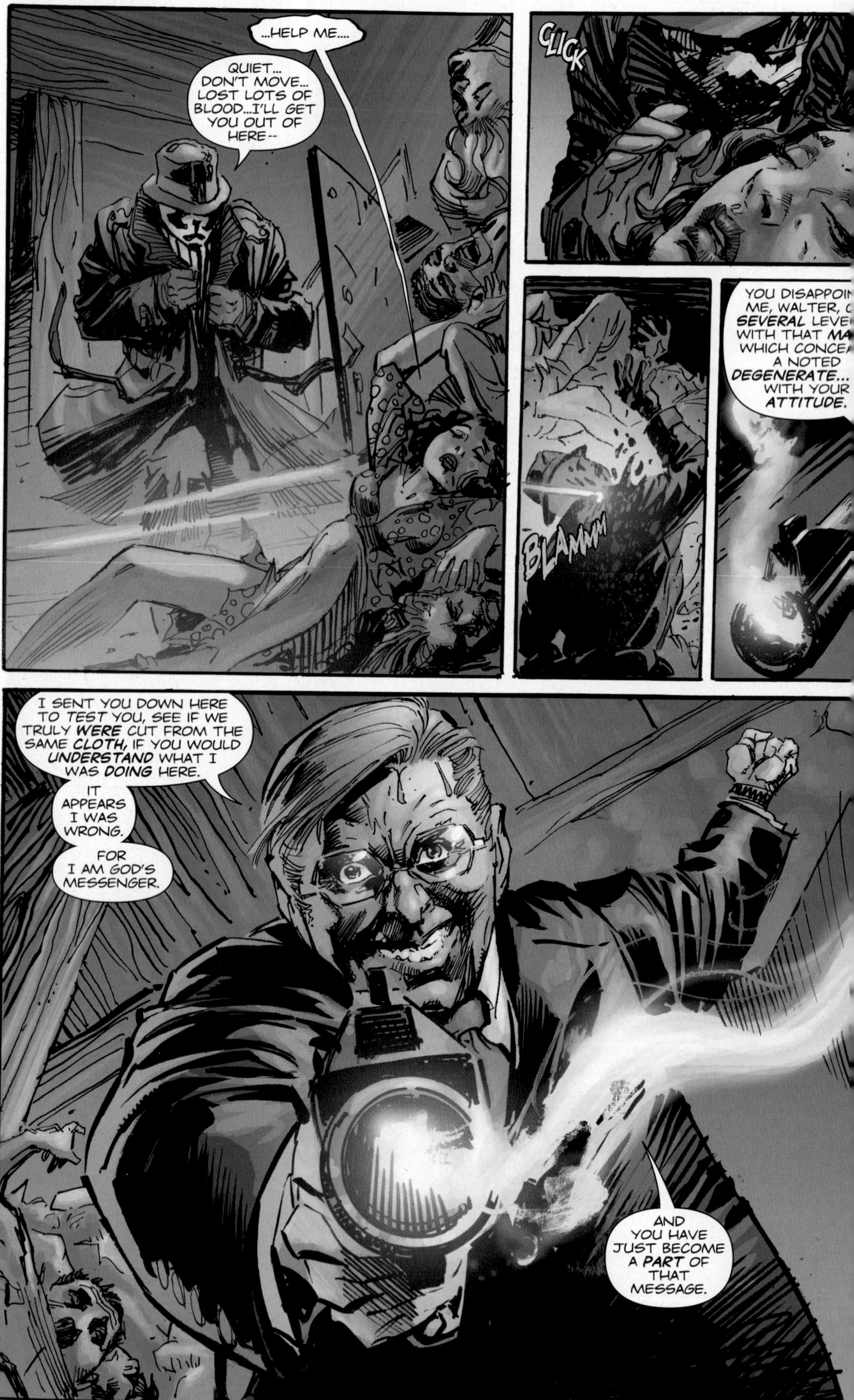
...HELP ME....
QUIET... DON'T MOVE... LOST LOTS OF BLOOD...I'LL GET YOU OUT OF HERE--
CLICK
BLAMMM
YOU DISAPPOIN ME, WALTER, O SEVERAL LEVE WITH THAT MA WHICH CONCEA A NOTED DEGENERATE... WITH YOUR ATTITUDE.
I SENT YOU DOWN HERE TO TEST YOU, SEE IF WE TRULY WERE CUT FROM THE SAME CLOTH, IF YOU WOULD UNDERSTAND WHAT I WAS DOING HERE.
IT APPEARS I WAS WRONG.
FOR I AM GOD'S MESSENGER.
AND YOU HAVE JUST BECOME A PART OF THAT MESSAGE.

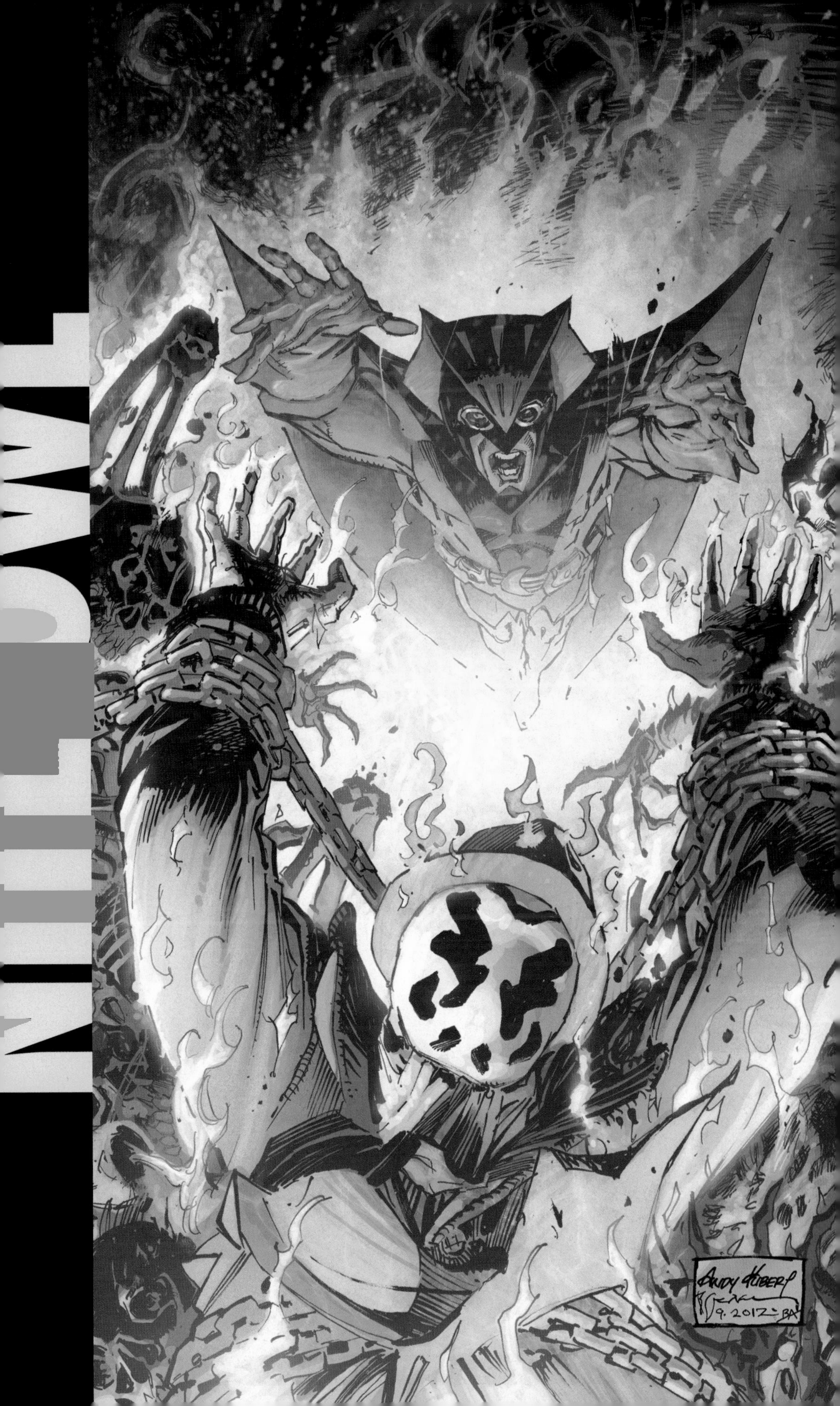
NITE OWL
ANDY KUBERT
9.2012-BA

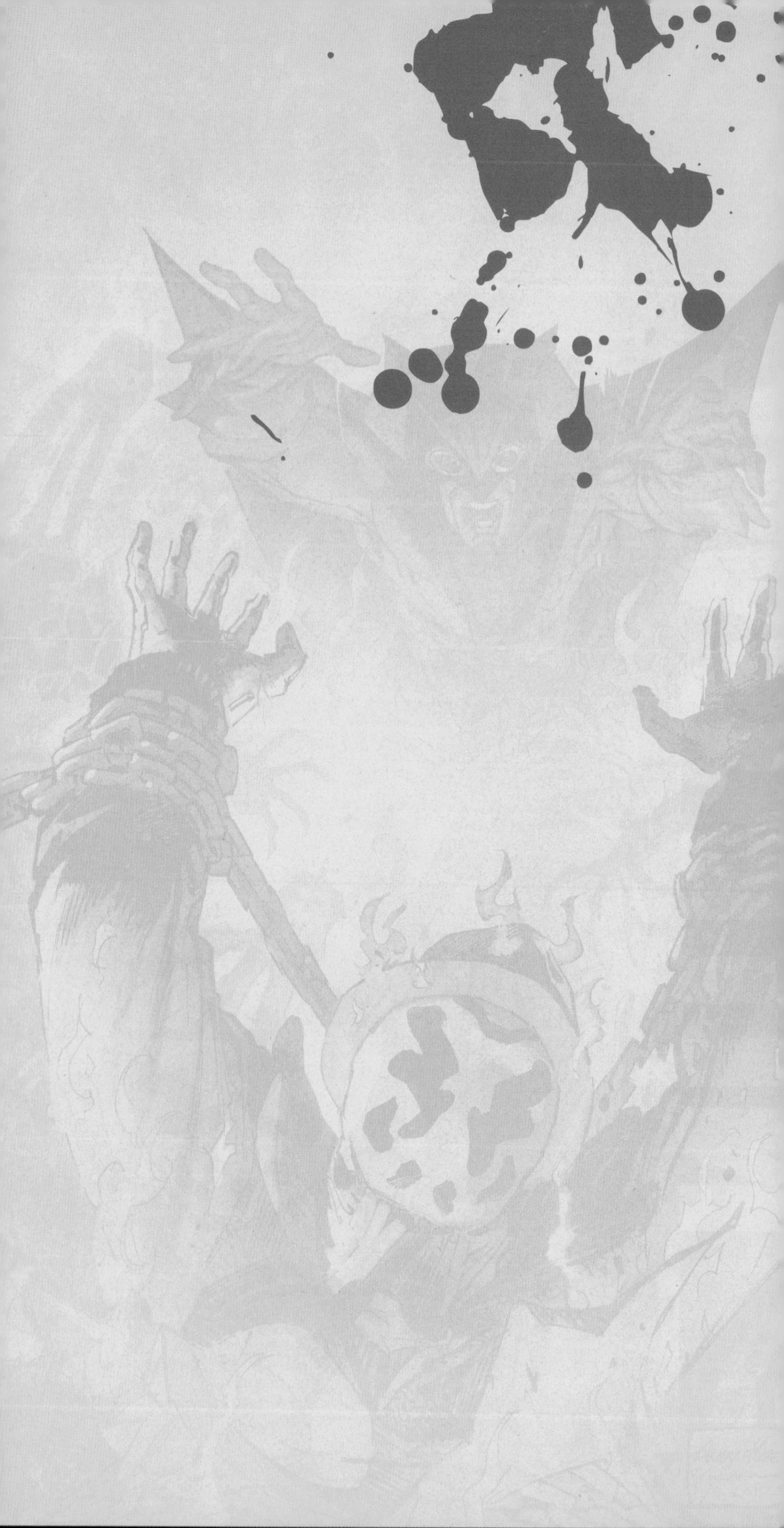

"LET IT BURN..."

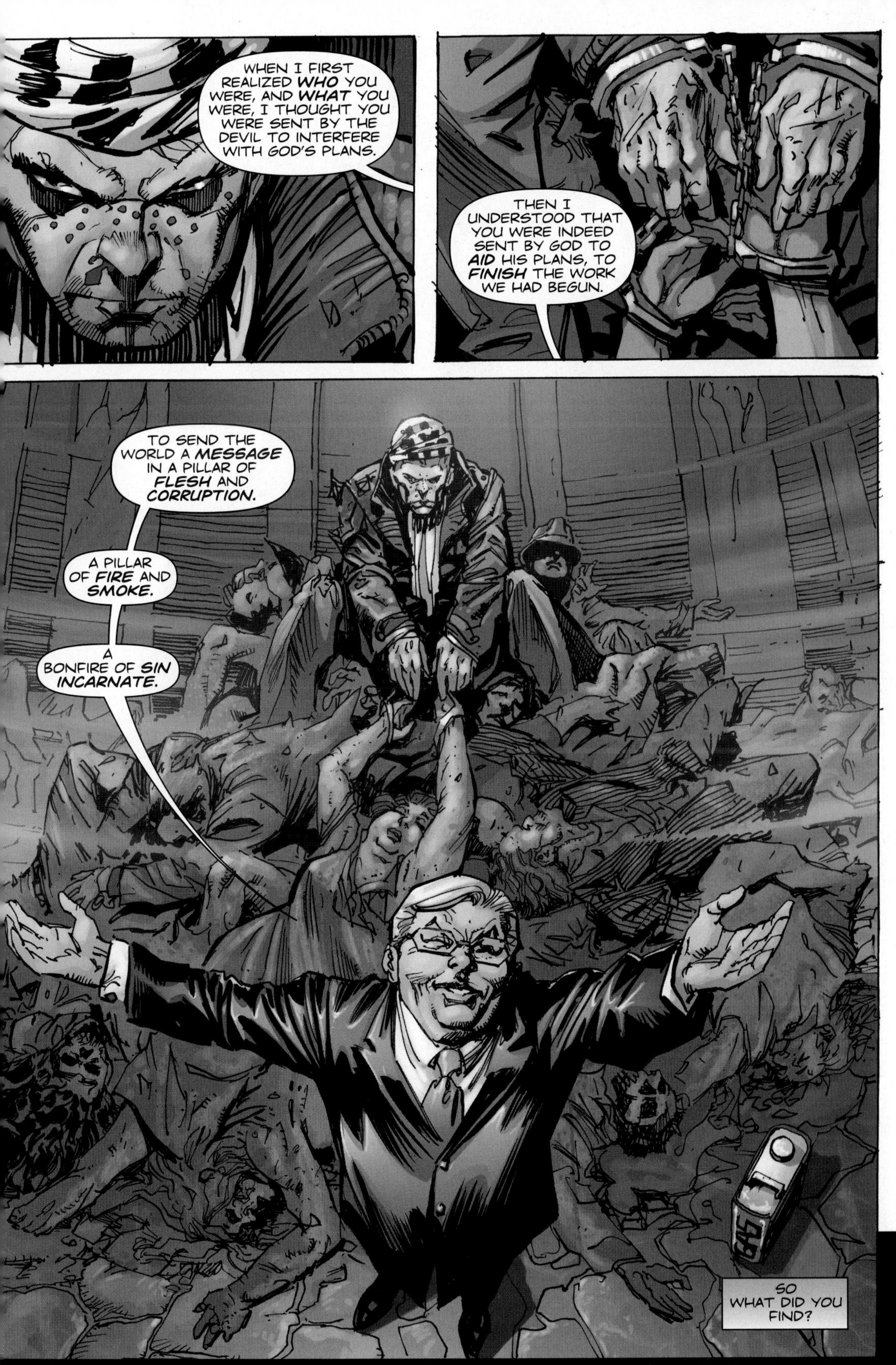
WHEN I FIRST REALIZED WHO YOU WERE, AND WHAT YOU WERE, I THOUGHT YOU WERE SENT BY THE DEVIL TO INTERFERE WITH GOD'S PLANS.
THEN I UNDERSTOOD THAT YOU WERE INDEED SENT BY GOD TO AID HIS PLANS, TO FINISH THE WORK WE HAD BEGUN.
TO SEND THE WORLD A MESSAGE IN A PILLAR OF FLESH AND CORRUPTION.
A PILLAR OF FIRE AND SMOKE.
A BONFIRE OF SIN INCARNATE.
SO WHAT DID YOU FIND?

ROM ONE NITE OWL TO ANOTHER

MICHAEL STRACZYNSKI–WRITER • ANDY KUBERT–PENCILS
BILL SIENKIEWICZ–INKS • BRAD ANDERSON–COLORS • NICK NAPOLITANO–LETTERS
CAMILLA ZHANG – ASST. EDITOR • MARK DOYLE – ASSOC. EDITOR • WILL DENNIS – EDITOR
ANDY KUBERT, BILL SIENKIEWICZ & BRAD ANDERSON–COVER • ETHAN VAN SCIVER & HI-FI–VARIANT COVER

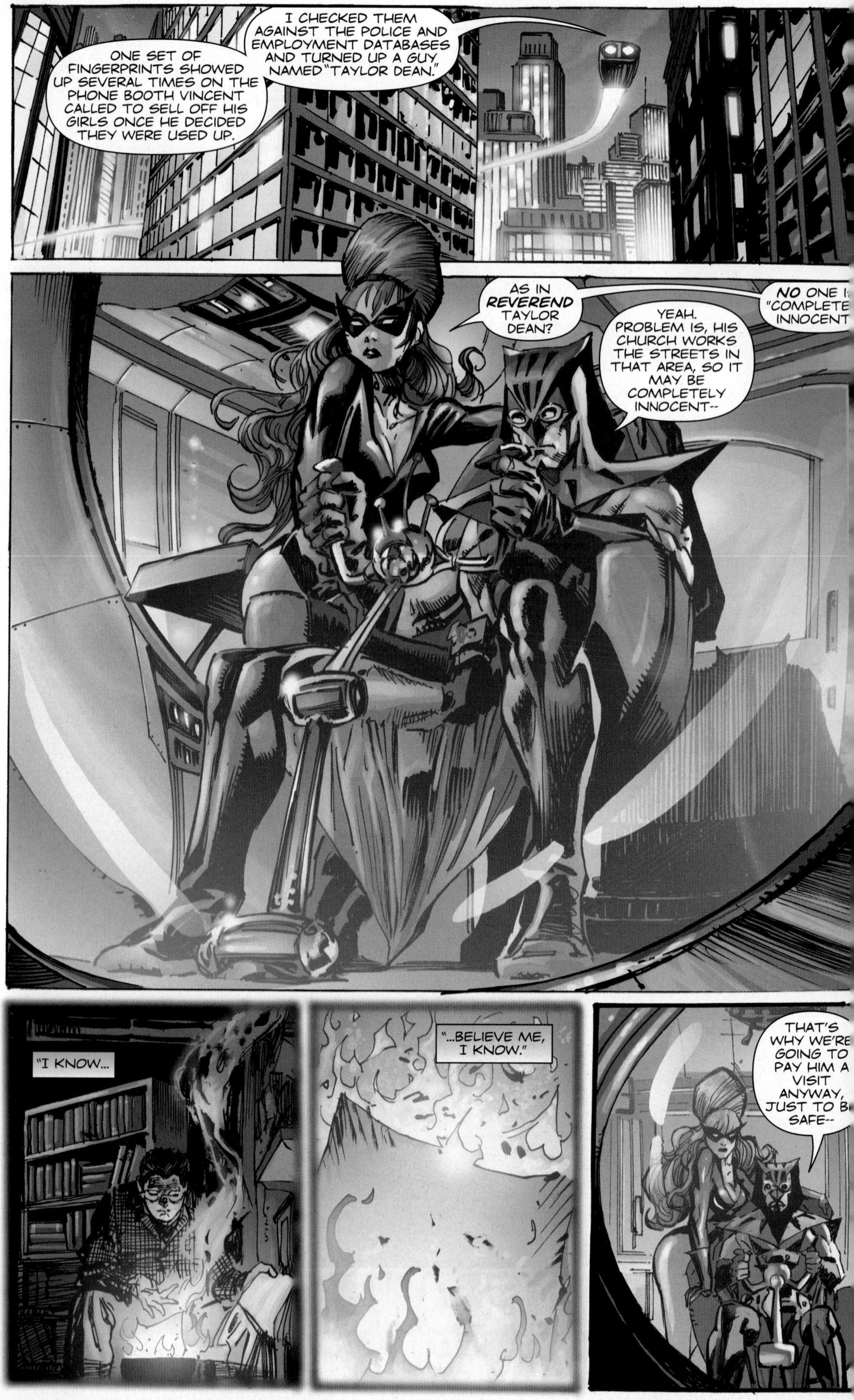
ONE SET OF FINGERPRINTS SHOWED UP SEVERAL TIMES ON THE PHONE BOOTH VINCENT CALLED TO SELL OFF HIS GIRLS ONCE HE DECIDED THEY WERE USED UP.
I CHECKED THEM AGAINST THE POLICE AND EMPLOYMENT DATABASES AND TURNED UP A GUY NAMED "TAYLOR DEAN."
AS IN REVEREND TAYLOR DEAN?
YEAH. PROBLEM IS, HIS CHURCH WORKS THE STREETS IN THAT AREA, SO IT MAY BE COMPLETELY INNOCENT--
NO ONE I "COMPLETE INNOCENT
"I KNOW...
"...BELIEVE ME, I KNOW."
THAT'S WHY WE'RE GOING TO PAY HIM A VISIT ANYWAY, JUST TO B SAFE--

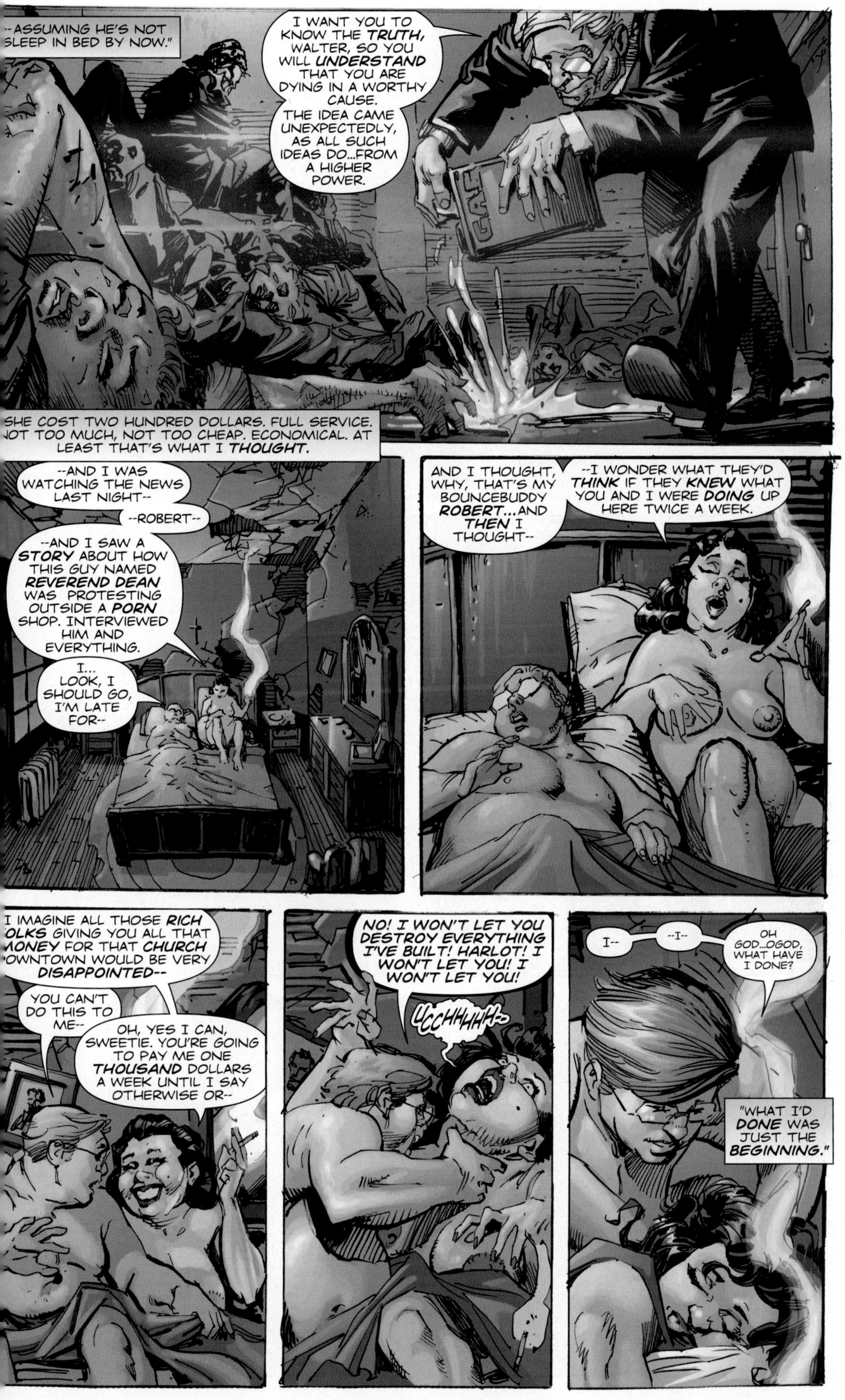
--ASSUMING HE'S NOT ASLEEP IN BED BY NOW."
I WANT YOU TO KNOW THE TRUTH, WALTER, SO YOU WILL UNDERSTAND THAT YOU ARE DYING IN A WORTHY CAUSE.
THE IDEA CAME UNEXPECTEDLY, AS ALL SUCH IDEAS DO...FROM A HIGHER POWER.
SHE COST TWO HUNDRED DOLLARS. FULL SERVICE. NOT TOO MUCH, NOT TOO CHEAP. ECONOMICAL. AT LEAST THAT'S WHAT I THOUGHT.
--AND I WAS WATCHING THE NEWS LAST NIGHT--
--ROBERT--
--AND I SAW A STORY ABOUT HOW THIS GUY NAMED REVEREND DEAN WAS PROTESTING OUTSIDE A PORN SHOP. INTERVIEWED HIM AND EVERYTHING.
I... LOOK, I SHOULD GO, I'M LATE FOR--
AND I THOUGHT, WHY, THAT'S MY BOUNCEBUDDY ROBERT...AND THEN I THOUGHT--
--I WONDER WHAT THEY'D THINK IF THEY KNEW WHAT YOU AND I WERE DOING UP HERE TWICE A WEEK.
I IMAGINE ALL THOSE RICH FOLKS GIVING YOU ALL THAT MONEY FOR THAT CHURCH DOWNTOWN WOULD BE VERY DISAPPOINTED--
YOU CAN'T DO THIS TO ME--
OH, YES I CAN, SWEETIE. YOU'RE GOING TO PAY ME ONE THOUSAND DOLLARS A WEEK UNTIL I SAY OTHERWISE OR--
NO! I WON'T LET YOU DESTROY EVERYTHING I'VE BUILT! HARLOT! I WON'T LET YOU! I WON'T LET YOU!
UCCHHHHH--
I--
--I--
OH GOD...OGOD, WHAT HAVE I DONE?
"WHAT I'D DONE WAS JUST THE BEGINNING."

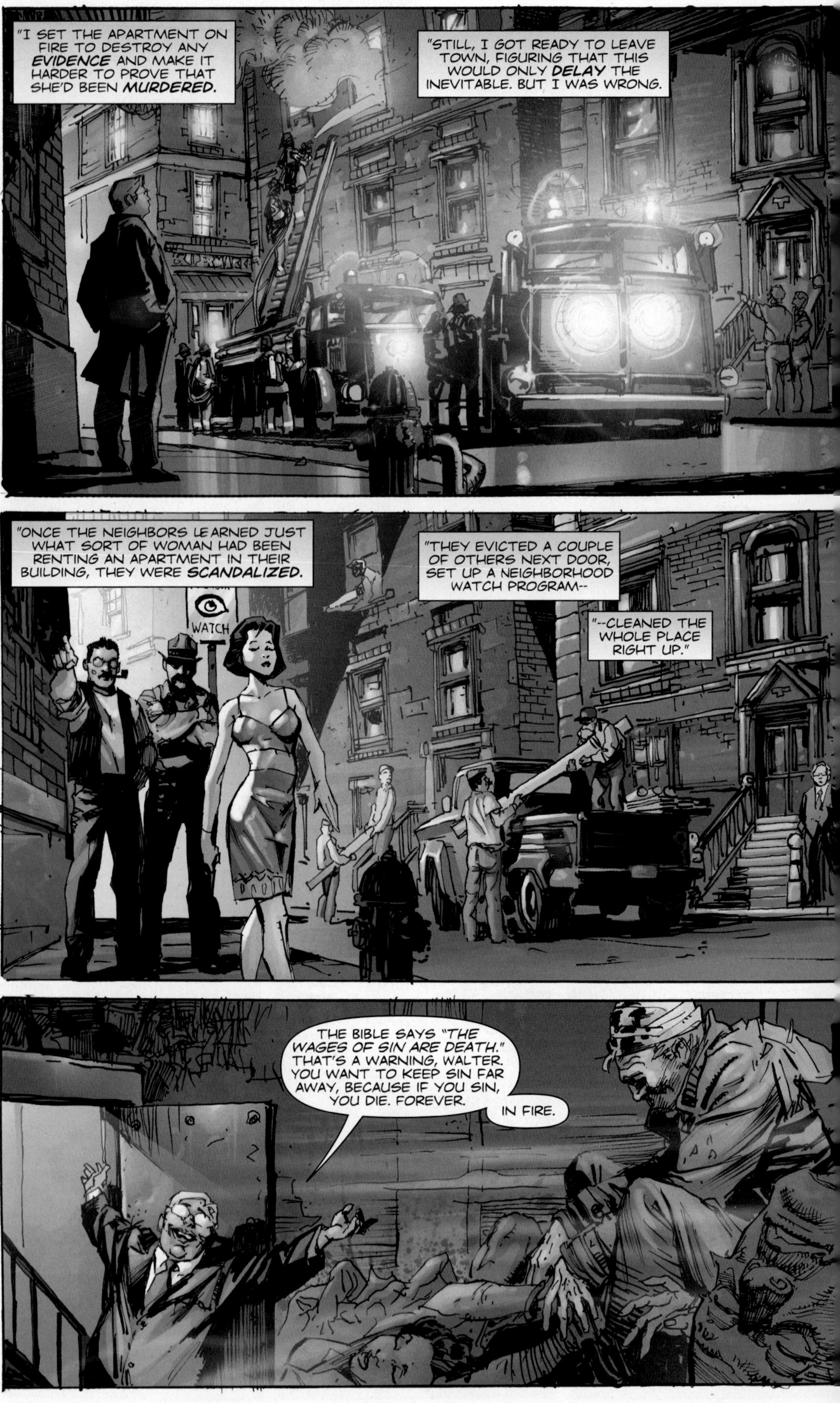
"I SET THE APARTMENT ON FIRE TO DESTROY ANY EVIDENCE AND MAKE IT HARDER TO PROVE THAT SHE'D BEEN MURDERED.
"STILL, I GOT READY TO LEAVE TOWN, FIGURING THAT THIS WOULD ONLY DELAY THE INEVITABLE. BUT I WAS WRONG.
"ONCE THE NEIGHBORS LEARNED JUST WHAT SORT OF WOMAN HAD BEEN RENTING AN APARTMENT IN THEIR BUILDING, THEY WERE SCANDALIZED.
WATCH
"THEY EVICTED A COUPLE OF OTHERS NEXT DOOR, SET UP A NEIGHBORHOOD WATCH PROGRAM--
"--CLEANED THE WHOLE PLACE RIGHT UP."
THE BIBLE SAYS "THE WAGES OF SIN ARE DEATH." THAT'S A WARNING, WALTER. YOU WANT TO KEEP SIN FAR AWAY, BECAUSE IF YOU SIN, YOU DIE. FOREVER.
IN FIRE.

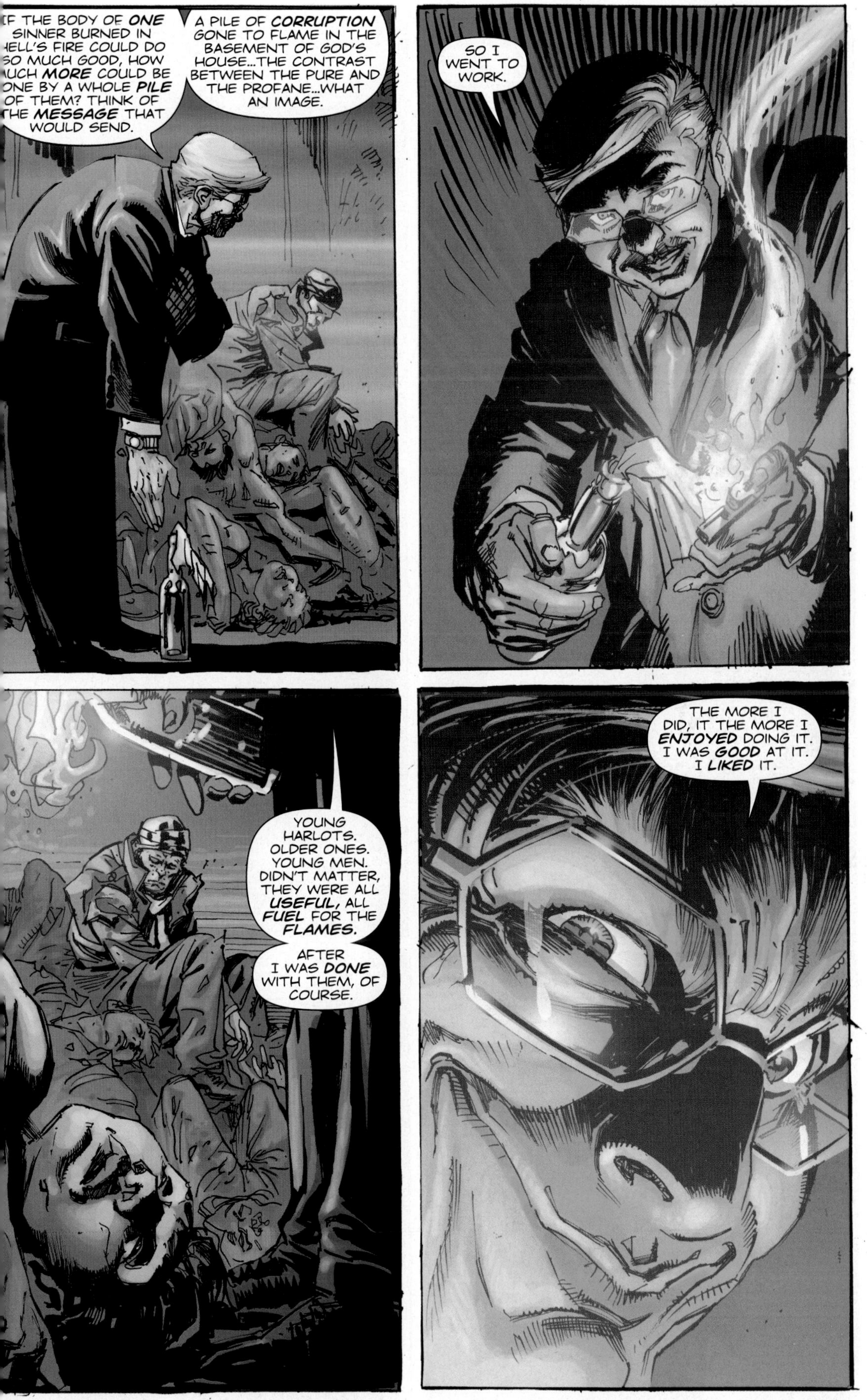

IF THE BODY OF ONE SINNER BURNED IN HELL'S FIRE COULD DO SO MUCH GOOD, HOW MUCH MORE COULD BE DONE BY A WHOLE PILE OF THEM? THINK OF THE MESSAGE THAT WOULD SEND.
A PILE OF CORRUPTION GONE TO FLAME IN THE BASEMENT OF GOD'S HOUSE...THE CONTRAST BETWEEN THE PURE AND THE PROFANE...WHAT AN IMAGE.
SO I WENT TO WORK.
YOUNG HARLOTS. OLDER ONES. YOUNG MEN. DIDN'T MATTER, THEY WERE ALL USEFUL, ALL FUEL FOR THE FLAMES.
AFTER I WAS DONE WITH THEM, OF COURSE.
THE MORE I DID, IT THE MORE I ENJOYED DOING IT. I WAS GOOD AT IT. I LIKED IT.

FOR A WHILE I EVEN ENJOYED THE RISK OF BRINGING THE BODIES *BACK* HERE, BUT I KNEW *GOD* WOULDN'T LET ME BE CAUGHT. I WAS DOING *GOD'S* WORK.

BUT I STILL HAD TO LEAVE MY *LAST* TASK EARLY, WHEN I FEARED SOMEONE MIGHT HAVE HEARD HER *SCREAMS* AND CALLED THE POLICE.

SLOPPY. UNFORTUNATE. STILL, HER HANDCUFFS PROVIDED A NICE WAY OF HANDLING *YOU*, WALTER.

I KNEW *GOD* WOULD SEND SOMEONE TO TAKE THE *BLAME* FOR WHAT I'D DONE, SOMEONE AS CORRUPT AS THE BODIES HE WOULD BE *FOUND* WITH...THE BODIES HE WOULD BE HELD *RESPONSIBLE* FOR.

BECAUSE ACCIDENTS HAPPEN TO PEOPLE LIKE YOU, WALTER.

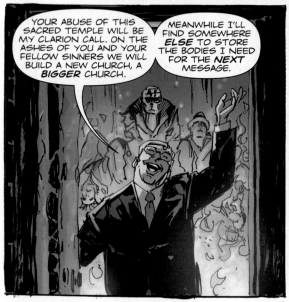

YOUR ABUSE OF THIS SACRED TEMPLE WILL BE MY CLARION CALL. ON THE ASHES OF YOU AND YOUR FELLOW SINNERS WE WILL BUILD A NEW CHURCH, A *BIGGER* CHURCH.

MEANWHILE I'LL FIND SOMEWHERE *ELSE* TO STORE THE BODIES I NEED FOR THE *NEXT* MESSAGE.

BECAUSE AS FOUR GOSPELS AND SIXTY-TWO *OTHER* BOOKS IN THE BIBLE CONFIRM, THERE'S *ALWAYS* ANOTHER MESSAGE IN NEED OF SENDING.

SLAM

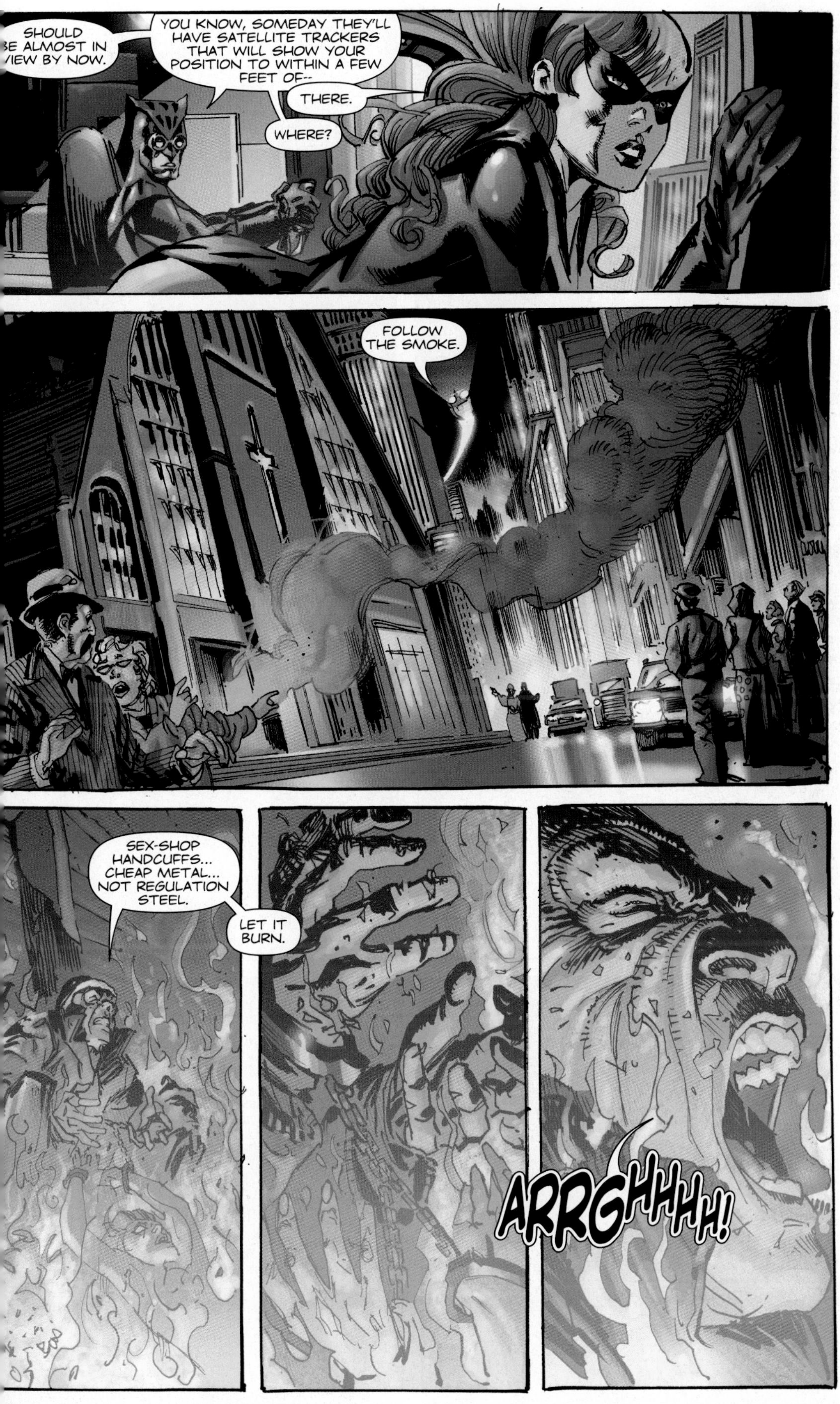
SHOULD BE ALMOST IN VIEW BY NOW.
YOU KNOW, SOMEDAY THEY'LL HAVE SATELLITE TRACKERS THAT WILL SHOW YOUR POSITION TO WITHIN A FEW FEET OF--
THERE.
WHERE?
FOLLOW THE SMOKE.
SEX-SHOP HANDCUFFS... CHEAP METAL... NOT REGULATION STEEL.
LET IT BURN.
ARRGHHHH!

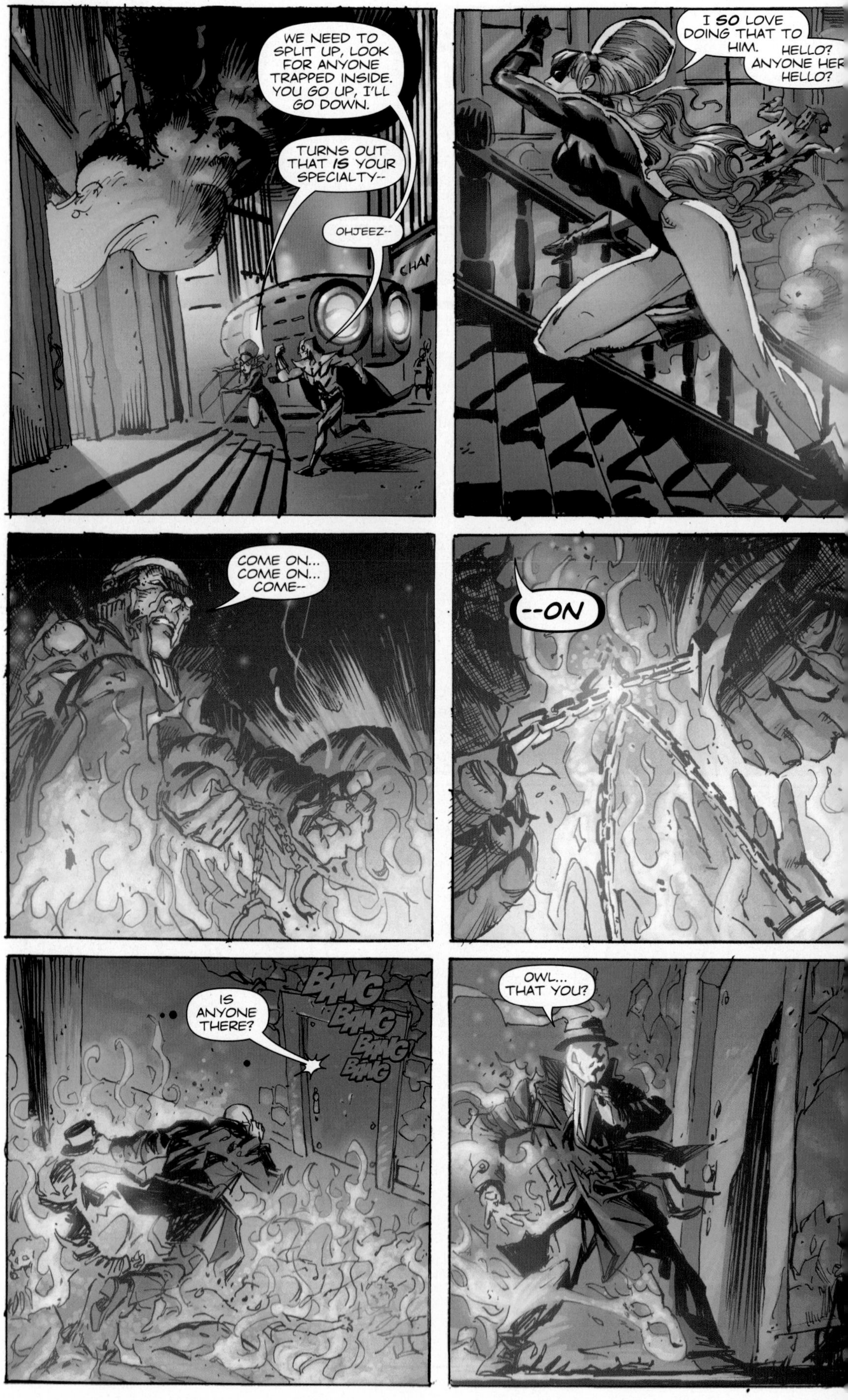
WE NEED TO SPLIT UP, LOOK FOR ANYONE TRAPPED INSIDE. YOU GO UP, I'LL GO DOWN.
TURNS OUT THAT IS YOUR SPECIALTY--
OHJEEZ--
I SO LOVE DOING THAT TO HIM.
HELLO? ANYONE HER HELLO?
COME ON... COME ON... COME--
--ON
BANG BANG BANG BANG
IS ANYONE THERE?
OWL... THAT YOU?

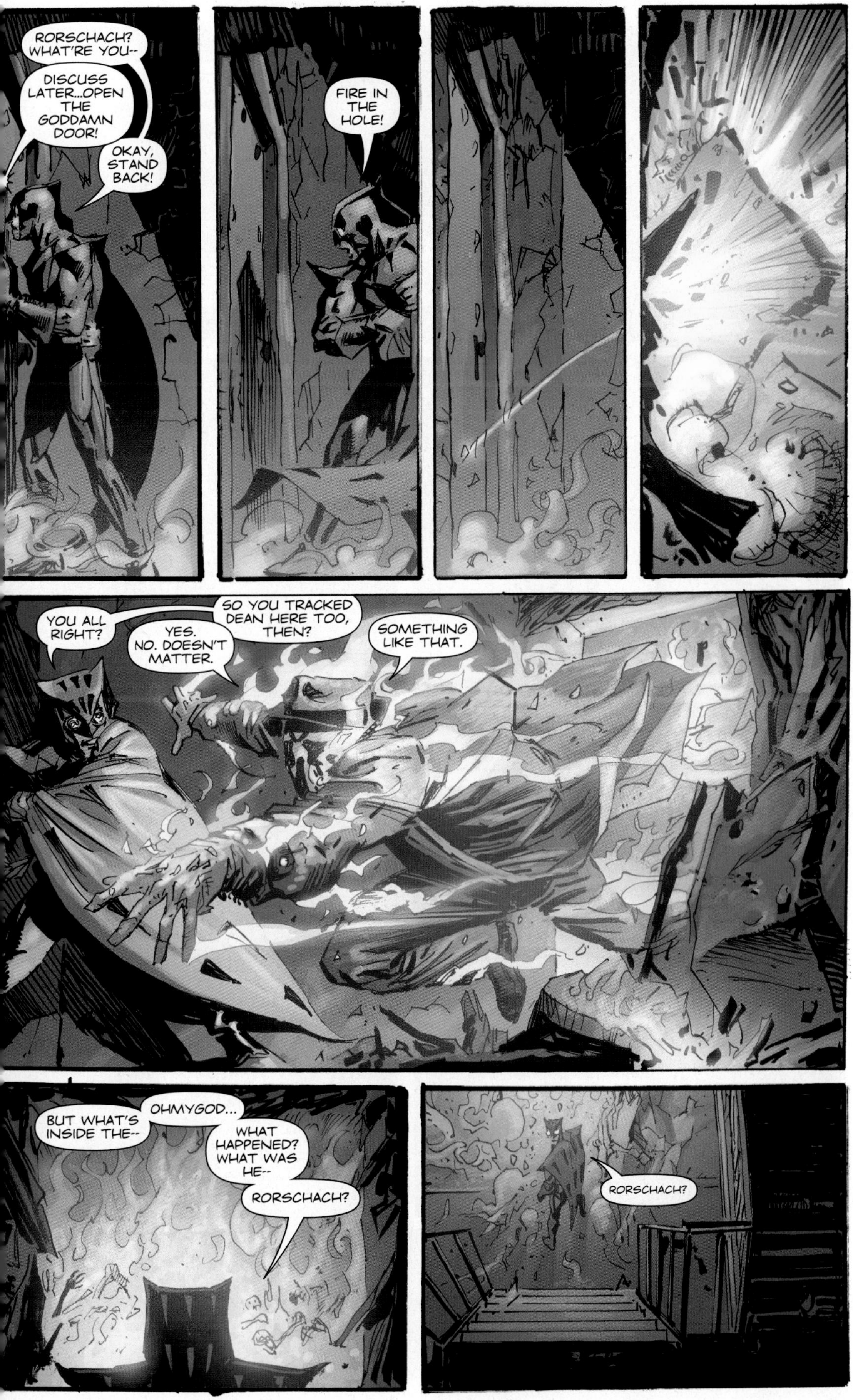
RORSCHACH? WHAT'RE YOU--
DISCUSS LATER...OPEN THE GODDAMN DOOR!
OKAY, STAND BACK!
FIRE IN THE HOLE!
YOU ALL RIGHT?
YES. NO. DOESN'T MATTER.
SO YOU TRACKED DEAN HERE TOO, THEN?
SOMETHING LIKE THAT.
BUT WHAT'S INSIDE THE--
OHMYGOD...
WHAT HAPPENED? WHAT WAS HE--
RORSCHACH?
RORSCHACH?

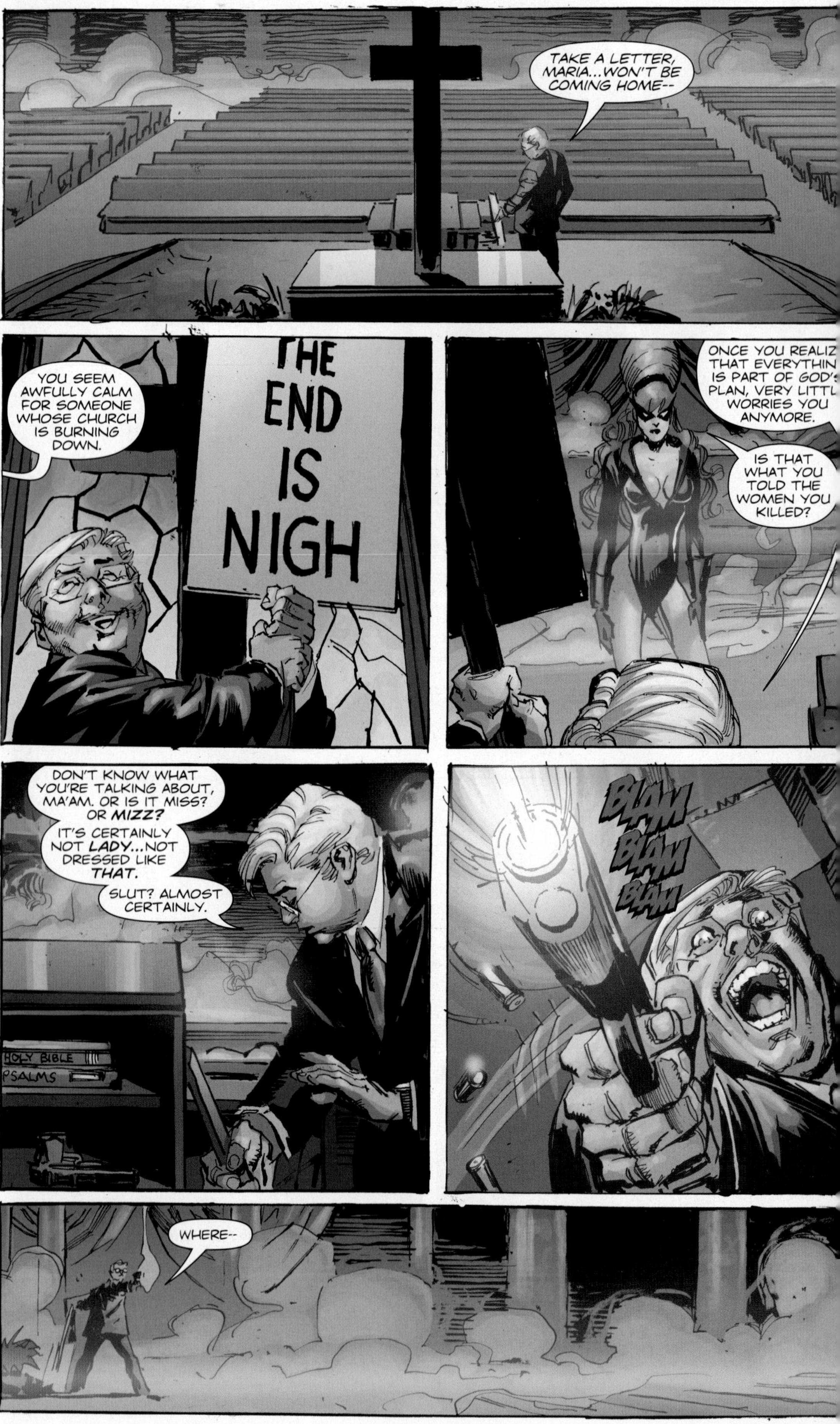
TAKE A LETTER, MARIA...WON'T BE COMING HOME--
THE END IS NIGH
YOU SEEM AWFULLY CALM FOR SOMEONE WHOSE CHURCH IS BURNING DOWN.
ONCE YOU REALIZ THAT EVERYTHIN IS PART OF GOD'S PLAN, VERY LITTL WORRIES YOU ANYMORE.
IS THAT WHAT YOU TOLD THE WOMEN YOU KILLED?
DON'T KNOW WHAT YOU'RE TALKING ABOUT, MA'AM. OR IS IT MISS? OR MIZZ?
IT'S CERTAINLY NOT LADY...NOT DRESSED LIKE THAT.
SLUT? ALMOST CERTAINLY.
HOLY BIBLE
PSALMS
BLAM BLAM BLAM
WHERE--

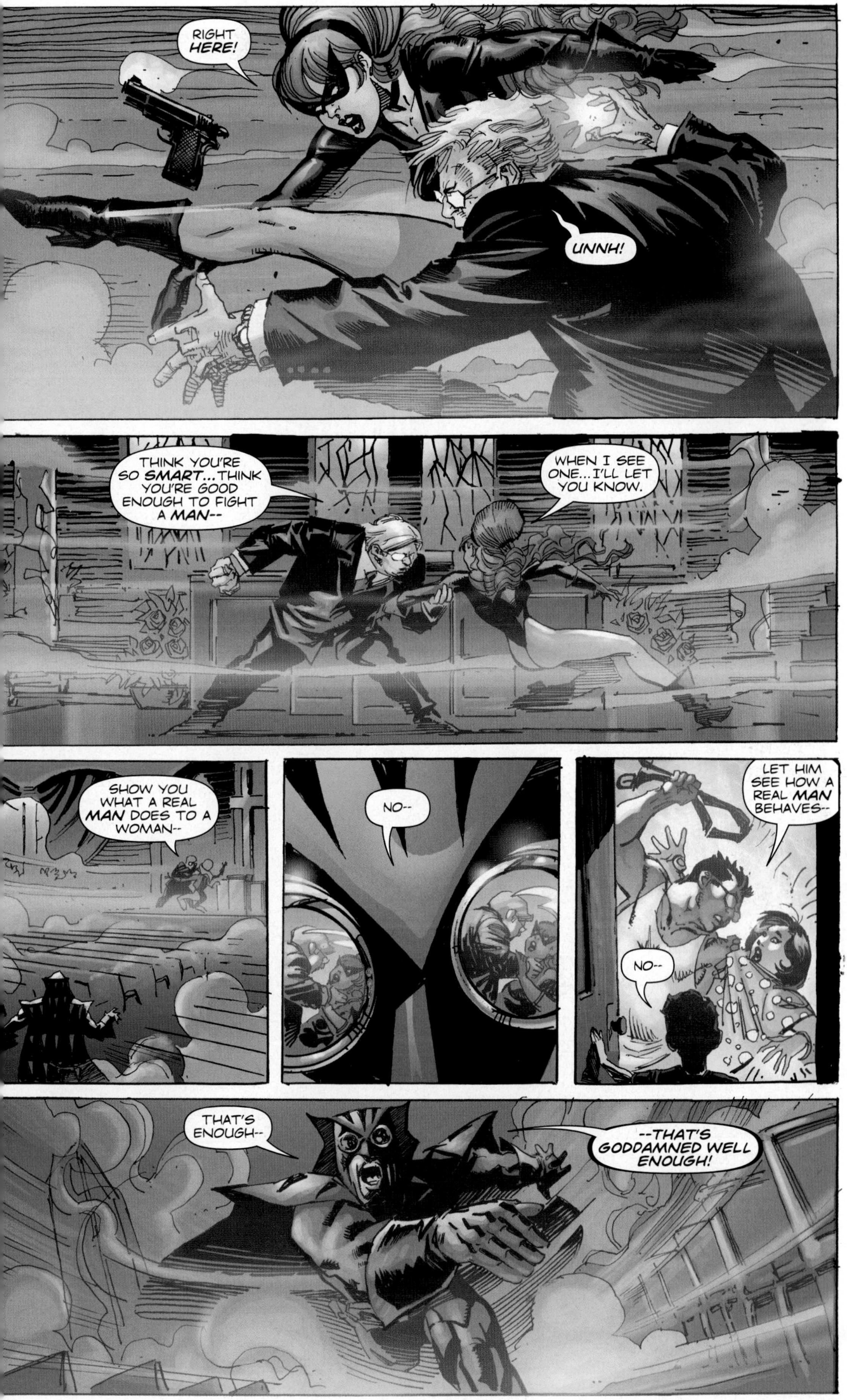
RIGHT HERE!
UNNH!
THINK YOU'RE SO SMART... THINK YOU'RE GOOD ENOUGH TO FIGHT A MAN--
WHEN I SEE ONE... I'LL LET YOU KNOW.
SHOW YOU WHAT A REAL MAN DOES TO A WOMAN--
NO--
LET HIM SEE HOW A REAL MAN BEHAVES--
NO--
THAT'S ENOUGH--
--THAT'S GODDAMNED WELL ENOUGH!

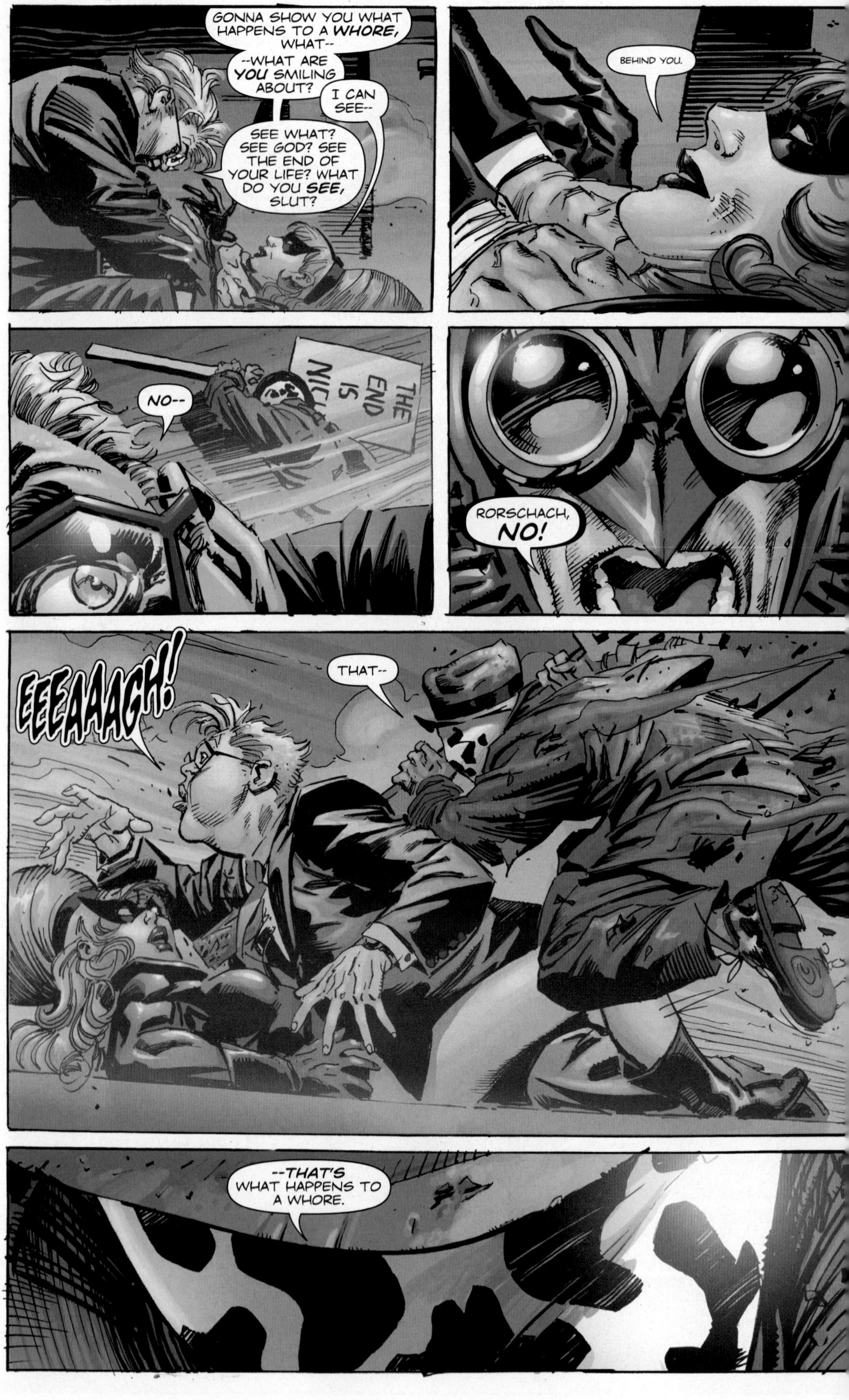
GONNA SHOW YOU WHAT HAPPENS TO A WHORE, WHAT--
--WHAT ARE YOU SMILING ABOUT?
I CAN SEE--
SEE WHAT? SEE GOD? SEE THE END OF YOUR LIFE? WHAT DO YOU SEE, SLUT?
BEHIND YOU.
NO--
THE END IS NIG
RORSCHACH, NO!
EEEAAAGH!
THAT--
--THAT'S WHAT HAPPENS TO A WHORE.

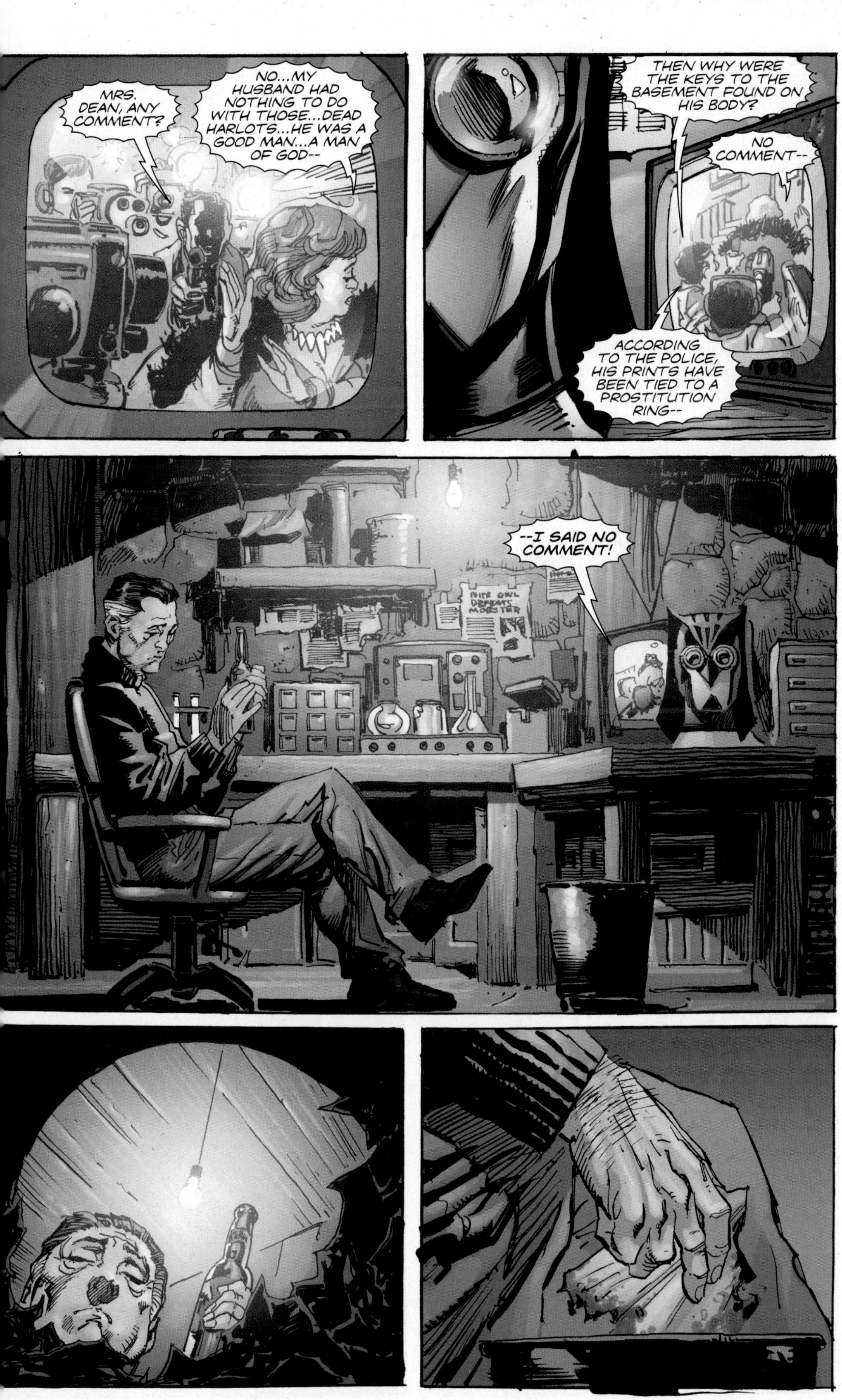

MRS. DEAN, ANY COMMENT?
NO...MY HUSBAND HAD NOTHING TO DO WITH THOSE...DEAD HARLOTS...HE WAS A GOOD MAN...A MAN OF GOD--
THEN WHY WERE THE KEYS TO THE BASEMENT FOUND ON HIS BODY?
NO COMMENT--
ACCORDING TO THE POLICE, HIS PRINTS HAVE BEEN TIED TO A PROSTITUTION RING--
--I SAID NO COMMENT!

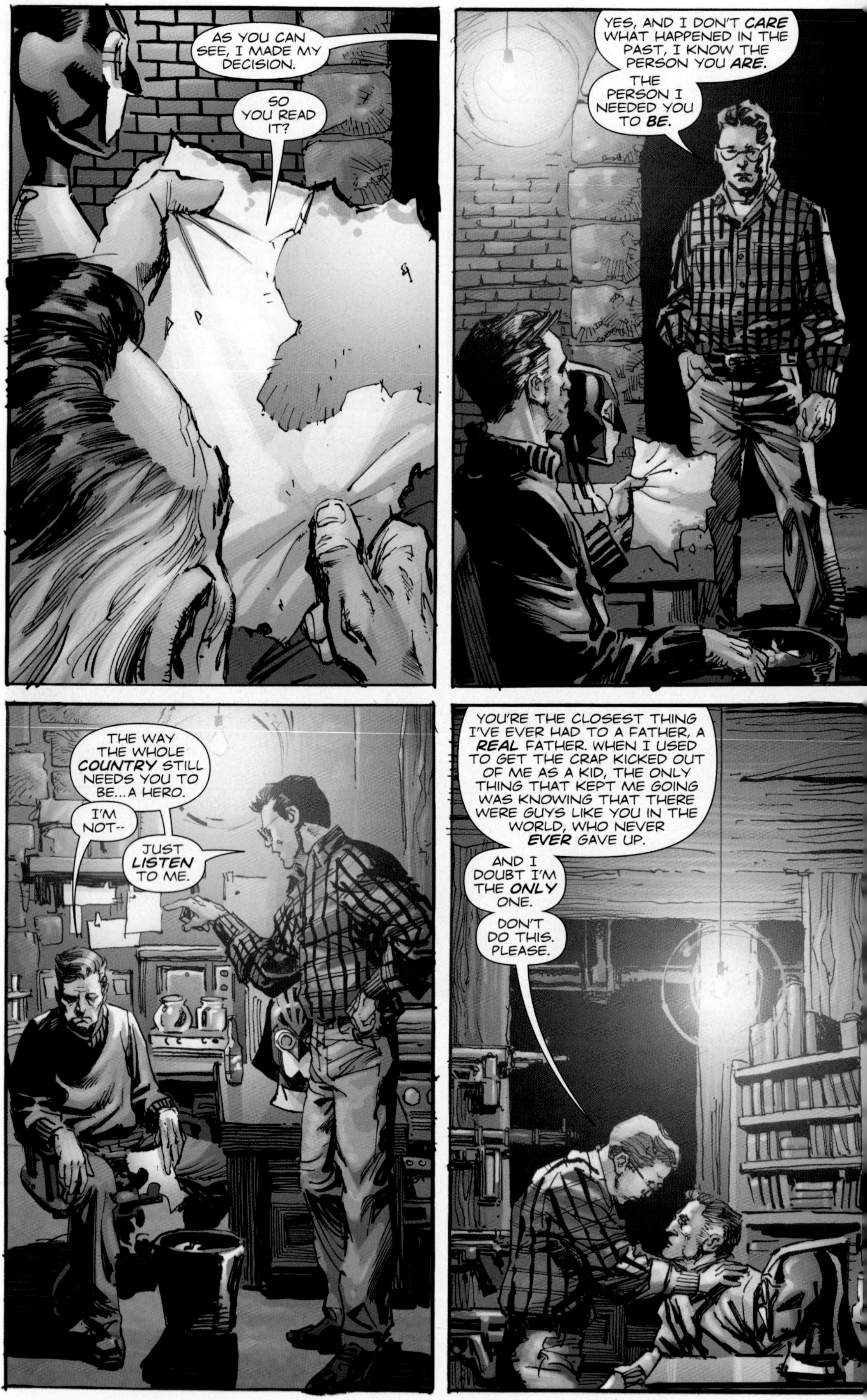

AS YOU CAN SEE, I MADE MY DECISION.
SO YOU READ IT?
YES, AND I DON'T CARE WHAT HAPPENED IN THE PAST, I KNOW THE PERSON YOU ARE.
THE PERSON I NEEDED YOU TO BE.
THE WAY THE WHOLE COUNTRY STILL NEEDS YOU TO BE...A HERO.
I'M NOT--
JUST LISTEN TO ME.
YOU'RE THE CLOSEST THING I'VE EVER HAD TO A FATHER, A REAL FATHER. WHEN I USED TO GET THE CRAP KICKED OUT OF ME AS A KID, THE ONLY THING THAT KEPT ME GOING WAS KNOWING THAT THERE WERE GUYS LIKE YOU IN THE WORLD, WHO NEVER EVER GAVE UP.
AND I DOUBT I'M THE ONLY ONE.
DON'T DO THIS. PLEASE.

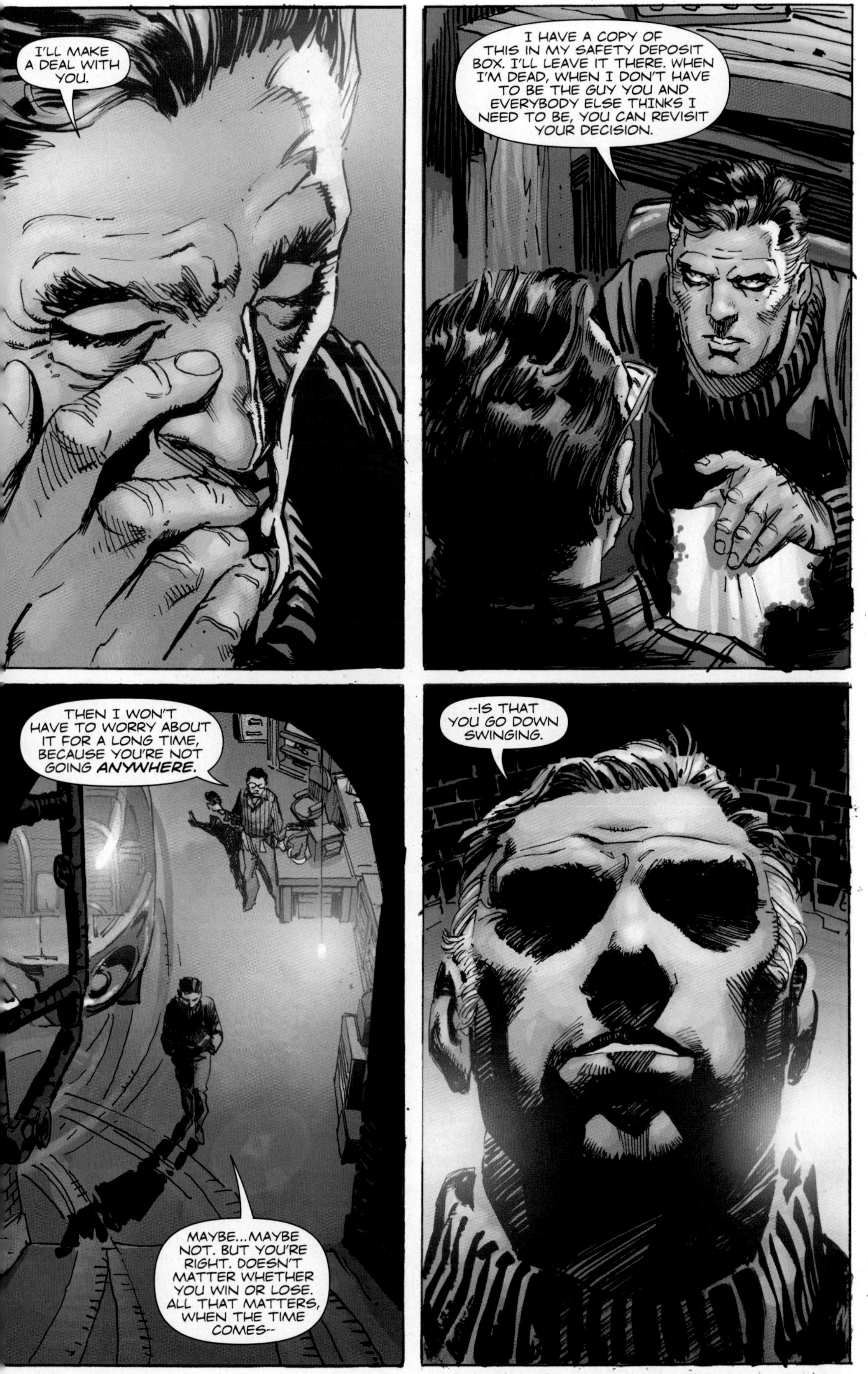
I'LL MAKE A DEAL WITH YOU.
I HAVE A COPY OF THIS IN MY SAFETY DEPOSIT BOX. I'LL LEAVE IT THERE. WHEN I'M DEAD, WHEN I DON'T HAVE TO BE THE GUY YOU AND EVERYBODY ELSE THINKS I NEED TO BE, YOU CAN REVISIT YOUR DECISION.
THEN I WON'T HAVE TO WORRY ABOUT IT FOR A LONG TIME, BECAUSE YOU'RE NOT GOING ANYWHERE.
MAYBE...MAYBE NOT. BUT YOU'RE RIGHT. DOESN'T MATTER WHETHER YOU WIN OR LOSE. ALL THAT MATTERS, WHEN THE TIME COMES--
--IS THAT YOU GO DOWN SWINGING.

I SHOULD TURN YOU IN TO THE POLICE, YOU **KNOW** THAT, RIGHT?

IF WE'D LET HIM GO HE WOULD'VE WALKED. MONEY. POWER. EXPENSIVE ATTORNEYS. WOULDN'T EVEN HAVE BEEN **CLOSE**.

YOU CAN'T JUST KILL PEOPLE--

YOU **SAW** WHAT HE DID--

I WOULD'VE--

YOU WOULD'VE **NOTHING**.

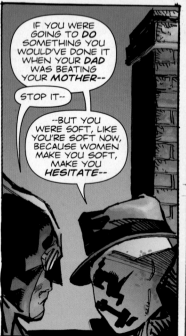

IF YOU WERE GOING TO **DO** SOMETHING YOU WOULD'VE DONE IT WHEN YOUR **DAD** WAS BEATING YOUR **MOTHER**--

STOP IT--

--BUT YOU WERE SOFT, LIKE YOU'RE SOFT NOW, BECAUSE WOMEN MAKE YOU SOFT, MAKE YOU **HESITATE**--

YEAH, YOU AND ME, WE'RE GONNA START ALL **OVER**...JUST GOTTA DEAL WITH THE **BRAT** IS ALL.

LITTLE ACCIDENT...KIDS HAVE 'EM ALL THE TIME. YEAH...GONNA HAVE A LATE TERM-- **REALLY** LATE TERM-- ABORTION.

WHAT THE--

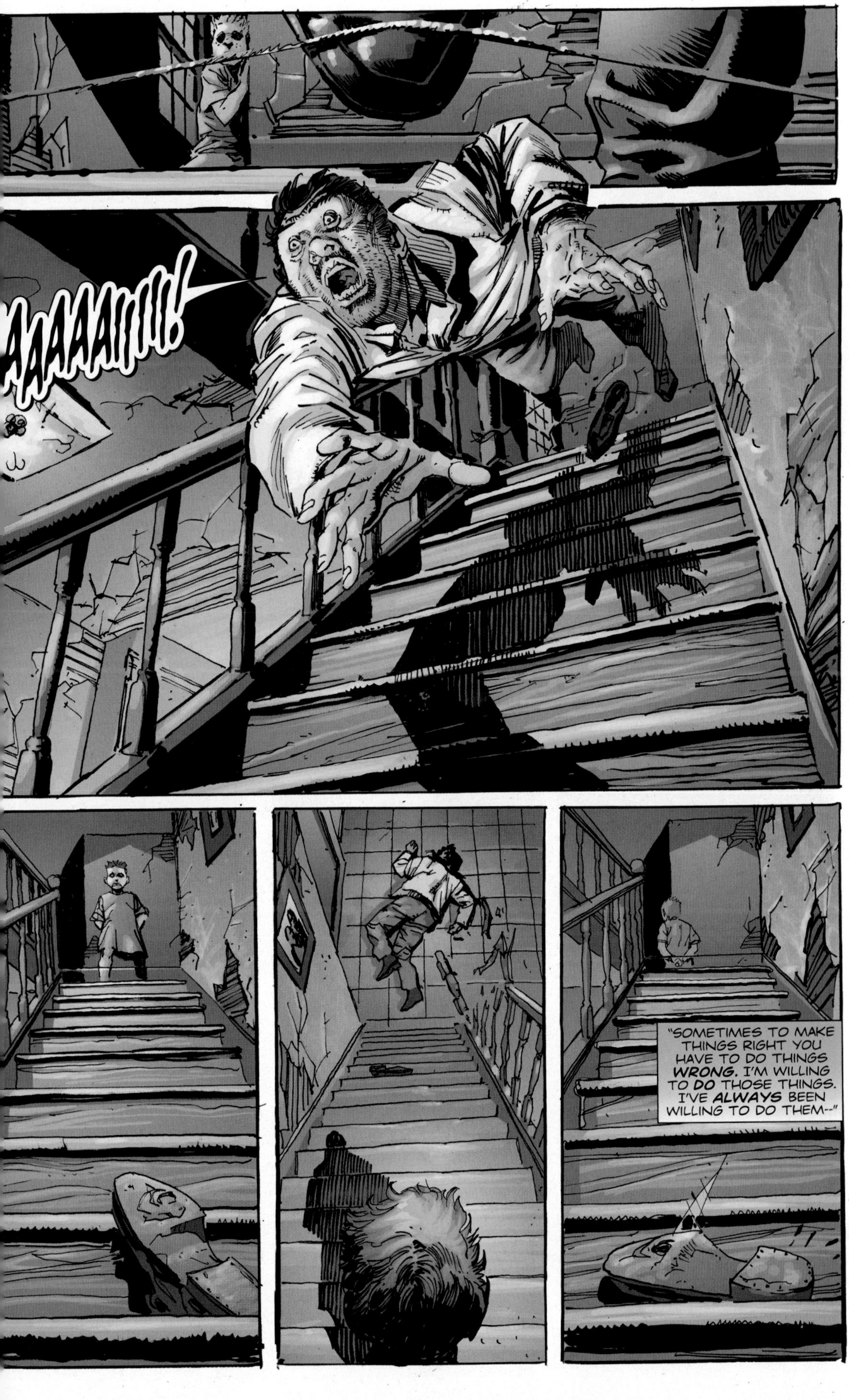
AAAAAIIII!
"SOMETIMES TO MAKE THINGS RIGHT YOU HAVE TO DO THINGS **WRONG**. I'M WILLING TO **DO** THOSE THINGS. I'VE **ALWAYS** BEEN WILLING TO DO THEM--"

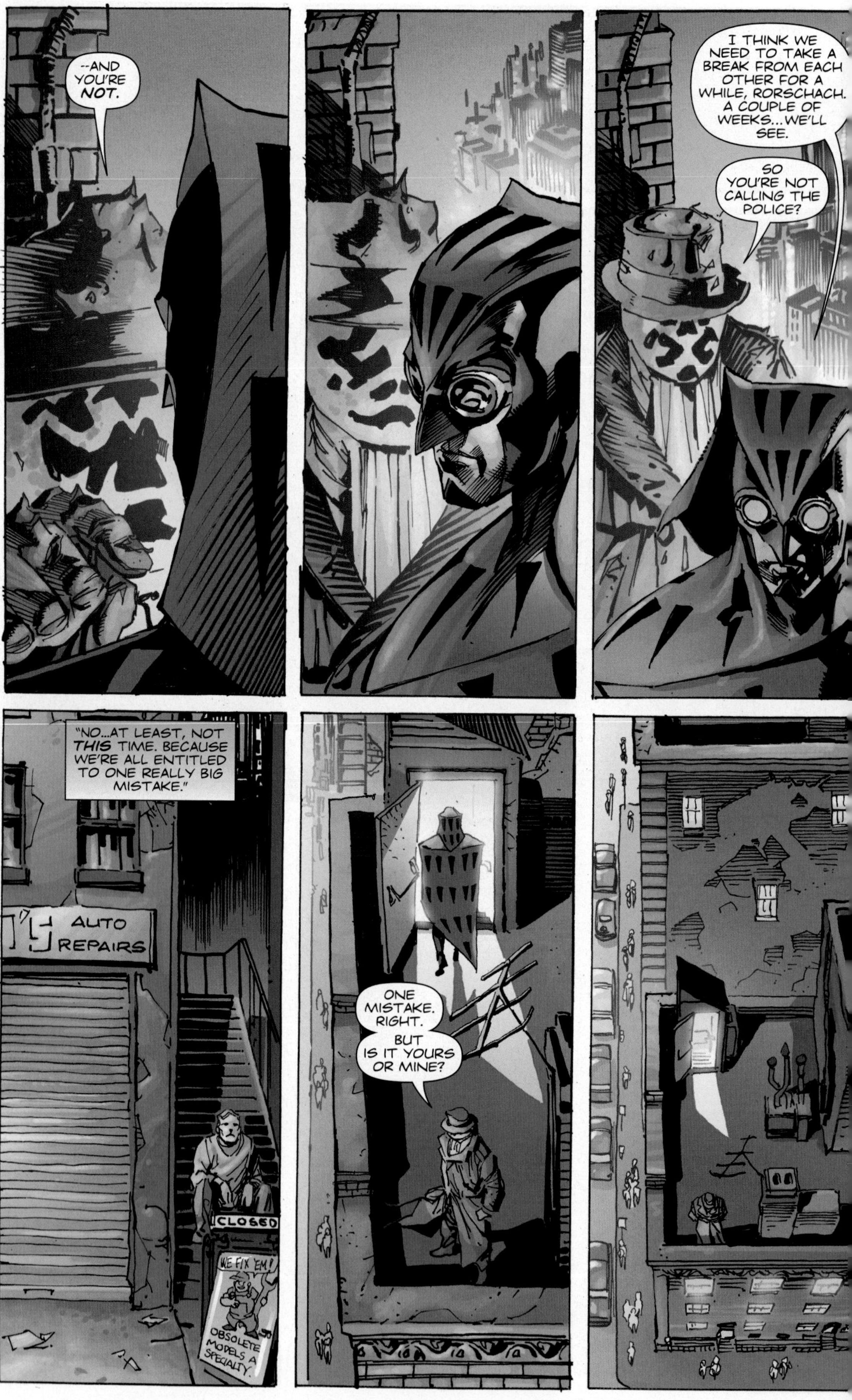
--AND YOU'RE NOT.
I THINK WE NEED TO TAKE A BREAK FROM EACH OTHER FOR A WHILE, RORSCHACH. A COUPLE OF WEEKS...WE'LL SEE.
SO YOU'RE NOT CALLING THE POLICE?
"NO...AT LEAST, NOT THIS TIME. BECAUSE WE'RE ALL ENTITLED TO ONE REALLY BIG MISTAKE."
AUTO REPAIRS
CLOSED
WE FIX 'EM!
OBSOLETE MODELS A SPECIALTY.
ONE MISTAKE. RIGHT.
BUT IS IT YOURS OR MINE?

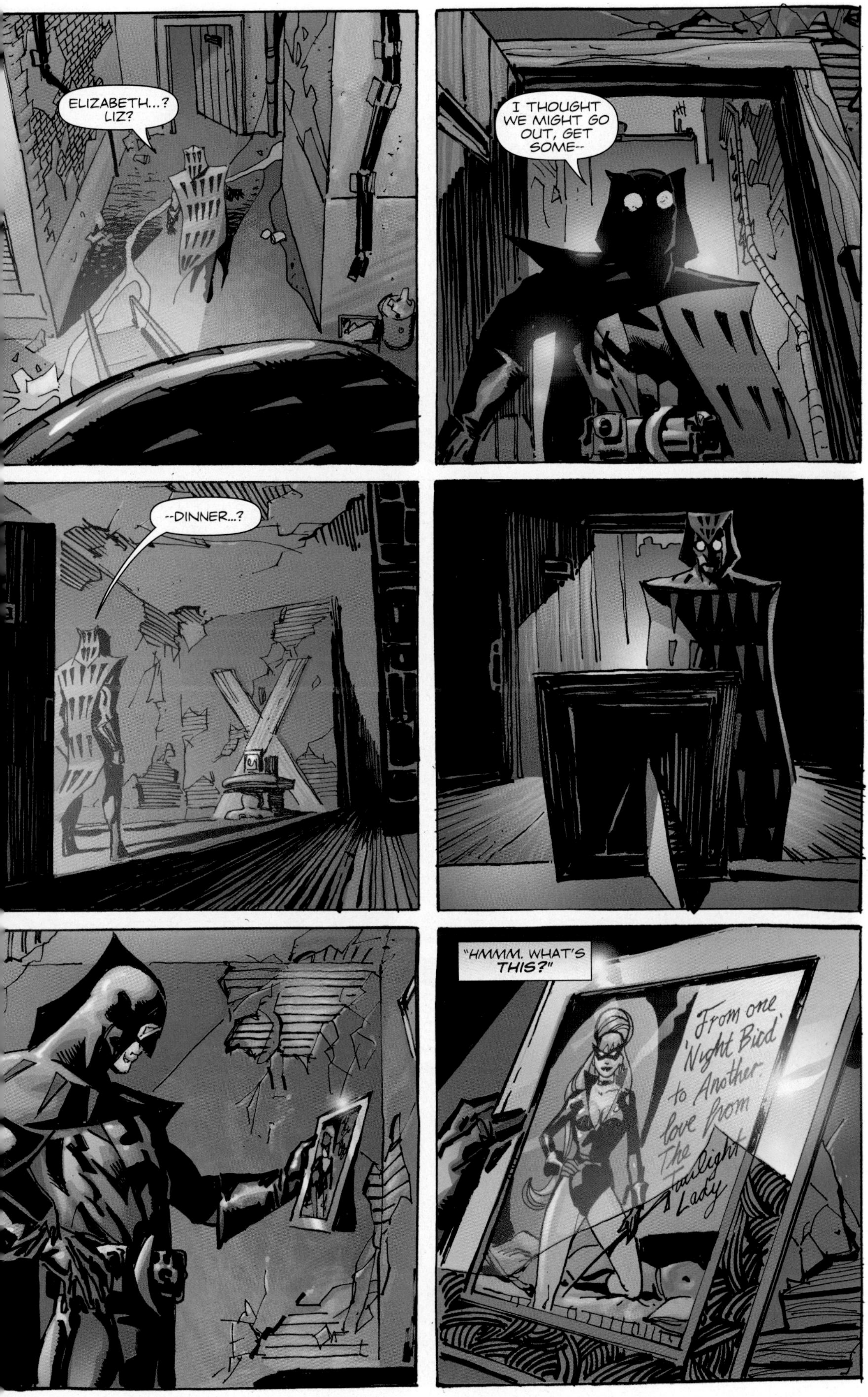
ELIZABETH...? LIZ?
I THOUGHT WE MIGHT GO OUT, GET SOME--
--DINNER...?
"HMMM. WHAT'S THIS?"
From one 'Night Bird' to Another love from The Twilight Lady

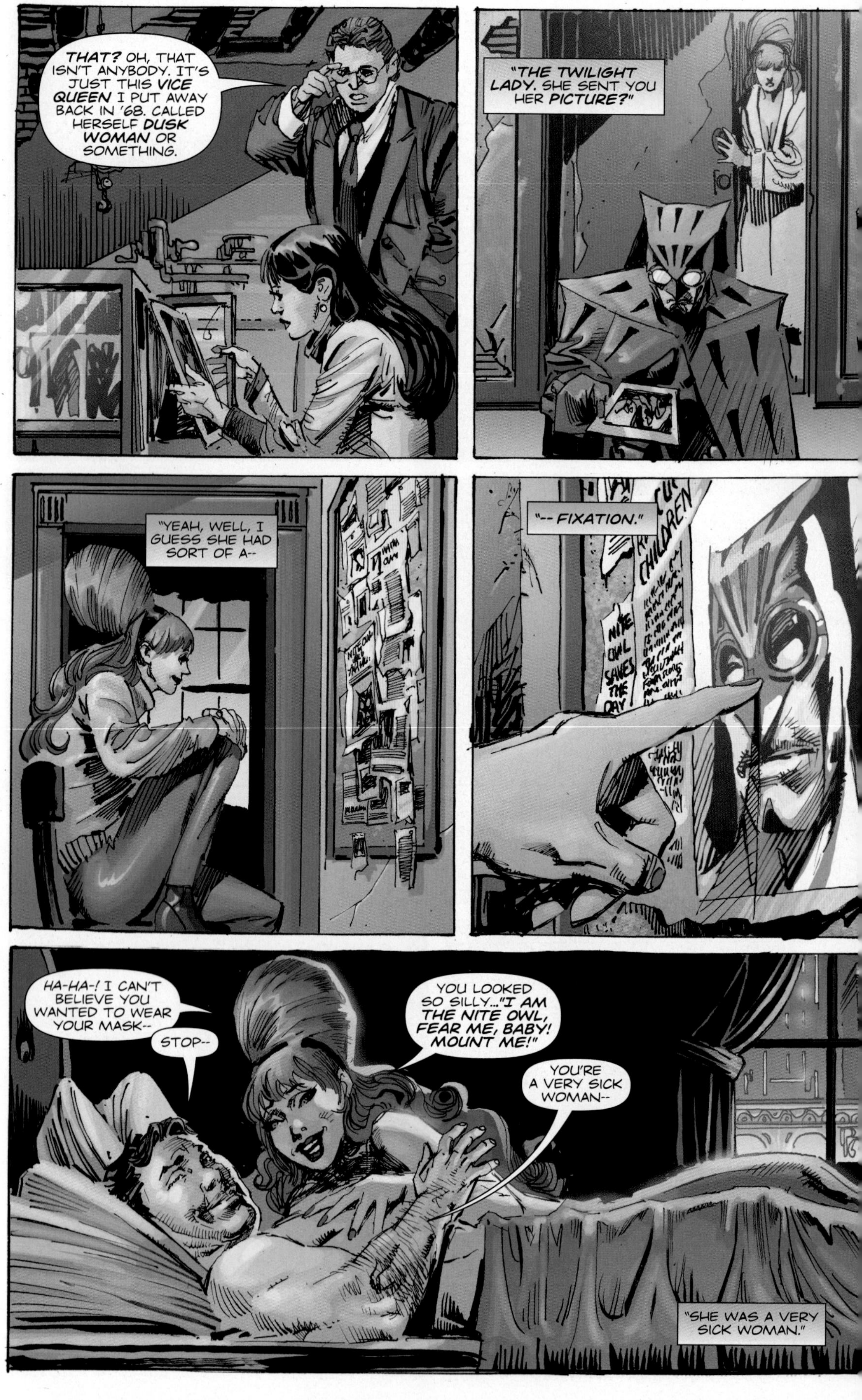
THAT? OH, THAT ISN'T ANYBODY. IT'S JUST THIS VICE QUEEN I PUT AWAY BACK IN '68. CALLED HERSELF DUSK WOMAN OR SOMETHING.
"THE TWILIGHT LADY. SHE SENT YOU HER PICTURE?"
"YEAH, WELL, I GUESS SHE HAD SORT OF A--
"--FIXATION."
CHILDREN
NITE OWL SAVES THE DAY
HA-HA-! I CAN'T BELIEVE YOU WANTED TO WEAR YOUR MASK--
STOP--
YOU LOOKED SO SILLY..."I AM THE NITE OWL, FEAR ME, BABY! MOUNT ME!"
YOU'RE A VERY SICK WOMAN--
"SHE WAS A VERY SICK WOMAN."

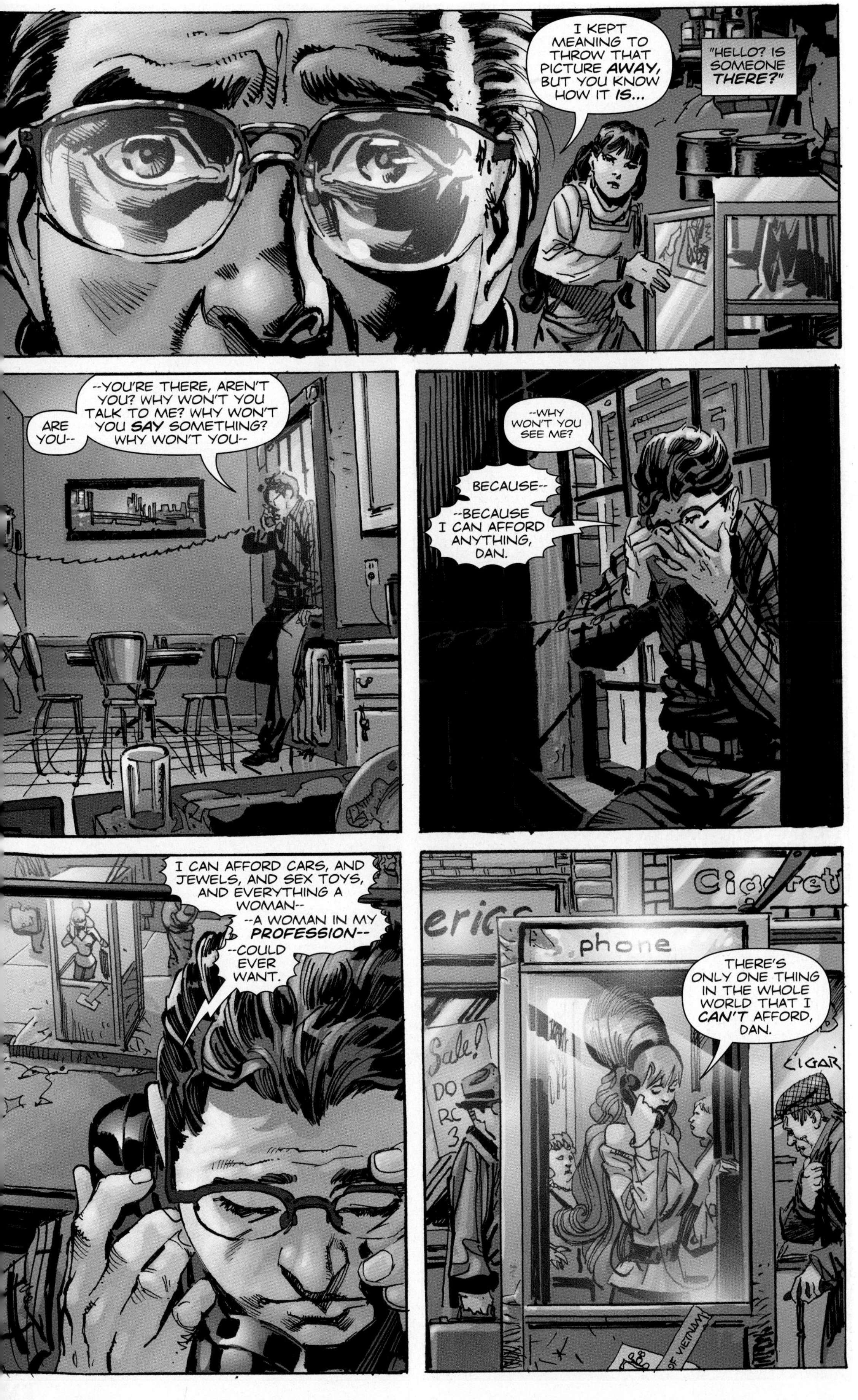

I KEPT MEANING TO THROW THAT PICTURE AWAY, BUT YOU KNOW HOW IT IS...
"HELLO? IS SOMEONE THERE?"
ARE YOU--
--YOU'RE THERE, AREN'T YOU? WHY WON'T YOU TALK TO ME? WHY WON'T YOU SAY SOMETHING? WHY WON'T YOU--
--WHY WON'T YOU SEE ME?
BECAUSE--
--BECAUSE I CAN AFFORD ANYTHING, DAN.
I CAN AFFORD CARS, AND JEWELS, AND SEX TOYS, AND EVERYTHING A WOMAN--
--A WOMAN IN MY PROFESSION--
--COULD EVER WANT.
Cigaret
phone
Sale!
CIGAR
THERE'S ONLY ONE THING IN THE WHOLE WORLD THAT I CAN'T AFFORD, DAN.

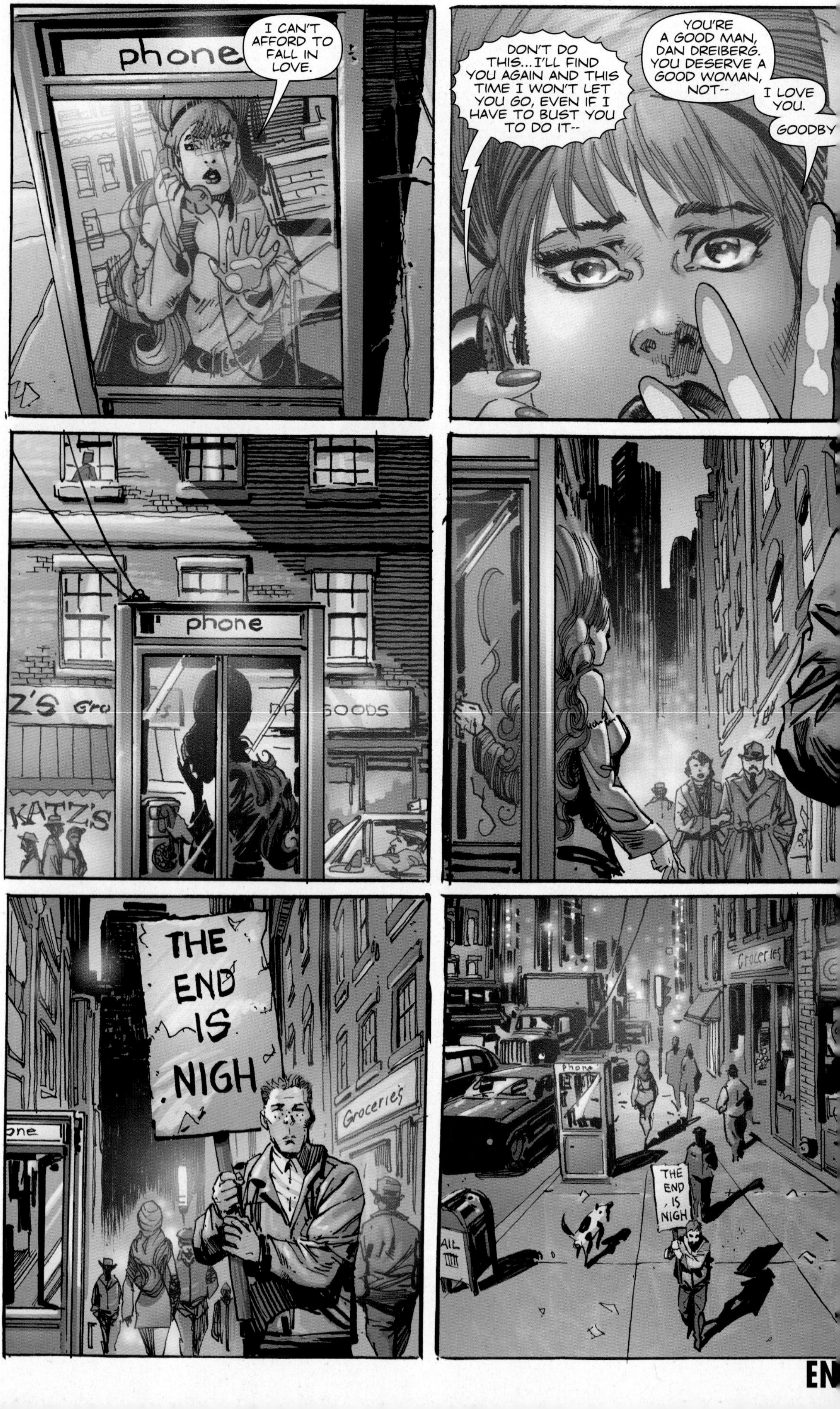
phone
I CAN'T AFFORD TO FALL IN LOVE.
DON'T DO THIS...I'LL FIND YOU AGAIN AND THIS TIME I WON'T LET YOU GO, EVEN IF I HAVE TO BUST YOU TO DO IT--
YOU'RE A GOOD MAN, DAN DREIBERG. YOU DESERVE A GOOD WOMAN, NOT--
I LOVE YOU.
GOODBY
phone
Z'S GRO
GOODS
KATZ'S
THE END IS NIGH
Groceries
Groceries
THE END IS NIGH
EN

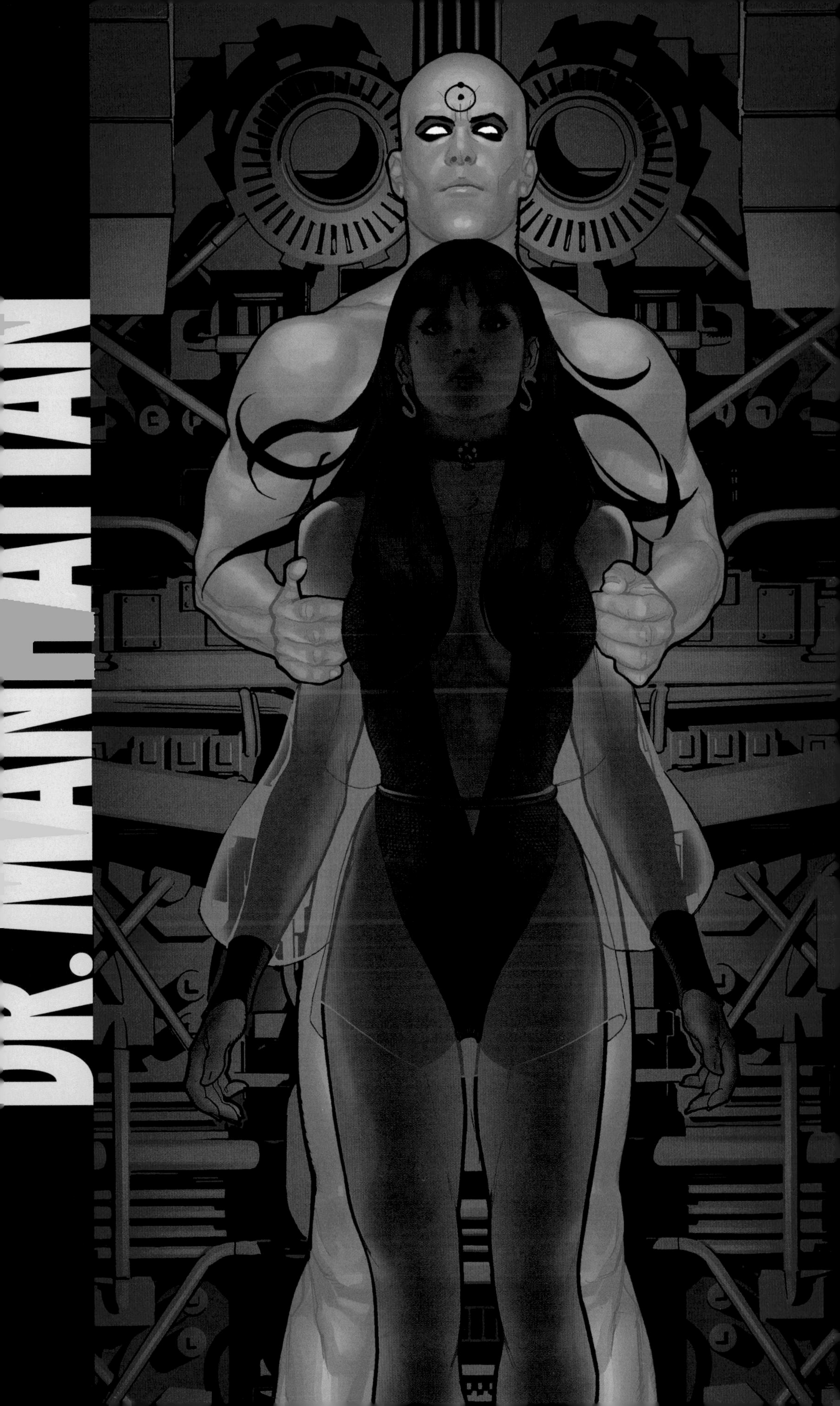
DR. MANHATTAN

DR. MANHATTAN

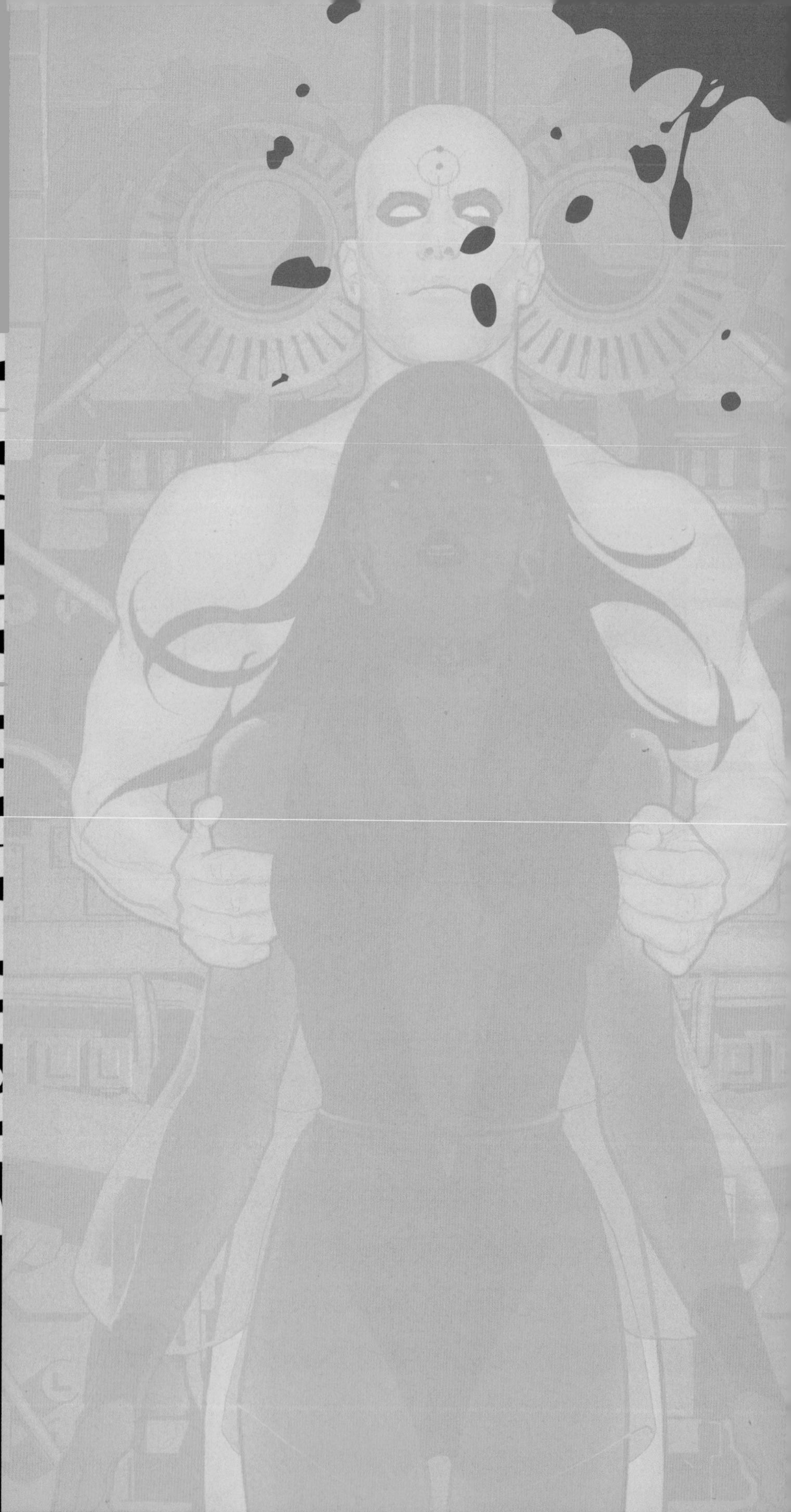

"I WATCH AS A BOX CONTAINING A MYSTERY IS LOWERED INTO THE SOIL."

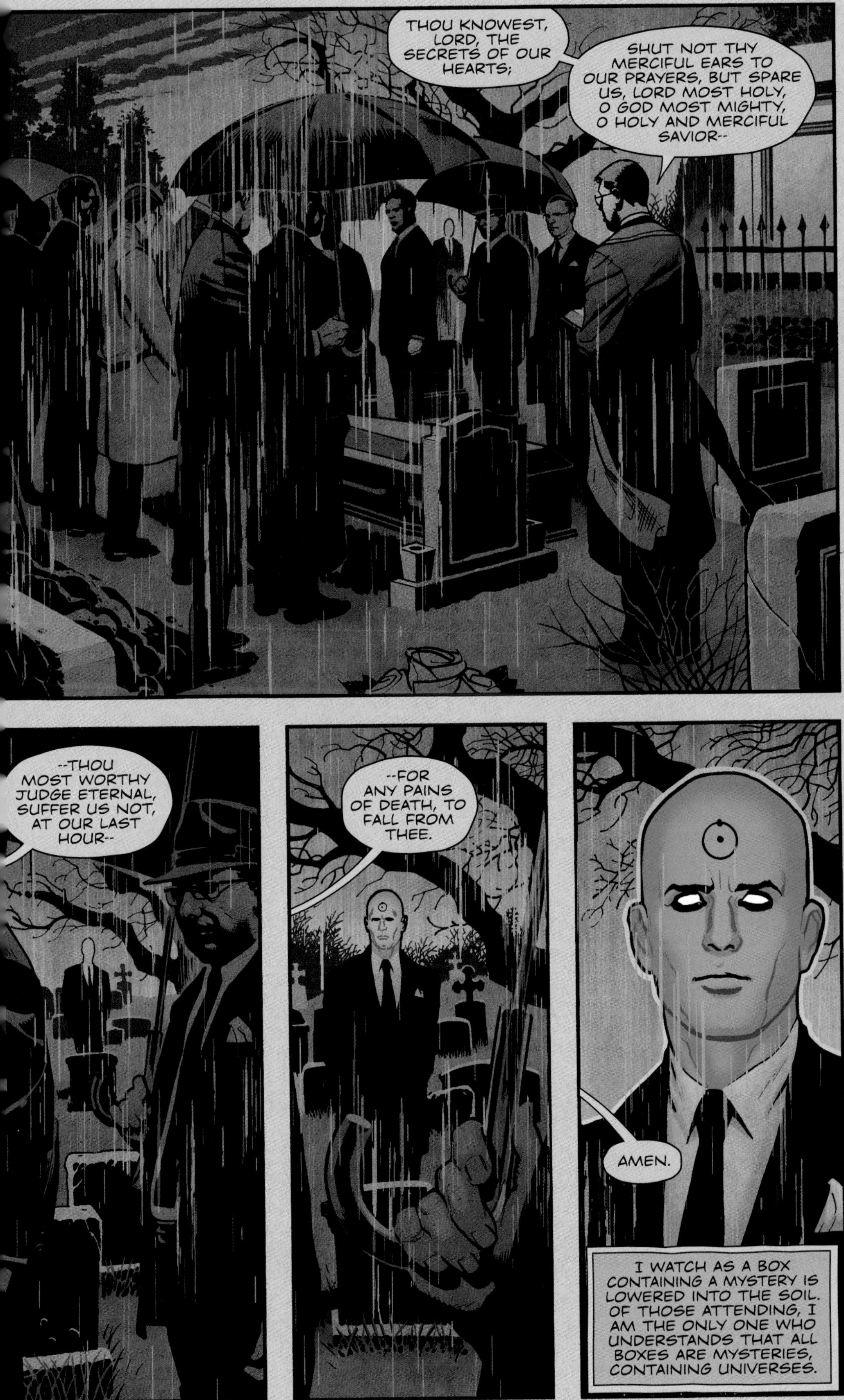
THOU KNOWEST, LORD, THE SECRETS OF OUR HEARTS;
SHUT NOT THY MERCIFUL EARS TO OUR PRAYERS, BUT SPARE US, LORD MOST HOLY, O GOD MOST MIGHTY, O HOLY AND MERCIFUL SAVIOR--
--THOU MOST WORTHY JUDGE ETERNAL, SUFFER US NOT, AT OUR LAST HOUR--
--FOR ANY PAINS OF DEATH, TO FALL FROM THEE.
AMEN.
I WATCH AS A BOX CONTAINING A MYSTERY IS LOWERED INTO THE SOIL. OF THOSE ATTENDING, I AM THE ONLY ONE WHO UNDERSTANDS THAT ALL BOXES ARE MYSTERIES, CONTAINING UNIVERSES.

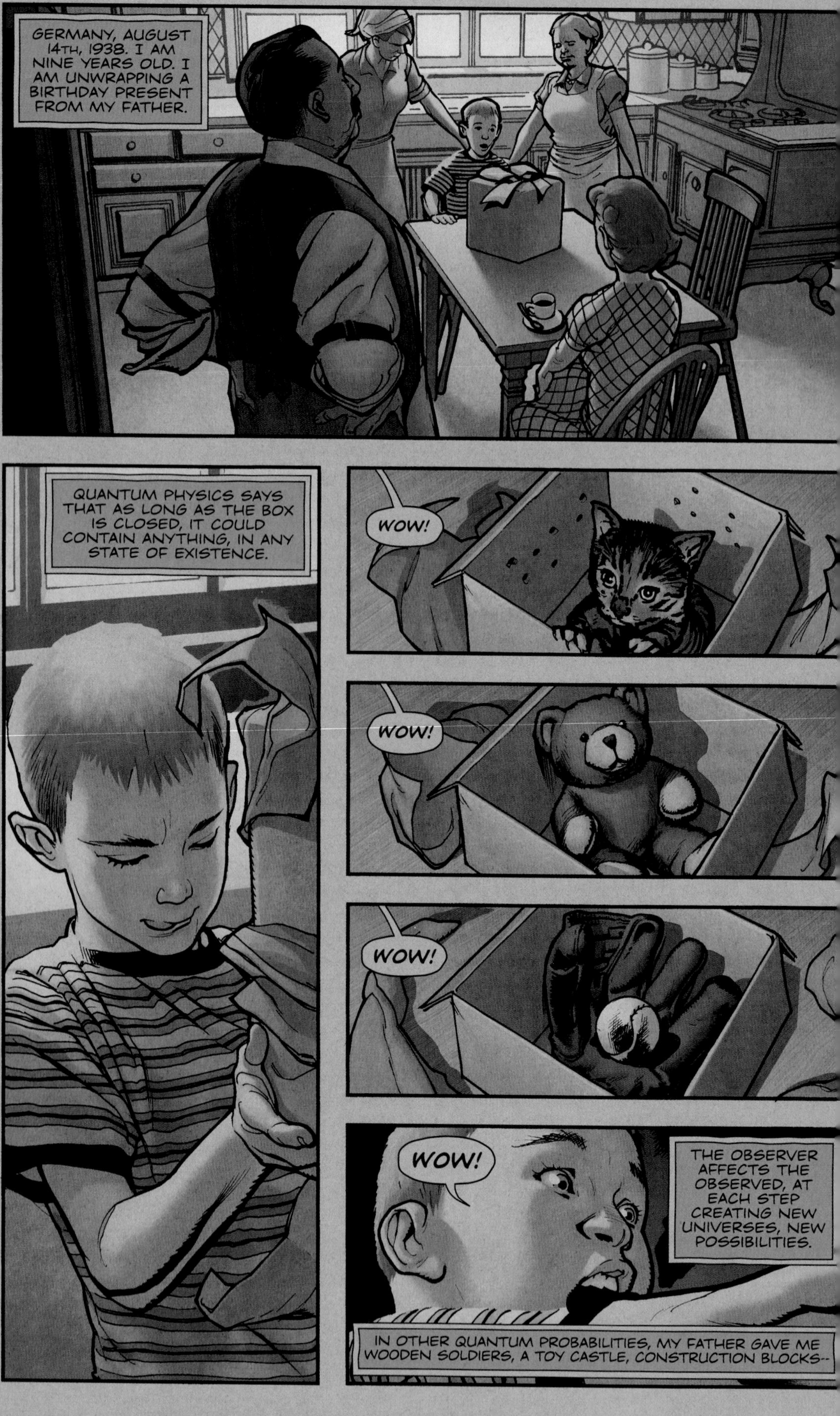
GERMANY, AUGUST 14TH, 1938. I AM NINE YEARS OLD. I AM UNWRAPPING A BIRTHDAY PRESENT FROM MY FATHER.
QUANTUM PHYSICS SAYS THAT AS LONG AS THE BOX IS CLOSED, IT COULD CONTAIN ANYTHING, IN ANY STATE OF EXISTENCE.
WOW!
WOW!
WOW!
WOW!
THE OBSERVER AFFECTS THE OBSERVED, AT EACH STEP CREATING NEW UNIVERSES, NEW POSSIBILITIES.
IN OTHER QUANTUM PROBABILITIES, MY FATHER GAVE ME WOODEN SOLDIERS, A TOY CASTLE, CONSTRUCTION BLOCKS--

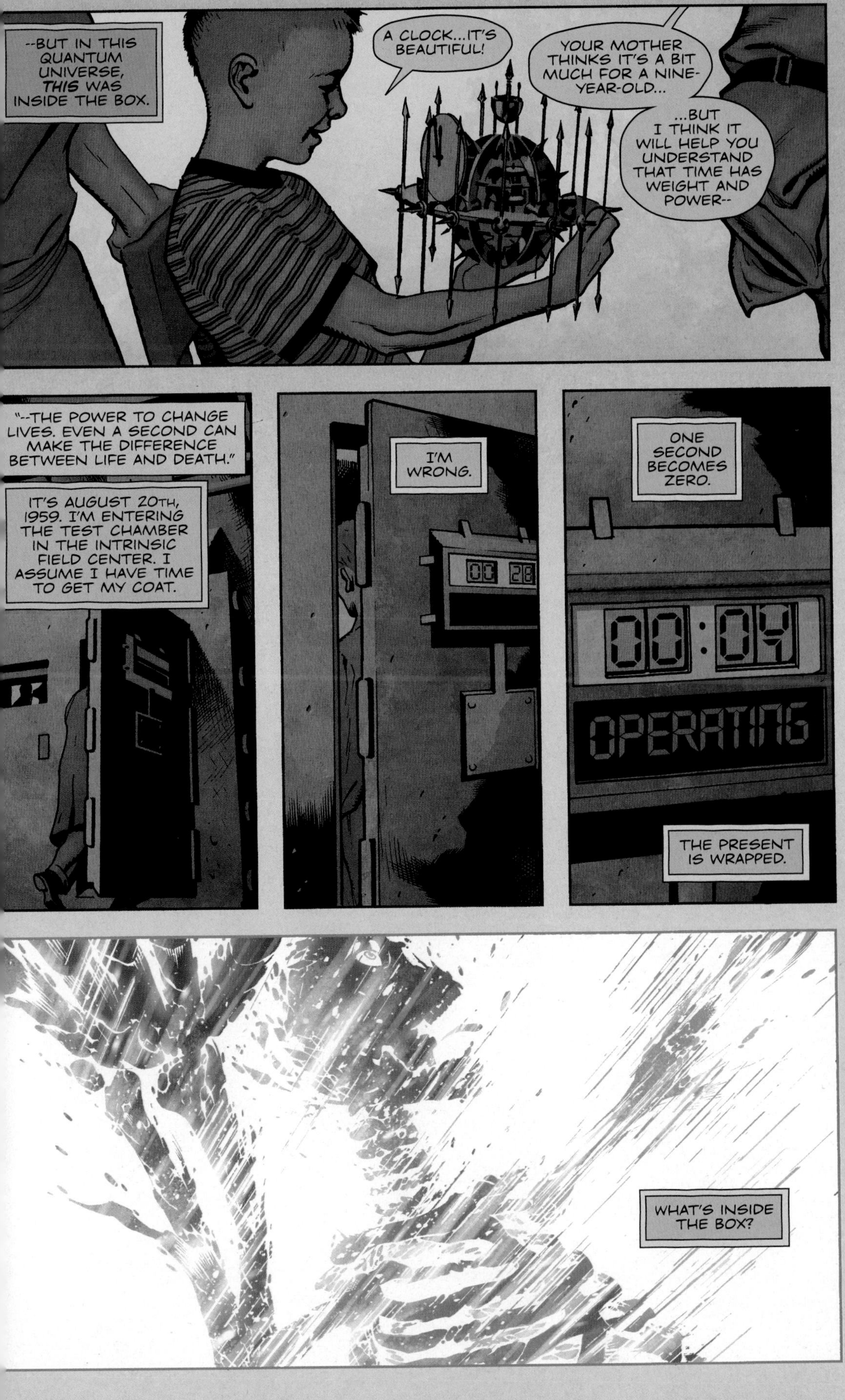
--BUT IN THIS QUANTUM UNIVERSE, THIS WAS INSIDE THE BOX.
A CLOCK...IT'S BEAUTIFUL!
YOUR MOTHER THINKS IT'S A BIT MUCH FOR A NINE-YEAR-OLD...
...BUT I THINK IT WILL HELP YOU UNDERSTAND THAT TIME HAS WEIGHT AND POWER--
"--THE POWER TO CHANGE LIVES. EVEN A SECOND CAN MAKE THE DIFFERENCE BETWEEN LIFE AND DEATH."
IT'S AUGUST 20TH, 1959. I'M ENTERING THE TEST CHAMBER IN THE INTRINSIC FIELD CENTER. I ASSUME I HAVE TIME TO GET MY COAT.
I'M WRONG.
ONE SECOND BECOMES ZERO.
00:04
OPERATING
THE PRESENT IS WRAPPED.
WHAT'S INSIDE THE BOX?

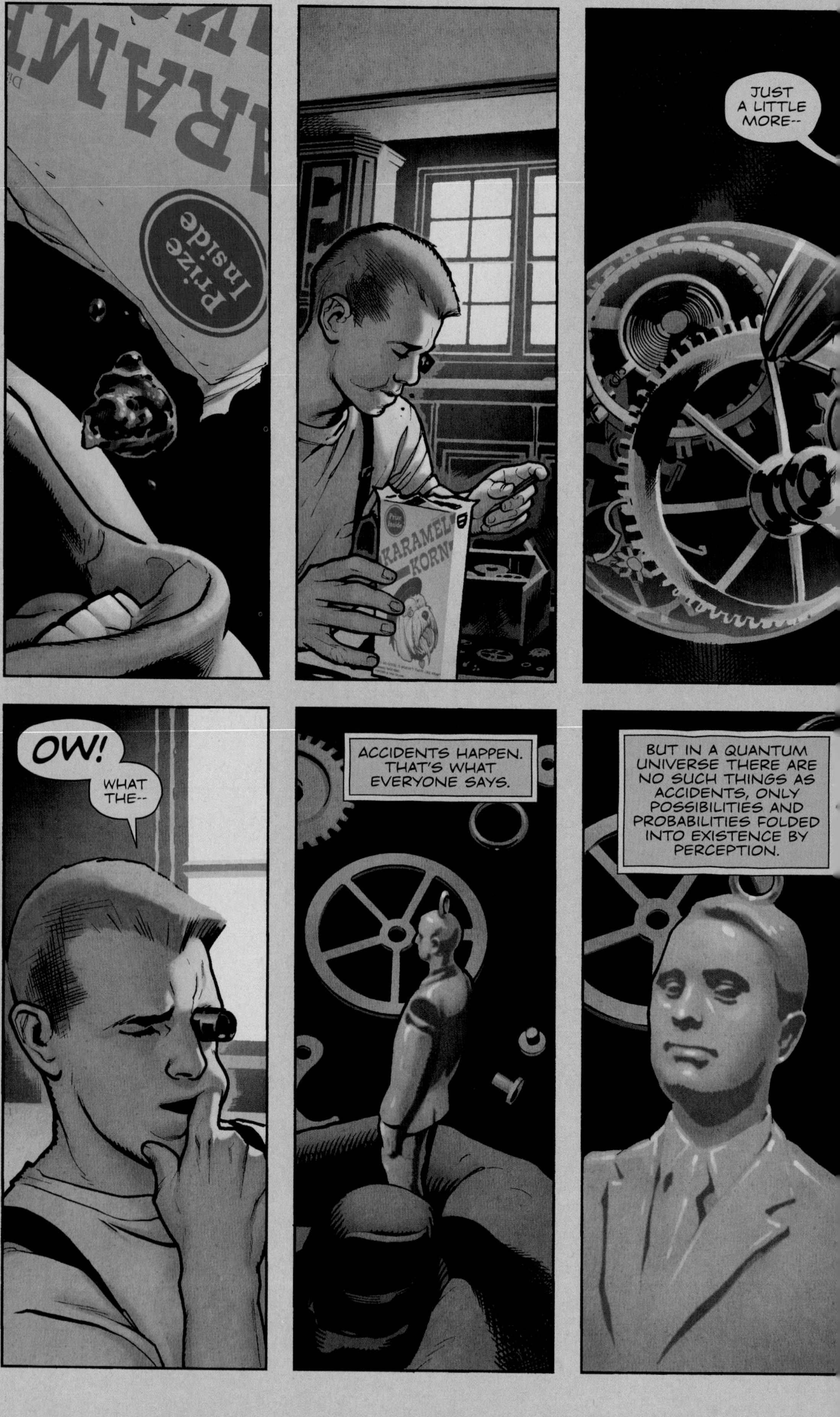
Prize Inside
KARAMEL KORN
JUST A LITTLE MORE--
OW!
WHAT THE--
ACCIDENTS HAPPEN. THAT'S WHAT EVERYONE SAYS.
BUT IN A QUANTUM UNIVERSE THERE ARE NO SUCH THINGS AS ACCIDENTS, ONLY POSSIBILITIES AND PROBABILITIES FOLDED INTO EXISTENCE BY PERCEPTION.

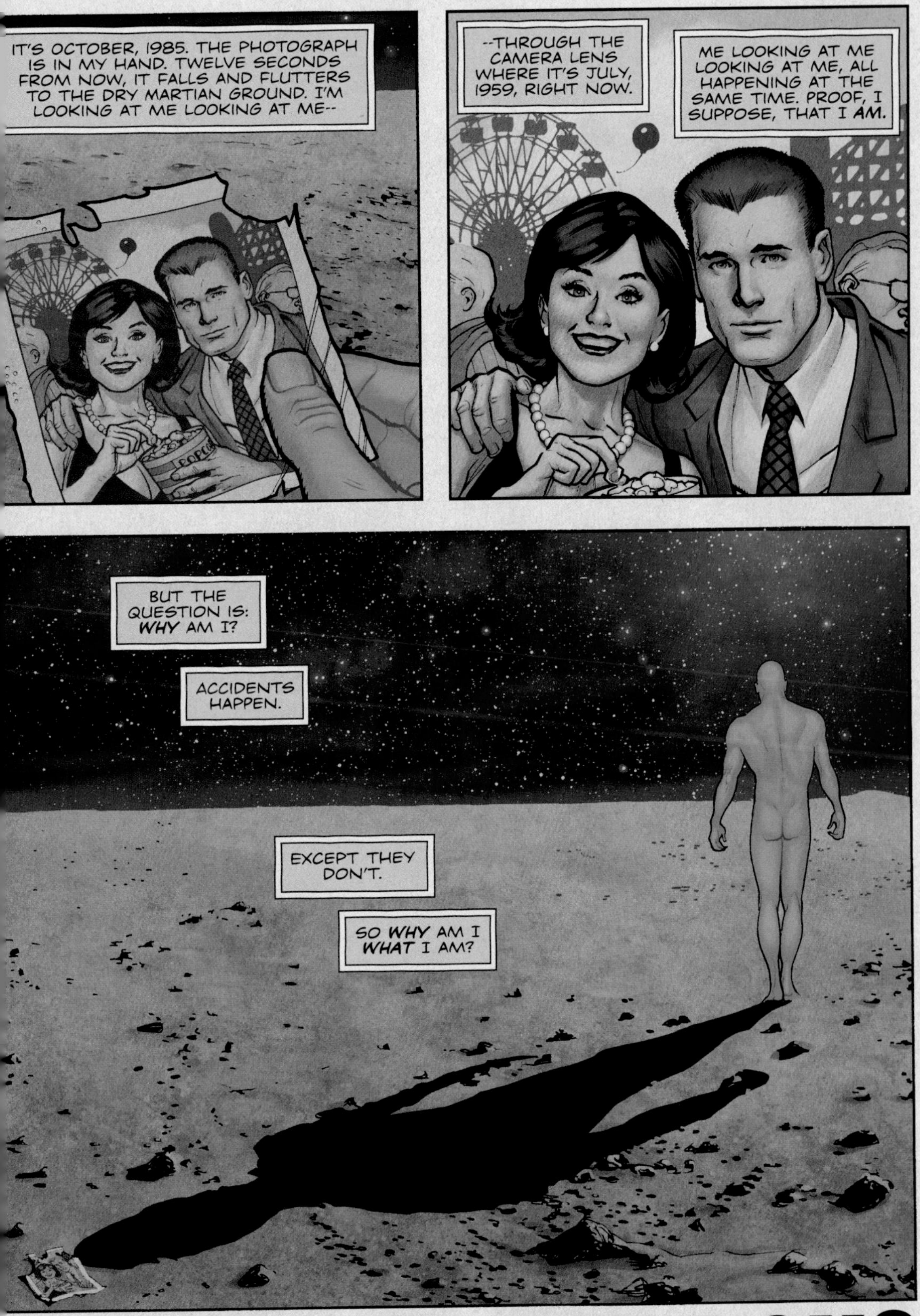
IT'S OCTOBER, 1985. THE PHOTOGRAPH IS IN MY HAND. TWELVE SECONDS FROM NOW, IT FALLS AND FLUTTERS TO THE DRY MARTIAN GROUND. I'M LOOKING AT ME LOOKING AT ME--
--THROUGH THE CAMERA LENS WHERE IT'S JULY, 1959, RIGHT NOW.
ME LOOKING AT ME LOOKING AT ME, ALL HAPPENING AT THE SAME TIME. PROOF, I SUPPOSE, THAT I *AM.*
BUT THE QUESTION IS: *WHY* AM I?
ACCIDENTS HAPPEN.
EXCEPT THEY DON'T.
SO *WHY* AM I *WHAT* I AM?

WHAT'S IN THE BOX?

J. MICHAEL STRACZYNSKI script ADAM HUGHES art
LAURA MARTIN colors STEVE WANDS letters ADAM HUGHES cover
PAUL POPE with LOVERN KINDZIERSKI and JIM LEE with SCOTT WILLIAMS & ALEX SINCLAIR variant covers
CAMILLA ZHANG asst. editor CHRIS CONROY assoc. editor MARK CHIARELLO editor
WATCHMEN created by ALAN MOORE and DAVE GIBBONS

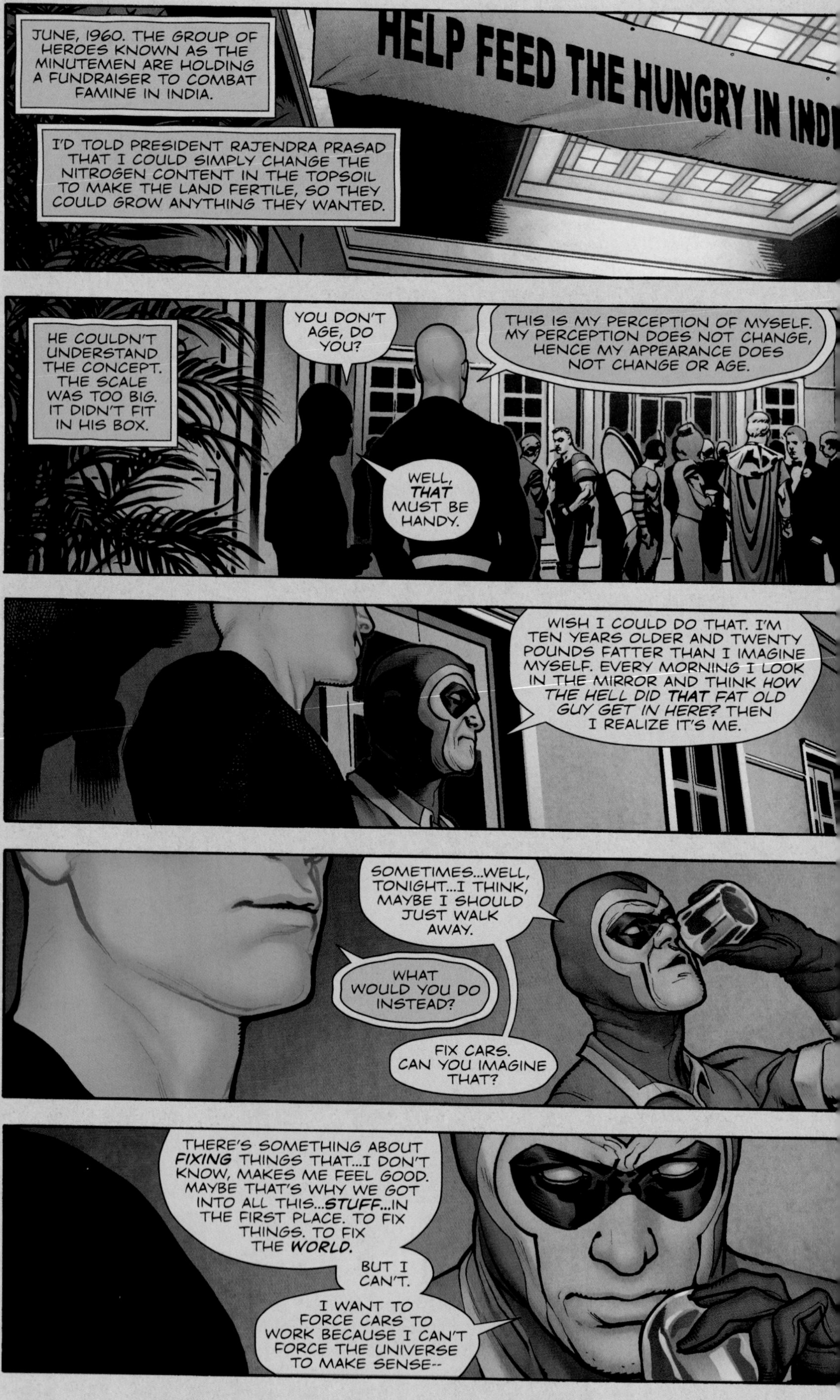
HELP FEED THE HUNGRY IN INDI
JUNE, 1960. THE GROUP OF HEROES KNOWN AS THE MINUTEMEN ARE HOLDING A FUNDRAISER TO COMBAT FAMINE IN INDIA.
I'D TOLD PRESIDENT RAJENDRA PRASAD THAT I COULD SIMPLY CHANGE THE NITROGEN CONTENT IN THE TOPSOIL TO MAKE THE LAND FERTILE, SO THEY COULD GROW ANYTHING THEY WANTED.
HE COULDN'T UNDERSTAND THE CONCEPT. THE SCALE WAS TOO BIG. IT DIDN'T FIT IN HIS BOX.
YOU DON'T AGE, DO YOU?
THIS IS MY PERCEPTION OF MYSELF. MY PERCEPTION DOES NOT CHANGE, HENCE MY APPEARANCE DOES NOT CHANGE OR AGE.
WELL, *THAT* MUST BE HANDY.
WISH I COULD DO THAT. I'M TEN YEARS OLDER AND TWENTY POUNDS FATTER THAN I IMAGINE MYSELF. EVERY MORNING I LOOK IN THE MIRROR AND THINK *HOW THE HELL DID* ***THAT*** *FAT OLD GUY GET IN HERE?* THEN I REALIZE IT'S ME.
SOMETIMES...WELL, TONIGHT...I THINK, MAYBE I SHOULD JUST WALK AWAY.
WHAT WOULD YOU DO INSTEAD?
FIX CARS. CAN YOU IMAGINE THAT?
THERE'S SOMETHING ABOUT ***FIXING*** THINGS THAT...I DON'T KNOW, MAKES ME FEEL GOOD. MAYBE THAT'S WHY WE GOT INTO ALL THIS...***STUFF***...IN THE FIRST PLACE. TO FIX THINGS. TO FIX THE ***WORLD.***
BUT I CAN'T.
I WANT TO FORCE CARS TO WORK BECAUSE I CAN'T FORCE THE UNIVERSE TO MAKE SENSE--

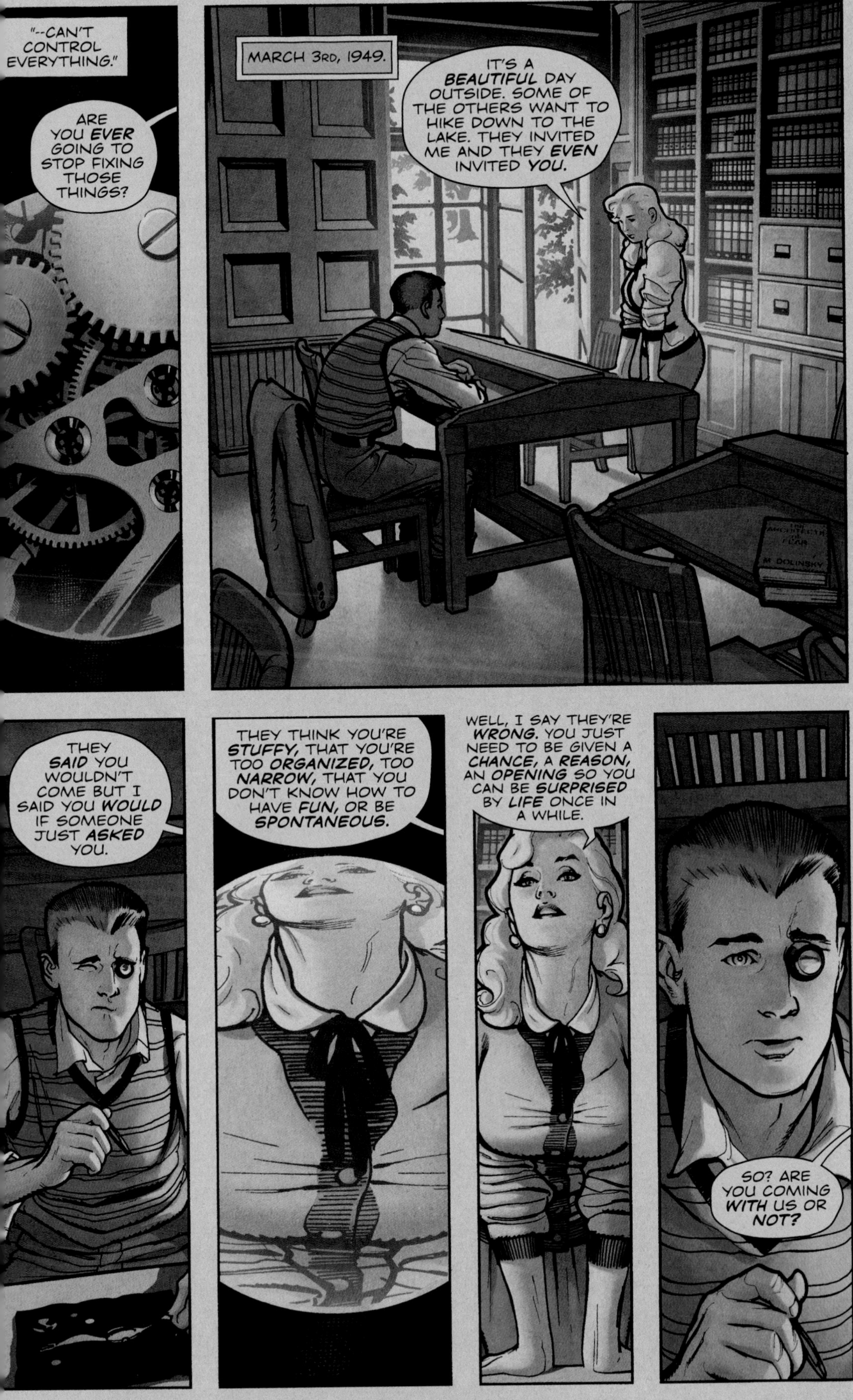
"--CAN'T CONTROL EVERYTHING."
ARE YOU EVER GOING TO STOP FIXING THOSE THINGS?
MARCH 3RD, 1949.
IT'S A BEAUTIFUL DAY OUTSIDE. SOME OF THE OTHERS WANT TO HIKE DOWN TO THE LAKE. THEY INVITED ME AND THEY EVEN INVITED YOU.
M DOLINSKY
THEY SAID YOU WOULDN'T COME BUT I SAID YOU WOULD IF SOMEONE JUST ASKED YOU.
THEY THINK YOU'RE STUFFY, THAT YOU'RE TOO ORGANIZED, TOO NARROW, THAT YOU DON'T KNOW HOW TO HAVE FUN, OR BE SPONTANEOUS.
WELL, I SAY THEY'RE WRONG. YOU JUST NEED TO BE GIVEN A CHANCE, A REASON, AN OPENING SO YOU CAN BE SURPRISED BY LIFE ONCE IN A WHILE.
SO? ARE YOU COMING WITH US OR NOT?

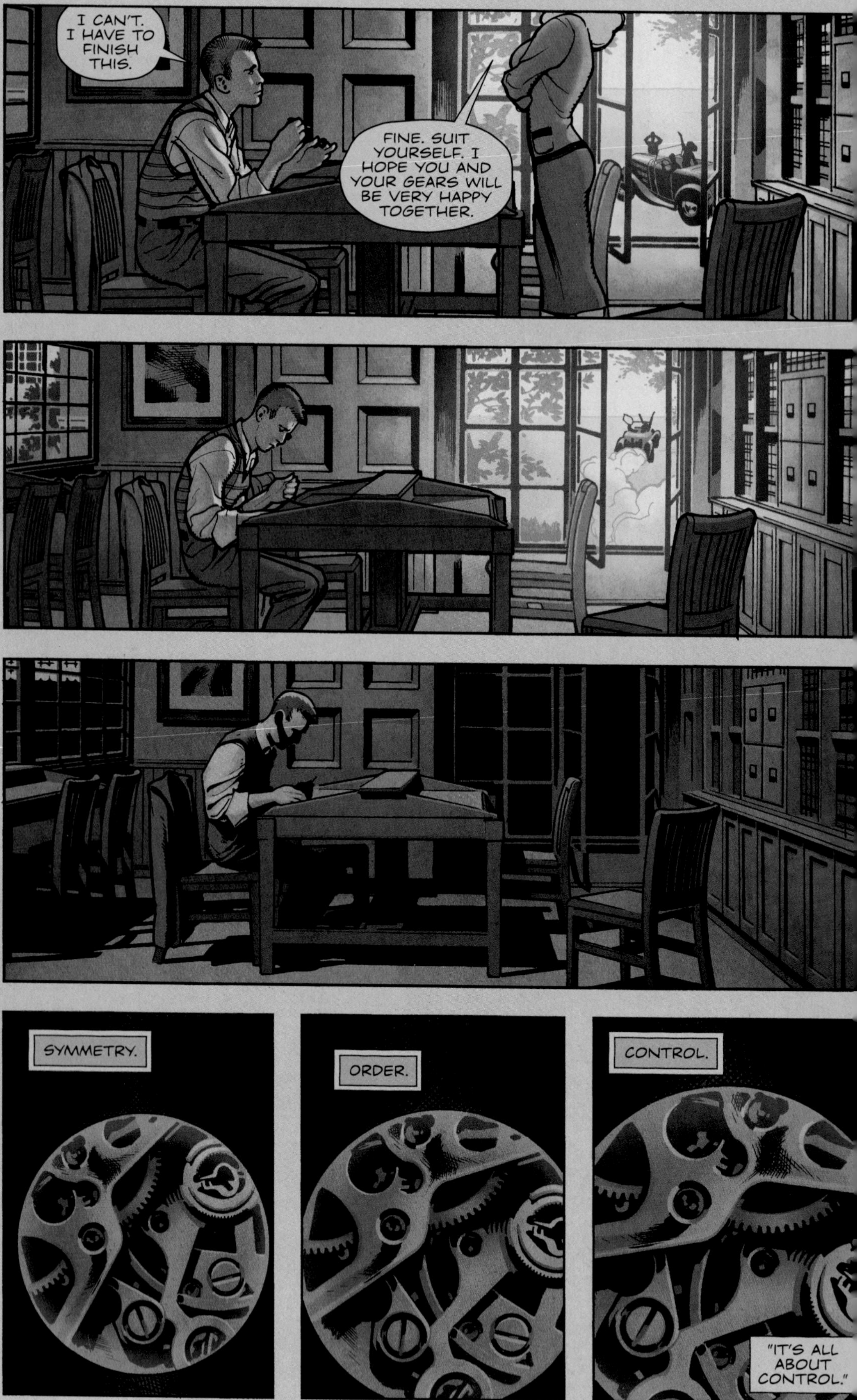
I CAN'T. I HAVE TO FINISH THIS.
FINE. SUIT YOURSELF. I HOPE YOU AND YOUR GEARS WILL BE VERY HAPPY TOGETHER.
SYMMETRY.
ORDER.
CONTROL.
"IT'S ALL ABOUT CONTROL."

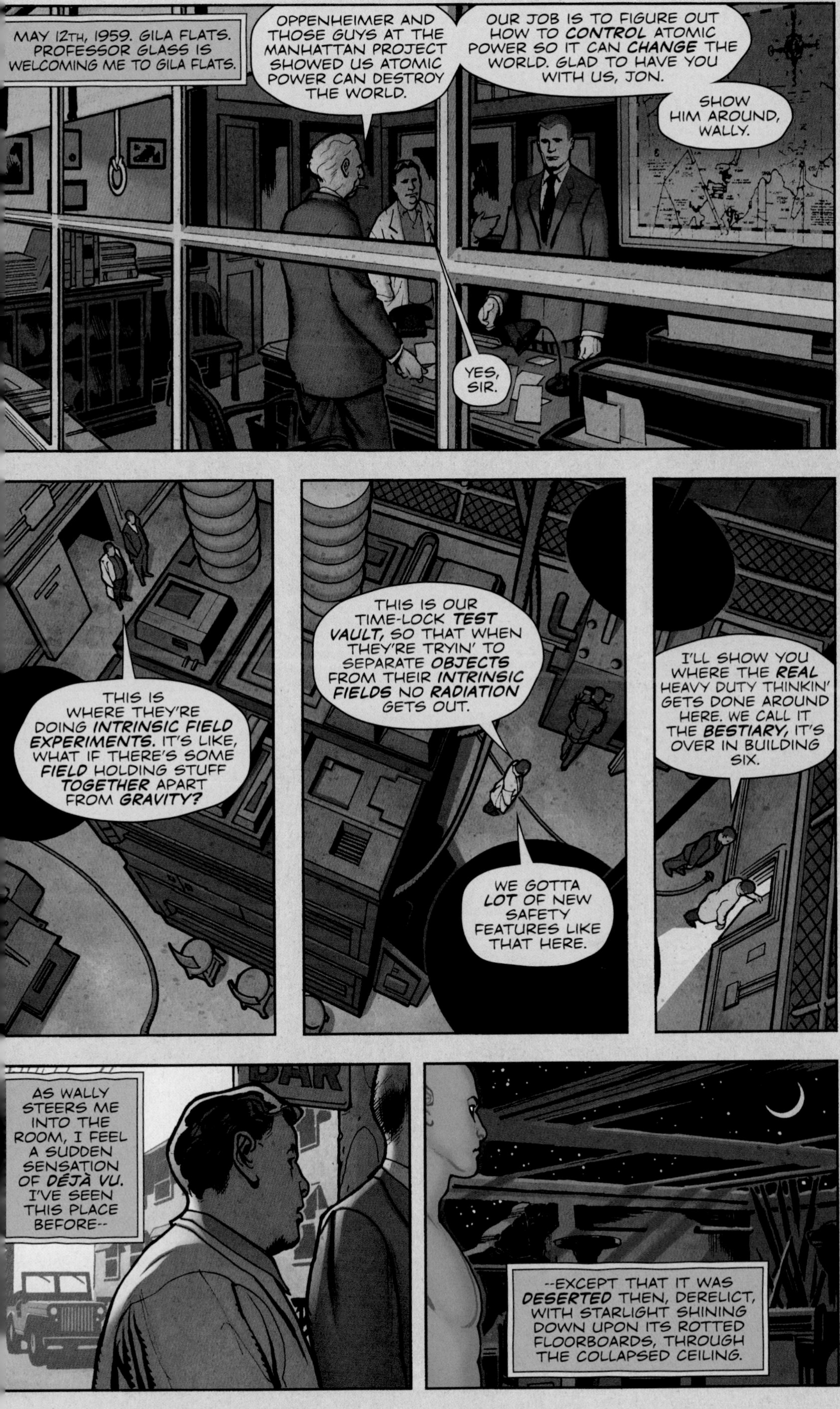

MAY 12TH, 1959. GILA FLATS. PROFESSOR GLASS IS WELCOMING ME TO GILA FLATS.
OPPENHEIMER AND THOSE GUYS AT THE MANHATTAN PROJECT SHOWED US ATOMIC POWER CAN DESTROY THE WORLD.
OUR JOB IS TO FIGURE OUT HOW TO CONTROL ATOMIC POWER SO IT CAN CHANGE THE WORLD. GLAD TO HAVE YOU WITH US, JON.
SHOW HIM AROUND, WALLY.
YES, SIR.
THIS IS WHERE THEY'RE DOING INTRINSIC FIELD EXPERIMENTS. IT'S LIKE, WHAT IF THERE'S SOME FIELD HOLDING STUFF TOGETHER APART FROM GRAVITY?
THIS IS OUR TIME-LOCK TEST VAULT, SO THAT WHEN THEY'RE TRYIN' TO SEPARATE OBJECTS FROM THEIR INTRINSIC FIELDS NO RADIATION GETS OUT.
WE GOTTA LOT OF NEW SAFETY FEATURES LIKE THAT HERE.
I'LL SHOW YOU WHERE THE REAL HEAVY DUTY THINKIN' GETS DONE AROUND HERE. WE CALL IT THE BESTIARY, IT'S OVER IN BUILDING SIX.
AS WALLY STEERS ME INTO THE ROOM, I FEEL A SUDDEN SENSATION OF DÉJÀ VU. I'VE SEEN THIS PLACE BEFORE--
BAR
--EXCEPT THAT IT WAS DESERTED THEN, DERELICT, WITH STARLIGHT SHINING DOWN UPON ITS ROTTED FLOORBOARDS, THROUGH THE COLLAPSED CEILING.

AND IN THAT MOMENT--

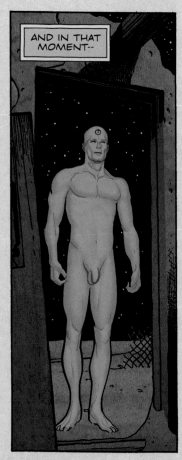

AND IN THAT MOMENT--

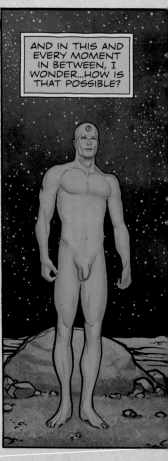

AND IN THIS AND EVERY MOMENT IN BETWEEN, I WONDER...HOW IS THAT POSSIBLE?

I HAD NOT YET CHANGED INTO WHAT I AM NOW. BUT I COULD STILL *SENSE* MYSELF IN THE FUTURE.

BECAUSE IT WAS STILL *ME,* STILL MY CONSCIOUSNESS, SLIDING UP AND DOWN THE TIMESTREAM.

STILL THE SAME QUANTUM OBSERVER.

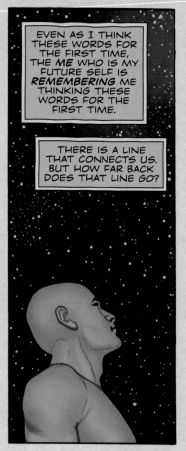

EVEN AS I THINK THESE WORDS FOR THE FIRST TIME, THE *ME* WHO IS MY FUTURE SELF IS *REMEMBERING* ME THINKING THESE WORDS FOR THE FIRST TIME.

THERE IS A LINE THAT CONNECTS US. BUT HOW FAR BACK DOES THAT LINE GO?

AND IS THAT FUTURE ME THE *SAME* FUTURE ME THAT WOULD HAVE EXISTED HAD I NOT MADE CERTAIN DECISIONS, CERTAIN--

--CHANGES?

"I GUESS I SHOULD *WELCOME* EVERYBODY TO THE FIRST EVER MEETING OF THE *CRIMEBUSTERS.*"

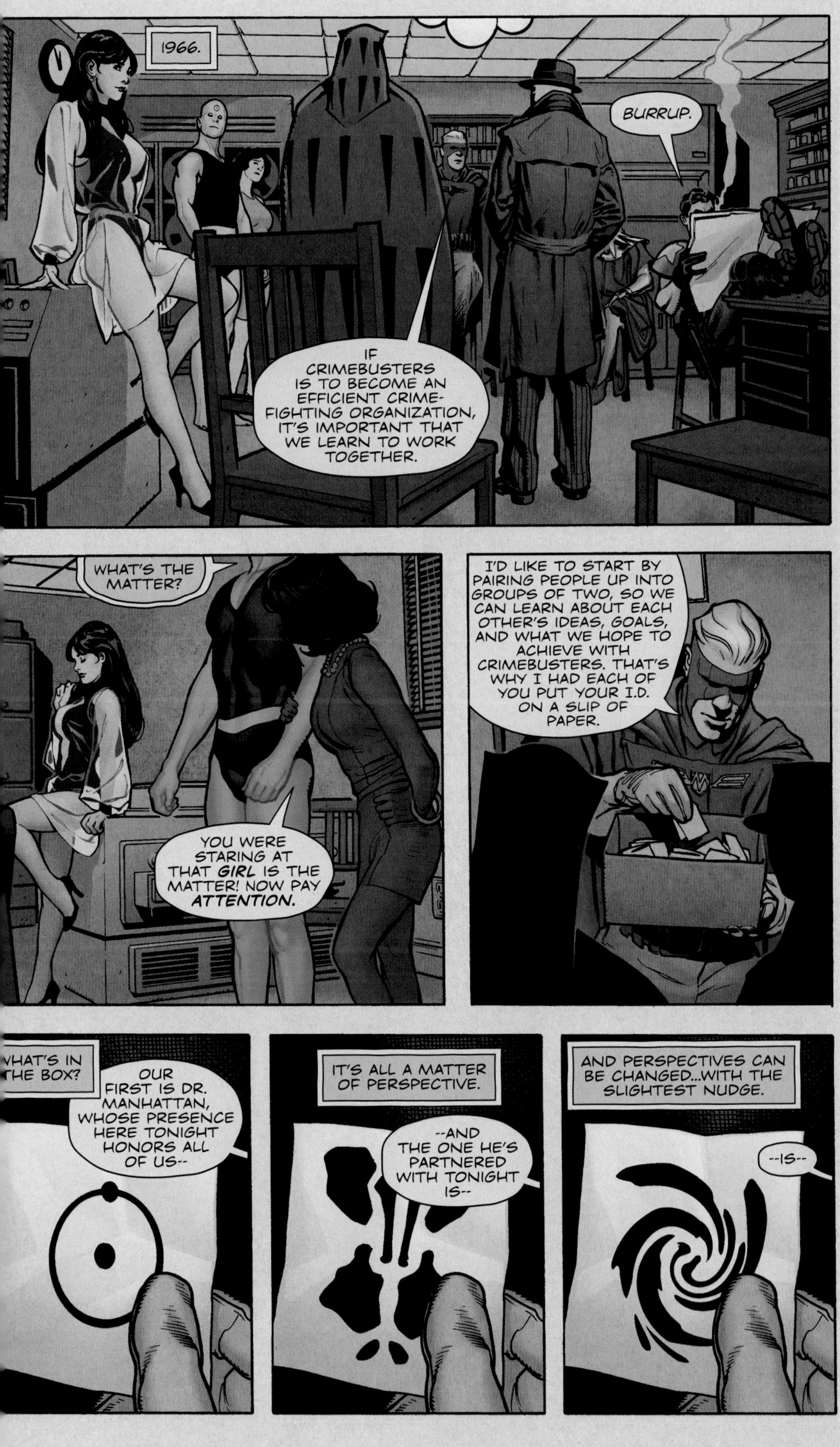
1966.
BURRUP.
IF CRIMEBUSTERS IS TO BECOME AN EFFICIENT CRIME-FIGHTING ORGANIZATION, IT'S IMPORTANT THAT WE LEARN TO WORK TOGETHER.
WHAT'S THE MATTER?
YOU WERE STARING AT THAT GIRL IS THE MATTER! NOW PAY ATTENTION.
I'D LIKE TO START BY PAIRING PEOPLE UP INTO GROUPS OF TWO, SO WE CAN LEARN ABOUT EACH OTHER'S IDEAS, GOALS, AND WHAT WE HOPE TO ACHIEVE WITH CRIMEBUSTERS. THAT'S WHY I HAD EACH OF YOU PUT YOUR I.D. ON A SLIP OF PAPER.
WHAT'S IN THE BOX?
OUR FIRST IS DR. MANHATTAN, WHOSE PRESENCE HERE TONIGHT HONORS ALL OF US--
IT'S ALL A MATTER OF PERSPECTIVE.
--AND THE ONE HE'S PARTNERED WITH TONIGHT IS--
AND PERSPECTIVES CAN BE CHANGED...WITH THE SLIGHTEST NUDGE.
--IS--

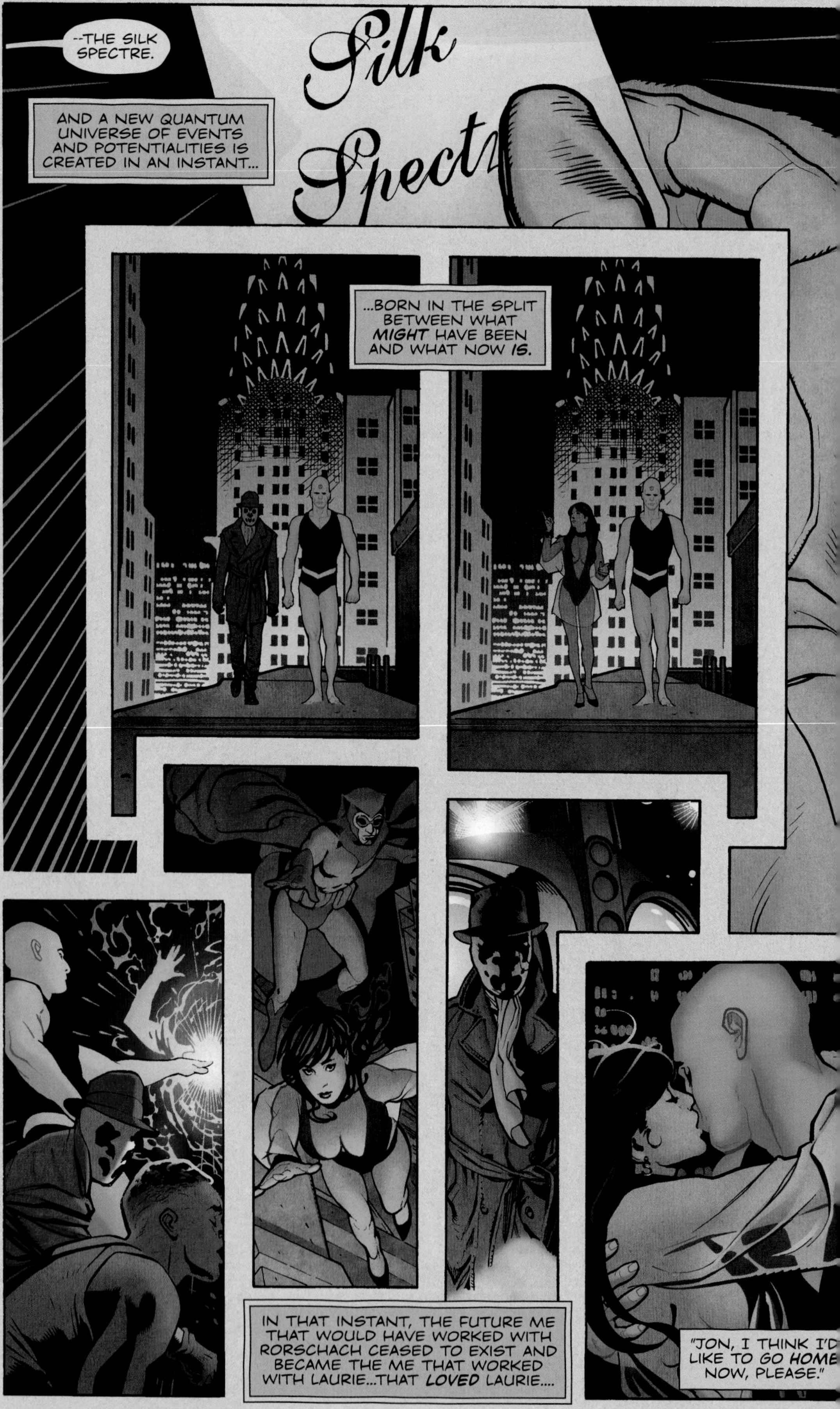
--THE SILK SPECTRE.
Silk Spectr
AND A NEW QUANTUM UNIVERSE OF EVENTS AND POTENTIALITIES IS CREATED IN AN INSTANT...
...BORN IN THE SPLIT BETWEEN WHAT MIGHT HAVE BEEN AND WHAT NOW IS.
IN THAT INSTANT, THE FUTURE ME THAT WOULD HAVE WORKED WITH RORSCHACH CEASED TO EXIST AND BECAME THE ME THAT WORKED WITH LAURIE...THAT LOVED LAURIE....
"JON, I THINK I'D LIKE TO GO HOME NOW, PLEASE."

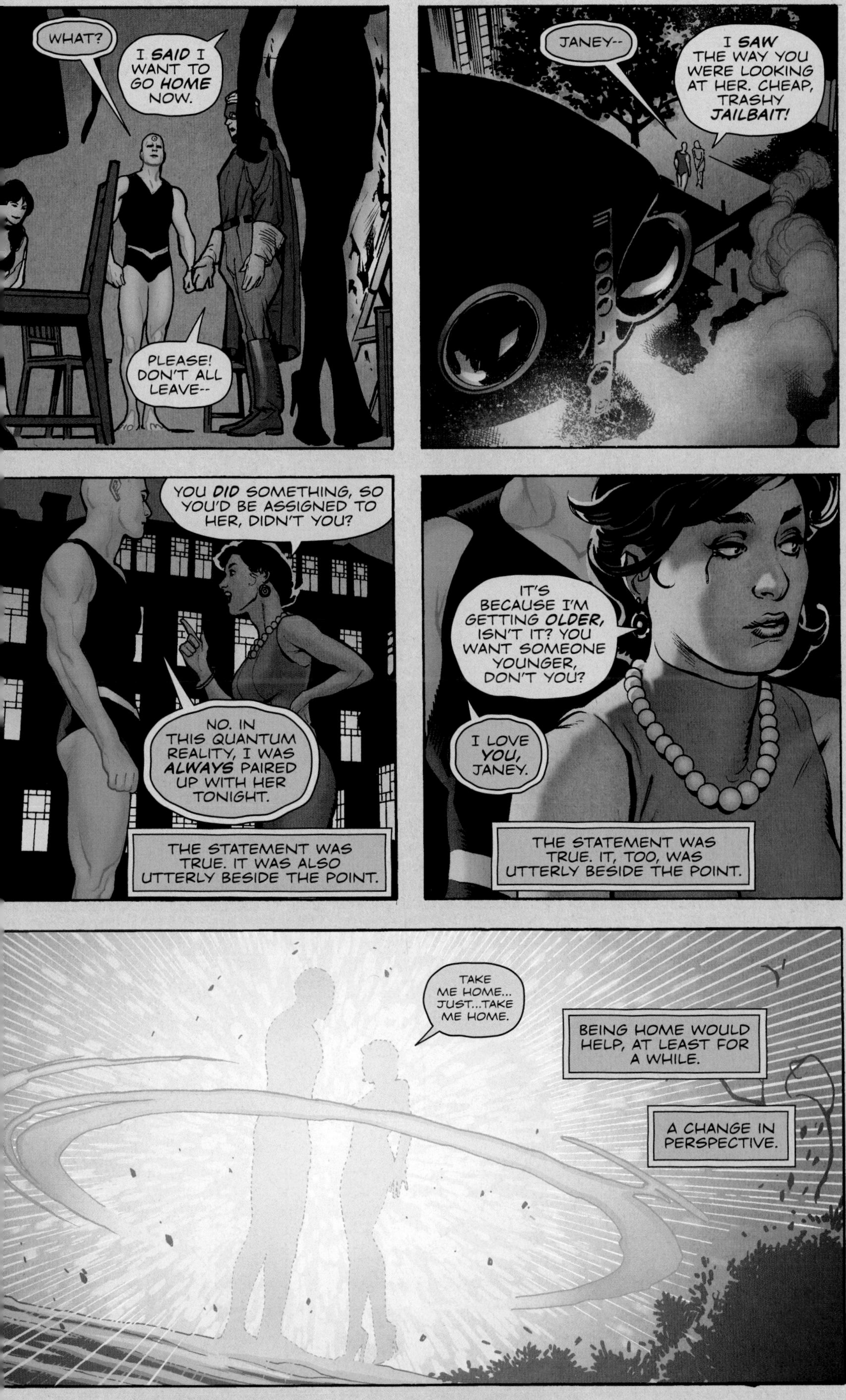
WHAT?
I SAID I WANT TO GO HOME NOW.
PLEASE! DON'T ALL LEAVE--
JANEY--
I SAW THE WAY YOU WERE LOOKING AT HER. CHEAP, TRASHY JAILBAIT!
YOU DID SOMETHING, SO YOU'D BE ASSIGNED TO HER, DIDN'T YOU?
NO. IN THIS QUANTUM REALITY, I WAS ALWAYS PAIRED UP WITH HER TONIGHT.
THE STATEMENT WAS TRUE. IT WAS ALSO UTTERLY BESIDE THE POINT.
IT'S BECAUSE I'M GETTING OLDER, ISN'T IT? YOU WANT SOMEONE YOUNGER, DON'T YOU?
I LOVE YOU, JANEY.
THE STATEMENT WAS TRUE. IT, TOO, WAS UTTERLY BESIDE THE POINT.
TAKE ME HOME... JUST...TAKE ME HOME.
BEING HOME WOULD HELP, AT LEAST FOR A WHILE.
A CHANGE IN PERSPECTIVE.

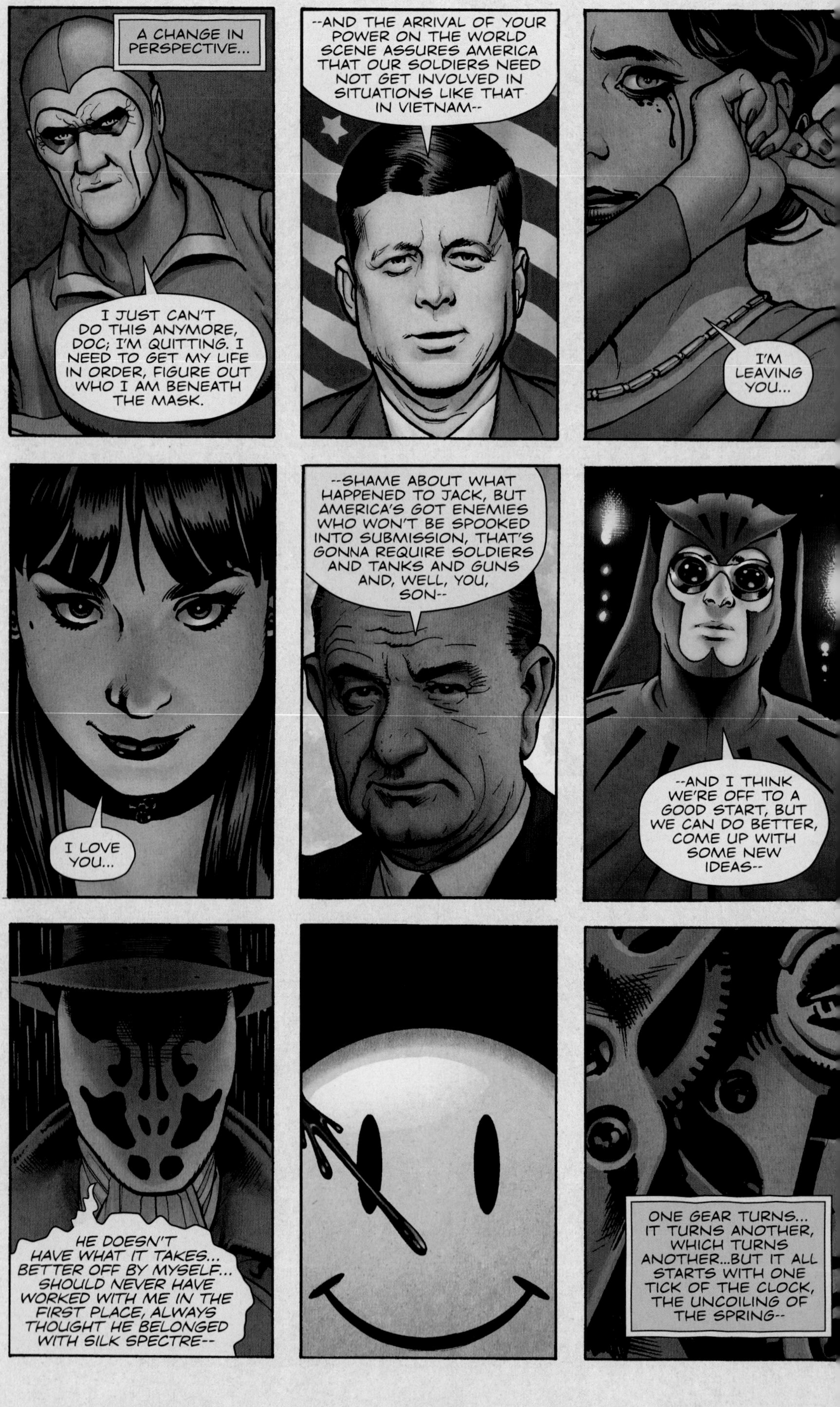
A CHANGE IN PERSPECTIVE...
I JUST CAN'T DO THIS ANYMORE, DOC; I'M QUITTING. I NEED TO GET MY LIFE IN ORDER, FIGURE OUT WHO I AM BENEATH THE MASK.
--AND THE ARRIVAL OF YOUR POWER ON THE WORLD SCENE ASSURES AMERICA THAT OUR SOLDIERS NEED NOT GET INVOLVED IN SITUATIONS LIKE THAT IN VIETNAM--
I'M LEAVING YOU...
I LOVE YOU...
--SHAME ABOUT WHAT HAPPENED TO JACK, BUT AMERICA'S GOT ENEMIES WHO WON'T BE SPOOKED INTO SUBMISSION, THAT'S GONNA REQUIRE SOLDIERS AND TANKS AND GUNS AND, WELL, YOU, SON--
--AND I THINK WE'RE OFF TO A GOOD START, BUT WE CAN DO BETTER, COME UP WITH SOME NEW IDEAS--
HE DOESN'T HAVE WHAT IT TAKES... BETTER OFF BY MYSELF... SHOULD NEVER HAVE WORKED WITH ME IN THE FIRST PLACE, ALWAYS THOUGHT HE BELONGED WITH SILK SPECTRE--
ONE GEAR TURNS... IT TURNS ANOTHER, WHICH TURNS ANOTHER...BUT IT ALL STARTS WITH ONE TICK OF THE CLOCK, THE UNCOILING OF THE SPRING--

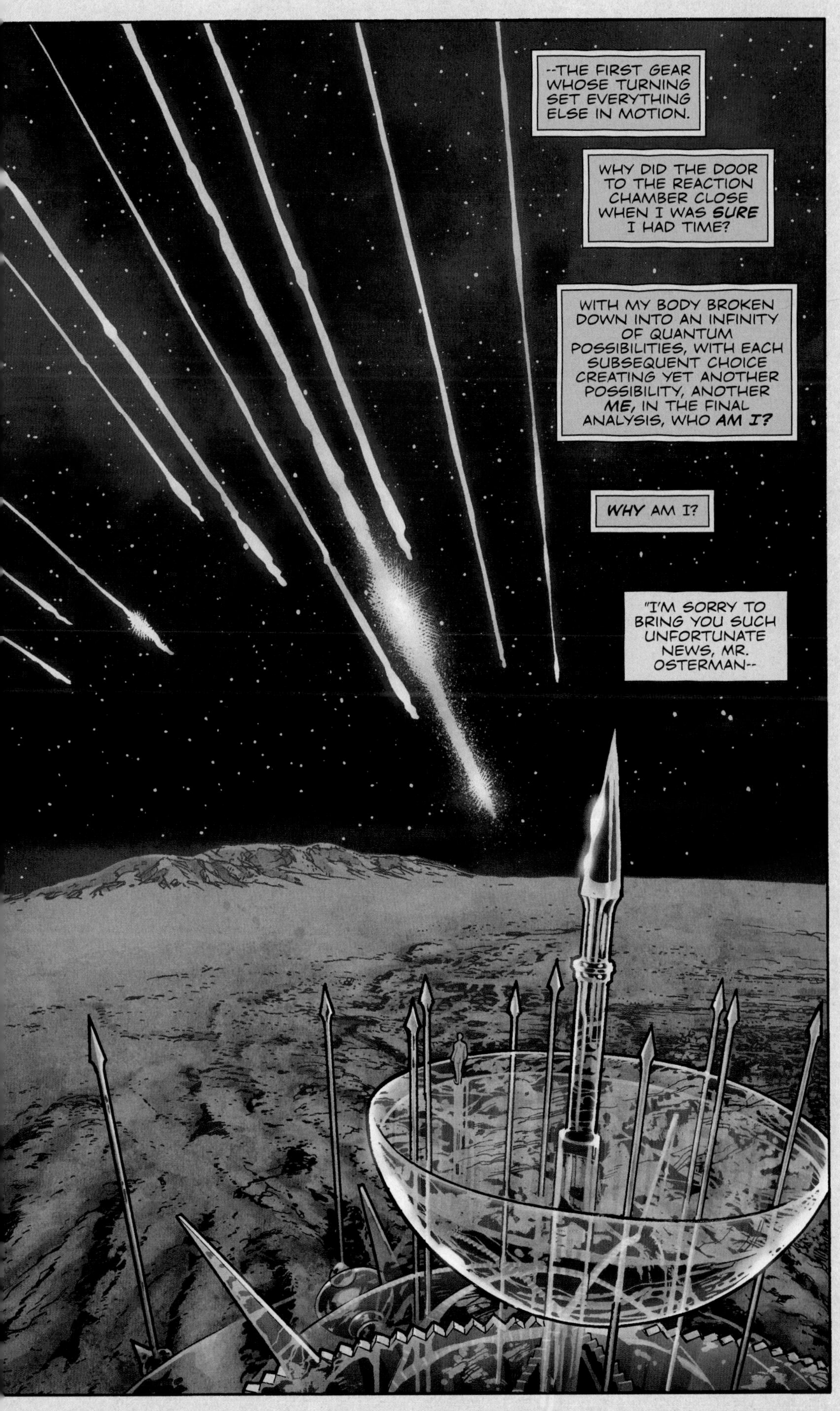
--THE FIRST GEAR WHOSE TURNING SET EVERYTHING ELSE IN MOTION.
WHY DID THE DOOR TO THE REACTION CHAMBER CLOSE WHEN I WAS **SURE** I HAD TIME?
WITH MY BODY BROKEN DOWN INTO AN INFINITY OF QUANTUM POSSIBILITIES, WITH EACH SUBSEQUENT CHOICE CREATING YET ANOTHER POSSIBILITY, ANOTHER **ME,** IN THE FINAL ANALYSIS, WHO **AM I?**
WHY AM I?
"I'M SORRY TO BRING YOU SUCH UNFORTUNATE NEWS, MR. OSTERMAN--

AUGUST, 1959.

--BUT THERE'S NOTHING WE CAN DO.

WE CAN HANDLE ALL THE ARRANGEMENTS FOR THE FUNERAL, EVEN THOUGH THERE'S NOTHING TECHNICALLY LEFT TO BURY--

MY SON...IS NOT DEAD.

MR. OSTERMAN--

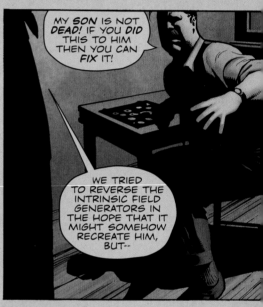

MY *SON* IS NOT *DEAD!* IF YOU *DID* THIS TO HIM THEN YOU CAN *FIX* IT!

WE TRIED TO REVERSE THE INTRINSIC FIELD GENERATORS IN THE HOPE THAT IT MIGHT SOMEHOW RECREATE HIM, BUT--

NO!

YOU JUST NEED...TO FIND THE PIECES... AND PUT THEM TOGETHER...TO *FIX* HIM...

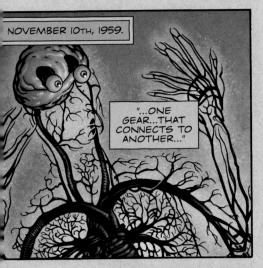

NOVEMBER 10TH, 1959.

"...ONE GEAR...THAT CONNECTS TO ANOTHER..."

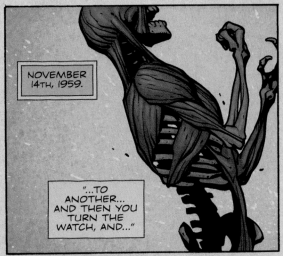

NOVEMBER 14TH, 1959.

"...TO ANOTHER... AND THEN YOU TURN THE WATCH, AND..."

HE'S NOT DEAD...JUST HAVE TO FIX HIM--

FATHER...IT'S ME...I'M RIGHT HERE.

IT'S ME...IT'S JON.

DAD...? WHAT'S WRONG? WHAT'S--

GOD HELP ME...GOD IN HEAVEN...MY SON IS DEAD...MY SON IS GONE...

...THEY'VE TAKEN HIM FROM ME.

HE WAS RIGHT. IT TOOK ME YEARS TO SEE THAT, BUT IN THE END, HE WAS RIGHT.

I AM NOT JON, BUT JON *BECAME* ME. HIS PERSPECTIVE *INFORMED* ME, HIS PERSPECTIVE--

--CREATED ME? IS THAT POSSIBLE? WHAT HAPPENED IN THAT MOMENT, THAT SURGE OF ENERGY THAT RESULTED IN MY BIRTH? IF I AM A QUANTUM *EFFECT*, WHAT WAS THE QUANTUM *CAUSE*?

WHATEVER IT WAS, DID IT HAPPEN *BEFORE* THE INCIDENT, OR *DURING* THE INCIDENT?

WHAT'S IN THE BOX?

I KNOW THAT I CAN RIDE THE TIMELINE BACK AND FORTH BETWEEN THE FUTURE AND THE MOMENT OF MY CREATION...

...AND THE MOMENT OF DÉJÀ VU IN GILA FLATS SHOWS THAT EVEN BEFORE THE INCIDENT MY CONSCIOUSNESS WAS ABLE TO RIDE THE TIMELINE FORWARD PAST THE POINT OF MY BODY'S DESTRUCTION.

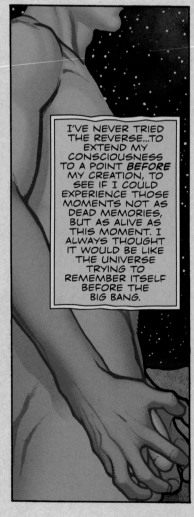

I'VE NEVER TRIED THE REVERSE...TO EXTEND MY CONSCIOUSNESS TO A POINT *BEFORE* MY CREATION, TO SEE IF I COULD EXPERIENCE THOSE MOMENTS NOT AS DEAD MEMORIES, BUT AS ALIVE AS THIS MOMENT. I ALWAYS THOUGHT IT WOULD BE LIKE THE UNIVERSE TRYING TO REMEMBER ITSELF BEFORE THE BIG BANG.

AND PERHAPS...IT IS TIME TO TRY.

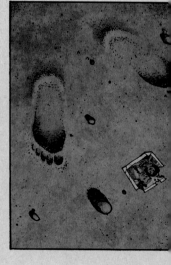

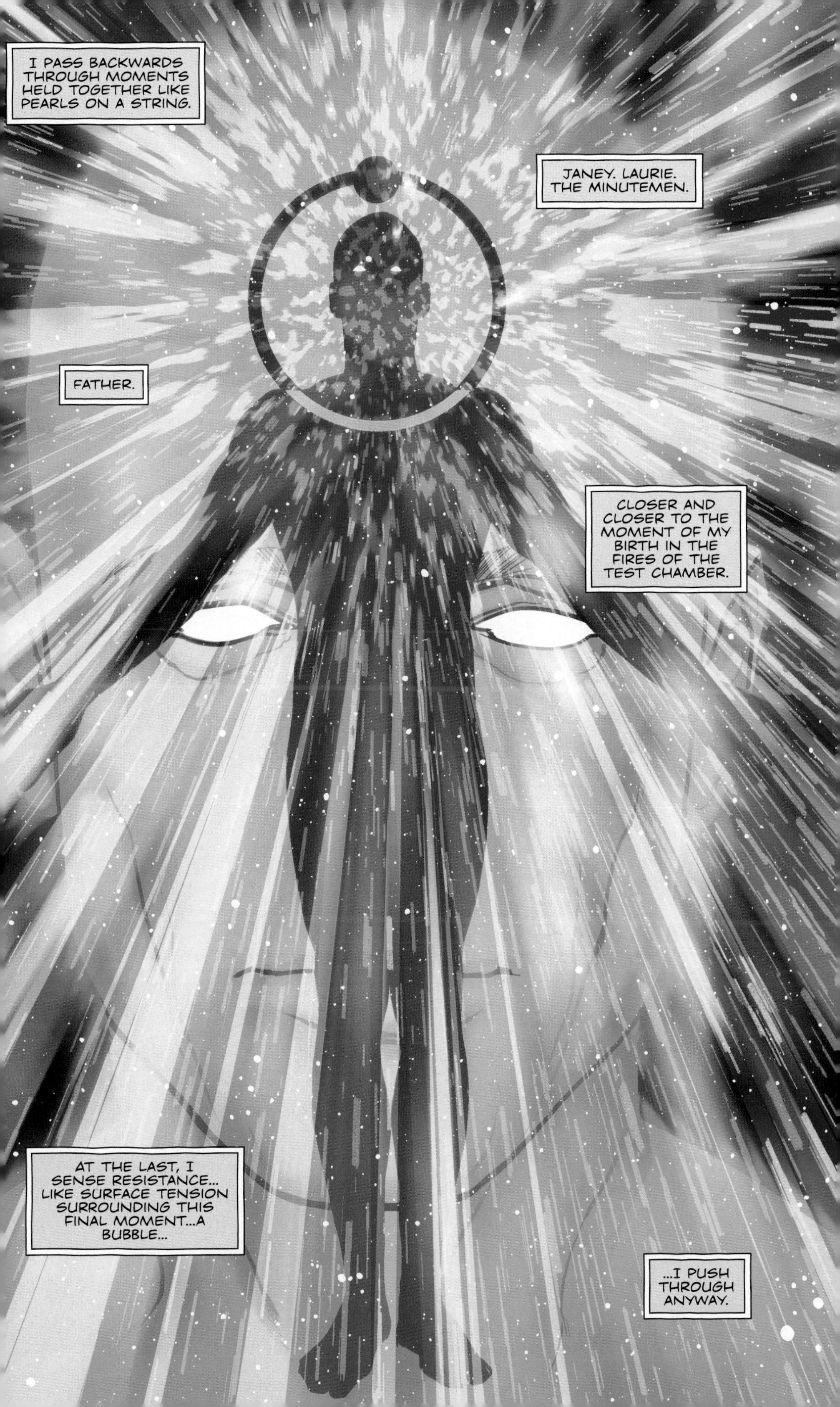
I PASS BACKWARDS THROUGH MOMENTS HELD TOGETHER LIKE PEARLS ON A STRING.
JANEY. LAURIE. THE MINUTEMEN.
FATHER.
CLOSER AND CLOSER TO THE MOMENT OF MY BIRTH IN THE FIRES OF THE TEST CHAMBER.
AT THE LAST, I SENSE RESISTANCE... LIKE SURFACE TENSION SURROUNDING THIS FINAL MOMENT...A BUBBLE...
...I PUSH THROUGH ANYWAY.

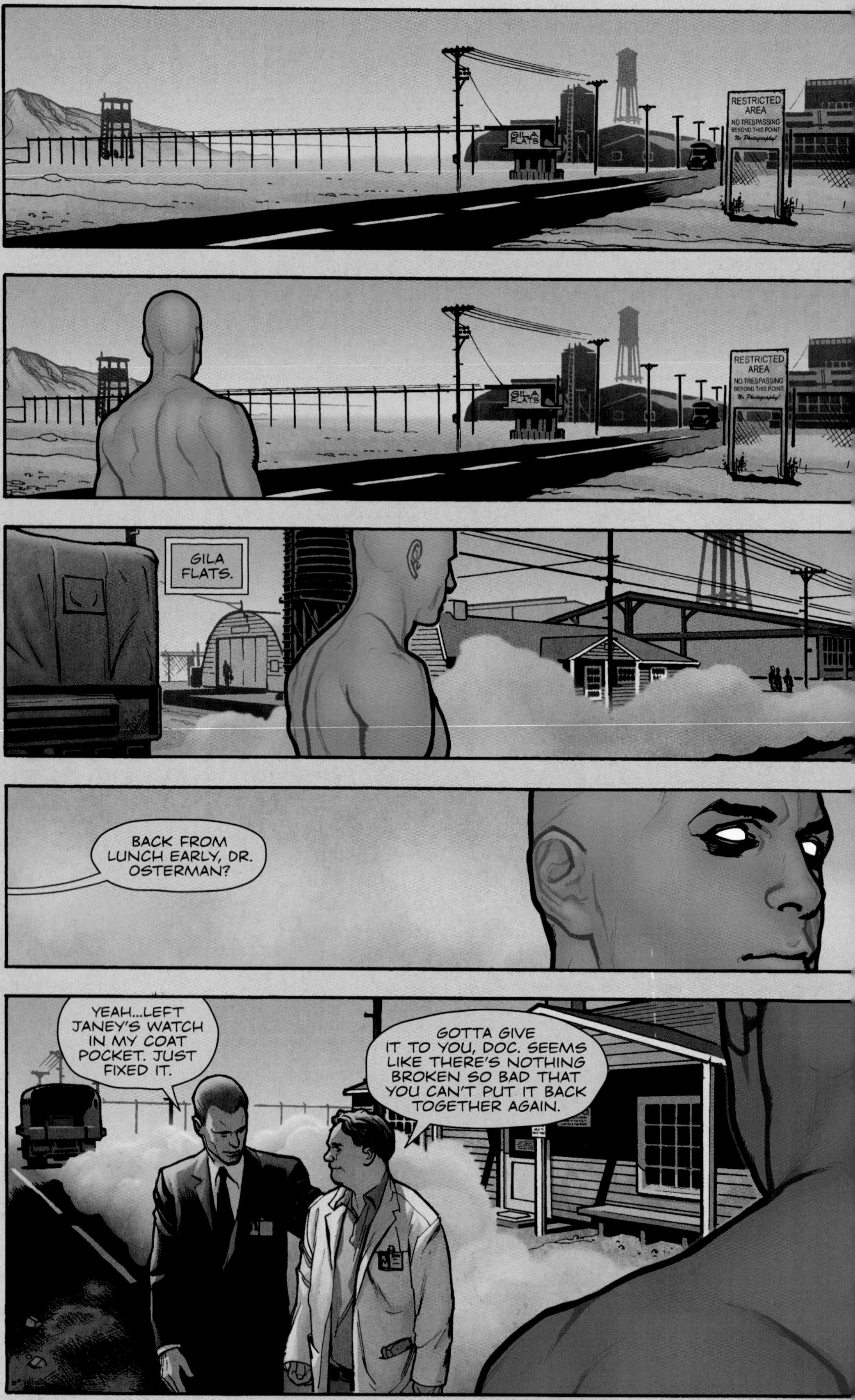
RESTRICTED AREA
NO TRESPASSING BEYOND THIS POINT
No Photography!
GILA FLATS
GILA FLATS.
BACK FROM LUNCH EARLY, DR. OSTERMAN?
YEAH...LEFT JANEY'S WATCH IN MY COAT POCKET. JUST FIXED IT.
GOTTA GIVE IT TO YOU, DOC. SEEMS LIKE THERE'S NOTHING BROKEN SO BAD THAT YOU CAN'T PUT IT BACK TOGETHER AGAIN.

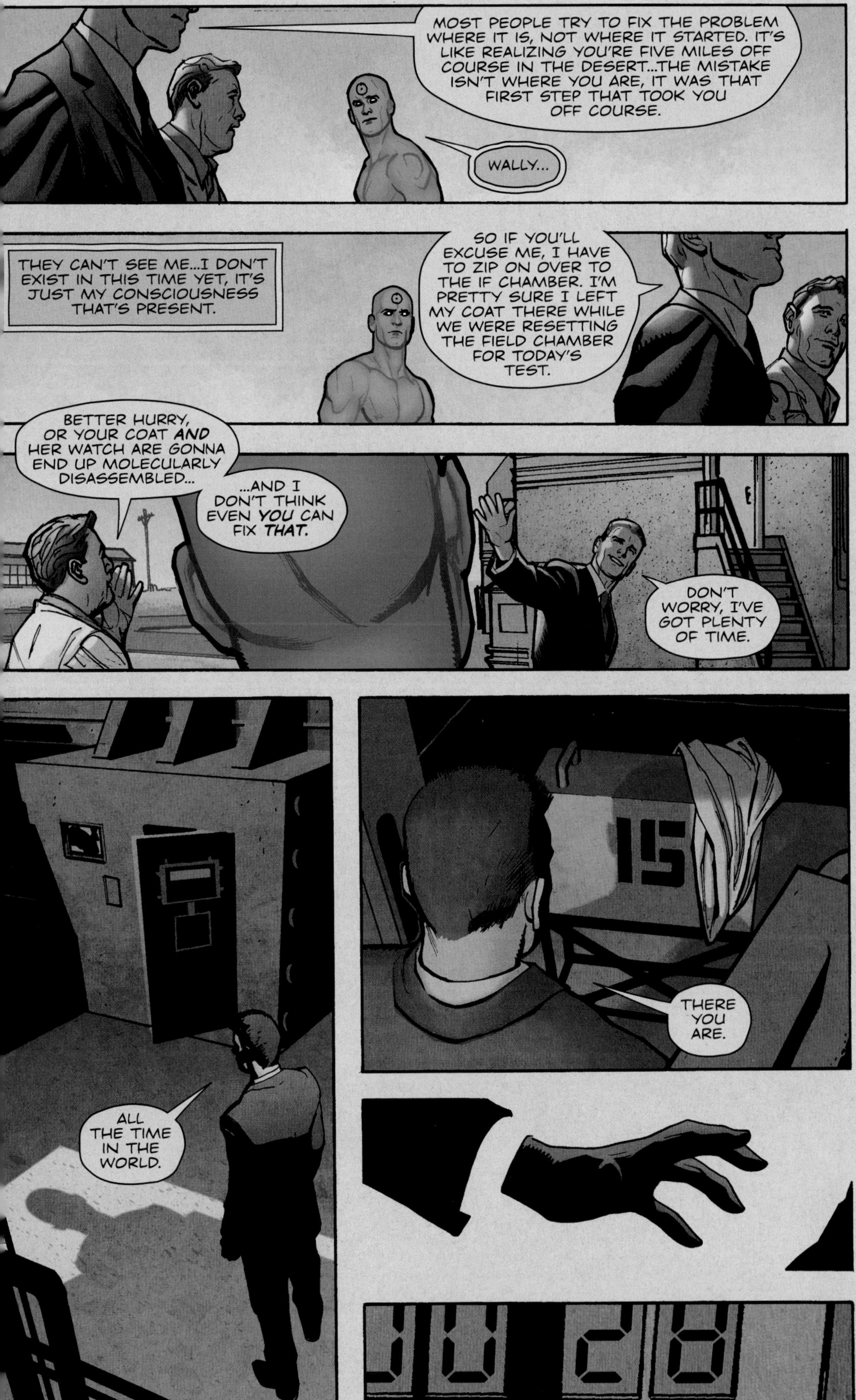
MOST PEOPLE TRY TO FIX THE PROBLEM WHERE IT IS, NOT WHERE IT STARTED. IT'S LIKE REALIZING YOU'RE FIVE MILES OFF COURSE IN THE DESERT...THE MISTAKE ISN'T WHERE YOU ARE, IT WAS THAT FIRST STEP THAT TOOK YOU OFF COURSE.
WALLY...
THEY CAN'T SEE ME...I DON'T EXIST IN THIS TIME YET, IT'S JUST MY CONSCIOUSNESS THAT'S PRESENT.
SO IF YOU'LL EXCUSE ME, I HAVE TO ZIP ON OVER TO THE IF CHAMBER. I'M PRETTY SURE I LEFT MY COAT THERE WHILE WE WERE RESETTING THE FIELD CHAMBER FOR TODAY'S TEST.
BETTER HURRY, OR YOUR COAT **AND** HER WATCH ARE GONNA END UP MOLECULARLY DISASSEMBLED...
...AND I DON'T THINK EVEN ***YOU*** CAN FIX ***THAT.***
DON'T WORRY, I'VE GOT PLENTY OF TIME.
ALL THE TIME IN THE WORLD.
15
THERE YOU ARE.

BUT... IT'S NOT POSSIBLE--

♪

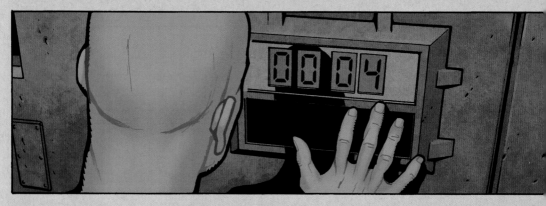

IT'S ONE-FIFTEEN P.M., AUGUST 20TH, 1959. THE MOMENT I WAS BORN. THE MOMENT OF THE ACCIDENT.

BECAUSE ACCIDENTS HAPPEN.

EXCEPT THIS ONE *DOESN'T* HAPPEN.

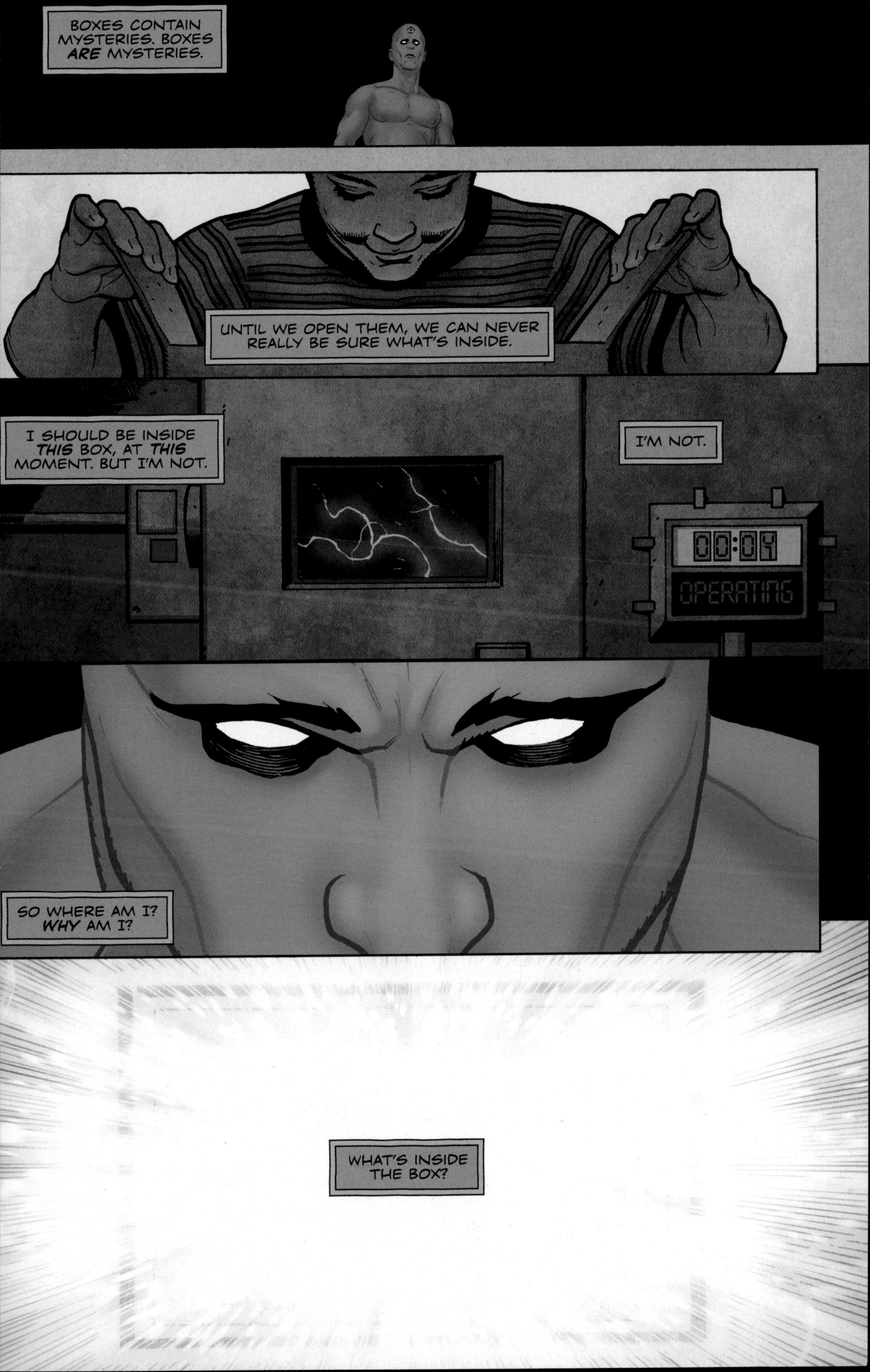

BOXES CONTAIN MYSTERIES. BOXES ***ARE*** MYSTERIES.
UNTIL WE OPEN THEM, WE CAN NEVER REALLY BE SURE WHAT'S INSIDE.
I SHOULD BE INSIDE ***THIS*** BOX, AT ***THIS*** MOMENT. BUT I'M NOT.
I'M NOT.
00:04
OPERATING
SO WHERE AM I? ***WHY*** AM I?
WHAT'S INSIDE THE BOX?

DR. MANHATTAN
15
MYSTE
AY
IT CAME FRO
DIMENSION
By MAX SHE
A THRILLING
PUBLICATION

DR. MANHATTAN

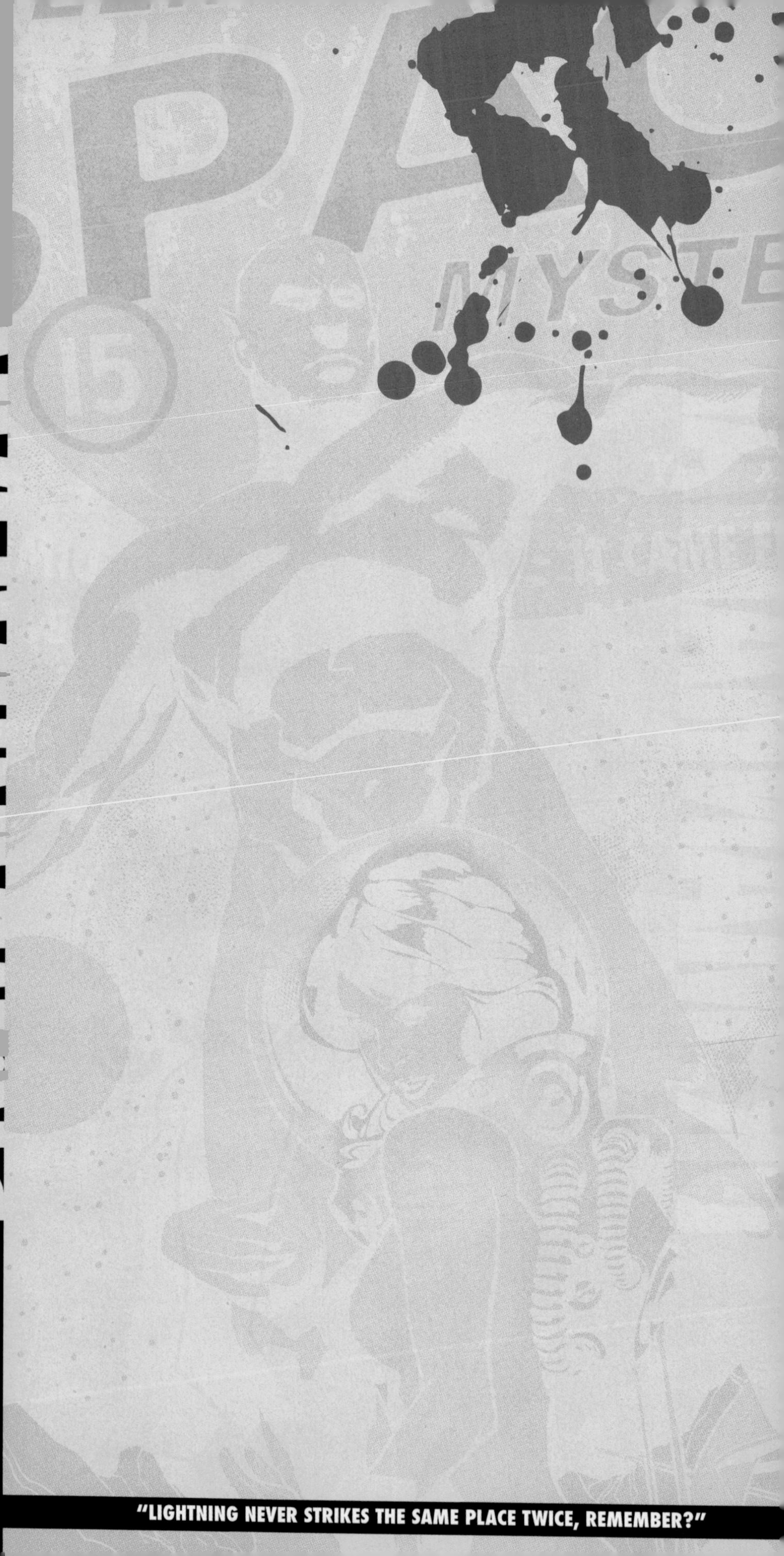

"LIGHTNING NEVER STRIKES THE SAME PLACE TWICE, REMEMBER?"

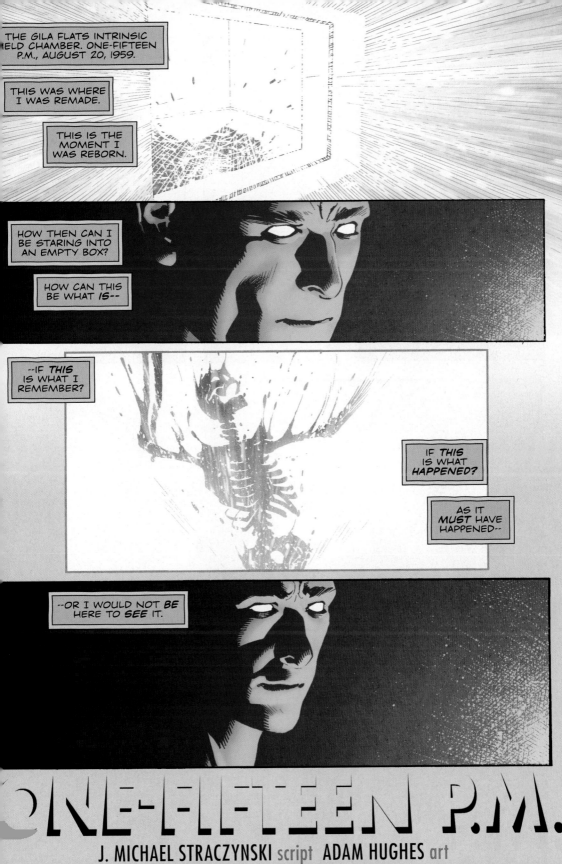

THE GILA FLATS INTRINSIC FIELD CHAMBER. ONE-FIFTEEN P.M., AUGUST 20, 1959.

THIS WAS WHERE I WAS REMADE.

THIS IS THE MOMENT I WAS REBORN.

HOW THEN CAN I BE STARING INTO AN EMPTY BOX?

HOW CAN THIS BE WHAT *IS*--

--IF *THIS* IS WHAT I REMEMBER?

IF *THIS* IS WHAT *HAPPENED*?

AS IT *MUST* HAVE HAPPENED--

--OR I WOULD NOT BE HERE TO *SEE* IT.

ONE-FIFTEEN P.M.

J. MICHAEL STRACZYNSKI script ADAM HUGHES art

LAURA MARTIN colors STEVE WANDS letters

ADAM HUGHES cover P. CRAIG RUSSELL variant cover

CAMILLA ZHANG asst. editor CHRIS CONROY assoc. editor MARK CHIARELLO editor

WATCHMEN created by ALAN MOORE and DAVE GIBBONS

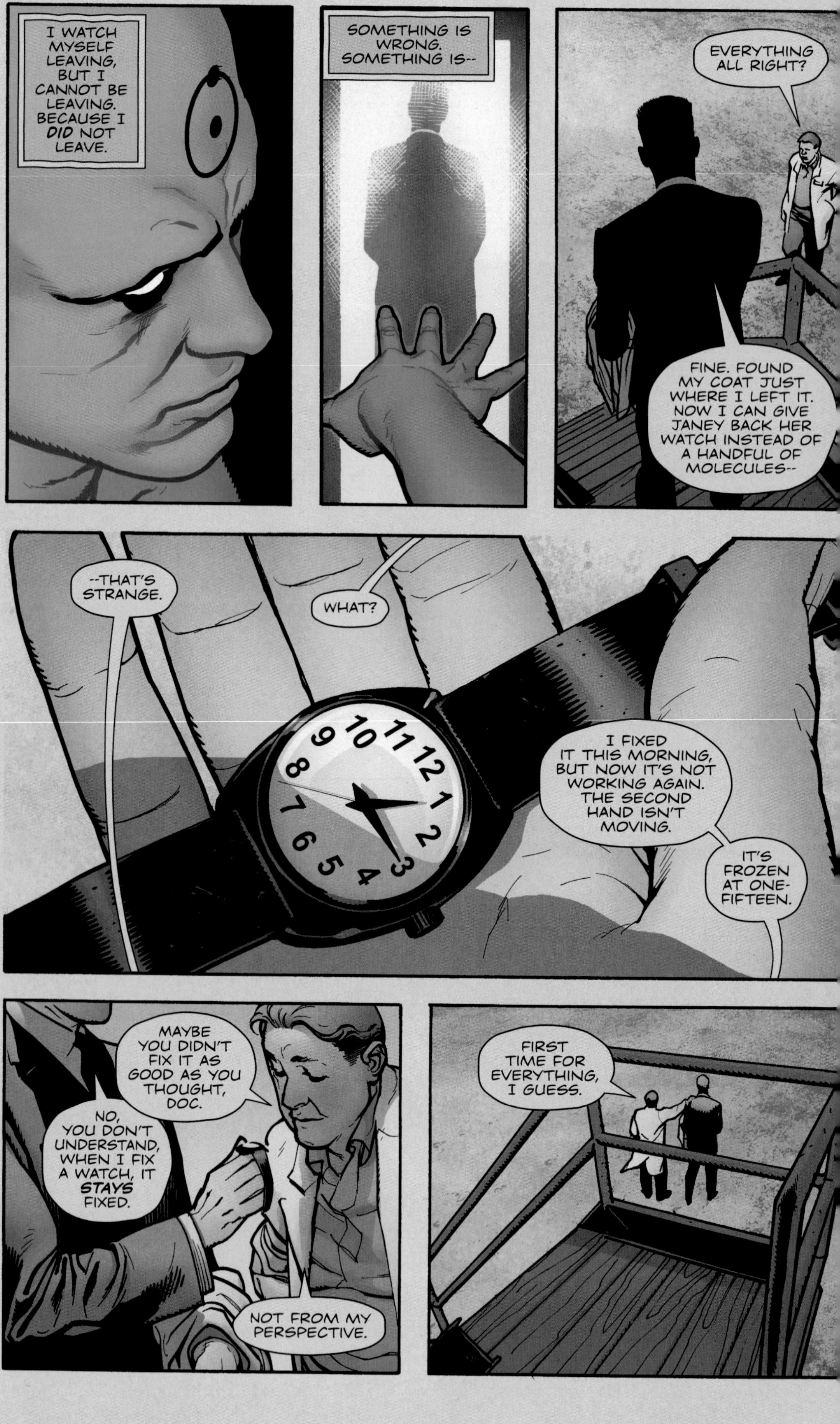
I WATCH MYSELF LEAVING, BUT I CANNOT BE LEAVING. BECAUSE I *DID* NOT LEAVE.
SOMETHING IS WRONG. SOMETHING IS--
EVERYTHING ALL RIGHT?
FINE. FOUND MY COAT JUST WHERE I LEFT IT. NOW I CAN GIVE JANEY BACK HER WATCH INSTEAD OF A HANDFUL OF MOLECULES--
--THAT'S STRANGE.
WHAT?
I FIXED IT THIS MORNING, BUT NOW IT'S NOT WORKING AGAIN. THE SECOND HAND ISN'T MOVING.
IT'S FROZEN AT ONE-FIFTEEN.
MAYBE YOU DIDN'T FIX IT AS GOOD AS YOU THOUGHT, DOC.
NO, YOU DON'T UNDERSTAND, WHEN I FIX A WATCH, IT **STAYS** FIXED.
NOT FROM MY PERSPECTIVE.
FIRST TIME FOR EVERYTHING, I GUESS.

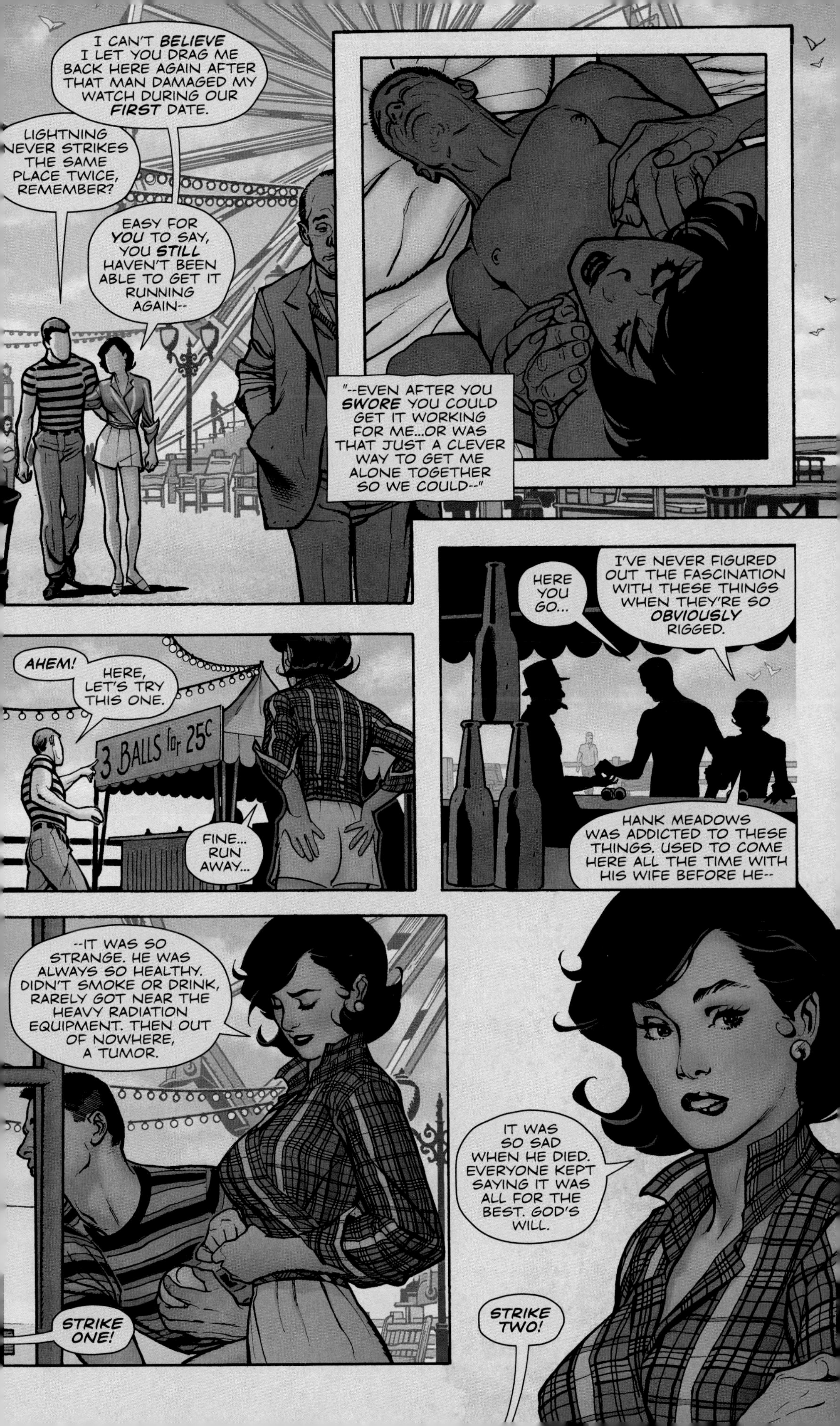
I CAN'T BELIEVE I LET YOU DRAG ME BACK HERE AGAIN AFTER THAT MAN DAMAGED MY WATCH DURING OUR FIRST DATE.
LIGHTNING NEVER STRIKES THE SAME PLACE TWICE, REMEMBER?
EASY FOR YOU TO SAY, YOU STILL HAVEN'T BEEN ABLE TO GET IT RUNNING AGAIN--
"--EVEN AFTER YOU SWORE YOU COULD GET IT WORKING FOR ME...OR WAS THAT JUST A CLEVER WAY TO GET ME ALONE TOGETHER SO WE COULD--"
AHEM!
HERE, LET'S TRY THIS ONE.
3 BALLS for 25c
FINE... RUN AWAY...
HERE YOU GO...
I'VE NEVER FIGURED OUT THE FASCINATION WITH THESE THINGS WHEN THEY'RE SO OBVIOUSLY RIGGED.
HANK MEADOWS WAS ADDICTED TO THESE THINGS. USED TO COME HERE ALL THE TIME WITH HIS WIFE BEFORE HE--
--IT WAS SO STRANGE. HE WAS ALWAYS SO HEALTHY. DIDN'T SMOKE OR DRINK, RARELY GOT NEAR THE HEAVY RADIATION EQUIPMENT. THEN OUT OF NOWHERE, A TUMOR.
STRIKE ONE!
IT WAS SO SAD WHEN HE DIED. EVERYONE KEPT SAYING IT WAS ALL FOR THE BEST. GOD'S WILL.
STRIKE TWO!

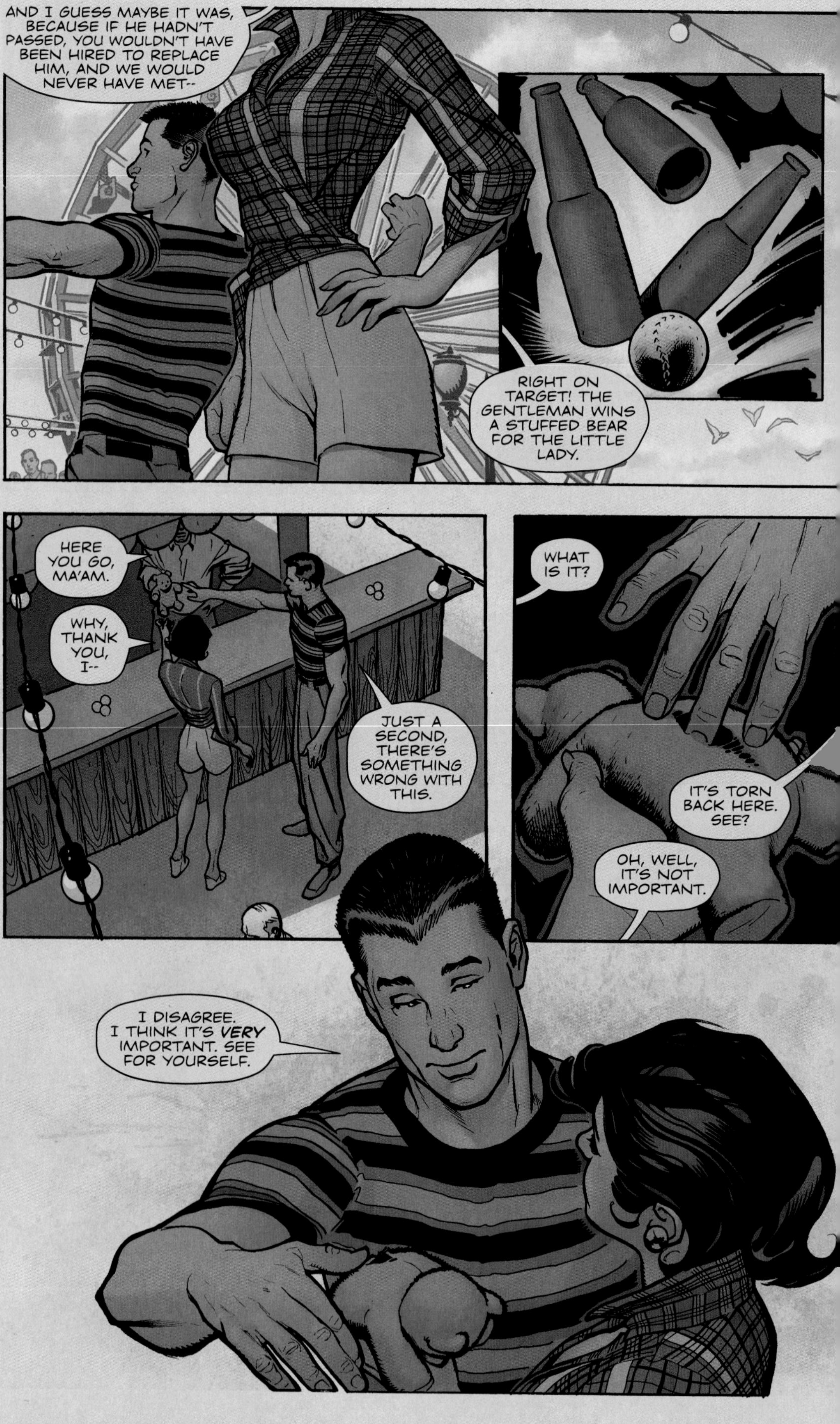
AND I GUESS MAYBE IT WAS, BECAUSE IF HE HADN'T PASSED, YOU WOULDN'T HAVE BEEN HIRED TO REPLACE HIM, AND WE WOULD NEVER HAVE MET--
RIGHT ON TARGET! THE GENTLEMAN WINS A STUFFED BEAR FOR THE LITTLE LADY.
HERE YOU GO, MA'AM.
WHY, THANK YOU, I--
JUST A SECOND, THERE'S SOMETHING WRONG WITH THIS.
WHAT IS IT?
IT'S TORN BACK HERE. SEE?
OH, WELL, IT'S NOT IMPORTANT.
I DISAGREE. I THINK IT'S *VERY* IMPORTANT. SEE FOR YOURSELF.

JON--

YES, LOVE?

--WHAT'S IN THE BOX?

COULD BE *ANYTHING*. WHY DON'T YOU OPEN IT AND LOOK INSIDE?

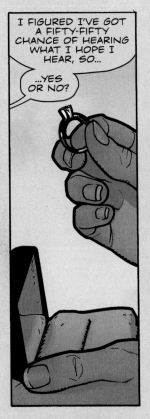

I FIGURED I'VE GOT A FIFTY-FIFTY CHANCE OF HEARING WHAT I HOPE I HEAR, SO...

...YES OR NO?

YES! OH, DARLING, MOST DEFINITELY YES!

THANKS AGAIN FOR YOUR HELP!

MY PLEASURE, PAL. THAT'S MY SPECIALTY...THAT'S WHAT *I DO*.

PROVIDING THE ILLUSION OF FREE WILL.

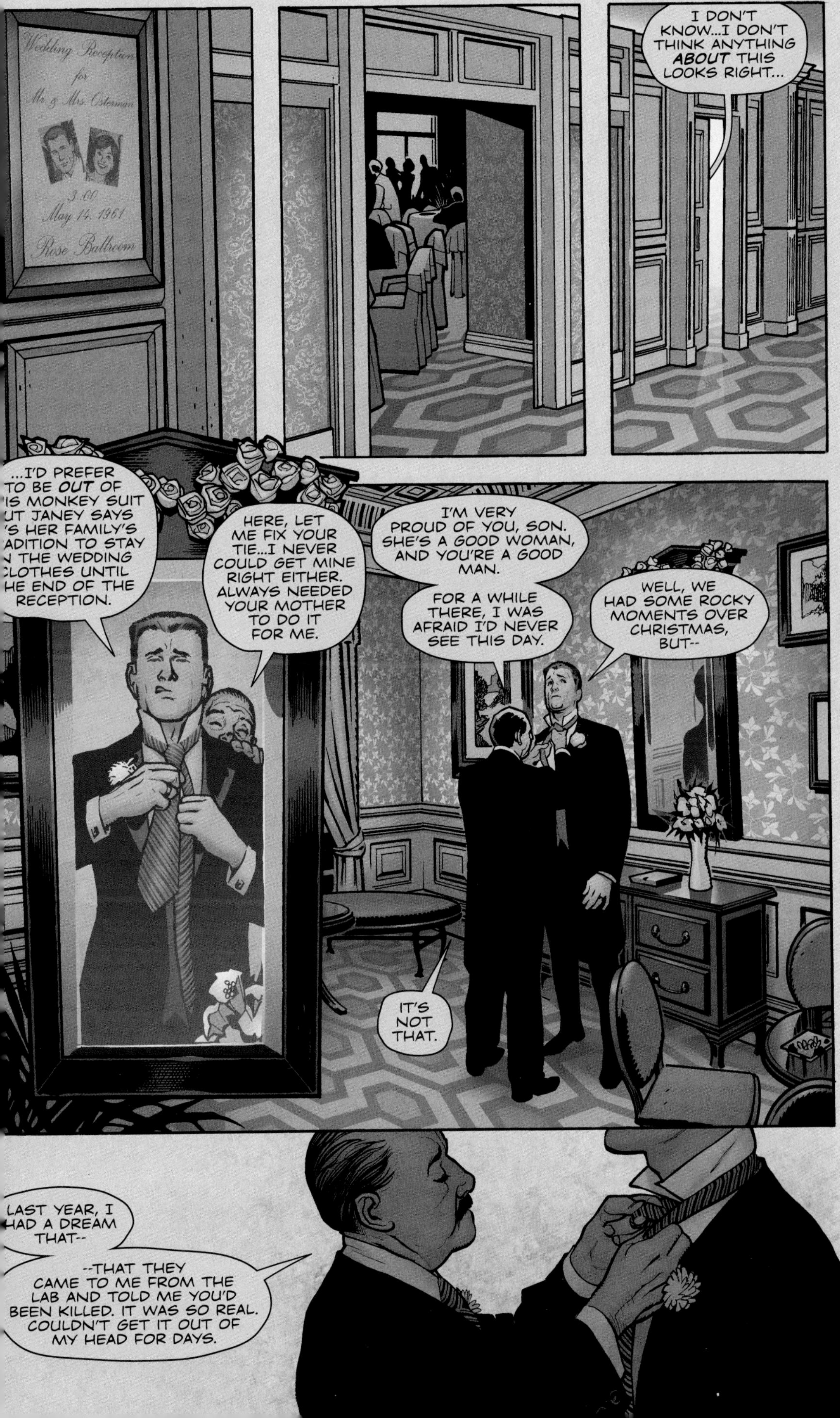

Wedding Reception for Mr. & Mrs. Osterman 3:00 May 14, 1961 Rose Ballroom
I DON'T KNOW...I DON'T THINK ANYTHING ABOUT THIS LOOKS RIGHT...
...I'D PREFER TO BE OUT OF IS MONKEY SUIT UT JANEY SAYS 'S HER FAMILY'S ADITION TO STAY N THE WEDDING CLOTHES UNTIL HE END OF THE RECEPTION.
HERE, LET ME FIX YOUR TIE...I NEVER COULD GET MINE RIGHT EITHER. ALWAYS NEEDED YOUR MOTHER TO DO IT FOR ME.
I'M VERY PROUD OF YOU, SON. SHE'S A GOOD WOMAN, AND YOU'RE A GOOD MAN.
FOR A WHILE THERE, I WAS AFRAID I'D NEVER SEE THIS DAY.
WELL, WE HAD SOME ROCKY MOMENTS OVER CHRISTMAS, BUT--
IT'S NOT THAT.
LAST YEAR, I HAD A DREAM THAT--
--THAT THEY CAME TO ME FROM THE LAB AND TOLD ME YOU'D BEEN KILLED. IT WAS SO REAL. COULDN'T GET IT OUT OF MY HEAD FOR DAYS.

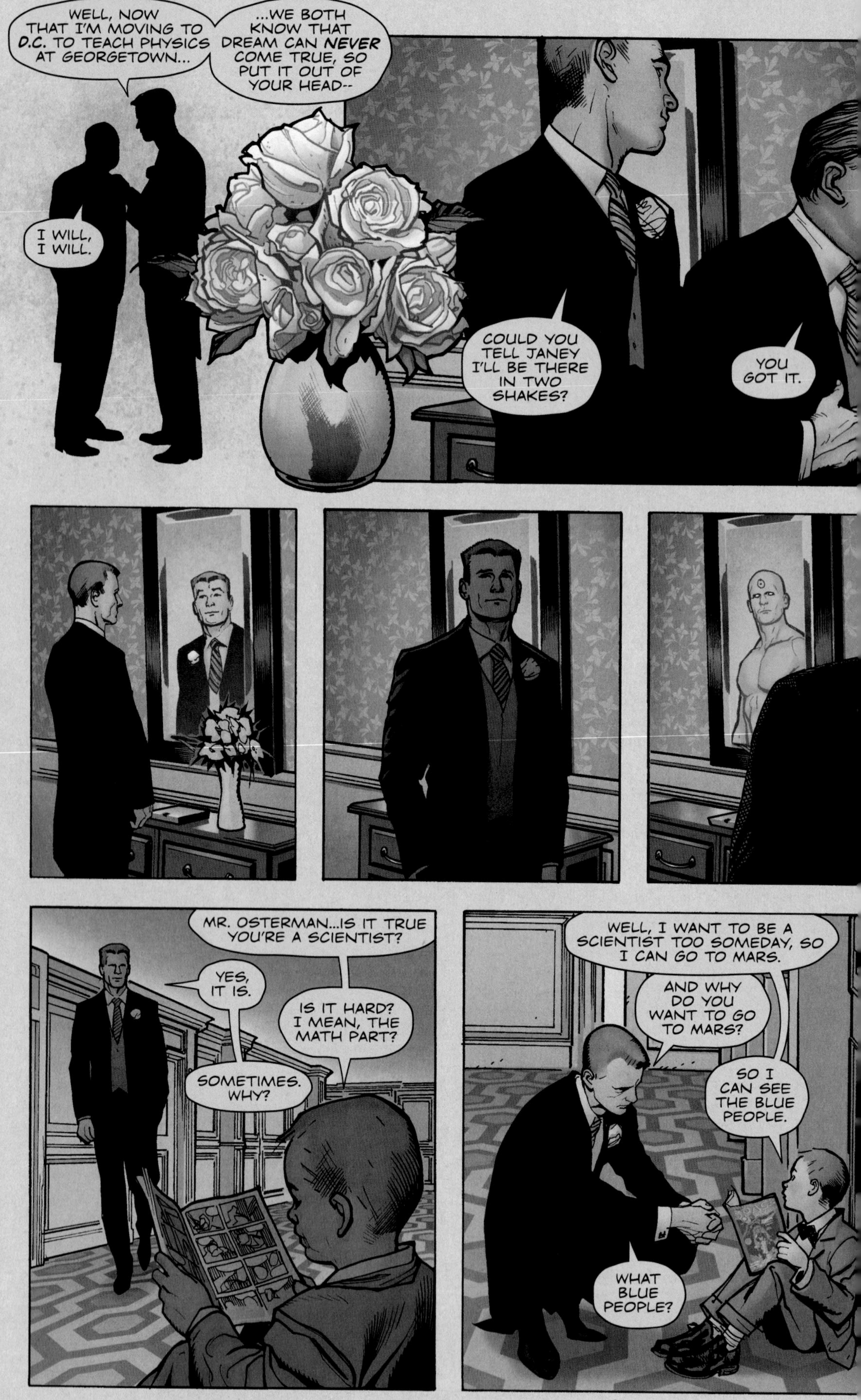
WELL, NOW THAT I'M MOVING TO D.C. TO TEACH PHYSICS AT GEORGETOWN...
...WE BOTH KNOW THAT DREAM CAN NEVER COME TRUE, SO PUT IT OUT OF YOUR HEAD--
I WILL, I WILL.
COULD YOU TELL JANEY I'LL BE THERE IN TWO SHAKES?
YOU GOT IT.
MR. OSTERMAN...IS IT TRUE YOU'RE A SCIENTIST?
YES, IT IS.
IS IT HARD? I MEAN, THE MATH PART?
SOMETIMES. WHY?
WELL, I WANT TO BE A SCIENTIST TOO SOMEDAY, SO I CAN GO TO MARS.
AND WHY DO YOU WANT TO GO TO MARS?
SO I CAN SEE THE BLUE PEOPLE.
WHAT BLUE PEOPLE?

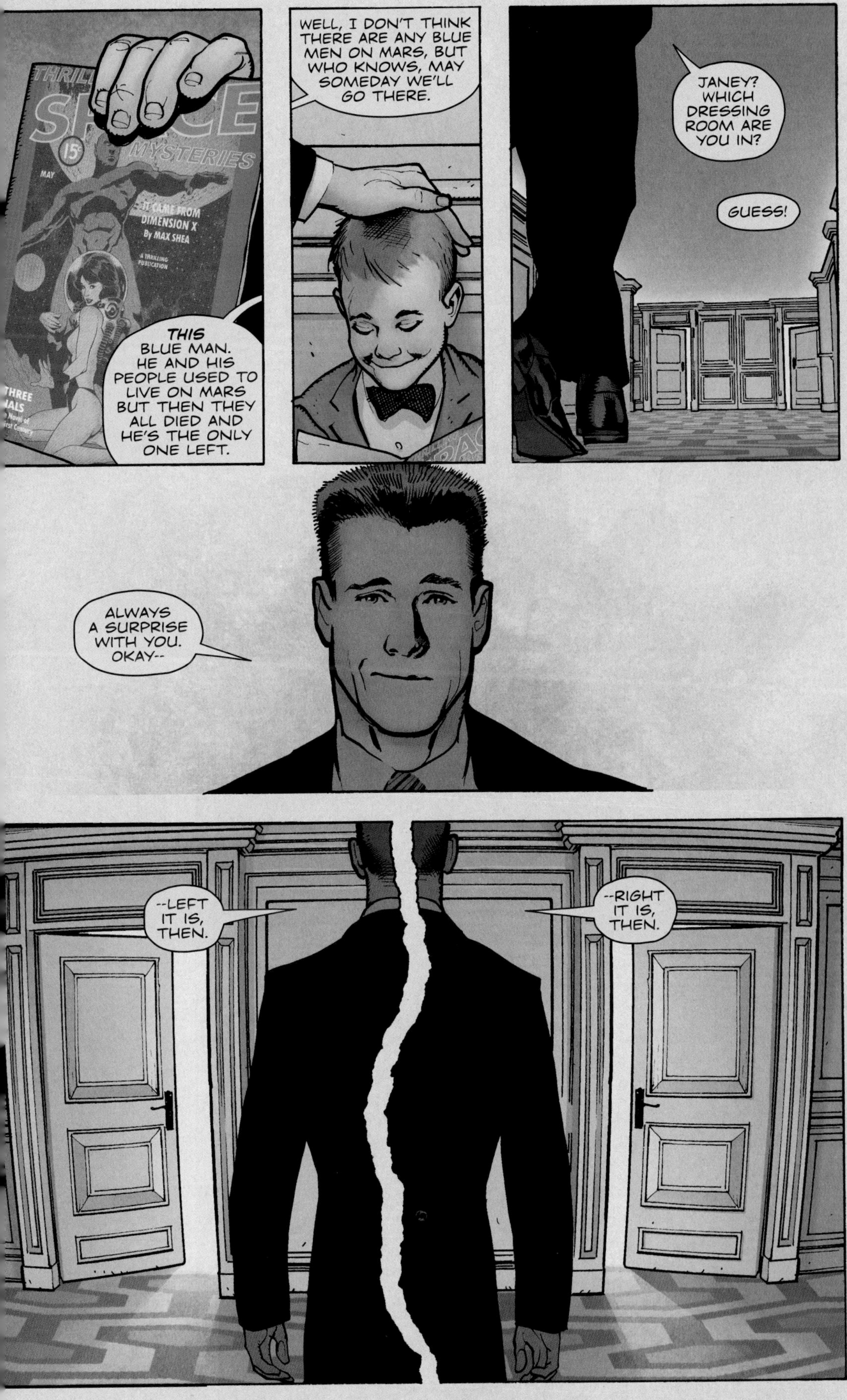
THRILLING SPACE MYSTERIES
15¢
MAY
IT CAME FROM DIMENSION X By MAX SHEA
A THRILLING PUBLICATION
THIS BLUE MAN. HE AND HIS PEOPLE USED TO LIVE ON MARS BUT THEN THEY ALL DIED AND HE'S THE ONLY ONE LEFT.
WELL, I DON'T THINK THERE ARE ANY BLUE MEN ON MARS, BUT WHO KNOWS, MAY SOMEDAY WE'LL GO THERE.
JANEY? WHICH DRESSING ROOM ARE YOU IN?
GUESS!
ALWAYS A SURPRISE WITH YOU. OKAY--
--LEFT IT IS, THEN.
--RIGHT IT IS, THEN.

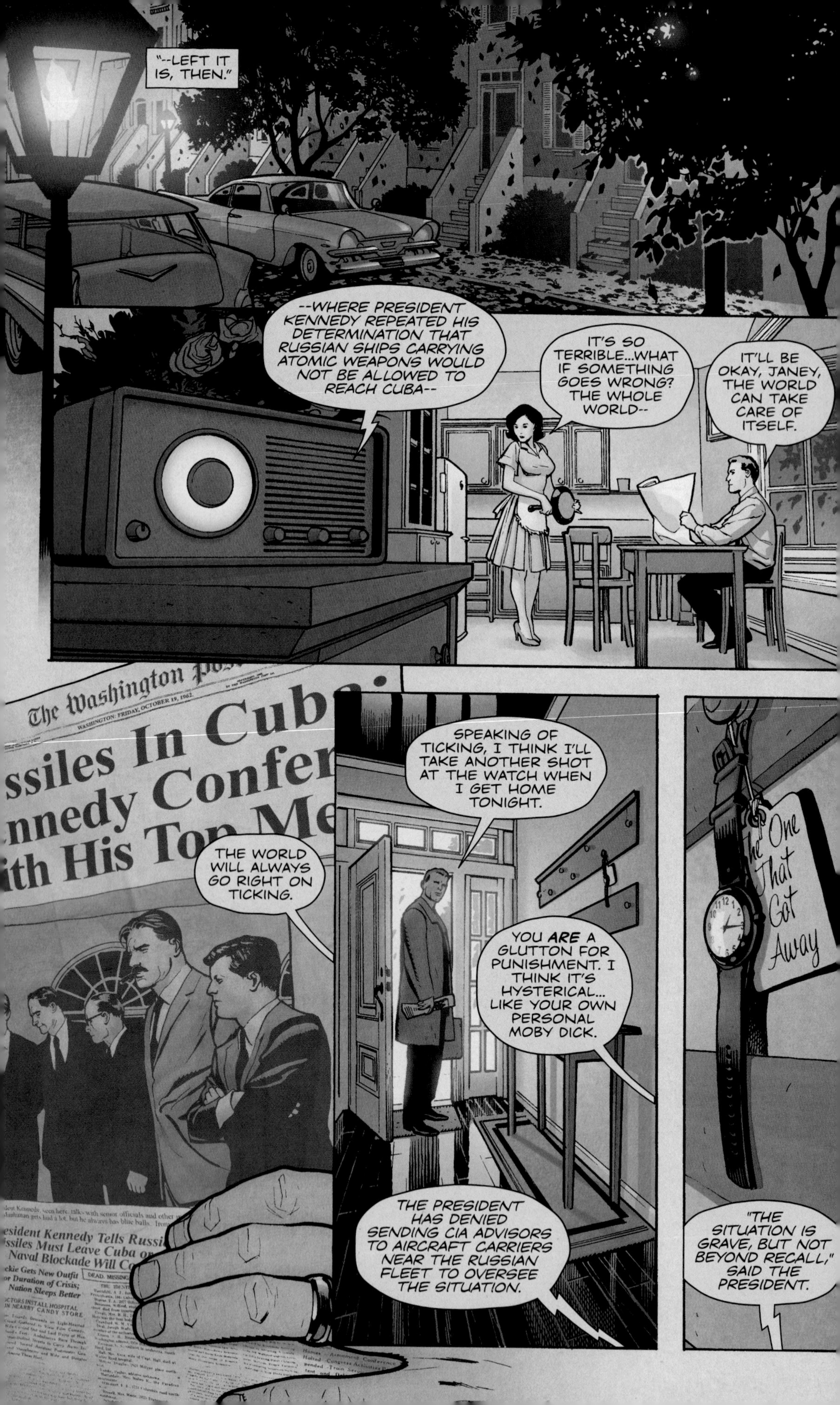
"--LEFT IT IS, THEN."
--WHERE PRESIDENT KENNEDY REPEATED HIS DETERMINATION THAT RUSSIAN SHIPS CARRYING ATOMIC WEAPONS WOULD NOT BE ALLOWED TO REACH CUBA--
IT'S SO TERRIBLE...WHAT IF SOMETHING GOES WRONG? THE WHOLE WORLD--
IT'LL BE OKAY, JANEY, THE WORLD CAN TAKE CARE OF ITSELF.
The Washington Post
WASHINGTON: FRIDAY, OCTOBER 19, 1962.
ssiles In Cub
nnedy Confer
ith His Top Me
THE WORLD WILL ALWAYS GO RIGHT ON TICKING.
esident Kennedy Tells Russi
ssiles Must Leave Cuba o
Naval Blockade Will Co
ckie Gets New Outfit
or Duration of Crisis;
Nation Sleeps Better
SPEAKING OF TICKING, I THINK I'LL TAKE ANOTHER SHOT AT THE WATCH WHEN I GET HOME TONIGHT.
YOU *ARE* A GLUTTON FOR PUNISHMENT. I THINK IT'S HYSTERICAL... LIKE YOUR OWN PERSONAL MOBY DICK.
THE PRESIDENT HAS DENIED SENDING CIA ADVISORS TO AIRCRAFT CARRIERS NEAR THE RUSSIAN FLEET TO OVERSEE THE SITUATION.
The One That Got Away
"THE SITUATION IS GRAVE, BUT NOT BEYOND RECALL," SAID THE PRESIDENT.

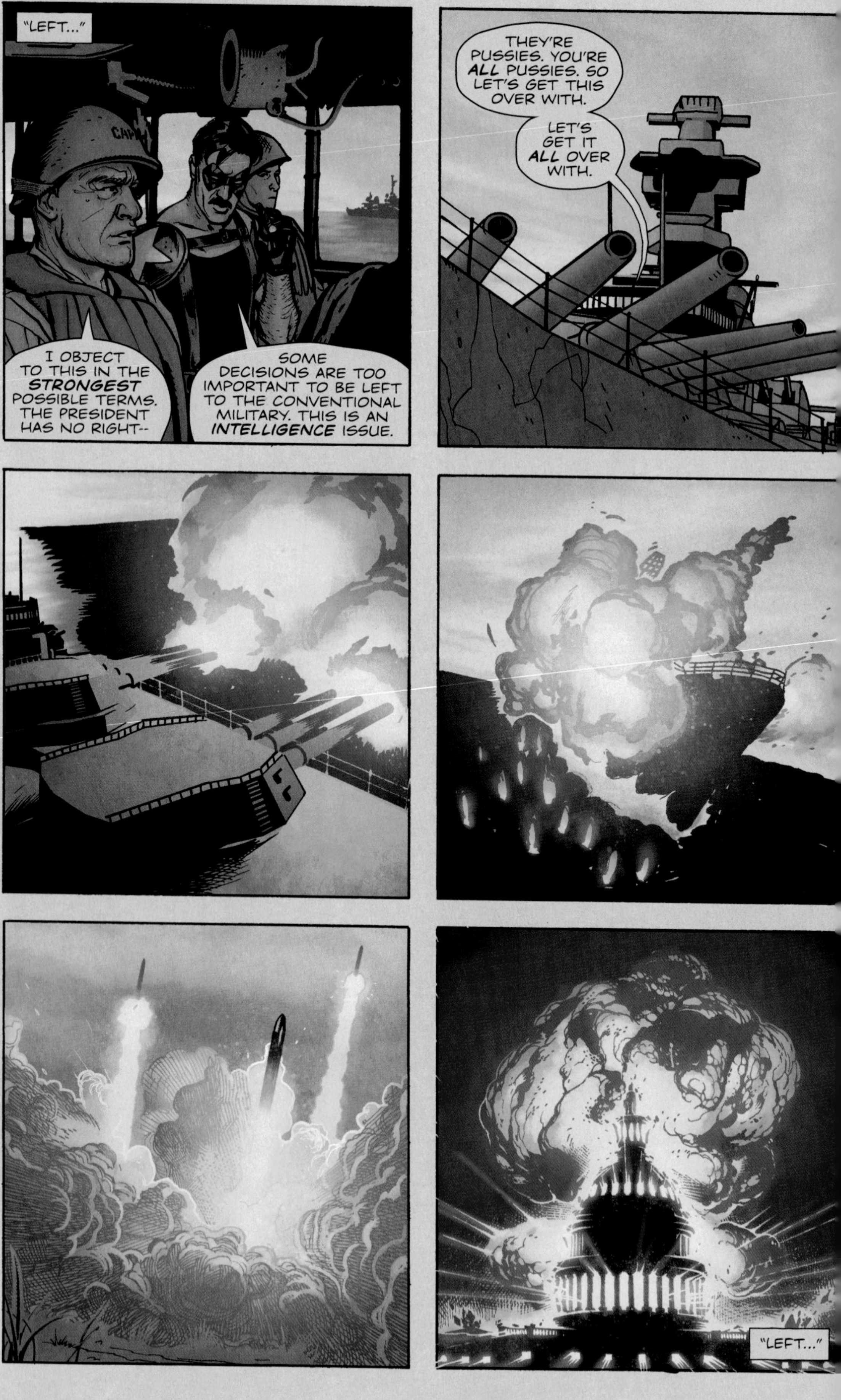
"LEFT..."
I OBJECT TO THIS IN THE STRONGEST POSSIBLE TERMS. THE PRESIDENT HAS NO RIGHT--
SOME DECISIONS ARE TOO IMPORTANT TO BE LEFT TO THE CONVENTIONAL MILITARY. THIS IS AN INTELLIGENCE ISSUE.
THEY'RE PUSSIES. YOU'RE ALL PUSSIES. SO LET'S GET THIS OVER WITH.
LET'S GET IT ALL OVER WITH.
"LEFT..."

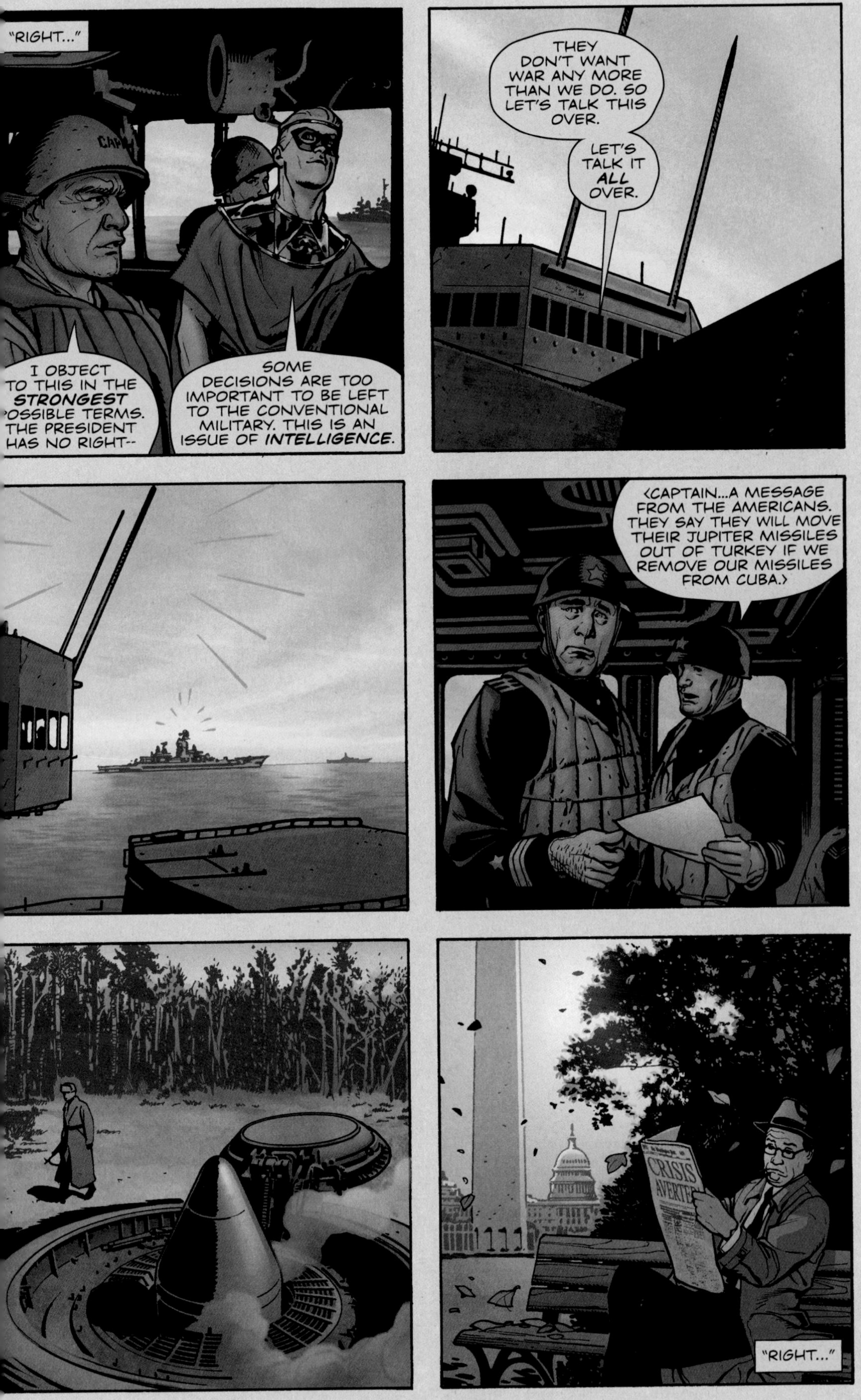
"RIGHT..."
I OBJECT TO THIS IN THE STRONGEST POSSIBLE TERMS. THE PRESIDENT HAS NO RIGHT--
SOME DECISIONS ARE TOO IMPORTANT TO BE LEFT TO THE CONVENTIONAL MILITARY. THIS IS AN ISSUE OF INTELLIGENCE.
THEY DON'T WANT WAR ANY MORE THAN WE DO. SO LET'S TALK THIS OVER.
LET'S TALK IT ALL OVER.
<CAPTAIN...A MESSAGE FROM THE AMERICANS. THEY SAY THEY WILL MOVE THEIR JUPITER MISSILES OUT OF TURKEY IF WE REMOVE OUR MISSILES FROM CUBA.>
CRISIS AVERTED
"RIGHT..."

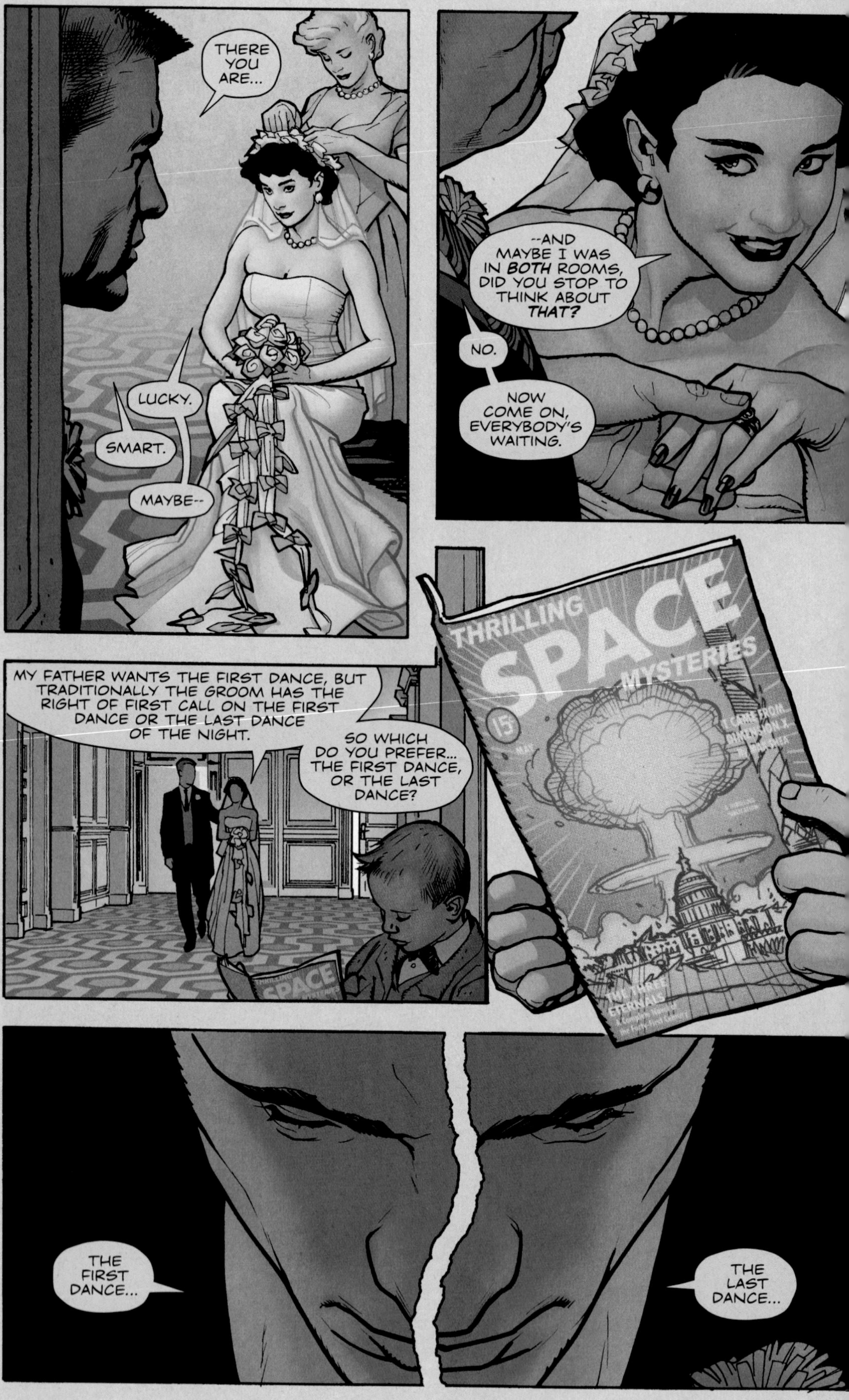

THERE YOU ARE...
LUCKY.
SMART.
MAYBE--
--AND MAYBE I WAS IN *BOTH* ROOMS, DID YOU STOP TO THINK ABOUT *THAT?*
NO.
NOW COME ON, EVERYBODY'S WAITING.
MY FATHER WANTS THE FIRST DANCE, BUT TRADITIONALLY THE GROOM HAS THE RIGHT OF FIRST CALL ON THE FIRST DANCE OR THE LAST DANCE OF THE NIGHT.
SO WHICH DO YOU PREFER... THE FIRST DANCE, OR THE LAST DANCE?
THRILLING SPACE MYSTERIES
15¢
THE FIRST DANCE...
THE LAST DANCE...

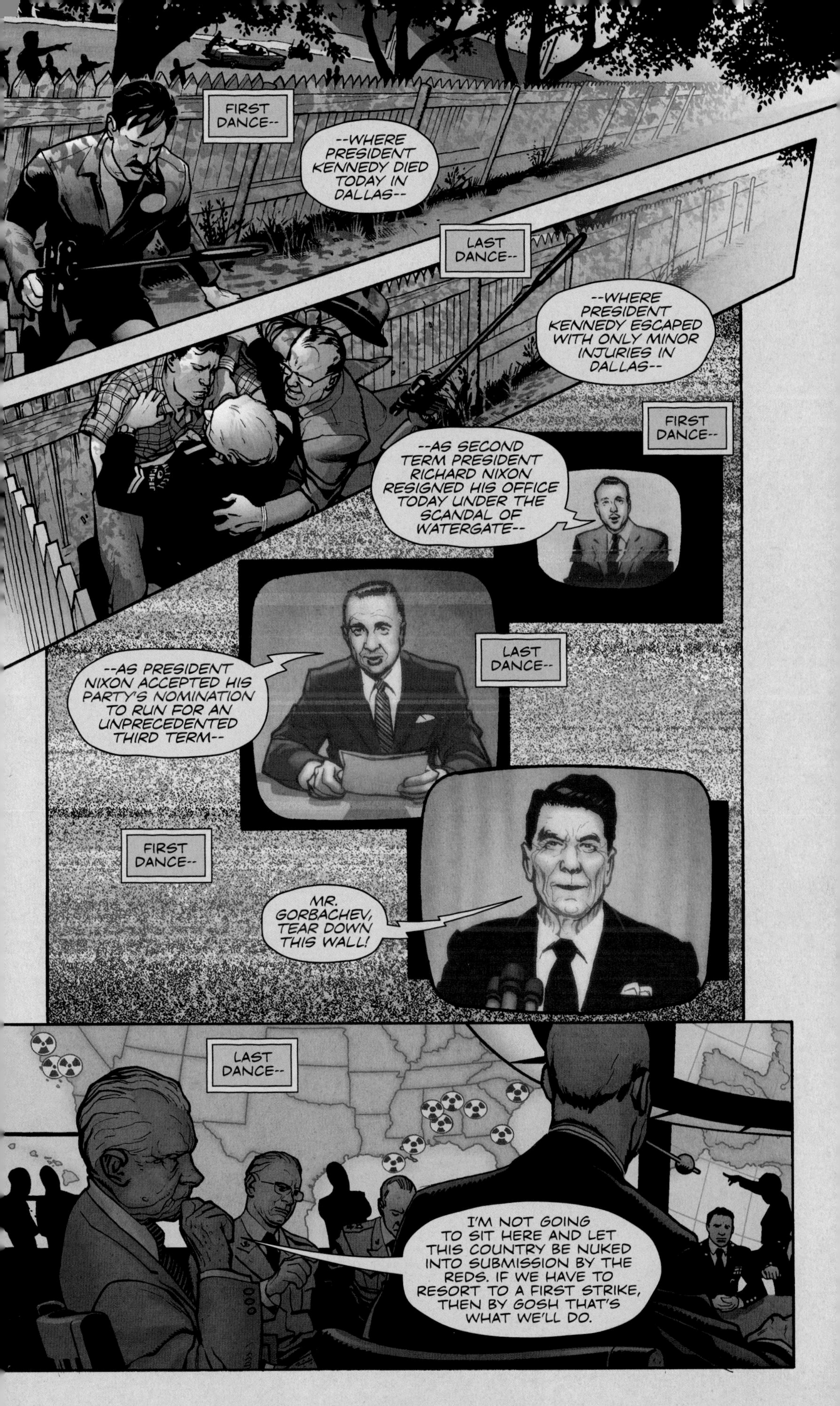
FIRST DANCE--
--WHERE PRESIDENT KENNEDY DIED TODAY IN DALLAS--
LAST DANCE--
--WHERE PRESIDENT KENNEDY ESCAPED WITH ONLY MINOR INJURIES IN DALLAS--
FIRST DANCE--
--AS SECOND TERM PRESIDENT RICHARD NIXON RESIGNED HIS OFFICE TODAY UNDER THE SCANDAL OF WATERGATE--
LAST DANCE--
--AS PRESIDENT NIXON ACCEPTED HIS PARTY'S NOMINATION TO RUN FOR AN UNPRECEDENTED THIRD TERM--
FIRST DANCE--
MR. GORBACHEV, TEAR DOWN THIS WALL!
LAST DANCE--
I'M NOT GOING TO SIT HERE AND LET THIS COUNTRY BE NUKED INTO SUBMISSION BY THE REDS. IF WE HAVE TO RESORT TO A FIRST STRIKE, THEN BY GOSH THAT'S WHAT WE'LL DO.

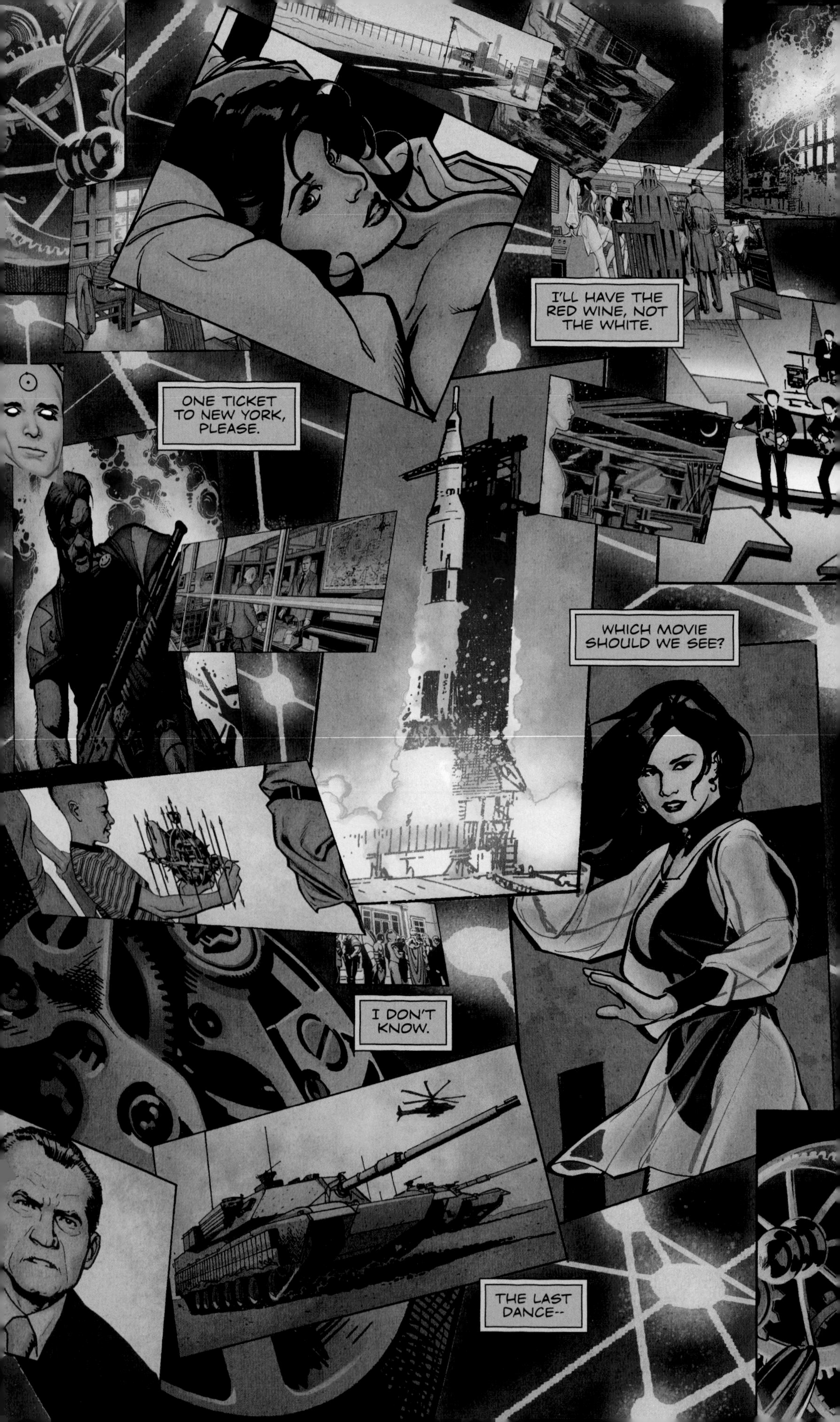
I'LL HAVE THE RED WINE, NOT THE WHITE.
ONE TICKET TO NEW YORK, PLEASE.
WHICH MOVIE SHOULD WE SEE?
I DON'T KNOW.
THE LAST DANCE--

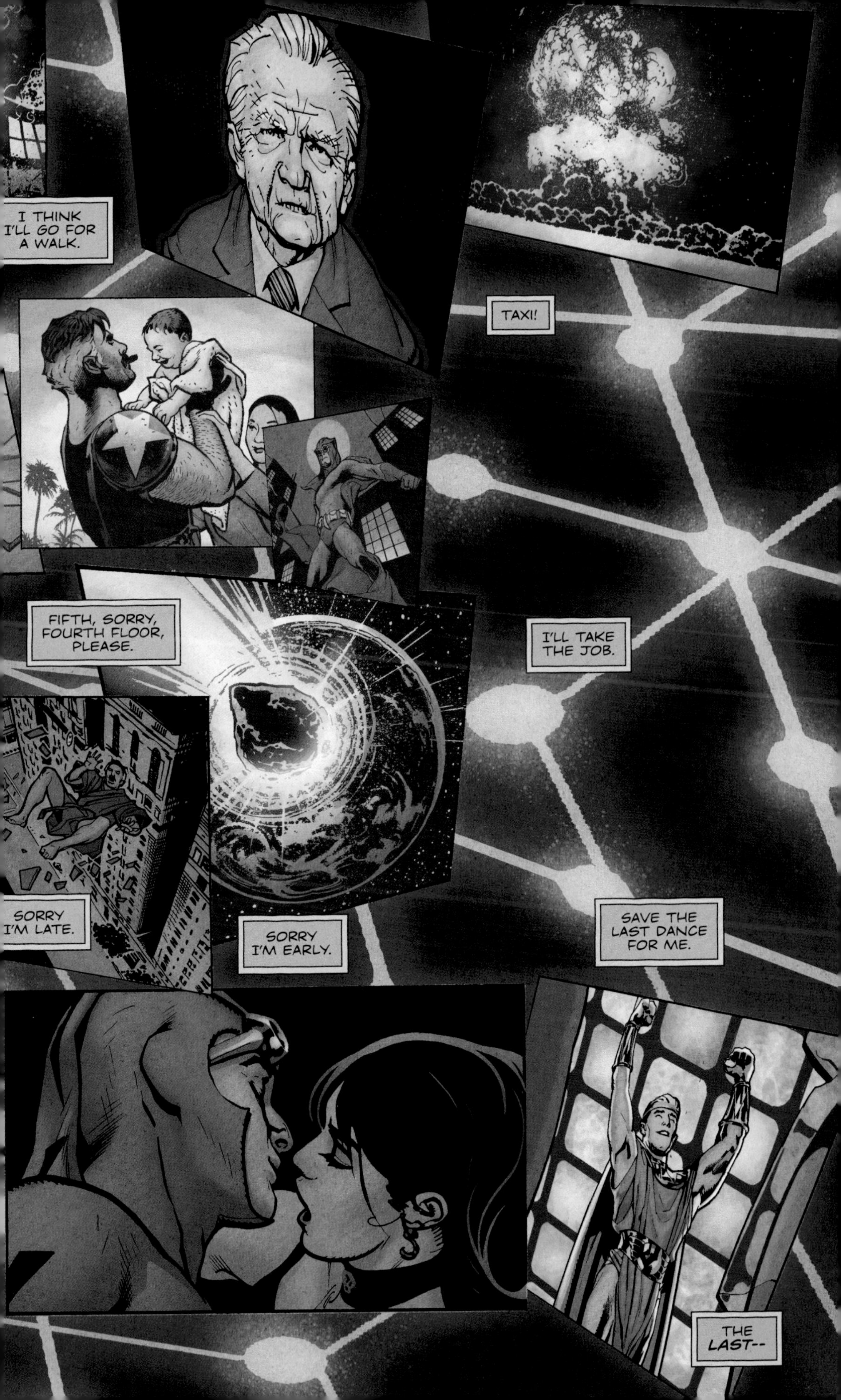

I THINK I'LL GO FOR A WALK.
TAXI!
FIFTH, SORRY, FOURTH FLOOR, PLEASE.
I'LL TAKE THE JOB.
SORRY I'M LATE.
SORRY I'M EARLY.
SAVE THE LAST DANCE FOR ME.
THE *LAST*--

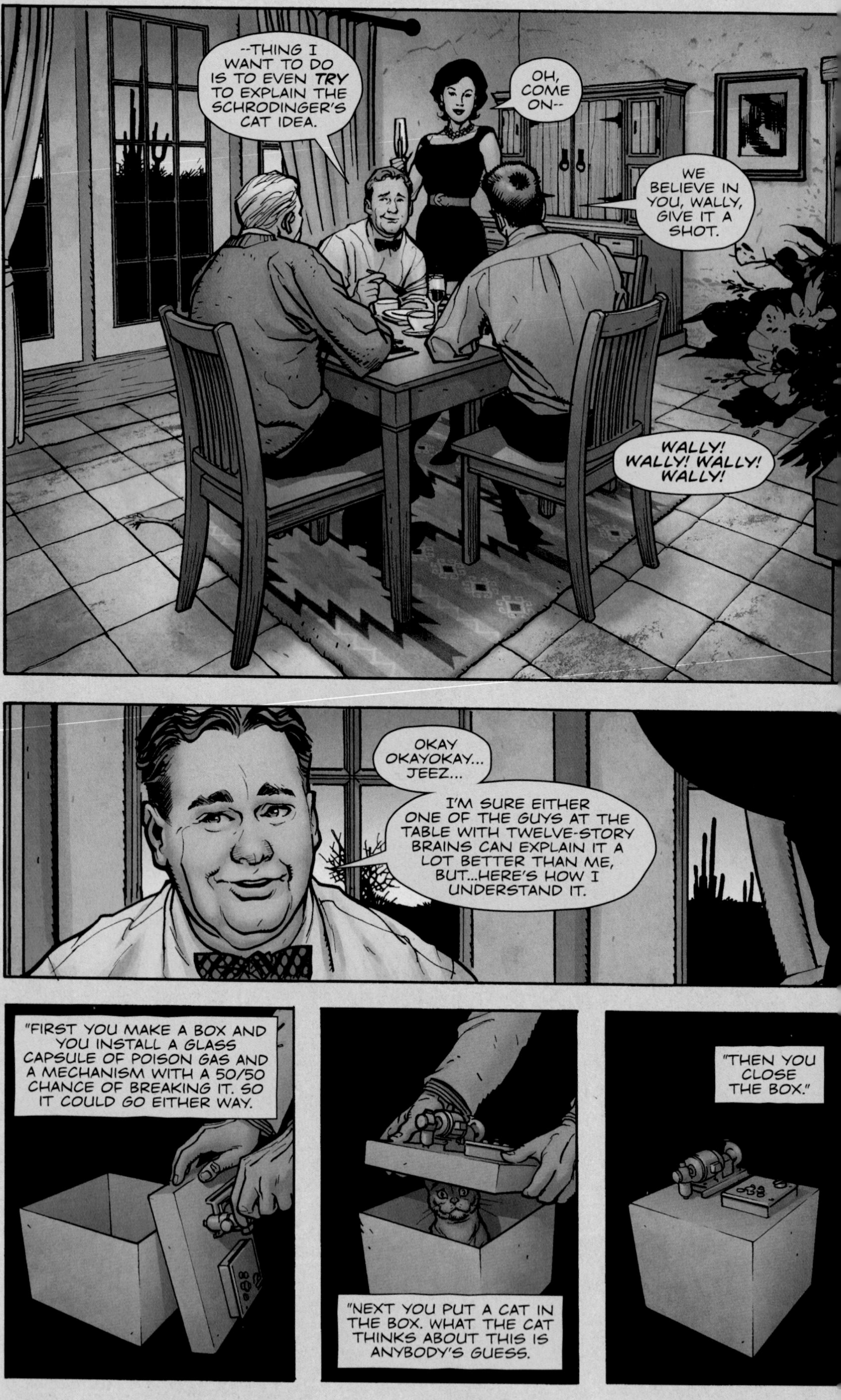
--THING I WANT TO DO IS TO EVEN TRY TO EXPLAIN THE SCHRODINGER'S CAT IDEA.
OH, COME ON--
WE BELIEVE IN YOU, WALLY, GIVE IT A SHOT.
WALLY! WALLY! WALLY! WALLY!
OKAY OKAYOKAY... JEEZ...
I'M SURE EITHER ONE OF THE GUYS AT THE TABLE WITH TWELVE-STORY BRAINS CAN EXPLAIN IT A LOT BETTER THAN ME, BUT...HERE'S HOW I UNDERSTAND IT.
"FIRST YOU MAKE A BOX AND YOU INSTALL A GLASS CAPSULE OF POISON GAS AND A MECHANISM WITH A 50/50 CHANCE OF BREAKING IT. SO IT COULD GO EITHER WAY.
"NEXT YOU PUT A CAT IN THE BOX. WHAT THE CAT THINKS ABOUT THIS IS ANYBODY'S GUESS.
"THEN YOU CLOSE THE BOX."

NOW, STANDING OUTSIDE THE BOX, ALL YOU KNOW IS THAT THERE'S A 50/50 CHANCE OF THE POISON BEING RELEASED.

SO THE CAT IN THE BOX IS EITHER ALIVE OR DEAD.

NO. ACCORDING TO QUANTUM PHYSICS, THE CAT IS BOTH ALIVE *AND* DEAD.

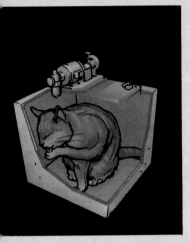

"IN QUANTUM PHYSICS, THE OBSERVER AFFECTS THE OBSERVED, THE WAY A PARTICLE IS A PARTICLE ONLY WHEN YOU'RE LOOKING AT IT. LOOK AWAY, IT BECOMES A WAVE. LOOK AT IT AGAIN, IT BECOMES A PARTICLE. SO THE CAT EXISTS IN BOTH STATES UNTIL THE QUANTUM OBSERVER OPENS THE BOX AND LOOKS INSIDE.

"THEN THE TWO QUANTUM POSSIBILITIES COLLAPSE INTO ONE REALITY.

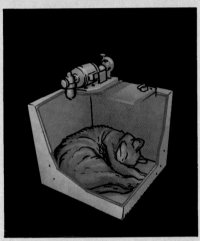

"A LIVE CAT--

"--OR A DEAD CAT.

"POINT BEING, WHATEVER YOU MAY *THINK* YOU KNOW, YOU DON'T *REALLY* KNOW WHAT'S IN THE BOX UNTIL YOU OPEN IT UP AND LOOK INSIDE."

OF COURSE, THAT RAISES A QUESTION.

WHAT HAPPENS IF YOU DON'T OPEN THE BOX?

WELL, DEPENDING ON HOW YOU SET THE CONDITIONS OF THE EXPERIMENT, THE LONGER THE BOX REMAINS CLOSED...THE LONGER THE QUANTUM OBSERVER DOESN'T, WELL, *OBSERVE*...

...UNANTICIPATED FACTORS COULD BEGIN TO ALTER THE RESULTS--

"--MULTIPLYING THE EFFECTS, CREATING MORE RANDOM QUANTUM PROBABILITIES AND POCKET UNIVERSES, ALL OF THEM EQUALLY REAL, JOCKEYING WITH ONE ANOTHER FOR THE MOMENT WHEN THE BOX IS OPENED--"

--AND ALL THOSE POSSIBILITIES FINALLY COLLAPSE INTO ONE REALITY.

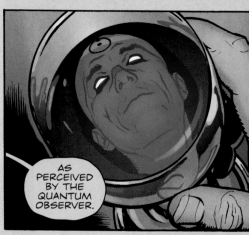

AS PERCEIVED BY THE QUANTUM OBSERVER.

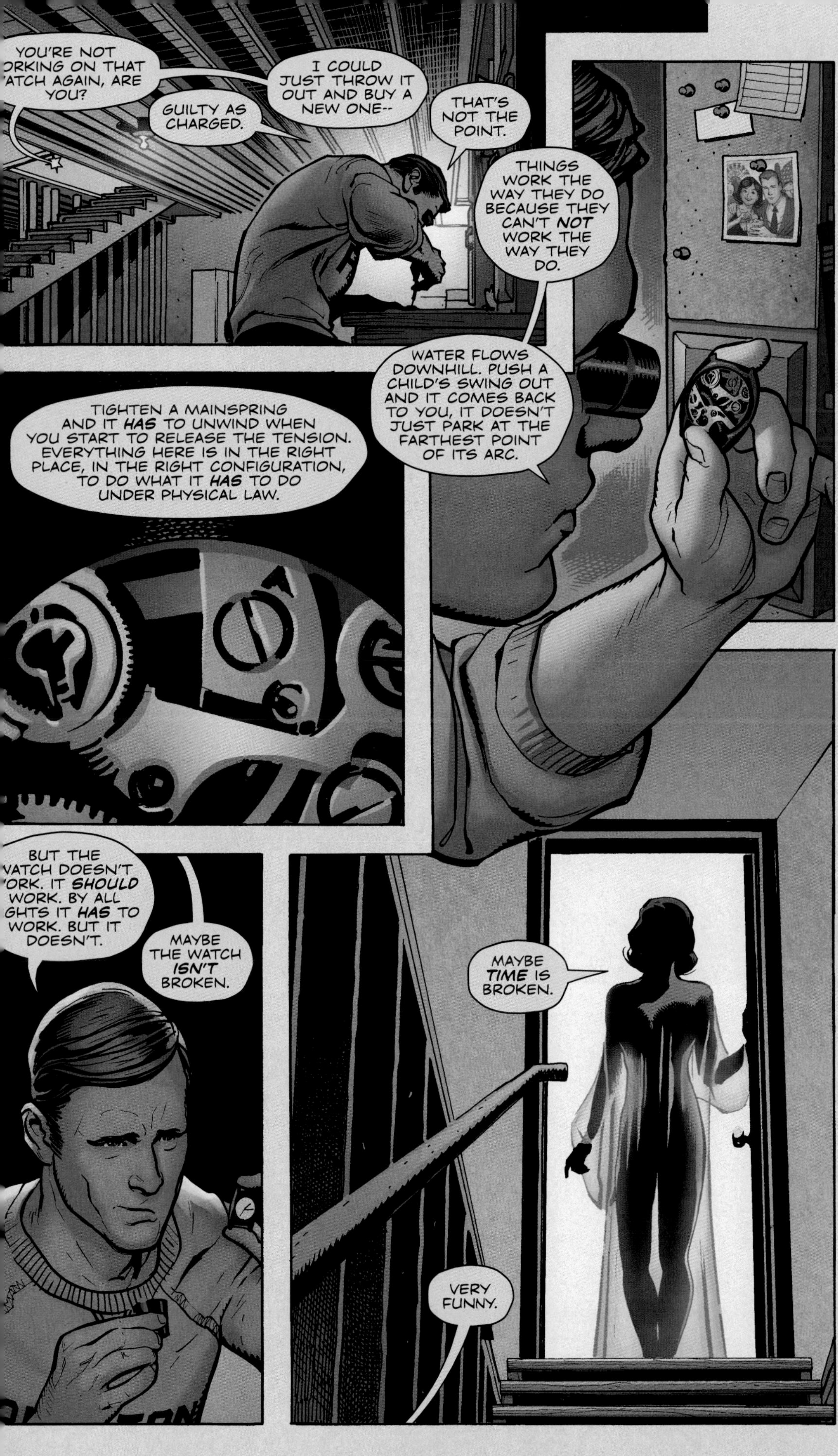
YOU'RE NOT ORKING ON THAT ATCH AGAIN, ARE YOU?
GUILTY AS CHARGED.
I COULD JUST THROW IT OUT AND BUY A NEW ONE--
THAT'S NOT THE POINT.
THINGS WORK THE WAY THEY DO BECAUSE THEY CAN'T NOT WORK THE WAY THEY DO.
WATER FLOWS DOWNHILL. PUSH A CHILD'S SWING OUT AND IT COMES BACK TO YOU, IT DOESN'T JUST PARK AT THE FARTHEST POINT OF ITS ARC.
TIGHTEN A MAINSPRING AND IT HAS TO UNWIND WHEN YOU START TO RELEASE THE TENSION. EVERYTHING HERE IS IN THE RIGHT PLACE, IN THE RIGHT CONFIGURATION, TO DO WHAT IT HAS TO DO UNDER PHYSICAL LAW.
BUT THE ATCH DOESN'T ORK. IT SHOULD WORK. BY ALL GHTS IT HAS TO WORK. BUT IT DOESN'T.
MAYBE THE WATCH ISN'T BROKEN.
MAYBE TIME IS BROKEN.
VERY FUNNY.

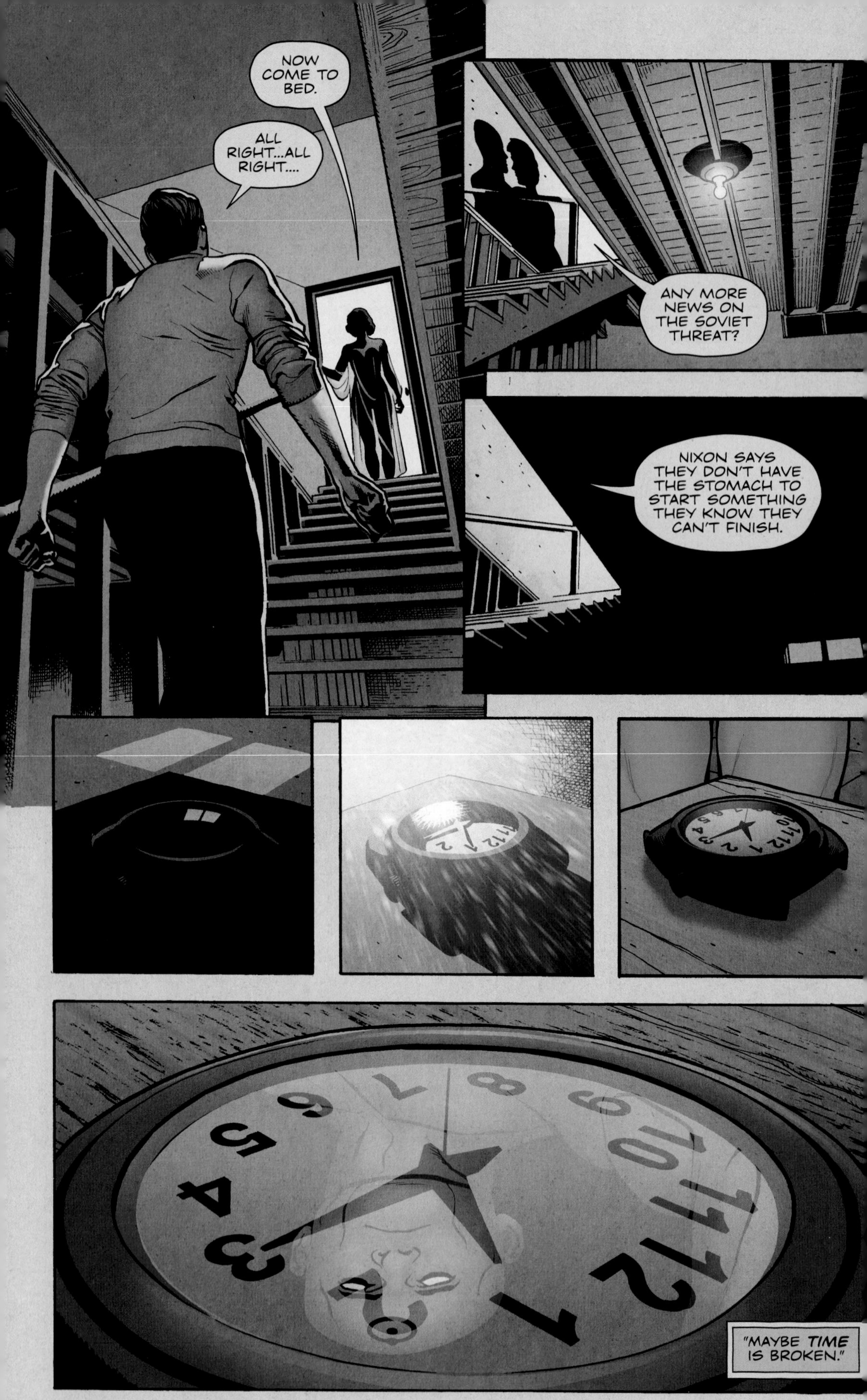
NOW COME TO BED.
ALL RIGHT...ALL RIGHT....
ANY MORE NEWS ON THE SOVIET THREAT?
NIXON SAYS THEY DON'T HAVE THE STOMACH TO START SOMETHING THEY KNOW THEY CAN'T FINISH.
"MAYBE *TIME* IS BROKEN."

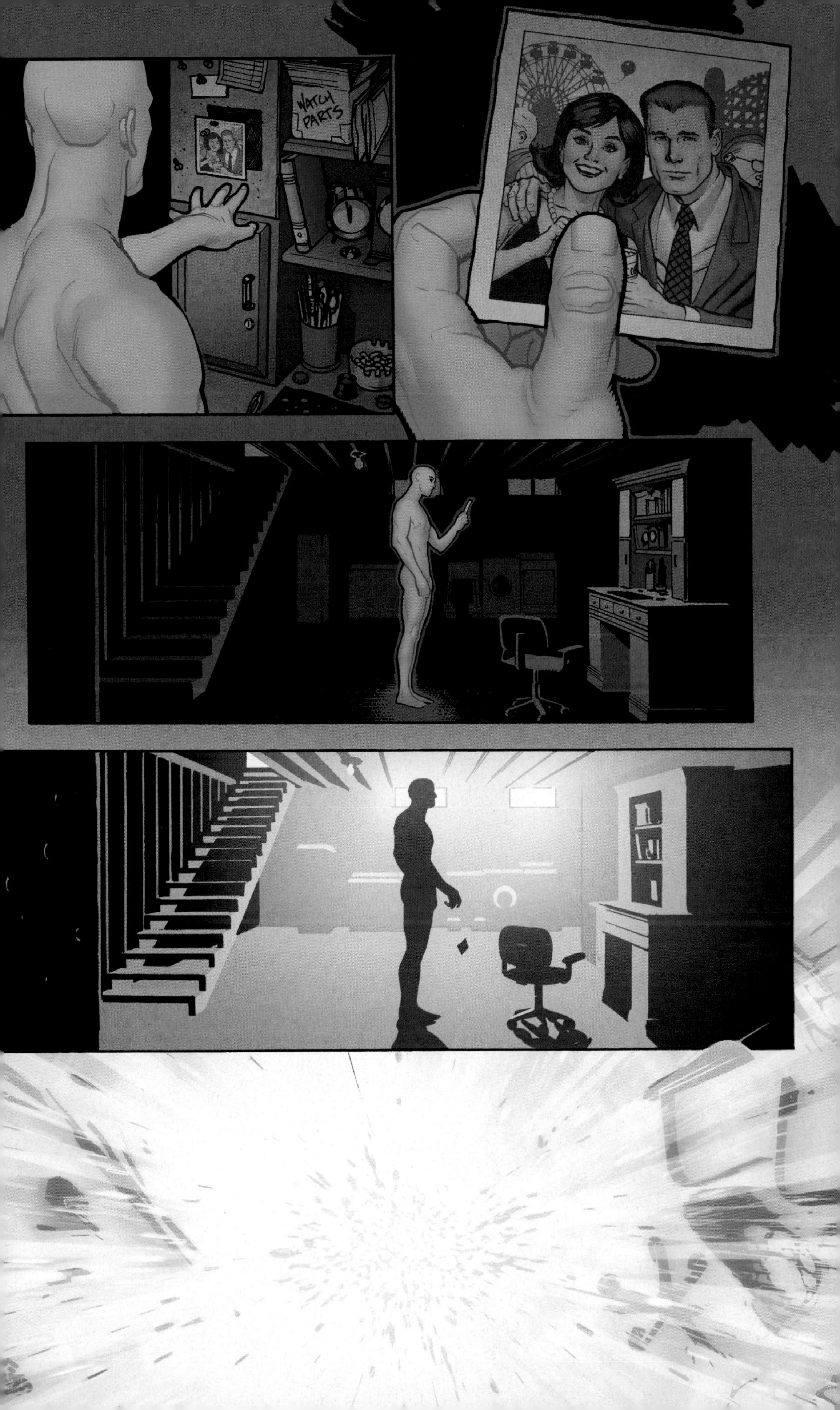
WATCH PARTS

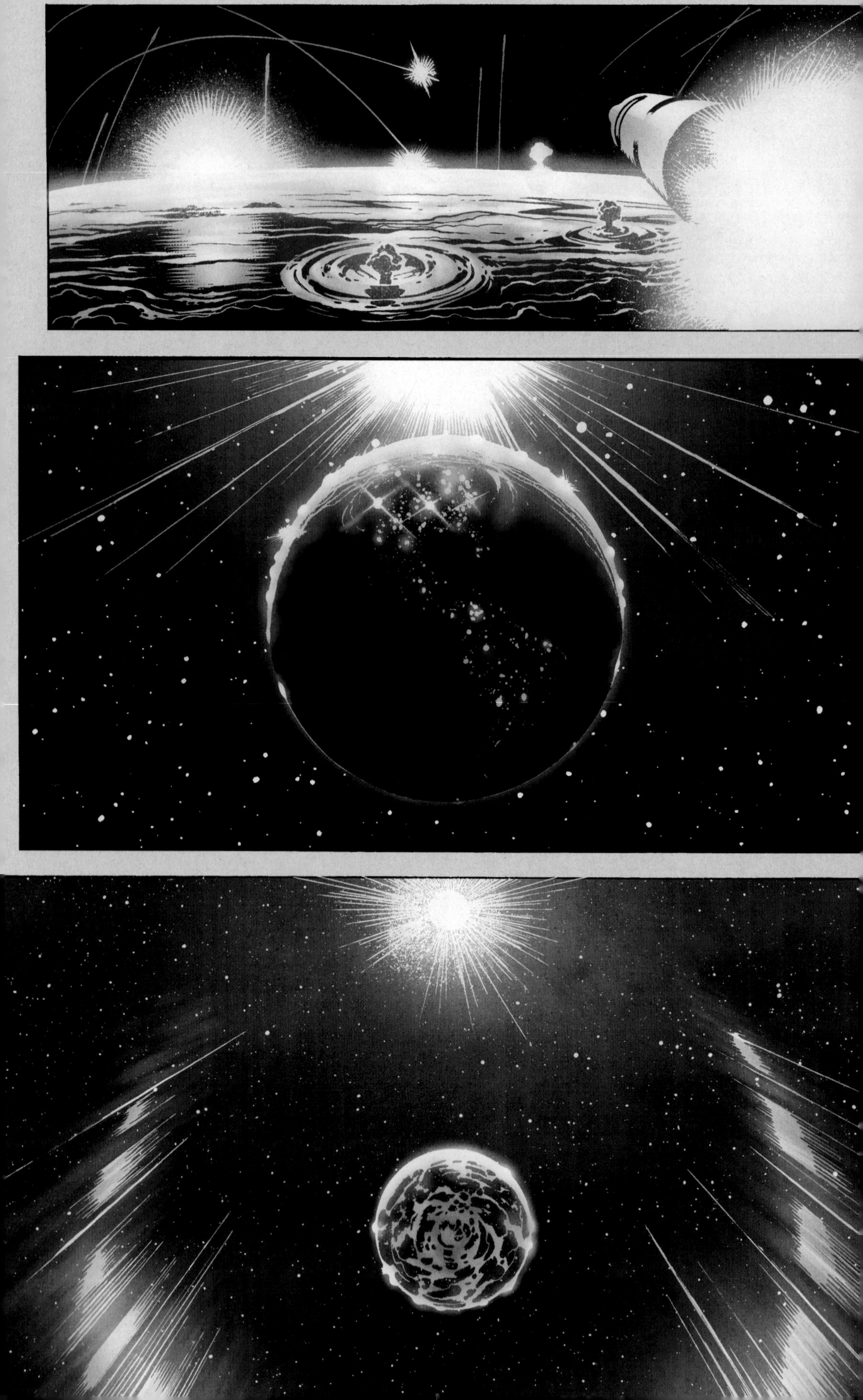

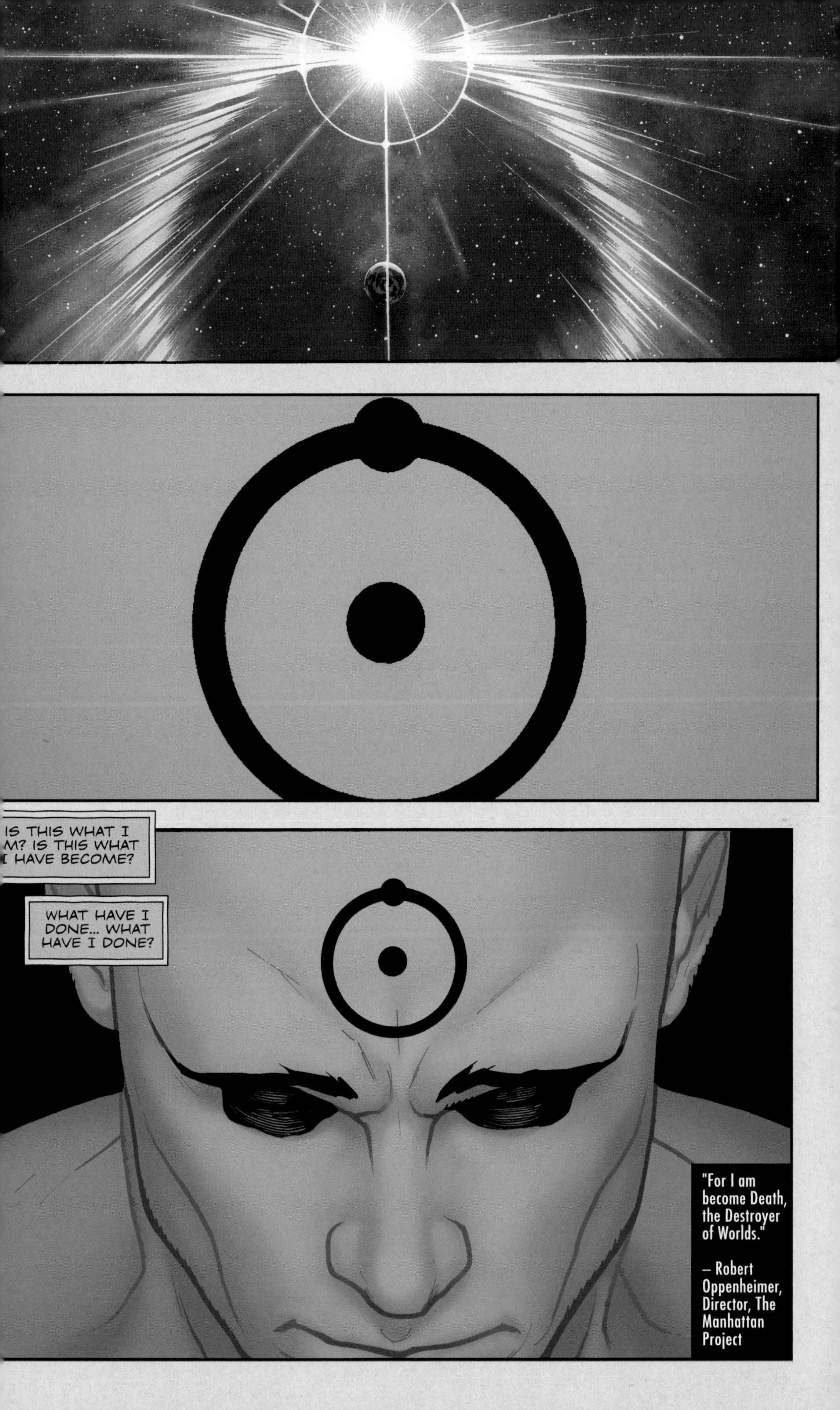

IS THIS WHAT I M? IS THIS WHAT I HAVE BECOME?
WHAT HAVE I DONE... WHAT HAVE I DONE?
"For I am become Death, the Destroyer of Worlds."
– Robert Oppenheimer, Director, The Manhattan Project

DR. MANHATTAN

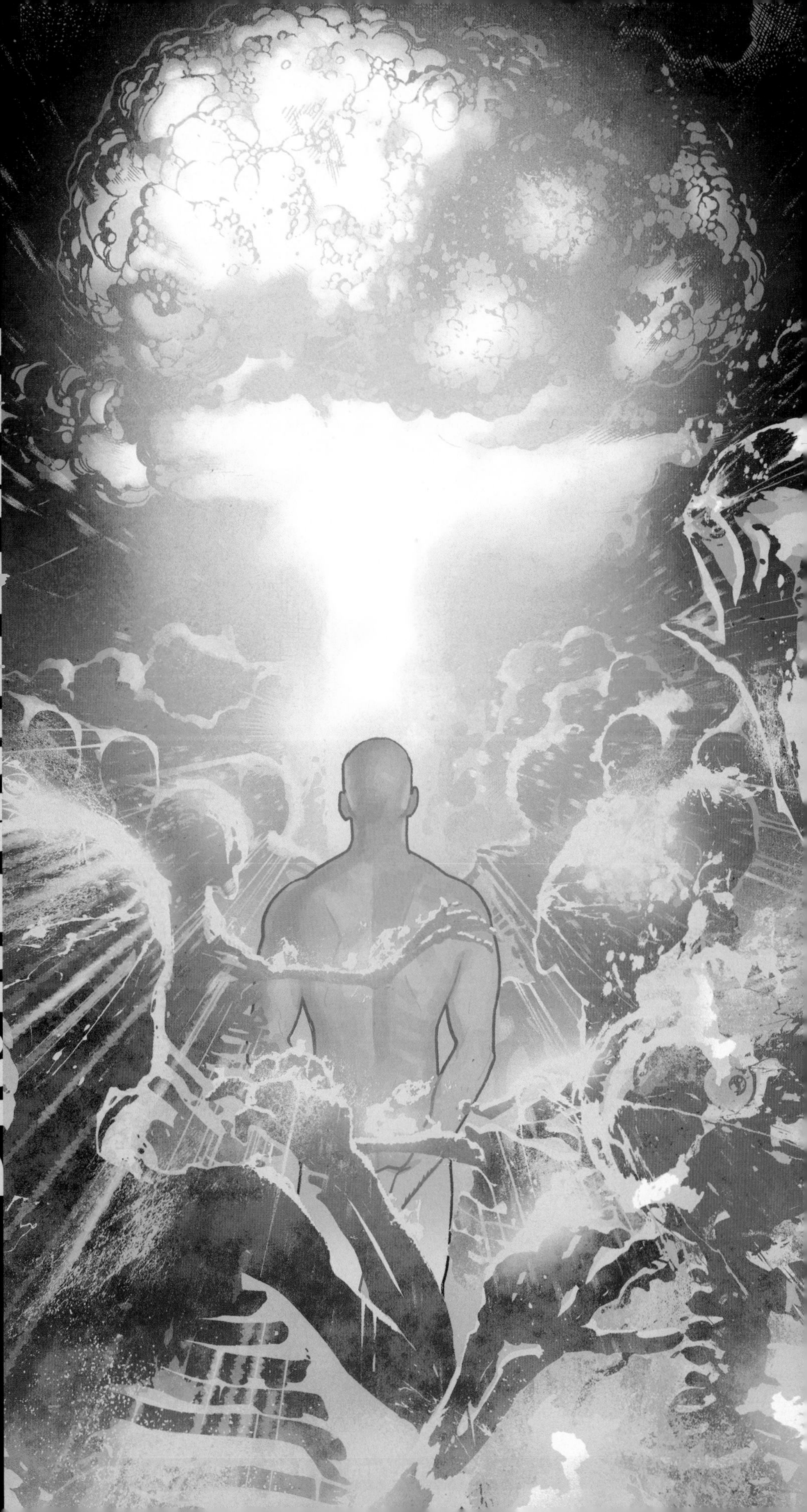

DR. MANHATTAN

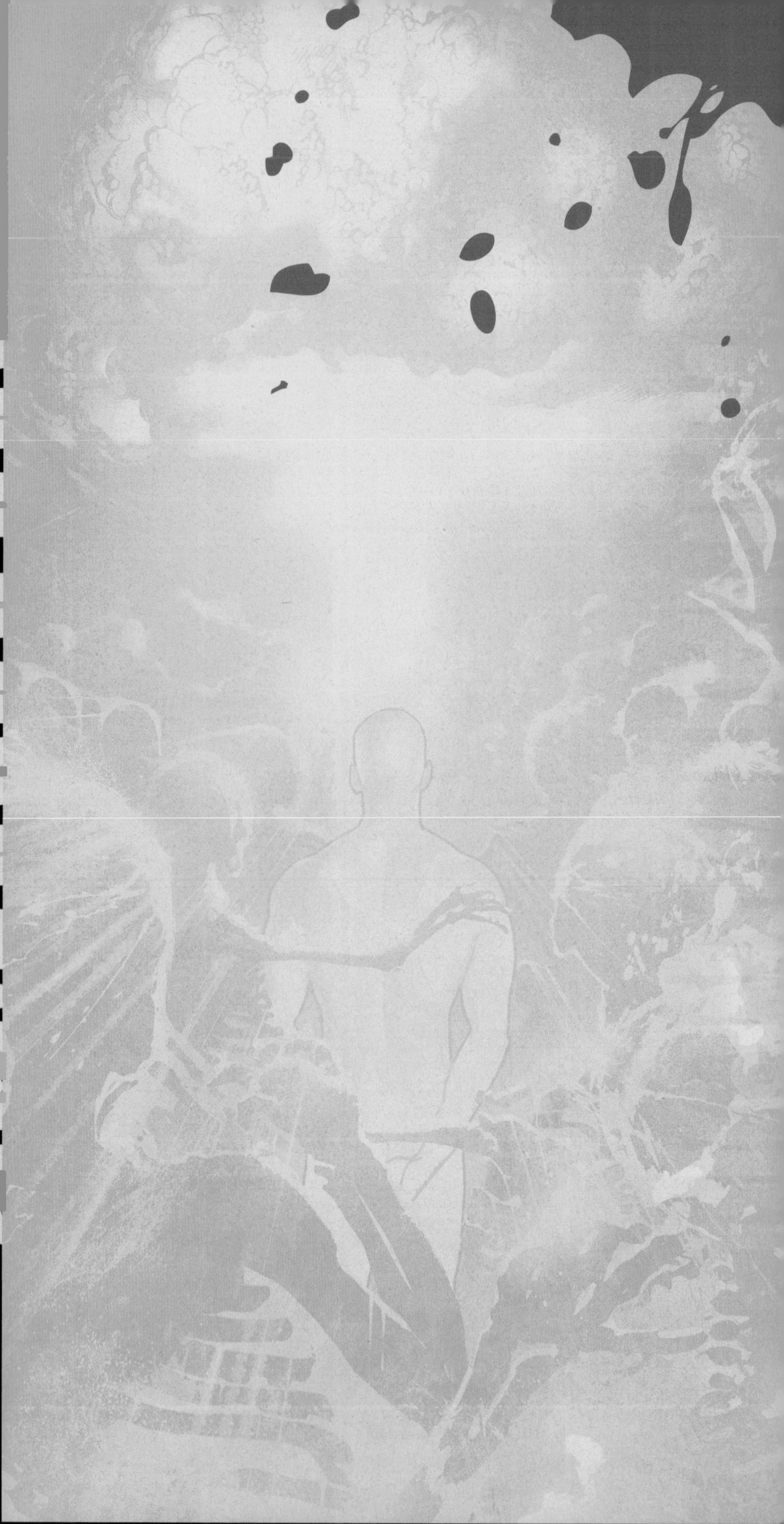

"I HAVE NAMED THE DISEASE. BUT WHAT IS THE CURE?"

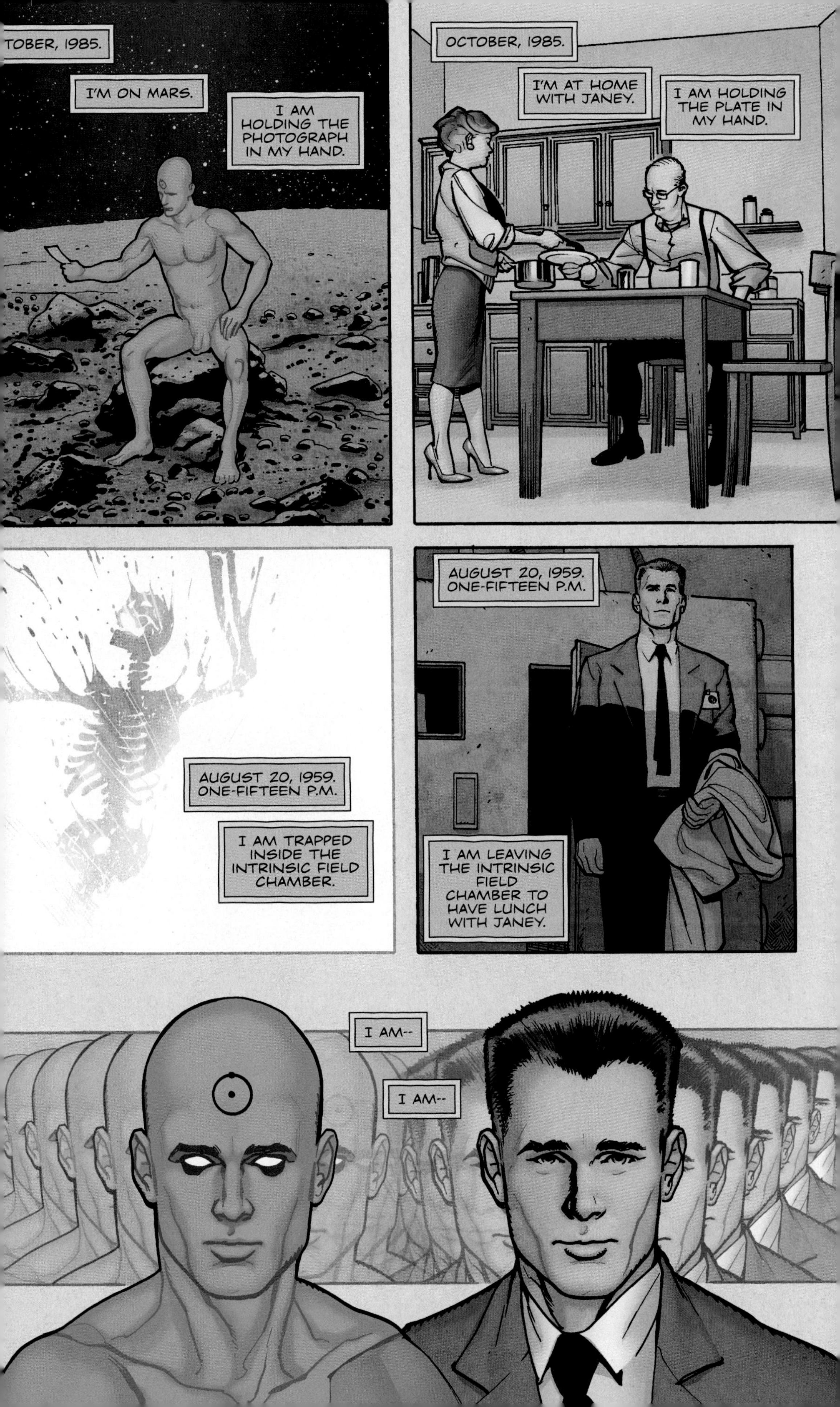
TOBER, 1985.
I'M ON MARS.
I AM HOLDING THE PHOTOGRAPH IN MY HAND.
OCTOBER, 1985.
I'M AT HOME WITH JANEY.
I AM HOLDING THE PLATE IN MY HAND.
AUGUST 20, 1959. ONE-FIFTEEN P.M.
I AM TRAPPED INSIDE THE INTRINSIC FIELD CHAMBER.
AUGUST 20, 1959. ONE-FIFTEEN P.M.
I AM LEAVING THE INTRINSIC FIELD CHAMBER TO HAVE LUNCH WITH JANEY.
I AM--
I AM--

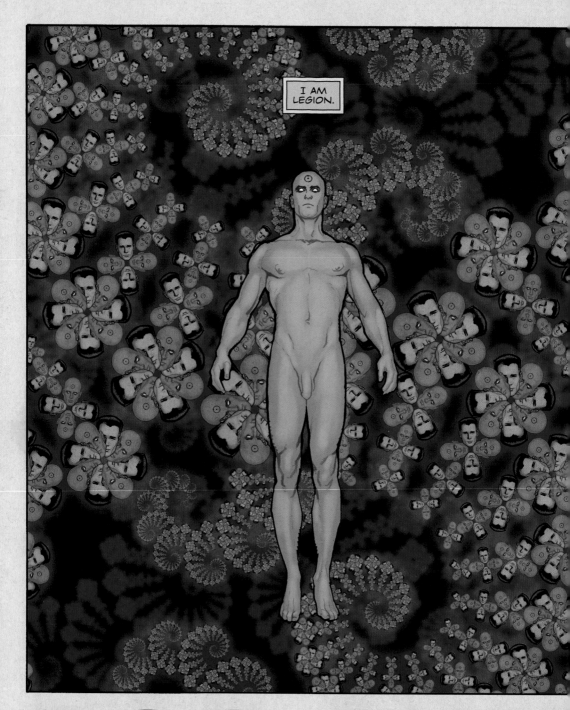

I AM LEGION.

EGO SUM

J. MICHAEL STRACZYNSKI script   ADAM HUGHES art

LAURA MARTIN colors   STEVE WANDS letters

ADAM HUGHES cover   NEAL ADAMS variant cover

CAMILLA ZHANG asst. editor   CHRIS CONROY assoc. editor   MARK CHIARELLO editor

WATCHMEN created by ALAN MOORE and DAVE GIBBONS

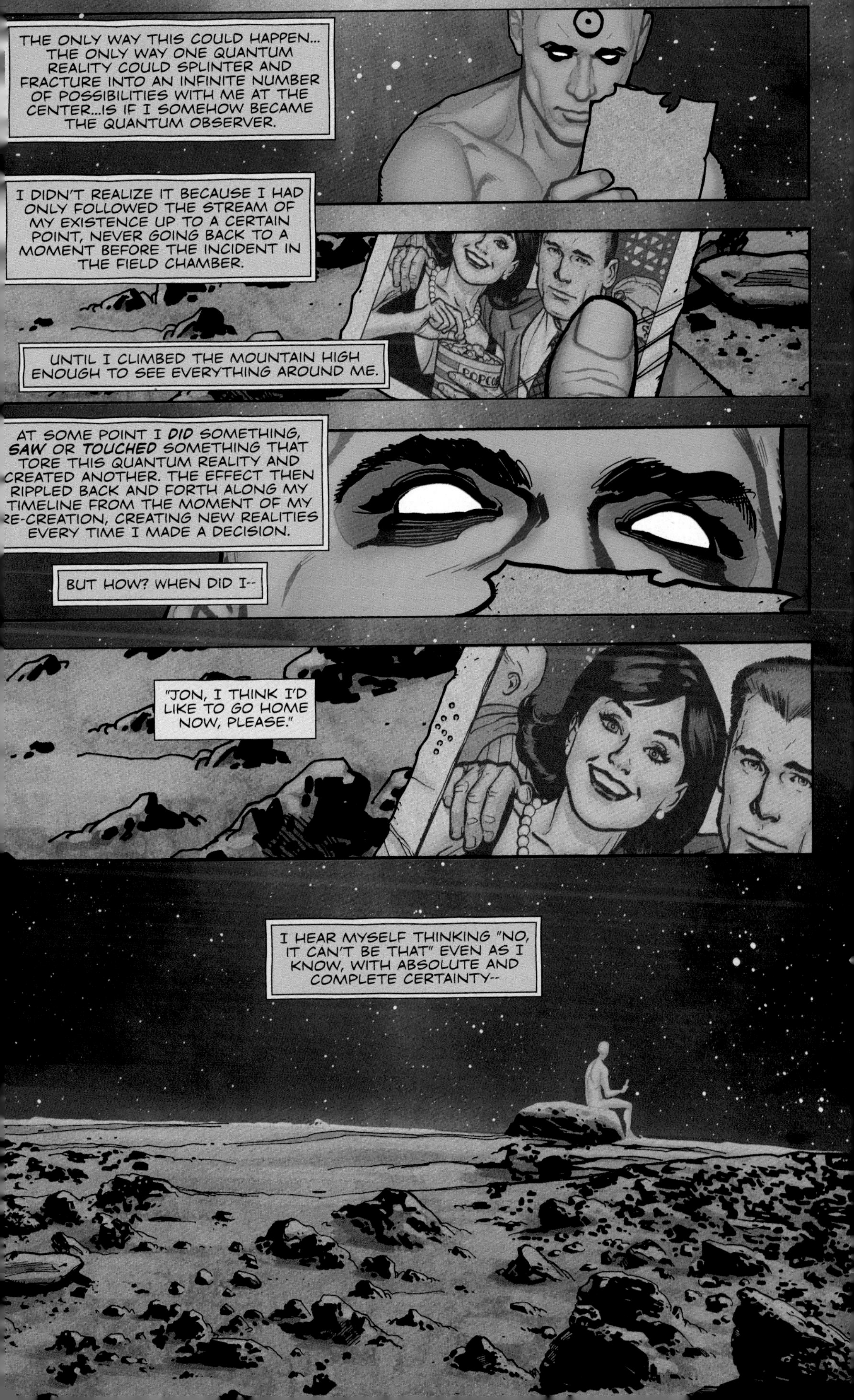
THE ONLY WAY THIS COULD HAPPEN... THE ONLY WAY ONE QUANTUM REALITY COULD SPLINTER AND FRACTURE INTO AN INFINITE NUMBER OF POSSIBILITIES WITH ME AT THE CENTER...IS IF I SOMEHOW BECAME THE QUANTUM OBSERVER.
I DIDN'T REALIZE IT BECAUSE I HAD ONLY FOLLOWED THE STREAM OF MY EXISTENCE UP TO A CERTAIN POINT, NEVER GOING BACK TO A MOMENT BEFORE THE INCIDENT IN THE FIELD CHAMBER.
UNTIL I CLIMBED THE MOUNTAIN HIGH ENOUGH TO SEE EVERYTHING AROUND ME.
AT SOME POINT I *DID* SOMETHING, *SAW* OR *TOUCHED* SOMETHING THAT TORE THIS QUANTUM REALITY AND CREATED ANOTHER. THE EFFECT THEN RIPPLED BACK AND FORTH ALONG MY TIMELINE FROM THE MOMENT OF MY RE-CREATION, CREATING NEW REALITIES EVERY TIME I MADE A DECISION.
BUT HOW? WHEN DID I--
"JON, I THINK I'D LIKE TO GO HOME NOW, PLEASE."
I HEAR MYSELF THINKING "NO, IT CAN'T BE THAT" EVEN AS I KNOW, WITH ABSOLUTE AND COMPLETE CERTAINTY--

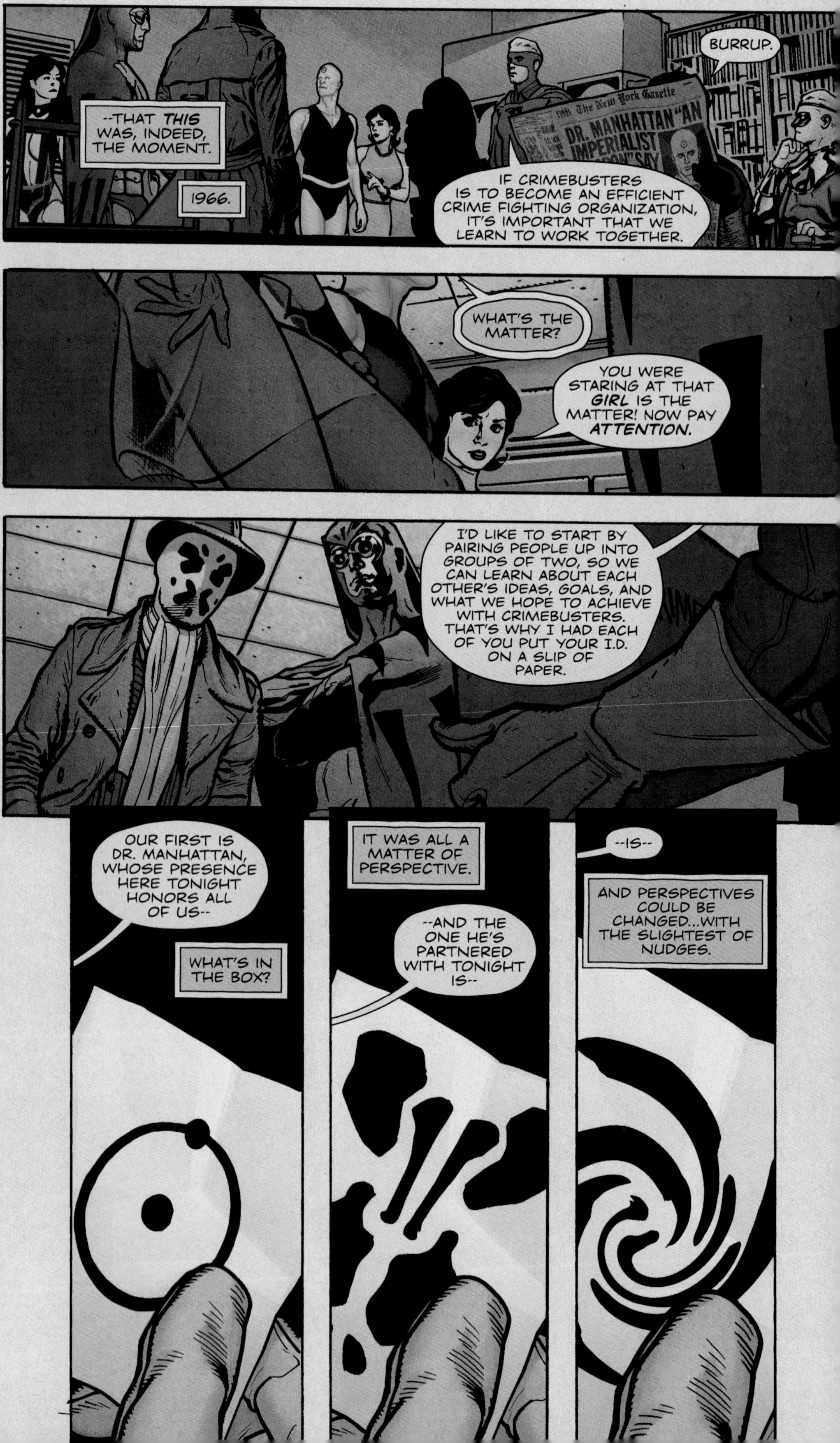

--THAT THIS WAS, INDEED, THE MOMENT.
1966.
BURRUP.
The New York Gazette
DR. MANHATTAN "AN IMPERIALIST
IF CRIMEBUSTERS IS TO BECOME AN EFFICIENT CRIME FIGHTING ORGANIZATION, IT'S IMPORTANT THAT WE LEARN TO WORK TOGETHER.
WHAT'S THE MATTER?
YOU WERE STARING AT THAT GIRL IS THE MATTER! NOW PAY ATTENTION.
I'D LIKE TO START BY PAIRING PEOPLE UP INTO GROUPS OF TWO, SO WE CAN LEARN ABOUT EACH OTHER'S IDEAS, GOALS, AND WHAT WE HOPE TO ACHIEVE WITH CRIMEBUSTERS. THAT'S WHY I HAD EACH OF YOU PUT YOUR I.D. ON A SLIP OF PAPER.
OUR FIRST IS DR. MANHATTAN, WHOSE PRESENCE HERE TONIGHT HONORS ALL OF US--
WHAT'S IN THE BOX?
IT WAS ALL A MATTER OF PERSPECTIVE.
--AND THE ONE HE'S PARTNERED WITH TONIGHT IS--
--IS--
AND PERSPECTIVES COULD BE CHANGED...WITH THE SLIGHTEST OF NUDGES.

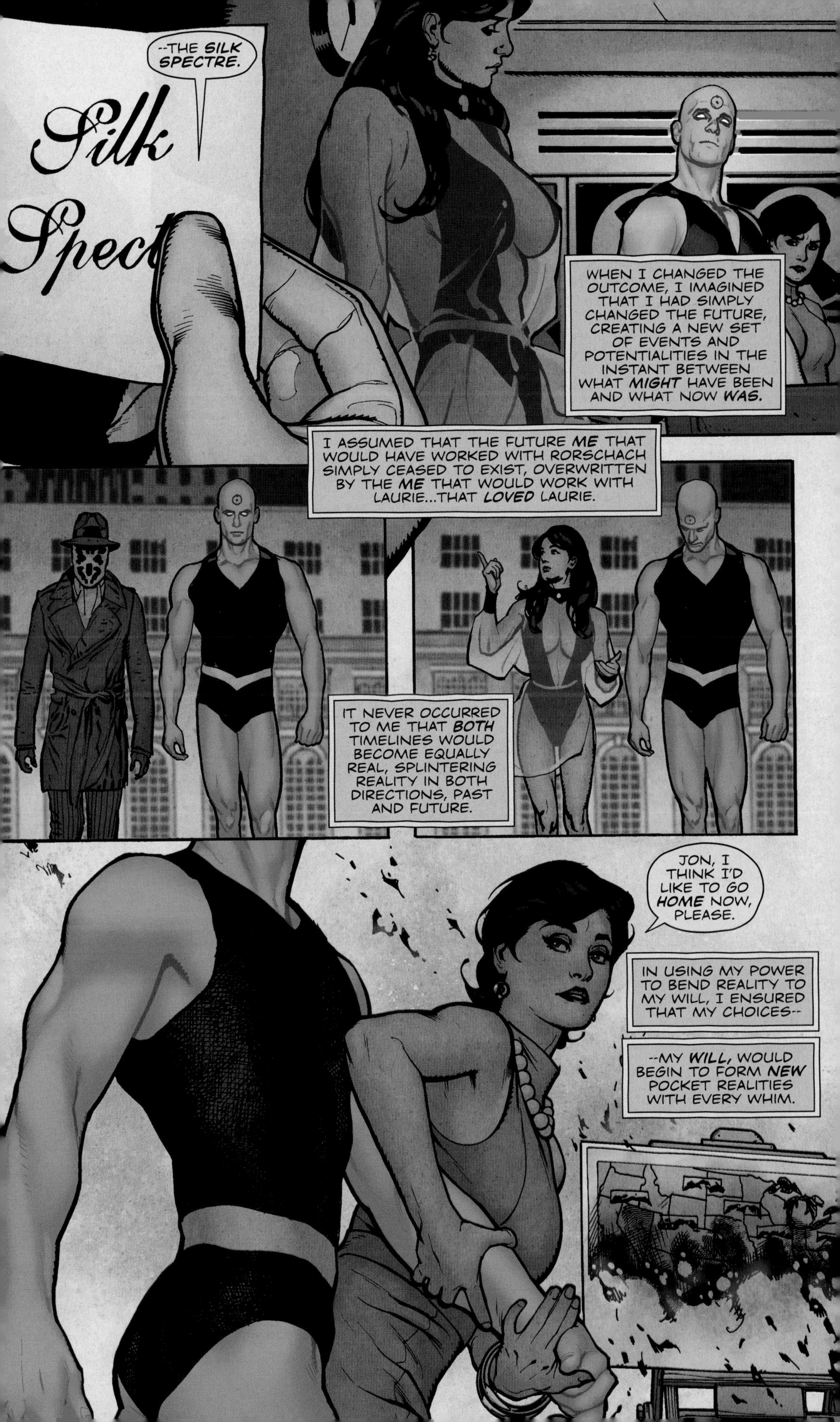

--THE SILK SPECTRE.
Silk Spect
WHEN I CHANGED THE OUTCOME, I IMAGINED THAT I HAD SIMPLY CHANGED THE FUTURE, CREATING A NEW SET OF EVENTS AND POTENTIALITIES IN THE INSTANT BETWEEN WHAT MIGHT HAVE BEEN AND WHAT NOW WAS.
I ASSUMED THAT THE FUTURE ME THAT WOULD HAVE WORKED WITH RORSCHACH SIMPLY CEASED TO EXIST, OVERWRITTEN BY THE ME THAT WOULD WORK WITH LAURIE...THAT LOVED LAURIE.
IT NEVER OCCURRED TO ME THAT BOTH TIMELINES WOULD BECOME EQUALLY REAL, SPLINTERING REALITY IN BOTH DIRECTIONS, PAST AND FUTURE.
JON, I THINK I'D LIKE TO GO HOME NOW, PLEASE.
IN USING MY POWER TO BEND REALITY TO MY WILL, I ENSURED THAT MY CHOICES--
--MY WILL, WOULD BEGIN TO FORM NEW POCKET REALITIES WITH EVERY WHIM.

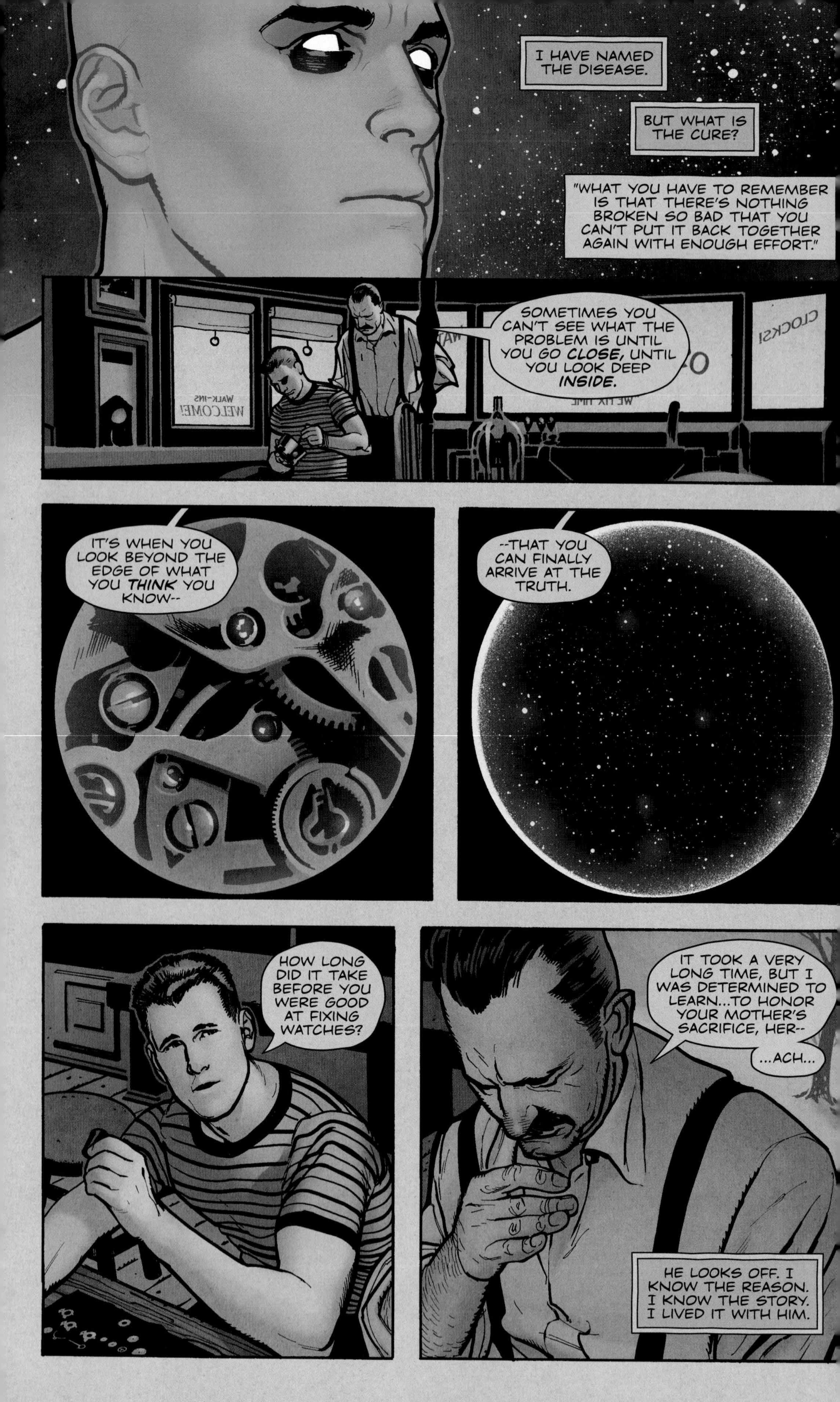

I HAVE NAMED THE DISEASE.
BUT WHAT IS THE CURE?
"WHAT YOU HAVE TO REMEMBER IS THAT THERE'S NOTHING BROKEN SO BAD THAT YOU CAN'T PUT IT BACK TOGETHER AGAIN WITH ENOUGH EFFORT."
WALK-INS WELCOME!
CLOCKS!
WE FIX TIME
SOMETIMES YOU CAN'T SEE WHAT THE PROBLEM IS UNTIL YOU GO CLOSE, UNTIL YOU LOOK DEEP INSIDE.
IT'S WHEN YOU LOOK BEYOND THE EDGE OF WHAT YOU THINK YOU KNOW--
--THAT YOU CAN FINALLY ARRIVE AT THE TRUTH.
HOW LONG DID IT TAKE BEFORE YOU WERE GOOD AT FIXING WATCHES?
IT TOOK A VERY LONG TIME, BUT I WAS DETERMINED TO LEARN...TO HONOR YOUR MOTHER'S SACRIFICE, HER--
...ACH...
HE LOOKS OFF. I KNOW THE REASON. I KNOW THE STORY. I LIVED IT WITH HIM.

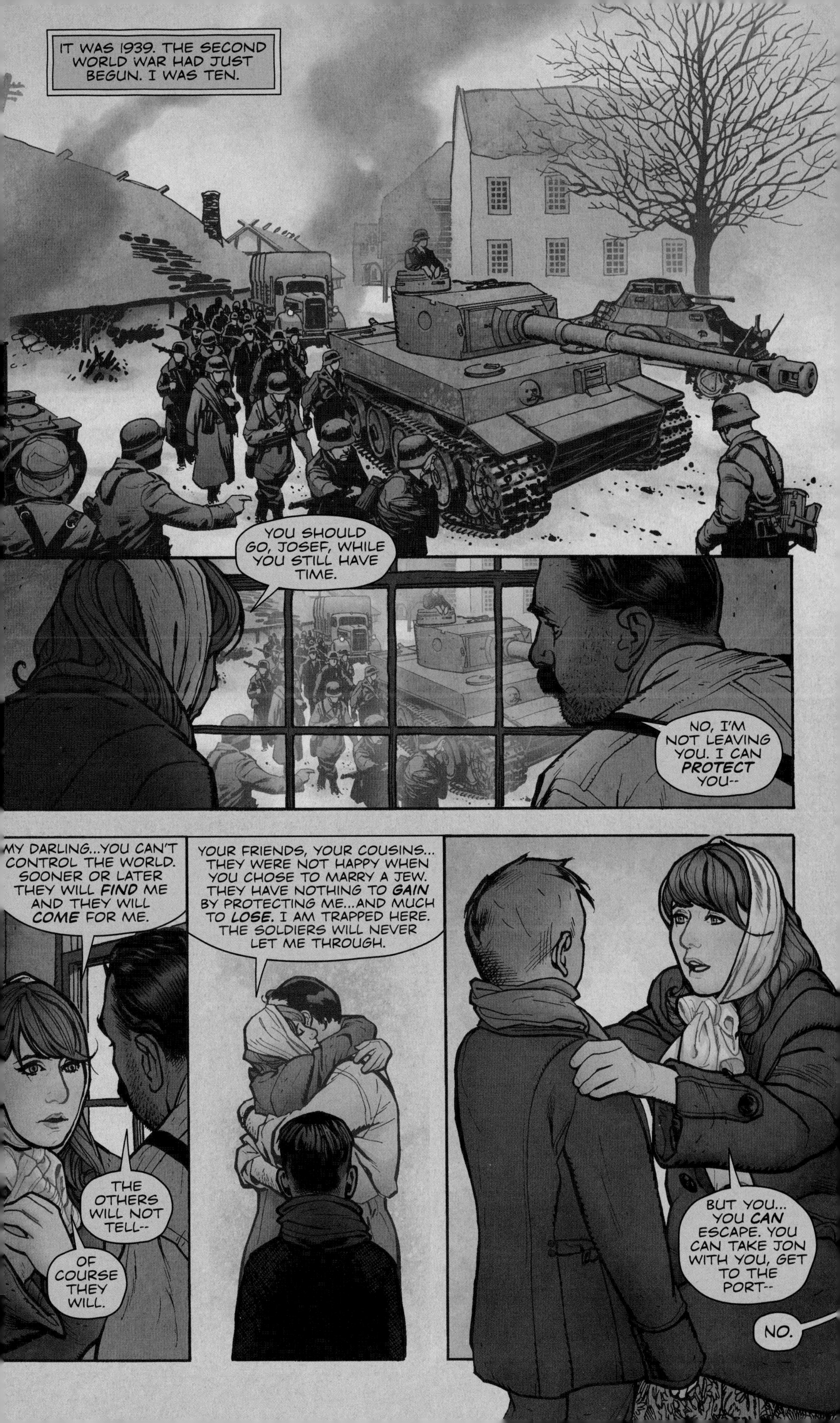
IT WAS 1939. THE SECOND WORLD WAR HAD JUST BEGUN. I WAS TEN.
YOU SHOULD GO, JOSEF, WHILE YOU STILL HAVE TIME.
NO, I'M NOT LEAVING YOU. I CAN PROTECT YOU--
MY DARLING...YOU CAN'T CONTROL THE WORLD. SOONER OR LATER THEY WILL FIND ME AND THEY WILL COME FOR ME.
THE OTHERS WILL NOT TELL--
OF COURSE THEY WILL.
YOUR FRIENDS, YOUR COUSINS... THEY WERE NOT HAPPY WHEN YOU CHOSE TO MARRY A JEW. THEY HAVE NOTHING TO GAIN BY PROTECTING ME...AND MUCH TO LOSE. I AM TRAPPED HERE. THE SOLDIERS WILL NEVER LET ME THROUGH.
BUT YOU... YOU CAN ESCAPE. YOU CAN TAKE JON WITH YOU, GET TO THE PORT--
NO.

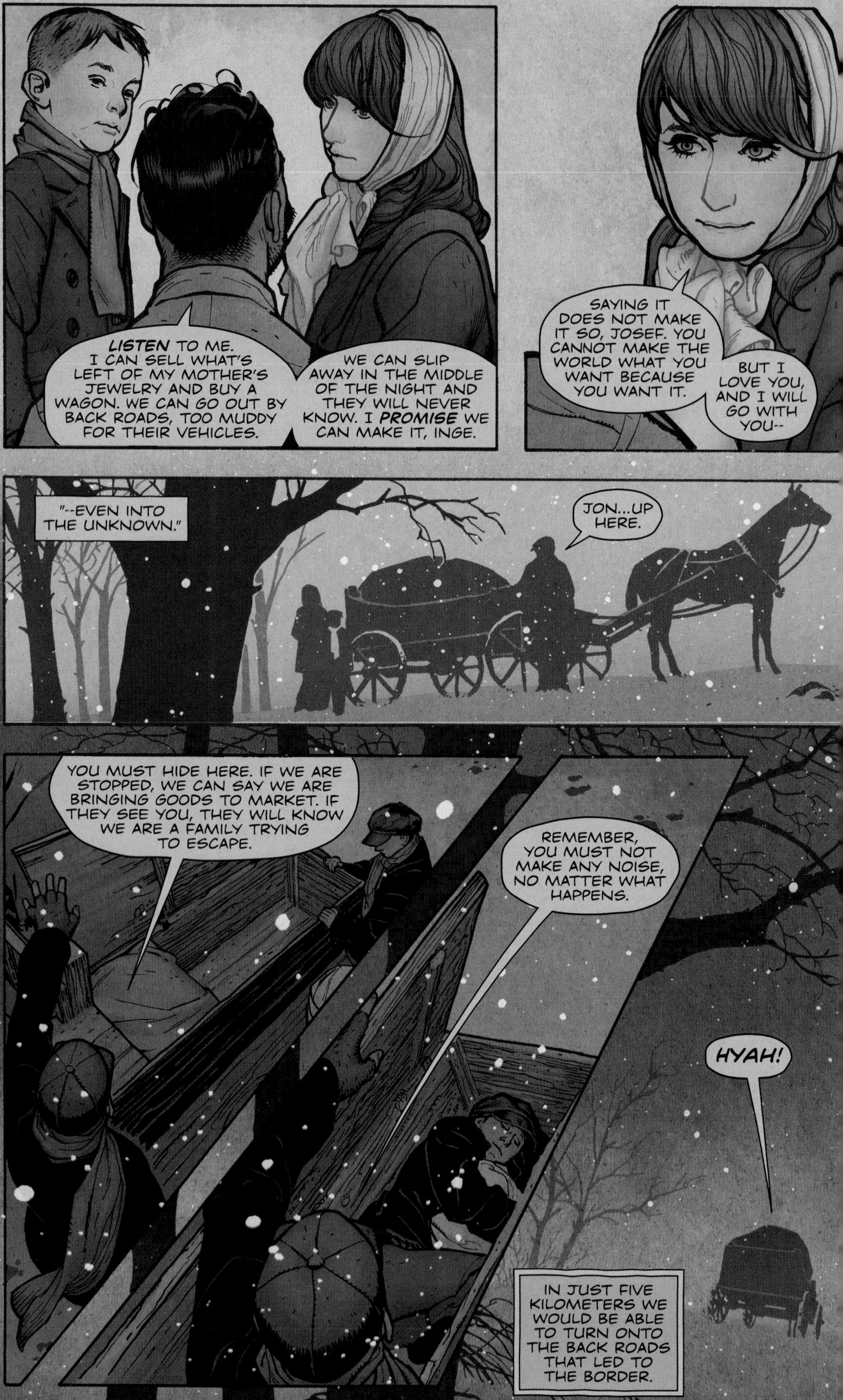
LISTEN TO ME. I CAN SELL WHAT'S LEFT OF MY MOTHER'S JEWELRY AND BUY A WAGON. WE CAN GO OUT BY BACK ROADS, TOO MUDDY FOR THEIR VEHICLES.
WE CAN SLIP AWAY IN THE MIDDLE OF THE NIGHT AND THEY WILL NEVER KNOW. I PROMISE WE CAN MAKE IT, INGE.
SAYING IT DOES NOT MAKE IT SO, JOSEF. YOU CANNOT MAKE THE WORLD WHAT YOU WANT BECAUSE YOU WANT IT.
BUT I LOVE YOU, AND I WILL GO WITH YOU--
"--EVEN INTO THE UNKNOWN."
JON...UP HERE.
YOU MUST HIDE HERE. IF WE ARE STOPPED, WE CAN SAY WE ARE BRINGING GOODS TO MARKET. IF THEY SEE YOU, THEY WILL KNOW WE ARE A FAMILY TRYING TO ESCAPE.
REMEMBER, YOU MUST NOT MAKE ANY NOISE, NO MATTER WHAT HAPPENS.
HYAH!
IN JUST FIVE KILOMETERS WE WOULD BE ABLE TO TURN ONTO THE BACK ROADS THAT LED TO THE BORDER.

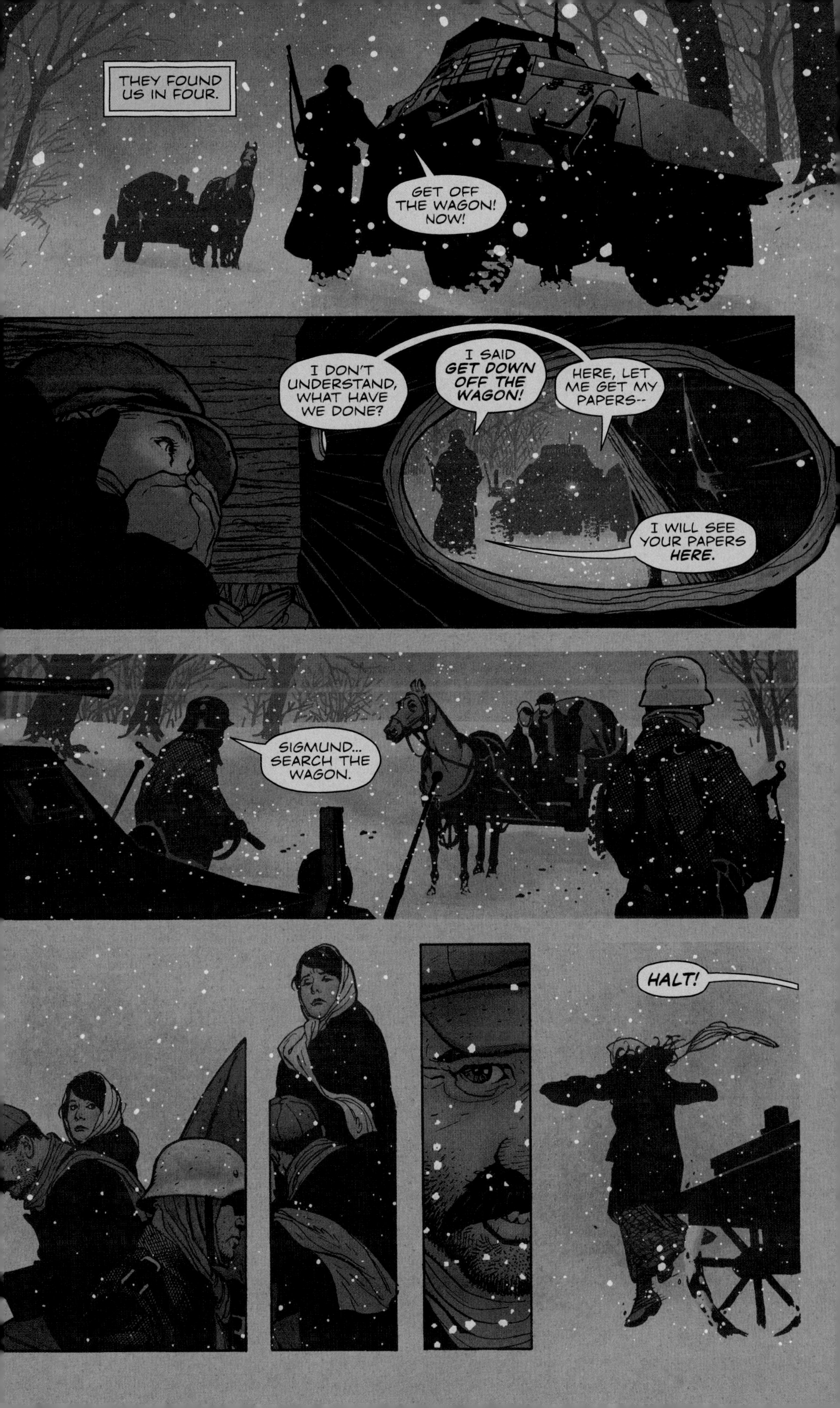

THEY FOUND US IN FOUR.
GET OFF THE WAGON! NOW!
I DON'T UNDERSTAND, WHAT HAVE WE DONE?
I SAID GET DOWN OFF THE WAGON!
HERE, LET ME GET MY PAPERS--
I WILL SEE YOUR PAPERS HERE.
SIGMUND... SEARCH THE WAGON.
HALT!

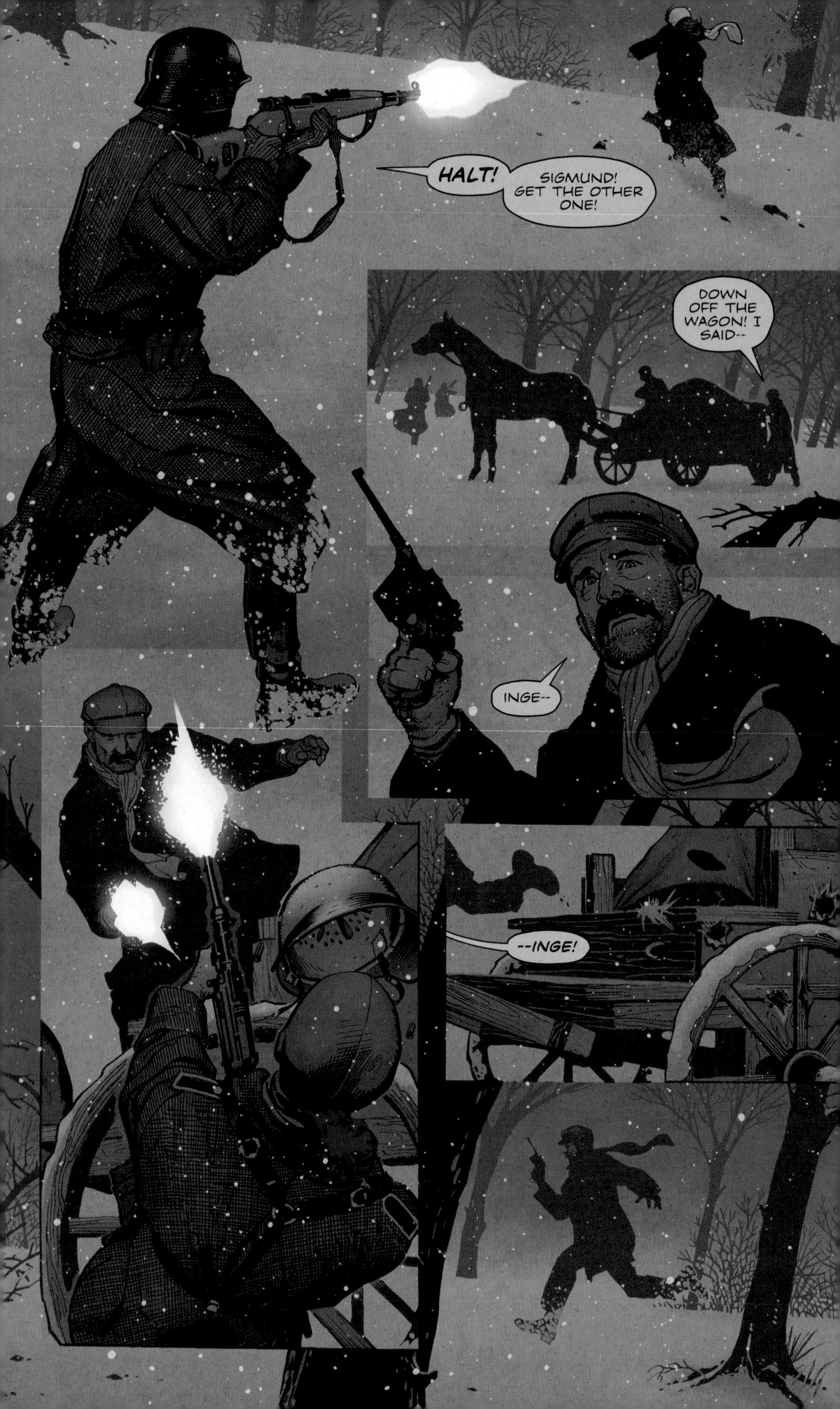
HALT!
SIGMUND! GET THE OTHER ONE!
DOWN OFF THE WAGON! I SAID--
INGE--
--INGE!

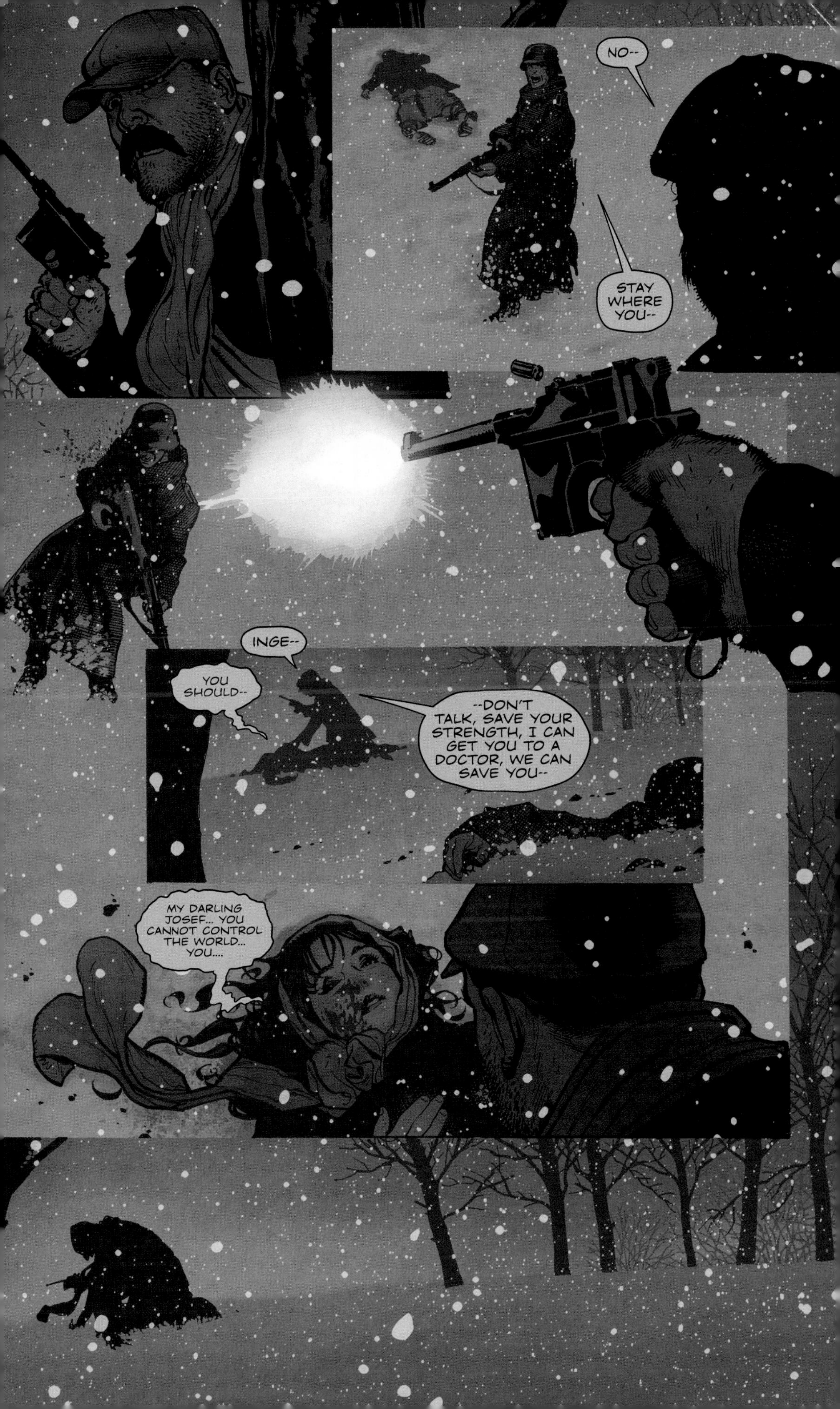
NO--
STAY WHERE YOU--
INGE--
YOU SHOULD--
--DON'T TALK, SAVE YOUR STRENGTH, I CAN GET YOU TO A DOCTOR, WE CAN SAVE YOU--
MY DARLING JOSEF... YOU CANNOT CONTROL THE WORLD... YOU....

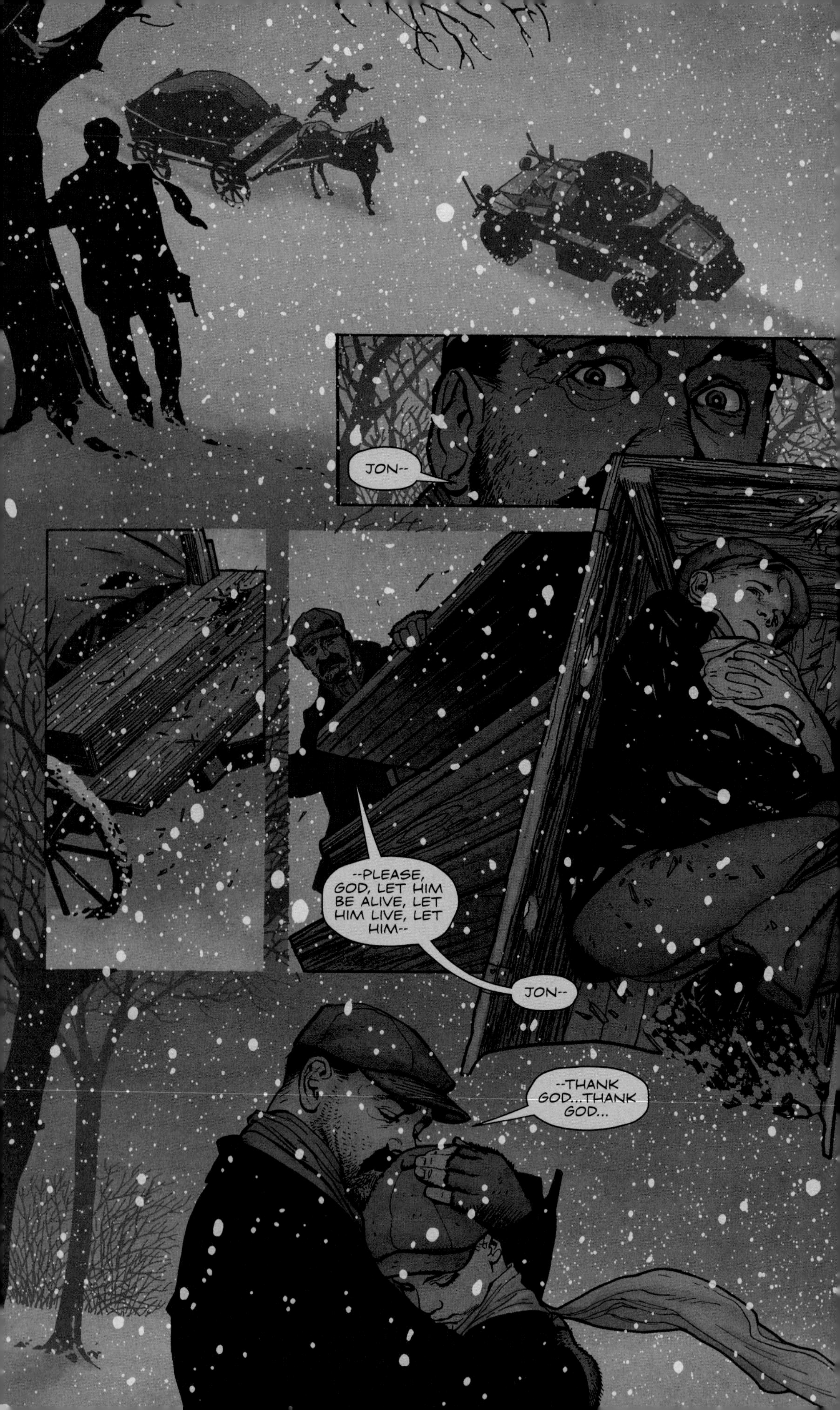
JON--
--PLEASE, GOD, LET HIM BE ALIVE, LET HIM LIVE, LET HIM--
JON--
--THANK GOD...THANK GOD...

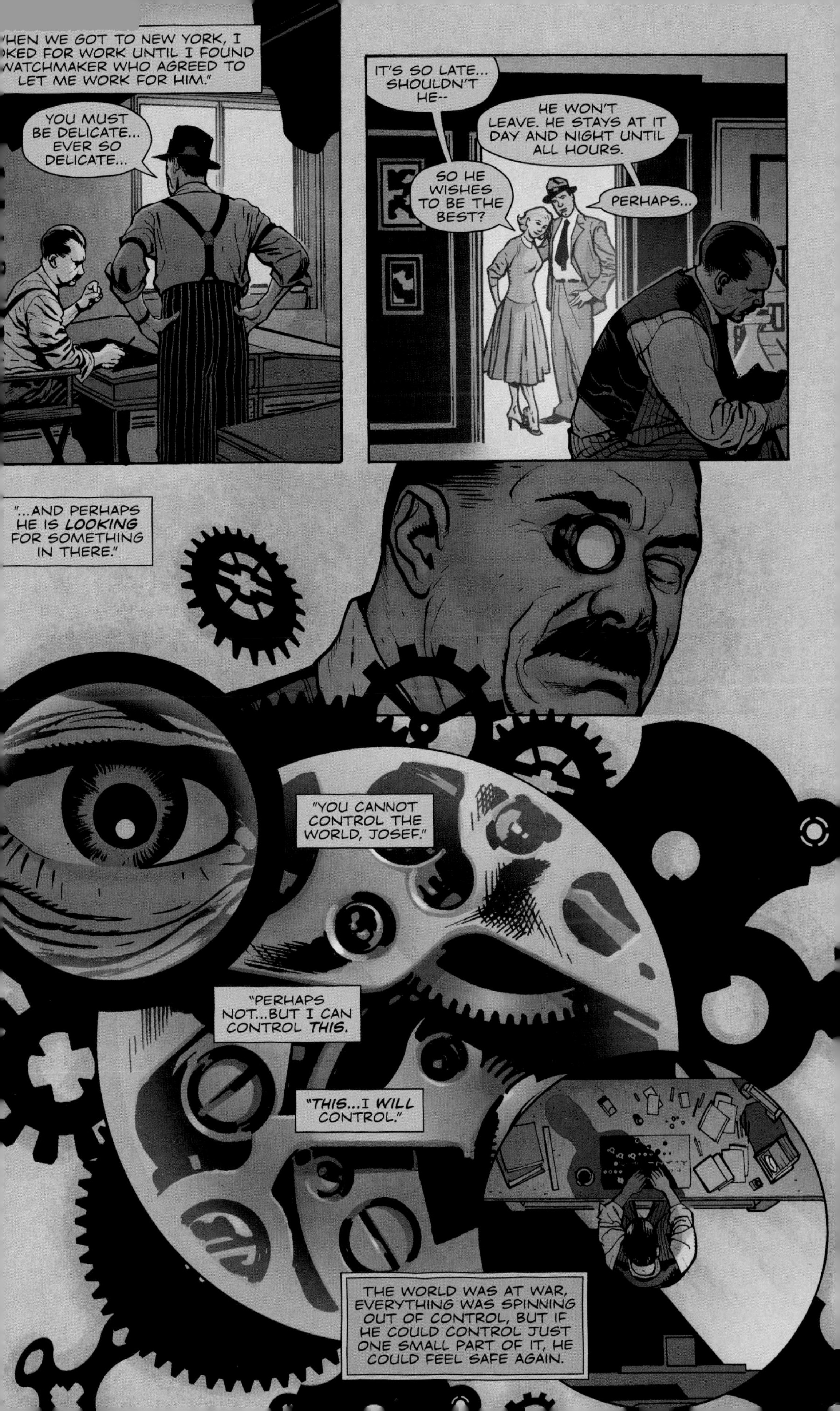

HEN WE GOT TO NEW YORK, I
KED FOR WORK UNTIL I FOUND
ATCHMAKER WHO AGREED TO
LET ME WORK FOR HIM."
YOU MUST BE DELICATE... EVER SO DELICATE...
IT'S SO LATE... SHOULDN'T HE--
HE WON'T LEAVE. HE STAYS AT IT DAY AND NIGHT UNTIL ALL HOURS.
SO HE WISHES TO BE THE BEST?
PERHAPS...
"...AND PERHAPS HE IS *LOOKING* FOR SOMETHING IN THERE."
"YOU CANNOT CONTROL THE WORLD, JOSEF."
"PERHAPS NOT...BUT I CAN CONTROL *THIS*.
"*THIS*...I *WILL* CONTROL."
THE WORLD WAS AT WAR, EVERYTHING WAS SPINNING OUT OF CONTROL, BUT IF HE COULD CONTROL JUST ONE SMALL PART OF IT, HE COULD FEEL SAFE AGAIN.

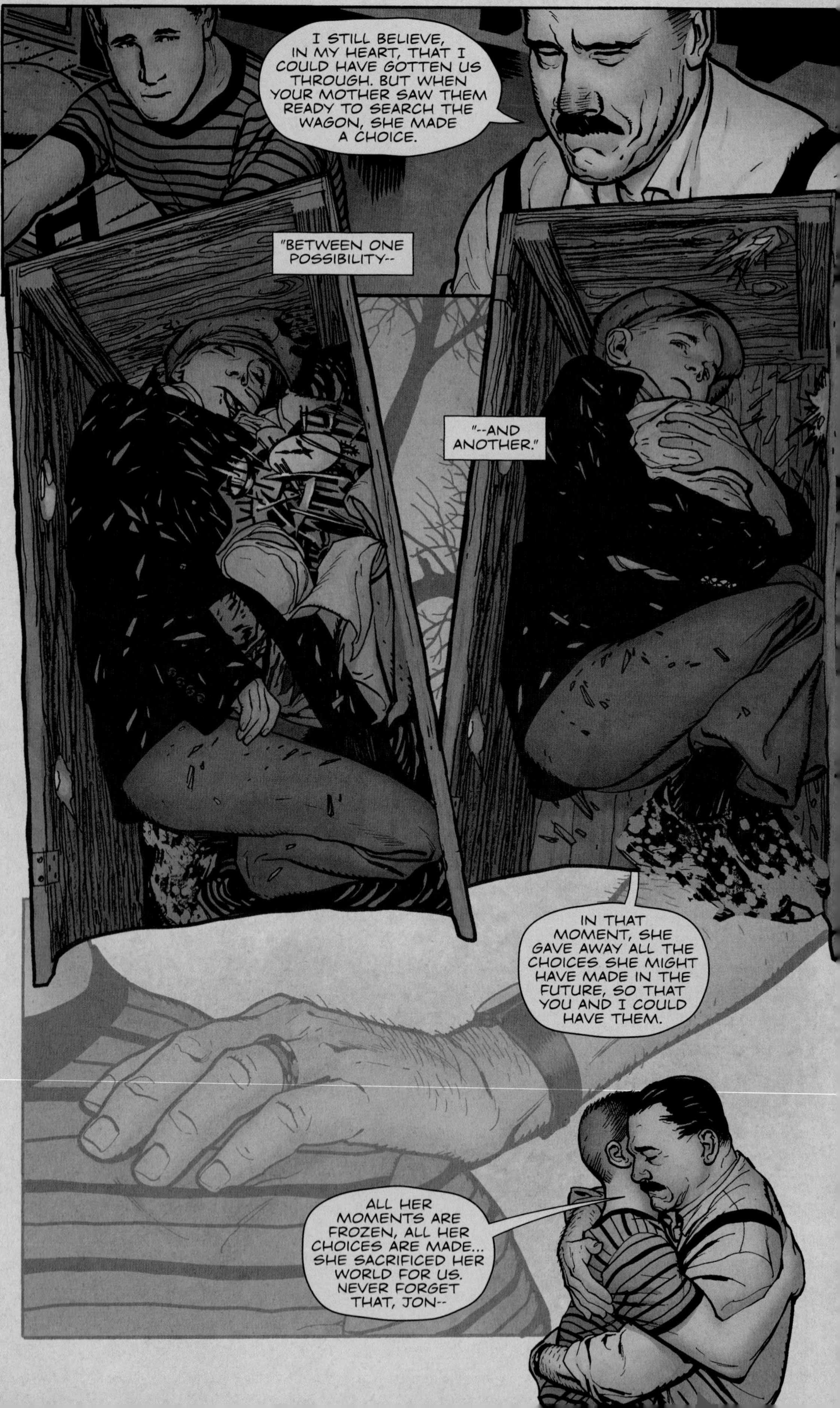
I STILL BELIEVE, IN MY HEART, THAT I COULD HAVE GOTTEN US THROUGH. BUT WHEN YOUR MOTHER SAW THEM READY TO SEARCH THE WAGON, SHE MADE A CHOICE.
"BETWEEN ONE POSSIBILITY--
"--AND ANOTHER."
IN THAT MOMENT, SHE GAVE AWAY ALL THE CHOICES SHE MIGHT HAVE MADE IN THE FUTURE, SO THAT YOU AND I COULD HAVE THEM.
ALL HER MOMENTS ARE FROZEN, ALL HER CHOICES ARE MADE... SHE SACRIFICED HER WORLD FOR US. NEVER FORGET THAT, JON--

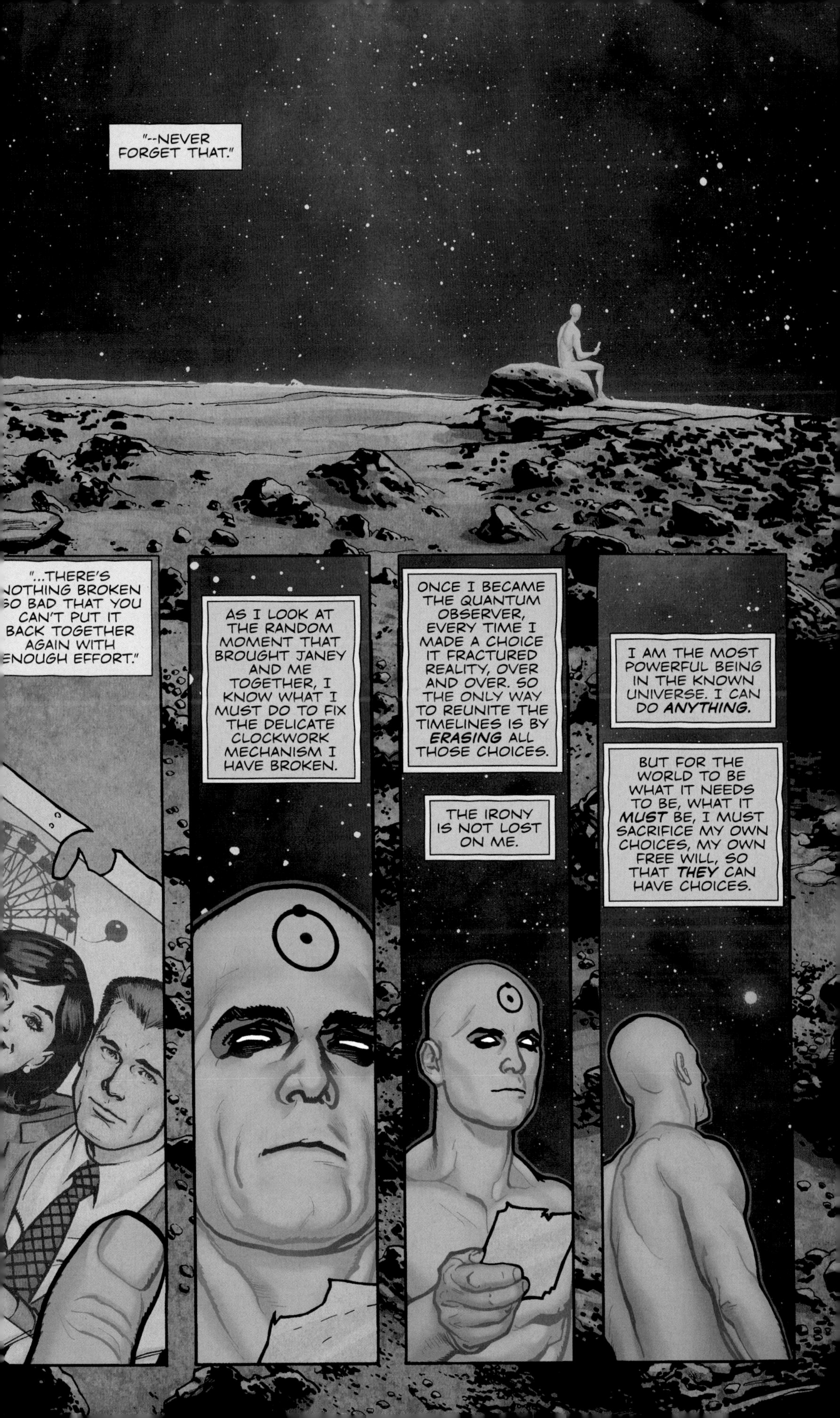
"--NEVER FORGET THAT."
"...THERE'S NOTHING BROKEN SO BAD THAT YOU CAN'T PUT IT BACK TOGETHER AGAIN WITH ENOUGH EFFORT."
AS I LOOK AT THE RANDOM MOMENT THAT BROUGHT JANEY AND ME TOGETHER, I KNOW WHAT I MUST DO TO FIX THE DELICATE CLOCKWORK MECHANISM I HAVE BROKEN.
ONCE I BECAME THE QUANTUM OBSERVER, EVERY TIME I MADE A CHOICE IT FRACTURED REALITY, OVER AND OVER. SO THE ONLY WAY TO REUNITE THE TIMELINES IS BY ERASING ALL THOSE CHOICES.
THE IRONY IS NOT LOST ON ME.
I AM THE MOST POWERFUL BEING IN THE KNOWN UNIVERSE. I CAN DO ANYTHING.
BUT FOR THE WORLD TO BE WHAT IT NEEDS TO BE, WHAT IT MUST BE, I MUST SACRIFICE MY OWN CHOICES, MY OWN FREE WILL, SO THAT THEY CAN HAVE CHOICES.

IN THIS NEW, UNITED TIMELINE, WHATEVER I HAVE DONE IN THE FUTURE IS DONE, THE DECISIONS ARE MADE, AND CANNOT BE CHANGED. THEY ARE AS IRREVOCABLE AS THE CHOICES I MADE IN THE PAST.

BECAUSE ALL THOSE MOMENTS ARE THE SAME MOMENT, ONE MOMENT, ETERNAL AND SIMULTANEOUS.

LIKE MY MOTHER, I MUST GIVE UP ALL OF MY CHOICES SO THAT THEY CAN MAKE OF THIS REALITY WHAT THEY WISH.

EDITED REPLAY

SO THAT I MUST FREEZE ETERNITY, LIKE A THAT FROZEN MOMENT, FLY IN THE AMBER.

BUT I MUST LET THIS LIMITED, MOST SURVIVE UNLESS BECOME THE UNITED WORLD'S ONE TRUE REALITY.

I AM LIMITLESS.

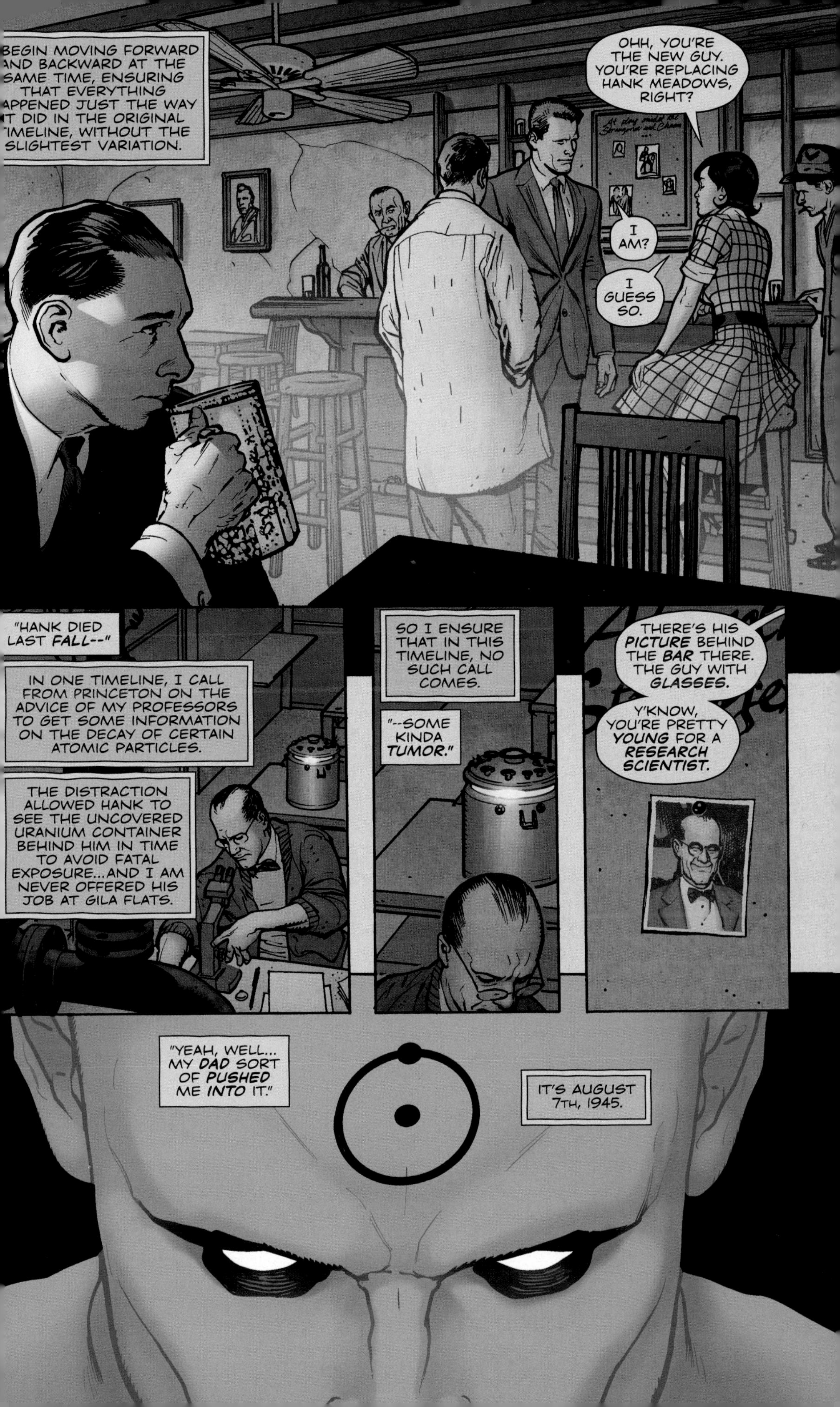

BEGIN MOVING FORWARD AND BACKWARD AT THE SAME TIME, ENSURING THAT EVERYTHING HAPPENED JUST THE WAY IT DID IN THE ORIGINAL TIMELINE, WITHOUT THE SLIGHTEST VARIATION.
OHH, YOU'RE THE NEW GUY. YOU'RE REPLACING HANK MEADOWS, RIGHT?
I AM?
I GUESS SO.
"HANK DIED LAST FALL--"
IN ONE TIMELINE, I CALL FROM PRINCETON ON THE ADVICE OF MY PROFESSORS TO GET SOME INFORMATION ON THE DECAY OF CERTAIN ATOMIC PARTICLES.
THE DISTRACTION ALLOWED HANK TO SEE THE UNCOVERED URANIUM CONTAINER BEHIND HIM IN TIME TO AVOID FATAL EXPOSURE...AND I AM NEVER OFFERED HIS JOB AT GILA FLATS.
SO I ENSURE THAT IN THIS TIMELINE, NO SUCH CALL COMES.
"--SOME KINDA TUMOR."
THERE'S HIS PICTURE BEHIND THE BAR THERE. THE GUY WITH GLASSES.
Y'KNOW, YOU'RE PRETTY YOUNG FOR A RESEARCH SCIENTIST.
"YEAH, WELL... MY DAD SORT OF PUSHED ME INTO IT."
IT'S AUGUST 7TH, 1945.

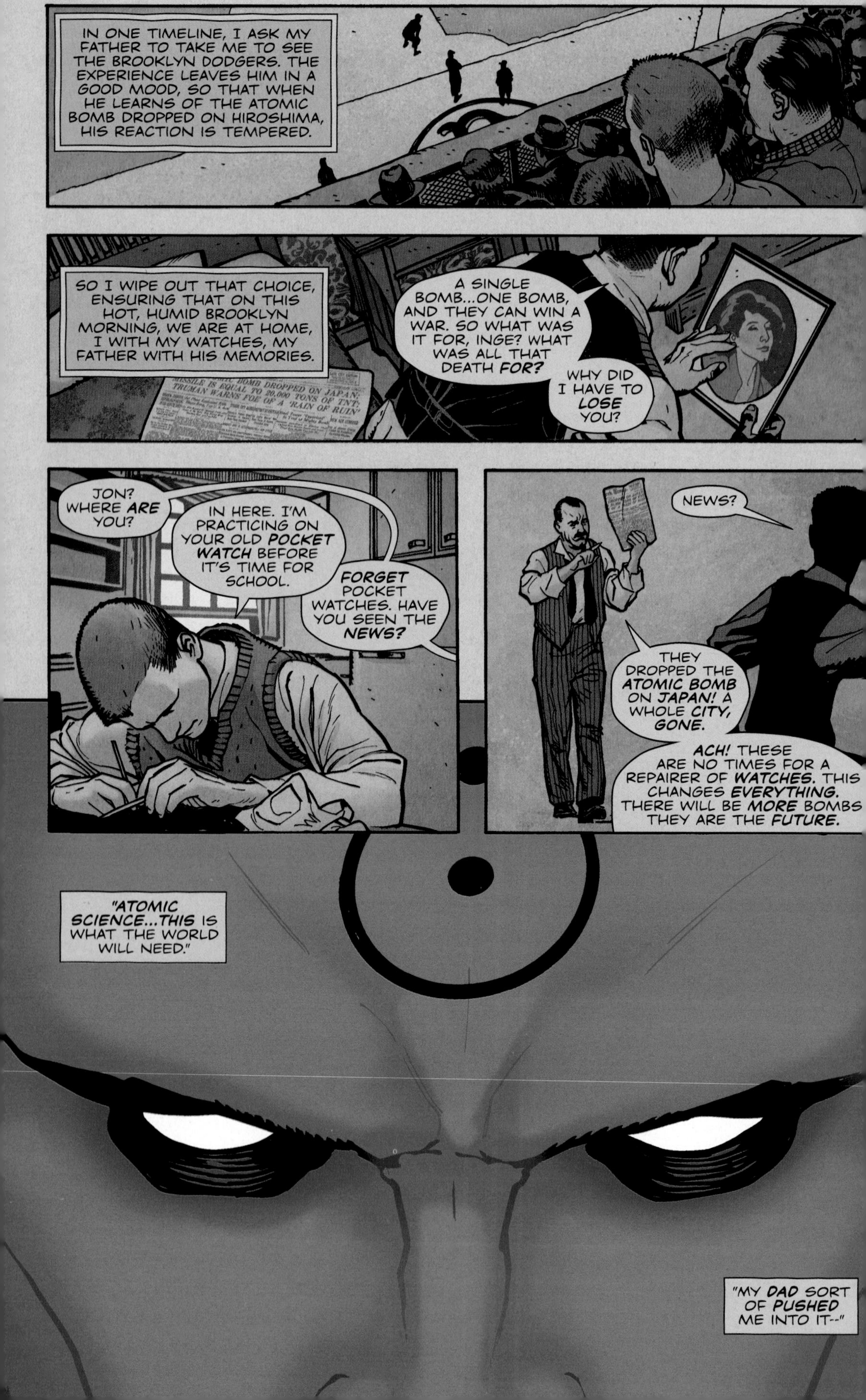

IN ONE TIMELINE, I ASK MY FATHER TO TAKE ME TO SEE THE BROOKLYN DODGERS. THE EXPERIENCE LEAVES HIM IN A GOOD MOOD, SO THAT WHEN HE LEARNS OF THE ATOMIC BOMB DROPPED ON HIROSHIMA, HIS REACTION IS TEMPERED.
SO I WIPE OUT THAT CHOICE, ENSURING THAT ON THIS HOT, HUMID BROOKLYN MORNING, WE ARE AT HOME, I WITH MY WATCHES, MY FATHER WITH HIS MEMORIES.
MISSILE IS EQUAL TO 20,000 TONS OF TNT; TRUMAN WARNS FOE OF A 'RAIN OF RUIN'
A SINGLE BOMB...ONE BOMB, AND THEY CAN WIN A WAR. SO WHAT WAS IT FOR, INGE? WHAT WAS ALL THAT DEATH FOR?
WHY DID I HAVE TO LOSE YOU?
JON? WHERE ARE YOU?
IN HERE. I'M PRACTICING ON YOUR OLD POCKET WATCH BEFORE IT'S TIME FOR SCHOOL.
FORGET POCKET WATCHES. HAVE YOU SEEN THE NEWS?
NEWS?
THEY DROPPED THE ATOMIC BOMB ON JAPAN! A WHOLE CITY, GONE.
ACH! THESE ARE NO TIMES FOR A REPAIRER OF WATCHES. THIS CHANGES EVERYTHING. THERE WILL BE MORE BOMBS. THEY ARE THE FUTURE.
"ATOMIC SCIENCE...THIS IS WHAT THE WORLD WILL NEED."
"MY DAD SORT OF PUSHED ME INTO IT--"

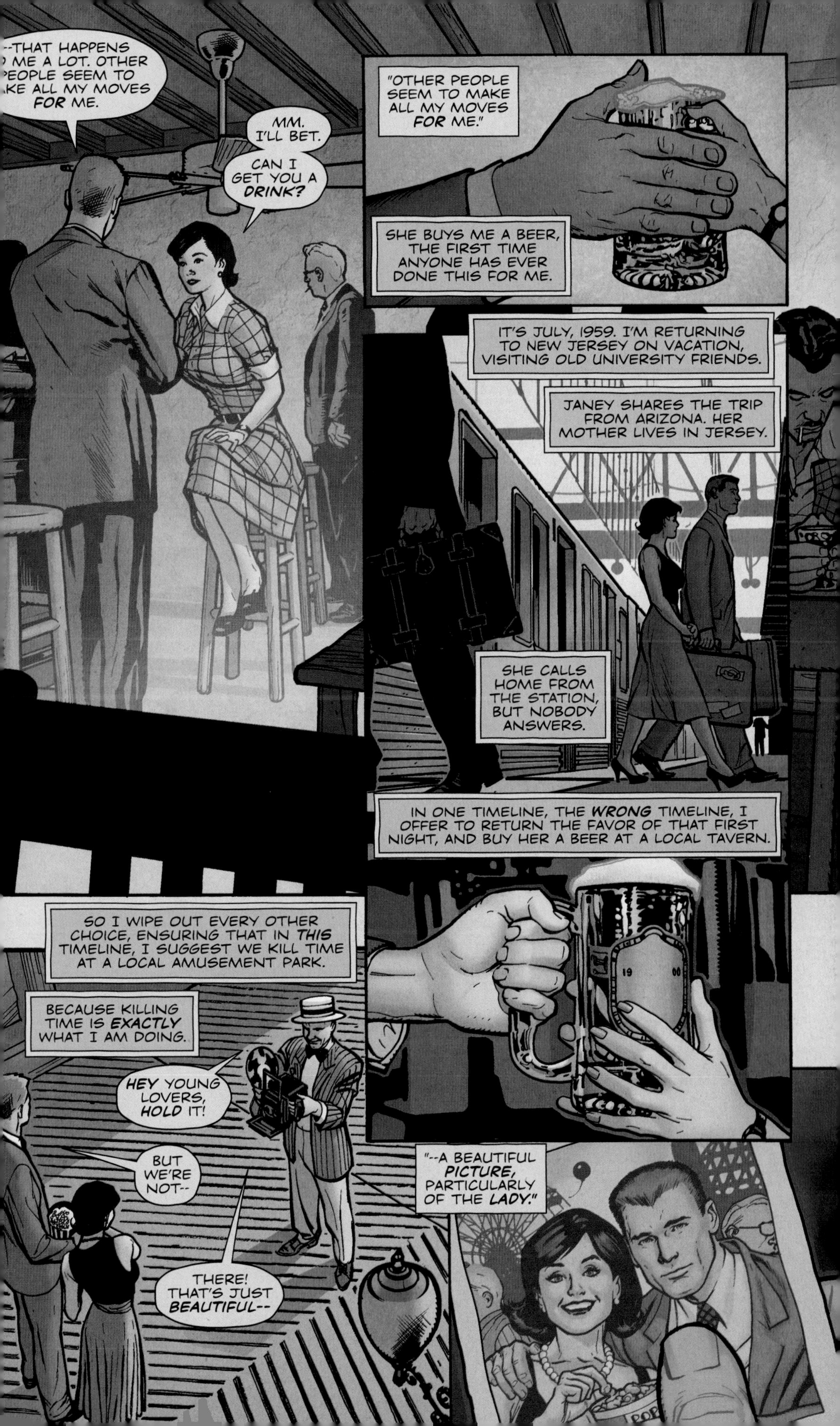
--THAT HAPPENS TO ME A LOT. OTHER PEOPLE SEEM TO MAKE ALL MY MOVES FOR ME.
MM. I'LL BET.
CAN I GET YOU A DRINK?
"OTHER PEOPLE SEEM TO MAKE ALL MY MOVES FOR ME."
SHE BUYS ME A BEER, THE FIRST TIME ANYONE HAS EVER DONE THIS FOR ME.
IT'S JULY, 1959. I'M RETURNING TO NEW JERSEY ON VACATION, VISITING OLD UNIVERSITY FRIENDS.
JANEY SHARES THE TRIP FROM ARIZONA. HER MOTHER LIVES IN JERSEY.
SHE CALLS HOME FROM THE STATION, BUT NOBODY ANSWERS.
IN ONE TIMELINE, THE WRONG TIMELINE, I OFFER TO RETURN THE FAVOR OF THAT FIRST NIGHT, AND BUY HER A BEER AT A LOCAL TAVERN.
SO I WIPE OUT EVERY OTHER CHOICE, ENSURING THAT IN THIS TIMELINE, I SUGGEST WE KILL TIME AT A LOCAL AMUSEMENT PARK.
BECAUSE KILLING TIME IS EXACTLY WHAT I AM DOING.
HEY YOUNG LOVERS, HOLD IT!
BUT WE'RE NOT--
THERE! THAT'S JUST BEAUTIFUL--
"--A BEAUTIFUL PICTURE, PARTICULARLY OF THE LADY."

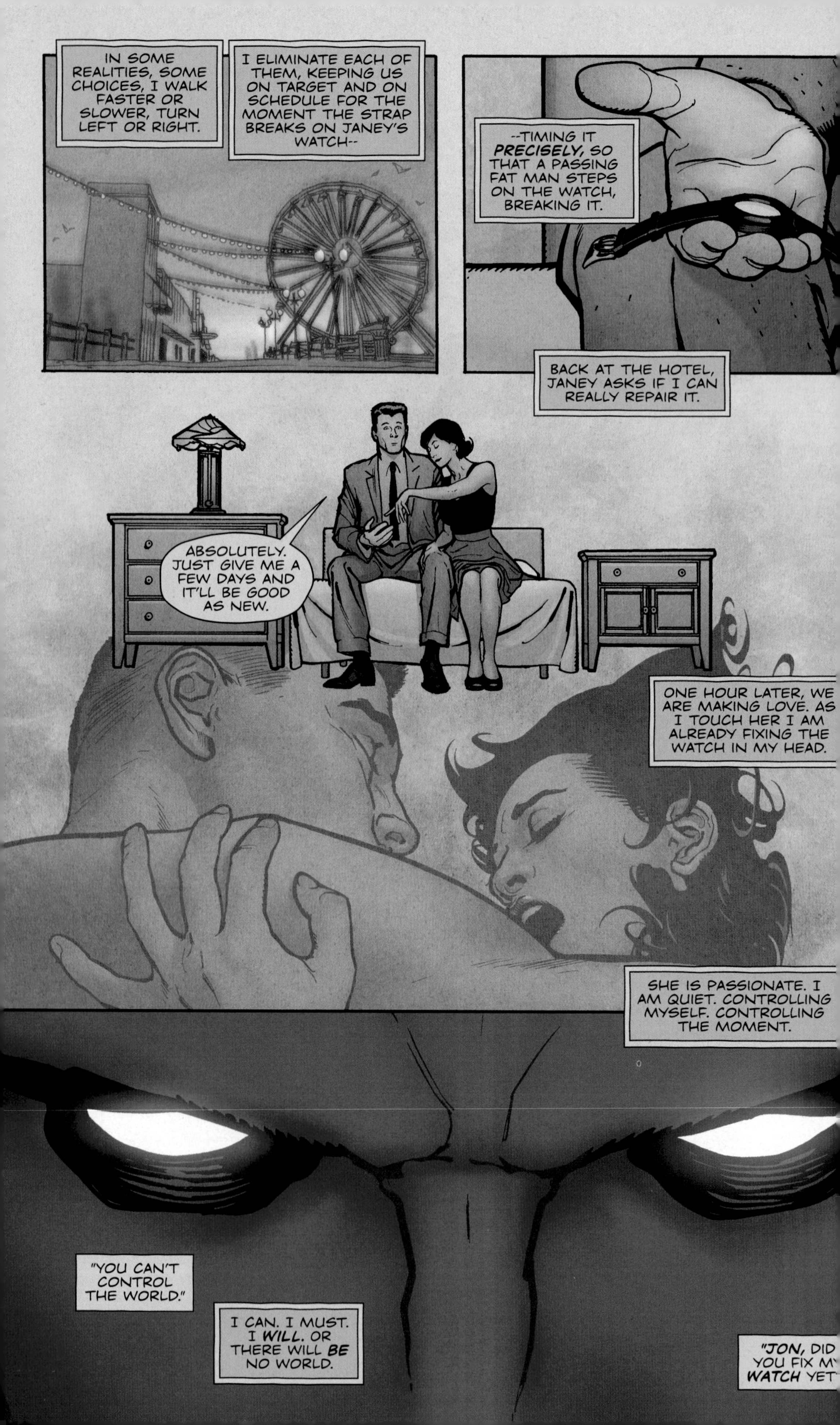
IN SOME REALITIES, SOME CHOICES, I WALK FASTER OR SLOWER, TURN LEFT OR RIGHT.
I ELIMINATE EACH OF THEM, KEEPING US ON TARGET AND ON SCHEDULE FOR THE MOMENT THE STRAP BREAKS ON JANEY'S WATCH--
--TIMING IT **PRECISELY,** SO THAT A PASSING FAT MAN STEPS ON THE WATCH, BREAKING IT.
BACK AT THE HOTEL, JANEY ASKS IF I CAN REALLY REPAIR IT.
ABSOLUTELY. JUST GIVE ME A FEW DAYS AND IT'LL BE GOOD AS NEW.
ONE HOUR LATER, WE ARE MAKING LOVE. AS I TOUCH HER I AM ALREADY FIXING THE WATCH IN MY HEAD.
SHE IS PASSIONATE. I AM QUIET. CONTROLLING MYSELF. CONTROLLING THE MOMENT.
"YOU CAN'T CONTROL THE WORLD."
I CAN. I MUST. I **WILL.** OR THERE WILL **BE** NO WORLD.
"**JON,** DID YOU FIX MY **WATCH** YET

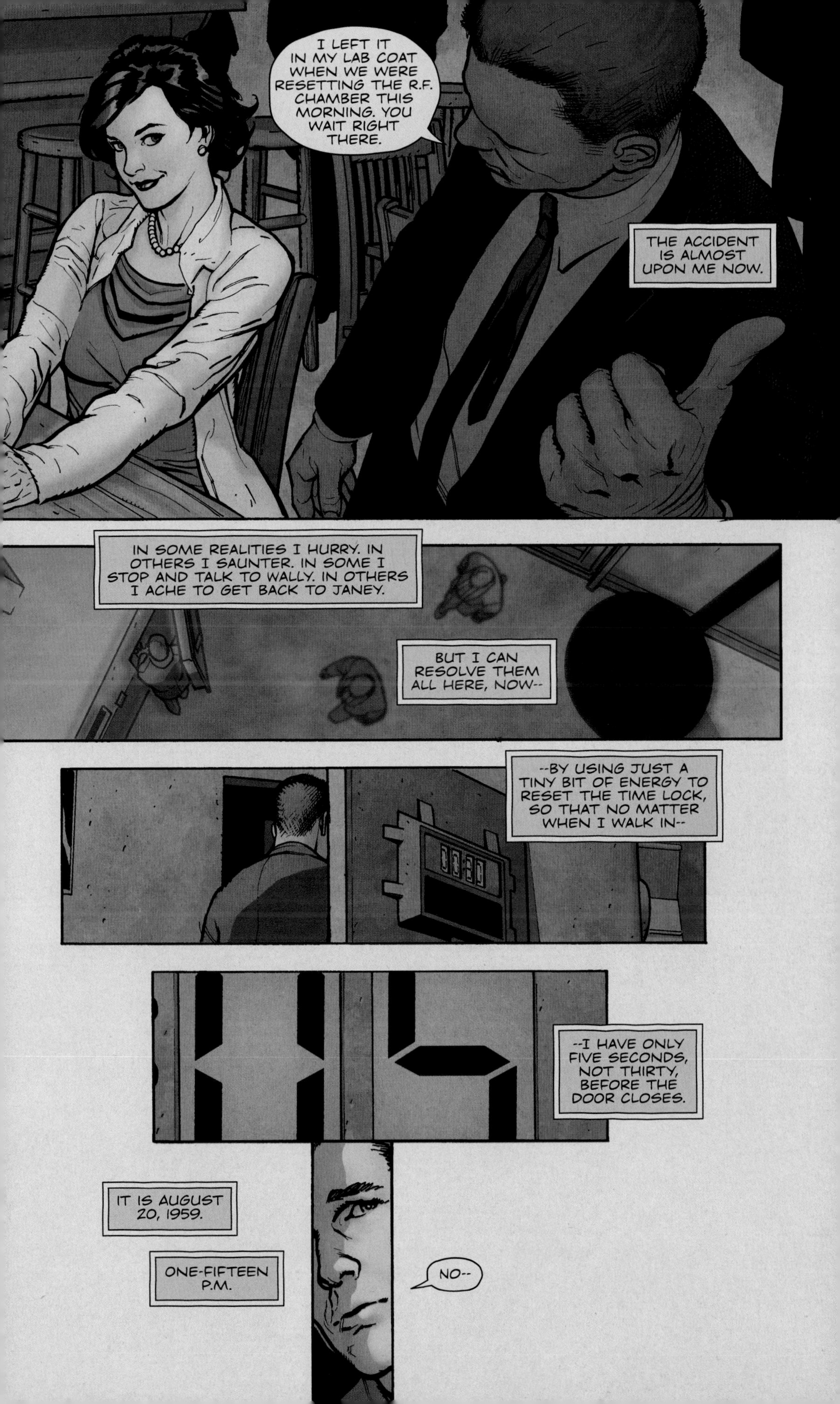

I LEFT IT IN MY LAB COAT WHEN WE WERE RESETTING THE R.F. CHAMBER THIS MORNING. YOU WAIT RIGHT THERE.
THE ACCIDENT IS ALMOST UPON ME NOW.
IN SOME REALITIES I HURRY. IN OTHERS I SAUNTER. IN SOME I STOP AND TALK TO WALLY. IN OTHERS I ACHE TO GET BACK TO JANEY.
BUT I CAN RESOLVE THEM ALL HERE, NOW--
--BY USING JUST A TINY BIT OF ENERGY TO RESET THE TIME LOCK, SO THAT NO MATTER WHEN I WALK IN--
--I HAVE ONLY FIVE SECONDS, NOT THIRTY, BEFORE THE DOOR CLOSES.
IT IS AUGUST 20, 1959.
ONE-FIFTEEN P.M.
NO--

"WHAT'S IN THE BOX?"

"WHAT'S IN THE BOX?"

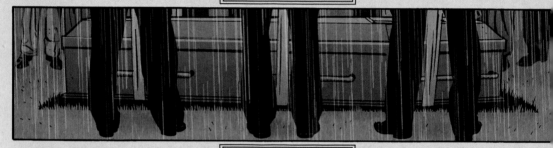

"WHAT'S IN THE BOX?"

"WHAT'S IN THE BOX?"

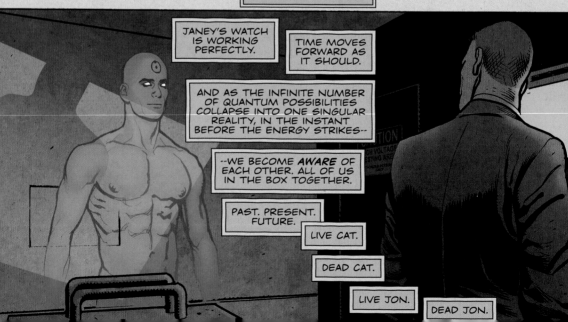

JANEY'S WATCH IS WORKING PERFECTLY.

TIME MOVES FORWARD AS IT SHOULD.

AND AS THE INFINITE NUMBER OF QUANTUM POSSIBILITIES COLLAPSE INTO ONE SINGULAR REALITY, IN THE INSTANT BEFORE THE ENERGY STRIKES--

--WE BECOME *AWARE* OF EACH OTHER. ALL OF US IN THE BOX TOGETHER.

PAST. PRESENT. FUTURE.

LIVE CAT.

DEAD CAT.

LIVE JON.

DEAD JON.

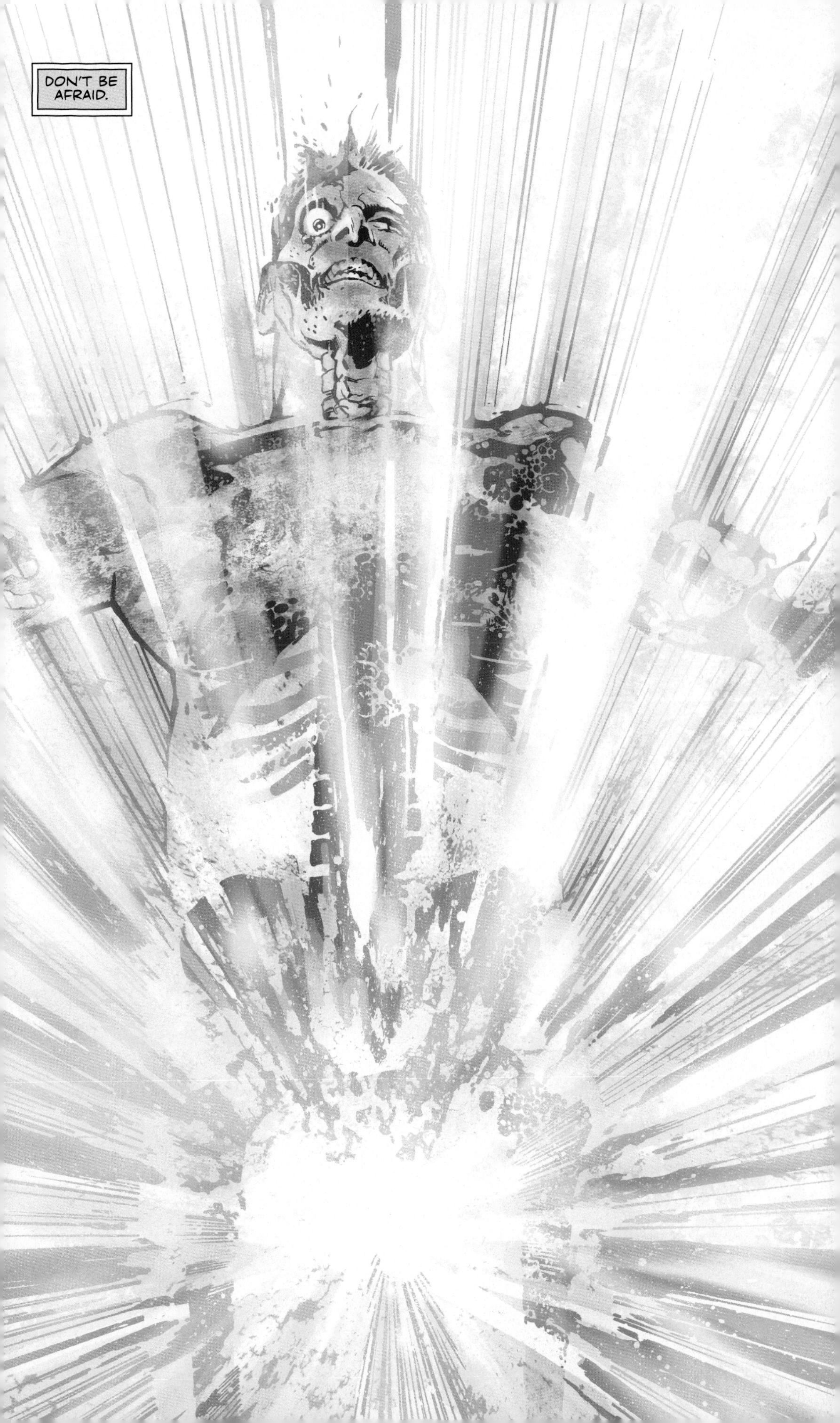
DON'T BE AFRAID.

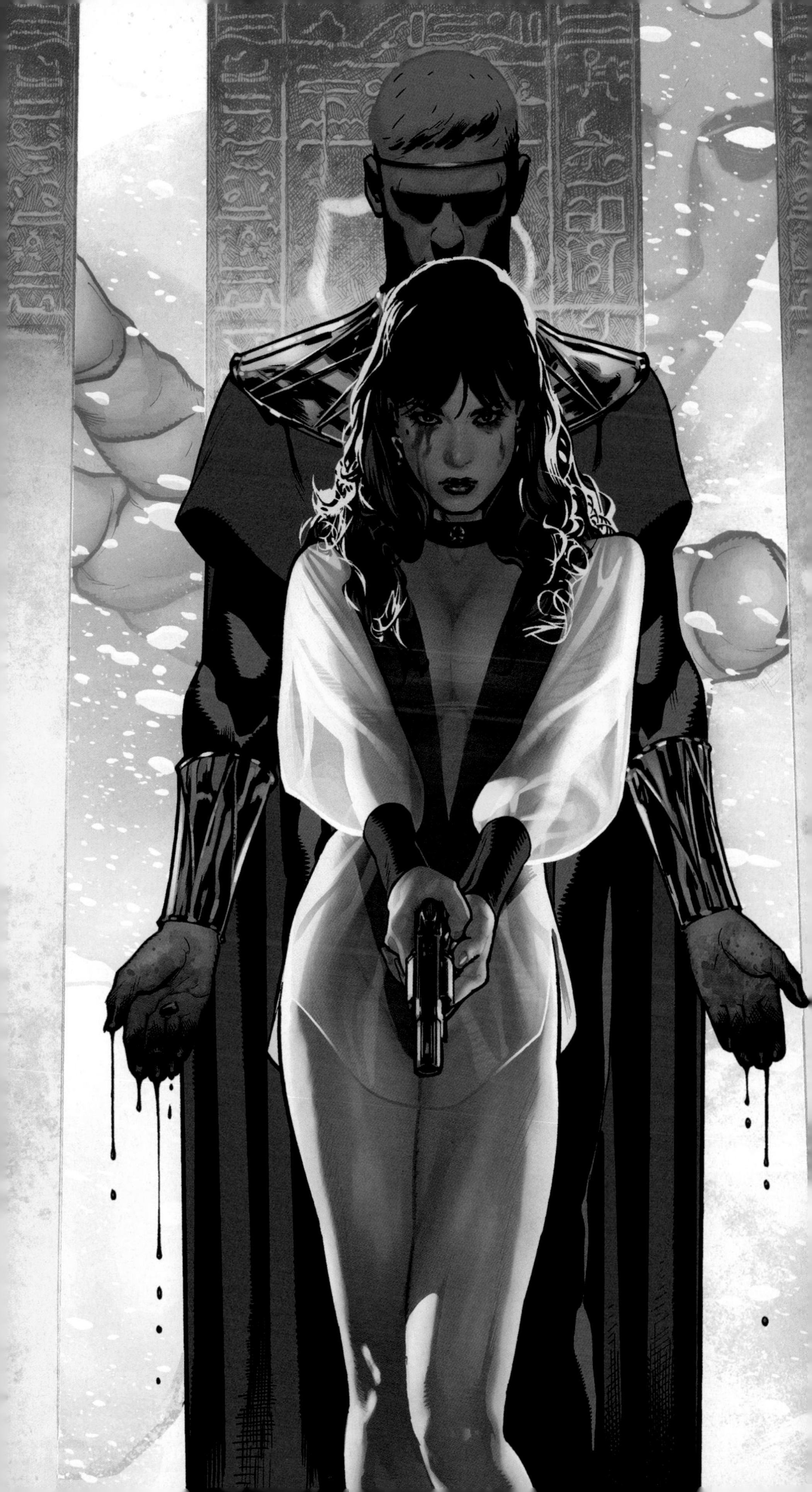

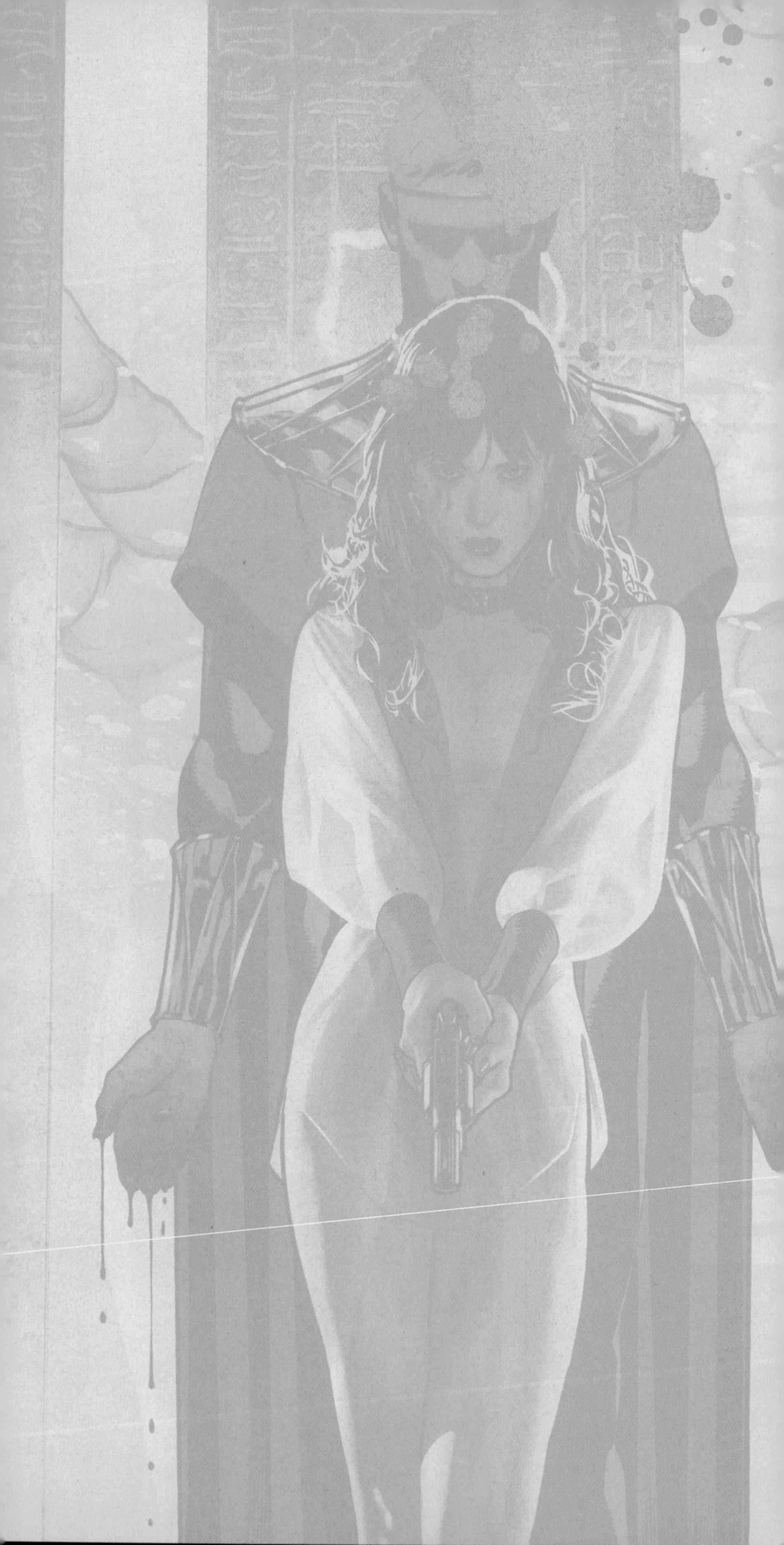

"I HAVE A SMALL SUGGESTION REGARDING THE DESTRUCTION OF EARTH."

AT ONE-FIFTEEN P.M., AUGUST 20, 1959, I ENTERED THE INTRINSIC FIELD CHAMBER IN THE HOPE THAT I HAD PUT TIME, SPACE AND THE UNIVERSE ITSELF BACK TOGETHER AGAIN AS IT NEEDED TO BE. AS IT MUST BE.

"THOU KNOWEST, LORD, THE SECRETS OF OUR HEARTS; SHUT NOT THY MERCIFUL EARS TO OUR PRAYERS, BUT SPARE US, LORD MOST HOLY, O GOD MOST MIGHTY, O HOLY AND MERCIFUL SAVIOR--"

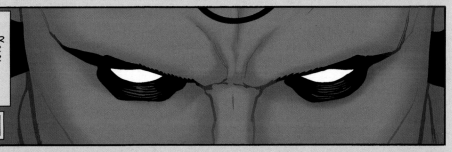

AND YET I'M AFRAID. AFRAID TO OPEN MY EYES. AFRAID THAT I DIDN'T GET IT RIGHT. AFRAID THAT I *MISSED* SOMETHING.

"--THOU MOST WORTHY JUDGE ETERNAL, SUFFER US NOT, AT OUR LAST HOUR, FOR ANY PAINS OF DEATH TO FALL FROM THEE. AMEN."

AMEN.

AMEN.

CHANGES IN PERSPECTIVE

. MICHAEL STRACZYNSKI script   ADAM HUGHES art

AURA MARTIN colors   STEVE WANDS letters

DAM HUGHES cover   BILL SIENKIEWICZ variant cover

AMILLA ZHANG asst. editor   CHRIS CONROY assoc. editor   MARK CHIARELLO editor

VATCHMEN created by ALAN MOORE and DAVE GIBBONS

I WATCH AS A BOX CONTAINING A MYSTERY IS LOWERED INTO THE SOIL.

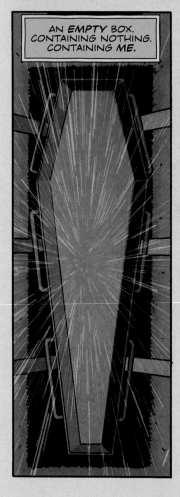

AN *EMPTY* BOX. CONTAINING NOTHING. CONTAINING *ME.*

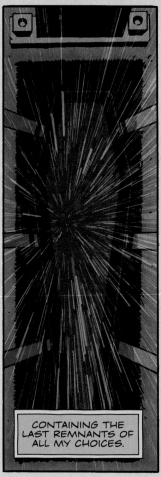

CONTAINING THE LAST REMNANTS OF ALL MY CHOICES.

JONATHAN OSTERMAN

MAY 5, 1929
AUGUST 30, 1959

DEAD. AND BURIED.

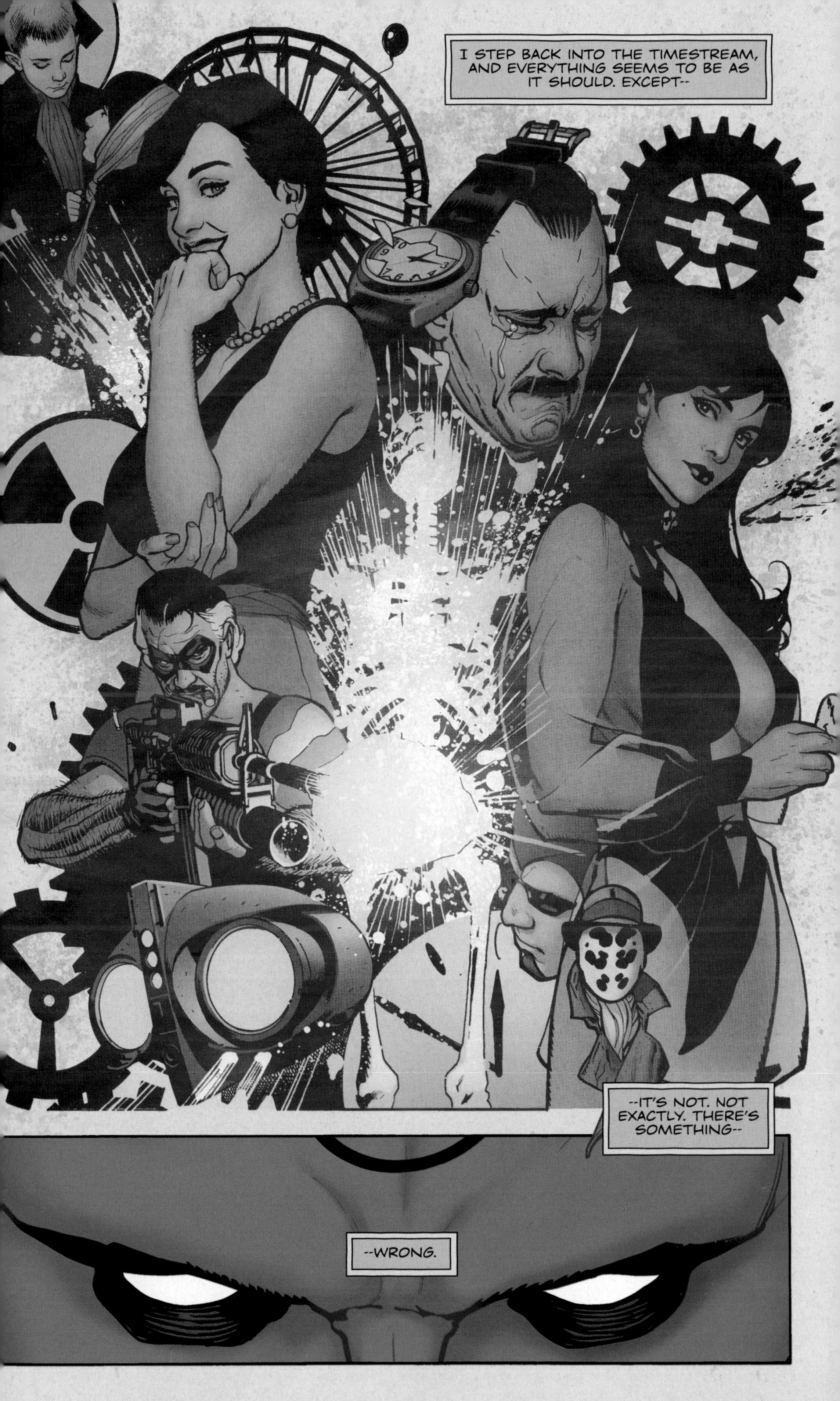
I STEP BACK INTO THE TIMESTREAM, AND EVERYTHING SEEMS TO BE AS IT SHOULD. EXCEPT--
--IT'S NOT. NOT EXACTLY. THERE'S SOMETHING--
--WRONG.

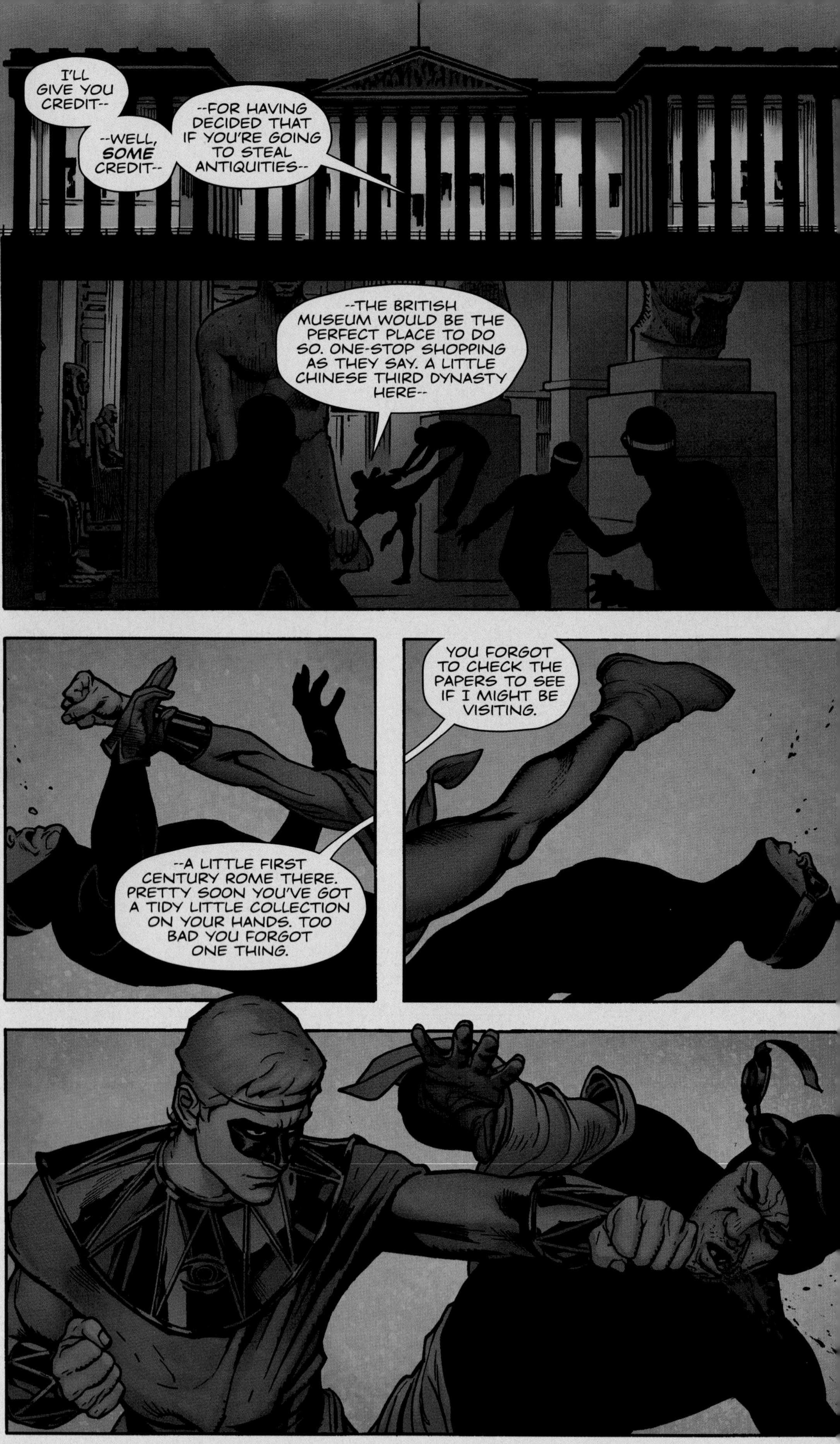
I'LL GIVE YOU CREDIT--
--WELL, SOME CREDIT--
--FOR HAVING DECIDED THAT IF YOU'RE GOING TO STEAL ANTIQUITIES--
--THE BRITISH MUSEUM WOULD BE THE PERFECT PLACE TO DO SO. ONE-STOP SHOPPING AS THEY SAY. A LITTLE CHINESE THIRD DYNASTY HERE--
--A LITTLE FIRST CENTURY ROME THERE. PRETTY SOON YOU'VE GOT A TIDY LITTLE COLLECTION ON YOUR HANDS. TOO BAD YOU FORGOT ONE THING.
YOU FORGOT TO CHECK THE PAPERS TO SEE IF I MIGHT BE VISITING.

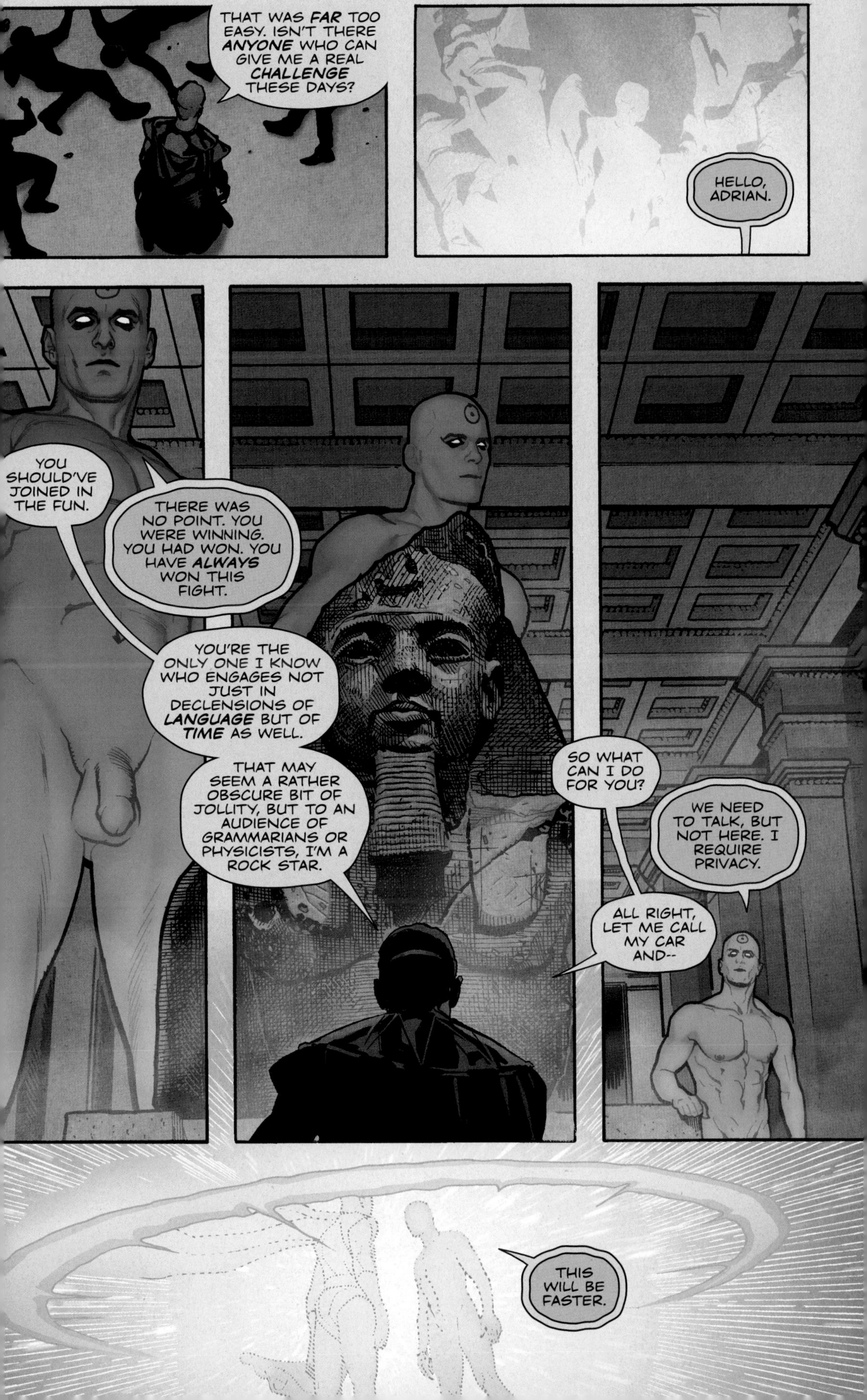
THAT WAS FAR TOO EASY. ISN'T THERE ANYONE WHO CAN GIVE ME A REAL CHALLENGE THESE DAYS?
HELLO, ADRIAN.
YOU SHOULD'VE JOINED IN THE FUN.
THERE WAS NO POINT. YOU WERE WINNING. YOU HAD WON. YOU HAVE ALWAYS WON THIS FIGHT.
YOU'RE THE ONLY ONE I KNOW WHO ENGAGES NOT JUST IN DECLENSIONS OF LANGUAGE BUT OF TIME AS WELL.
THAT MAY SEEM A RATHER OBSCURE BIT OF JOLLITY, BUT TO AN AUDIENCE OF GRAMMARIANS OR PHYSICISTS, I'M A ROCK STAR.
SO WHAT CAN I DO FOR YOU?
WE NEED TO TALK, BUT NOT HERE. I REQUIRE PRIVACY.
ALL RIGHT, LET ME CALL MY CAR AND--
THIS WILL BE FASTER.

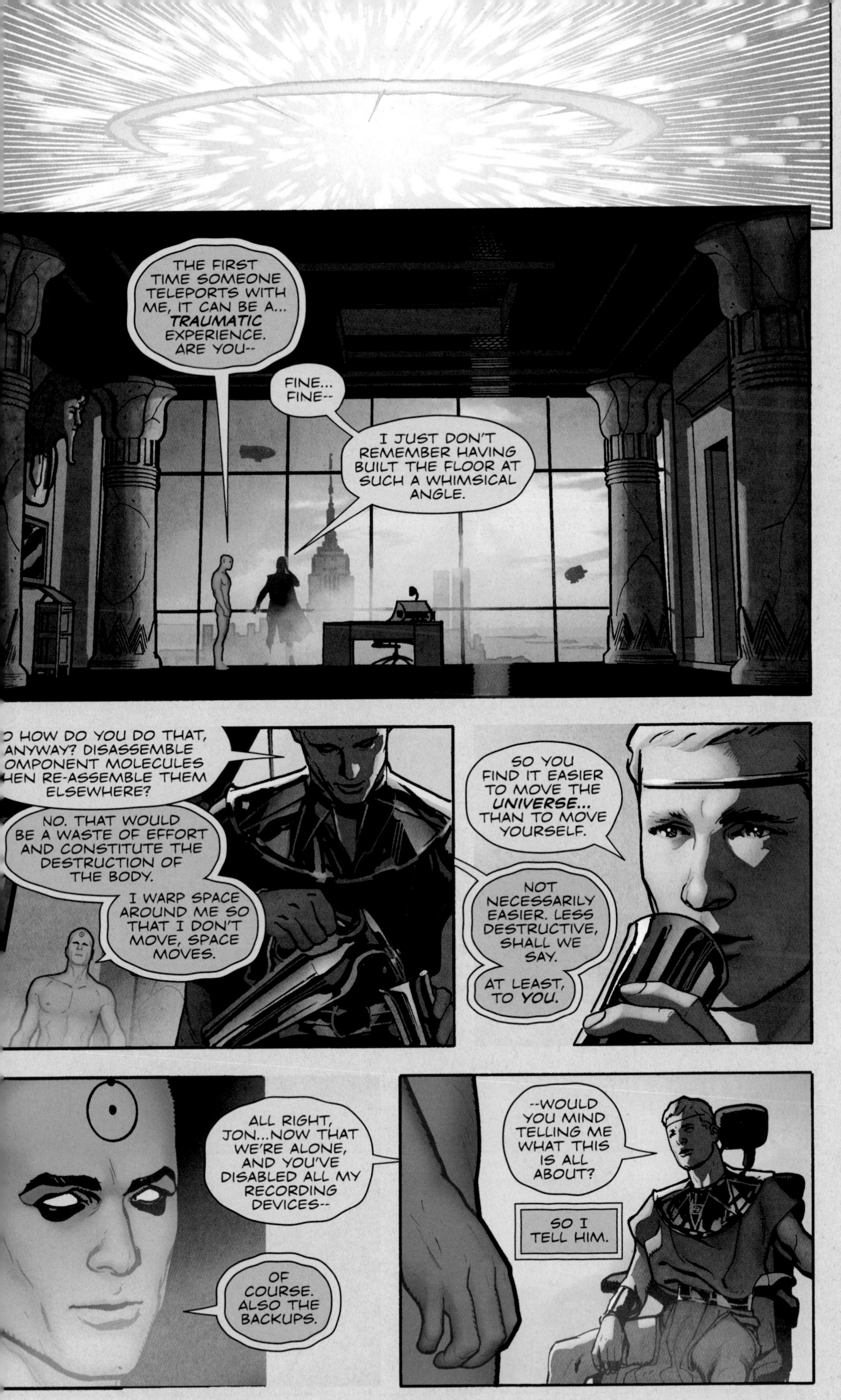
THE FIRST TIME SOMEONE TELEPORTS WITH ME, IT CAN BE A... TRAUMATIC EXPERIENCE. ARE YOU--
FINE... FINE--
I JUST DON'T REMEMBER HAVING BUILT THE FLOOR AT SUCH A WHIMSICAL ANGLE.
O HOW DO YOU DO THAT, ANYWAY? DISASSEMBLE OMPONENT MOLECULES HEN RE-ASSEMBLE THEM ELSEWHERE?
NO. THAT WOULD BE A WASTE OF EFFORT AND CONSTITUTE THE DESTRUCTION OF THE BODY.
I WARP SPACE AROUND ME SO THAT I DON'T MOVE, SPACE MOVES.
SO YOU FIND IT EASIER TO MOVE THE UNIVERSE... THAN TO MOVE YOURSELF.
NOT NECESSARILY EASIER. LESS DESTRUCTIVE, SHALL WE SAY.
AT LEAST, TO YOU.
ALL RIGHT, JON...NOW THAT WE'RE ALONE, AND YOU'VE DISABLED ALL MY RECORDING DEVICES--
OF COURSE. ALSO THE BACKUPS.
--WOULD YOU MIND TELLING ME WHAT THIS IS ALL ABOUT?
SO I TELL HIM.

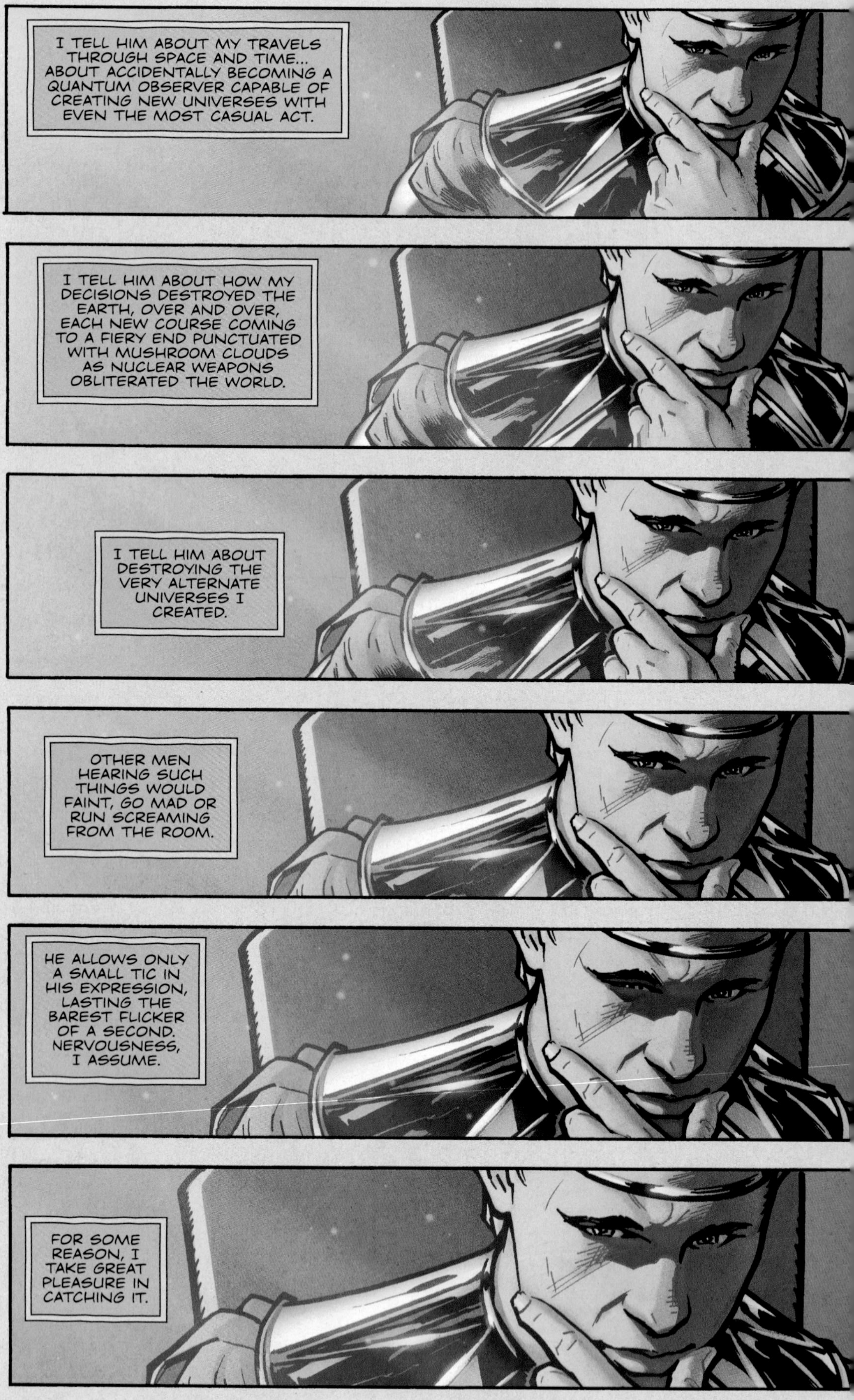

I TELL HIM ABOUT MY TRAVELS THROUGH SPACE AND TIME... ABOUT ACCIDENTALLY BECOMING A QUANTUM OBSERVER CAPABLE OF CREATING NEW UNIVERSES WITH EVEN THE MOST CASUAL ACT.
I TELL HIM ABOUT HOW MY DECISIONS DESTROYED THE EARTH, OVER AND OVER, EACH NEW COURSE COMING TO A FIERY END PUNCTUATED WITH MUSHROOM CLOUDS AS NUCLEAR WEAPONS OBLITERATED THE WORLD.
I TELL HIM ABOUT DESTROYING THE VERY ALTERNATE UNIVERSES I CREATED.
OTHER MEN HEARING SUCH THINGS WOULD FAINT, GO MAD OR RUN SCREAMING FROM THE ROOM.
HE ALLOWS ONLY A SMALL TIC IN HIS EXPRESSION, LASTING THE BAREST FLICKER OF A SECOND. NERVOUSNESS, I ASSUME.
FOR SOME REASON, I TAKE GREAT PLEASURE IN CATCHING IT.

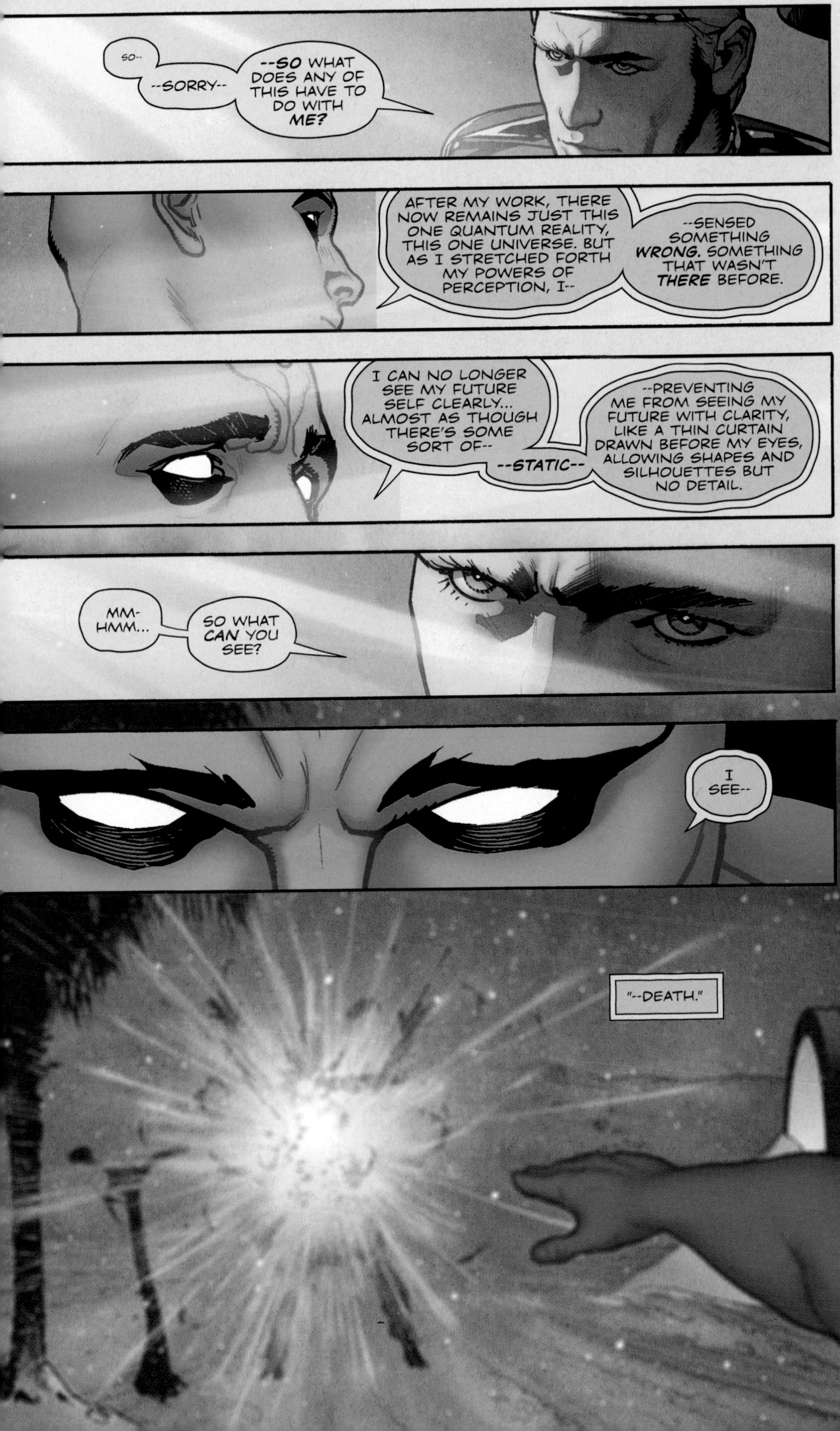

SO--
--SORRY--
--SO WHAT DOES ANY OF THIS HAVE TO DO WITH ME?
AFTER MY WORK, THERE NOW REMAINS JUST THIS ONE QUANTUM REALITY, THIS ONE UNIVERSE. BUT AS I STRETCHED FORTH MY POWERS OF PERCEPTION, I--
--SENSED SOMETHING WRONG. SOMETHING THAT WASN'T THERE BEFORE.
I CAN NO LONGER SEE MY FUTURE SELF CLEARLY... ALMOST AS THOUGH THERE'S SOME SORT OF--
--STATIC--
--PREVENTING ME FROM SEEING MY FUTURE WITH CLARITY, LIKE A THIN CURTAIN DRAWN BEFORE MY EYES, ALLOWING SHAPES AND SILHOUETTES BUT NO DETAIL.
MM-HMM...
SO WHAT CAN YOU SEE?
I SEE--
"--DEATH."

I SEE--
"--DESTRUCTION."
AND I FEEL--
"--RESPONSIBLE."

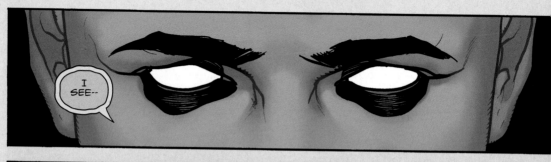

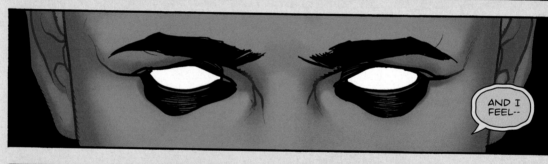

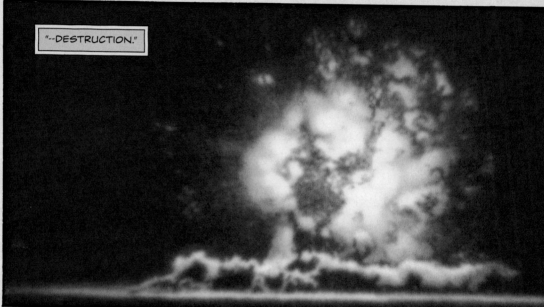

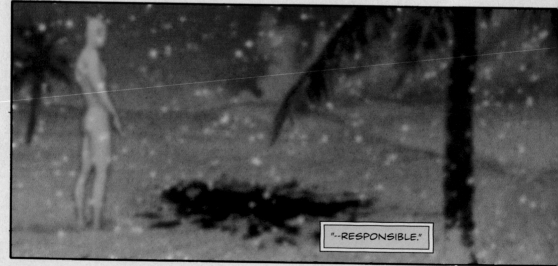

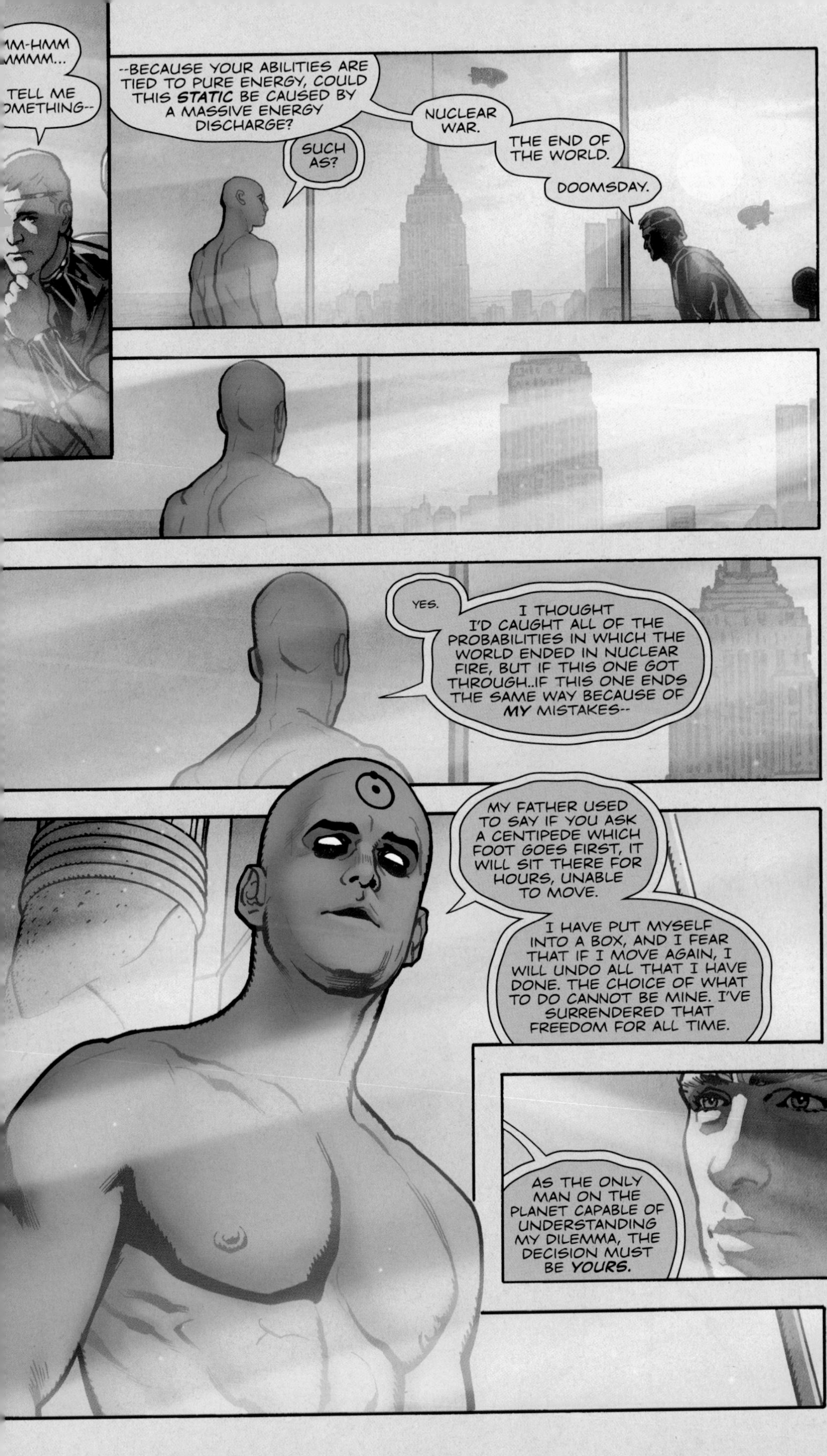
MM-HMM
MMMM...
TELL ME
OMETHING--
--BECAUSE YOUR ABILITIES ARE TIED TO PURE ENERGY, COULD THIS STATIC BE CAUSED BY A MASSIVE ENERGY DISCHARGE?
SUCH AS?
NUCLEAR WAR.
THE END OF THE WORLD.
DOOMSDAY.
YES.
I THOUGHT I'D CAUGHT ALL OF THE PROBABILITIES IN WHICH THE WORLD ENDED IN NUCLEAR FIRE, BUT IF THIS ONE GOT THROUGH..IF THIS ONE ENDS THE SAME WAY BECAUSE OF MY MISTAKES--
MY FATHER USED TO SAY IF YOU ASK A CENTIPEDE WHICH FOOT GOES FIRST, IT WILL SIT THERE FOR HOURS, UNABLE TO MOVE.
I HAVE PUT MYSELF INTO A BOX, AND I FEAR THAT IF I MOVE AGAIN, I WILL UNDO ALL THAT I HAVE DONE. THE CHOICE OF WHAT TO DO CANNOT BE MINE. I'VE SURRENDERED THAT FREEDOM FOR ALL TIME.
AS THE ONLY MAN ON THE PLANET CAPABLE OF UNDERSTANDING MY DILEMMA, THE DECISION MUST BE YOURS.

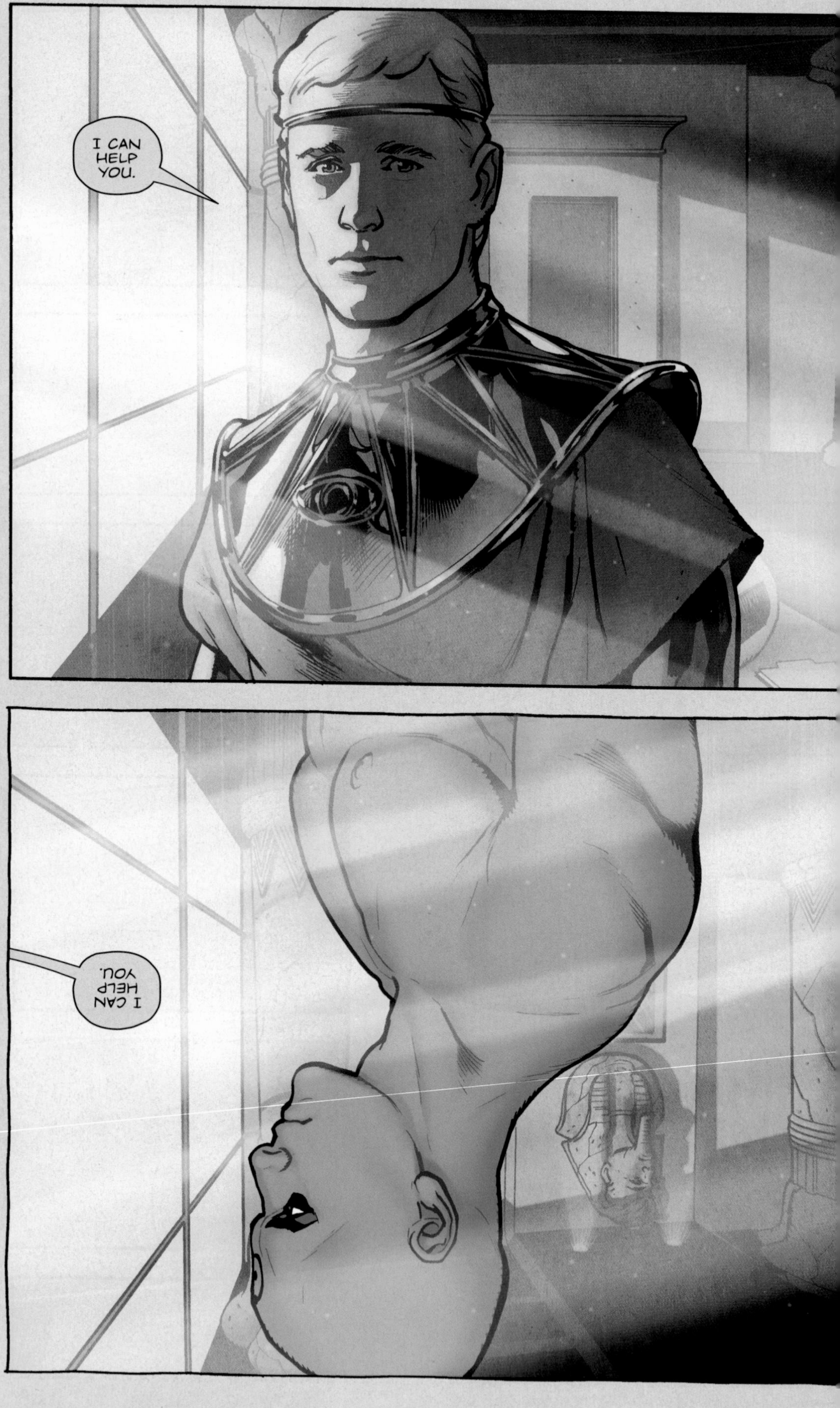

I CAN HELP YOU.
I CAN HELP YOU.

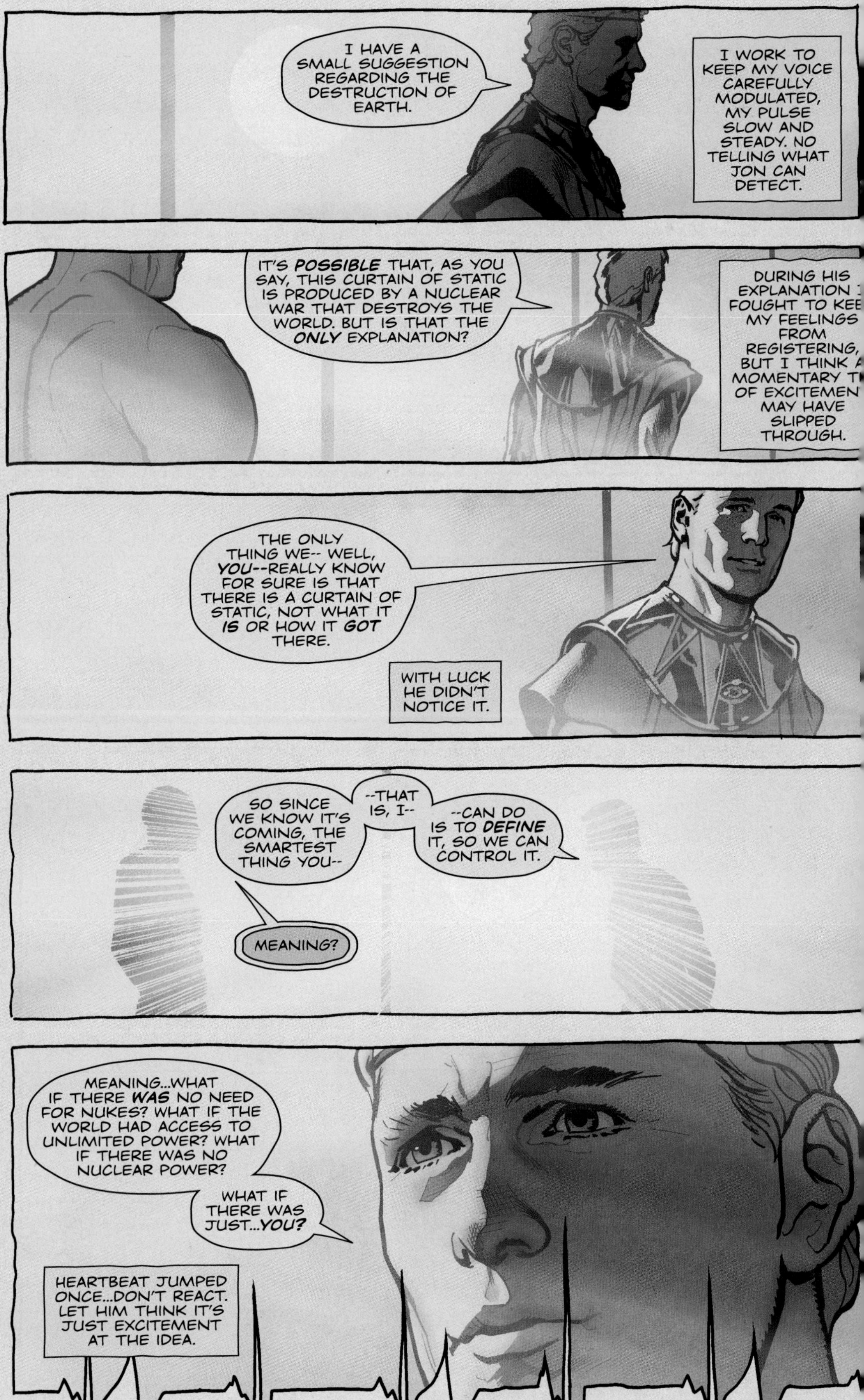
I WORK TO KEEP MY VOICE CAREFULLY MODULATED, MY PULSE SLOW AND STEADY. NO TELLING WHAT JON CAN DETECT.
I HAVE A SMALL SUGGESTION REGARDING THE DESTRUCTION OF EARTH.
IT'S **POSSIBLE** THAT, AS YOU SAY, THIS CURTAIN OF STATIC IS PRODUCED BY A NUCLEAR WAR THAT DESTROYS THE WORLD. BUT IS THAT THE **ONLY** EXPLANATION?
DURING HIS EXPLANATION FOUGHT TO KEE MY FEELINGS FROM REGISTERING, BUT I THINK MOMENTARY OF EXCITEMEN MAY HAVE SLIPPED THROUGH.
THE ONLY THING WE-- WELL, **YOU**--REALLY KNOW FOR SURE IS THAT THERE IS A CURTAIN OF STATIC, NOT WHAT IT **IS** OR HOW IT **GOT** THERE.
WITH LUCK HE DIDN'T NOTICE IT.
SO SINCE WE KNOW IT'S COMING, THE SMARTEST THING YOU--
--THAT IS, I--
--CAN DO IS TO **DEFINE** IT, SO WE CAN CONTROL IT.
MEANING?
MEANING...WHAT IF THERE **WAS** NO NEED FOR NUKES? WHAT IF THE WORLD HAD ACCESS TO UNLIMITED POWER? WHAT IF THERE WAS NO NUCLEAR POWER?
WHAT IF THERE WAS JUST...**YOU?**
HEARTBEAT JUMPED ONCE...DON'T REACT. LET HIM THINK IT'S JUST EXCITEMENT AT THE IDEA.

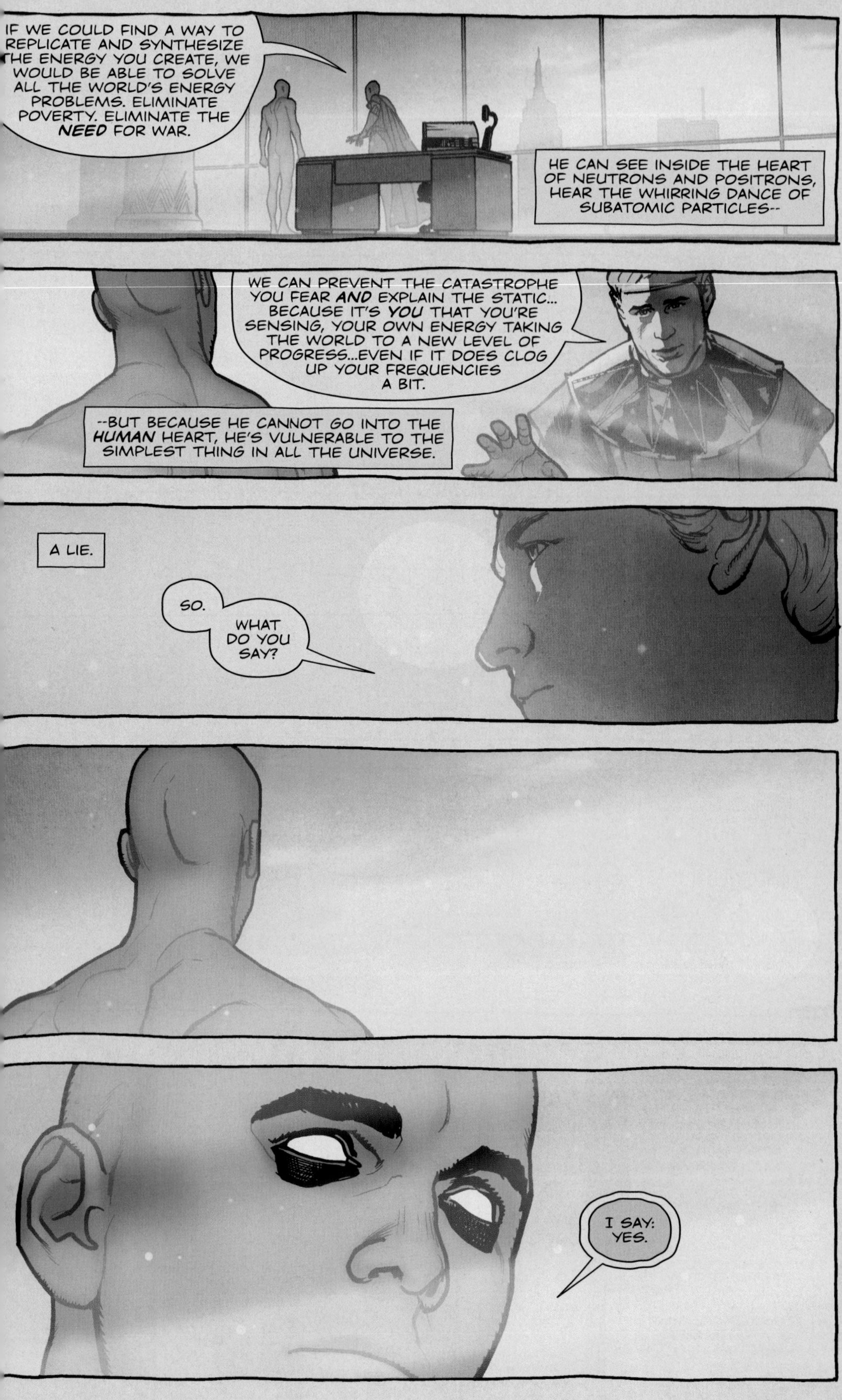
IF WE COULD FIND A WAY TO REPLICATE AND SYNTHESIZE THE ENERGY YOU CREATE, WE WOULD BE ABLE TO SOLVE ALL THE WORLD'S ENERGY PROBLEMS. ELIMINATE POVERTY. ELIMINATE THE NEED FOR WAR.
HE CAN SEE INSIDE THE HEART OF NEUTRONS AND POSITRONS, HEAR THE WHIRRING DANCE OF SUBATOMIC PARTICLES--
WE CAN PREVENT THE CATASTROPHE YOU FEAR AND EXPLAIN THE STATIC... BECAUSE IT'S YOU THAT YOU'RE SENSING, YOUR OWN ENERGY TAKING THE WORLD TO A NEW LEVEL OF PROGRESS...EVEN IF IT DOES CLOG UP YOUR FREQUENCIES A BIT.
--BUT BECAUSE HE CANNOT GO INTO THE HUMAN HEART, HE'S VULNERABLE TO THE SIMPLEST THING IN ALL THE UNIVERSE.
A LIE.
SO.
WHAT DO YOU SAY?
I SAY: YES.

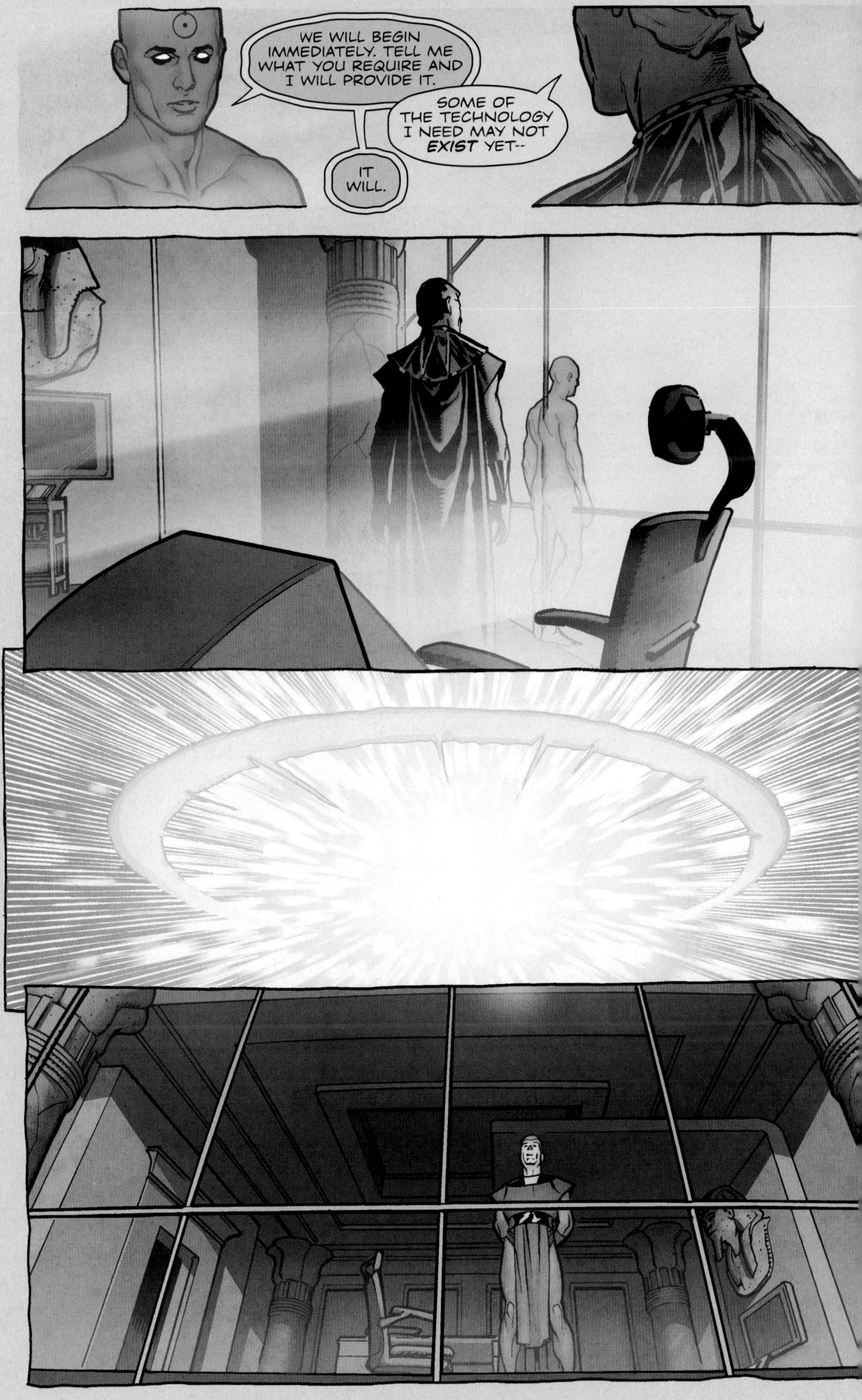
WE WILL BEGIN IMMEDIATELY. TELL ME WHAT YOU REQUIRE AND I WILL PROVIDE IT.
SOME OF THE TECHNOLOGY I NEED MAY NOT **EXIST** YET--
IT WILL.

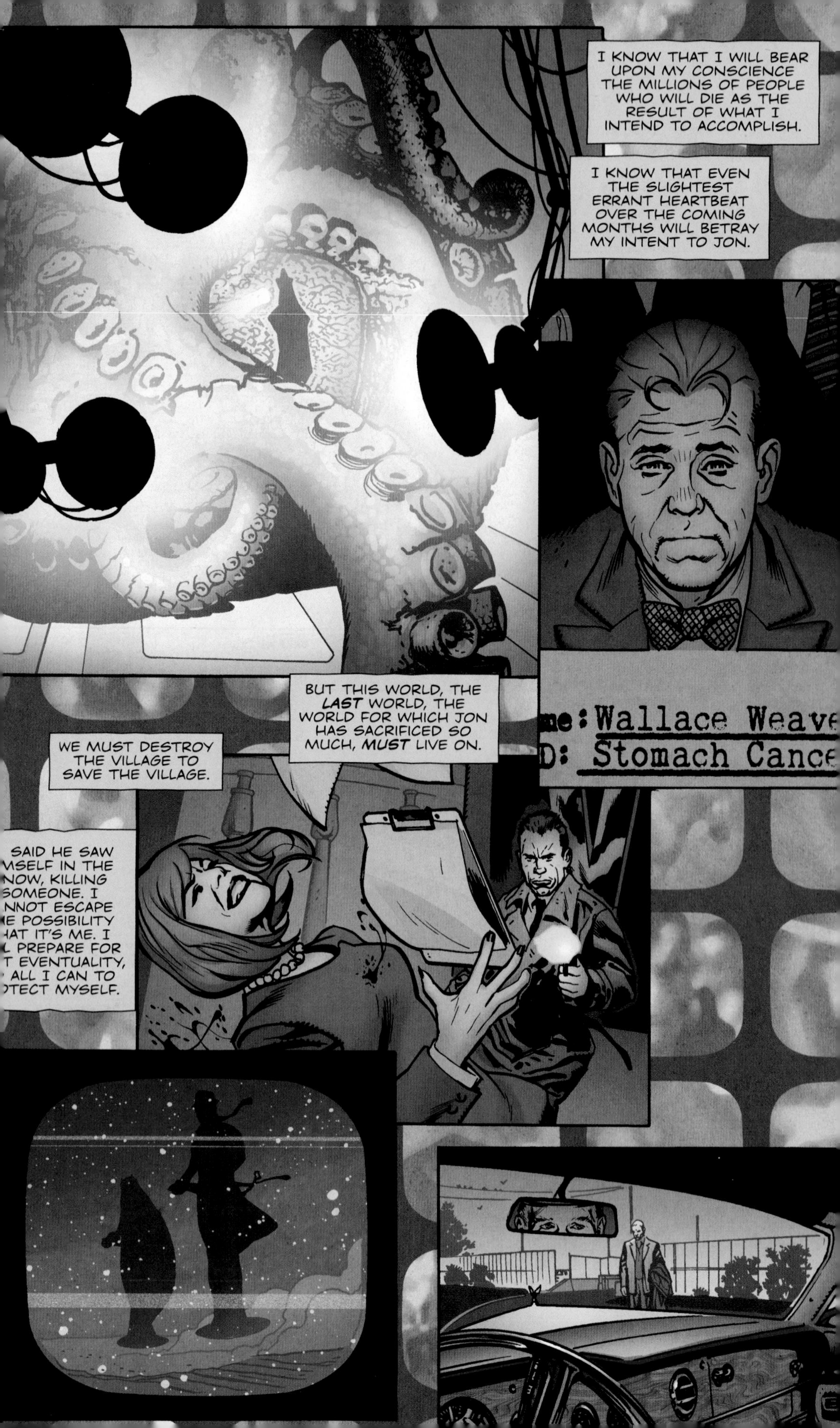
I KNOW THAT I WILL BEAR UPON MY CONSCIENCE THE MILLIONS OF PEOPLE WHO WILL DIE AS THE RESULT OF WHAT I INTEND TO ACCOMPLISH.
I KNOW THAT EVEN THE SLIGHTEST ERRANT HEARTBEAT OVER THE COMING MONTHS WILL BETRAY MY INTENT TO JON.
me:Wallace Weave
D: Stomach Cance
BUT THIS WORLD, THE ***LAST*** WORLD, THE WORLD FOR WHICH JON HAS SACRIFICED SO MUCH, ***MUST*** LIVE ON.
WE MUST DESTROY THE VILLAGE TO SAVE THE VILLAGE.
SAID HE SAW MSELF IN THE NOW, KILLING SOMEONE. I NNOT ESCAPE E POSSIBILITY HAT IT'S ME. I L PREPARE FOR T EVENTUALITY, ALL I CAN TO OTECT MYSELF.

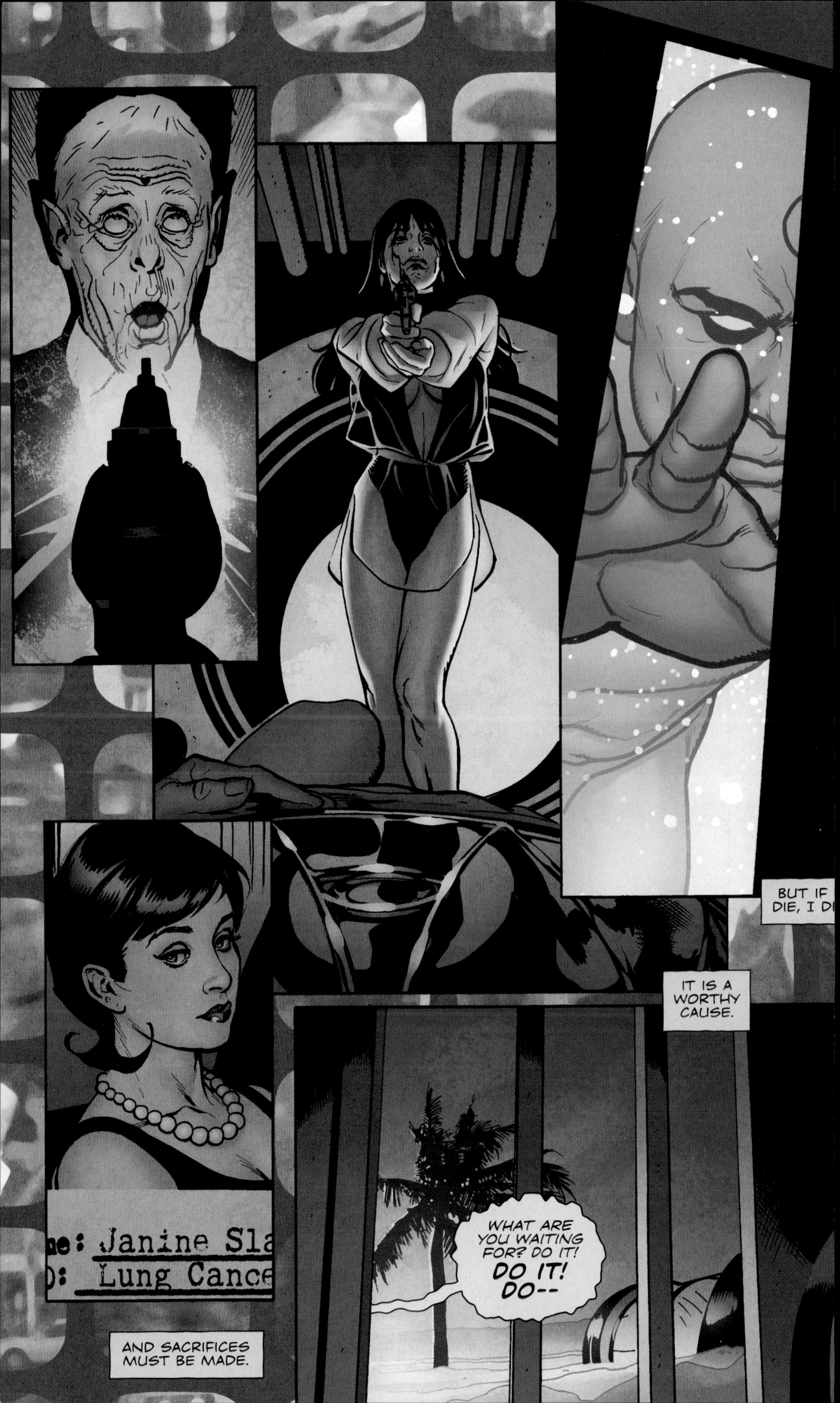
BUT IF
DIE, I D
IT IS A WORTHY CAUSE.
ne: Janine Sla
D: Lung Cance
WHAT ARE YOU WAITING FOR? DO IT! DO IT! DO--
AND SACRIFICES MUST BE MADE.

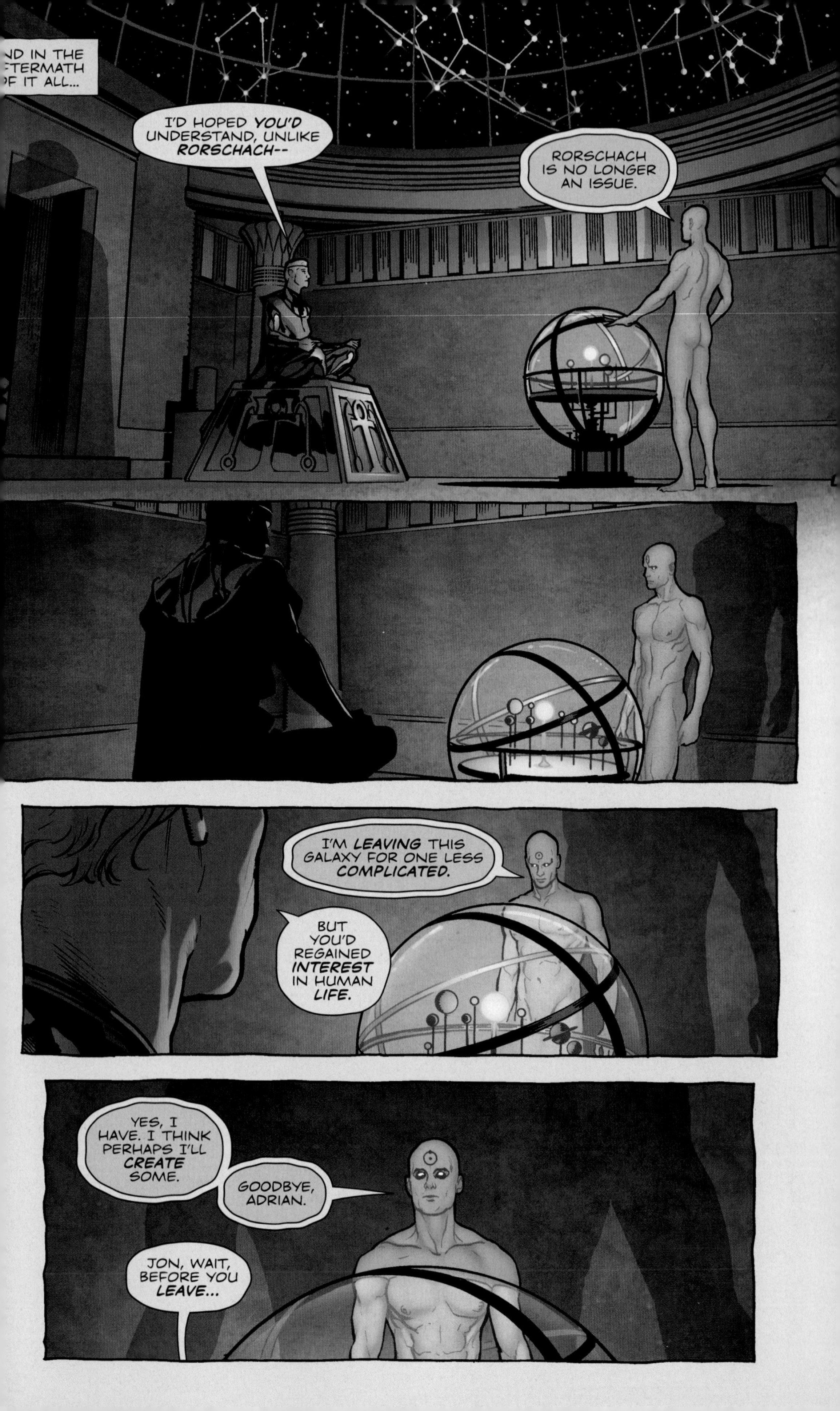
ND IN THE
TERMATH
F IT ALL...
I'D HOPED ***YOU'D*** UNDERSTAND, UNLIKE ***RORSCHACH--***
RORSCHACH IS NO LONGER AN ISSUE.
I'M ***LEAVING*** THIS GALAXY FOR ONE LESS ***COMPLICATED.***
BUT YOU'D REGAINED ***INTEREST*** IN HUMAN ***LIFE.***
YES, I HAVE. I THINK PERHAPS I'LL ***CREATE*** SOME.
GOODBYE, ADRIAN.
JON, WAIT, BEFORE YOU ***LEAVE...***

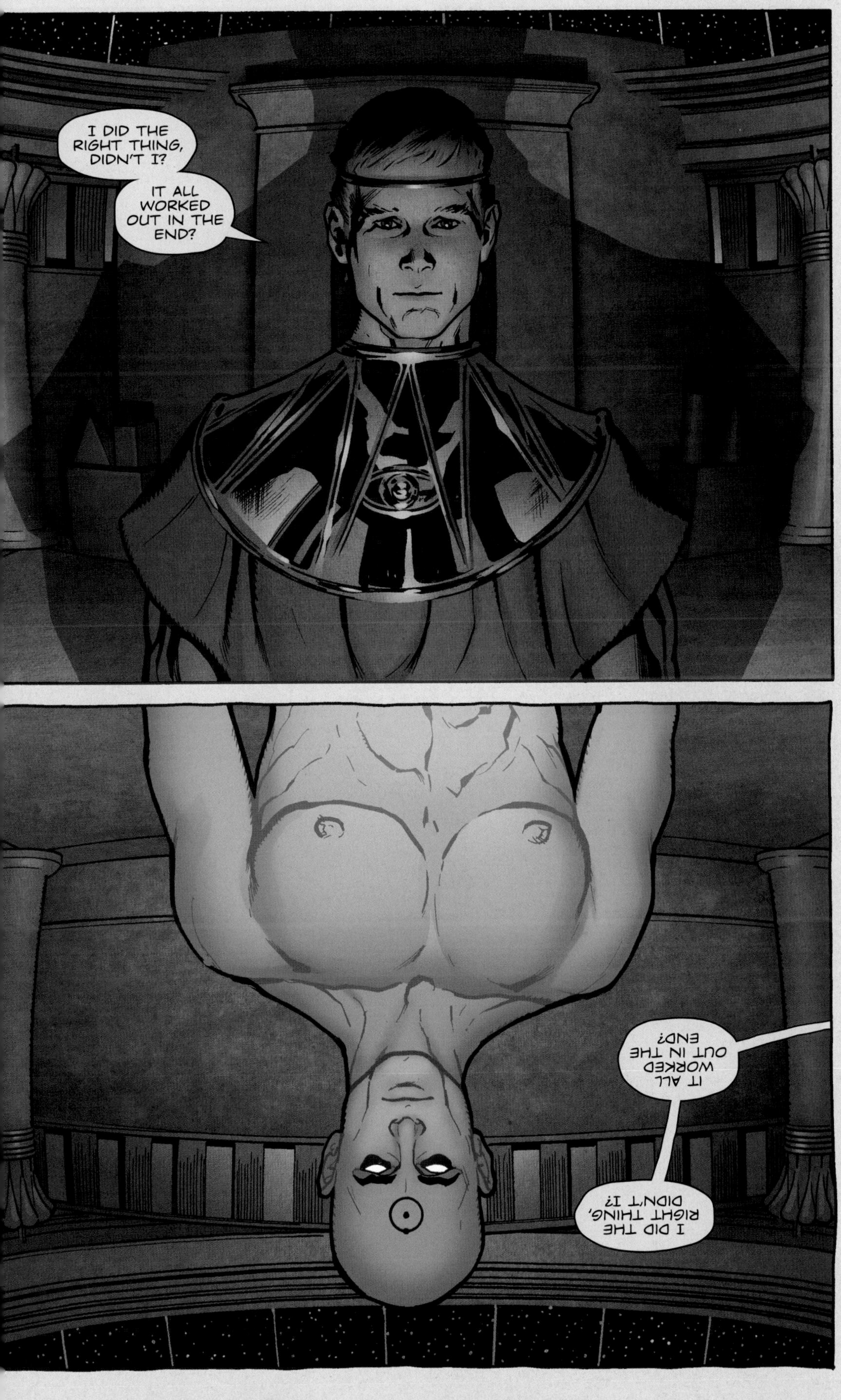
I DID THE RIGHT THING, DIDN'T I?
IT ALL WORKED OUT IN THE END?
I DID THE RIGHT THING, DIDN'T I?
IT ALL WORKED OUT IN THE END?

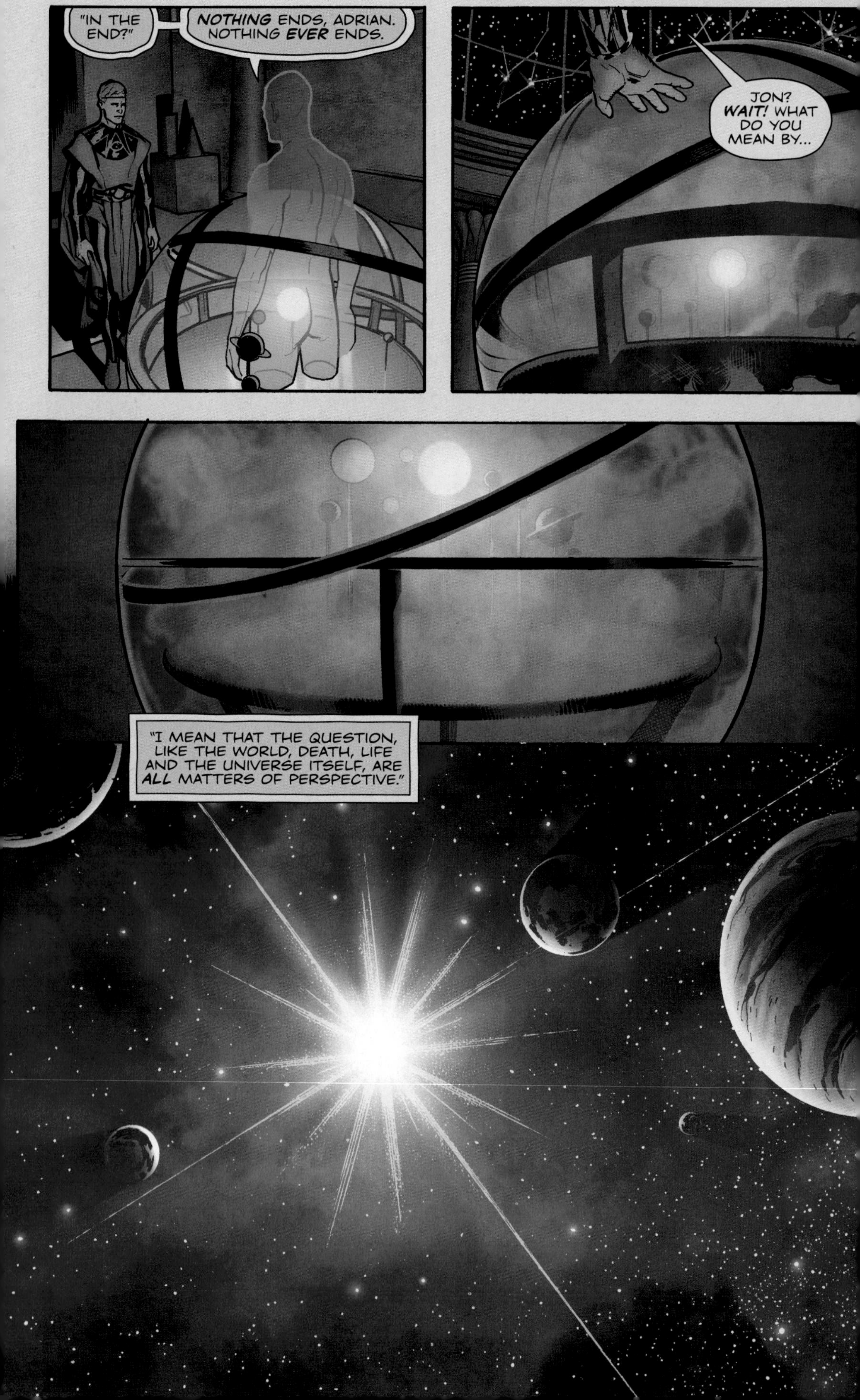
"IN THE END?"
NOTHING ENDS, ADRIAN. NOTHING EVER ENDS.
JON? WAIT! WHAT DO YOU MEAN BY...
"I MEAN THAT THE QUESTION, LIKE THE WORLD, DEATH, LIFE AND THE UNIVERSE ITSELF, ARE ALL MATTERS OF PERSPECTIVE."

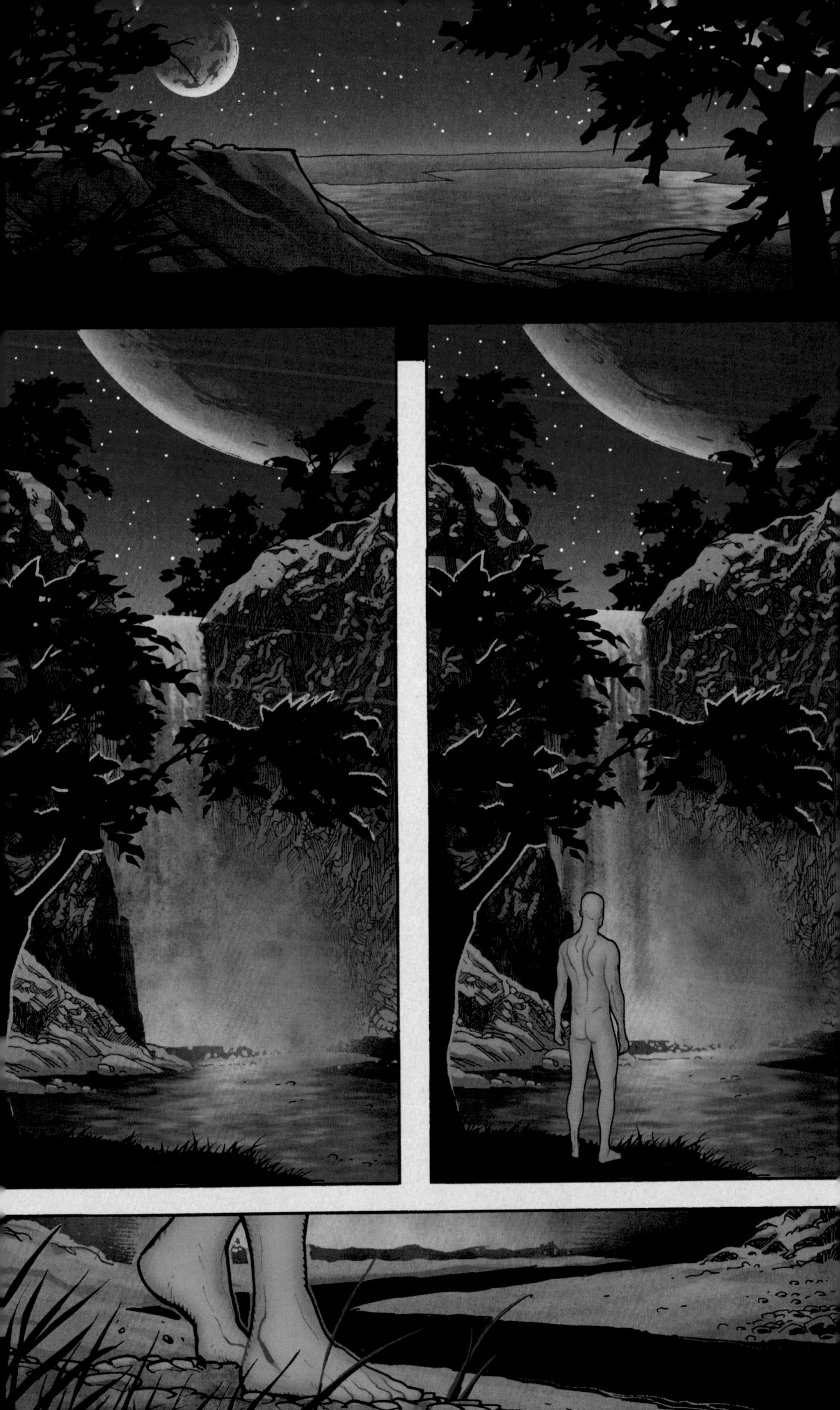

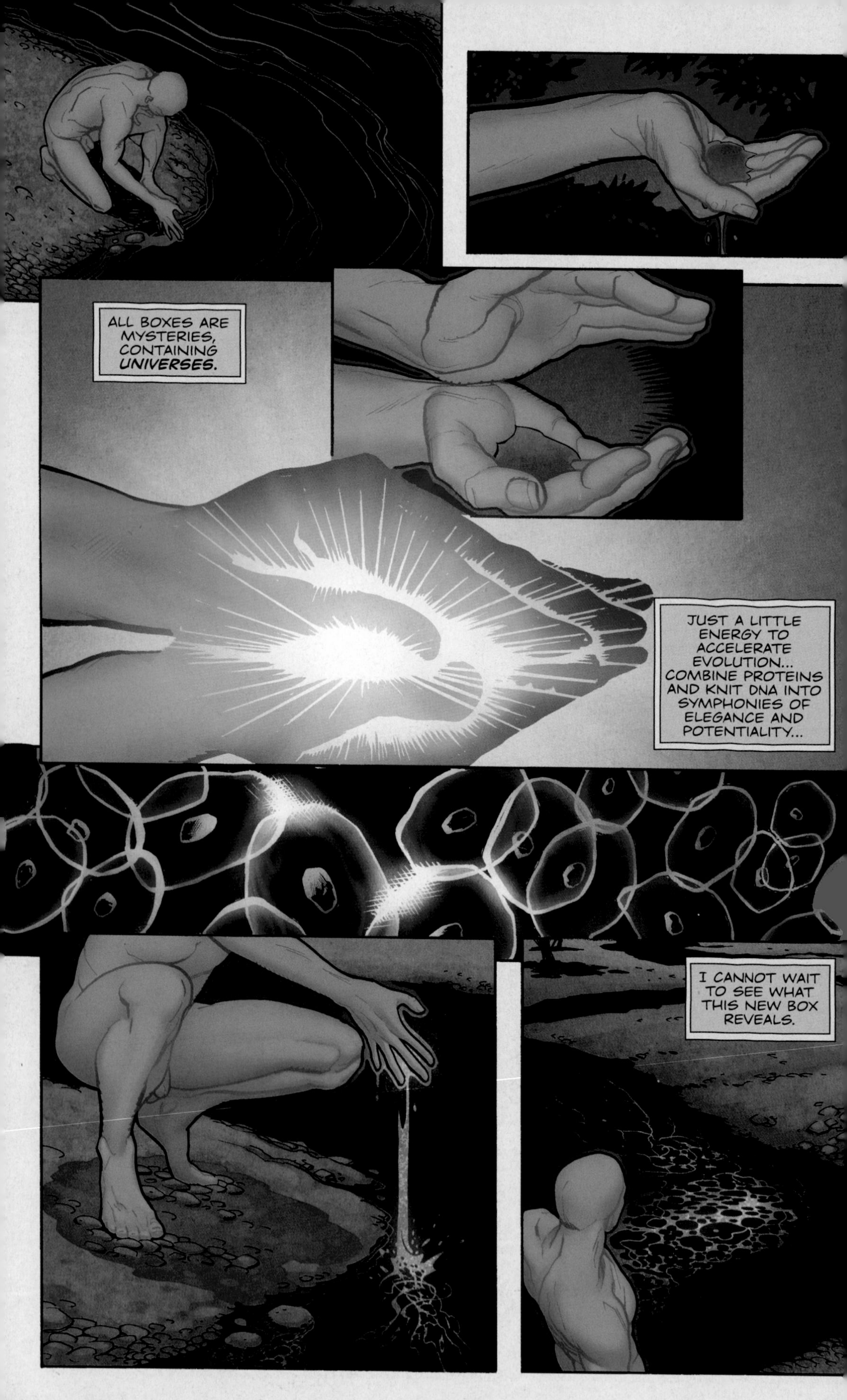
ALL BOXES ARE MYSTERIES, CONTAINING *UNIVERSES.*
JUST A LITTLE ENERGY TO ACCELERATE EVOLUTION... COMBINE PROTEINS AND KNIT DNA INTO SYMPHONIES OF ELEGANCE AND POTENTIALITY...
I CANNOT WAIT TO SEE WHAT THIS NEW BOX REVEALS.

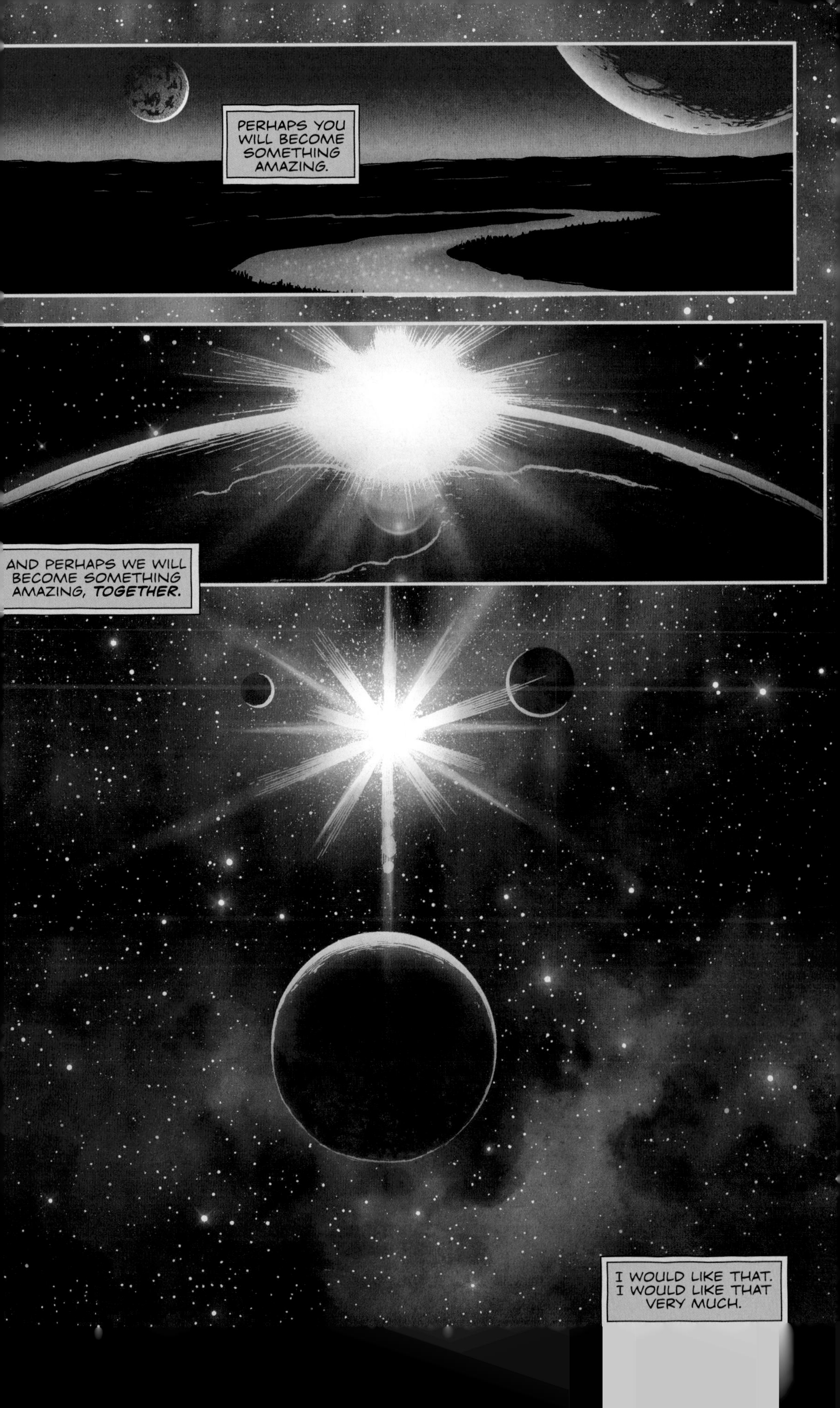
PERHAPS YOU WILL BECOME SOMETHING AMAZING.
AND PERHAPS WE WILL BECOME SOMETHING AMAZING, TOGETHER.
I WOULD LIKE THAT. I WOULD LIKE THAT VERY MUCH.

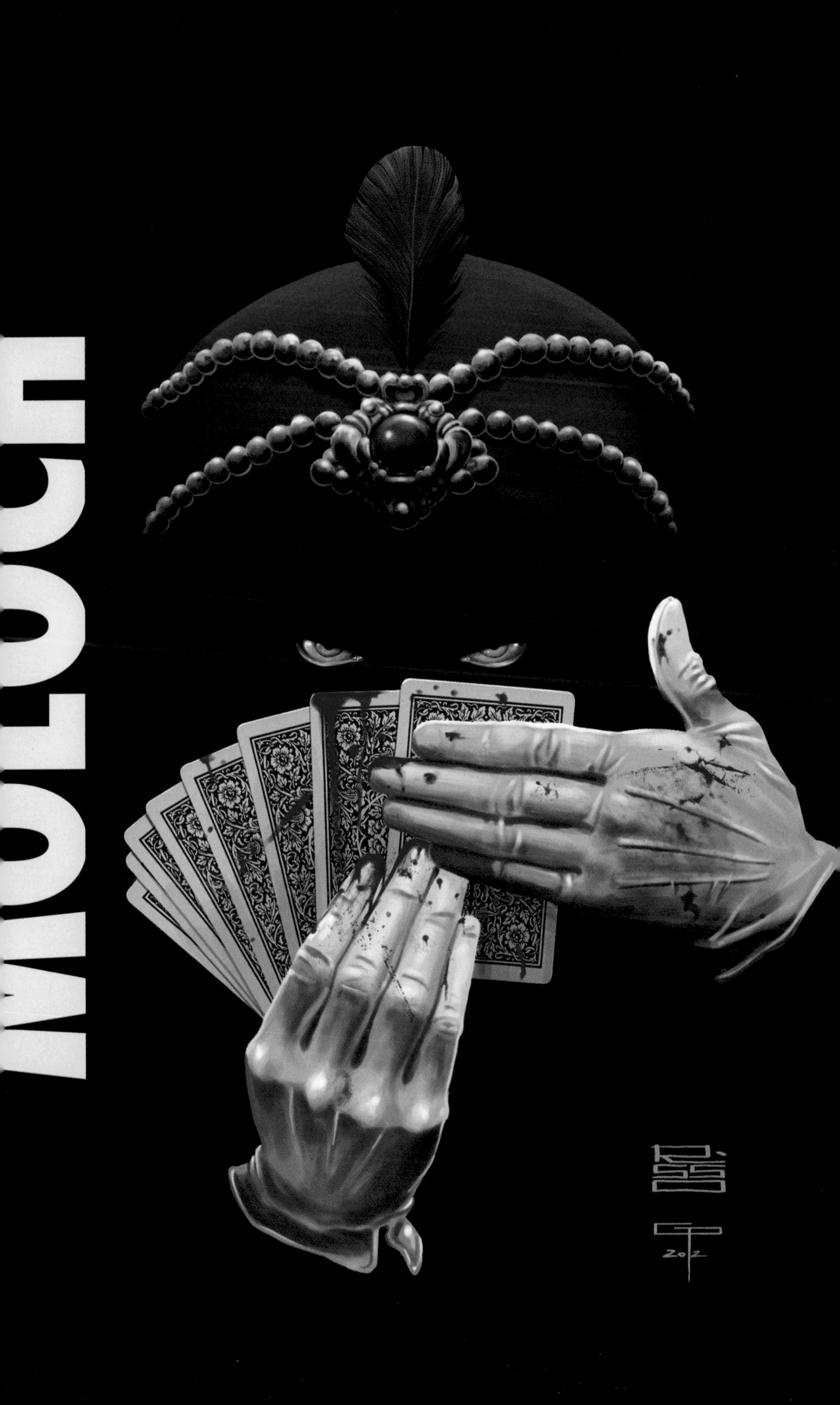
MOLOCH

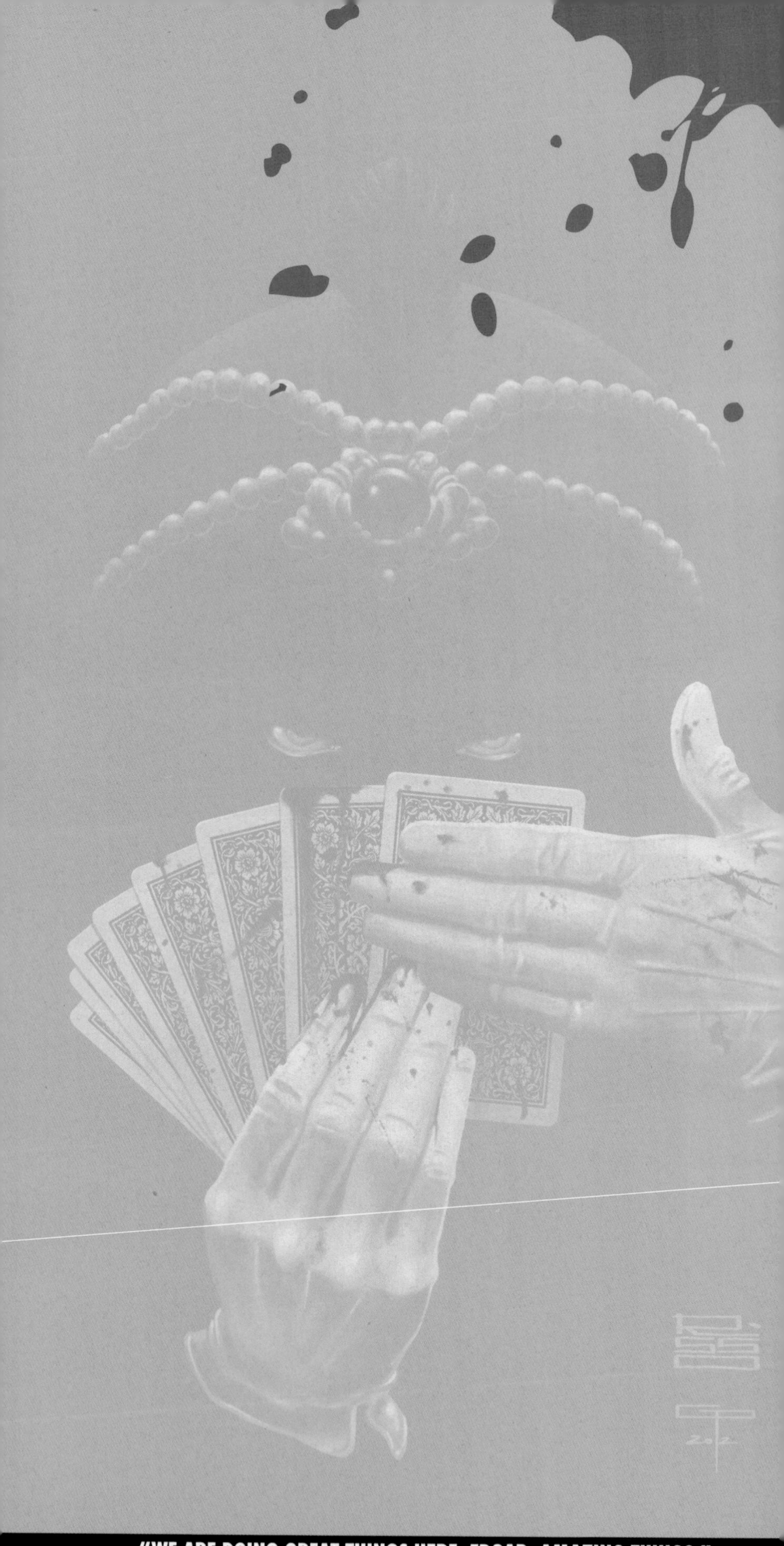

"WE ARE DOING GREAT THINGS HERE, EDGAR. AMAZING THINGS."

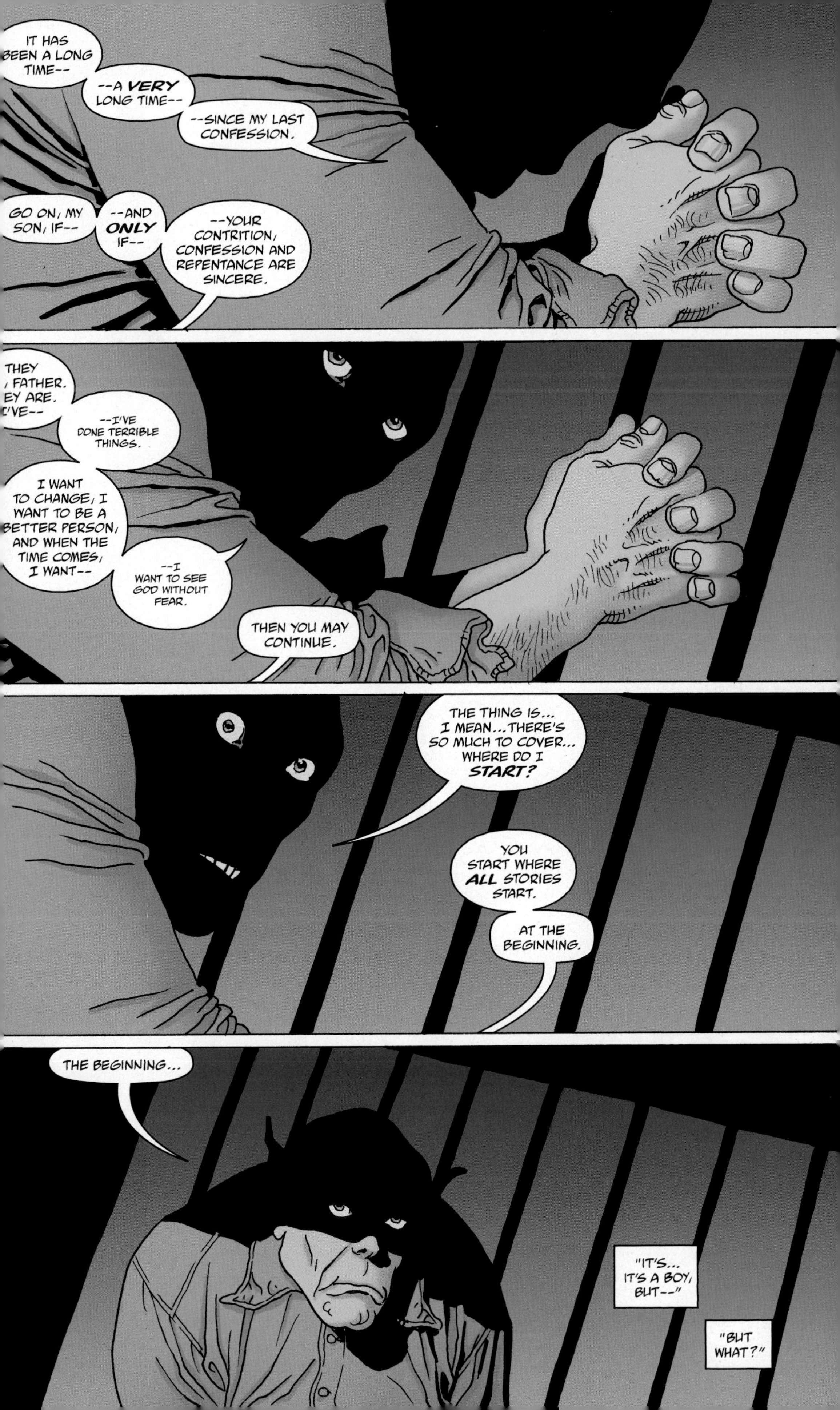

IT HAS BEEN A LONG TIME--
--A VERY LONG TIME--
--SINCE MY LAST CONFESSION.
GO ON, MY SON, IF--
--AND ONLY IF--
--YOUR CONTRITION, CONFESSION AND REPENTANCE ARE SINCERE.
THEY , FATHER. EY ARE. I'VE--
--I'VE DONE TERRIBLE THINGS.
I WANT TO CHANGE, I WANT TO BE A BETTER PERSON, AND WHEN THE TIME COMES, I WANT--
--I WANT TO SEE GOD WITHOUT FEAR.
THEN YOU MAY CONTINUE.
THE THING IS... I MEAN...THERE'S SO MUCH TO COVER... WHERE DO I START?
YOU START WHERE ALL STORIES START.
AT THE BEGINNING.
THE BEGINNING...
"IT'S... IT'S A BOY, BUT--"
"BUT WHAT?"

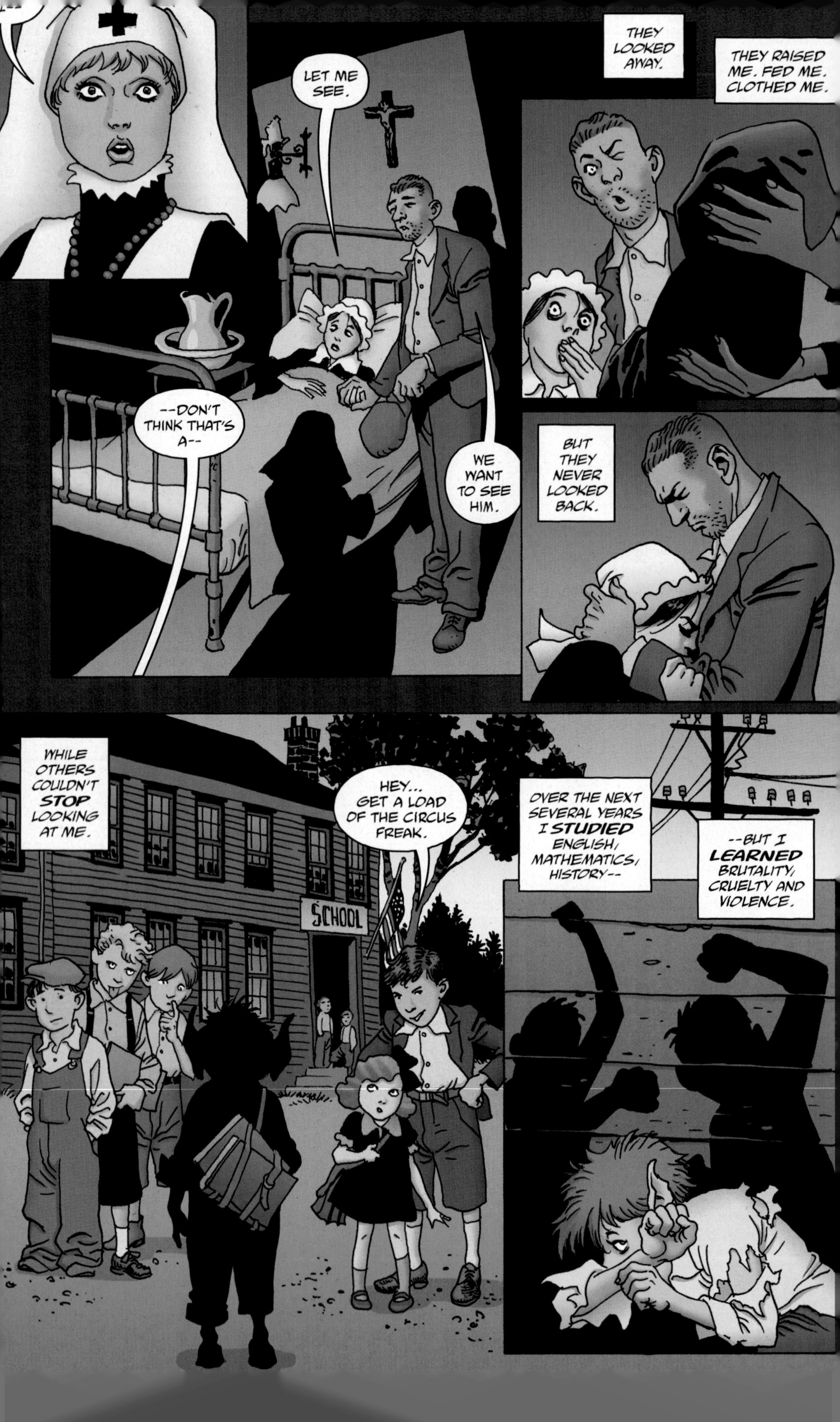

LET ME SEE.
THEY LOOKED AWAY.
THEY RAISED ME. FED ME. CLOTHED ME.
--DON'T THINK THAT'S A--
WE WANT TO SEE HIM.
BUT THEY NEVER LOOKED BACK.
WHILE OTHERS COULDN'T STOP LOOKING AT ME.
HEY... GET A LOAD OF THE CIRCUS FREAK.
SCHOOL
OVER THE NEXT SEVERAL YEARS I STUDIED ENGLISH, MATHEMATICS, HISTORY--
--BUT I LEARNED BRUTALITY, CRUELTY AND VIOLENCE.

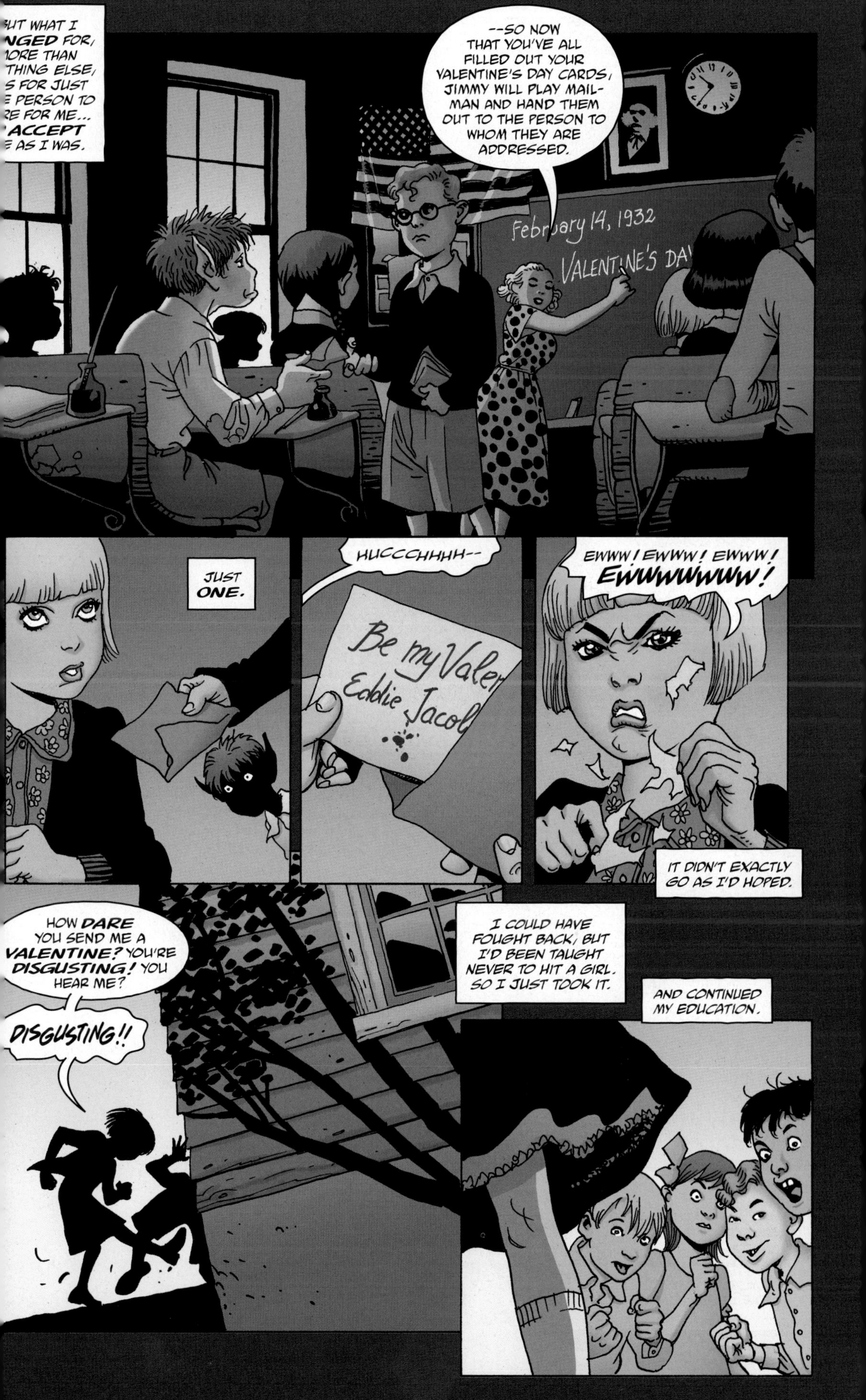

BUT WHAT I NGED FOR, MORE THAN THING ELSE, S FOR JUST E PERSON TO RE FOR ME... ACCEPT E AS I WAS.
--SO NOW THAT YOU'VE ALL FILLED OUT YOUR VALENTINE'S DAY CARDS, JIMMY WILL PLAY MAIL-MAN AND HAND THEM OUT TO THE PERSON TO WHOM THEY ARE ADDRESSED.
February 14, 1932
VALENTINE'S DA
JUST ONE.
HUCCCHHHH--
Be my Valen
Eddie Jacol
EWWW! EWWW! EWWW! EWWWWWW!
IT DIDN'T EXACTLY GO AS I'D HOPED.
HOW DARE YOU SEND ME A VALENTINE? YOU'RE DISGUSTING! YOU HEAR ME?
DISGUSTING!!
I COULD HAVE FOUGHT BACK, BUT I'D BEEN TAUGHT NEVER TO HIT A GIRL. SO I JUST TOOK IT.
AND CONTINUED MY EDUCATION.

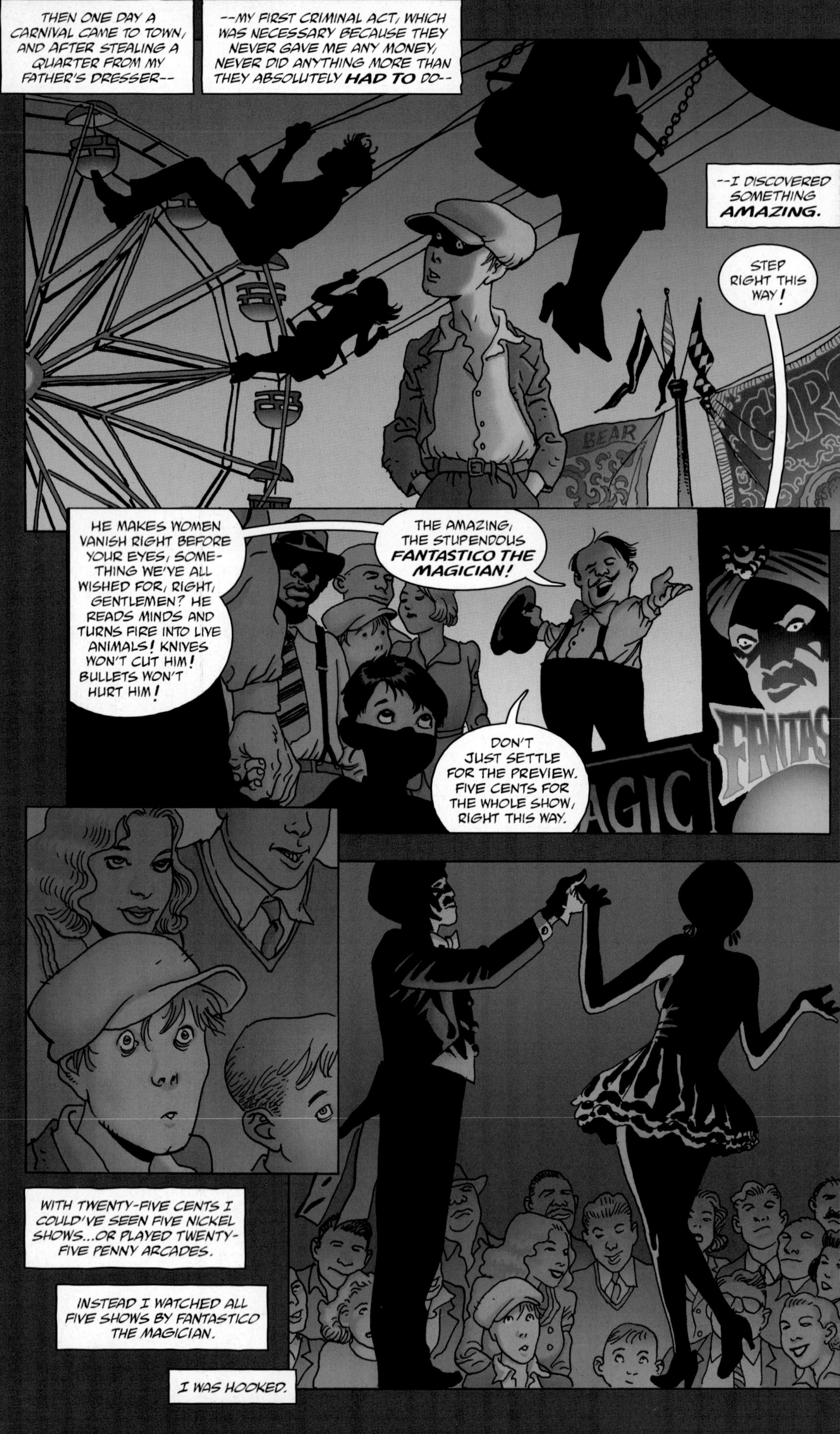
THEN ONE DAY A CARNIVAL CAME TO TOWN, AND AFTER STEALING A QUARTER FROM MY FATHER'S DRESSER--
--MY FIRST CRIMINAL ACT, WHICH WAS NECESSARY BECAUSE THEY NEVER GAVE ME ANY MONEY, NEVER DID ANYTHING MORE THAN THEY ABSOLUTELY **HAD TO** DO--
--I DISCOVERED SOMETHING **AMAZING.**
STEP RIGHT THIS WAY!
BEAR
THE AMAZING, THE STUPENDOUS **FANTASTICO THE MAGICIAN!**
HE MAKES WOMEN VANISH RIGHT BEFORE YOUR EYES, SOMETHING WE'VE ALL WISHED FOR, RIGHT, GENTLEMEN? HE READS MINDS AND TURNS FIRE INTO LIVE ANIMALS! KNIVES WON'T CUT HIM! BULLETS WON'T HURT HIM!
DON'T JUST SETTLE FOR THE PREVIEW. FIVE CENTS FOR THE WHOLE SHOW, RIGHT THIS WAY.
WITH TWENTY-FIVE CENTS I COULD'VE SEEN FIVE NICKEL SHOWS...OR PLAYED TWENTY-FIVE PENNY ARCADES.
INSTEAD I WATCHED ALL FIVE SHOWS BY FANTASTICO THE MAGICIAN.
I WAS HOOKED.

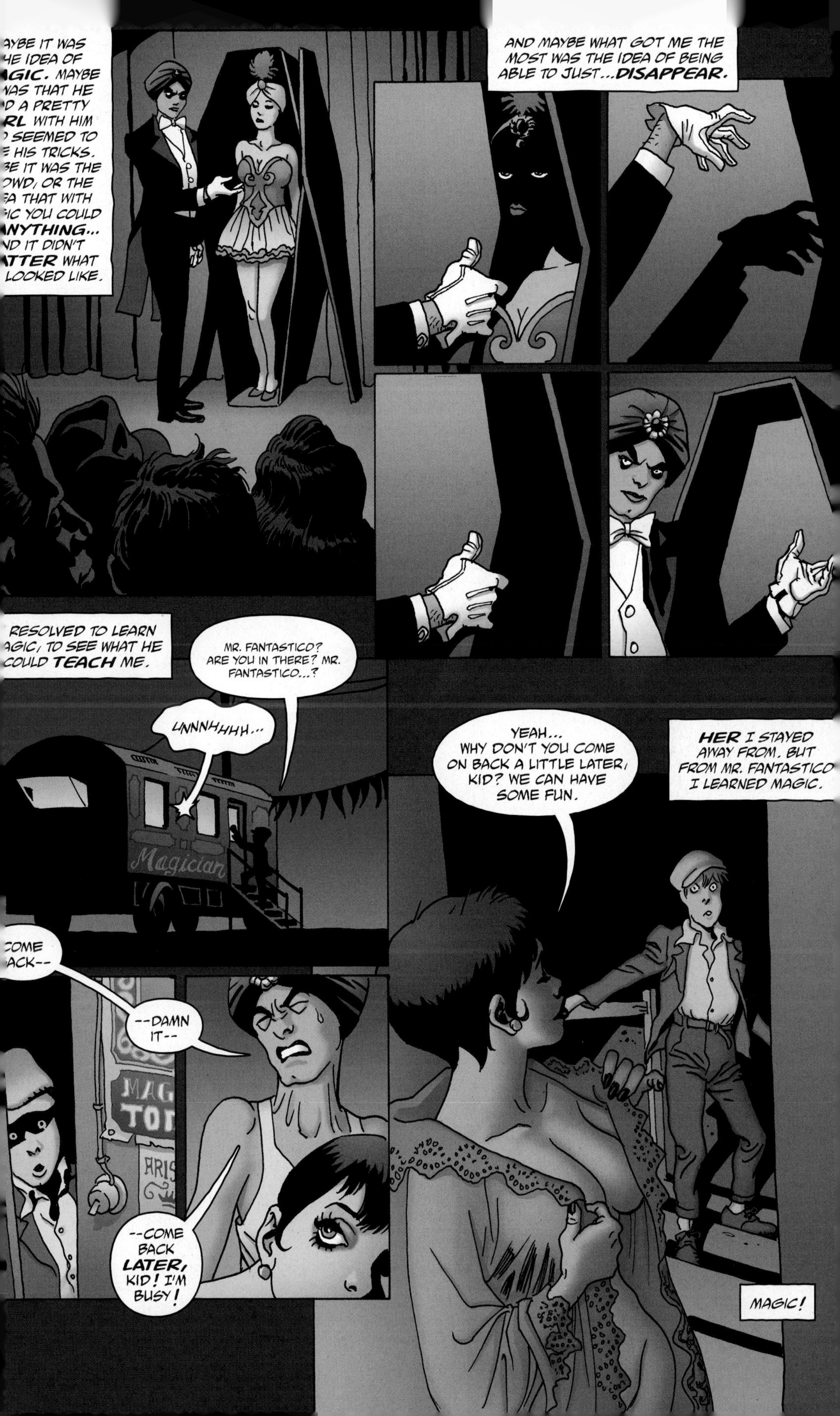

AYBE IT WAS HE IDEA OF AGIC. MAYBE WAS THAT HE D A PRETTY RL WITH HIM SEEMED TO E HIS TRICKS. BE IT WAS THE OWD, OR THE EA THAT WITH IC YOU COULD ANYTHING... ND IT DIDN'T ATTER WHAT LOOKED LIKE.
AND MAYBE WHAT GOT ME THE MOST WAS THE IDEA OF BEING ABLE TO JUST...DISAPPEAR.
RESOLVED TO LEARN AGIC, TO SEE WHAT HE COULD TEACH ME.
MR. FANTASTICO? ARE YOU IN THERE? MR. FANTASTICO...?
UNNNHHHH...
Magician
COME ACK--
--DAMN IT--
--COME BACK LATER, KID! I'M BUSY!
MAG TOD
ARIS
YEAH... WHY DON'T YOU COME ON BACK A LITTLE LATER, KID? WE CAN HAVE SOME FUN.
HER I STAYED AWAY FROM. BUT FROM MR. FANTASTICO I LEARNED MAGIC.
MAGIC!

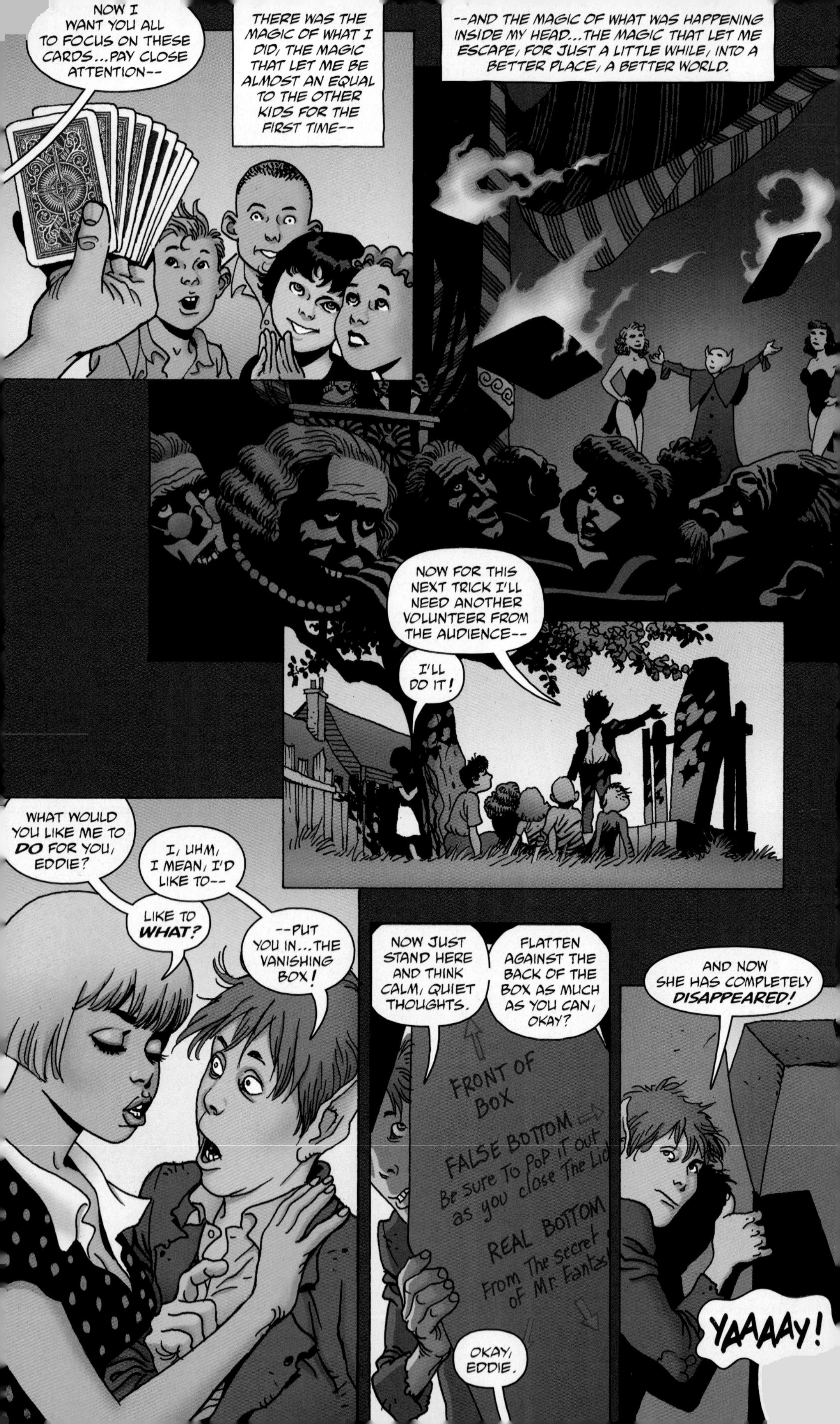
NOW I WANT YOU ALL TO FOCUS ON THESE CARDS...PAY CLOSE ATTENTION--
THERE WAS THE MAGIC OF WHAT I DID, THE MAGIC THAT LET ME BE ALMOST AN EQUAL TO THE OTHER KIDS FOR THE FIRST TIME--
--AND THE MAGIC OF WHAT WAS HAPPENING INSIDE MY HEAD...THE MAGIC THAT LET ME ESCAPE, FOR JUST A LITTLE WHILE, INTO A BETTER PLACE, A BETTER WORLD.
NOW FOR THIS NEXT TRICK I'LL NEED ANOTHER VOLUNTEER FROM THE AUDIENCE--
I'LL DO IT!
WHAT WOULD YOU LIKE ME TO DO FOR YOU, EDDIE?
I, UHM, I MEAN, I'D LIKE TO--
LIKE TO WHAT?
--PUT YOU IN...THE VANISHING BOX!
NOW JUST STAND HERE AND THINK CALM, QUIET THOUGHTS.
FLATTEN AGAINST THE BACK OF THE BOX AS MUCH AS YOU CAN, OKAY?
FRONT OF BOX
FALSE BOTTOM
Be sure To PoP it out as you close The Lid
REAL BOTTOM
From The Secret of Mr. Fantas!
OKAY, EDDIE.
AND NOW SHE HAS COMPLETELY DISAPPEARED!
YAAAAY!

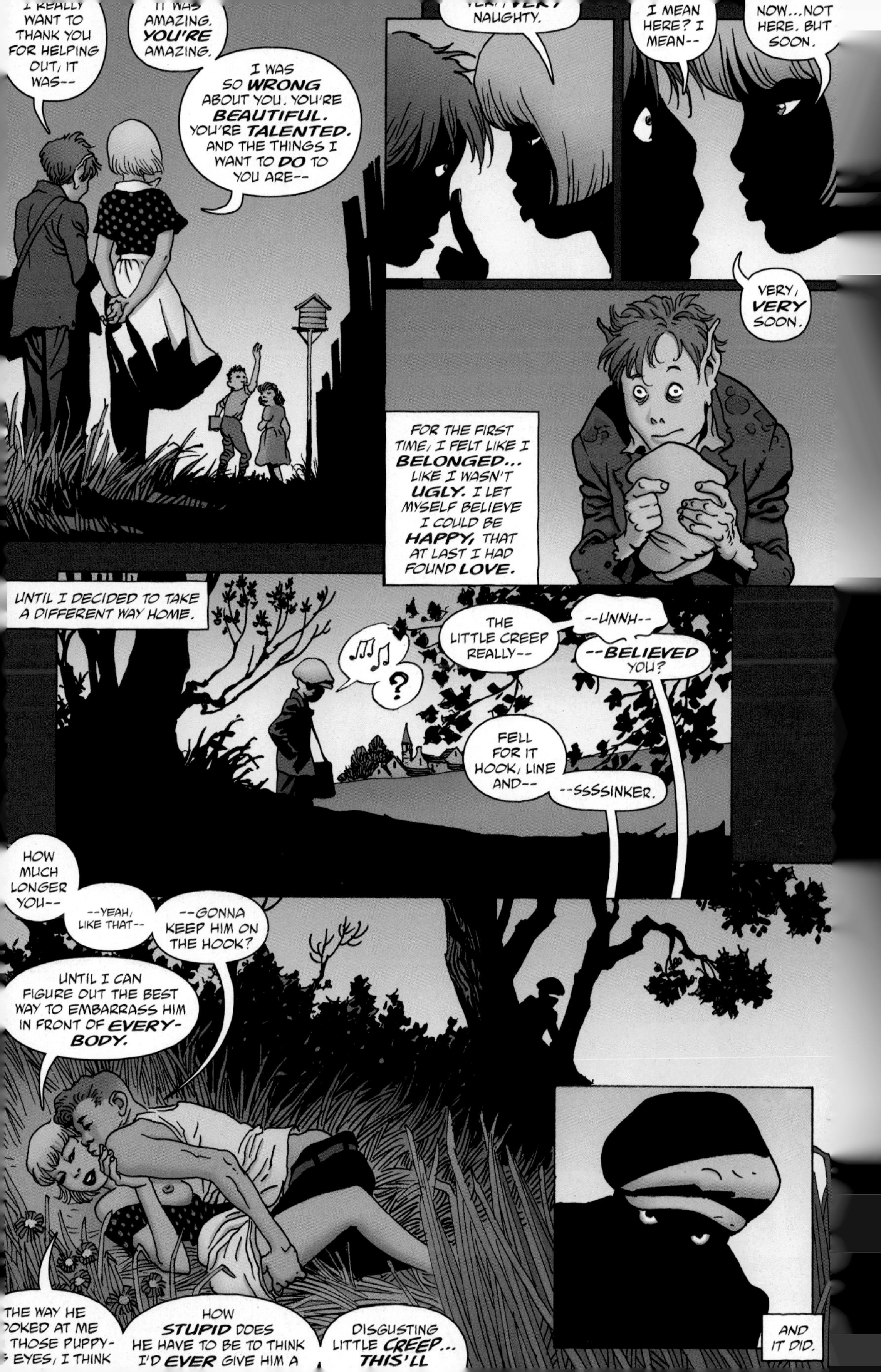
I REALLY WANT TO THANK YOU FOR HELPING OUT, IT WAS--
IT WAS AMAZING. YOU'RE AMAZING.
I WAS SO WRONG ABOUT YOU. YOU'RE BEAUTIFUL. YOU'RE TALENTED. AND THE THINGS I WANT TO DO TO YOU ARE--
NAUGHTY.
I MEAN HERE? I MEAN--
NOW...NOT HERE. BUT SOON.
VERY, VERY SOON.
FOR THE FIRST TIME, I FELT LIKE I BELONGED... LIKE I WASN'T UGLY. I LET MYSELF BELIEVE I COULD BE HAPPY, THAT AT LAST I HAD FOUND LOVE.
UNTIL I DECIDED TO TAKE A DIFFERENT WAY HOME.
?
THE LITTLE CREEP REALLY--
--UNNH--
--BELIEVED YOU?
FELL FOR IT HOOK, LINE AND--
--SSSSINKER.
HOW MUCH LONGER YOU--
--YEAH, LIKE THAT--
--GONNA KEEP HIM ON THE HOOK?
UNTIL I CAN FIGURE OUT THE BEST WAY TO EMBARRASS HIM IN FRONT OF EVERY-BODY.
THE WAY HE OOKED AT ME THOSE PUPPY- EYES, I THINK
HOW STUPID DOES HE HAVE TO BE TO THINK I'D EVER GIVE HIM A
DISGUSTING LITTLE CREEP... THIS'LL
AND IT DID.

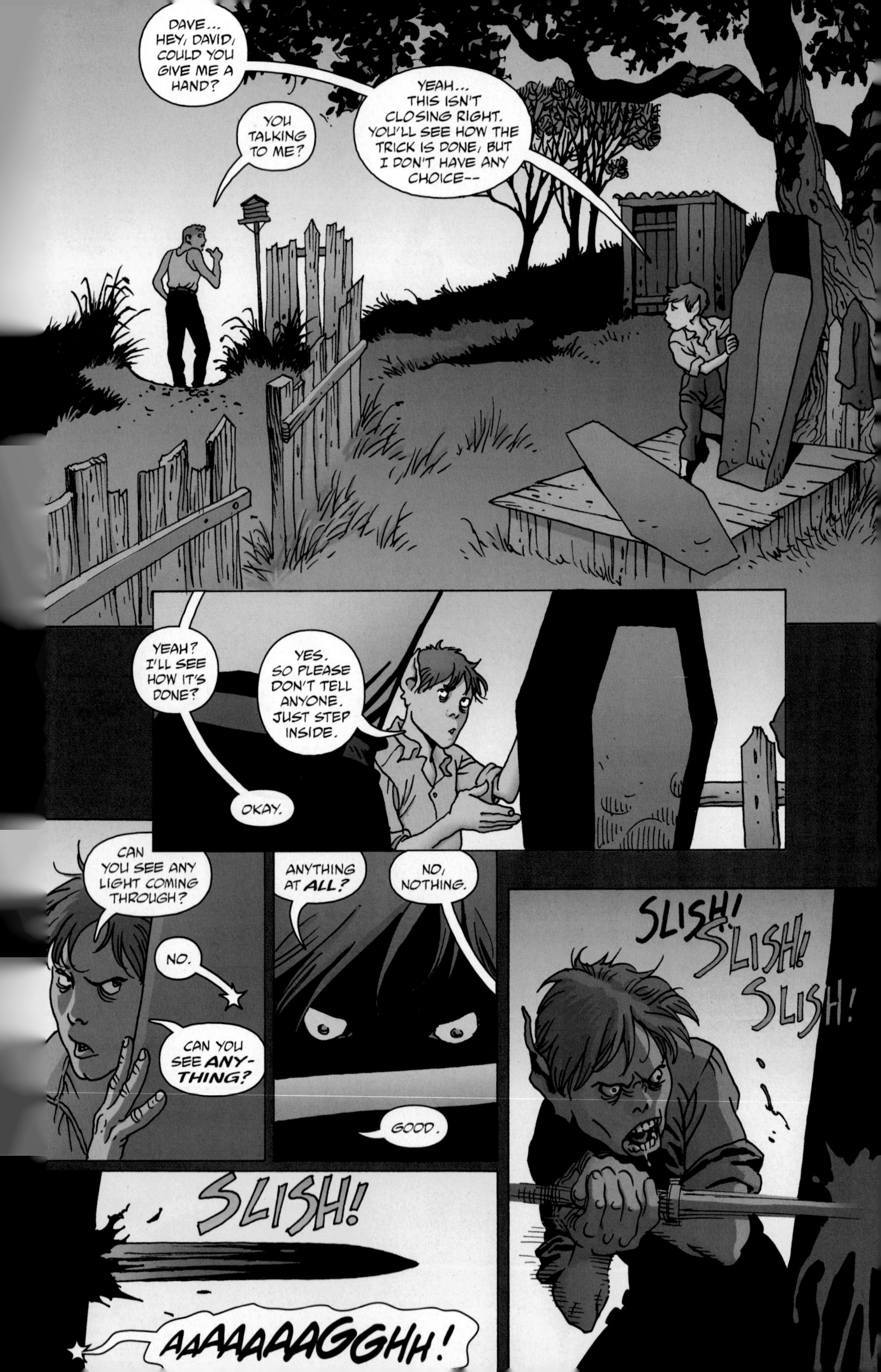
DAVE... HEY, DAVID, COULD YOU GIVE ME A HAND?
YOU TALKING TO ME?
YEAH... THIS ISN'T CLOSING RIGHT. YOU'LL SEE HOW THE TRICK IS DONE, BUT I DON'T HAVE ANY CHOICE--
YEAH? I'LL SEE HOW IT'S DONE?
YES. SO PLEASE DON'T TELL ANYONE. JUST STEP INSIDE.
OKAY.
CAN YOU SEE ANY LIGHT COMING THROUGH?
NO.
CAN YOU SEE ANYTHING?
ANYTHING AT ALL?
NO, NOTHING.
GOOD.
SLISH! SLISH! SLISH!
SLISH!
AAAAAAAGGHH!

MARIE... TIME TO GET UP....

JUST FIVE MORE MINUTES, MOM.

HAD THE WEIRDEST DREAMS...SO HARD TO WAKE UP--

WHAT WAS THAT, MARIE?

I--

--HUUUHHRRR!

EEEEEEEEEEEEEEEEEEEEEEEEEEEEEEEEEE

FWEEEEEEEEEEEEEE

I HEARD, THROUGH THE GRAPEVINE, THAT THE INCIDENT *UNHINGED* HER...AND SHE SPENT THE NEXT TEN *YEARS* IN AN *ASYLUM*.

I GUESS IT STRAIGHTENED OUT *BOTH* OF US.

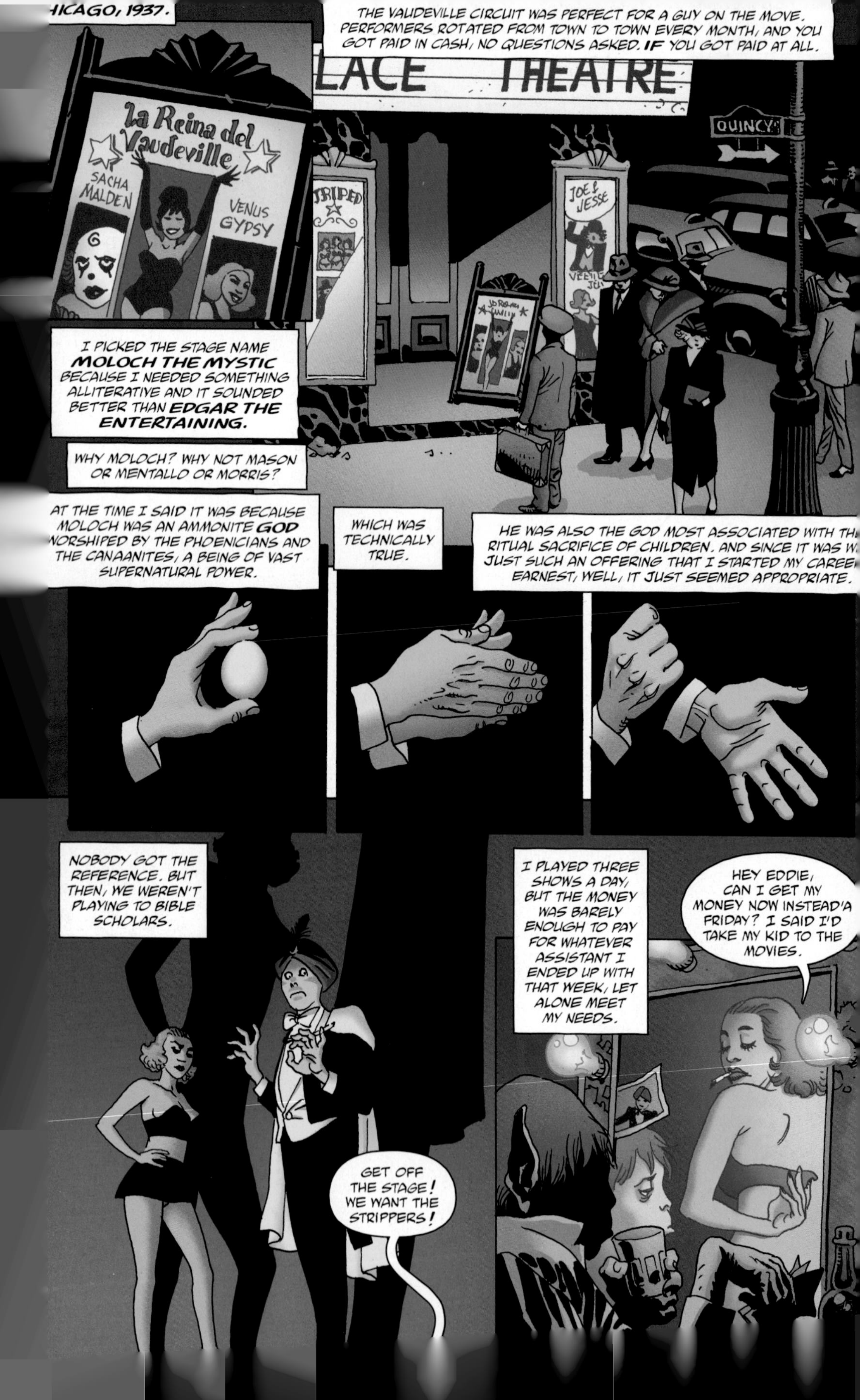

HICAGO, 1937.
THE VAUDEVILLE CIRCUIT WAS PERFECT FOR A GUY ON THE MOVE. PERFORMERS ROTATED FROM TOWN TO TOWN EVERY MONTH, AND YOU GOT PAID IN CASH, NO QUESTIONS ASKED. IF YOU GOT PAID AT ALL.
LACE THEATRE
La Reina del Vaudeville
SACHA MALDEN
VENUS GYPSY
QUINCY
STRIPED
JOE & JESSE
I PICKED THE STAGE NAME MOLOCH THE MYSTIC BECAUSE I NEEDED SOMETHING ALLITERATIVE AND IT SOUNDED BETTER THAN EDGAR THE ENTERTAINING.
WHY MOLOCH? WHY NOT MASON OR MENTALLO OR MORRIS?
AT THE TIME I SAID IT WAS BECAUSE MOLOCH WAS AN AMMONITE GOD WORSHIPED BY THE PHOENICIANS AND THE CANAANITES, A BEING OF VAST SUPERNATURAL POWER.
WHICH WAS TECHNICALLY TRUE.
HE WAS ALSO THE GOD MOST ASSOCIATED WITH THE RITUAL SACRIFICE OF CHILDREN. AND SINCE IT WAS W JUST SUCH AN OFFERING THAT I STARTED MY CAREE EARNEST, WELL, IT JUST SEEMED APPROPRIATE.
NOBODY GOT THE REFERENCE. BUT THEN, WE WEREN'T PLAYING TO BIBLE SCHOLARS.
GET OFF THE STAGE! WE WANT THE STRIPPERS!
I PLAYED THREE SHOWS A DAY, BUT THE MONEY WAS BARELY ENOUGH TO PAY FOR WHATEVER ASSISTANT I ENDED UP WITH THAT WEEK, LET ALONE MEET MY NEEDS.
HEY EDDIE, CAN I GET MY MONEY NOW INSTEAD'A FRIDAY? I SAID I'D TAKE MY KID TO THE MOVIES.

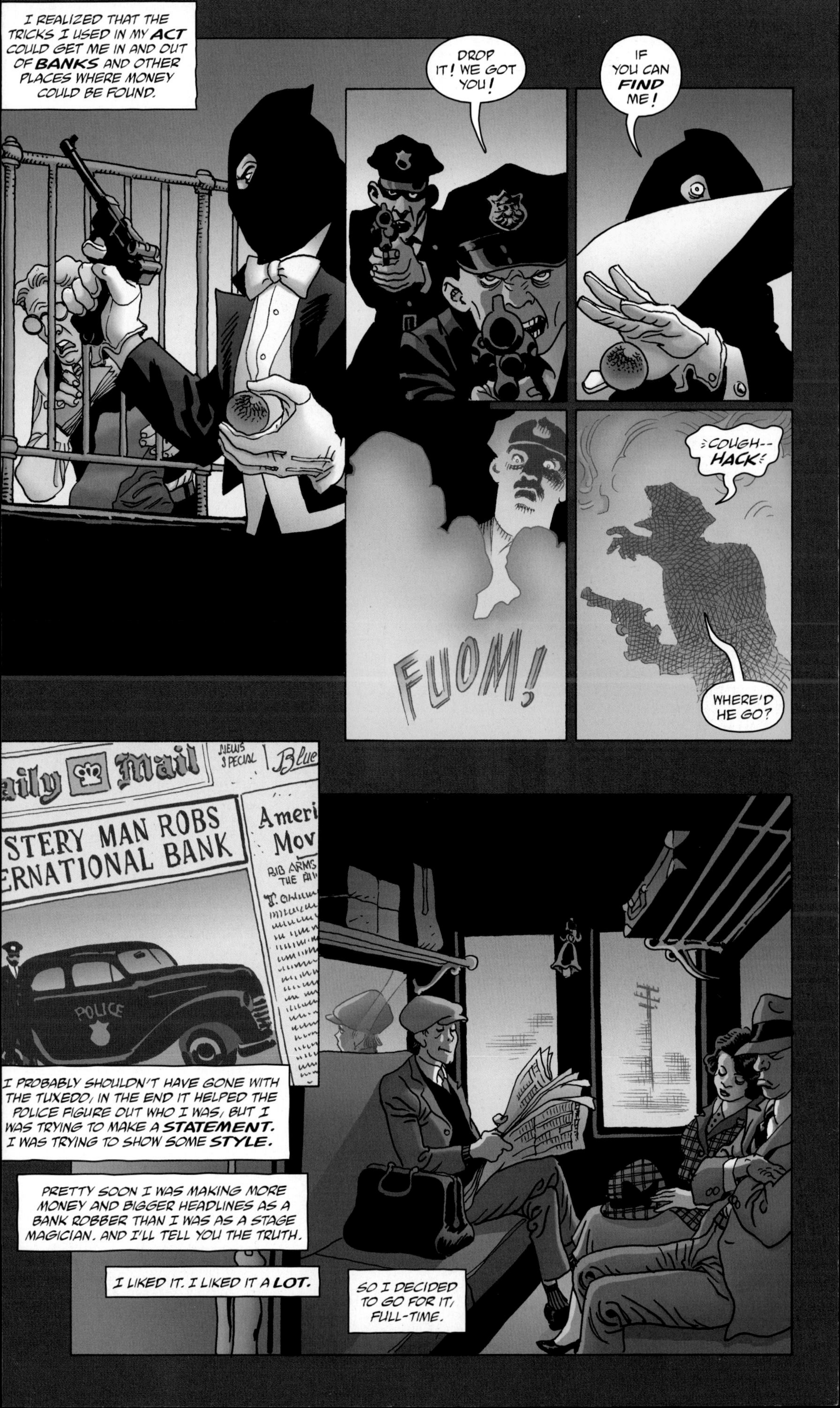

I REALIZED THAT THE TRICKS I USED IN MY ACT COULD GET ME IN AND OUT OF BANKS AND OTHER PLACES WHERE MONEY COULD BE FOUND.
DROP IT! WE GOT YOU!
IF YOU CAN FIND ME!
FUOM!
COUGH-- HACK
WHERE'D HE GO?
Daily Mail
NEWS SPECIAL
STERY MAN ROBS
ERNATIONAL BANK
Ameri
Mov
POLICE
I PROBABLY SHOULDN'T HAVE GONE WITH THE TUXEDO; IN THE END IT HELPED THE POLICE FIGURE OUT WHO I WAS, BUT I WAS TRYING TO MAKE A STATEMENT. I WAS TRYING TO SHOW SOME STYLE.
PRETTY SOON I WAS MAKING MORE MONEY AND BIGGER HEADLINES AS A BANK ROBBER THAN I WAS AS A STAGE MAGICIAN. AND I'LL TELL YOU THE TRUTH.
I LIKED IT. I LIKED IT A LOT.
SO I DECIDED TO GO FOR IT, FULL-TIME.

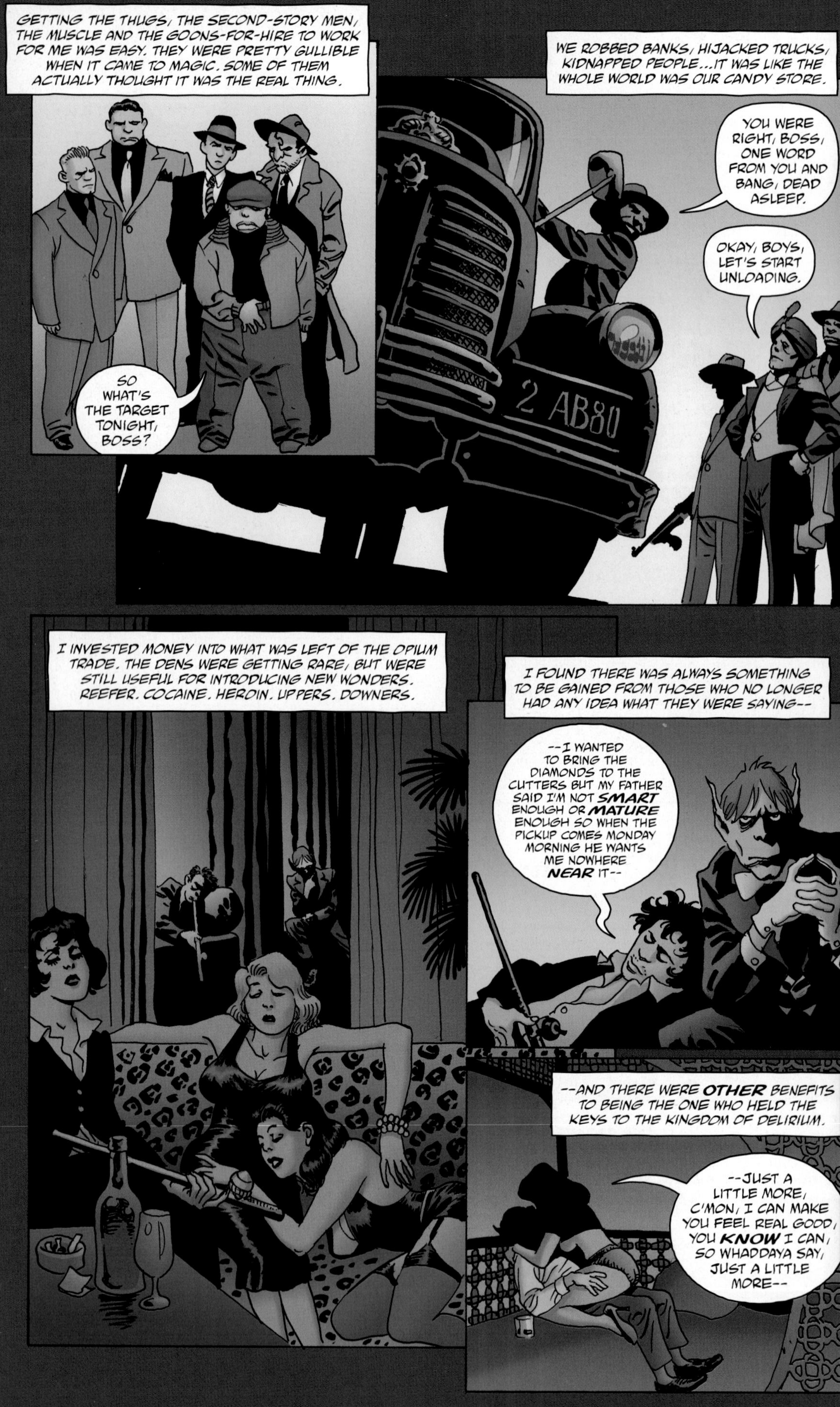
GETTING THE THUGS, THE SECOND-STORY MEN, THE MUSCLE AND THE GOONS-FOR-HIRE TO WORK FOR ME WAS EASY. THEY WERE PRETTY GULLIBLE WHEN IT CAME TO MAGIC. SOME OF THEM ACTUALLY THOUGHT IT WAS THE REAL THING.
SO WHAT'S THE TARGET TONIGHT, BOSS?
WE ROBBED BANKS, HIJACKED TRUCKS, KIDNAPPED PEOPLE...IT WAS LIKE THE WHOLE WORLD WAS OUR CANDY STORE.
YOU WERE RIGHT, BOSS, ONE WORD FROM YOU AND BANG, DEAD ASLEEP.
OKAY, BOYS, LET'S START UNLOADING.
2 AB80
I INVESTED MONEY INTO WHAT WAS LEFT OF THE OPIUM TRADE. THE DENS WERE GETTING RARE, BUT WERE STILL USEFUL FOR INTRODUCING NEW WONDERS. REEFER. COCAINE. HEROIN. UPPERS. DOWNERS.
I FOUND THERE WAS ALWAYS SOMETHING TO BE GAINED FROM THOSE WHO NO LONGER HAD ANY IDEA WHAT THEY WERE SAYING--
--I WANTED TO BRING THE DIAMONDS TO THE CUTTERS BUT MY FATHER SAID I'M NOT **SMART** ENOUGH OR **MATURE** ENOUGH SO WHEN THE PICKUP COMES MONDAY MORNING HE WANTS ME NOWHERE **NEAR** IT--
--AND THERE WERE **OTHER** BENEFITS TO BEING THE ONE WHO HELD THE KEYS TO THE KINGDOM OF DELIRIUM.
--JUST A LITTLE MORE, C'MON, I CAN MAKE YOU FEEL REAL GOOD, YOU **KNOW** I CAN, SO WHADDAYA SAY, JUST A LITTLE MORE--

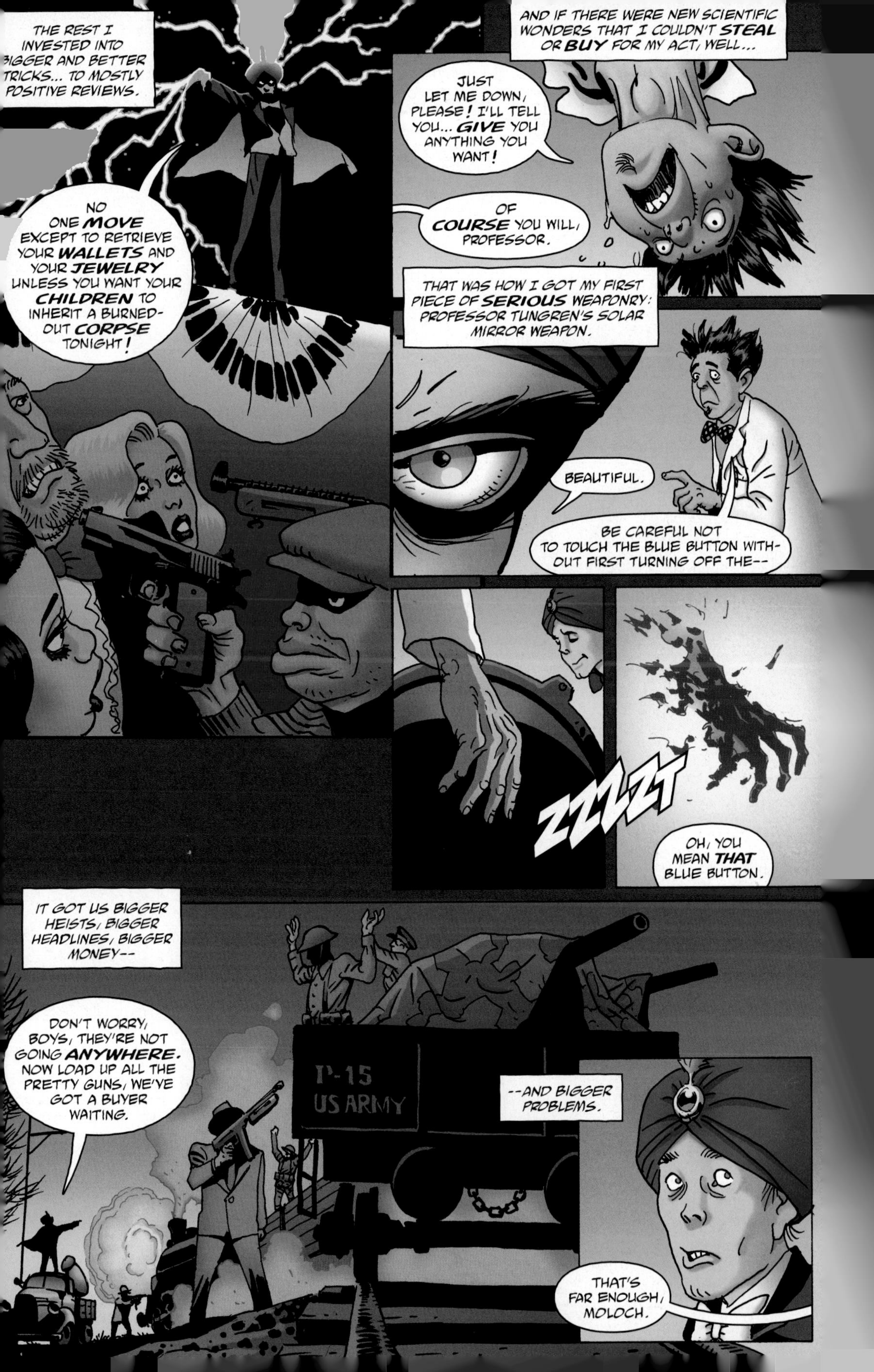
THE REST I INVESTED INTO BIGGER AND BETTER TRICKS... TO MOSTLY POSITIVE REVIEWS.
NO ONE MOVE EXCEPT TO RETRIEVE YOUR WALLETS AND YOUR JEWELRY UNLESS YOU WANT YOUR CHILDREN TO INHERIT A BURNED-OUT CORPSE TONIGHT!
AND IF THERE WERE NEW SCIENTIFIC WONDERS THAT I COULDN'T STEAL OR BUY FOR MY ACT, WELL...
JUST LET ME DOWN, PLEASE! I'LL TELL YOU... GIVE YOU ANYTHING YOU WANT!
OF COURSE YOU WILL, PROFESSOR.
THAT WAS HOW I GOT MY FIRST PIECE OF SERIOUS WEAPONRY: PROFESSOR TUNGREN'S SOLAR MIRROR WEAPON.
BEAUTIFUL.
BE CAREFUL NOT TO TOUCH THE BLUE BUTTON WITH-OUT FIRST TURNING OFF THE--
ZZZZT
OH, YOU MEAN THAT BLUE BUTTON.
IT GOT US BIGGER HEISTS, BIGGER HEADLINES, BIGGER MONEY--
DON'T WORRY, BOYS, THEY'RE NOT GOING ANYWHERE. NOW LOAD UP ALL THE PRETTY GUNS, WE'VE GOT A BUYER WAITING.
P-15
US ARMY
--AND BIGGER PROBLEMS.
THAT'S FAR ENOUGH, MOLOCH.

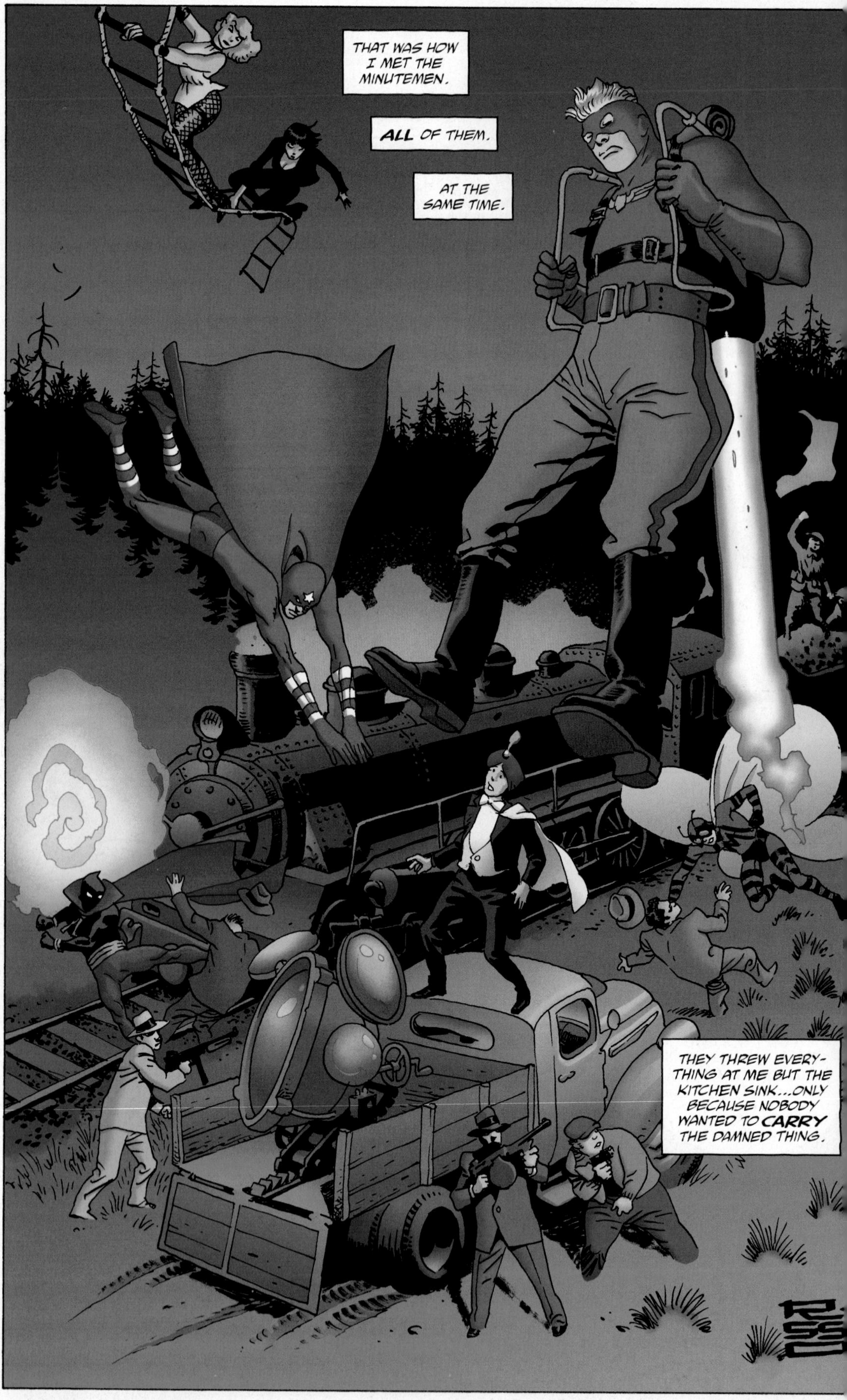
THAT WAS HOW I MET THE MINUTEMEN.
ALL OF THEM.
AT THE SAME TIME.
THEY THREW EVERY-THING AT ME BUT THE KITCHEN SINK...ONLY BECAUSE NOBODY WANTED TO CARRY THE DAMNED THING.

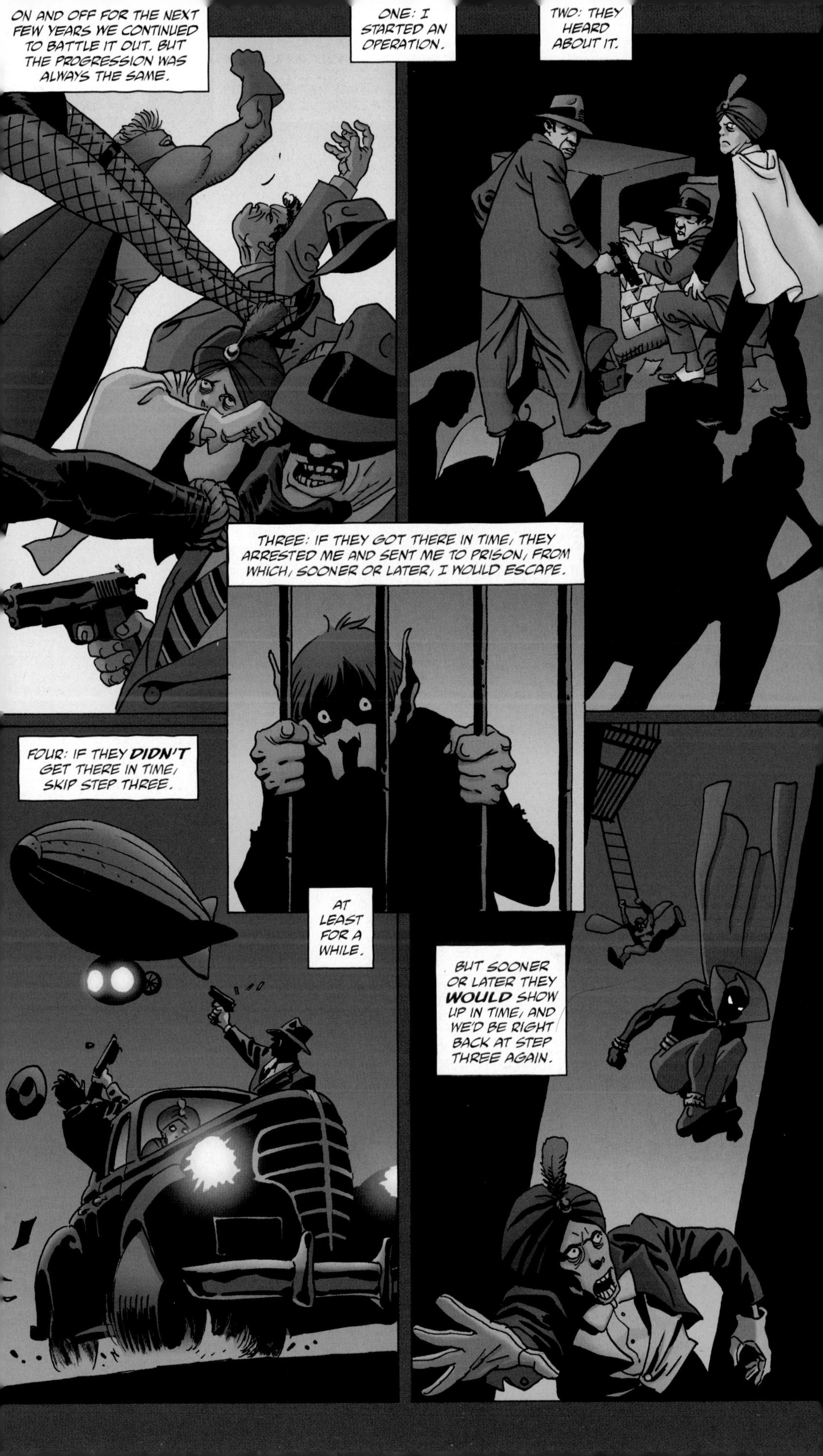
ON AND OFF FOR THE NEXT FEW YEARS WE CONTINUED TO BATTLE IT OUT. BUT THE PROGRESSION WAS ALWAYS THE SAME.
ONE: I STARTED AN OPERATION.
TWO: THEY HEARD ABOUT IT.
THREE: IF THEY GOT THERE IN TIME, THEY ARRESTED ME AND SENT ME TO PRISON, FROM WHICH, SOONER OR LATER, I WOULD ESCAPE.
FOUR: IF THEY DIDN'T GET THERE IN TIME, SKIP STEP THREE.
AT LEAST FOR A WHILE.
BUT SOONER OR LATER THEY WOULD SHOW UP IN TIME, AND WE'D BE RIGHT BACK AT STEP THREE AGAIN.

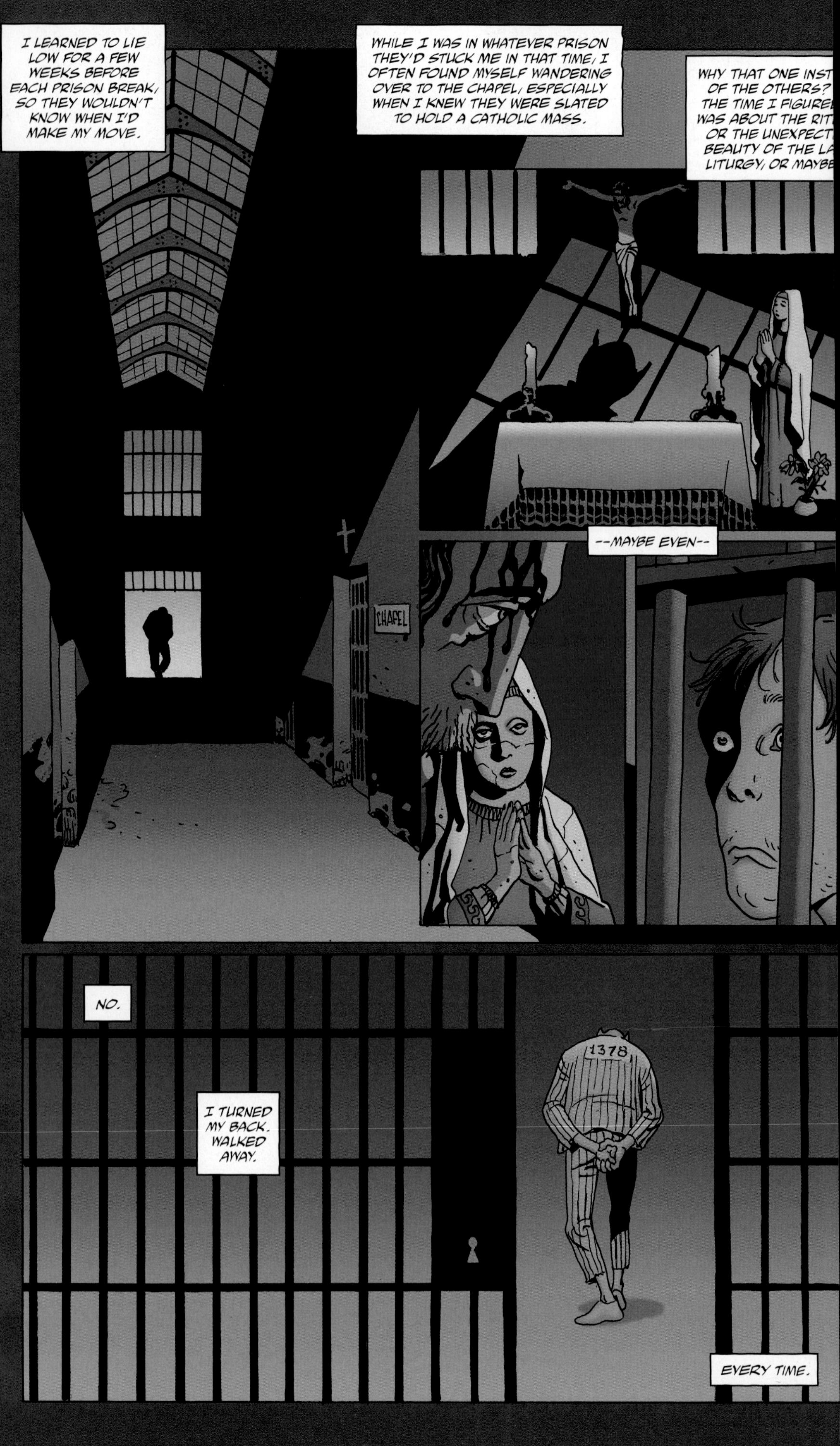
I LEARNED TO LIE LOW FOR A FEW WEEKS BEFORE EACH PRISON BREAK, SO THEY WOULDN'T KNOW WHEN I'D MAKE MY MOVE.
WHILE I WAS IN WHATEVER PRISON THEY'D STUCK ME IN THAT TIME, I OFTEN FOUND MYSELF WANDERING OVER TO THE CHAPEL, ESPECIALLY WHEN I KNEW THEY WERE SLATED TO HOLD A CATHOLIC MASS.
CHAPEL
WHY THAT ONE INST OF THE OTHERS? THE TIME I FIGURE WAS ABOUT THE RIT OR THE UNEXPECT BEAUTY OF THE LA LITURGY, OR MAYBE
--MAYBE EVEN--
NO.
I TURNED MY BACK. WALKED AWAY.
1378
EVERY TIME.

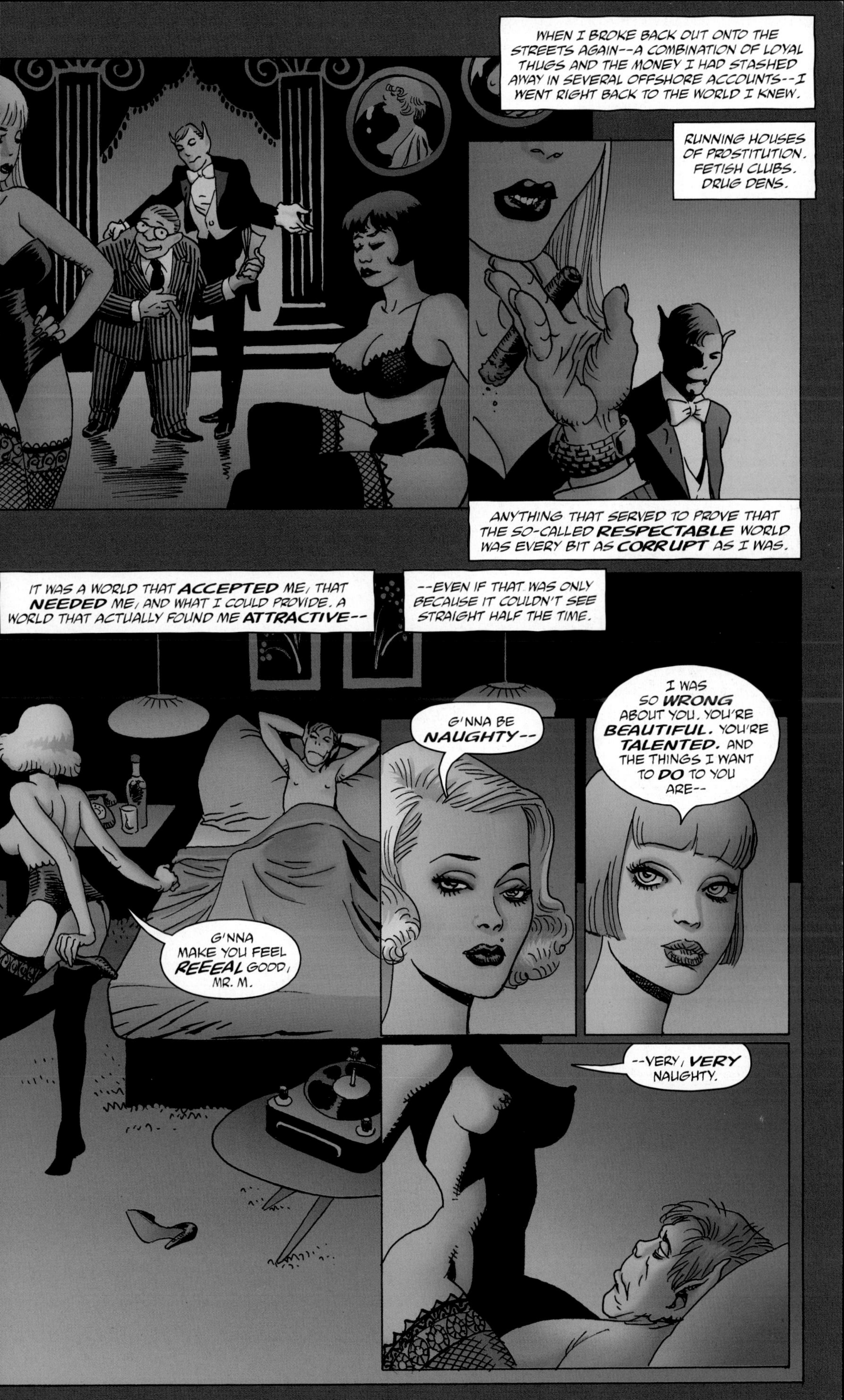
WHEN I BROKE BACK OUT ONTO THE STREETS AGAIN--A COMBINATION OF LOYAL THUGS AND THE MONEY I HAD STASHED AWAY IN SEVERAL OFFSHORE ACCOUNTS--I WENT RIGHT BACK TO THE WORLD I KNEW.
RUNNING HOUSES OF PROSTITUTION. FETISH CLUBS. DRUG DENS.
ANYTHING THAT SERVED TO PROVE THAT THE SO-CALLED **RESPECTABLE** WORLD WAS EVERY BIT AS **CORRUPT** AS I WAS.
IT WAS A WORLD THAT **ACCEPTED** ME, THAT **NEEDED** ME, AND WHAT I COULD PROVIDE. A WORLD THAT ACTUALLY FOUND ME **ATTRACTIVE**--
--EVEN IF THAT WAS ONLY BECAUSE IT COULDN'T SEE STRAIGHT HALF THE TIME.
G'NNA MAKE YOU FEEL **REEEAL** GOOD, MR. M.
G'NNA BE **NAUGHTY**--
I WAS SO **WRONG** ABOUT YOU. YOU'RE **BEAUTIFUL**. YOU'RE **TALENTED**. AND THE THINGS I WANT TO **DO** TO YOU ARE--
--VERY, **VERY** NAUGHTY.

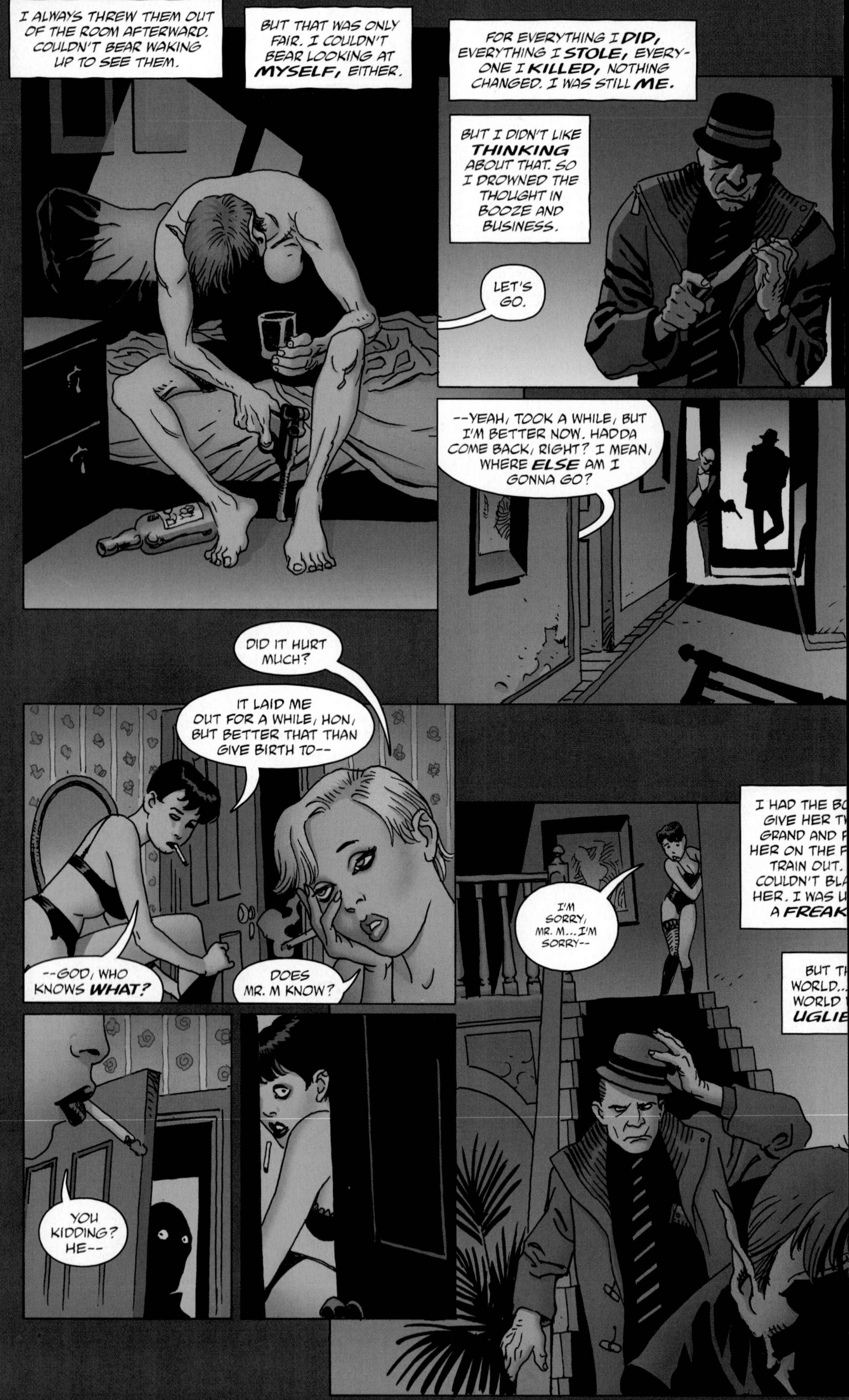
I ALWAYS THREW THEM OUT OF THE ROOM AFTERWARD. COULDN'T BEAR WAKING UP TO SEE THEM.
BUT THAT WAS ONLY FAIR. I COULDN'T BEAR LOOKING AT MYSELF, EITHER.
FOR EVERYTHING I DID, EVERYTHING I STOLE, EVERYONE I KILLED, NOTHING CHANGED. I WAS STILL ME.
BUT I DIDN'T LIKE THINKING ABOUT THAT. SO I DROWNED THE THOUGHT IN BOOZE AND BUSINESS.
LET'S GO.
--YEAH, TOOK A WHILE, BUT I'M BETTER NOW. HADDA COME BACK, RIGHT? I MEAN, WHERE ELSE AM I GONNA GO?
DID IT HURT MUCH?
IT LAID ME OUT FOR A WHILE, HON, BUT BETTER THAT THAN GIVE BIRTH TO--
--GOD, WHO KNOWS WHAT?
DOES MR. M KNOW?
YOU KIDDING? HE--
I'M SORRY, MR. M...I'M SORRY--
I HAD THE BO GIVE HER TW GRAND AND P HER ON THE F TRAIN OUT. COULDN'T BLA HER. I WAS LI A FREAK
BUT TH WORLD... WORLD UGLIE

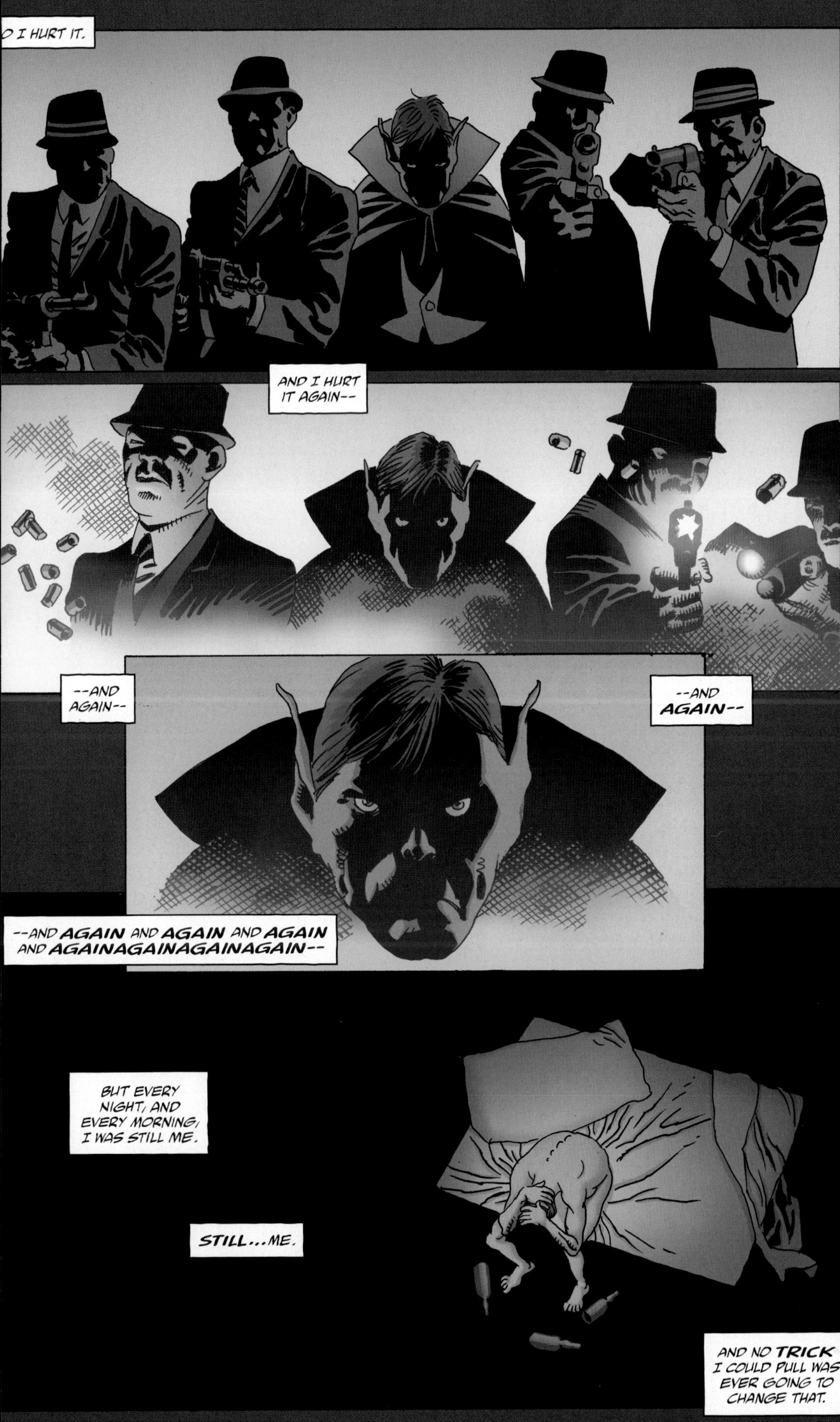
O I HURT IT.
AND I HURT IT AGAIN--
--AND AGAIN--
--AND AGAIN--
--AND AGAIN AND AGAIN AND AGAIN AND AGAINAGAINAGAINAGAIN--
BUT EVERY NIGHT, AND EVERY MORNING, I WAS STILL ME.
STILL...ME.
AND NO TRICK I COULD PULL WAS EVER GOING TO CHANGE THAT.

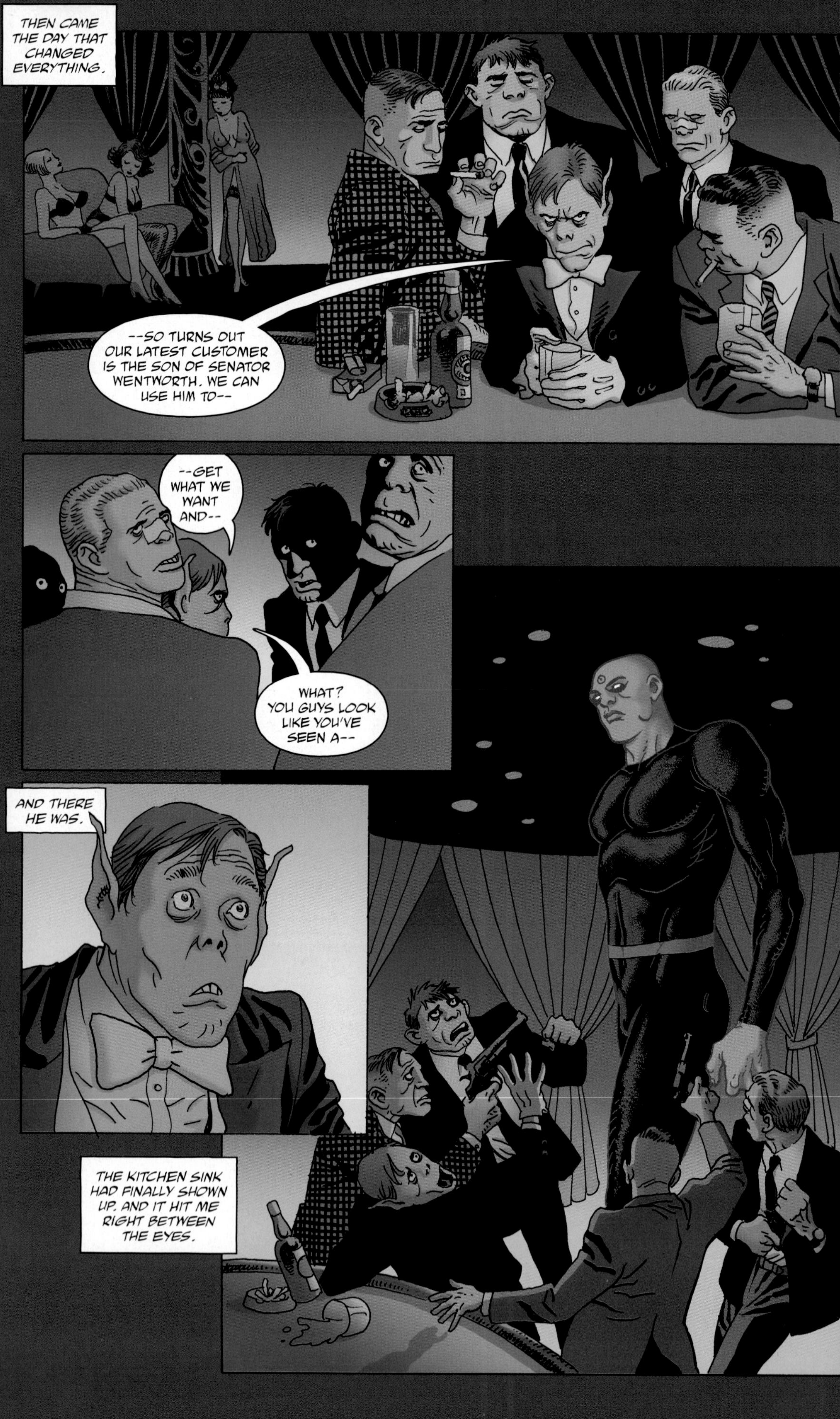
THEN CAME THE DAY THAT CHANGED EVERYTHING.
--SO TURNS OUT OUR LATEST CUSTOMER IS THE SON OF SENATOR WENTWORTH. WE CAN USE HIM TO--
--GET WHAT WE WANT AND--
WHAT? YOU GUYS LOOK LIKE YOU'VE SEEN A--
AND THERE HE WAS.
THE KITCHEN SINK HAD FINALLY SHOWN UP. AND IT HIT ME RIGHT BETWEEN THE EYES.

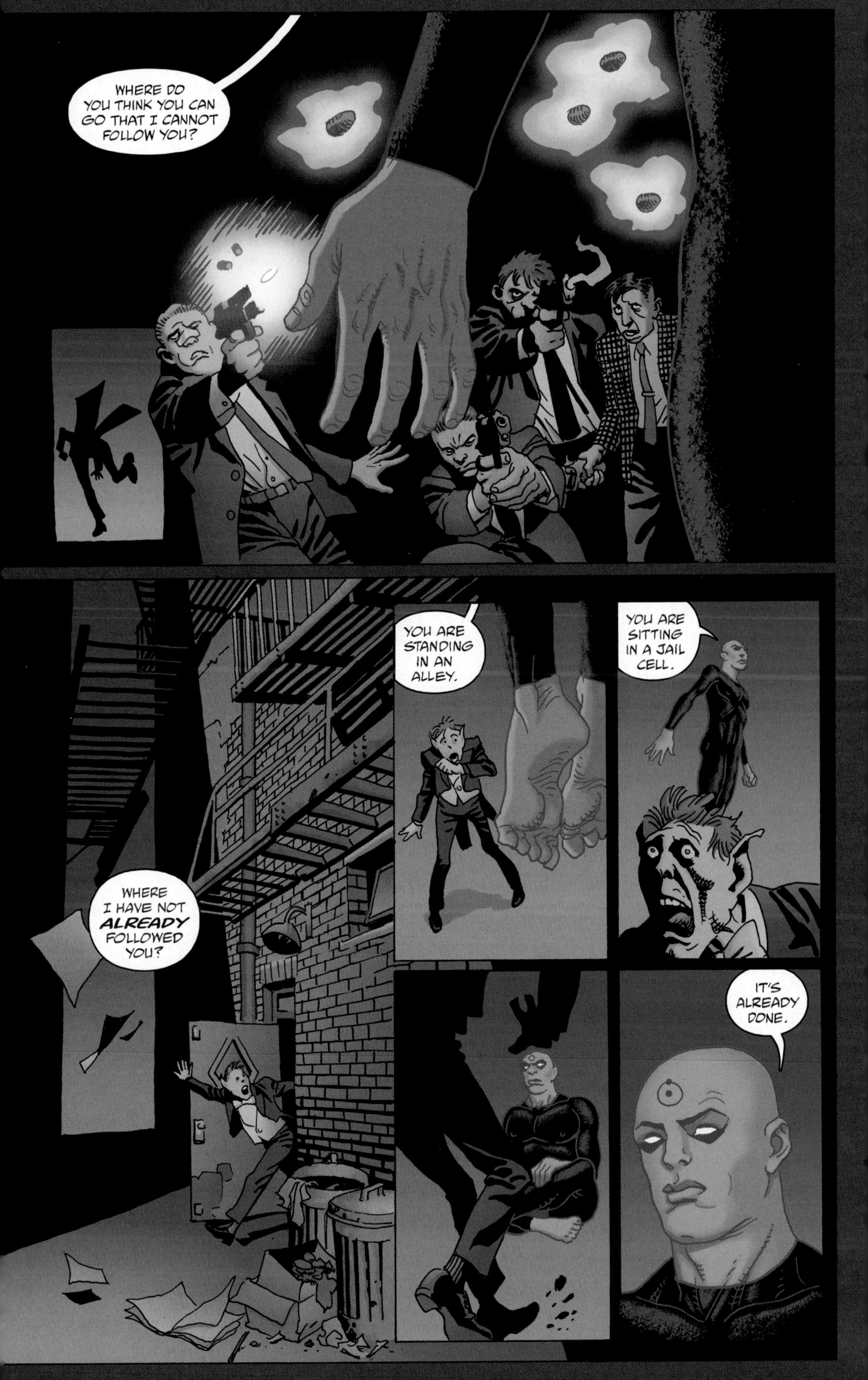
WHERE DO YOU THINK YOU CAN GO THAT I CANNOT FOLLOW YOU?
WHERE I HAVE NOT ALREADY FOLLOWED YOU?
YOU ARE STANDING IN AN ALLEY.
YOU ARE SITTING IN A JAIL CELL.
IT'S ALREADY DONE.

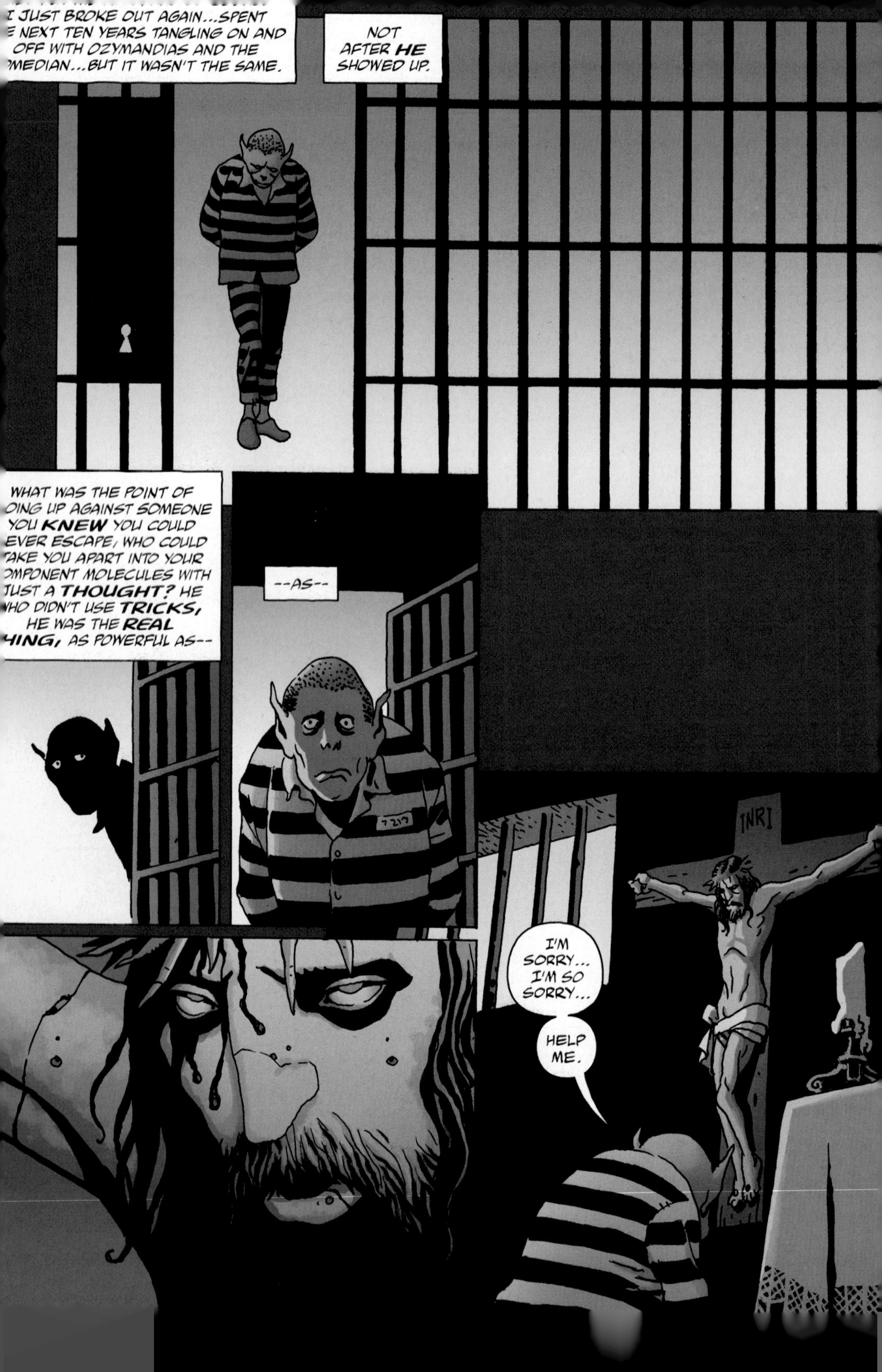
I JUST BROKE OUT AGAIN...SPENT E NEXT TEN YEARS TANGLING ON AND OFF WITH OZYMANDIAS AND THE OMEDIAN...BUT IT WASN'T THE SAME.
NOT AFTER HE SHOWED UP.
WHAT WAS THE POINT OF OING UP AGAINST SOMEONE YOU KNEW YOU COULD EVER ESCAPE, WHO COULD AKE YOU APART INTO YOUR OMPONENT MOLECULES WITH JUST A THOUGHT? HE WHO DIDN'T USE TRICKS, HE WAS THE REAL HING, AS POWERFUL AS--
--AS--
INRI
I'M SORRY... I'M SO SORRY...
HELP ME.

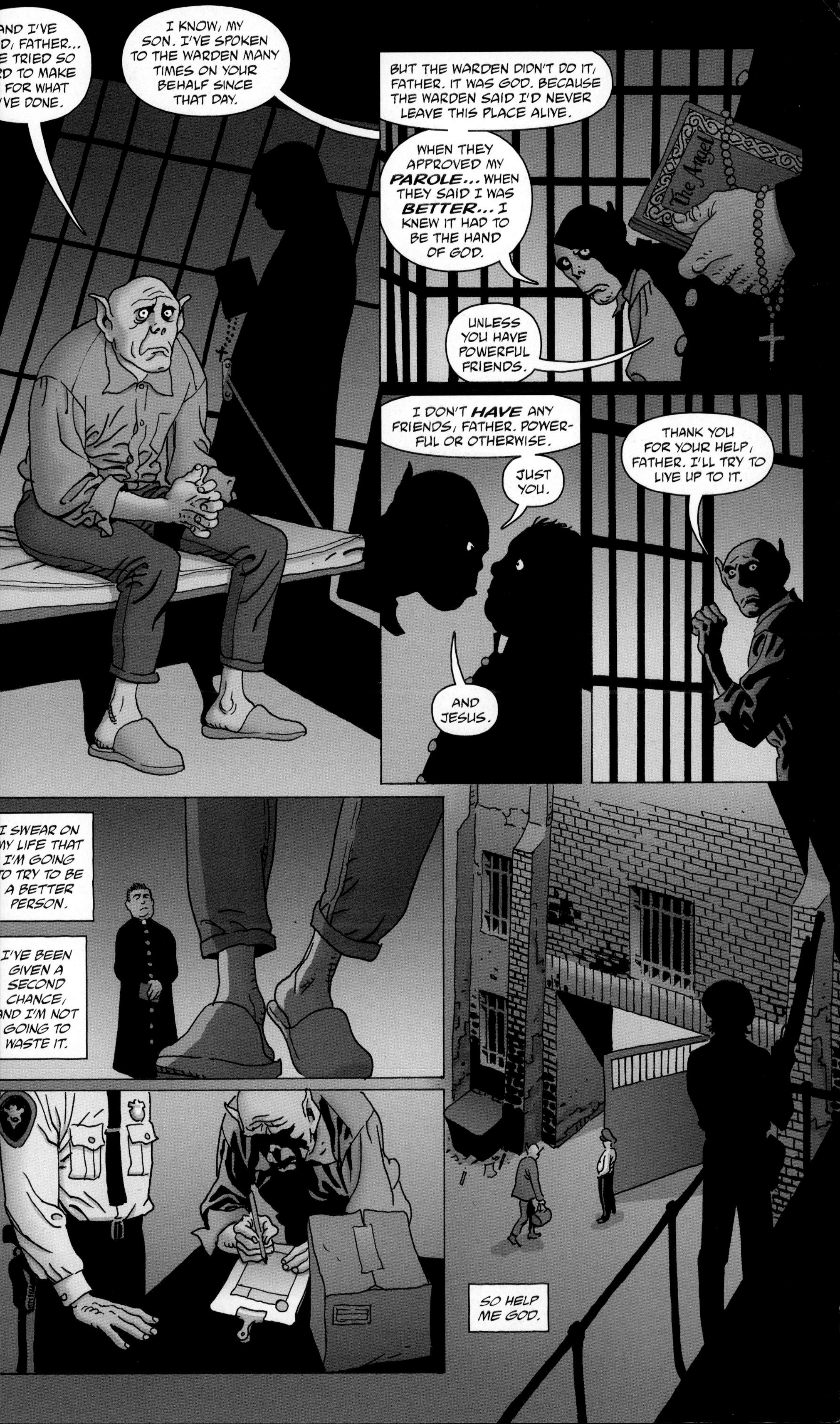

AND I'VE
D, FATHER...
E TRIED SO
RD TO MAKE
FOR WHAT
'VE DONE.
I KNOW, MY SON. I'VE SPOKEN TO THE WARDEN MANY TIMES ON YOUR BEHALF SINCE THAT DAY.
BUT THE WARDEN DIDN'T DO IT, FATHER. IT WAS GOD. BECAUSE THE WARDEN SAID I'D NEVER LEAVE THIS PLACE ALIVE.
WHEN THEY APPROVED MY PAROLE... WHEN THEY SAID I WAS BETTER... I KNEW IT HAD TO BE THE HAND OF GOD.
The Angel
UNLESS YOU HAVE POWERFUL FRIENDS.
I DON'T HAVE ANY FRIENDS, FATHER. POWER-FUL OR OTHERWISE.
JUST YOU.
AND JESUS.
THANK YOU FOR YOUR HELP, FATHER. I'LL TRY TO LIVE UP TO IT.
I SWEAR ON MY LIFE THAT I'M GOING TO TRY TO BE A BETTER PERSON.
I'VE BEEN GIVEN A SECOND CHANCE, AND I'M NOT GOING TO WASTE IT.
SO HELP ME GOD.

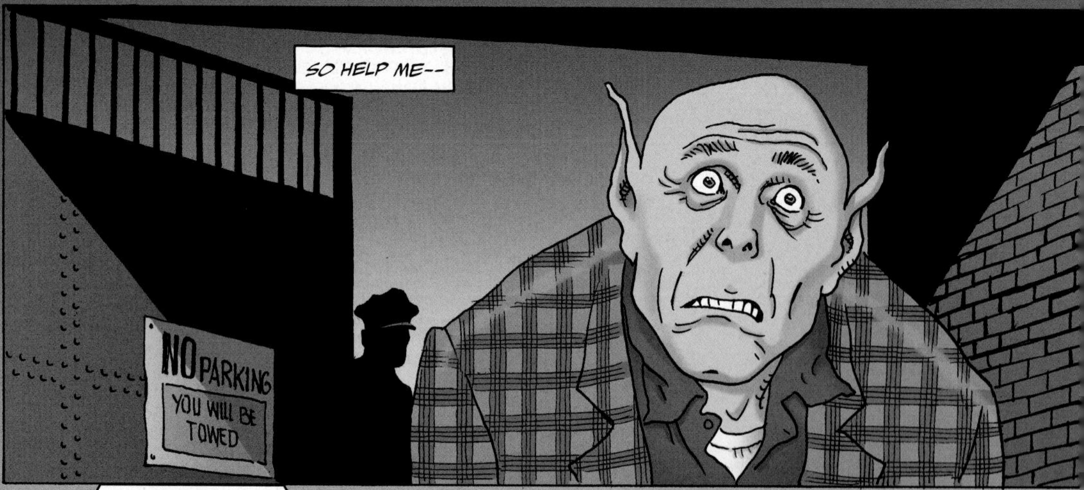
SO HELP ME--
NO PARKING
YOU WILL BE TOWED

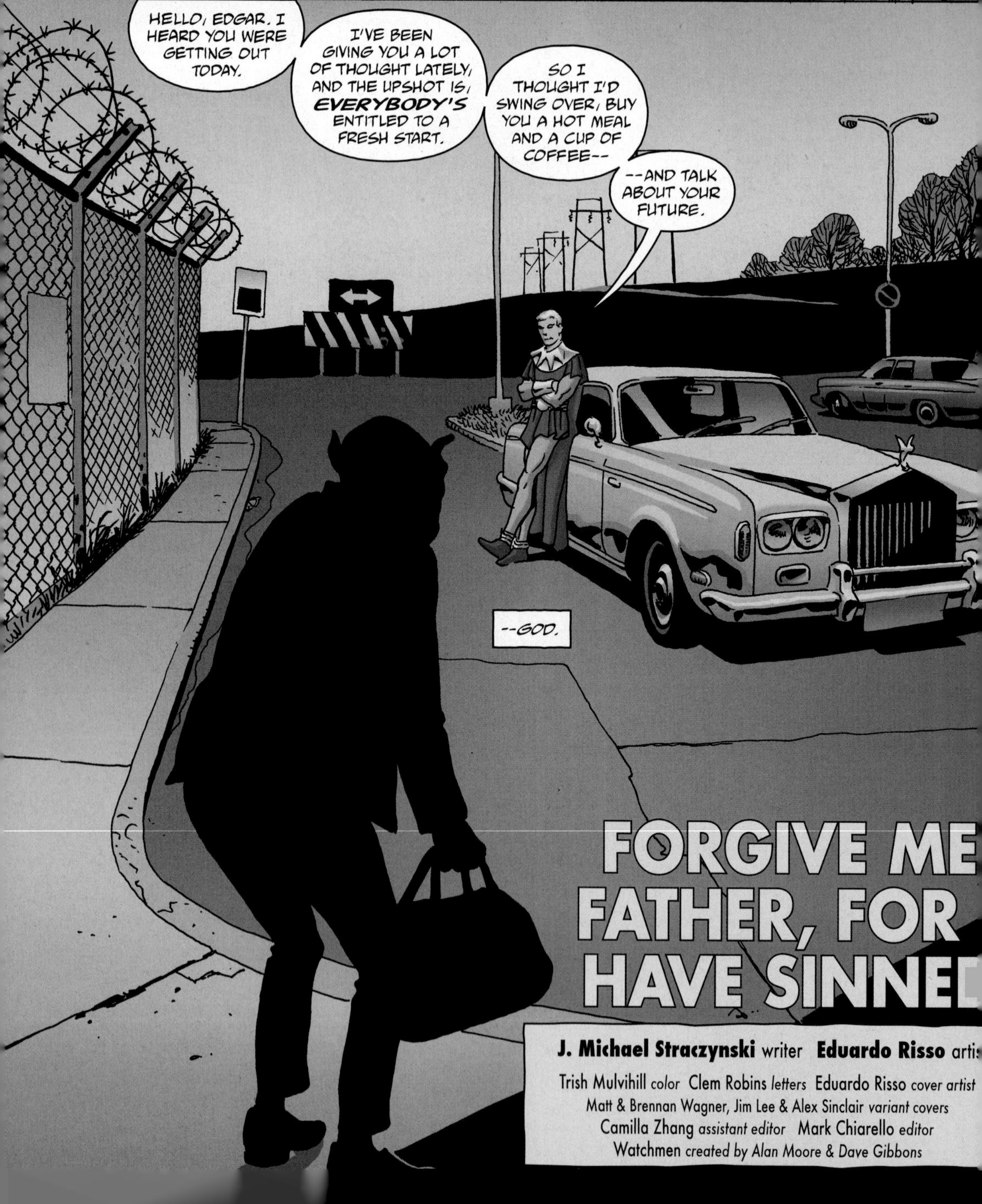
HELLO, EDGAR. I HEARD YOU WERE GETTING OUT TODAY.
I'VE BEEN GIVING YOU A LOT OF THOUGHT LATELY, AND THE UPSHOT IS, EVERYBODY'S ENTITLED TO A FRESH START.
SO I THOUGHT I'D SWING OVER, BUY YOU A HOT MEAL AND A CUP OF COFFEE--
--AND TALK ABOUT YOUR FUTURE.
--GOD.
FORGIVE ME FATHER, FOR HAVE SINNED
J. Michael Straczynski writer Eduardo Risso artis
Trish Mulvihill color Clem Robins letters Eduardo Risso cover artist
Matt & Brennan Wagner, Jim Lee & Alex Sinclair variant covers
Camilla Zhang assistant editor Mark Chiarello editor
Watchmen created by Alan Moore & Dave Gibbons

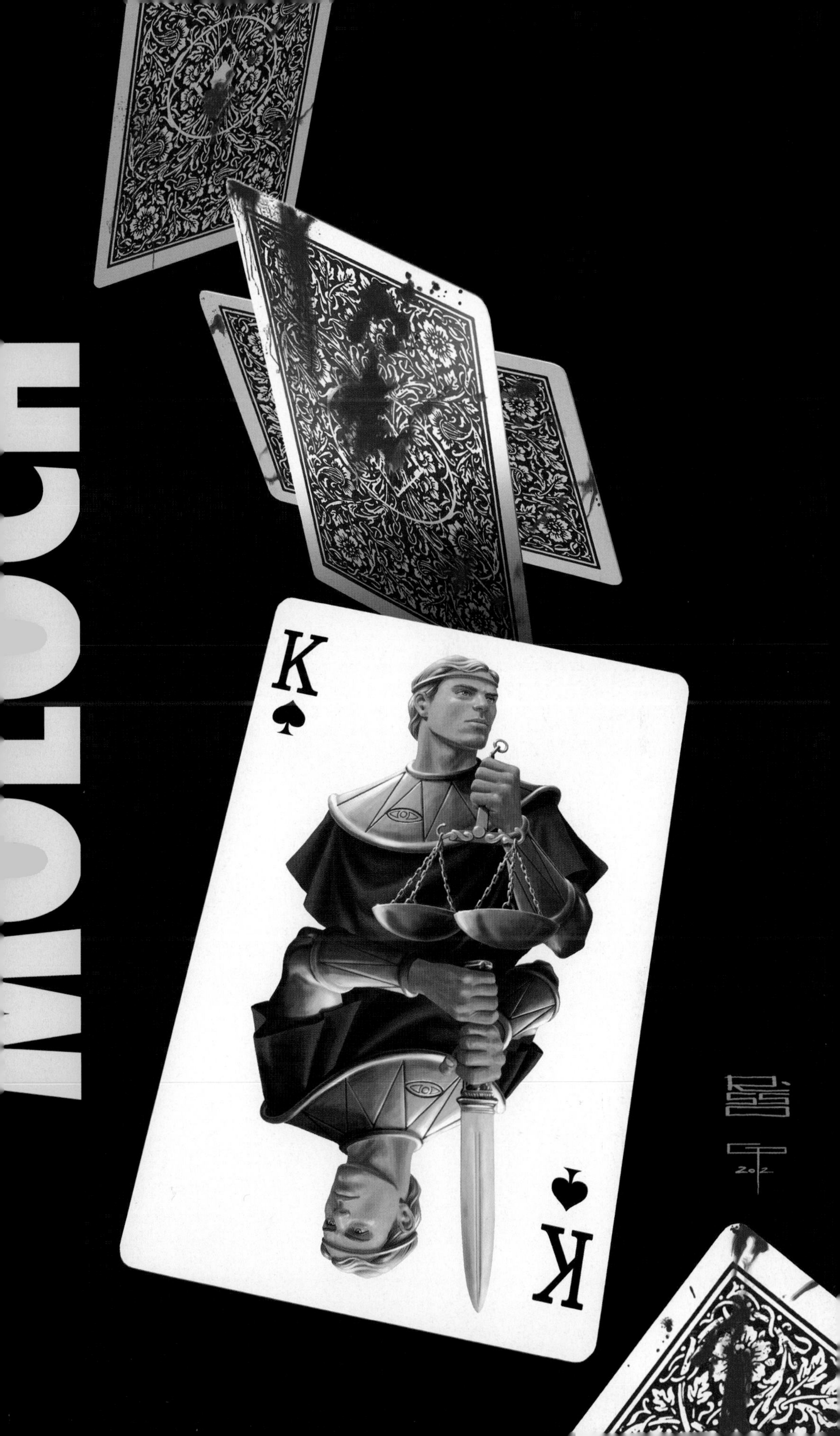
K
K

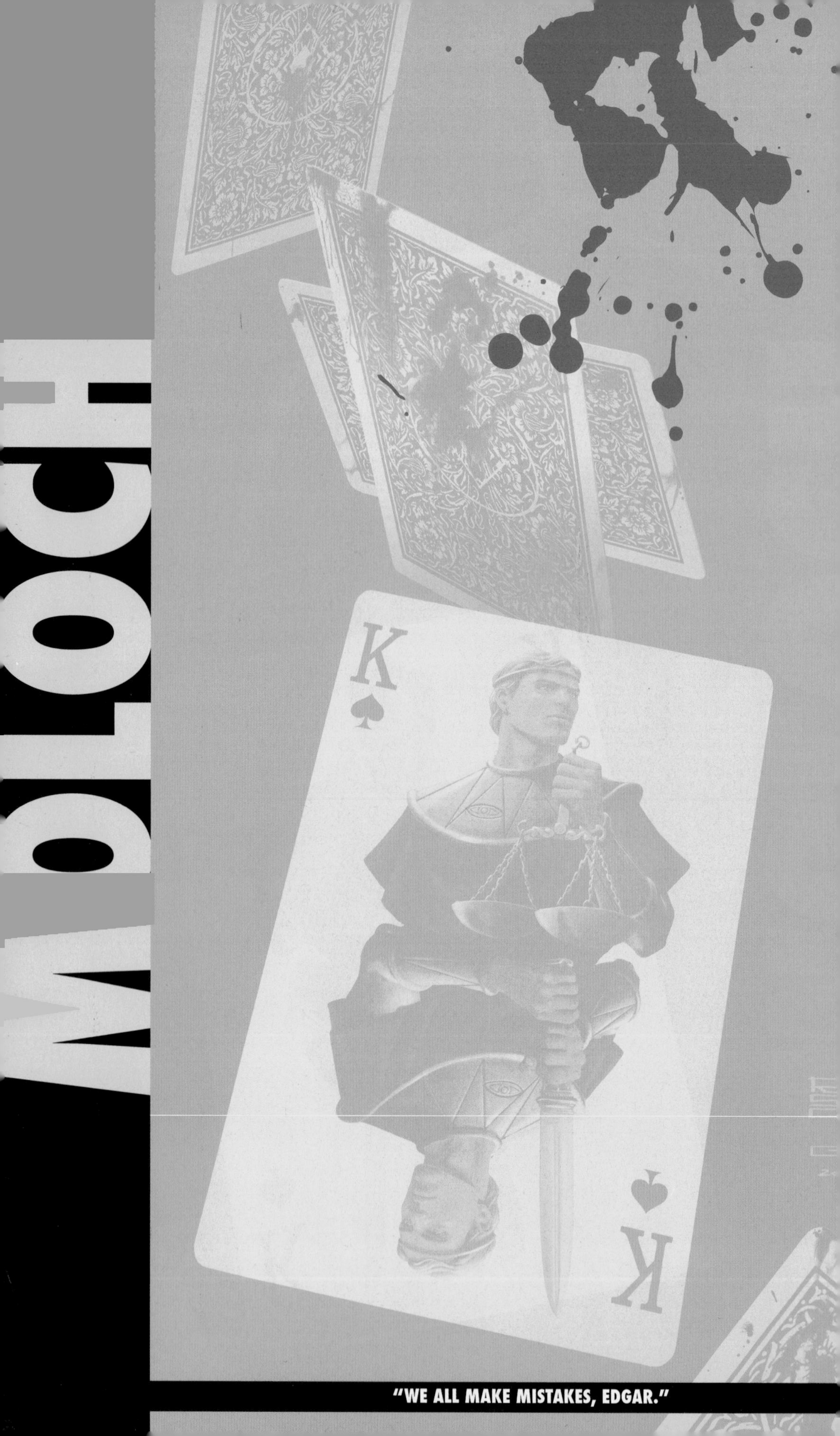
MOLOCH
"WE ALL MAKE MISTAKES, EDGAR."

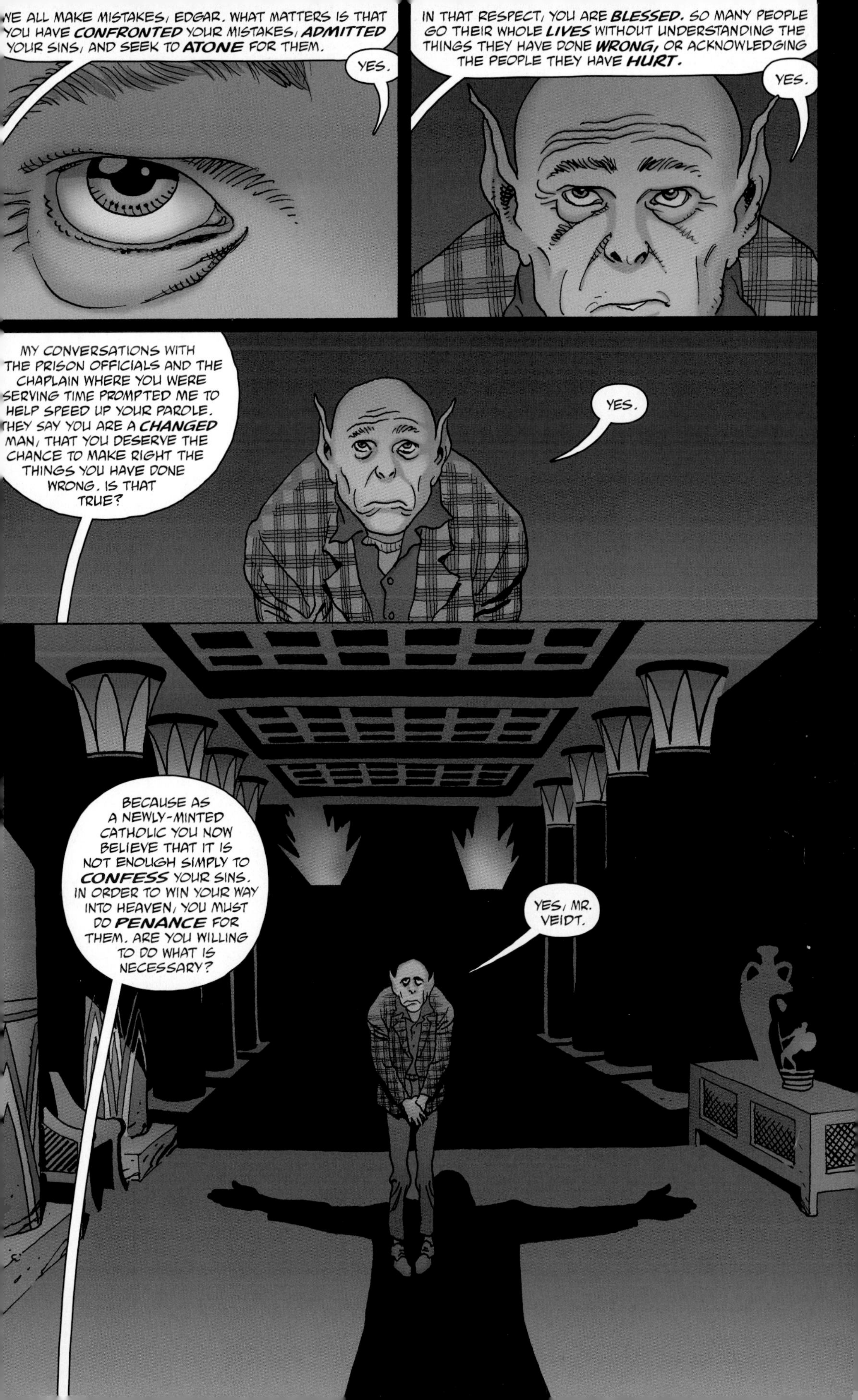
WE ALL MAKE MISTAKES, EDGAR. WHAT MATTERS IS THAT YOU HAVE CONFRONTED YOUR MISTAKES, ADMITTED YOUR SINS, AND SEEK TO ATONE FOR THEM.
YES.
IN THAT RESPECT, YOU ARE BLESSED. SO MANY PEOPLE GO THEIR WHOLE LIVES WITHOUT UNDERSTANDING THE THINGS THEY HAVE DONE WRONG, OR ACKNOWLEDGING THE PEOPLE THEY HAVE HURT.
YES.
MY CONVERSATIONS WITH THE PRISON OFFICIALS AND THE CHAPLAIN WHERE YOU WERE SERVING TIME PROMPTED ME TO HELP SPEED UP YOUR PAROLE. THEY SAY YOU ARE A CHANGED MAN, THAT YOU DESERVE THE CHANCE TO MAKE RIGHT THE THINGS YOU HAVE DONE WRONG. IS THAT TRUE?
YES.
BECAUSE AS A NEWLY-MINTED CATHOLIC YOU NOW BELIEVE THAT IT IS NOT ENOUGH SIMPLY TO CONFESS YOUR SINS. IN ORDER TO WIN YOUR WAY INTO HEAVEN, YOU MUST DO PENANCE FOR THEM. ARE YOU WILLING TO DO WHAT IS NECESSARY?
YES, MR. VEIDT.

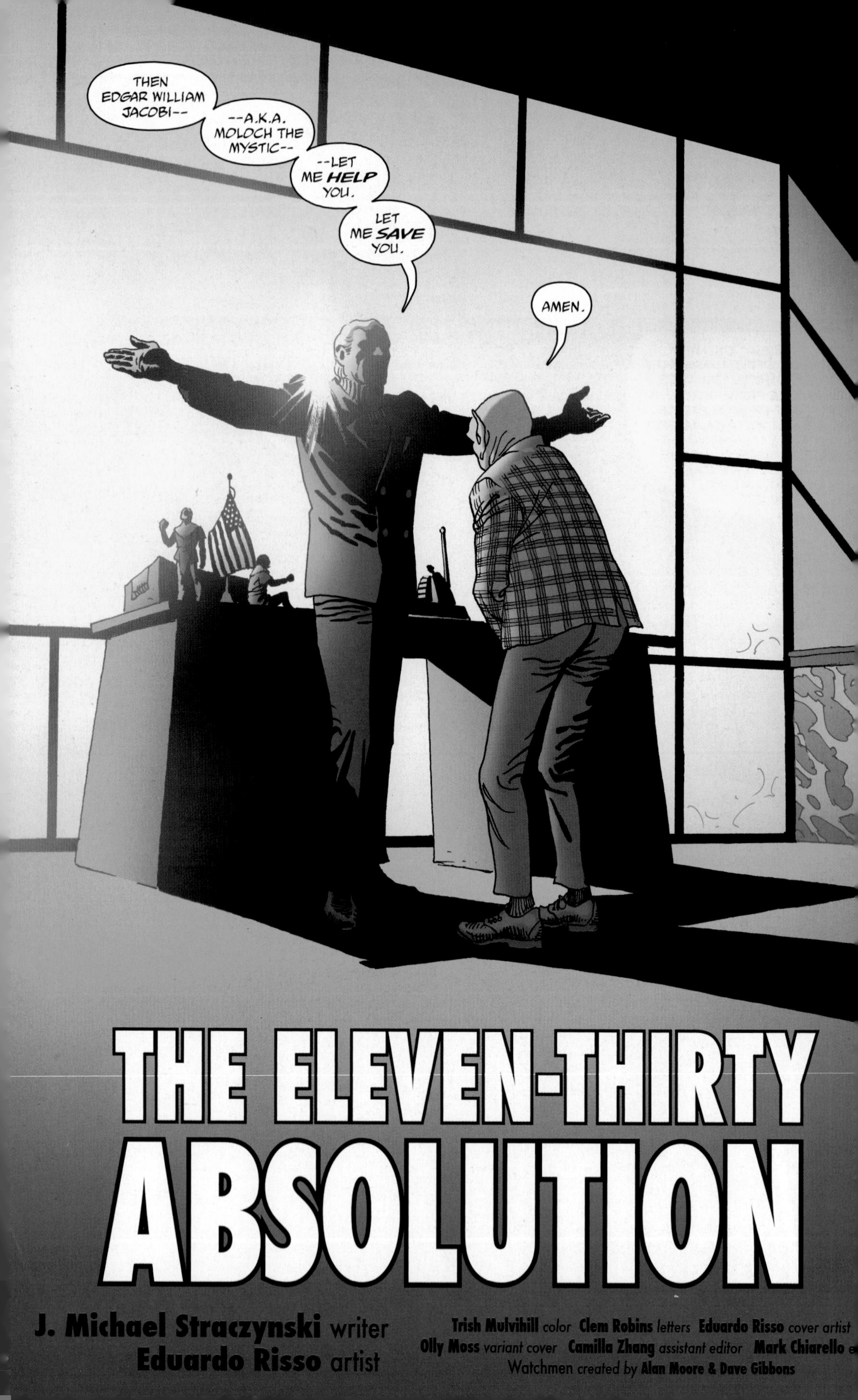
THEN EDGAR WILLIAM JACOBI--
--A.K.A. MOLOCH THE MYSTIC--
--LET ME HELP YOU.
LET ME SAVE YOU.
AMEN.

THE ELEVEN-THIRTY ABSOLUTION

J. Michael Straczynski writer
Eduardo Risso artist

Trish Mulvihill color **Clem Robins** letters **Eduardo Risso** cover artist
Olly Moss variant cover **Camilla Zhang** assistant editor **Mark Chiarello** e
Watchmen created by **Alan Moore & Dave Gibbons**

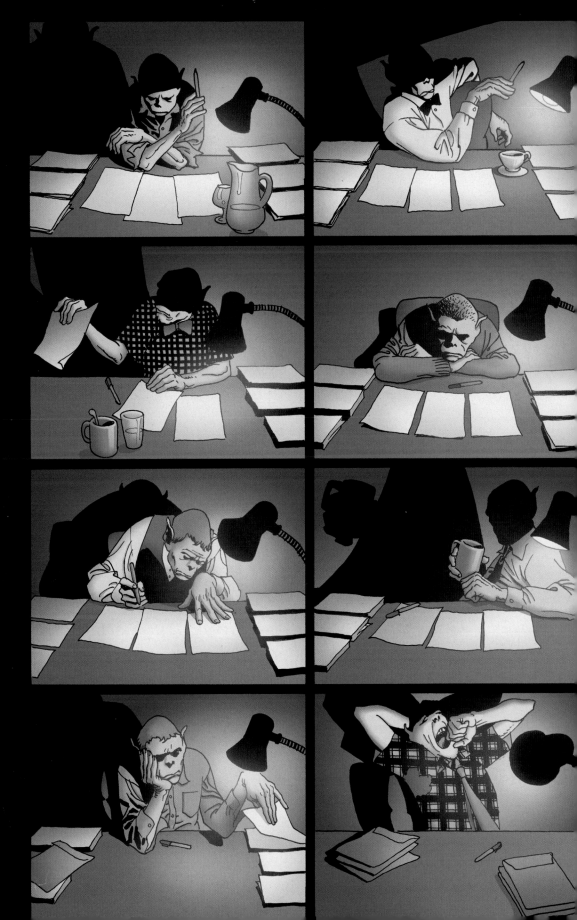

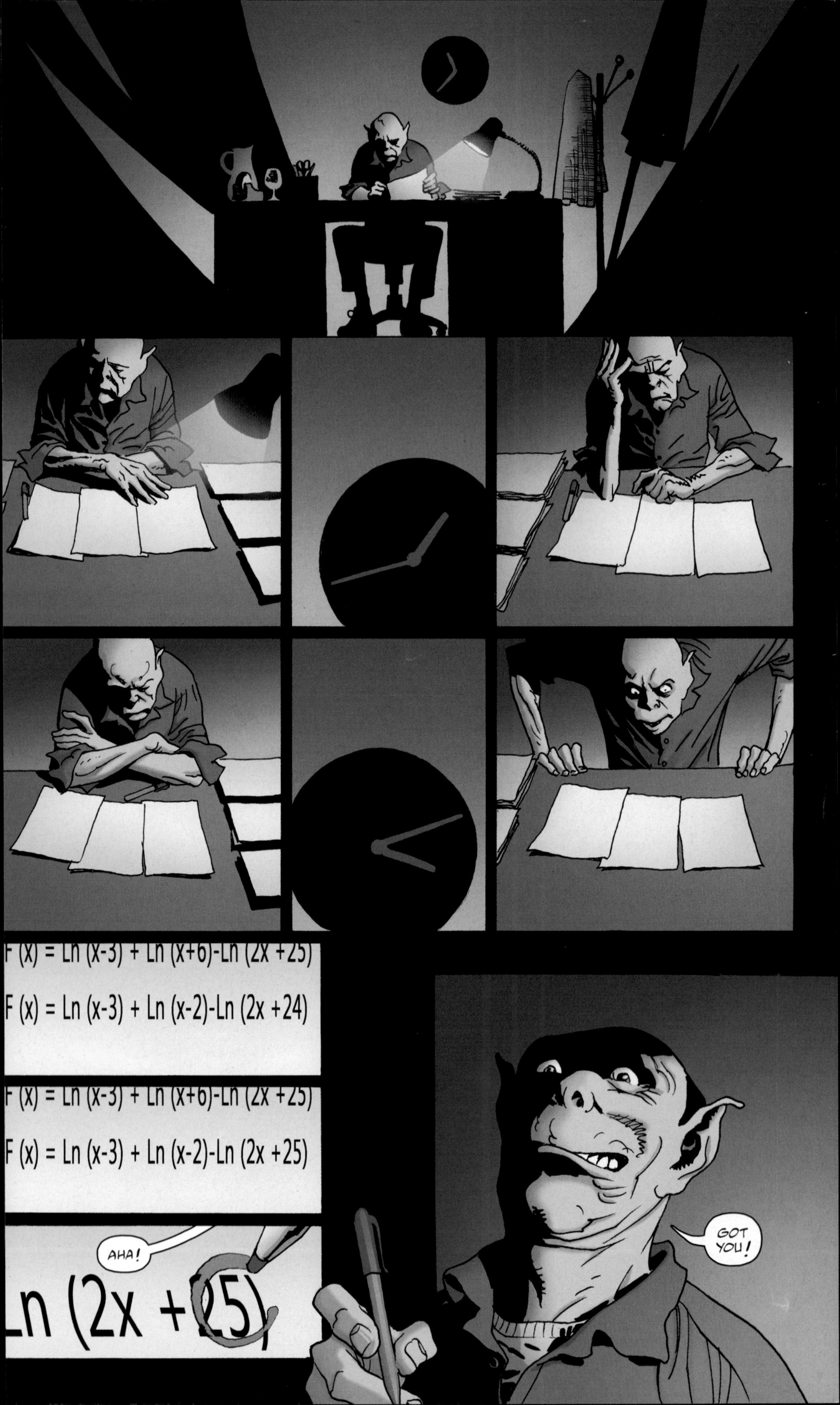
F (x) = Ln (x-3) + Ln (x+6)-Ln (2x +25)
F (x) = Ln (x-3) + Ln (x-2)-Ln (2x +24)
F (x) = Ln (x-3) + Ln (x+6)-Ln (2x +25)
F (x) = Ln (x-3) + Ln (x-2)-Ln (2x +25)
AHA!
Ln (2x +25)
GOT YOU!

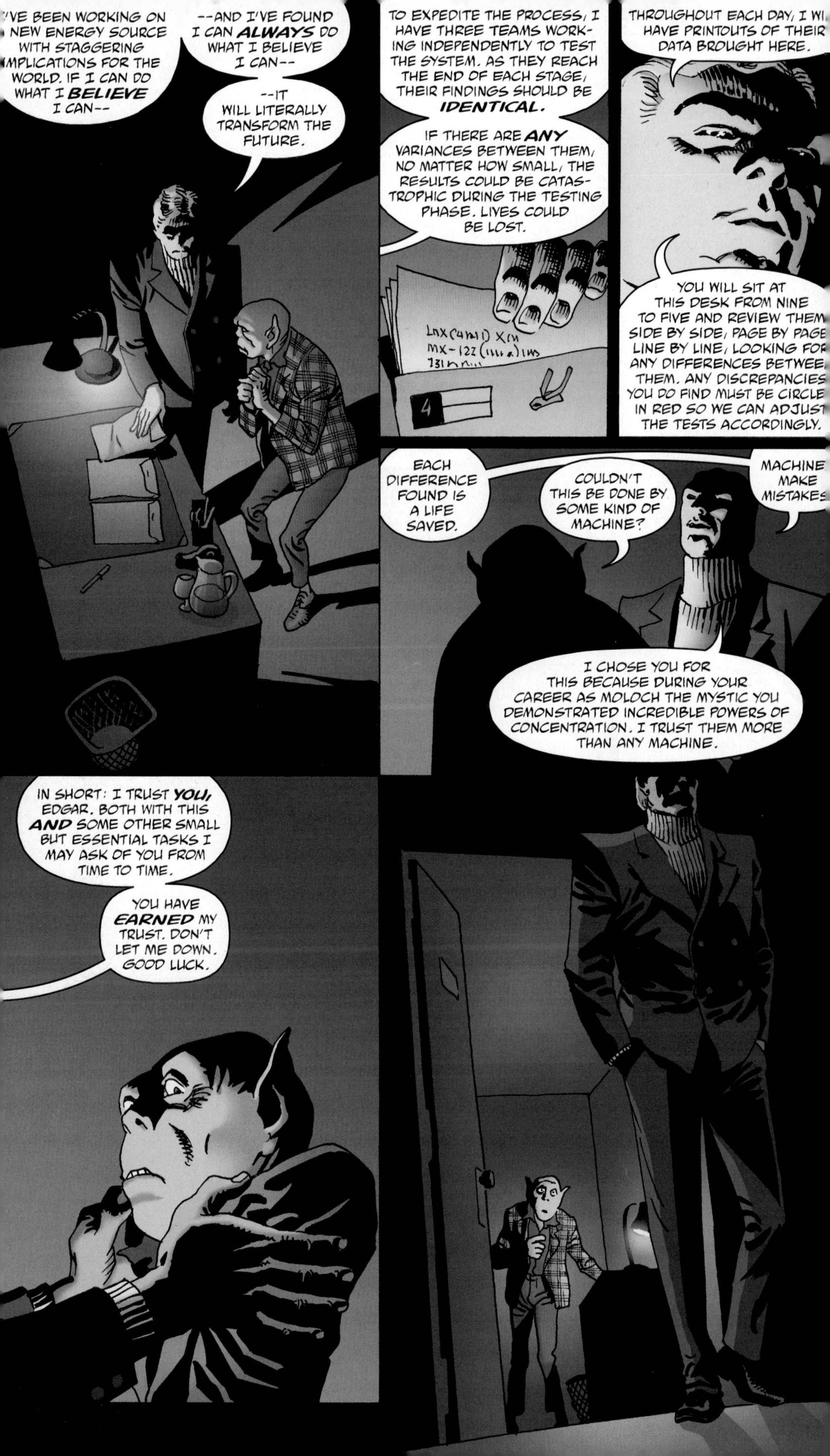

I'VE BEEN WORKING ON NEW ENERGY SOURCE WITH STAGGERING IMPLICATIONS FOR THE WORLD. IF I CAN DO WHAT I BELIEVE I CAN--
--AND I'VE FOUND I CAN ALWAYS DO WHAT I BELIEVE I CAN--
--IT WILL LITERALLY TRANSFORM THE FUTURE.
TO EXPEDITE THE PROCESS, I HAVE THREE TEAMS WORKING INDEPENDENTLY TO TEST THE SYSTEM. AS THEY REACH THE END OF EACH STAGE, THEIR FINDINGS SHOULD BE IDENTICAL.
IF THERE ARE ANY VARIANCES BETWEEN THEM, NO MATTER HOW SMALL, THE RESULTS COULD BE CATASTROPHIC DURING THE TESTING PHASE. LIVES COULD BE LOST.
THROUGHOUT EACH DAY, I WI HAVE PRINTOUTS OF THEIR DATA BROUGHT HERE.
YOU WILL SIT AT THIS DESK FROM NINE TO FIVE AND REVIEW THEM SIDE BY SIDE, PAGE BY PAGE LINE BY LINE, LOOKING FOR ANY DIFFERENCES BETWEE THEM. ANY DISCREPANCIES YOU DO FIND MUST BE CIRCLE IN RED SO WE CAN ADJUST THE TESTS ACCORDINGLY.
EACH DIFFERENCE FOUND IS A LIFE SAVED.
COULDN'T THIS BE DONE BY SOME KIND OF MACHINE?
MACHINE MAKE MISTAKES
I CHOSE YOU FOR THIS BECAUSE DURING YOUR CAREER AS MOLOCH THE MYSTIC YOU DEMONSTRATED INCREDIBLE POWERS OF CONCENTRATION. I TRUST THEM MORE THAN ANY MACHINE.
IN SHORT: I TRUST YOU, EDGAR. BOTH WITH THIS AND SOME OTHER SMALL BUT ESSENTIAL TASKS I MAY ASK OF YOU FROM TIME TO TIME.
YOU HAVE EARNED MY TRUST. DON'T LET ME DOWN. GOOD LUCK.

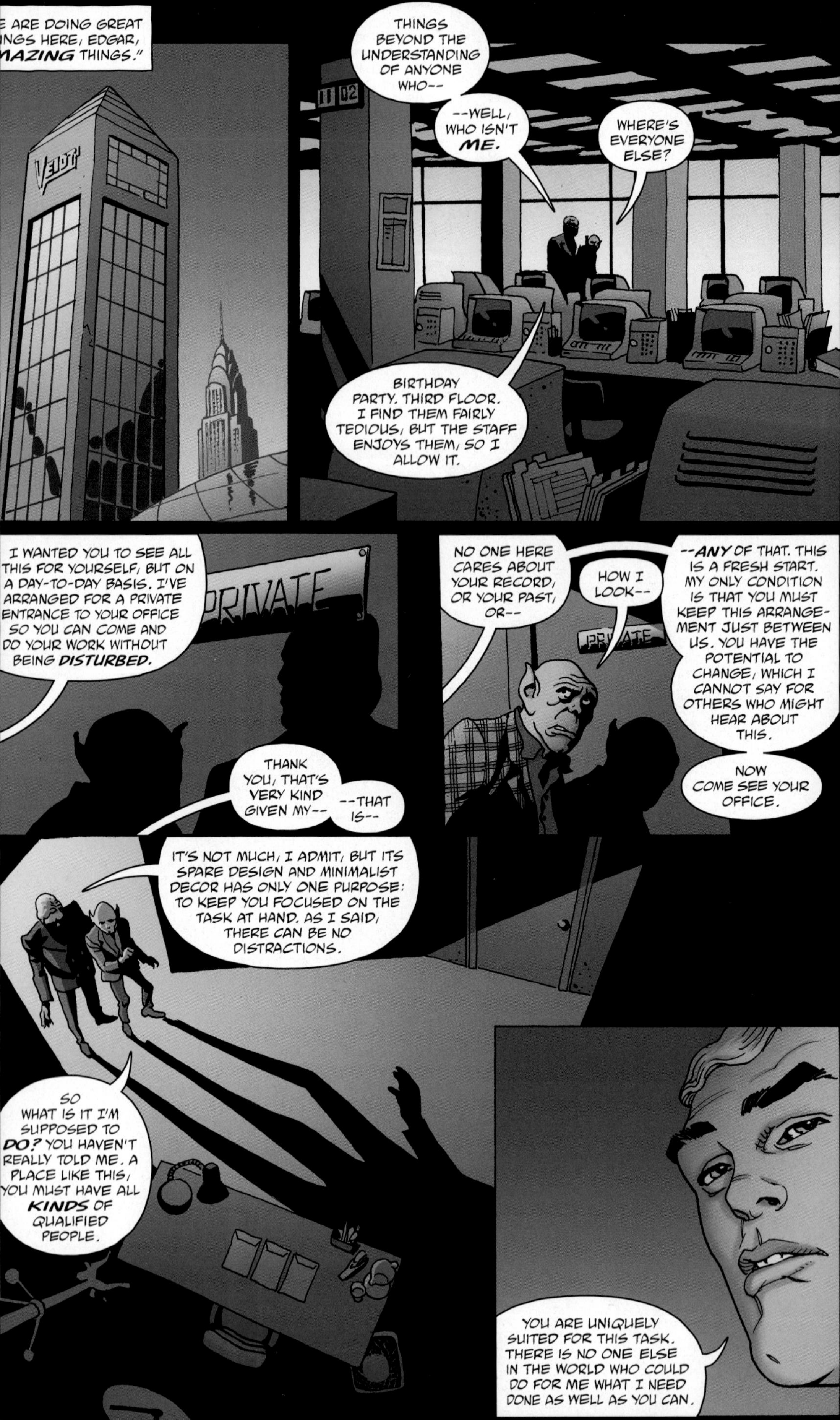

E ARE DOING GREAT
INGS HERE, EDGAR,
MAZING THINGS."
THINGS BEYOND THE UNDERSTANDING OF ANYONE WHO--
--WELL, WHO ISN'T ME.
WHERE'S EVERYONE ELSE?
BIRTHDAY PARTY. THIRD FLOOR. I FIND THEM FAIRLY TEDIOUS, BUT THE STAFF ENJOYS THEM, SO I ALLOW IT.
I WANTED YOU TO SEE ALL THIS FOR YOURSELF, BUT ON A DAY-TO-DAY BASIS. I'VE ARRANGED FOR A PRIVATE ENTRANCE TO YOUR OFFICE SO YOU CAN COME AND DO YOUR WORK WITHOUT BEING DISTURBED.
PRIVATE
THANK YOU, THAT'S VERY KIND GIVEN MY--
--THAT IS--
NO ONE HERE CARES ABOUT YOUR RECORD, OR YOUR PAST, OR--
HOW I LOOK--
--ANY OF THAT. THIS IS A FRESH START. MY ONLY CONDITION IS THAT YOU MUST KEEP THIS ARRANGEMENT JUST BETWEEN US. YOU HAVE THE POTENTIAL TO CHANGE, WHICH I CANNOT SAY FOR OTHERS WHO MIGHT HEAR ABOUT THIS.
NOW COME SEE YOUR OFFICE.
IT'S NOT MUCH, I ADMIT, BUT ITS SPARE DESIGN AND MINIMALIST DECOR HAS ONLY ONE PURPOSE: TO KEEP YOU FOCUSED ON THE TASK AT HAND. AS I SAID, THERE CAN BE NO DISTRACTIONS.
SO WHAT IS IT I'M SUPPOSED TO DO? YOU HAVEN'T REALLY TOLD ME. A PLACE LIKE THIS, YOU MUST HAVE ALL KINDS OF QUALIFIED PEOPLE.
YOU ARE UNIQUELY SUITED FOR THIS TASK. THERE IS NO ONE ELSE IN THE WORLD WHO COULD DO FOR ME WHAT I NEED DONE AS WELL AS YOU CAN.

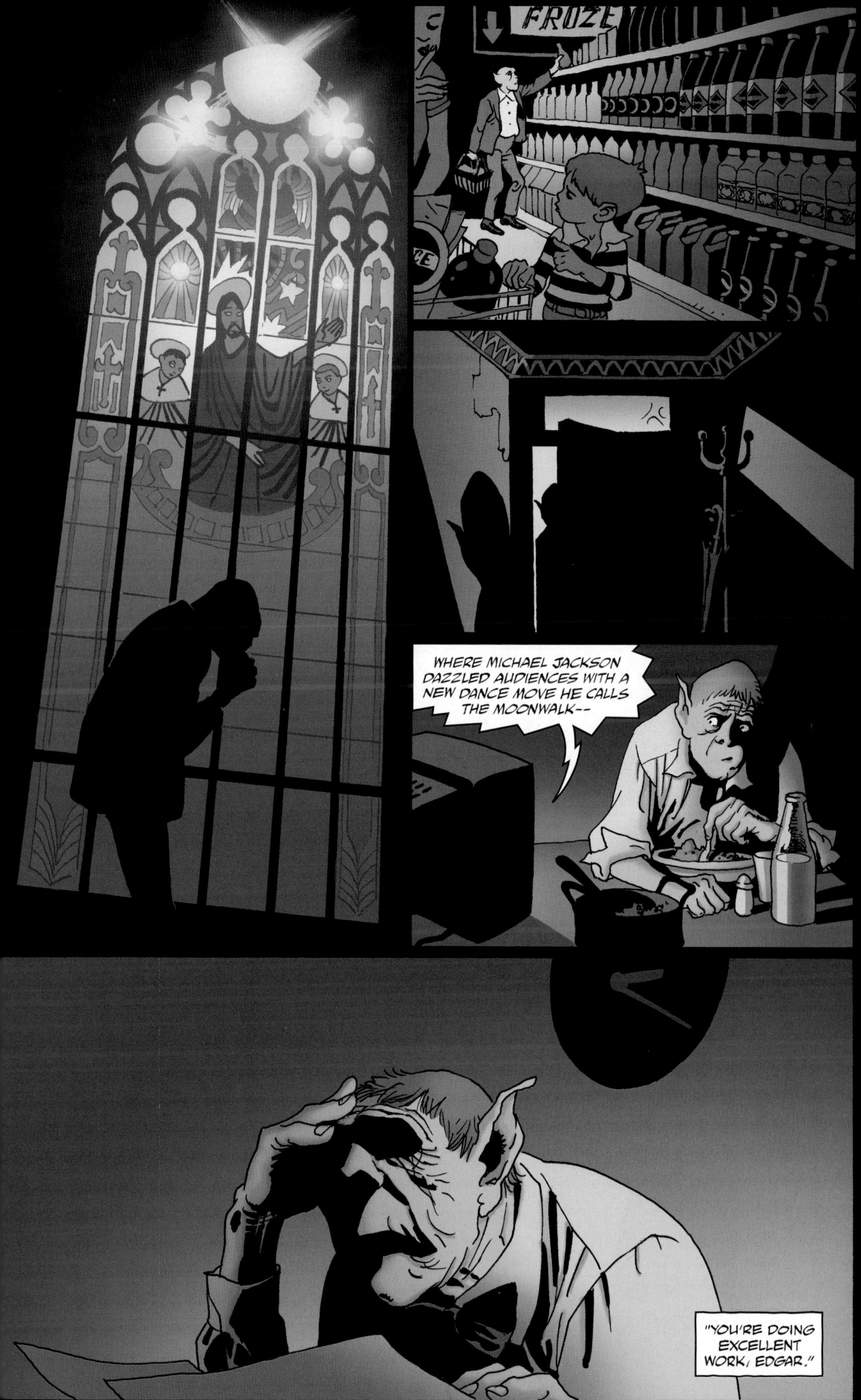
FROZE
WHERE MICHAEL JACKSON DAZZLED AUDIENCES WITH A NEW DANCE MOVE HE CALLS THE MOONWALK--
"YOU'RE DOING EXCELLENT WORK, EDGAR."

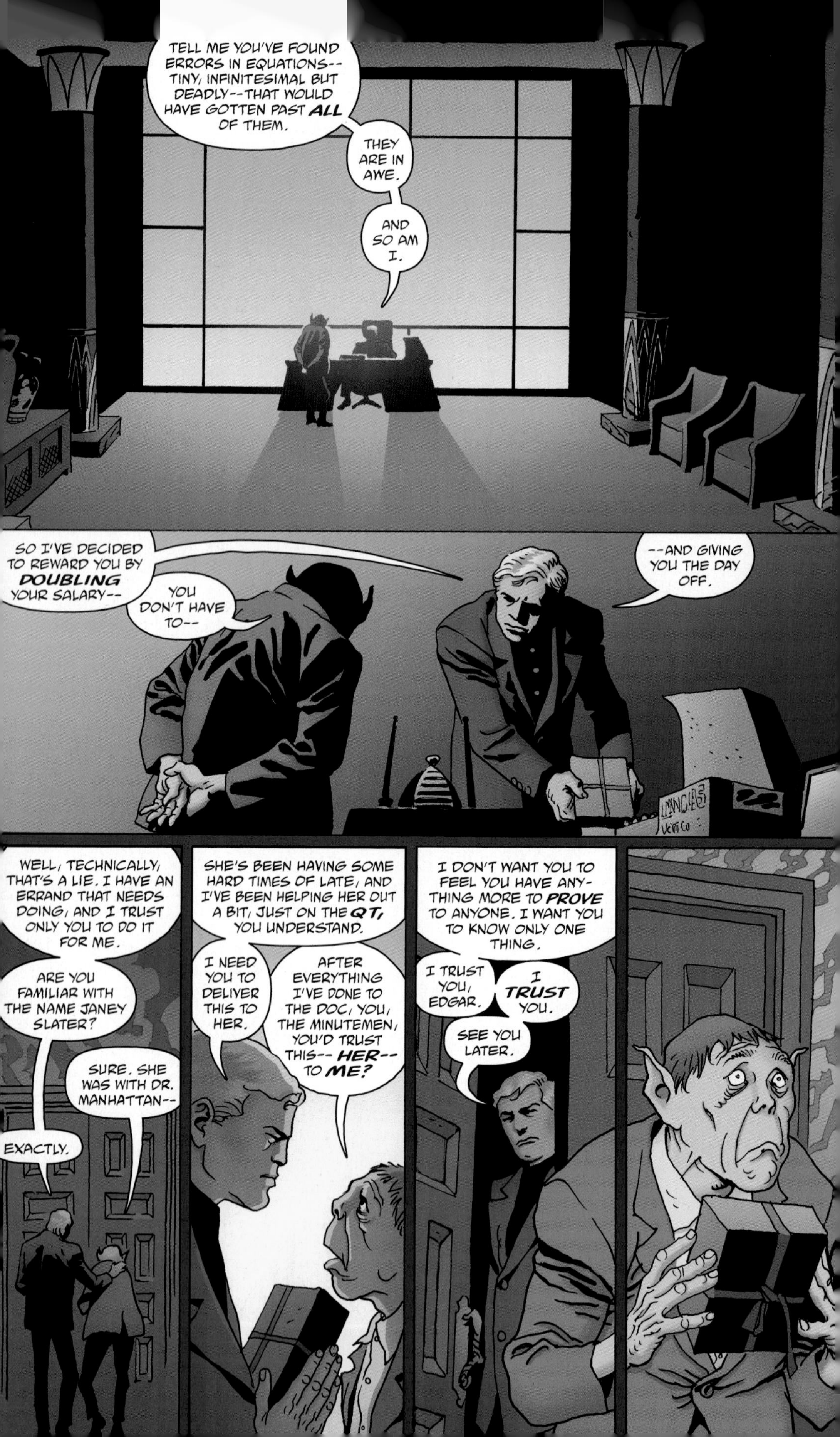

TELL ME YOU'VE FOUND ERRORS IN EQUATIONS-- TINY, INFINITESIMAL BUT DEADLY--THAT WOULD HAVE GOTTEN PAST ALL OF THEM.
THEY ARE IN AWE.
AND SO AM I.
SO I'VE DECIDED TO REWARD YOU BY DOUBLING YOUR SALARY--
YOU DON'T HAVE TO--
--AND GIVING YOU THE DAY OFF.
WELL, TECHNICALLY, THAT'S A LIE. I HAVE AN ERRAND THAT NEEDS DOING, AND I TRUST ONLY YOU TO DO IT FOR ME.
ARE YOU FAMILIAR WITH THE NAME JANEY SLATER?
SURE. SHE WAS WITH DR. MANHATTAN--
EXACTLY.
SHE'S BEEN HAVING SOME HARD TIMES OF LATE, AND I'VE BEEN HELPING HER OUT A BIT, JUST ON THE QT, YOU UNDERSTAND.
I NEED YOU TO DELIVER THIS TO HER.
AFTER EVERYTHING I'VE DONE TO THE DOC, YOU, THE MINUTEMEN, YOU'D TRUST THIS-- HER-- TO ME?
I DON'T WANT YOU TO FEEL YOU HAVE ANY-THING MORE TO PROVE TO ANYONE. I WANT YOU TO KNOW ONLY ONE THING.
I TRUST YOU, EDGAR.
I TRUST YOU.
SEE YOU LATER.

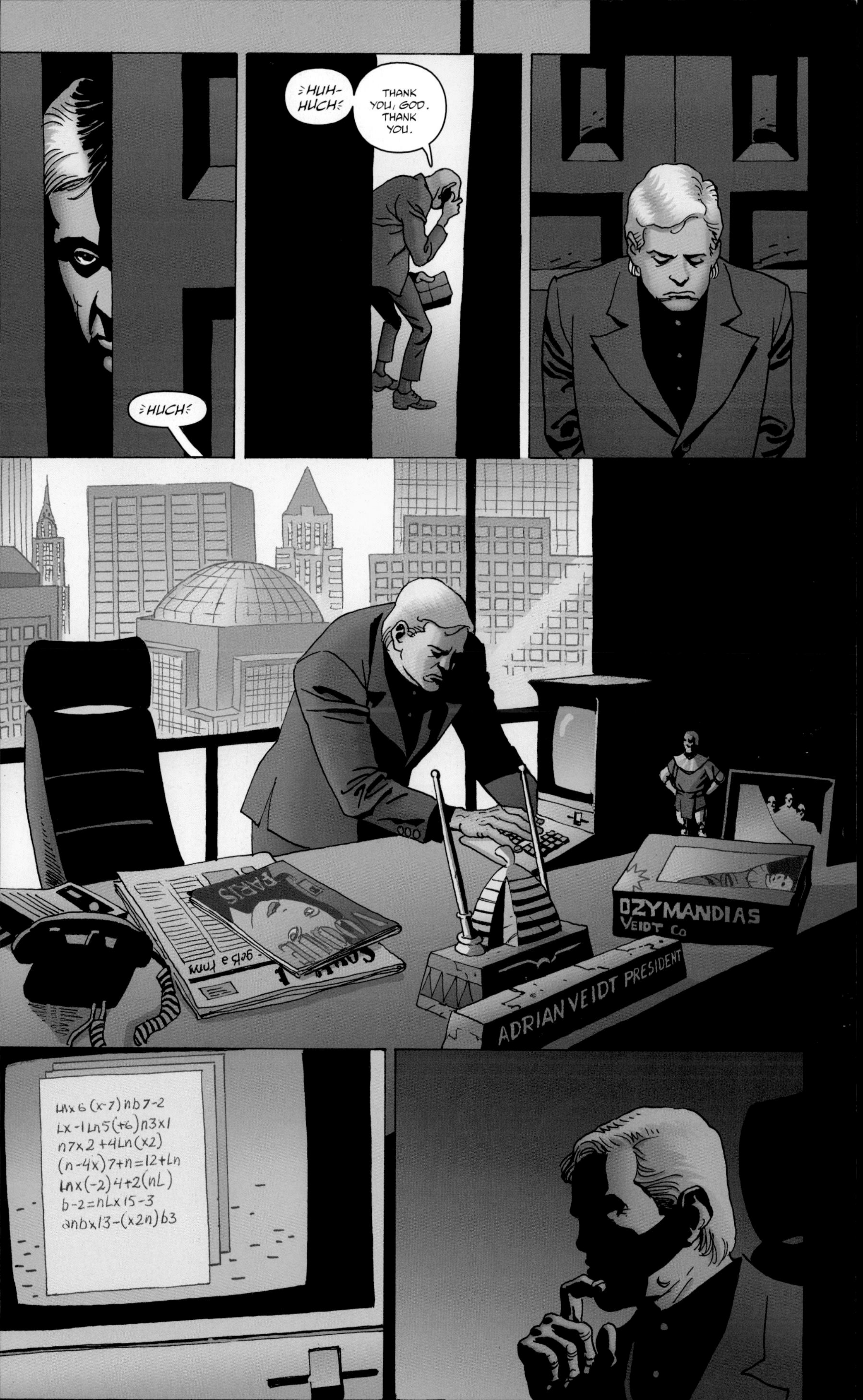
HUH-HUCH
THANK YOU, GOD. THANK YOU.
HUCH
PARIS
OZYMANDIAS
VEIDT CO
ADRIAN VEIDT PRESIDENT
Lnx6 (x-7) nb7-2
Lx-1Ln5(+6) n3x1
n7x2 +4Ln(x2)
(n-4x)7+n=12+Ln
Lnx(-2)4+2(nL)
b-2=nLx15-3
anbx13-(x2n)b3

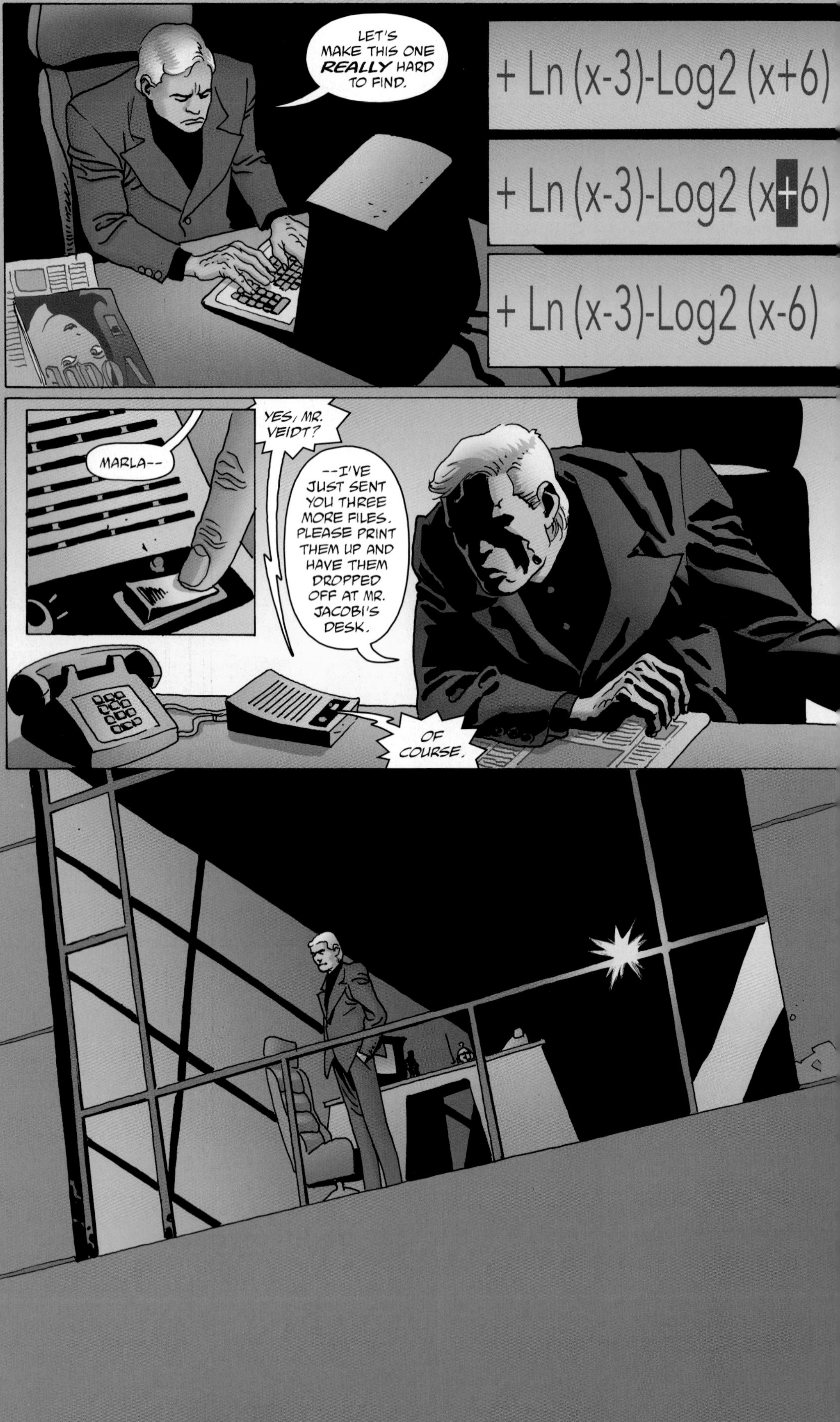
LET'S MAKE THIS ONE REALLY HARD TO FIND.
+ Ln (x-3)-Log2 (x+6)
+ Ln (x-3)-Log2 (x+6)
+ Ln (x-3)-Log2 (x-6)
MARLA--
YES, MR. VEIDT?
--I'VE JUST SENT YOU THREE MORE FILES. PLEASE PRINT THEM UP AND HAVE THEM DROPPED OFF AT MR. JACOBI'S DESK.
OF COURSE.

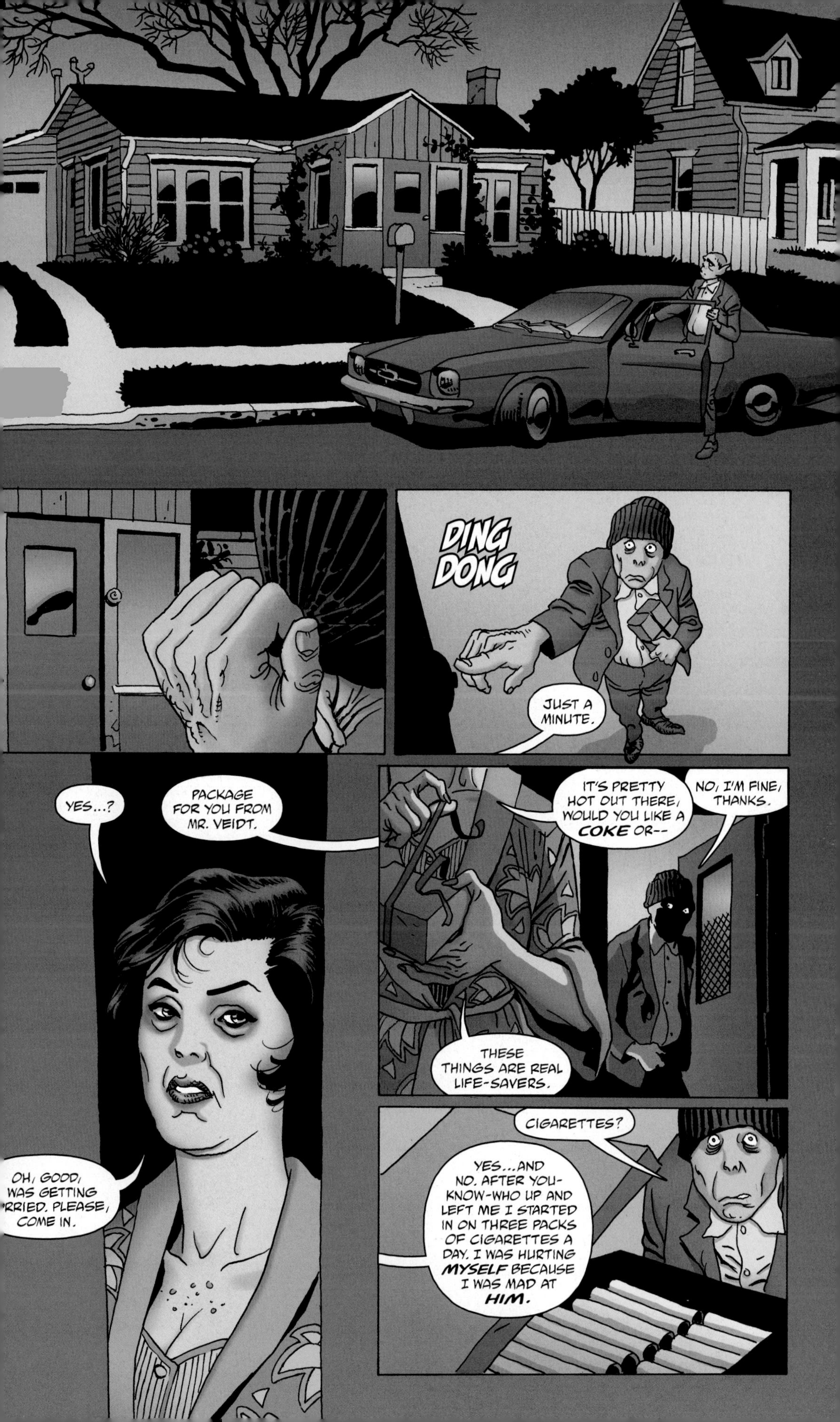
DING DONG
JUST A MINUTE.
YES...?
PACKAGE FOR YOU FROM MR. VEIDT.
OH, GOOD, WAS GETTING RRIED. PLEASE, COME IN.
IT'S PRETTY HOT OUT THERE, WOULD YOU LIKE A COKE OR--
NO, I'M FINE, THANKS.
THESE THINGS ARE REAL LIFE-SAVERS.
CIGARETTES?
YES...AND NO. AFTER YOU-KNOW-WHO UP AND LEFT ME I STARTED IN ON THREE PACKS OF CIGARETTES A DAY. I WAS HURTING MYSELF BECAUSE I WAS MAD AT HIM.

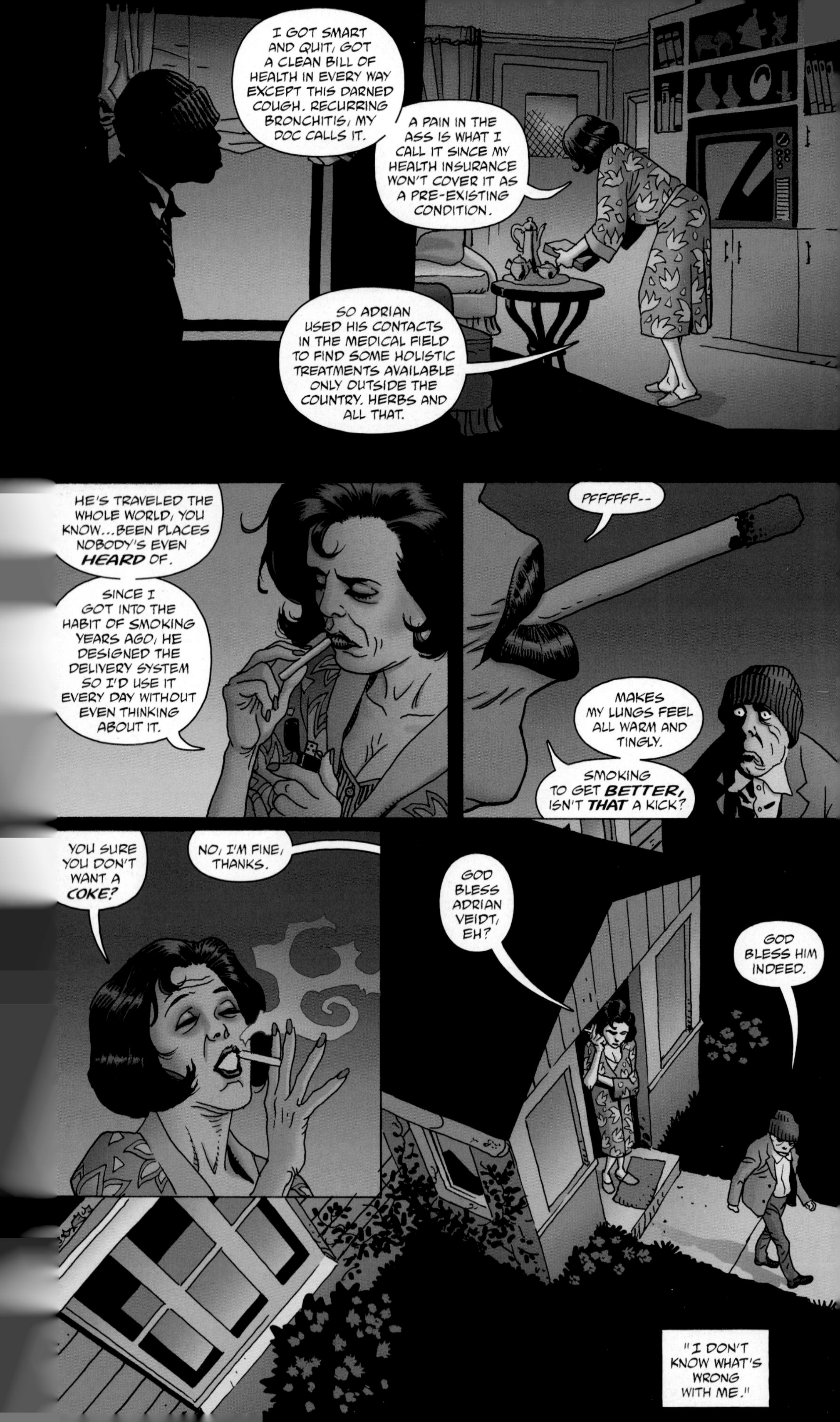
I GOT SMART AND QUIT, GOT A CLEAN BILL OF HEALTH IN EVERY WAY EXCEPT THIS DARNED COUGH. RECURRING BRONCHITIS, MY DOC CALLS IT.
A PAIN IN THE ASS IS WHAT I CALL IT SINCE MY HEALTH INSURANCE WON'T COVER IT AS A PRE-EXISTING CONDITION.
SO ADRIAN USED HIS CONTACTS IN THE MEDICAL FIELD TO FIND SOME HOLISTIC TREATMENTS AVAILABLE ONLY OUTSIDE THE COUNTRY. HERBS AND ALL THAT.
HE'S TRAVELED THE WHOLE WORLD, YOU KNOW...BEEN PLACES NOBODY'S EVEN **HEARD** OF.
SINCE I GOT INTO THE HABIT OF SMOKING YEARS AGO, HE DESIGNED THE DELIVERY SYSTEM SO I'D USE IT EVERY DAY WITHOUT EVEN THINKING ABOUT IT.
PFFFFFF--
MAKES MY LUNGS FEEL ALL WARM AND TINGLY.
SMOKING TO GET **BETTER,** ISN'T **THAT** A KICK?
YOU SURE YOU DON'T WANT A **COKE?**
NO, I'M FINE, THANKS.
GOD BLESS ADRIAN VEIDT, EH?
GOD BLESS HIM INDEED.
"I DON'T KNOW WHAT'S WRONG WITH ME."

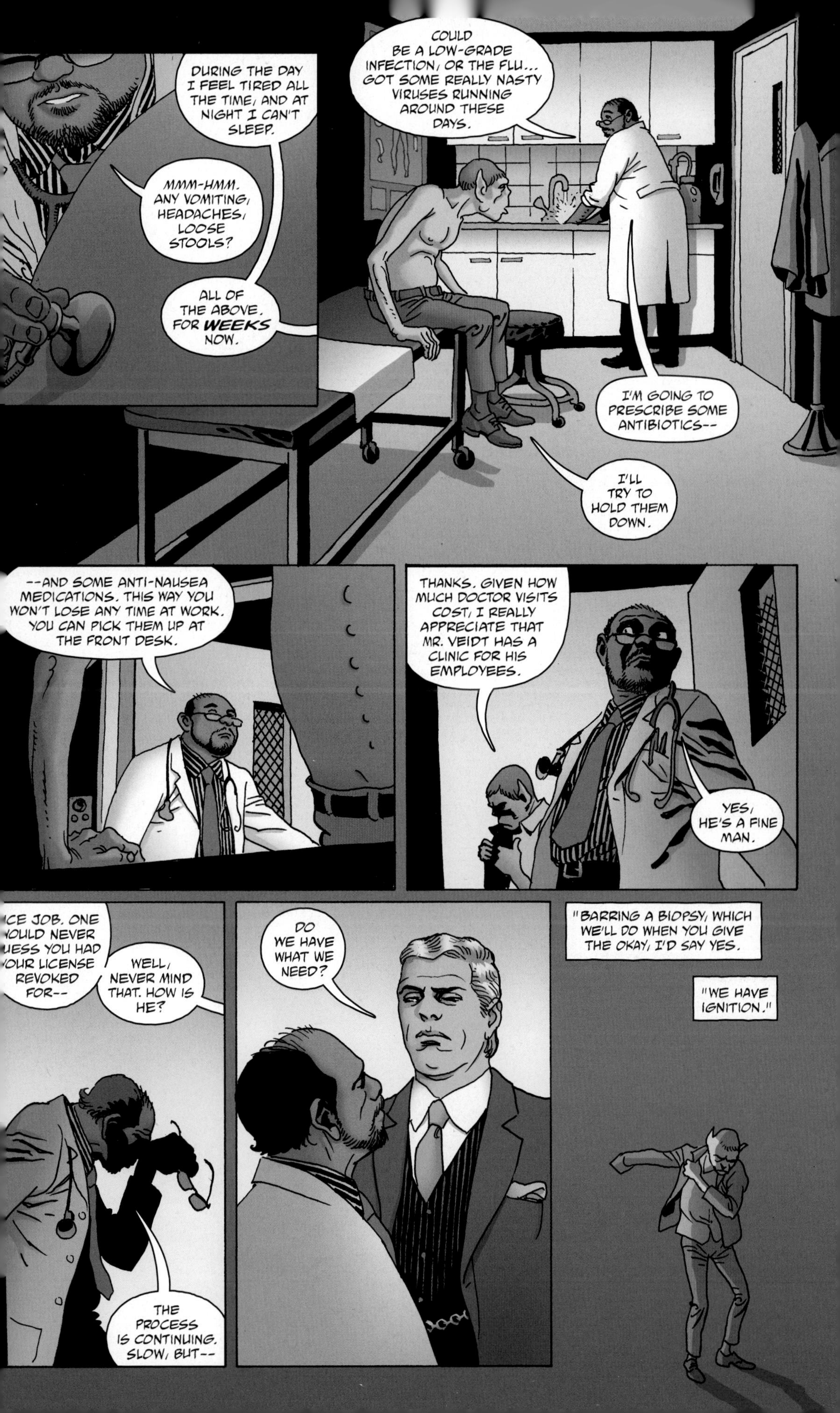
DURING THE DAY I FEEL TIRED ALL THE TIME, AND AT NIGHT I CAN'T SLEEP.
MMM-HMM. ANY VOMITING, HEADACHES, LOOSE STOOLS?
ALL OF THE ABOVE. FOR WEEKS NOW.
COULD BE A LOW-GRADE INFECTION, OR THE FLU... GOT SOME REALLY NASTY VIRUSES RUNNING AROUND THESE DAYS.
I'M GOING TO PRESCRIBE SOME ANTIBIOTICS--
I'LL TRY TO HOLD THEM DOWN.
--AND SOME ANTI-NAUSEA MEDICATIONS. THIS WAY YOU WON'T LOSE ANY TIME AT WORK. YOU CAN PICK THEM UP AT THE FRONT DESK.
THANKS. GIVEN HOW MUCH DOCTOR VISITS COST, I REALLY APPRECIATE THAT MR. VEIDT HAS A CLINIC FOR HIS EMPLOYEES.
YES, HE'S A FINE MAN.
ICE JOB. ONE OULD NEVER UESS YOU HAD OUR LICENSE REVOKED FOR--
WELL, NEVER MIND THAT. HOW IS HE?
THE PROCESS IS CONTINUING. SLOW, BUT--
DO WE HAVE WHAT WE NEED?
"BARRING A BIOPSY, WHICH WE'LL DO WHEN YOU GIVE THE OKAY, I'D SAY YES.
"WE HAVE IGNITION."

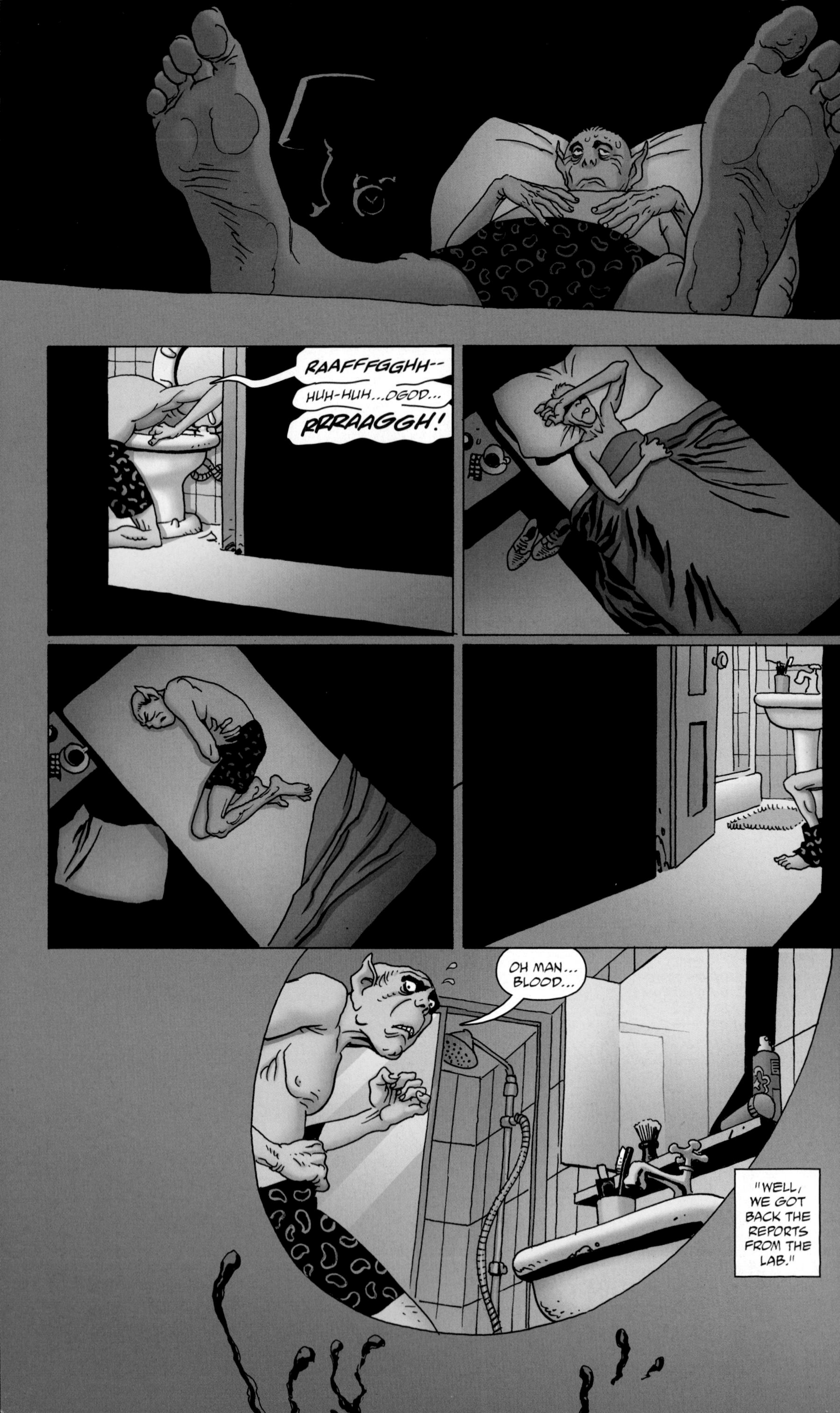

RAAFFFGGHH--
HUH-HUH...OGOD...
RRRAAGGH!
OH MAN... BLOOD...
"WELL, WE GOT BACK THE REPORTS FROM THE LAB."

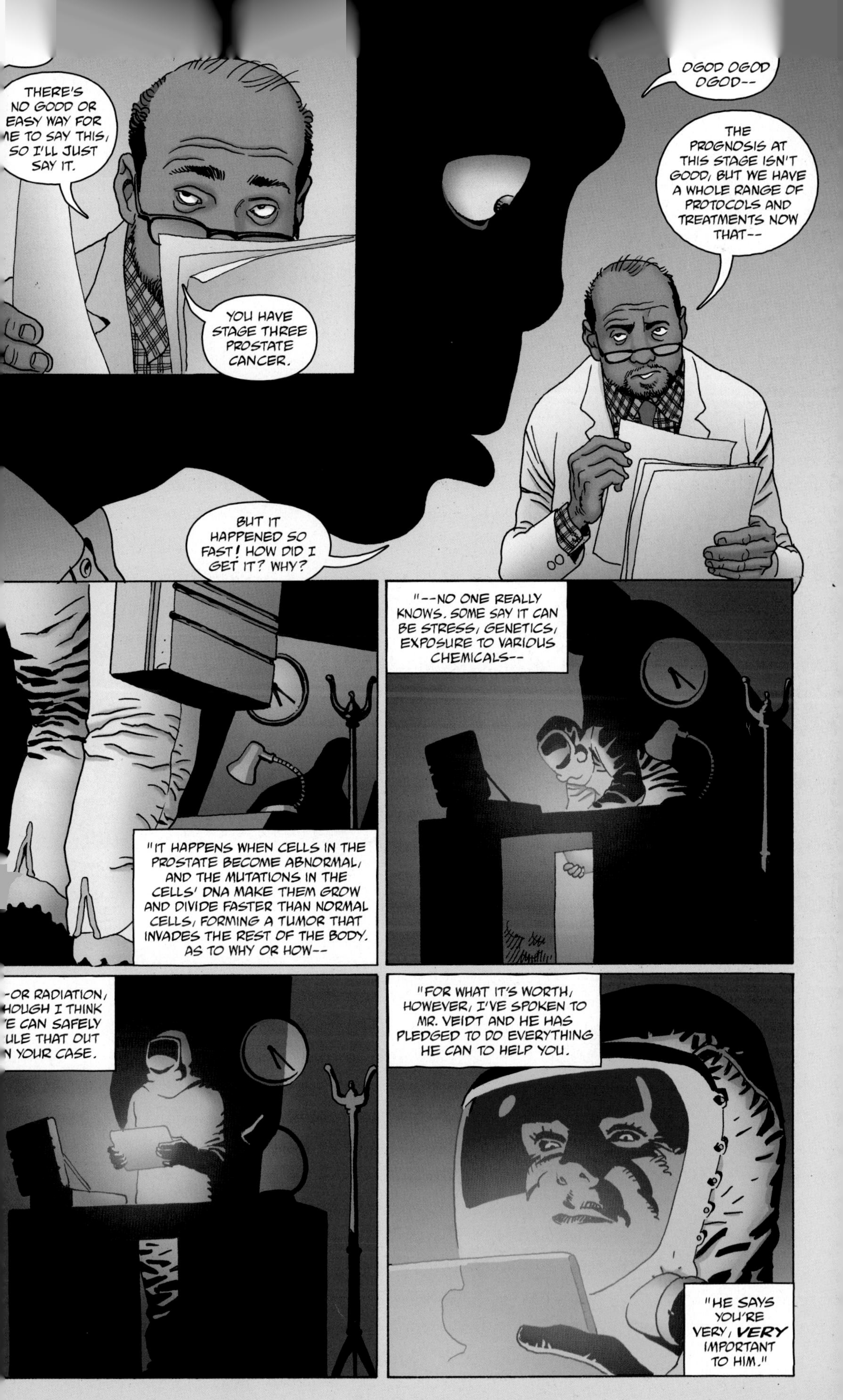
THERE'S NO GOOD OR EASY WAY FOR ME TO SAY THIS, SO I'LL JUST SAY IT.
YOU HAVE STAGE THREE PROSTATE CANCER.
OGOD OGOD OGOD--
THE PROGNOSIS AT THIS STAGE ISN'T GOOD, BUT WE HAVE A WHOLE RANGE OF PROTOCOLS AND TREATMENTS NOW THAT--
BUT IT HAPPENED SO FAST! HOW DID I GET IT? WHY?
"IT HAPPENS WHEN CELLS IN THE PROSTATE BECOME ABNORMAL, AND THE MUTATIONS IN THE CELLS' DNA MAKE THEM GROW AND DIVIDE FASTER THAN NORMAL CELLS, FORMING A TUMOR THAT INVADES THE REST OF THE BODY. AS TO WHY OR HOW--
"--NO ONE REALLY KNOWS. SOME SAY IT CAN BE STRESS, GENETICS, EXPOSURE TO VARIOUS CHEMICALS--
-OR RADIATION, HOUGH I THINK E CAN SAFELY ULE THAT OUT N YOUR CASE.
"FOR WHAT IT'S WORTH, HOWEVER, I'VE SPOKEN TO MR. VEIDT AND HE HAS PLEDGED TO DO EVERYTHING HE CAN TO HELP YOU.
"HE SAYS YOU'RE VERY, VERY IMPORTANT TO HIM."

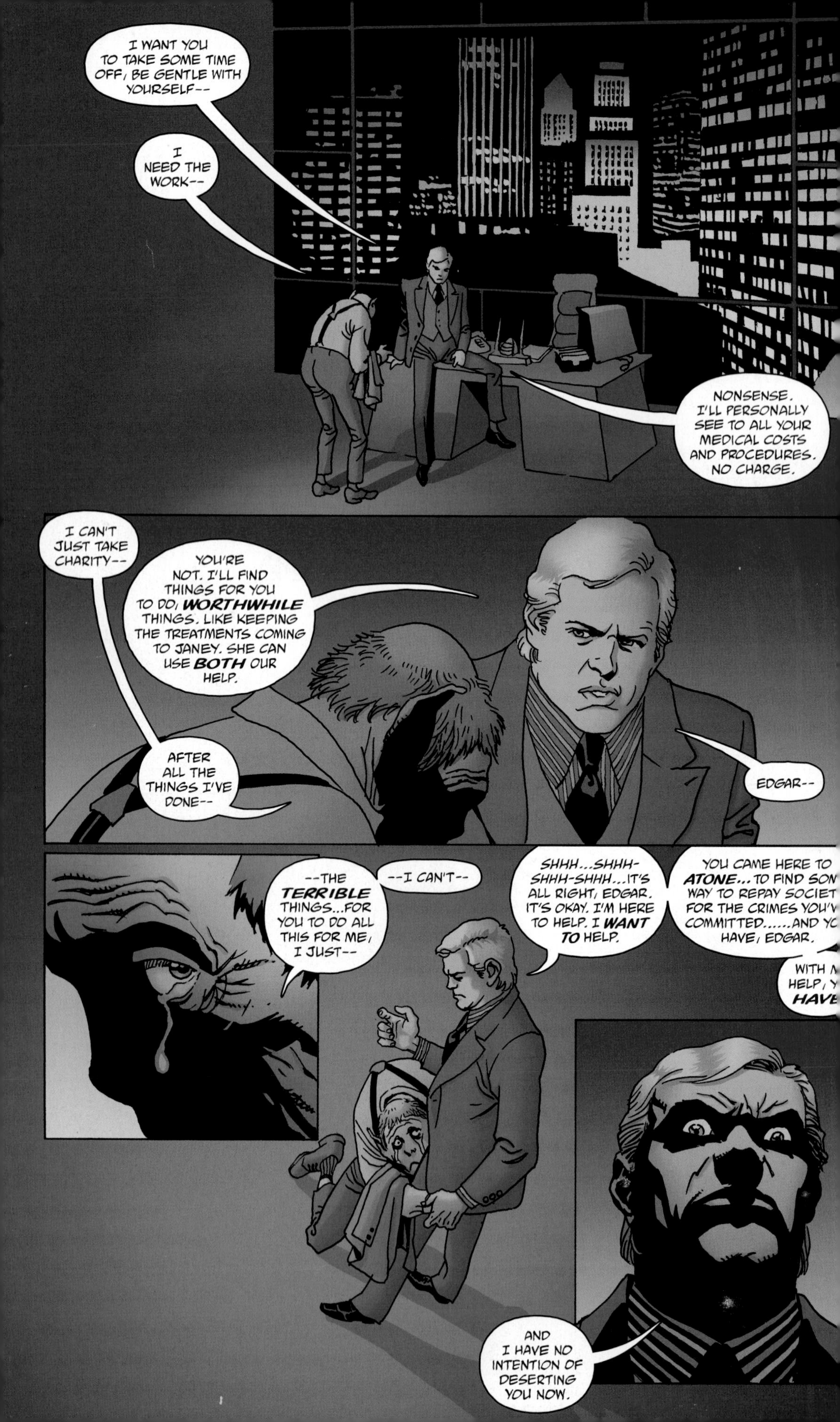
I WANT YOU TO TAKE SOME TIME OFF, BE GENTLE WITH YOURSELF--
I NEED THE WORK--
NONSENSE. I'LL PERSONALLY SEE TO ALL YOUR MEDICAL COSTS AND PROCEDURES. NO CHARGE.
I CAN'T JUST TAKE CHARITY--
YOU'RE NOT. I'LL FIND THINGS FOR YOU TO DO, WORTHWHILE THINGS. LIKE KEEPING THE TREATMENTS COMING TO JANEY. SHE CAN USE BOTH OUR HELP.
AFTER ALL THE THINGS I'VE DONE--
EDGAR--
--THE TERRIBLE THINGS...FOR YOU TO DO ALL THIS FOR ME, I JUST--
--I CAN'T--
SHHH...SHHH-SHHH-SHHH...IT'S ALL RIGHT, EDGAR. IT'S OKAY. I'M HERE TO HELP. I WANT TO HELP.
YOU CAME HERE TO ATONE...TO FIND SOM WAY TO REPAY SOCIET FOR THE CRIMES YOU'V COMMITTED......AND YO HAVE, EDGAR.
WITH HELP, Y HAVE
AND I HAVE NO INTENTION OF DESERTING YOU NOW.

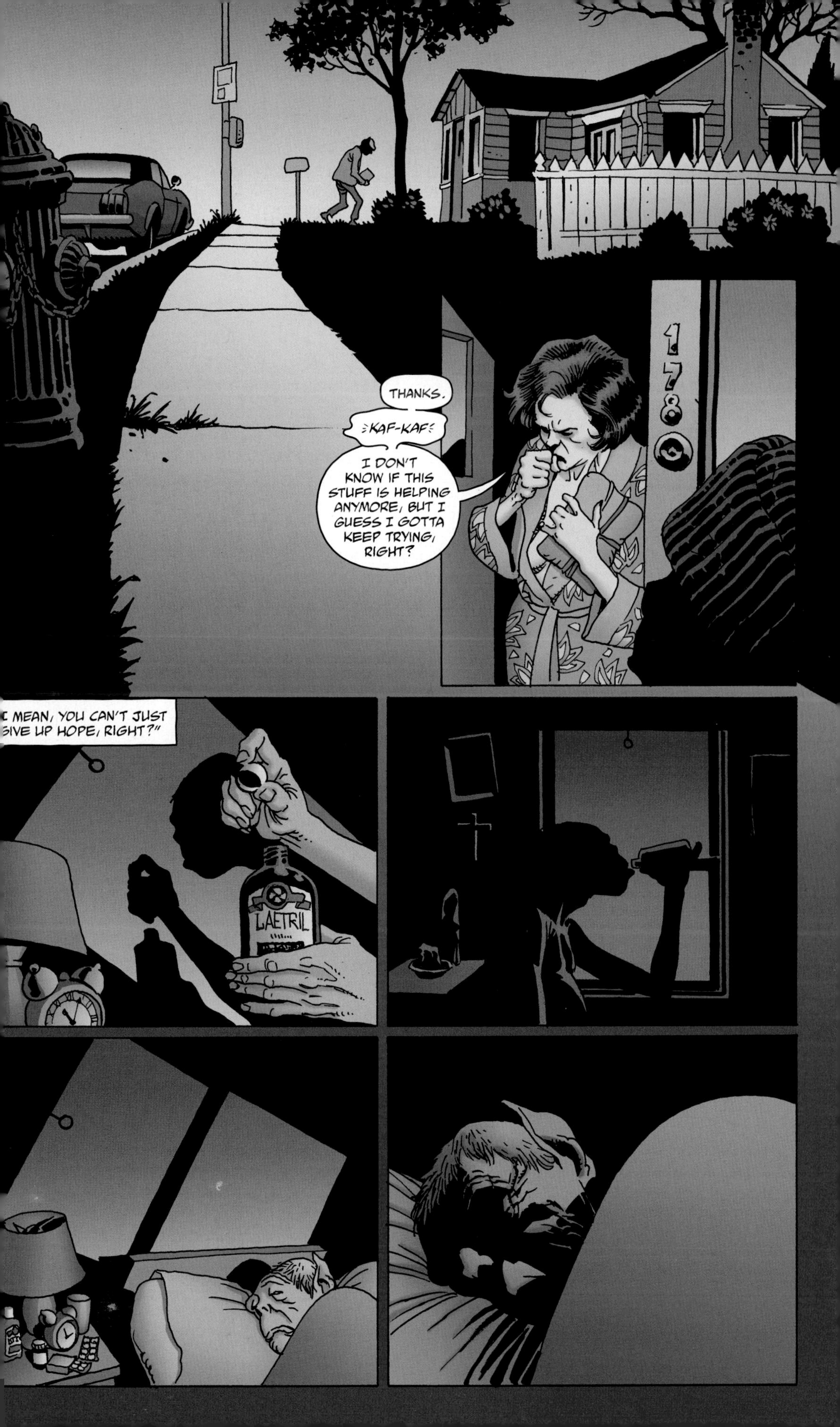
THANKS.
KAF-KAF
I DON'T KNOW IF THIS STUFF IS HELPING ANYMORE, BUT I GUESS I GOTTA KEEP TRYING, RIGHT?
I MEAN, YOU CAN'T JUST GIVE UP HOPE, RIGHT?"
LAETRIL
1780

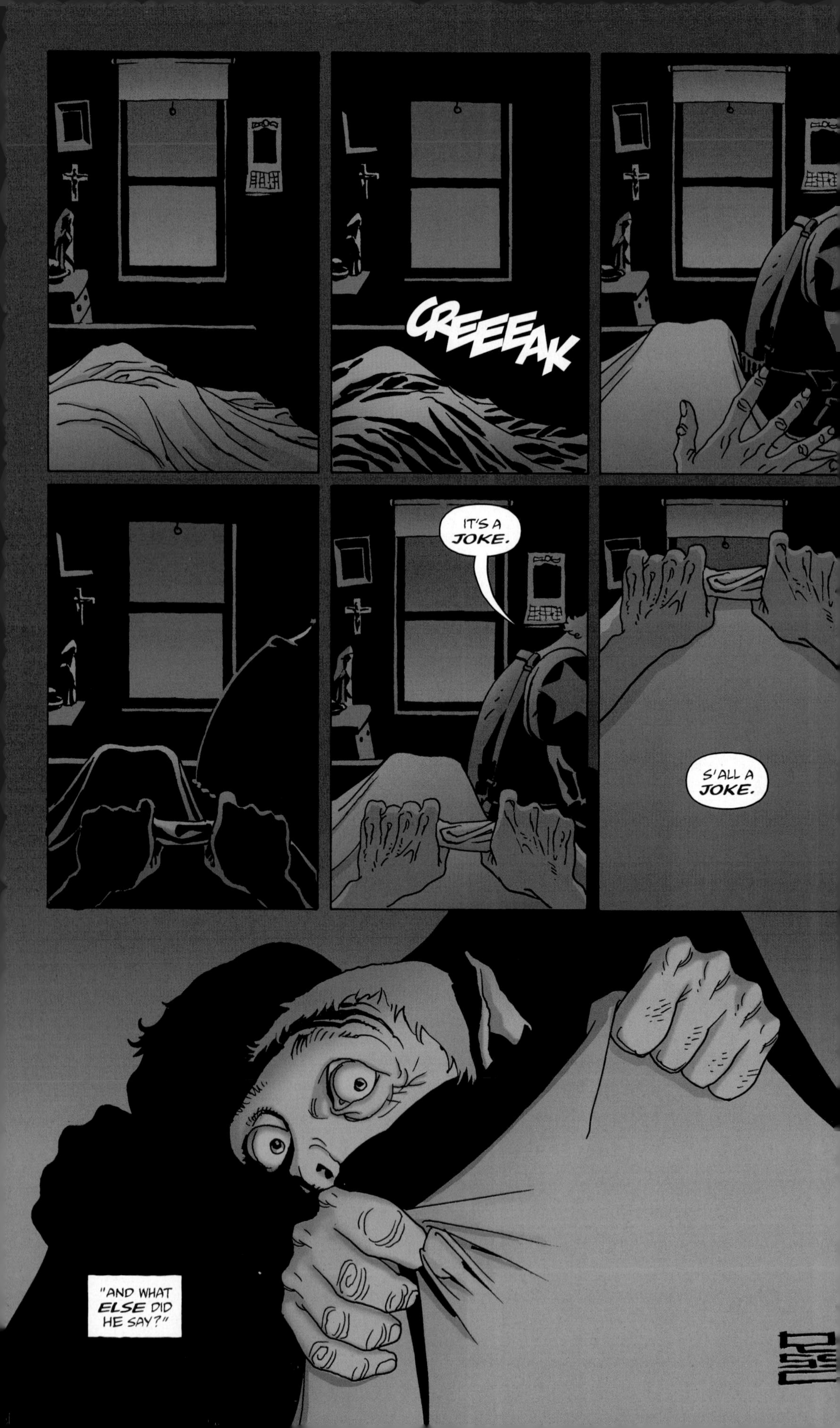
CREEEAK
IT'S A JOKE.
S'ALL A JOKE.
"AND WHAT ELSE DID HE SAY?"

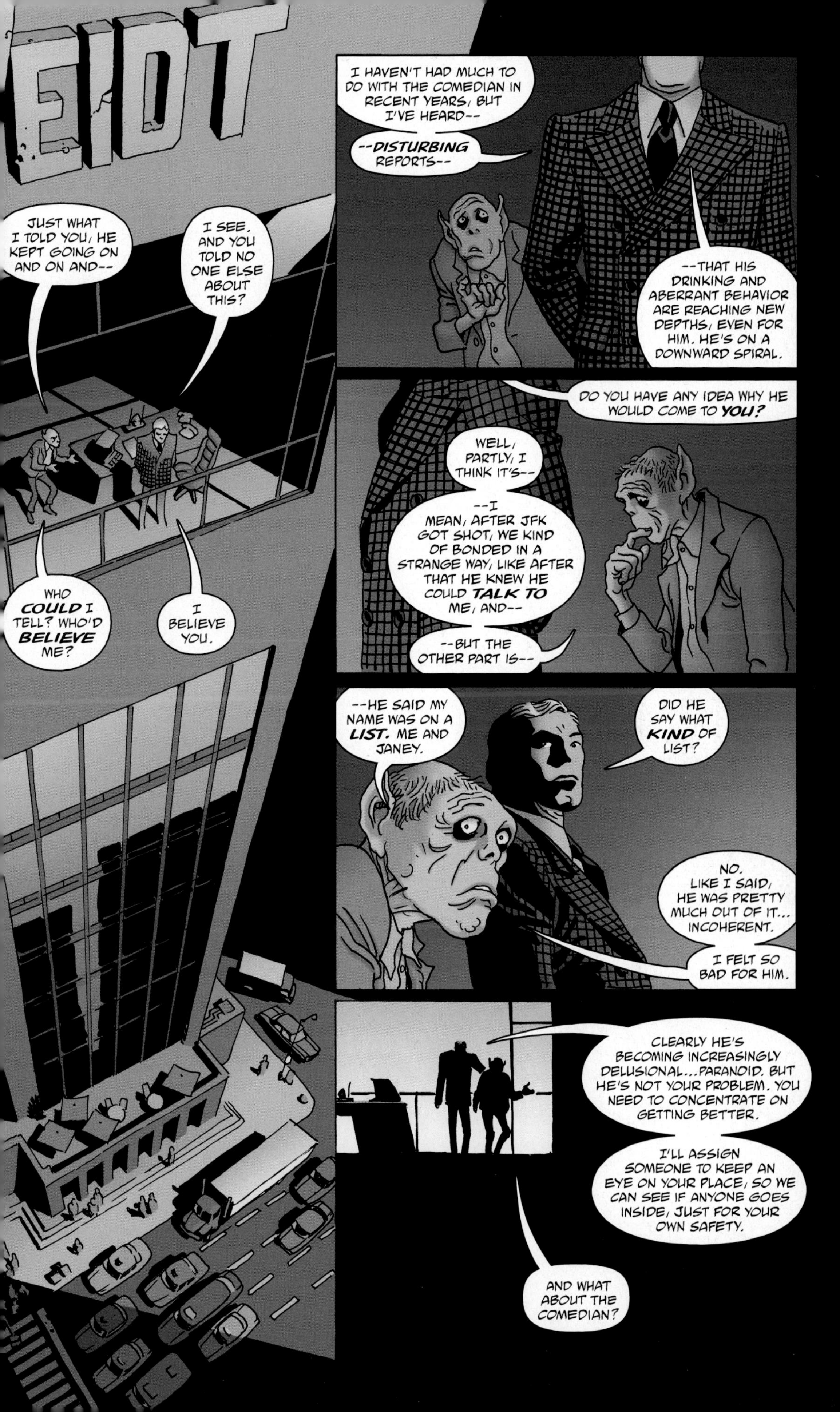
EIDT
JUST WHAT I TOLD YOU, HE KEPT GOING ON AND ON AND--
I SEE. AND YOU TOLD NO ONE ELSE ABOUT THIS?
WHO COULD I TELL? WHO'D BELIEVE ME?
I BELIEVE YOU.
I HAVEN'T HAD MUCH TO DO WITH THE COMEDIAN IN RECENT YEARS, BUT I'VE HEARD--
--DISTURBING REPORTS--
--THAT HIS DRINKING AND ABERRANT BEHAVIOR ARE REACHING NEW DEPTHS, EVEN FOR HIM. HE'S ON A DOWNWARD SPIRAL.
DO YOU HAVE ANY IDEA WHY HE WOULD COME TO YOU?
WELL, PARTLY, I THINK IT'S--
--I MEAN, AFTER JFK GOT SHOT, WE KIND OF BONDED IN A STRANGE WAY, LIKE AFTER THAT HE KNEW HE COULD TALK TO ME, AND--
--BUT THE OTHER PART IS--
--HE SAID MY NAME WAS ON A LIST. ME AND JANEY.
DID HE SAY WHAT KIND OF LIST?
NO. LIKE I SAID, HE WAS PRETTY MUCH OUT OF IT... INCOHERENT.
I FELT SO BAD FOR HIM.
CLEARLY HE'S BECOMING INCREASINGLY DELUSIONAL...PARANOID. BUT HE'S NOT YOUR PROBLEM. YOU NEED TO CONCENTRATE ON GETTING BETTER.
I'LL ASSIGN SOMEONE TO KEEP AN EYE ON YOUR PLACE, SO WE CAN SEE IF ANYONE GOES INSIDE, JUST FOR YOUR OWN SAFETY.
AND WHAT ABOUT THE COMEDIAN?

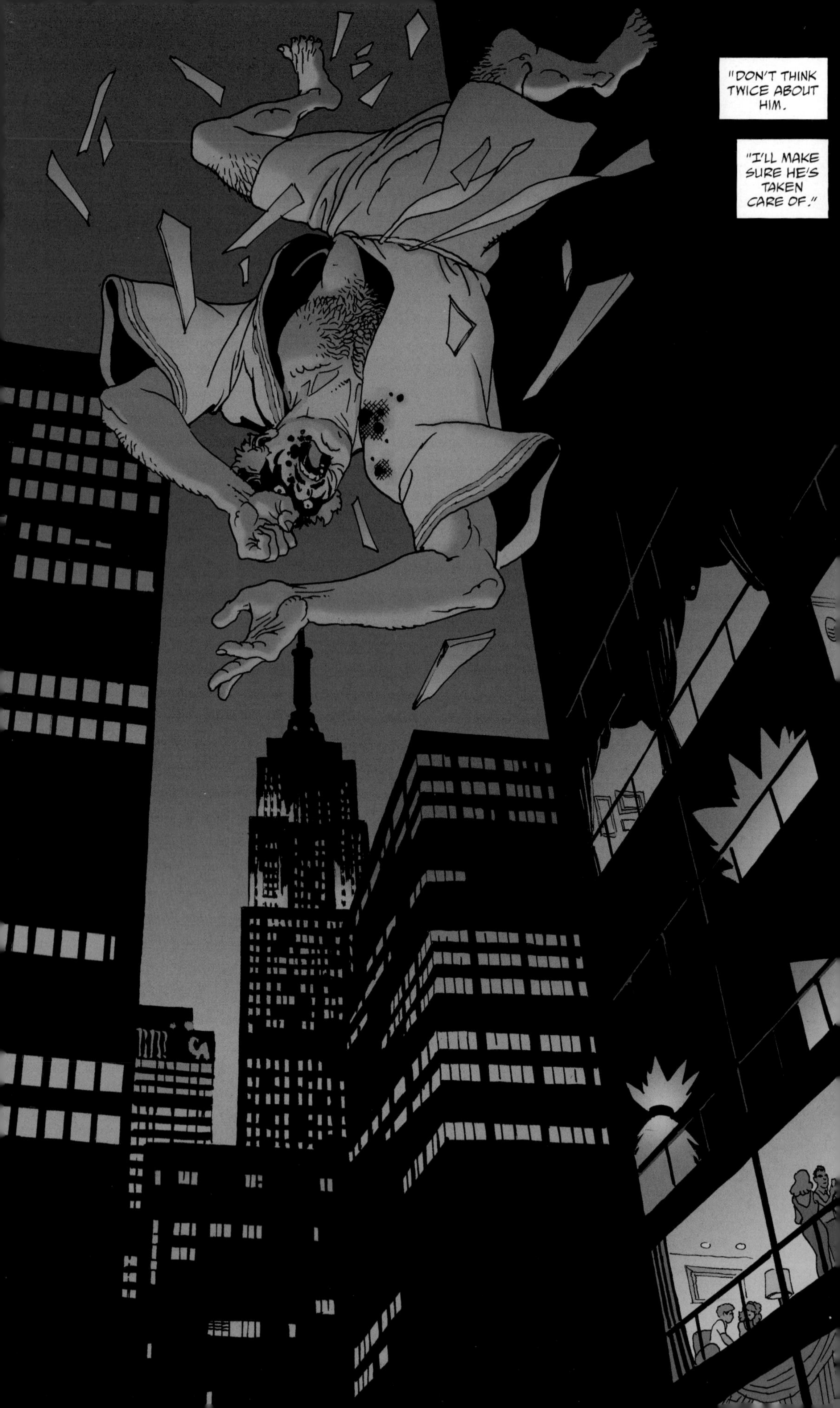
"DON'T THINK TWICE ABOUT HIM.
"I'LL MAKE SURE HE'S TAKEN CARE OF."

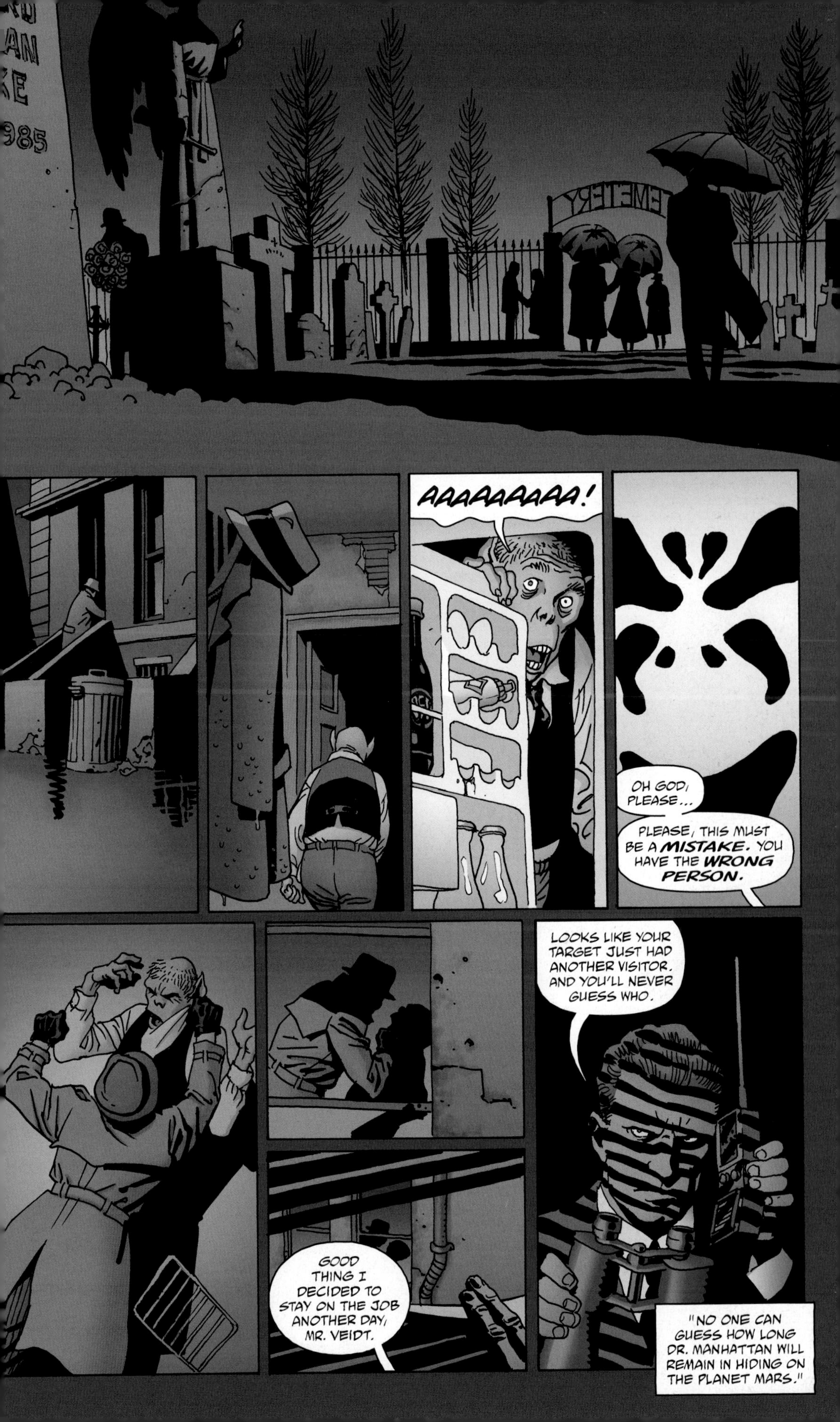
985
EMETERY
AAAAAAAAA!
OH GOD, PLEASE...
PLEASE, THIS MUST BE A **MISTAKE.** YOU HAVE THE **WRONG PERSON.**
LOOKS LIKE YOUR TARGET JUST HAD ANOTHER VISITOR. AND YOU'LL NEVER GUESS WHO.
GOOD THING I DECIDED TO STAY ON THE JOB ANOTHER DAY, MR. VEIDT.
"NO ONE CAN GUESS HOW LONG DR. MANHATTAN WILL REMAIN IN HIDING ON THE PLANET MARS."

THE MAN DESCRIBED AS THE MOST POWERFUL FORCE IN THE UNIVERSE WAS LAST SEEN ERUPTING IN A RAGE DURING A TALK SHOW ON **ABC**.

FOR THOSE WHO MISSED IT, HERE'S ANOTHER LOOK.

I WONDER IF YOU REMEMBER **WALLY WEAVER**. BACK IN THE EARLY SIXTIES THE NEWSPAPERS CALLED HIM **DR. MANHATTAN'S BUDDY**.

HE DIED OF **CANCER** IN 1971.

I BELIEVE IT WAS **SUDDEN** AND QUITE **PAINFUL**.

I REMEMBER WALLY AS A GOOD FRIEND. I ATTENDED HIS **FUNERAL**.

HOW ABOUT **EDWARD W. JACOBI**, ALSO KNOWN AS **MOLOCH?** YOU ENCOUNTERED **HIM SEVERAL** TIMES DURING THE SIXTIES IN **BATTLES**, **CONFLICTS**, WHATEVER IT IS YOU SUPER-PEOPLE **DO**.

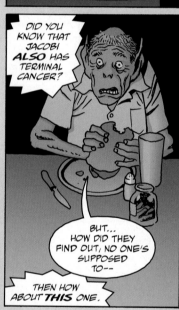

DID YOU KNOW THAT JACOBI **ALSO** HAS TERMINAL CANCER?

BUT... HOW DID THEY FIND OUT, NO ONE'S SUPPOSED TO--

THEN HOW ABOUT **THIS** ONE.

DID YOU KNOW THAT MISS **JANEY SLATER**, LINKED ROMANTICALLY WITH YOU IN THE SIXTIES, IS CURRENTLY SUFFERING FROM LUNG CANCER?

"DOCTORS HAVE GIVEN HER SIX MONTHS TO LIVE."

BUT SHE SAID SHE HAD A CLEAN BILL OF HEALTH, SHE--

THE CIGARETTES... OH GOD...OH GOD, NO--

NOTICE ANY **CONNECTION?**

BECAUSE FROM WHERE **I'M** STANDING, IT'S STARTING TO LOOK PRETTY **CONCLUSIVE**.

HELLO, EDGAR.

DON'T BE AFRAID. I'M HERE TO TELL YOU WHAT THIS IS ALL ABOUT.

I'M HERE TO TELL YOU THE TRUTH.

SO HELP ME GOD.

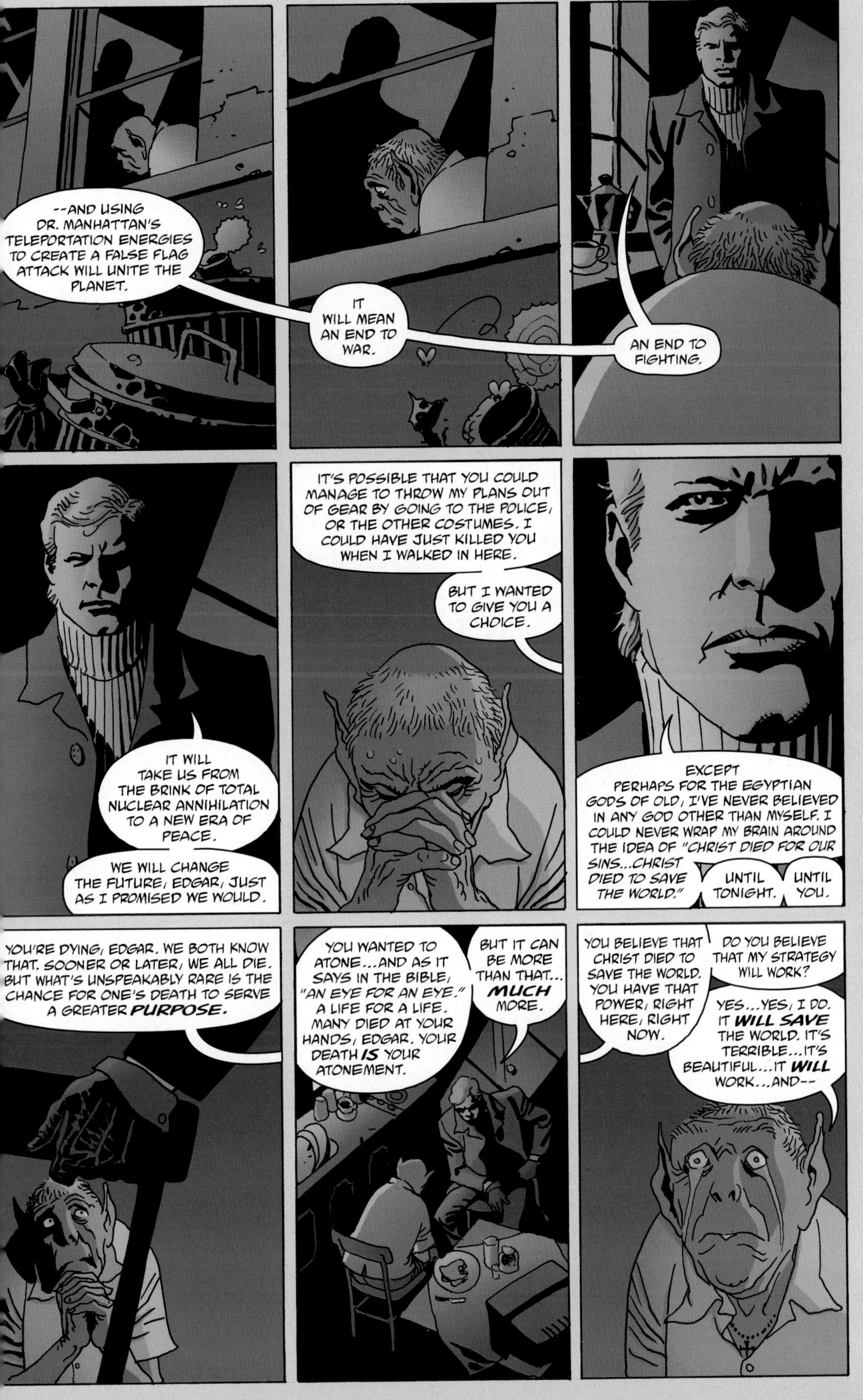
--AND USING DR. MANHATTAN'S TELEPORTATION ENERGIES TO CREATE A FALSE FLAG ATTACK WILL UNITE THE PLANET.
IT WILL MEAN AN END TO WAR.
AN END TO FIGHTING.
IT'S POSSIBLE THAT YOU COULD MANAGE TO THROW MY PLANS OUT OF GEAR BY GOING TO THE POLICE, OR THE OTHER COSTUMES. I COULD HAVE JUST KILLED YOU WHEN I WALKED IN HERE.
BUT I WANTED TO GIVE YOU A CHOICE.
IT WILL TAKE US FROM THE BRINK OF TOTAL NUCLEAR ANNIHILATION TO A NEW ERA OF PEACE.
WE WILL CHANGE THE FUTURE, EDGAR, JUST AS I PROMISED WE WOULD.
EXCEPT PERHAPS FOR THE EGYPTIAN GODS OF OLD, I'VE NEVER BELIEVED IN ANY GOD OTHER THAN MYSELF. I COULD NEVER WRAP MY BRAIN AROUND THE IDEA OF "CHRIST DIED FOR OUR SINS...CHRIST DIED TO SAVE THE WORLD."
UNTIL TONIGHT.
UNTIL YOU.
YOU'RE DYING, EDGAR. WE BOTH KNOW THAT. SOONER OR LATER, WE ALL DIE. BUT WHAT'S UNSPEAKABLY RARE IS THE CHANCE FOR ONE'S DEATH TO SERVE A GREATER **PURPOSE.**
YOU WANTED TO ATONE...AND AS IT SAYS IN THE BIBLE, "AN EYE FOR AN EYE." A LIFE FOR A LIFE. MANY DIED AT YOUR HANDS, EDGAR. YOUR DEATH **IS** YOUR ATONEMENT.
BUT IT CAN BE MORE THAN THAT... **MUCH** MORE.
YOU BELIEVE THAT CHRIST DIED TO SAVE THE WORLD. YOU HAVE THAT POWER, RIGHT HERE, RIGHT NOW.
DO YOU BELIEVE THAT MY STRATEGY WILL WORK?
YES...YES, I DO. IT **WILL SAVE** THE WORLD. IT'S TERRIBLE...IT'S BEAUTIFUL...IT **WILL** WORK...AND--

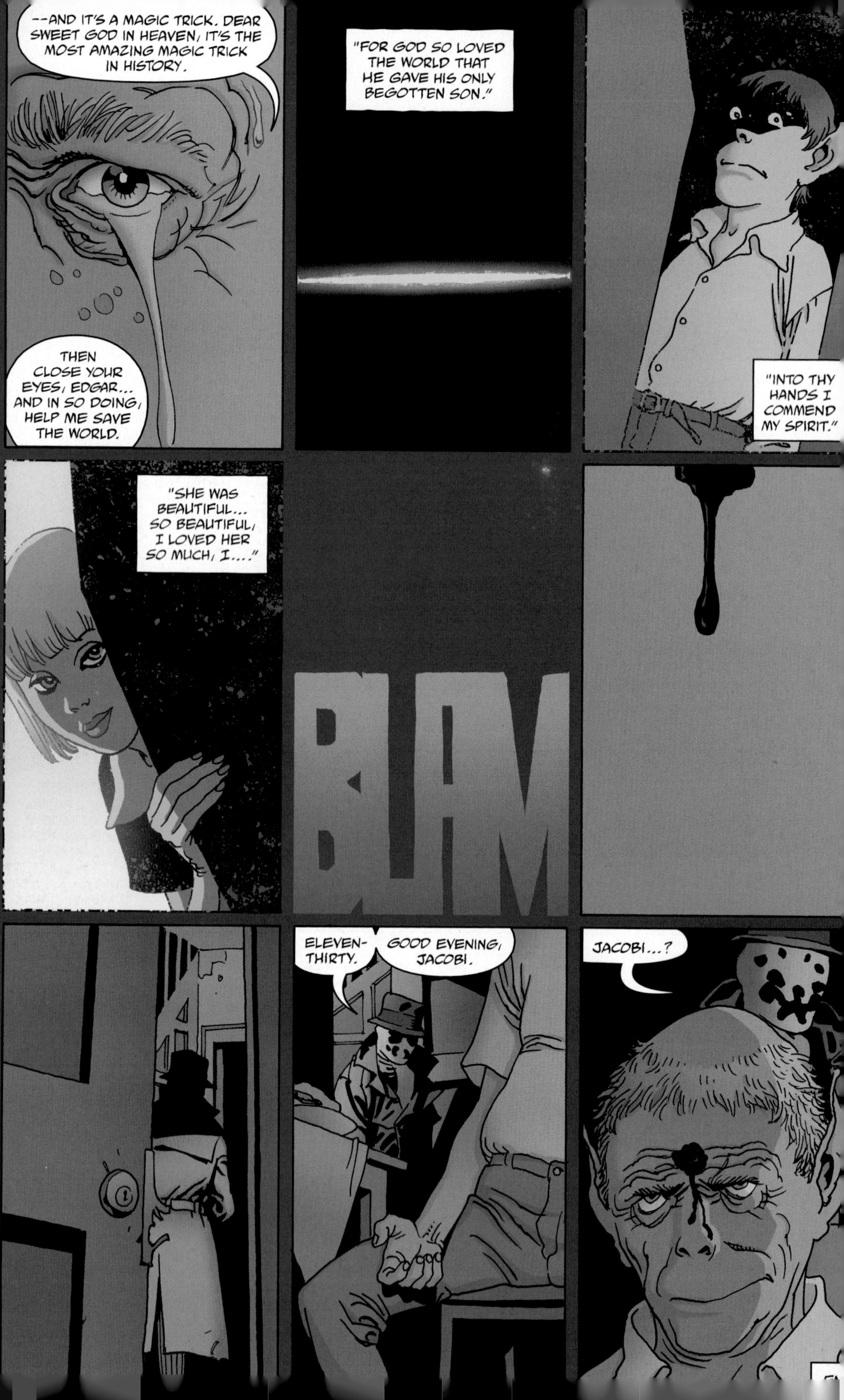
--AND IT'S A MAGIC TRICK. DEAR SWEET GOD IN HEAVEN, IT'S THE MOST AMAZING MAGIC TRICK IN HISTORY.
THEN CLOSE YOUR EYES, EDGAR... AND IN SO DOING, HELP ME SAVE THE WORLD.
"FOR GOD SO LOVED THE WORLD THAT HE GAVE HIS ONLY BEGOTTEN SON."
"INTO THY HANDS I COMMEND MY SPIRIT."
"SHE WAS BEAUTIFUL... SO BEAUTIFUL, I LOVED HER SO MUCH, I...."
BLAM
ELEVEN-THIRTY.
GOOD EVENING, JACOBI.
JACOBI...?

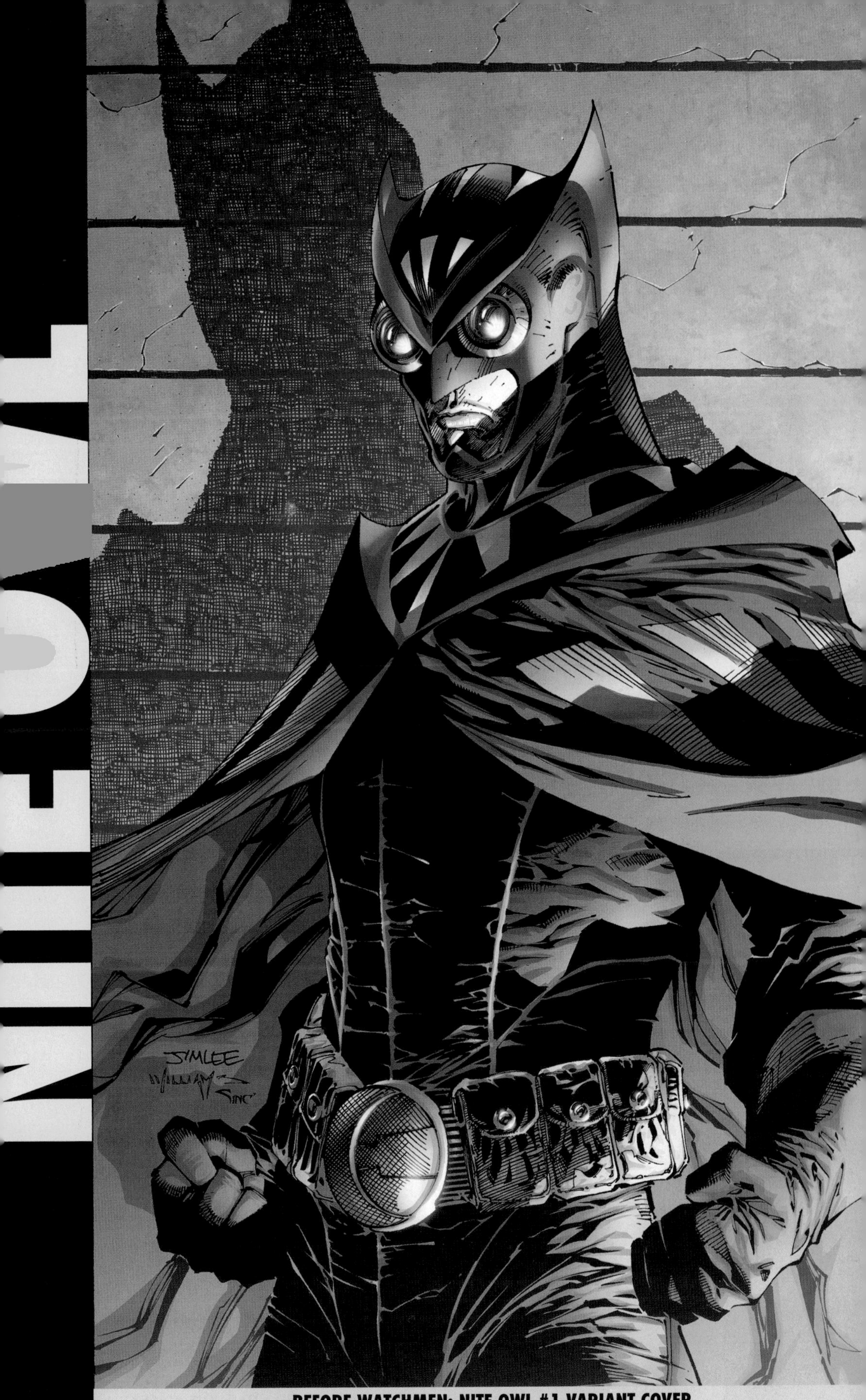
NITE OWL

BEFORE WATCHMEN: NITE OWL #1 VARIANT COVER
Art by JIM LEE with SCOTT WILLIAMS & ALEX SINCLAIR

NITE OWL

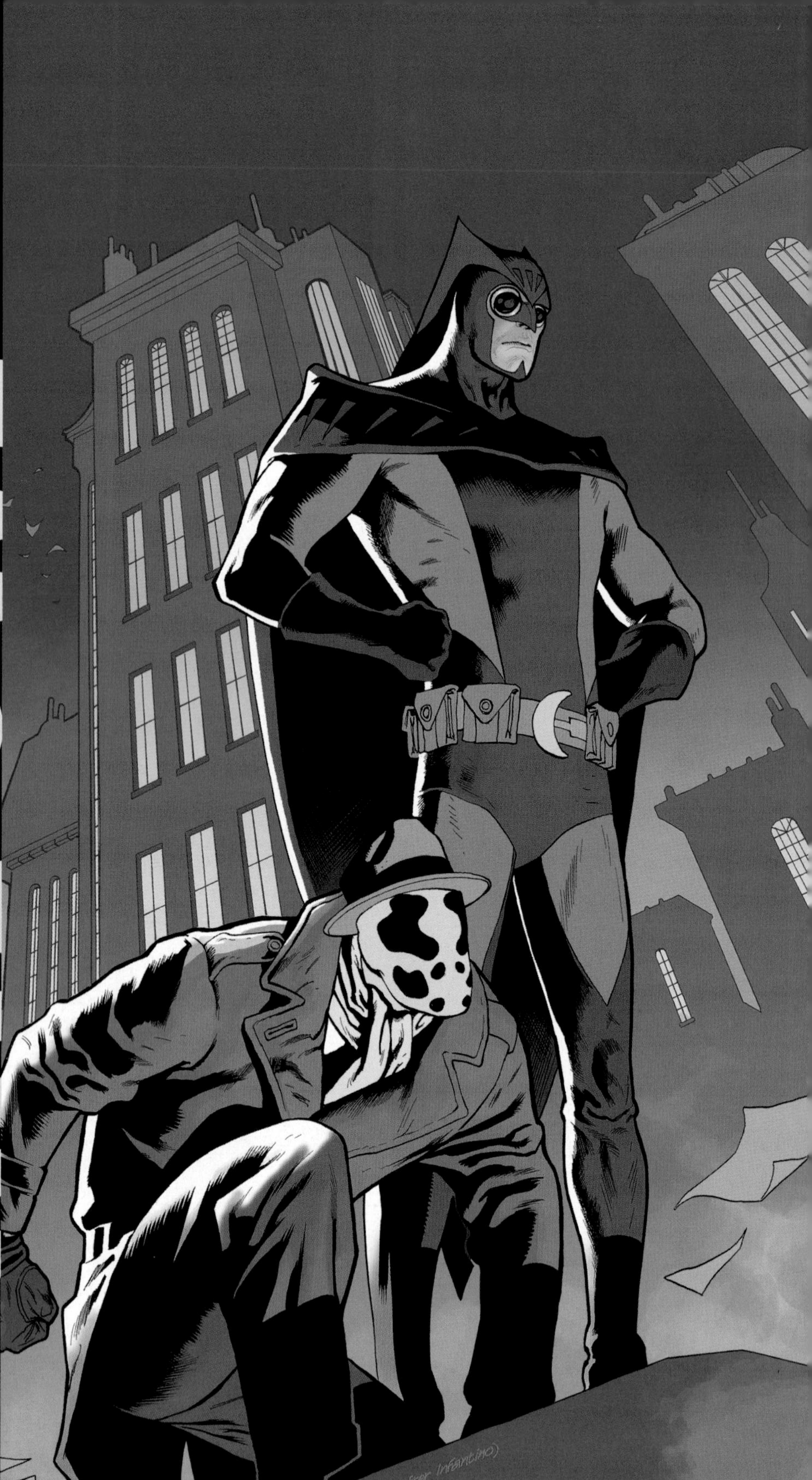

BEFORE WATCHMEN: NITE OWL #1 VARIANT COVER
Art by KEVIN NOWLAN

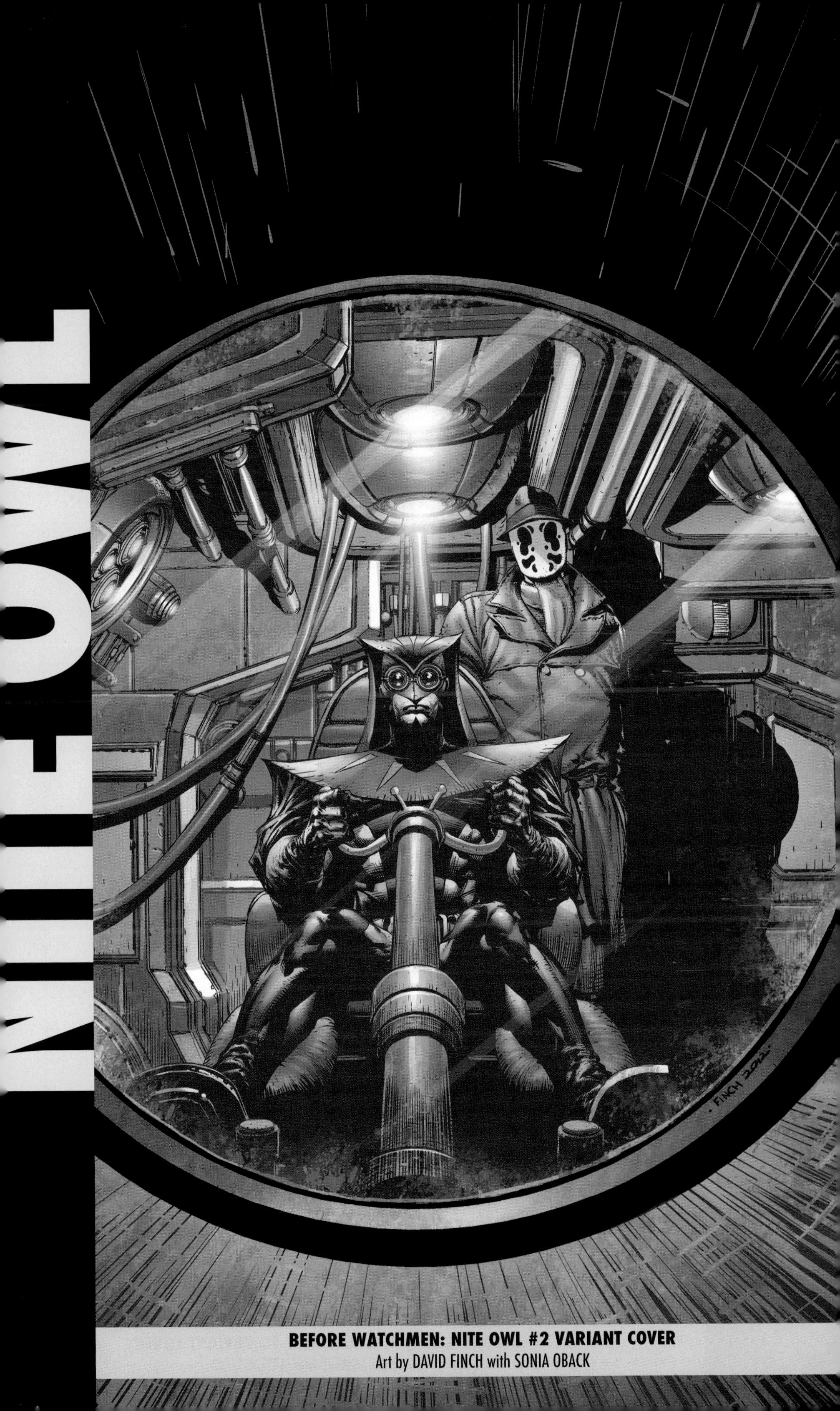
NITE OWL
FINCH 2012

BEFORE WATCHMEN: NITE OWL #2 VARIANT COVER
Art by DAVID FINCH with SONIA OBACK

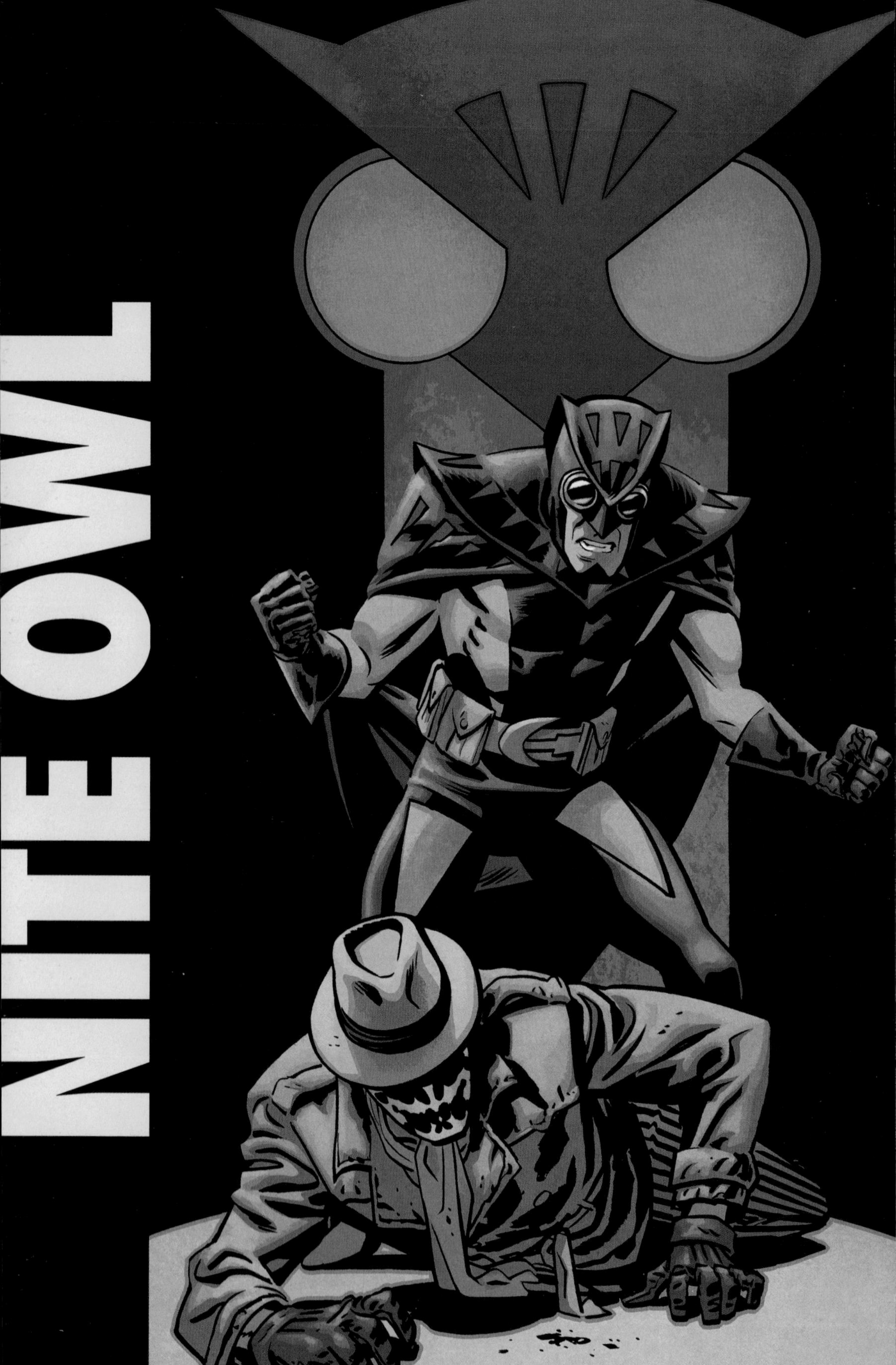
NITE OWL

BEFORE WATCHMEN: NITE OWL #3 VARIANT COVER
Art by CHRIS SAMNEE with MATT WILSON

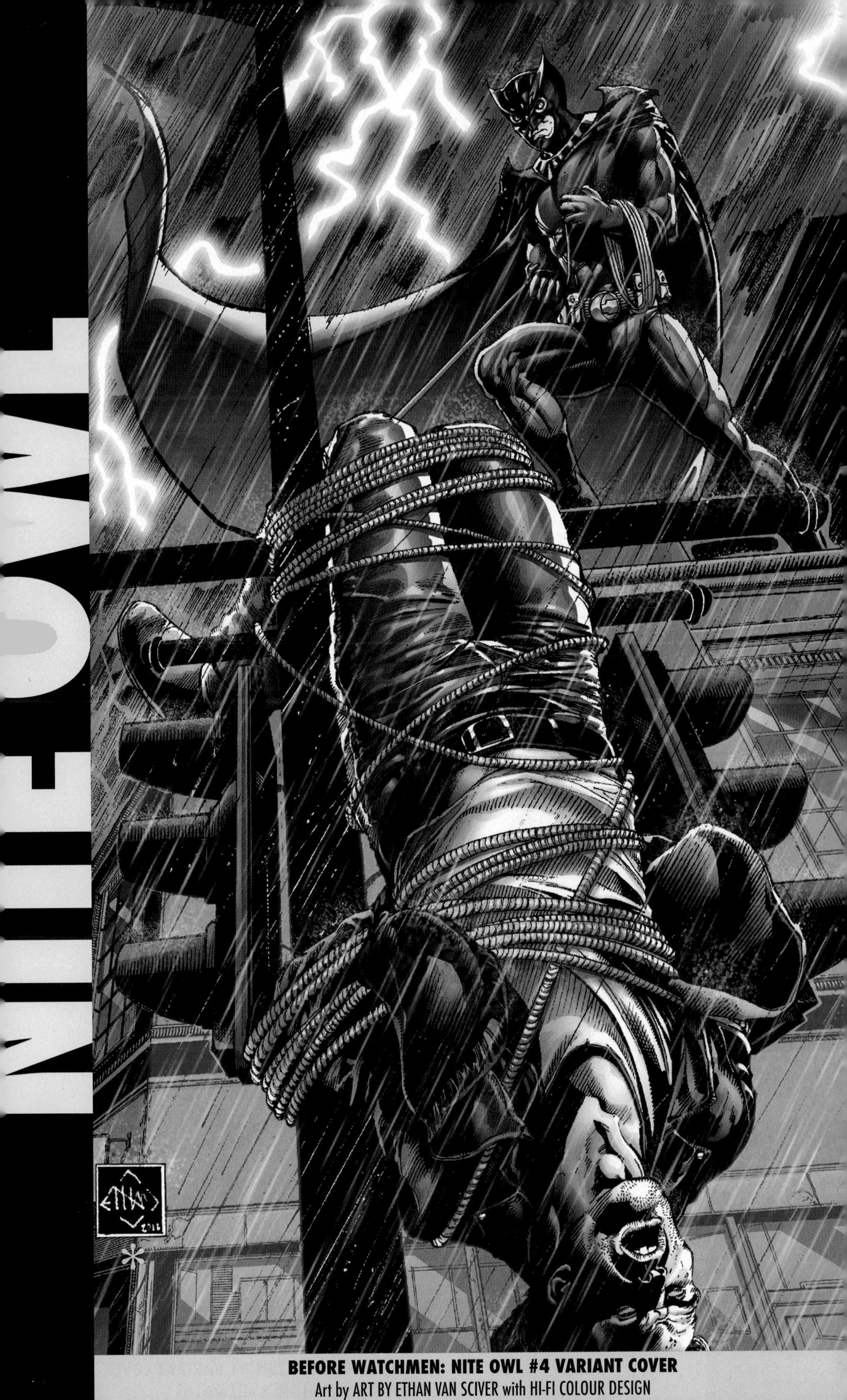
NITE OWL

BEFORE WATCHMEN: NITE OWL #4 VARIANT COVER

Art by ART BY ETHAN VAN SCIVER with HI-FI COLOUR DESIGN

DR. MANHATTAN

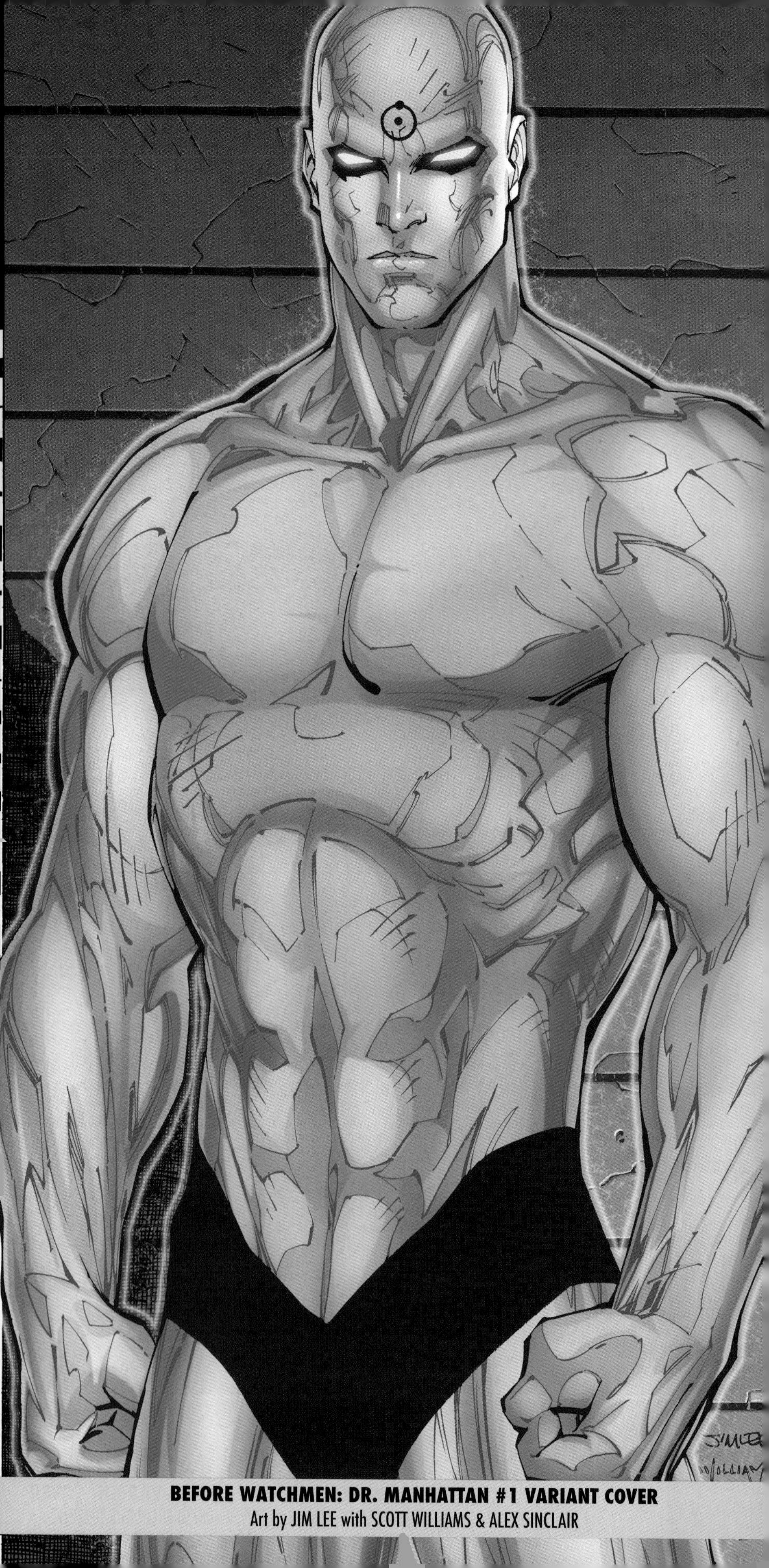

BEFORE WATCHMEN: DR. MANHATTAN #1 VARIANT COVER
Art by JIM LEE with SCOTT WILLIAMS & ALEX SINCLAIR

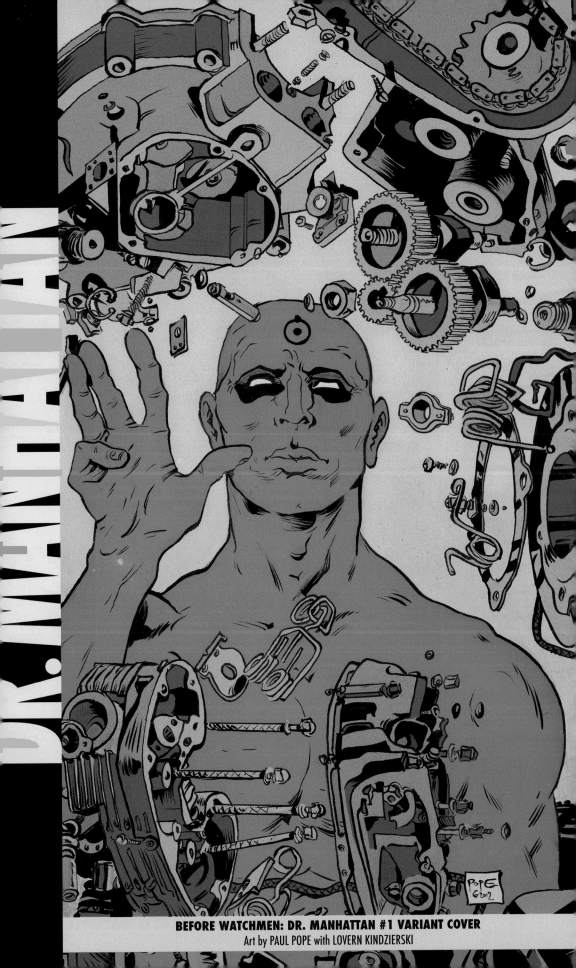

BEFORE WATCHMEN: DR. MANHATTAN #1 VARIANT COVER
Art by PAUL POPE with LOVERN KINDZIERSKI

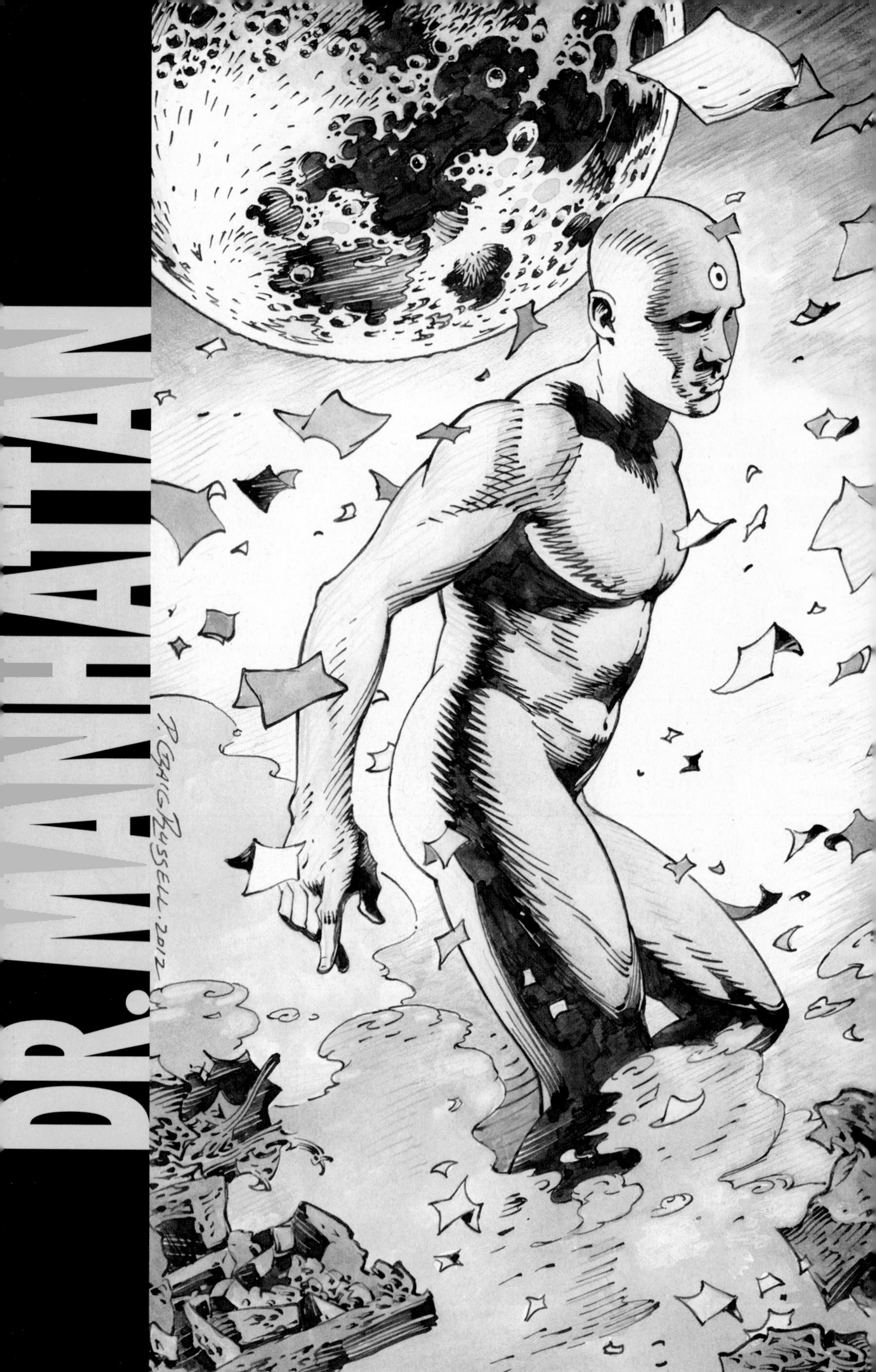
DR. MANHATTAN
P. CRAIG RUSSELL. 2012

BEFORE WATCHMEN: DR. MANHATTAN #2 VARIANT COVER
Art by P. CRAIG RUSSELL

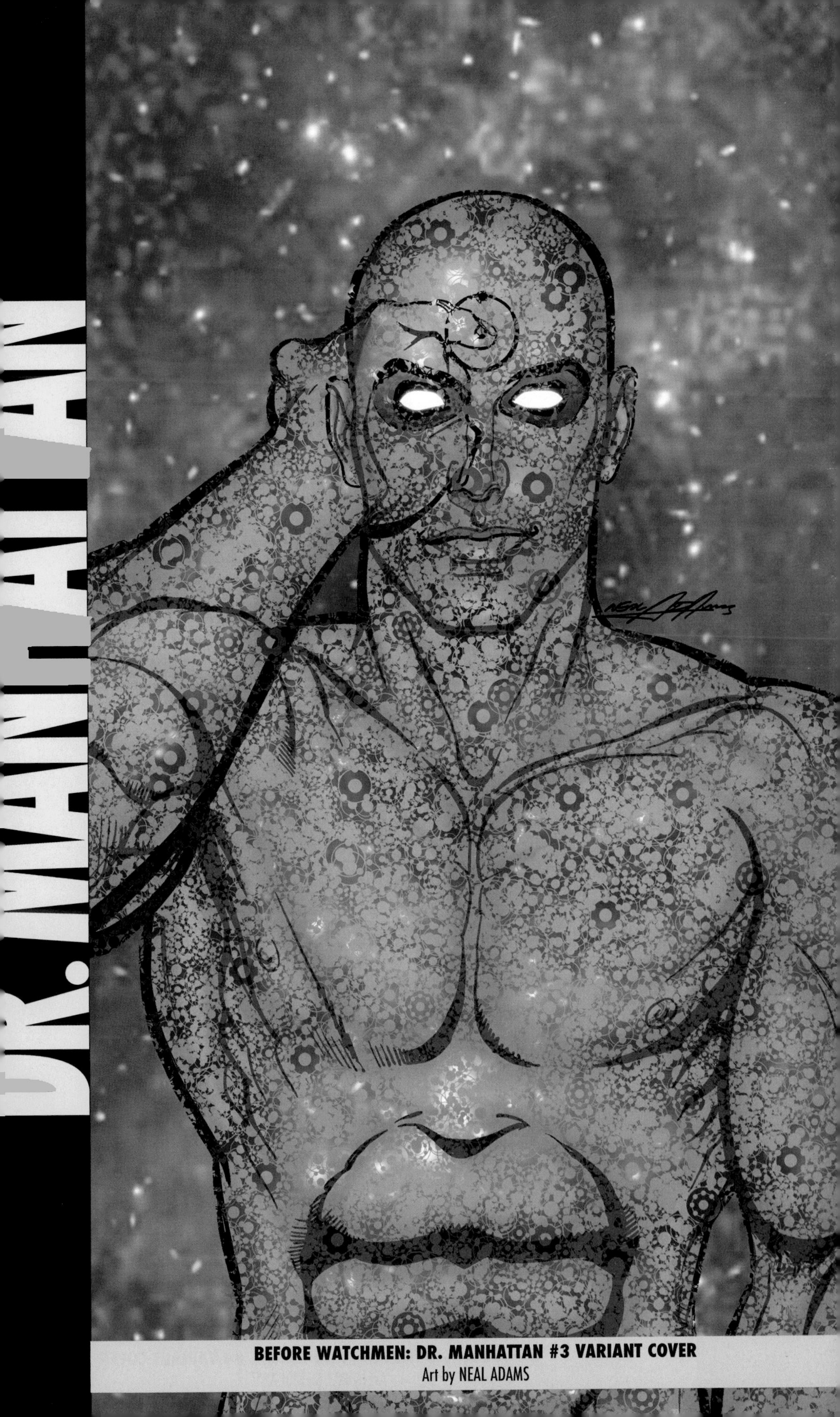
DR. MANHATTAN

BEFORE WATCHMEN: DR. MANHATTAN #3 VARIANT COVER
Art by NEAL ADAMS

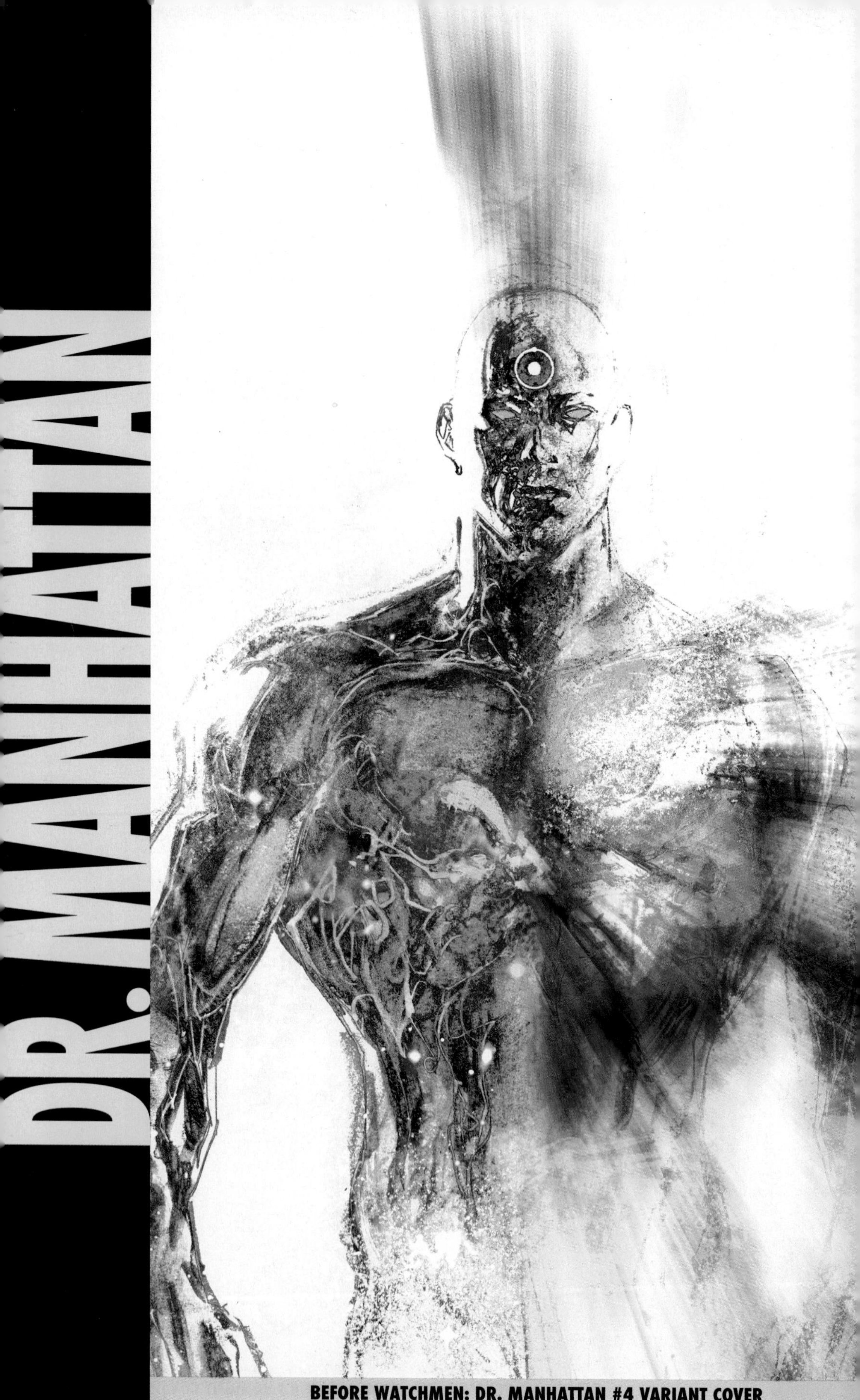
DR. MANHATTAN

BEFORE WATCHMEN: DR. MANHATTAN #4 VARIANT COVER
Art by BILL SIENKIEWICZ